Luminous Heart

The Nitartha Institute Series

published by Snow Lion Publications

Nitartha Institute was founded in 1996 by The Dzogchen Ponlop Rinpoche, under the guidance of Khenchen Thrangu Rinpoche and Khenpo Tsültrim Gyamtso Rinpoche, the leading contemporary teachers of the Karma Kagyü tradition of Tibetan Buddhism. The Institute, under the aegis of Nitartha *international*, aims to fully transmit the Buddhist tradition of contemplative inquiry and learning; it offers Western students training in advanced Buddhist view and practice, as taught by the Karma Kagyü and Nyingma lineages of Tibet.

The Institute is pleased to ally with Snow Lion Publications in presenting this series of important works offering a wide range of graded educational materials that include authoritative translations of key texts from the Buddhist tradition, both those unique to the Kagyü and Nyingma lineages and those common to the wider scope of Indo-Tibetan Buddhism; modern commentaries by notable lineage scholar-practitioners; manuals for contemplative practice; and broader studies that deepen understanding of particular aspects of the Buddhist view. The initial releases are from the Kagyü tradition and will be followed by publications from the Nyingma tradition.

This publication is an Intermediate Level Nitartha book.

LUMINOUS HEART

Essential Writings of
Rangjung Dorje, the Third Karmapa

With Jamgön Kongtrul Lodrö Thayé and others

TRANSLATED AND INTRODUCED BY
Karl Brunnhölzl

Snow Lion

Snow Lion
An imprint of Shambhala Publications, Inc.
4720 Walnut Street
Boulder, Colorado 80301
www.shambhala.com

This edition published 2021

Cover art: Chris Banigan and Peratek / Shutterstock.com
Cover design: Kate Huber-Parker
Interior design: Stephanie Johnston, based on a design by Gopa & Ted2, Inc.

9 8 7 6 5 4 3 2 1

First paperback edition
Printed in United States of America

♾ This edition is printed on acid-free paper that meets the American National Standards Institute Z39.48 Standard.
♻ This book is printed on 30% postconsumer recycled paper.
For more information please visit www.shambhala.com.
Snow Lion is distributed worldwide by
Penguin Random House, Inc., and its subsidiaries.

Library of Congress Cataloging-in-Publication Data
Names: Rang-byung-rdo-rje, Karma-pa III, 1284–1339 author. | Rang-byung-rdo-rje, Karma-pa III, 1284–1339 Criticism and interpretation. | Rang-byung-rdo-rje, Karma-pa III, 1284–1339 Poems. Selections. | Kong-sprul Blo-gros-mtha'-yas, 1813–1899, writer of commentary. | Brunnhölzl, Karl, translator.
Title: Luminous heart: essential writings of Rangjung Dorje, the third Karmapa / with Jamgön Kongtrul Lodrö Thayé and others ; translated and introduced by Karl Brunnhölzl.
Description: Boulder : Shambhala, 2021.
Identifiers: LCCN 2021001590 | ISBN 9781559395007 (trade paperback)
Subjects: LCSH: Enlightenment (Buddhism) | Buddhist philosophy. | Mādhyamika (Buddhism) | Yogācāra (Buddhism) | Buddhist literature, Tibetan—Translations into English.
Classification: LCC BQ4398 .R36 2021 | DDC 294.3/923092—dc23
LC record available at https://lccn.loc.gov/2021001590

Table of Contents

Abbreviations:

AC	Rangjung Dorje's autocommentary on his *Profound Inner Reality*
AS	*Asiatische Studien*
D	Derge Tibetan Tripiṭaka
DSC	Rangjung Dorje's commentary on the *Dharmadhātustava*
J	Johnston's Sanskrit edition of the *Ratnagotravibhāgavyākhyā*
JAOS	*Journal of the American Oriental Society*
JIABS	*Journal of the International Association of Buddhist Studies*
JIBS	*Journal of Indian and Buddhist Studies (Indogaku Bukkyōgakku Kenkyū)*
JIP	*Journal of Indian Philosophy*
JNS	Mikyö Dorje's commentary on the *Abhisamayālaṃkāra*
LTWA	Library of Tibetan Works and Archives
MM	Rangjung Dorje's *Aspiration Prayer of Mahāmudrā*
NT	Rangjung Dorje's *Treatise on Pointing Out the Tathāgata Heart*
NTC	Jamgön Kongtrul Lodrö Tayé's commentary on NT
NTKD	Kakyab Dorje's commentary on NT
NTKY	Göncho Yenla's annotations to NT
NY	Rangjung Dorje's *Treatise on the Distinction between Consciousness and Wisdom*
NYC	Jamgön Kongtrul Lodrö Tayé's commentary on NY
NYKD	Kakyab Dorje's commentary on NY
OED	Rangjung Dorje's *Ornament That Explains the* Dharmadharmatāvibhāga
P	Peking Tibetan Tripiṭaka
PEW	*Philosophy East and West*
T	A Complete Catalogue of the Tibetan Buddhist Canons. Tohoku Imperial University, 1934
Taishō	Taishō Shinshū Daizōkyō (The Chinese Buddhist Canon). Ed. J. Takakusu, K. Watanabe. Tokyo: Taishō Shinshū Daizōkyō Kanko kai, 1970

TBRC The Tibetan Buddhist Resource Center (www.tbrc.org)
TOK Jamgön Kongtrul Lodrö Tayé's *Treasury of Knowledge*
WZKS *Wiener Zeitschrift für die Kunde Südasiens*
ZDC Jamgön Kongtrul Lodrö Tayé's commentary on ZMND
ZDKT Karma Trinlépa's commentary on ZMND
ZMND Rangjung Dorje's *Profound Inner Reality*
ZZB Trimkang Lotsāwa's commentary on *The Profound Inner Reality*

An Aspiration
by H.H. the Seventeenth Karmapa, Ogyen Trinley Dorje

You realize that whatever appears dawns within the play of the mind
And that this mind is the dharmakāya free from clinging.
Through the power of that, you supreme siddhas master apparent existence.
Precious ones of the Kagyü lineage, please bring about excellent virtue.

Through the heart of a perfect Buddha having awoken in you,
You are endowed with the blossoming of the glorious qualities of supreme insight.
You genuine holder of the teachings by the name Dzogchen Ponlop,
Through your merit, the activity of virtue,

You publish the hundreds of flawless dharma paintings
That come from the protectors of beings, the Takpo Kagyü,
As a display of books that always appears
As a feast for the mental eyes of persons without bias.

While the stream of the Narmadā[1] river of virtue
Washes away the stains of the mind,
With the waves of the virtues of the two accumulations rolling high,
May it merge with the ocean of the qualities of the victors.

This was composed by Karmapa Ogyen Trinley Dorje as an auspicious aspiration for the publication of the precious teachings called The Eight Great Texts of Sūtra and Tantra *by the supreme Dzogchen Ponlop Karma Sungrap Ngedön Tenpé Gyaltsen on April 18, 2004 (Buddhist Era 2548). May it be auspicious.*

Foreword
by H.H. the Seventeenth Karmapa, Ogyen Trinley Dorje

In Tibet, all the ravishing and beautiful features of a self-arisen realm—being encircled by ranges of snow mountains adorned by superb white snowflakes and being filled with Sal trees, abundant herbs, and cool clear rivers—are wonderfully assembled in a single place. These wonders make our land endowed with the dharma the sole pure realm of human beings in this world. In it, all aspects of the teachings of the mighty sage, the greatly compassionate teacher skilled in means, are perfectly complete—the greater and lesser yānas as well as the mantrayāna. They are as pure and unblemished as the most refined pure gold; they accord with reasoning through the power of things; they dispel the darkness of the minds of all beings; and they are a great treasury bestowing all benefit and happiness one could wish for, just as desired. Not having vanished, these teachings still exist as the great treasure of the *Kangyur*, the *Tengyur*, and the sciences as well as the excellent teachings of the Tibetan scholars and siddhas who have appeared over time. Their sum equals the size of the mighty king of mountains, and their words and meanings are like a sip of the nectar of immortality. Headed by Dzogchen Ponlop Rinpoche with his utterly virtuous and pure intention to solely cherish the welfare of the teachings and beings, many dedicated workers of Nitartha *international*, striving with devotion, diligence, and prajñā, undertook hardships and made efforts over many years to preserve these teachings and further their transmission, and restore them. In particular, they worked toward the special purpose of propagating the excellent stream of teachings and practices of the unequaled Marpa Kagyü lineage, the great family of siddhas, in all directions and times, like the flow of a river in summertime. Through these efforts, the *Eight Great Texts of Sūtra and Tantra* publication series, inclusive of all the essential meanings of the perfectly complete teachings of the victor is magically manifesting as a great harvest for the teachings and beings. Bearing this in mind, I rejoice in this activity from the bottom of my heart and toss flowers of praise into the sky. Through this excellent activity, may the intentions of our noble forefathers may be fulfilled in the expanse of peace.

Karmapa Ogyen Trinley Dorje
Gyütö Ramoche Temple
July 19, 2002 (Buddhist Era 2547)

Foreword by The Dzogchen Ponlop Rinpoche

The Third Karmapa, Rangjung Dorje, is regarded as the architect of the Karma Kagyü interpretations of the view on buddha nature and other key topics that later became central to the philosophical school known as *Shentong* ("empty of other"). His writings became the authoritative basis for the standard Karma Kagyü position on buddha nature and the touchstone for the writings of subsequent lineage authors on the subject of buddha nature and *shentong*, such as the Eighth Karmapa, Mikyö Dorje. Rangjung Dorje's three most renowned treatises are *The Profound Inner Reality* (Tib. zab mo nang don), *The Distinction between Consciousness and Wisdom* (Tib. rnam shes ye shes 'byed pa), and *Pointing Out the Tathāgata Heart* (Tib. snying po bstan pa). His main work, *The Profound Inner Reality*, is one of the most complete elucidations of the Buddhist teachings on the completion stage practices of the Anuttarayogatantra. *The Distinction between Consciousness and Wisdom* explains the mahāyāna theory of eight consciousnesses and their transformation into the five wisdoms. *Pointing Out the Tathāgata Heart* clarifies the Buddha's teachings on *tathāgathagarbha*. The latter two texts are known as "the two lesser treatises of Rangjung Dorje."

The teachings from these three treatises play an essential role for practitioners of vajrayāna Buddhism by providing an overview which enriches the meditator's understanding of the complete transformative path of vajrayāna. The Karma Kagyü lineage is heir to both of the great mahāyāna traditions of emptiness—*Rangtong* Madhyamaka ("Empty-of-self Middle Way") and *Shentong* Madhyamaka ("Empty-of-other Middle Way"). It is commonly understood in this lineage that the *rangtong* approach is needed to determine and gain certainty in the right view, while *shentong* is required for the practice of meditation. This combination of the right view of emptiness and the meditative experience of luminous buddha nature is considered to be jointly necessary for complete awakening

While the Eighth Karmapa, Mikyö Dorje, and his followers emphasized the view of genuine emptiness that comes from the Madhyamaka teachings of the great Indian master Nāgārjuna, Rangjung Dorje and, later, Jamgön Kongtrul Lodrö Tayé emphasized the luminous empty mind of buddha nature, which is mainly presented in the treatises of the great Indian masters Maitreya and Asaṅga. Thus, the Karma Kagyü lineage inherits the great treasure of the complete teachings of both mahāyāna lineages.

It is my great delight that Dr. Brunnhölzl has translated the crucial passages on the view in *The Profound Reality* as well as the two lesser treatises with their commentaries. Karl has been studying and practicing Buddhism for many decades under the guidance of great Buddhist masters, such as the Venerable Khenchen Tsültrim Gyatso Rinpoche. An accomplished translator, Karl is also skilled in presenting the most complicated and intricate subjects in a clear and direct manner, as well as in leading meditation trainings. This work is an invaluable gift and great contribution to Western Buddhism. I trust that this book will bring great insight and genuine benefit for all readers.

Dzogchen Ponlop Rinpoche
Nalanda West
Seattle, Washington
September 22, 2008

Preface

IN AN ONGOING EFFORT to create a body of English translations of essential works by the Karmapas and other major lineage figures of the Tibetan Karma Kagyü School, I present here a volume with some of the main writings of the Third Karmapa, Rangjung Dorje[2] (1284–1339), on buddha nature, the origin and permutations of ordinary deluded consciousness, its transition to nonconceptual nondual wisdom, and the characteristics and functions of buddhahood together with its enlightened activity. These materials primarily include:

- Chapter 1 and excerpts from chapters 6 and 9 of *The Profound Inner Reality* with its autocommentary
- *Pointing Out the Tathāgata Heart*
- *The Distinction between Consciousness and Wisdom*
- Excerpts from *The Ornament That Explains the* Dharmadharmatāvibhāga

In addition, this volume contains four shorter poems by the Third Karmapa:

- *The Wisdom Lamp That Illuminates the Basic Nature*
- *Proclaiming Mind's Way of Being Mistaken*
- *Stanzas That Express Realization*
- *A Song on the Ālaya*

These texts by the Third Karmapa are supplemented by:

- Two commentaries on *Pointing Out the Tathāgata Heart* and *The Distinction between Consciousness and Wisdom* by Jamgön Kongtrul Lodrö Tayé[3] (1813–1899)
- Excerpts from a commentary by the First Karma Trinlépa, Choglé Namgyal[4] (1456–1539) on the first chapter of the autocommentary on *The Profound Inner Reality*

Excerpts from Pawo Tsugla Trengwa's[5] (1504–1566) presentation of buddhahood, kāyas, wisdoms, and enlightened activity in his commentary on the *Bodhicaryāvatāra*.

As for the view of Karmapa Rangjung Dorje, this book may be regarded as a continuation of, and elaboration on, the remarks thereon in *In Praise of Dharmadhātu* (which also contains the Third Karmapa's commentary on this text), providing translations of more of the still-extant materials that describe his unique approach to both Yogācāra and Madhyamaka. In the Kagyü tradition, it is generally said that its distinct outlook on Madhyamaka was primarily presented by the Eighth Karmapa, Mikyö Dorje[6] (1507–1554), while its position on buddha nature (and the tantras) was mainly put forth by the Third Karmapa. As the following will show, the Yogācāra tradition of Maitreya, Asaṅga, and Vasubandhu may well be included in the scope of the Third Karmapa's explanations, which generally present a creative synthesis of Yogācāra, Madhyamaka, and the teachings on buddha nature. In addition, all of the above materials are not only scholarly documents, but bear great significance for practicing the Buddhist path and making what is described in them a living experience.

My wish to publish these texts in English dates far back, and the work on them has been in progress for about fifteen years, but had to be postponed many times due to other responsibilities, so I am truly delighted that this project finally comes to fruition. It would not have been possible without all the Tibetan masters from whom I received oral explanations on most of the above texts over the last two decades. In this regard, my heartfelt gratitude goes to Khenchen Tsultrim Gyamtso Rinpoche, Tenga Rinpoche, Dzogchen Ponlop Rinpoche, Sangyé Nyenpa Rinpoche, Ringu Tulku, and the late Khenpo Lama Thubten. I am also very grateful to all the Western scholars, particularly Professor Lambert Schmithausen and Dr. Klaus-Dieter Mathes, who opened many doors to the Indian sources of the Yogācāra tradition.

Sincere thanks go to Sidney Piburn and Jeff Cox from Snow Lion Publications for their continuous support and readiness to publish this work, and to Michael Wakoff for being a meticulous and caring editor. I am also very grateful to Stephanie Johnston, who read through the entire manuscript, offered many helpful suggestions, and produced both the layout and the index. As for Jamgön Kongtrul Lodrö Tayé's commentary on *Distinction between Consciousness and Wisdom*, its first-draft translation was prepared together with Anna Johnson, Christine McKenna, Gelong Karma Jinpa, and Karma Chögyal during a three-month Tibetan Intensive at Gampo Abbey, Canada.

May this book be a contributing cause for the buddha heart of H.H. the Seventeenth Gyalwang Karmapa Ogyen Trinley Drodul Dorje swiftly embracing all sentient beings in whatever ways suitable. May it in particular contribute to planting and sustaining both the great scholarly and meditative traditions of the Karma Kagyü lineage in the English-speaking world, since they were founded and fostered by all the Karmapas as a means to introduce all beings into their true nature.

Fremont, Seattle, September 11, 2007

INTRODUCTION

The Indian Yogācāra Background

In certain parts of the Eastern as well as the Western academic traditions, the Yogācāra School has often been neglected or misrepresented, usually in favor of assigning the "pole position" among Buddhist schools to Madhyamaka (in particular, to its Prāsaṅgika brand). There are many reasons for this, but two of the main ones are (1) making superficial and out-of-context judgments based on a unidimensional understanding and discussion of what seem to be stereotypical "buzz words" (such as *cittamātra*) and (2) not treating the concepts and explanations of Yogācāra in their own terms, but looking at them through the lenses of other philosophical systems. As Nguyen says:

> It is a truism in modern studies of systems of meaning (such as cultures, languages, religions, mythology) that it is necessary first to see such a system of meaning from within, in terms of its own categories and concepts, and its own inherent logic. If on the contrary, we set out by attempting to view a system of meaning in terms of categories fundamentally alien to it, we are in danger of misconstruing the system and constructing a distorted interpretation of it that overlooks its basic meanings and inherent structure. This mistake has often been made in the past in studies of Yogācāra philosophy. . . .
>
> In Buddhist literature itself, texts like the *Mahāyānasūtrālaṃkāra*, *Madhyāntavibhāga*, and *Mahāyānasaṃgraha* are always careful to consider all particular concepts in their integral relationship to the thought-system as a whole. Each of these texts deserves careful study.[7]

Hall adds:

> The argument over whether Vijñānavāda is idealistic or realistic bears a marked resemblance to the controversy as to whether Madhyamaka is nihilism or transcendental absolutism.
>
> Mistaking taxonomy for understanding is a fault not limited to modern writers on Buddhism. A similar excessive concern for and trust in doctrinal labels can be seen in ancient Indian philosophers and Tibetan scholastics, and even in the Abhidharma itself. The identification of one school with another (such as that of Vijñānavāda with some Western form of idealism) is not only likely to be misleading; it is only all too often the point at which the argument stops. A more fruitful approach to comparative philosophy would begin by tentatively accepting several comparable philosophies as coherent systems in their own terms, and would proceed to apply their several viewpoints to specific problems of philosophy.[8]

As should be evidenced by many of the following quotes from Yogācāra texts, this school was definitely not advocating some kind of naïve idealism or psychologism, nor an ultimately and truly existing consciousness.[9] King says:

> It should be made clear from the outset then that the Yogācāra school is far more complex in its understanding of the nature of experience than is usually acknowledged.[10]

Lusthaus elaborates:

> Buddhism is not a psychologism. Even Yogācāra, which does propose to reduce karma and the entirety of the triple world to cognitive factors, is not a psychologism. This is because the point of Buddhist analysis is not the reification of a mental structure or theory of mind, but its erasure. Vasubandhu highlights the closure of cognitive horizons not because such a closure is either desirable or unalterable, but because the closure can only be opened once its all-encompassing complexity and ubiquity is understood and recognized. Yogācāra uses psychological arguments to overcome psychological closure, not to enhance it.[11]

The Yogācāras were also not immune or oblivious to notions such as "emptiness," "lack of nature," and "identitylessness" (which are often wrongly considered to belong solely and uniquely to Madhyamaka), but included and greatly used them as parts of their own explanations too. Specifically, hermeneutic frameworks such as the three natures, the threefold lack of nature, and the three emptinesses (see below) are not at all presented in order to contradict the prajñāpāramitā sūtras or Nāgārjuna, but equally serve to explain emptiness, just within a further developed hermeneutical system. As King says:

> As a Mahāyāna school, the Yogācāra developed as a response to the insights of those same [prajñāpāramitā] sūtras. Under such circumstances, it would have been difficult indeed to have ignored the centrality of the notion of *śūnyatā* to these texts. In fact, the idea that the early classical Yogācāra of Asaṅga and Vasubandhu found any difficulty whatsoever in embracing the basic insights of the Madhyamaka school disregards both the historical and textual evidence, which, on the contrary, displays a spirit of underlying continuity and acceptance.[12]

However, in contrast to the Mādhyamikas' reluctance to speak about the specifics of seeming reality and the Buddhist path of purifying the deluded mind (or mind at all), the Yogācāra system, besides presenting sophisticated analyses of ultimate reality, also elaborates on how the deluded mind operates, how it can make the transition to the unmistaken wisdom that sees this mind's own ultimate nature, and what the characteristics and the fruition of this wisdom are. Thus, Yogācāra not only investigates the definitive meaning of the scriptures in a nonreifying manner, but also what happens experientially in the minds of those who study and practice this meaning. At the same time, it provides broader contextualizing comments on the sūtras and addresses typical misconceptions about emptiness and Madhyamaka, such as it being pure nihilism (which was a very common concern even among Buddhists since the time of Nāgārjuna). Consequently, one could even argue that the Yogācāra system is not only not inferior to the Madhyamaka approach, but exhibits a much more encompassing outlook on human experience and the soteriological[13] issues of the Buddhist path than the almost exclusively one-way deconstructive approach of the Mādhyamikas. This seems to have occurred already to some people in India, as the following verse attributed to the audience of the seven-year debate between Candragomī and Candrakīrti illustrates.

> Ah, the treatises of noble Nāgārjuna
> Are medicine for some and poison for others.
> The treatises of Ajita[14] and noble Asaṅga
> Are nectar for all people.[15]

King elaborates:

> Thus, we find in the Yogācāra, as in the Madhyamaka school, a pointed refusal to become involved in an ontological debate. It is interesting that this type of analysis is something of a bridge-building exercise between what might be seen as an undue emphasis upon negative language (via negativa) in the exposition of emptiness by (some?) Mādhyamikas on the one hand, and the overarching realism (via positiva) of the Abhidharma schools on the other hand. As such, the Yogācāra movement can be seen as a "re-forming" of the Middle Path. This is not to say that such a reformation is necessarily out of step with the understanding of *śūnyatā* as systematized in the *śāstras* of Nāgārjuna (who is clearly neither a nihilist nor a realist in the accepted senses of the terms), but merely that, in its emphasis upon the "given" of meditative and so-called "normative" perception, the Yogācāra aim is to establish the appropriate parameters of linguistic usage and a rigorous logic for the establishment of the Mahāyāna position on experientially verifiable grounds.[16]

In addition, quite a number of Tibetan masters emphasize that Yogācāra (whether it is called that way or *shentong*) is more in harmony with the vajrayāna. For example, Śākya Chogden (1428–1507) says:

> As for the reasonings that ascertain all phenomena as lacking a nature, the other one [that is, Niḥsvabhāvavāda] is vaster, while the [description of] the definitive meaning of what is to be experienced through meditation is more profound in this system. Because its explanation of nothing but nondual wisdom as what is to be experienced as a result of meditation very greatly accords with the vajrayāna [systems], this [latter] system is more profound.[17]

and

> In the uncommon texts of mantra,
> There is no explanation whatsoever

About what is to be experienced through the view
That is not in accord with the texts of Maitreya.[18]

. . .

The Maitreya dharmas accord with the mantra[yāna],
Because they assert solely nondual wisdom
As what is to be realized after [all] phenomena
In terms of apprehender and apprehended have been realized to be empty.

For all these reasons, let alone the Buddhist perspective proper, Yogācāra presentations of mental processes also have great potential to significantly contribute to the modern cognitive sciences. Nguyen suggests:

> In modern studies of comparative philosophy and religion, Yogācāra thought, once adequately understood, should provoke major interest, given its startling parallels with the most modern developments in Western thought about cognition and epistemology. Just as the modern researchers now acknowledge that the modern world has much to learn from the medical lore of traditional cultures, the same could be said of classical Buddhist philosophical pyschology.[19]

In sum, the Yogācāra tradition considered itself as a continuation of all the preceding developments in Buddhism and not as a radical departure from them or even as a distinct new school per se. To retain what was regarded as useful in other schools of Buddhism did not mean to be ignorant of the pervasive Madhyamaka cautions against reifications of any kind. Thus, the vast range of Yogācāra writings represents a digest of virtually everything that previous Buddhist masters had developed, including intricate abhidharma analyses, charting the grounds of the many levels of the paths in the three yānas, subtle descriptions of meditative processes, presentations of epistemology and reasoning, explorations of mind and its functions in both its ignorant and enlightened modes, and commentaries on major mahāyāna sūtras. Thus, any linear or one-dimensional presentation of this Buddhist school seems not only misguided, but highly inconsiderate, due to the rich variety of this school's sources and explanatory models (in itself, this variety and its development are nice examples of key Yogācāra notions, which usually describe processes rather than states or things). Nevertheless, a brief overview, in the Yogācāra School's own terms, of the main topics addressed in the following texts by the Third Karmapa is indispensable to demonstrate how firmly he is steeped in the view and explanations of this school.

The Major Yogācāra Masters and Their Works

Let's begin with the Indian masters (in roughly chronological order) and their major texts[20] that are at the core of the Yogācāra tradition. First and foremost, we have Maitreya and his five seminal works, which are the foundations for all subsequent Yogācāra scriptures:

Abhisamayālaṃkāra[21]
Mahāyānasūtrālaṃkāra[22]
Madhyāntavibhāga
Dharmadharmatāvibhāga
Ratnagotravibhāga (Uttaratantra)[23]

Nāgamitra (third/fourth century?) composed a *Kāyatrayāvatāramukha*, which discusses dharmakāya, sambhogakāya, and nirmāṇakāya in terms of the three natures.

Asaṅga and Vasubandhu (both fourth century CE) were the two earliest commentators on the five texts by Maitreya and also composed many texts of their own. The following main Yogācāra texts are attributed to Asaṅga:

Saṃdhinirmocanasūtravyākhyāna (commentary)
Ratnagotravibhāgavyākhyā (commentary)[24]
Yogācārabhūmi (consisting of the *Bahubhūmivastu*, *Viniścayasaṃgrahaṇī*, *Vivaraṇasaṃgrahaṇī*, *Paryāyasaṃgrahaṇī*, and *Vastusaṃgrahaṇī*)
Abhidharmasamucchaya
Mahāyānasaṃgraha

Vasubandhu's main Yogācara works consist of:

Mahāyānasūtrālaṃkārabhāṣya
Madhyāntavibhāgabhāṣya
Dharmadharmatāvibhāgavṛtti
Mahāyānasaṃgrahabhāṣya[25]
Viṃśatikākārikā
Triṃśikākārikā
Trisvabhāvanirdeśa
Karmasiddhiprakaraṇa
Pañcaskandhaprakaraṇa
Vyākhyāyukti

Guṇabhadra (394–468) was greatly active in translating and teaching mahāyāna sūtras as well as Yogācāra and *tathāgatagarbha*[26] materials in China. He is credited with the first translation of the *Laṅkāvatārasūtra*.

Dignāga (c. 480–540) is said to have taught at the Indian Buddhist University of Nālandā and is mainly famous for his logico-epistemological texts. However, as many studies have shown, these works (such as the *Pramāṇasamucchaya*) are generally grounded in the Yogācāra system. In addition, he also wrote a few more explicitly Yogācāra texts, such as the *Ālambanaparīkṣā* with its autocommentary.[27]

Ratnamati (fifth–sixth century) was another Indian active in China, who greatly emphasized the *tathāgatagarbha* teachings. He translated the *Uttaratantra*, Vasubandhu's commentary on the *Daśabhūmikasūtra*, and many other such texts.

Bodhiruci's collaboration with Ratnamati (and Buddhasānta) in translating Vasubandhu's above commentary came to an end over their disagreement as to whether *tathāgatagarbha* represents classical Yogācāra thought or not. Bodhiruci translated thirty-nine texts into Chinese, among them the *Laṅkāvatārasūtra*, the *Anūnatvāpūrṇatvanirdeśasūtra*, and the *Mahāyānasaṃgraha*.

Kambala (also fifth–sixth century) wrote a brilliant poetic treatise, called *Ālokamālāprakaraṇanāma*, which represents an unusually early and unique approach of synthesizing Madhyamaka and Yogācāra. Combining the framework of the three natures with that of the two realities, Kambala clearly assimilates Madhyamaka to Yogācāra and not vice versa (as, for example, Śāntarakṣita and Kamalaśīla did much later). Also the autocommentary on his *Bhagavatīprajñāpāramitānavaślokapiṇḍārtha* (better known as *Navaślokī*) exhibits typical Yogācāra features.

Guṇamati (sixth century) wrote a commentary on Vasubandhu's *Vyākhyāyukti* and is renowned as Sthiramati's main teacher. Both were active at the Buddhist University of Valabhi (in present-day Gujarat).

Sthiramati (c. 510–570) is often unduly ignored, but he not only composed important commentaries on several of the above texts by Maitreya, Asaṅga, and Vasubandhu, but also systematized and elaborated many classical Yogācāra themes. Especially his large commentaries on Maitreya's *Mahāyānasūtrālaṃkāra* and *Madhyāntavibhāga* as well as his shorter one on Vasubandhu's *Triṃśikā* can be considered as landmarks in Yogācāra writing in their own right. His Yogācāra works include:

Mahāyānasūtrālaṃkāravṛttibhāṣya
Madhyāntavibhāgaṭīkā
Viṃśatikābhāṣya

Triṃśikābhāṣya
Abhidharmasamucchayavyākhyā[28]
Pañcaskandhaprakaraṇavaibhāsa

Paramārtha (499–569) traveled to China in 546 and remained there until the end of his life, being the first one to widely teach and translate Yogācāra (and *tathāgatagarbha*) materials there. The Chinese canon contains thirty-two texts attributed to him, either works authored by him or translations (partially with significant embedded comments). The latter include several sūtras, Asaṅga's *Viniṣcayasaṃgrahaṇī* and *Mahāyānasaṃgraha*, Vasubandhu's *Madhyāntavibhāgabhāṣya* and *Mahāyānasaṃgrahabhāṣya* (Paramārtha's most complex and significant work), and Vasubandhu's *Viṃśatikā* and *Triṃśikā*.[29] He also translated, if not authored, the famous *Awakening of Faith in the Mahāyāna*.[30] In addition, he is considered as the author (or at least the commentator and redactor) of the *Buddhagotraśāstra* (*Fo Xing Lun*),[31] which is one of the rare texts that synthesizes explicitly and in detail many classical Yogācāra materials, such as the three natures, with the notion of *tathāgatagarbha*. Among Paramārtha's novel interpretations of Yogācāra concepts, the best known is his theory of a ninth consciousness, called *amalavijñāna* (see below). This is primarily found in his commentary on Vasubandhu's *Triṃśikā*, called *Evolution of Consciousness* (*Chuan Shi Lun*),[32] and the comments embedded in his translations of the *Viniṣcayasaṃgrahaṇī*, the *Mahāyānasaṃgraha*, and its *Bhāṣya*.[33] Together with Kumārajīva (344–413) and Hsüan-tsang (602–664), he is considered to be one of the greatest translators of Buddhist scriptures into Chinese.[34]

Dharmapāla (530–561) was an abbot of Nālandā University. His works are only extant in Chinese, and Hsüan-tsang, who was instrumental in bringing Yogācāra teachings to China, greatly relies on Dharmapāla's views (primarily in his *Vijñaptimātratāsiddhi*, which compiles the commentaries by ten Indian Yogācāras on Vasubandhu's *Viṃśatikā* and *Triṃśikā*). Dharmapāla also composed a commentary on Dignāga's *Ālambanaparīkṣā* and had a famous written debate with Bhāvaviveka, which is found in the former's commentaries on Āryadeva's *Catuḥśataka* and *Śataśāstra* from a Yogācāra point of view.

Another sixth-century Yogācāra is Asvabhāva, who often closely follows Sthiramati and wrote the following commentaries on texts by Maitreya, Asaṅga, and Kambala:

Mahāyānasūtrālaṃkāraṭīkā
Mahāyānasaṃgrahopanibandhana
Ālokamālāṭīkāhṛdānandajananī

Śīlabhadra (529–645) followed Dharmapāla as the abbot of Nālandā and taught Hsüan-tsang for fifteen months during the latter's stay there. He is the author of the *Buddhabhūmivyākhyāna*, one of two extant commentaries on the *Buddhabhūmisūtra* (the other one being the *Buddhabhūmyupadeśa*).[35] His text greatly relies on the *Mahāyānasūtrālaṃkāra* and its *Bhāṣya*, as well as on the *Mahāyānasaṃgraha*.

Guṇaprabha (sixth century) is of course most famous for his *Vinayasūtra*, but he also wrote a commentary on the *Bodhisattvabhūmi*, a *Bodhisattvabhūmiśīlaparivartabhāṣya*, and a commentary on Vasubandhu's *Pañcaskandhaprakaraṇa*.

Jinaputra (second half of sixth century) wrote a commentary on the *Abhidharmasamucchaya* and a short part of the *Yogācārabhūmi*, called *Bodhisattvabhūmiśīlaparivartaṭīkā*.

Prasenajit (sixth/seventh century) is reported to have studied with Sthiramati, Śīlabhadra, and many other masters, being highly erudite in all Indian Buddhist and non-Buddhist fields of knowledge. However, he preferred to live as a hermit outside of the Buddhist institutional mainstream and repeatedly refused to become the personal teacher of the then king of Magadha, instead dwelling with many hundreds of students on a mountainside. Though he is not known to have composed any texts of his own, he was highly influential in teaching Hsüan-tsang a great number of both Madhyamaka and Yogācāra texts, particularly providing the final clarifications on the *Yogācārabhūmi*, for two years after the latter had been taught by Śīlabhadra. When Hsüan-tsang returned to Nālandā thereafter, he debated some Mādhyamikas and finally even composed a (lost) Sanskrit treatise in three thousand stanzas on Yogācāra and Madhyamaka not being mutually exclusive, but in harmony.[36]

Candragomī (sixth/seventh century) was a disciple of Sthiramati. In his early adulthood, he had been married to a princess, but left her to spend the rest of his life keeping the five Buddhist precepts of a layman. He was very erudite in all Buddhist and non-Buddhist fields of learning and also a great poet. After being invited to Nālandā by Candrakīrti, he had an ongoing debate with the latter for seven years, defending the Yogācāra view. His teachings are reported to have been focused mainly on the *Daśabhūmikasūtra*, the *Laṅkāvatārasūtra*, the *Samādhirājasūtra*, the *Gaṇḍālaṃkāradhāraṇī*, and the prajñāpāramitā sūtras, of which he also composed synopses. Among his works, the most famous are the *Candravyākaraṇa* (a work on Sanskrit grammar), the *Śiṣyalekha*, and the *Bodhisattvasaṃvaraviṃsaka* (a mnemonic summary of the Ethics chapter of the *Bodhisattvabhūmi*). Many other texts by him (such as a **Pradīpamālā* on the stages of the bodhisattva path) are mentioned in various sources, with some of them being more specifically Yogācāra, but none of them have survived.[37]

Dharmakīrti (c. 600–660), like Dignāga, is best known for his contributions to epistemology and logic through his seven texts on valid cognition (such as the *Pramāṇavārttika*), but these texts also clearly exhibit many Yogācara traits.

Vinītadeva (c. 645–715) composed commentaries on Vasubandhu's *Viṃśatikā* and *Triṃśika* and Dignāga's *Ālambanaparīkśā* (as well as on several of Dharmakīrti's treatises on valid cognition).

Pṛthivībandhu (seventh century?) wrote a detailed commentary on Vasubandhu's *Pañcaskandhaprakaraṇa*.

Jñānacandra (eighth century) composed a brief meditation manual, called *Yogacaryābhāvanātātparyārthanirdeśa*, and a commentary on Nāgamitra's *Kāyatrayāvatāramukha*.

Sāgaramegha (eighth century) wrote a massive commentary on the *Bodhisattvabhūmi*, called *Yogācārabhūmaubodhisattvabhūmivyākhyā*.

Sumatiśīla (late eighth century) authored a detailed commentary on Vasubandhu's *Karmasiddhiprakaraṇa*.

Late Yogācāras (all tenth–eleventh century) include Dharmakīrti of Sumatra[38] (one of the main teachers of Atiśa); Jñānaśrīmitra (*Sākarasiddhi*, *Sākarasaṃgraha*, and *Sarvajñāsiddhi*); Ratnakīrti (*Ratnakīrtinibandhāvalī* and *Sarvajñāsiddhi*); and Jñānaśrībhadra (commentary on the *Laṅkāvatārasūtra*, summary of the *Mahāyānasūtrālaṃkāra*, and commentary on the *Pramāṇavārttika*). Ratnākāraśānti is variously considered a Yogācāra or Mādhyamika. In any case, most of his works (such as *Vijñaptimātratāsiddhi*, *Triyānavyavasthāna*, *Madhyamakālaṃkāravṛtti-Madhyamapratipadāsiddhi*, *Prajñāpāramitopadeśa*, and *Madhyamakālaṃkāropadeśa*) exhibit a synthesis of both these systems, often referred to as "Vijñapti-Madhyamaka."[39]

Several other Indian Mādhyamikas, such as Śrīgupta (seventh century?), Śāntarakṣita, Kamalaśīla, Haribhadra (all eighth century), Viydākaraprabha (eighth/ninth century), Jetāri (tenth/eleventh century), and Nandaśrī, indeed used a lot of Yogācāra materials, but clearly upheld the Madhyamaka view as their final position.

In brief, the main classical Indian exponents of Yogācāra are no doubt Maitreya, Asaṅga, Vasubandhu, and Sthiramati. As will be seen in the following, it is also primarily their works that provide the roadmap for the discussions of the eight consciousnesses, the four wisdoms, the three kāyas, and buddha nature in the Third Karmapa's texts translated below.

In terms of its contents, it should be noted that the Yogācāra system is by no means some kind of speculative philosophy that starts from a priori axioms and then constructs a magnificent edifice of abstract concepts in order to define what is true. On the contrary, the Yogācāra School proceeds from observing and analyzing a wide range of meditative experiences (hence its name), which reveal both the deluded and nondeluded processes of the mind. Through exploring and outlining the perceptual and conceptual structures of such processes, the Yogācāra system works out primarily their epistemological and soteriological implications (and only secondarily their ontological ones). As common in the Buddhist tradition (and many Indian spiritual traditions in general), Yogācāra treats epistemological analysis (a purely philosophical discipline for Western minds) as inseparable from, and being most relevant for, soteriological concerns (a religious matter for Western minds). In other words, the delusion about a truly existent self and phenomena and its resultant suffering are basically taken to be a cognitive error, while liberation or buddhahood is nothing but the removal of this error. As *Mahāyānasūtrālaṃkāra* VI.2 says:

> In itself, the view about a self lacks the characteristic of a self,
> As do its deformities—their characteristics differ [from a self].
> Nor is there another [self] apart from these two, so it arises as a mere error.
> Therefore, liberation is the termination of this mere error.

Vasubandhu's *Bhāṣya* and Sthiramati[40] comment that neither "the view about a self" (the mind that entertains the various beliefs related to "me" and "mine") nor its "deformities" (the five skandhas produced by afflictions and impregnations of negative tendencies) have the characteristics of a self, since their characteristics differ from those of a self, which on their view is purely imaginary (both the grasping at a self and the skandhas are multiple, conditioned, impermanent, not all-pervading, and so on, while the self is said to have the opposite characteristics). Nor is there a self outside of this grasping and the skandhas. Therefore, such grasping is nothing but an error, just as is mistaking a rope for a snake. And since there is no self that is in bondage, liberation is simply the termination of this error—there isn't anybody or anything that is liberated. *Madhyāntavibhāga* I.4 agrees, saying that liberation is nothing but the extinction of the false imagination that does not exist as it appears, yet seemingly exists and operates within a mind that is ignorant about its own true nature, in the form of projecting the fundamentally delusive duality of subject and object, upon which we then act.

The following is a brief outline of some of the main Yogācāra notions and pedagogic templates that are employed toward the end of terminating mind's self-delusion and revealing its natural state.

The World Is Merely Mind's Own Play

One of the most inclusive notions in Buddhism in general and Yogācāra in particular is *vikalpa* (Tib. rnam rtog), with the related *kalpanā* (Tib. rtog pa), *parikalpa* (Tib. kun rtog), and their cognates. All of them have the basic sense of "constructing," "forming," "manufacturing," or "inventing." Thus, in terms of mind, they mean "creating in the mind," "forming in the imagination," and even "assuming to be real," "feigning," and "fiction." This shows that their usual translation as "thought" or "concept" is not wrong, but—particularly in a Yogācāra context—far too narrow. Fundamentally—and this is to be kept in mind throughout Buddhist texts—these terms refer to the continuous, constructive yet deluded activity of the mind that never tires of producing all kinds of dualistic appearances and experiences, thus literally building its own world.[41] Obviously, what is usually understood by "conception" or "conceptual thinking" is just a small part of this dynamic, since, from a Buddhist point of view, *vikalpa* also includes nonconceptual imagination and even what appears as outer objects and sense consciousnesses—literally everything that goes on in a dualistic mind, be it an object or a subject, conscious or not.[42] Vasubandhu's *Triṃśikā* 20–21ab says:

> Whichever entity is imagined
> By whichever imagination
> Is the imaginary nature,
> Which is unfindable.
>
> But the other-dependent nature
> Is the imagination that arises from conditions.

The meaning of "imagination" as an essentially deluded, dualistic, and illusory mental activity is particularly highlighted by the classical Yogācāra terms *abhūtaparikalpa* ("false imagination," lit. "imagination of what is unreal")[43] and *parikalpita* ("the imaginary," one of the three natures), with the latter being everything that appears as the division into subject and object that is produced by false imagination. The following passages serve to identify what false imagination is and its extent. For example, *Madhyāntavibhāga* I.8ab says:

> False imagination [consists of]
> The minds and mental factors of the three realms.

Vasubandhu's *Madhyāntavibhāgabhāṣya* on I.1 states:

> Here, false imagination is the imagination of apprehender and apprehended.[44]

Sthiramati's *Ṭīkā* elaborates on this:

> False imagination means that duality is unreal (or false) in it, or that [duality] is imagined by it. The word "false" indicates that it does not exist as it imagines [itself] in the form of being apprehender and apprehended. The word "imagination" indicates that referents are not found as they are imagined. Thus, being free from apprehender and apprehended is explained to be the characteristic of this [false imagination]. So, what is this [false imagination]? Without further differentiation, false imagination consists of the minds and mental factors of past, present, and future, which serve as causes and results, comprise the three realms, are beginningless, terminated by nirvāṇa, and conform with saṃsāra. But when differentiated, it is the imagination of the apprehender and the apprehended. Here, the imagination of the apprehended is consciousness appearing as [outer] referents and sentient beings. The imagination of the apprehender is consciousness appearing as a self and cognition. "Duality" refers to apprehender and apprehended, with the apprehended being forms and so on, and the apprehender being the eye consciousness and so on.[45]

Rongtön Shéja Künrig's[46] (1367–1449) commentary on the *Abhisamayālaṃkāra* explains:

> All the many kinds of conceptions that are mentioned in the scriptures are included in false imagination, because they have the aspects of the three realms appearing as the duality of apprehender and apprehended under the sway of latent tendencies. False imagination is threefold—the conceptions that are the mere appearance as the duality of apprehender and apprehended; those that have the aspect of coarse states of mind; and those that have the aspect of the appearance of terms and their referents. The first

> consists of the mere appearance, under the sway of latent tendencies, of apprehender and apprehended being different. The second is what the abhidharma explains as the confused mental chatter that is included in the portions of [the mental factors of] intention and prajñā. The third is the clinging to referents through following names.[47]

In sum, this means that "imagination" includes all eight consciousnesses with their accompanying mental factors as well as their respective objects. As for all of this appearing, but actually being unreal, the mind's own confused play, *Mahāyānasūtrālaṃkāra* XI.15 states:

> False imagination is explained
> To be just like an illusion.
> Just as the aspect in which an illusion [appears],
> It is explained as the mistakenness of duality.

The *Bhāṣya* adds that false imagination should be known to be the other-dependent nature, which is also stated in XI.40cd. Furthermore, verses 4–5 of the *Triṃśikā* declare:

> What appears here? The imagination of what is nonexistent.[48]
> How does it appear? By way of having the character of duality.
> What is its nonexistence with that [duality]?
> The very nature of nonduality in it.
>
> What is the imagination of the nonexistent here?
> It is the mind that imagines in certain ways what [does not exist],
> [But its] referents, which it imagines like that,
> Are absolutely never found in these ways.

Sometimes, the opposite of false imagination—correct imagination—is also presented. The latter refers to the mind being engaged in cultivating the antidotes for false imagination on the Buddhist path. "Correct imagination" refers to increasingly more refined—but still more or less dualistic—mental processes or creations that serve as the remedies for respectively coarser kinds of obscuring mental creations, perceptions, and misconceptions (false imagination). Initially, on the paths of accumulation and preparation, such remedial activities are conceptual in a rather obvious way, such as meditating on the repulsiveness of the body as an antidote against desire, or cultivating bodhicitta through contemplating the kindness of one's parents and so on. More subtle approaches would include familiarizing with momentary impermanence or personal and phenomenal identitylessness. From the path of seeing onward, all coarse conceptions of ordinary sentient beings (even the remedial ones) have ceased. However, during the first seven bhūmis, there are still subtle concepts about true reality, and on the last three bhūmis, about attaining the final fruition of buddhahood. In other words, though phenomena are not taken as real anymore, on the first seven bhūmis, there is still the apprehending of characteristics, and on the last three bhūmis, there is still a subtle tendency of duality. In brief, since the remedial wisdom that consumes what is to be relinquished still depends on what it relinquishes and still entails subtle reference points with regard to the dharmadhātu,[49] it must eventually and naturally subside too, once even its most subtle fuel (the apprehending of characteristics and duality) is burnt up. Using the example of washing a stained shirt, remedial wisdom would correspond to the detergent used to wash away the stains. Obviously, after the detergent performed its function, both it and the stains would need to be removed from the shirt in order for it to be considered clean—from the perspective of the clean shirt itself, both stains and detergent are dirt. Thus, though correct imagination is the remedy for false imagination, both are still "imagination" in the sense that, from the perspective of the sole unmistaken cognition of a buddha, even the realizations on the bhūmis are not final and have to be transcended. As for the "nonconceptual wisdom" of buddhahood, it is the mind's ultimate cognitive capacity that is not impaired by any imaginations or mental fictions—in it, there is no delusional need or impulse to construct anything. Thus, a more literal rendering of the term would be "nonimaginative" or "nonconstructive" wisdom, whose facets or functions are the four wisdoms explained below.[50]

"Mind-Only?"

Everything being mind's imagination leads to the most well-known, but also most misunderstood notions of the Yogācāra School—*cittamātra* or *vijñaptimātra*. Very often, it is still said that these terms mean that outer objects do not exist and everything is "only mind," with "mind" being the only thing that really or ultimately exists. However, when looking at what the Yogācāra texts themselves say, this is a gross misrepresentation. The beginning of Vasubandhu's *Viṃśatikāvṛtti* says:

> In the mahāyāna, the three realms are presented as being mere cognizance (*vijñaptimātra*). The sūtras say, "O sons of the Victor, all three realms are mere mind (*cittamātra*)." . . . Here, the word "mind" has the sense of [mind] being associated with [its mental factors]. "Mere" has the meaning of excluding referents.
>
> All this is mere cognizance
> Because of the appearance of nonexistent referents,
> Just as the seeing of nonexistent strands of hair
> In someone with blurred vision.

Like many other Yogācāra texts, Vasubandu's indeed continues by denying the existence of material outer objects, but the full purpose of teaching *cittamātra* is much vaster—realizing phenomenal identitylessness. Moreover, in this process, mere mind itself is no exception to being identityless. The *Viṃśatikāvṛtti* on verse 10 says:

> How does the teaching on mere cognizance serve as the entrance to phenomenal identitylessness? It is to be understood that mere cognizance makes the appearances of form and so on arise, but that there is no phenomenon whatsoever that has the characteristic of form and so on. "But if there is no phenomenon in any respect at all, then also mere cognizance does not exist, so how can it be presented as such?" Entering into phenomenal identitylessness does not mean that there is no phenomenon in any respect at all. . . . It refers to the identitylessness in the sense of an imaginary identity, that is, a nature of phenomena as imagined by childish beings, which is the imaginary [nature, consisting of fictional identities] such as apprehender and apprehended. But it is not [meant] in the sense of [the nonexistence of] the inexpressible identity that is the object of the buddhas.[51] Likewise, one enters into the identitylessness of this very mere cognizance as well, in the sense of [it lacking] any identity imagined by yet another cognizance. It is for this reason that, through the presentation of mere cognizance, one enters into the identitylessness of all phenomena, but not through the complete denial of their [relative] existence. Also, otherwise, [mere] cognizance would be the referent of another cognizance, and thus [a state of] mere cognizance would not be established, since it [still] has a referent.[52]

Hall further comments on this as follows:

> *Vijñapti* designates the basic phenomenon of conscious experience, without requiring its separation into object, subject, and act of cognition. . . . To translate *vijñapti* as "representation" conveys its "public" aspect, but seems to imply representation of something. . . . On the contrary, . . . when *vijñapti* is qualified as "*vijñapti*-only," it cannot be meant as a representation of anything else, especially not of an external object. . . . As is so often the case in Buddhist philosophy, Vasubandhu is consciously navigating between two extremes, which in this case may be called realism and idealism.
>
> In negative terms, *vijñapti-mātra* rules out the realist extreme: substantial external objects of cognition are denied. However, *vijñapti-mātra* has also a positive connotation, and the fact that Vasubandhu here affirms precisely *vijñapti*—rather than *vijñāna* or *citta*, which might be more easily misunderstood—seems to indicate an intent to avoid the idealist extreme as well. What is exclusively affirmed is not consciousness as an abiding entity, but the content of momentary acts of consciousness. When this *vijñapti* is equated with *citta*, *manas*, and *vijñāna*, it follows that mind itself is *vijñapti-mātra*: it consists of nothing else than the contents of momentary mental acts. The intention here is not to reduce the material to the mental, but to deny the dichotomy, while affirming that the basic reality is more usefully discussed in the terms belonging to a correct understanding of the mental.
>
> . . . Vasubandhu points out that this teaching of *dharma-nairātmya* works only when *vijñapti-mātra* itself is understood to be *vijñapti*-only. Clearly, no reification of consciousness is intended here. . . .
>
> The doctrine of *vijñapti-mātra* is not the metaphysical assertion of a transcendental reality consisting of "mind-only." It is a practical injunction to suspend judgment: "Stop at the bare percept; no need to posit any entity behind it."
>
> Rather than asserting "mind-only" as the true nature of unconditioned reality, Vasubandhu presents "mind-only" as a description of our delusion: the dreams of this sleep from which the Buddha has awakened. It is, after all, saṃsāra that is declared to be *vijñapti-*

> *mātra*. Yet if "mind-only" is merely skepticism about reified external entities, how does it avoid the opposite extreme of reductionism? The world is neither completely real, nor completely unreal, but like a dream. A dream has its own presence and continuity, but its objects lack the substantiality of external objects. Whether common-sense things or Abhidharmic dharmas, dream-objects are bare percepts. If the dream-world saṃsāra is "mind-only" then freedom and the Buddhist path are possible—we can "change our minds." If the realms of meditation are "mind-only" then one can create a counter-dream within the dream of the world's delusion. Most important, one can awaken from a dream.[53]

Thus, that "mere mind" is being constantly referred to in Yogācāra texts as the delusional perception of what does not exist (these texts moreover abounding with dreams, illusions, and so on as examples for it) hardly suggests that said momentary mental activities exist in a real or ultimate way. In addition, Asvabhāva's *Mahāyānasaṃgrahopanibandhana* explicitly says that "mere mind" refers only to the mistaken minds and mental factors of saṃsāra (the realities of suffering and its origin), but not to the reality of the path:

> As for [the statement in the sūtras], "[All three realms are] mere mind," "mind" and "cognizance" are equivalent. The word "only" eliminates [the existence of] referents, and by virtue of [such referents] not existing, [the existence of] an apprehender is eliminated too, because [both] are imaginary. [However,] since this [mind] does not arise without the mental factors, these mental factors are not negated. As it is said, "Without mental factors, mind never arises." . . . "All three realms" refer to cognizance appearing as the three realms. Through saying, "all three realms," it is held that the minds and mental factors that are associated with craving, such as desire, and contained in the three realms are just mere cognizance. However, this does not refer to [the minds and mental factors in meditative equipoise] that constitute the reality of the path (those that focus on suchness and those that focus on the other-dependent [nature]) and those during subsequent attainment. For, they are not made into what is "mine" through the cravings of engaging in the three realms, are remedies, and are unmistaken.[54]

Moreover, many Yogācāra works proceed by explicitly and repeatedly making it clear that "mere mind" does not exist and is to be relinquished in order to attain the full realization of buddhahood. For example, *Mahāyānasūtrālaṃkāra* VI.7–8 says:

> Understanding that referents are mere [mental] chatter,
> [Bodhisattvas] dwell in mere mind appearing as these.
> Then, they directly perceive the dharmadhātu,
> Thus being free from the characteristic of duality.
>
> The mind is aware that nothing other than mind exists.
> Then, it is realized that mind does not exist either.
> The intelligent ones are aware that both do not exist
> And abide in the dharmadhātu, in which these are absent.[55]

The *Bhāṣya* on these verses comments that, once bodhisattvas realize that referents are nothing but mental chatter, they dwell in mere mind appearing as such referents. This represents the four levels of the path of preparation. Subsequently, on the path of seeing, bodhisattvas directly perceive the dharmadhātu free from the characteristic of the duality of apprehender and apprehended. As for directly perceiving the dharmadhātu, having realized that there is no apprehended object that is other than mind, bodhisattvas realize that mere mind does not exist either, because without something apprehended, there is no apprehender.[56] Also *Abhisamayālaṃkāra* V.7 says on the culmination of the path of seeing:

> If apprehended referents do not exist like that,
> Can these two be asserted as the apprehenders of anything?
> Thus, their characteristic is the emptiness
> Of a nature of an apprehender.

The above two verses from the *Mahāyānasūtrālaṃkāra* represent one of the classic descriptions of the "four yogic practices" found in many mahāyāna texts in general and Yogācāra works in particular. These four steps of realization are:

(1) Outer objects are observed to be nothing but mind (*upalambhaprayoga, dmigs pa'i sbyor ba*)

(2) Thus, outer objects are not observed as such (*anupalambhaprayoga mi, dmigs pa'i sbyor ba*)

(3) With outer objects being unobservable, a mind cognizing them is not observed either (*upalambhānupalambhaprayoga, dmigs pa mi dmigs pa'i sbyor ba*)

(4) Not observing both, nonduality is observed (*nopalambhopalambha-prayoga, mi dmigs dmigs pa'i sbyor ba*).

Thus, stages (1)–(3)—and thus the notion of *cittamātra*—are progressively dealt with on the bodhisattva path only up through the end of the path of preparation. Stage (4) marks the path of seeing (the first bhūmi), on which bodhisattvas have to let go of the notion of *cittamātra* as well. This progression is also clearly expressed in *Mahāyānasaṃgraha* III.11–14, specifically matching these four stages with the four stages of the path of preparation (heat, peak, poised readiness, and the supreme mundane dharma). Here too, the notion of *cittamātra* is said to be relinquished:

> After this [stage of poised readiness], the destruction of the discriminating notion of mere cognizance represents the samādhi that immediately precedes [the path of seeing]. This is to be regarded as the stage of the supreme mundane dharma.[57]

The text also speaks about the ultimate purpose and function of the notion of mere cognizance:

> Why do [bodhisattvas] engage in mere cognizance? The cognitions of [nonconceptual and unmistaken] supramundane calm abiding and superior insight focus on [all] the miscellaneous dharmas [of the mahāyāna, whose general characteristic is suchness], and the subsequently attained [nonconceptual] cognition in terms of various kinds of cognizance [realizes all phenomena to be nothing but imaginations of apprehender and apprehended]. Through these [cognitions], they relinquish all seeds in the ālaya-consciousness together with their causes, and thus increase the seeds of making contact with the dharmakāya [—cultivating the latent tendencies for listening of the mahāyāna. Finally,] through undergoing the fundamental change of state, they perfectly accomplish all the buddhadharmas and thus attain omniscient wisdom. This is why they engage [in mere cognizance].
>
> Since the subsequently attained cognition regards everything that arises in the ālaya-consciousness and all characteristics of mere cognizance as being like illusions and such, it arises in a naturally unmistaken way. Therefore, these bodhisattvas are always unmistaken in their teachings on causes and results, just as illusionists are with regard to the phenomena in the illusions they produced.[58]

In other words, like so many other general Buddhist and specific Yogācāra notions, *cittamātra* (or *vijñaptimātra*) is no exception to simply being an expedient pedagogic tool to realize a certain level on the path. However, it is neither the final realization, nor to be reified in any way (thus becoming an obstacle to this very realization), but—as in the above example of cleaning a shirt—to be discarded once its intended function has been accomplished. In connection with the four yogic practices, the same crucial point is expressed in many other Yogācāra texts too, such as *Madhyāntavibhāga* I.6–7:

> Based on observation,
> Nonobservation arises.
> Based on nonobservation,
> Nonobservation arises.
>
> Thus, observation is established
> As the nature of nonobservation.
> Therefore, observation and nonobservation
> Are to be understood as equal.

Sthiramati's *Ṭīkā* comments:

> There is no difference between the nonobservation of referents and the observation as mere cognizance in that [both] do not exist. Thus, they are to be understood as equal. . . . [The latter] is just called "observation," since an unreal object appears [for it]. However, since there is no [actual] referent, nothing is observed by this ["observation"]. Therefore, ultimately, its nature is nonobservation. . . . Hence, it is said that it does not exist as the nature of observation. In such observation, neither is the nature of observation to be eliminated, nor is the nature of nonobservation to be established. They are the same in that they are undifferentiable. . . . "So why is [mere] cognition called 'observation' then?" In its nature, it is nonobservation, but [it is designated] in this way, since an unreal object appears [for it], as this is the convention in the world and the treatises.[59]

The *Dharmadharmatāvibhāga* states:

> Through [referents] being observed in this way, they are observed as mere cognizance.

By virtue of observing them as mere cognizance,
Referents are not observed,
And through not observing referents,
Mere cognizance is not observed [either].
Through not observing this [mere cognizance],
One enters into the observation of both being without difference.
This nonobservation of a difference between these two
Is nonconceptual wisdom.
It is without object and without observing,
Since it is characterized
By the nonobservation of all characteristics.[60]

Verses 36–38 of Vasubandhu's *Trisvabhāvanirdeśa* agree:

Through the observation of it being merely mind,
A knowable object is not observed.
Through not observing a knowable object,
Mind is not observed [either].

Through not observing both,
The dharmadhātu is observed.
Through observing the dharmadhātu,
Mastery is observed.[61]

Having gained mastery,
Through accomplishing the welfare of oneself and others,
The wise attain unsurpassable enlightenment
With its nature of the three kāyas.

Verses 26–30 of his *Triṃśikā* say:

For as long as consciousness
Does not dwell in mere cognizance,
The aftereffects of dualistic apprehension
Will not come to a halt.

But "all this is mere cognizance"
Refers to this observing too—
Anything that is propped up in front [of one's mind]
Means not dwelling in "merely that [cognizance]."

When consciousness itself
Does not observe any focal object,
It rests in the very being of mere consciousness,
Since there is no apprehender without something apprehended.[62]

Then, it is no-mind and nonreferential—
It is supramundane wisdom.
This is the fundamental change of state
And the relinquishment of the twofold impregnations of negative tendencies.

It is the uncontaminated dhātu
That is inconceivable, virtuous, stable,
And blissful—the vimuktikāya
Called the dharma[kāya] of the great sage.

As in line 28c above, sometimes, Yogācāras differentiate between "mere mind" (*cittamātra*), "mere consciousness" (*vijñānamātra*), and "mere cognizance" (*vijñaptimātra*) on the one hand, and "the very being or nature of mere mind, consciousness, and cognizance" (adding the suffixes *-tā* or *-tva* to the former terms), with the latter indicating the actual nature of the former, that is, the nondual dharmadhātu or nonconceptual wisdom. Another way to put this is that *cittamātra* and so on usually just correspond to false imagination or the other-dependent nature, while *cittamātratā* and such refer to its true nature—the perfect nature.

Also, as Sthiramati states in his introduction to the *Triṃśikābhāṣya*, one of the main objectives of the *Triṃśikā* is to help those who do not correctly understand *cittamātra*, due to their attachment to the supposed reality of persons and phenomena, to fully realize the actuality of personal and phenomenal identitylessness in order to accomplish the true fruition of the teaching of *cittamātra*.[63] In general, Sthiramati explains that demonstrating that phenomena do not exist permanently (that is, as having an intrinsic nature of their own) means to avoid the extreme of superimposition, while to say that they are "mere cognizance" serves to avoid the extreme of utter denial. Thus, there is also a difference in Yogācāra texts between mind, consciousness, and cognizance on the one hand, and "mere mind," and so on on the other hand. Mind or consciousness stands for the delusive activity of mental construction itself as well as the fictional reality it constructs, while "mere mind" and so on denote the realization that this supposed reality is not ultimately real, but only the plethora of one's own ongoing mental chatter. Thus, on the path, what appears as one's personal projected universe of the false duality of subject and object is first reduced to seeing the projector of this illusory world—one's very own mind, called "false imagination," "*cittamātra*," or "the other-dependent nature." Then, once the "bare structure" of the latter without the overlay of delusional fictions (the imaginary nature) is seen, the truth of *cittamātra* is realized, since to realize the true nature of false imagination or the other-dependent nature as always being free from such overlay is called the attainment of the perfect nature, which is nothing but the nonconceptual wisdom of seeing the ultimate essence of the other-dependent nature. This is also the attainment of suchness, the dharmadhātu, and so on as the final true realization of *cittamātra*. Hsüan-tsang states in his *Vijñaptimātratāsiddhi*:

> Since *citta* and *caittas*[64] depend on other things to arise (*paratantra*), they are like a magician's trick, not truly substantial ("real") entities. But so as to oppose false attachments to the view that external to *citta* and *caittas* there are perceptual-objects (ching, *viśaya*) [composed of] real, substantial entities, we say that the only existent is consciousness. But if you become attached to the view that *vijñapti-mātra* is something truly real and existent, that's the same as being attached to external perceptual-objects, i.e., it becomes just another dharma-attachment [and definitely not liberating].[65]

Paramārtha says the following in his commentary on verses 17–18 of Vasubandhu's *Triṃśikā*:

> What does it mean to establish the principle of Consciousness-Only? The meaning, fundamentally, is to dispense with sense objects and to dispense with the mind. Now if the objective world does not exist, Consciousness-Only would also be destroyed. This is what I mean by "the principle of Consciousness-Only is upheld." This is called the pure component [of consciousness] because both defilements and the objective world do not exist [in the system of Consciousness-Only]. . . .
>
> For this reason, outside of consciousness no events can take place. This is why it is called the impure component, for only the prior sense object is dispensed with but not consciousness itself. . . .
>
> Q: If one dispenses with sense objects but retains consciousness, then one can say that there is a principle of Consciousness-Only.

> But if both the sense object and consciousness are to be dispensed with, how can consciousness [of any kind] be maintained?
>
> A: One establishes that Consciousness-Only temporarily dispenses with the sense object but retains the [existence of] mind. In the final analysis, however, one dispenses with sense objects in order to empty the mind. This is the correct meaning. Therefore, [when] both the sense object and consciousness are dissolved, this principle is upheld. [When] both the sense object and consciousness are dissolved, this [state] is identical to the true nature [*tattva* or *tathatā*]. The true nature is identical to Pure Consciousness (*amala-vijñāna*). Additionally, we can say in the final analysis that this is Pure Consciousness.[66]

In his comments on verses 21–22 and 28,[67] Paramārtha repeats his stance of *cittamātra* meaning the nonexistence of both objects and consciousness. On verses 23–25, where the imaginary, the other-dependent, and the perfect natures are described as the threefold lack of nature (see below), he concludes that the principle of *cittamātra* is explained in order to indicate this threefold lack of nature.[68]

In the light of all this, it seems as (un)justified to call the Yogācāra School "Mind-Only School" or "Mere Mentalism" (*sems tsam pa*) as it would be to refer to the Madhyamaka School as the "Name-Only School" (*ming tsam pa*). Just as the notions of *cittamātra* or *vijñaptimātra* play a significant role in the Yogācāra School, the notions of *nāmamātra* (name-only) and *prajñaptimātra* (imputation-only) play a significant role in Madhyamaka, describing the fact that all phenomena are merely nominal and imputed, but they neither represent the ultimate or most essential feature of Madhyamaka, nor encompass its much larger scope. Rather, all the above notions are explicitly to be transcended in their respective systems and not to be reified, or even to be put forth as ultimate reality. In fact, all four standard Indian Buddhist schools (Vaibhāṣika, Sautrāntika, Yogācāra, and Madhyamaka) were named after their most essential or encompassing features and not after something that they themselves explain to be relinquished.

Mind's Play Has Many Faces

In Yogācāra texts, false imagination, as the most general term for mind's deluded mode of operation, is further divided in several ways in terms of its various specific functions. In all of these cases (and this is also true for most other notions, such as the skandhas, in Buddhism in general), it cannot be overemphasized that what is described are dynamic processes and not any kinds of static entities or states. Thus, when Yogācāras speak about two, three, or eight consciousnesses (or three natures, five wisdoms, and three kāyas, for that matter), they in no way mean two, three, or eight distinct "minds," or even just static properties of a single mind. Rather, different numbers of consciousness stand for different functions of the mind, all of which operate as momentarily impermanent and changing processes (like constantly moving, changing, and interacting currents in the ocean), none of which is truly existent. *Madhyāntavibhāga* I.3 speaks of mind displaying as all kinds of seeming expressions in terms of subject and object:

> Consciousness arises as the appearance of referents,
> Sentient beings, a self, and cognizance,
> [But] it does not have an [external] referent.
> Since that does not exist, it does not exist either.

Madhyāntavibhāga I.9 specifies the subjective side of this further:

> A single one is the conditioning consciousness.
> The remaining entail experience.
> Experience, delimitation,
> And setting in motion are the mental factors.[69]

Thus, there are two main kinds of consciousness—the ālaya-consciousness, as the most basic ground of mind, and the other seven consciousnesses that operate out of this ground and engage their respective objects (which are also nothing but different aspects of this basic ground). According to the *Madhyāntavibhāgabhāṣya*, the ālaya-consciousness is the "conditioning consciousness," because it is the foundation of all other consciousnesses, which entail experiencing their respective objects. Among mental factors, feeling refers to pleasant, unpleasant, and indifferent experiences; discrimination delimits the characteristics of objects; and the other mental factors set consciousness in motion to engage objects.

Vasubandhu's *Triṃśikā* presents a threefold model of the dynamic evolution or display of saṃsāric mind:

> [Mind's] behavior in terms of self and phenomena
> Operates in many different ways

In the modulation of consciousness.
This modulation is threefold—

Maturation, what is called "thinking,"
And the cognition of objects.
Here, maturation is the "ālaya-consciousness,"
Which contains all the seeds.
. . .
What operates by resting on the [ālaya-consciousness]
Is the consciousness called "mentation,"
Which has it as its focal object, its nature being self-centeredness.

It is always associated with the four afflictions,
And obscured yet neutral.
. . .
This is the second modulation.
The third is the observation
Of the six kinds of objects . . .[70]

Thus, Vasubandhu's three basic modulations (*pariṇāma*) of consciousness are the ālaya-consciousness, the afflicted mind,[71] and the remaining six consciousnesses (the five sense consciousnesses and the mental consciousness). In Yogācāra texts, these are also referred to as the triad of "mind" (Skt. citta, Tib. sems), "mentation" (Skt. manas, Tib. yid),[72] and "consciousness" (Skt. vijñāna, Tib. rnam shes), respectively. As for the eight consciousnesses, they are described in detail in AC and NYC below, which also provide copious quotations. So, to highlight some of the essential features here, the ālaya-consciousness is nothing but the sum total of the virtuous, nonvirtuous, and neutral tendencies that make up the mind stream of a sentient being. Thus, it is not like a container separate from its contents, but resembles the constant flow of all the water drops that are labeled "a river." In other words, there is no other underlying, permanent substratum or entity apart from the momentary mental impulses that constitute this ever-changing stream of various latent mental tendencies. Due to certain conditions—mainly the stirring of the afflicted mind (comparable to stirring by a wind or strong current)—various momentary appearances of subject and object manifest. What seem to be external (objects), internal (mind and the sense faculties), or both (the body) are not so, but just different aspects of the ālaya-consciousness appearing as if close or far. Right after each moment of this dualistic interaction of subjects and objects, the imprints created by them merge back into—or are "stored"—in the ālaya, just as waves on the surface of a river emerge from and remerge into it, every time interacting and criss-crossing with other such waves, and thus changing the overall current. In this way, the ālaya-consciousness is both the cause for saṃsāric appearances and their result, that is, their imprints that reemerge later. This does not mean that the ālaya actively creates anything, it is just the dynamic network of various causes and conditions interacting, which is otherwise known as dependent origination. In this way, it is said to be equivalent to fundamental ignorance and the karma accumulated by it, thus serving as the basis for all appearances and experiences in saṃsāra, which at the same time represent the sum of all factors to be relinquished in order to attain nirvāṇa. Thus, the ālaya-consciousness fully ceases to exist only upon the attainment of buddhahood. As the *Laṅkāvatārasūtra* and others say, because of all of this, it is not to be misconceived as an ātman or a creator.[73]

The afflicted mind is simply another expression for mind not recognizing its own nature. Technically speaking, it is the consciousness that solely focuses inwardly and thus mistakes the empty aspect of the ālaya-consciousness as being a self and its lucid aspect as what is "other." It is said to be so close to the ālaya that it misperceives it in this way, very much like when one cannot see a table clearly or even recognize it as a table, when one presses one's eye against its surface. Usually, we think that not seeing or recognizing something is due to being too far away from it, but, as in this example, the afflicted mind is the most fundamental case of not recognizing something due to being too close to it. This is the starting point of fundamental subject-object duality, which then ramifies into the appearances of the remaining six consciousnesses and their objects, all of them being constantly filtered and afflicted through this basic self-concern. Thus, these consciousnesses are always accompanied by the three primary mental afflictions (desire for what seems pleasurable, aversion toward what seems unpleasurable, and indifference toward what seems to be neither) as well as countless secondary mental disturbances based on these afflictions. Karmic actions (trying to obtain what seems desirable and get rid of what seems not) ensue, inevitably leading to various kinds of suffering sooner or later. Thus, the wheel of saṃsāra spins.[74] Asaṅga's *Mahāyānasaṃgraha* describes "mentation" as follows:

> Among those [consciousnesses], mentation is twofold. Since it is the support that acts as the immediate condition, the "mentation which is [any] consciousness that has just ceased" is the support for [the arising of] consciousness. The second is the afflicted mind, which is always congruently associated[75] with the four afflictions of

> the views about a real personality, self-conceit, attachment to the self, and ignorance. This is the support for the afflictedness of consciousness. [Thus,] consciousness is produced by virtue of the first [aspect of mentation] as its support, while the second one makes it afflicted. [Mentation] is a consciousness, because it cognizes objects. Since it is [both] immediately preceding and self-centered, mentation has two aspects.[76]

Thus, the part of mentation that is the afflicted mind constantly entails a set of four subtle afflictions. Just as is the afflicted mind itself, these four are largely instinctive and unconscious, with any conscious thinking such as, "I am so and so" belonging to the conceptual part of the sixth consciousness, which superimposes more conscious and coarse layers of ego-clinging, based on the gut-level sense of "me" that constitutes the afflicted mind. Being a consciousness, it is moreover constantly associated with the five neutral omnipresent mental factors: impulse, feeling, discrimination, contact, and mental engagement (as is the ālaya-consciousness). However, despite being accompanied by these four afflictions, in itself, the afflicted mind is neutral in the sense of being neither virtuous nor nonvirtuous. For example, if we think, "I will help my sick mother," the ensuing action will be virtuous, and if we think, "I will kill someone," the ensuing action will be nonvirtuous. Still, in both cases, the clinging to "I" is the same. Thus, the very fact that the afflicted mind is essentially neutral makes it at all possible to accumulate virtue (at least in its still-contaminated form), despite one's grasping at a self. Finally, however, since the afflicted mind—the grasping at "me" and "mine"—is the root of all other afflictions, such as desire and anger, it must be relinquished. In other words, since this clinging to a self is the opposite of the prajñā that realizes the lack of a self, it obscures liberation from saṃsāra.[77]

As for the term "mentation," despite being primarily used for the afflicted mind in Yogācāra texts, it is also generally used for the mental-sense faculty (equivalent to the immediate condition) as well as the sixth consciousness. Matters are further complicated by texts that provide overlapping descriptions and functions of all these terms. When the Indian Yogācāra texts (as does the *Mahāyānasaṃgraha* above) speak of the "immediate condition," they discuss it as either being related to the afflicted mind (as above), or in the context of the four conditions (causal, dominant, immediate, and object condition). Thus, the commentaries on the above quote from the *Mahāyānasaṃgraha* say that the first kind of mentation corresponds to the "dhātu of mentation" and the "āyatana of mentation" (as in the *Abhidharmakośa*), there being thus no mentation distinct from the six consciousnesses—any one of these six having just ceased is mentation. The first five consciousnesses have the five physical sense faculties as their supports, but the sixth consciousness does not have such a support. Consequently, in order to attribute a support to this consciousness too, mentation (or the mental-sense faculty) is what serves as its support (which is nothing but a previous moment of any one of the six consciousnesses having ceased and thus triggering the next one). In relation to the mental consciousness which immediately follows one of these consciousnesses that have just passed, they serve as its immediate condition and the support for its arising. It is in this sense that Sthiramati's commentary on *Mahāyānasūtrālaṃkāra* IX.42 says that the arising of the mental consciousness relies on the afflicted mind, just as the arising of an eye consciousness relies on the eye sense faculty. Also, Sthiramati's *Pañcaskandhaprakaraṇavaibhāṣya* states:

> Any one of the six consciousnesses, such as the eye [consciousness], that has ceased is present as the entity which is the support for the arising of the immediately following consciousnesses. Therefore, since they function as the supports for the immediately following minds, they are called "mentation." . . . The immediate condition is consciousness immediately upon its having ceased.[78]

Guṇaprabha's *Pañcaskandhavivaraṇa* says:

> As for [mentation] "functioning as a mental support," this refers to what is present in being the six operating consciousnesses. As [*Abhidharmakośa* I.17ab] explains:
>
> > Mentation is the consciousness
> > Immediately after [any of] the six [consciousnesses] have passed.
>
> Any of these [six] having ceased is what is called "mentation." For example, a certain son is called the "father" of someone else, and a certain fruition is called the "seed" of something else. Likewise, when the six results that consist of the operating consciousnesses having ceased serve as the support for the arising of other [subsequent] consciousnesses, they are referred to as "functioning as mental supports."[79]

Thus, "mentation" can either designate the mental-sense faculty (which equals the immediate condition), the afflicted mind, or the seventh consciousness as consisting of both the afflicted mind and the immediate condition (or immediate mind).[80] However, in specific Yogācāra terminology, what mentation actually refers to is only the afflicted mind. As Sthiramati comments on Vasubandhu's *Pañcaskandhaprakaraṇa*:

> "In actual fact, mentation is what focuses on the ālaya-consciousness" means that the afflicted mind permanently focuses on the ālaya-consciousness as being a self, because it is congruently associated with focusing on a self in terms of being ignorant about it, [entertaining] views about it, being proud of it, and being attached to it. It always exists by virtue of having the character of self-centeredness. In actual fact, this is what is called "mentation." To refer to [the state of] consciousness immediately upon the six collections of consciousnesses, such as the eye [consciousness], having ceased as "mentation" is in order to establish [this state] as the location of [the arising of] the sixth—the mental—consciousness, but not because it has the aspect of self-centeredness. Therefore, in actual fact, it is not mentation per se.[81]

As the *Abhidharmasamucchaya* and many other texts explain, the afflicted mind is the ever-present ego-clinging in saṃsāric beings and even in those on the Buddhist path of learning:

> Except for when the path [of seeing] has become manifest [in one's mind stream], in the meditative absorption of cessation,[82] and the level of nonlearning, it is always present in virtuous, nonvirtuous, and neutral states.[83]

In terms of the hīnayāna path, this means that the afflicted mind is not present in the meditative equipoises of all noble beings from stream-enterers up through arhats, since the realization of the ultimate is incompatible with views about a self, and since arhats have relinquished all afflicted phenomena of the three realms.[84] In terms of the mahāyāna path, the afflicted mind is out of function during the meditative equipoises of bodhisattvas from the first bhūmi onward, because both personal and phenomenal identitylessness are directly realized. However, by virtue of habitual latent tendencies, it still operates during the subsequent attainment of the first seven bhūmis (therefore, they are called "impure"). On the eighth bhūmi, the afflicted mind is fully relinquished. From a mahāyāna perspective, the afflicted mind is inactive in the meditative equipoise of arhats with remainder, but its latent tendencies still show in their phases of subsequent attainment. In arhats without remainder, these tendencies are not manifest, since such arhats are in constant meditative equipoise. However, together with the remaining cognitive obscurations, they constitute what the mahāyāna calls "the ground of the latent tendencies of ignorance."

There is not much to say on the remaining six consciousnesses, except for the sixth one being explained as twofold in the teachings on valid cognition (*pramāṇa*). These two are the (more commonly known) thinking mind and what is called "mental valid perception." The latter refers to the part of the sixth consciousness that, like the five sense consciousnesses, is able to directly perceive sense objects (such as visible forms) upon being triggered by a preceding moment of sense consciousness (such as a visual consciousness). Together with the five sense consciousnesses, mental perception represents the outwardly oriented consciousnesses, while the thinking mind focuses on (more or less) conceptual mental images, which may or may not be triggered by preceding sense perceptions (such as seeing, reading, or hearing about something, and then thinking about it).

In general, it is said that the sense consciousnesses and the mental consciousness are "unstable" consciousnesses, that is, they do not operate at all times (such as when being fast asleep). The afflicted mind and the ālaya-consciousness are "stable" (they operate even during deep sleep and coma). However, in certain meditative states, even the afflicted mind temporarily sinks back into the ālaya-consciousness, but rearises from it once one rises from such meditations. In a way, the ālaya-consciousness can be understood as referring to nothing but the ever-unimpeded underlying stream of the vivid clarity aspect of mind, otherwise mind would be like a stone, or would have to be switched on again out of nothing upon waking up in the morning, or coming out of a coma or deep meditation.

Several texts by Paramārtha speak about the *amalavijñāna* ("pure or stainless consciousness") as a ninth kind of consciousness.[85] It refers to the unconditioned, changeless, permanent mind unaffected by any impurities, identical with suchness as the ultimate. This *amalavijñāna* is said to be the foundation of the Buddhist path, while the ālaya-consciousness is the foundation of all defilements and eventually eliminated. Paramārtha also equates this *amalavijñāna* with suchness, nonconceptual wisdom, and mind's luminosity. He says that it is unmistaken and free from both the imaginary and the other-dependent natures (which comprise the manifestations of mistaken consciousness), thus being reminiscent of typical *shentong* positions.[86]

Mind Operates on Three Levels

The three "natures" or "characteristics" are the main Yogācāra pedagogic template to explain mind's operational modes when deluded and undeluded. They are the imaginary nature, the other-dependent nature, and the perfect nature.[87] In Indian, Tibetan, and Chinese texts, one finds a great number of sometimes very different presentations of what these three natures are and how they are interrelated.[88] However, if one keeps in mind that all of these models describe processes rather than three clearly separate and fixed things or realities, their descriptions are not contradictory, but just emphasize different aspects of the same dynamics. For example, it is much easier to describe the features of a book, a CD, or a flower that lie still in front of oneself than the ever-changing and interacting movements of waves on the ocean. The fluid character of all three natures is shown in the following passages from the *Mahāyānasaṃgraha*:

> In one sense, the other-dependent nature is other-dependent; in another sense, it is imaginary; and in yet another sense, it is perfect. In what sense is the other-dependent nature called "other-dependent"? It is other-dependent in that it originates from the seeds of other-dependent latent tendencies. In what sense is it called "imaginary"? Because it is both the cause of [false] imagination and what is imagined by it. In what sense is it called "perfect"? Because it does not at all exist in the way it is imagined.[89]

and

> Thus, in terms of its imaginary aspect, this very other-dependent nature is saṃsāra. In terms of its perfect aspect, it is nirvāṇa.[90]

In this vein, the other-dependent nature is the process or experiential structure in which the world presents itself as a seeming (delusive) reality for beings whose minds have a dualistic perceptual structure (which is the imaginary nature). The perfect nature is the underlying fundamental process or structure of mind's true nature and its own expressions as they are unwarped by said dualistic perceptual structure. In more technical terms, the other-dependent nature is the basic "stuff" or stratum of which all our saṃsāric experiences and appearances consist. It is the mistaken imagination that appears as the unreal entities of subject and object, because these are appearances under the sway of something "other," that is, triggered by the latent tendencies of ignorance. The other-dependent nature appears as the outer world with its various beings and objects; as one's own body; as the sense consciousnesses that perceive these objects and the conceptual consciousness that thinks about them; as the clinging to a personal self and real phenomena; and as the mental events, such as feelings, that accompany all these consciousnesses. Thus, false imagination is what creates the basic split of bare experience into seemingly real perceivers that apprehend seemingly real objects. The duality of subject and object—the imaginary nature—does not even exist on the level of seeming reality, but the mind that creates this split does exist and functions on this level. However, the other-dependent nature in no way exists ultimately, since the Yogācāra texts repeatedly describe it as illusionlike and so on, and also state that it is to be relinquished, while the perfect nature is what is to be revealed (see below).

The imaginary nature covers the entire range of what is superimposed—consciously or unconsciously—by false imagination onto the various appearances of the other-dependent nature. This starts from the most basic gut-level sense of subject-object duality—the very fact that, for example, sense objects naturally seem to appear to be "out there" and the perceiver is "here"; people naturally thinking and instinctively acting in terms of "me" and "others"; and standard notions such as "me and my body," or "me and my mind," all of which represent the imaginary nature. Progressively coarser levels of mistaken overlay include more reified conscious notions of a self and really existent phenomena up through the most rigid belief systems about what we and the world are. In other words, what appear as one's own body and mind form the bases for imputing a personal self. What appear as other beings, outer objects, and the consciousnesses that relate to them provide the bases for imputing really existent phenomena. In detail, the imaginary nature includes the aspects that appear as conceptual objects (such as the mental image of a form); the connections of names and referents (the notion that a name is the corresponding referent and the mistaking of a referent for the corresponding name); all that is apprehended through mental superimposition (such as direction, time, outer, inner, big, small, good, bad, and so on); and all nonentities (such as space). All of these exist only conventionally, as nominal objects for the dualistic consciousnesses of ordinary sentient beings, but are not established as really existent. *Mahāyānasūtrālaṃkāra* XIII.17 says:

> Just as there are neither depths nor heights
> In a perfect painting, but are seen there,
> There is never any duality in any respect
> In false imagination, but it is seen there.

The perfect nature is emptiness in the sense that what appears as other-dependent false imagination is primordially never established as the imaginary nature. As the ultimate object and the true nature of the other-dependent nature, this emptiness is the sphere of nonconceptual wisdom, and it is nothing other than phenomenal identitylessness. It is called "perfect," because it never changes into something else, is the supreme among all dharmas, and is the focal object of prajñā during the process of purifying the mind from adventitious stains. Since the dharmas of the noble ones are attained through realizing it, it is called "dharmadhātu." By virtue of its quality of never changing into something else, it is termed "suchness." Just as space, it is without any distinctions, but conventionally, the perfect nature may be presented as twofold—the unchanging perfect nature (suchness) and the unmistaken perfect nature (the nondual nonconceptual wisdom that realizes this suchness). At times, the perfect nature is also equated with the luminous nature of mind free from adventitious stains, or buddha nature. The *Mahāyānasaṃgraha* characterizes the three natures as follows:

> "In this . . . very extensive teaching of the mahāyāna . . ., how should the imaginary nature be understood?" It should be understood through the teachings on the synonyms of nonexistents. "How should the other-dependent nature be understood?" It should be understood to be like an illusion, a mirage, an optical illusion, a reflection, an echo, [the reflection of] the moon in water, and a magical creation. "How should the perfect nature be understood?" It should be understood through the teachings on the four kinds of pure dharmas. As for these four kinds of pure dharmas, (1) natural purity means suchness, emptiness, the true end, signlessness, and the ultimate. Also the dharmadhātu is just this. (2) Unstained purity refers to [the state of] this very [natural purity] not having any obscurations. (3) The purity of the path to attain this [unstained purity] consists of all the dharmas concordant with enlightenment, such as the pāramitās. (4) The pure object in order to generate this [path] is the teaching of the genuine dharma of the mahāyāna. In this way, since this [dharma] is the cause for purity, it is not the imaginary [nature]. Since it is the natural outflow of the pure dharmadhātu, it is not the other-dependent [nature either]. All completely pure dharmas are included in these four kinds [of purity].[91]

As in this passage, many Yogācāra texts emphasize the unreal nature of the other-dependent nature and that it is definitely not the ultimate existent.[92] Nevertheless, the other-dependent nature's lack of reality does not prevent the mere appearance and functioning of various seeming manifestations for the mind. The *Mahāyānasaṃgraha* continues:

> Why is the other-dependent nature taught in such a way as being like an illusion and so on? In order to eliminate the mistaken doubts of others about the other-dependent nature. . . . In order to eliminate the doubts of those others who think, "How can nonexistents become objects?" it is [taught] to be like an illusion. In order to eliminate the doubts of those who think, "How can mind and mental events arise without [outer] referents?" it is [taught] to be like a mirage. In order to eliminate the doubts of those who think, "How can likes and dislikes be experienced if there are no referents?" it is [taught] to be like a dream. In order to eliminate the doubts of those who think, "If there are no referents, how can the desired and undesired results of positive and negative actions be accomplished?" it is [taught] to be like a reflection. In order to eliminate the doubts of those who think, "How can various consciousnesses arise if there are no referents?" it is [taught to be] like an optical illusion. In order to eliminate the doubts of those who think, "How can various conventional expressions come about if there are no referents?" it is [taught] to be like an echo. In order to eliminate the doubts of those who think, "If there are no referents, how can the sphere of the meditative concentration that apprehends true actuality come about?" it is [taught] to be like [a reflection of] the moon in water. In order to eliminate the doubts of those who think, "If there are no referents, how can unerring bodhisattvas be reborn as they wish in order to accomplish their activity for sentient beings?" it is [taught] to be like a magical creation.[93]

These passages also highlight that the template of the three natures is not so much an ontological model, but primarily a soteriological one. This is also expressed in the *Mahāyānasūtrālaṃkārabhāṣya* on XIX.77–78, which says that the realization of the three natures is the special realization of bodhisattvas. As Nguyen says:

> The close association between ontology and soteriology is indeed one of the distinctive features of Buddhism as a whole, and a topic

> that was given a most thorough analytical treatment in the Yogācāra tradition. . . . In fact, from the perspective of Mahāyāna Buddhism in general and the Yogācāra School in particular, the realization of Reality in itself implies the attainment of enlightenment, that is, nirvana, or in other words, the attainment of buddhahood. This is because in Mahāyāna Buddhology, buddhahood is synonymous with Ultimate or True Reality. Put differently, within the Yogācāra world view, ontological realization is not different from soteriological attainment. Thus the realization of True Reality in this context is more than just an ontological insight into reality; it also carries broader implications and ramifications from the practical perspective of soteriology.[94]

This becomes even clearer when the three natures are also referred to as "lack of nature" and "emptiness." The *Laṅkāvatārasūtra* says:

> When scrutinized with insight,
> Neither the dependent, nor the imaginary,
> Nor the perfect [natures] exist.
> So how could insight imagine any entity?[95]

The way in which *Mahāyānasūtrālaṃkāra* XI.50–51 speaks about the lack of nature of all phenomena in general sounds exactly like what is found in prajñāpāramitā or Madhyamaka texts:

> Because [phenomena] do not exist as themselves or through an identity of their own,
> Do not dwell in a nature of their own,
> And do not exist as they are apprehended,
> Their lack of nature is asserted.
>
> The lack of nature establishes,
> With each one being the basis of the following one,
> Nonarising, nonceasing,
> Primordial peace, and parinirvāṇa.

More specifically, the *Saṃdhinirmocanasūtra*'s seventh chapter speaks at length about the lack of nature in terms of characteristics, the lack of nature in terms of arising, and the ultimate lack of nature as representing the imaginary, other-dependent, and perfect natures, respectively. Asaṅga's

Saṃdhinirmocanasūtrabhāṣya says that this threefold lack of nature is taught as a remedy for four wrong ideas about the meaning of what is taught through the lack of nature in general. For example, it is a misconception to think that the lack of nature is mere nonexistence, or to believe that what is without nature cannot arise even as a mere appearance on the level of seeming reality.[96]

In their discussions on establishing the mahāyāna sūtras as the words of the Buddha, chapters 3 and 4 of Vasubandhu's *Vyākhyāyukti* not only defend the prajñāpāramitā sūtras against the charge of nihilism, but point out that these sūtras themselves criticize nihilism as the activity of māras[97] and that their key notion "lack of nature" is not to be understood literally in the sense of nothing existing at all. Rather, it has to be interpreted in the correct way, which is accomplished through the threefold lack of nature as presented in the *Saṃdhinirmocanasūtra*.[98] In particular, the lack of nature of all phenomena must be clarified in this way in order to relinquish the extremes of superimposition and denial, that is, in order to (1) prevent childish beings from clinging to the existence of the imaginary nature and (2) prevent those who do not understand, when just the main points are being discussed, from clinging to the nonexistence of those phenomena whose nature it is to be inexpressible. When discussing the levels and modes of existence of what are described by the three natures themselves, the *Vyākhyāyukti* matches them with the framework of the two realities:

> It may be said, "The Bhagavat taught in the *Pāramārthaśūnyatā[sūtra]*, 'Both karmic actions and their maturations exist, but an agent is not observable.'[99] How is this [statement to be understood]—in terms of the ultimate or the seeming? . . . If it is in terms of the ultimate, how could all phenomena lack a nature? If it is in terms of the seeming, it should not be said that an agent is not observable, since an agent too exists on the level of the seeming." To start, [one needs to know] what this "seeming" and what the ultimate is. By virtue of this, one will know what exists on the level of the seeming and what exists ultimately. Some [śrāvakas] may say, "The seeming consists of names, expressions, designations, and conventions, while the specific characteristics of phenomena are the ultimate." However, in this case, since both karmic actions and their maturations exist as both names and specific characteristics, [whether they pertain to the ultimate or not] depends on one's concept of existence, [that is, on] how one asserts these two [—karma and maturation—as being either names or specifically characterized phenomena].

> I hold that a person is something that exists on the level of the seeming, but not as something substantial, because it is [just a] name that is labeled onto the skandhas. Karmic actions and their maturations exist substantially on the level of the seeming, but do not exist ultimately, because they are the objects of mundane cognition. [*Paramārtha* means] being the object of the ultimate, because the ultimate (*parama*) is supramundane wisdom and it is the object (*artha*) of the latter.[100] The specific characteristics of the [above] two [karmic actions and their maturations] are not the sphere of this [wisdom], since its sphere is the inexpressible general characteristic [that is suchness]. Here, you may wonder, "Is it mundane cognition or supramundane [wisdom] that represents valid cognition?" There is only one [ultimately valid cognition]—supramundane [wisdom]. Mundane cognition has divisions—being attained subsequently to supramundane [wisdom], it is not [ultimate] valid cognition. [Needless to say then that any] other [cognitions] are not valid cognition [either]. Thus, this accords with a verse of the Mahāsaṃghikas:
>
> Neither the eye, the ear, nor the nose is valid cognition,
> Nor is the tongue, the body, or mentation valid cognition.
> If these sense faculties were valid cognition,
> Whom would the path of noble ones do any good?[101]
>
> . . . If one speaks about "the seeming" and states that "what accords with afflicted phenomena is explained as flaws" and "what accords with purified phenomena is explained to be excellent" [and yet claims that] these are nothing but mere verbiage, how could one explain anything to be excellent, explain anything as a flaw, or actually accept any seeming phenomena without doubt? In other words, if these too were [utterly] nonexistent, how could [the Buddha] speak of existence on the level of the seeming? Through denying all afflicted and purified phenomena, one could not express anything, since one would not abide in [knowing] what is the case and what is not the case and moreover refute one's own statements.[102]

This points to two of the main misconceptions that explain why the Yogācāras saw a need to interpret the message of the prajñāpāramitā sūtras in terms of the three natures. Obviously, since these sūtras themselves teach one to reject what is afflicted and practice or adopt what is pure, in terms of the path, it makes no sense to simply take emptiness as meaning that nothing whatsoever exists on any level of reality, because then there is nothing to adopt or to reject. Thus, given the emptiness of all phenomena on the ultimate level, the existence of skandhas, karmic actions, a person, adopting, rejecting, and so on can only be, and must be accepted on, the level of seeming reality. However, within that level, one needs to further distinguish clearly between mere imaginary labels (such as the person) and the functional phenomena (such as skandhas and actions) that are taken as the bases for such labeling and perform the functions to be worked with on the path, even though both do not exist ultimately (neither does the path that nevertheless leads to the realization of the ultimate). Thus, verses 23–24 of Vasubandhu's *Triṃśikā* state:

> Based on the three kinds of lack of nature
> Of the three kinds of nature,
> It is taught that all phenomena
> Are without nature.
>
> The first one lacks a nature
> In terms of characteristics; the next one
> Lacks existence on its own,
> And the following is the lack of nature as such.

Sthiramati's commentary explains:

> "The first one" is the imaginary nature. It "lacks a nature in terms of characteristics," because its characteristics are imputed. [For example,] form has the characteristic of form, feeling has the characteristic of experience, and so on. Thus, since [the imaginary nature] has no character of its own (*svarūpa*), just as a sky-flower, it is the lack of nature of any character of its own. "The next one" refers to the other-dependent nature. It does not exist by itself (*na svayaṃbhāva*), because it arises through other conditions, just as an illusion. Thus, as shown, there is no arising of it, which is why it is referred to as "the lack of nature in terms of arising." Because the perfect nature is the ultimate of all phenomena, which are other-dependent in nature, it is referred to as their true nature (*dharmatā*). Therefore, the perfect nature is the ultimate lack of nature, because the nature of the perfect [nature] is to not be any entity (*abhāvasvabhāvatvāt*).[103]

In brief, just as when mistaking the moving colors and shapes in a movie for a story line with actual persons with all their emotions and so on, the imaginary nature stands for the illusory display of dualistic appearances that actually do not exist in the first place, let alone having any characteristics of their own. Therefore, it is called "the lack of nature in terms of characteristics." Just as the mere movement of said shapes and colors on the screen, the other-dependent nature consists of dependently originating appearances which means that they appear in an illusionlike manner, but are without any nature of their own and do not "really" arise. Thus, the other-dependent nature is called "the lack of nature in terms of arising." The perfect nature is "the ultimate lack of nature," which has two aspects. First, although there is no personal identity, the perfect nature is what functions as the path that remedies the notion of a personal identity. Just as an illusory ship can be used to cross an illusory ocean, it serves as the means to cross the ocean of saṃsāra to the other shore of nirvāṇa. In terms of dependent origination, this remedial or path aspect is actually contained within the other-dependent nature, but since it is the cause for realizing the ultimate, it is included in the category of "the ultimate lack of nature." The second aspect of the perfect nature is the one by virtue of which enlightenment is attained through actively engaging in it and is undifferentiable from phenomenal identitylessness. Like space, it is omnipresent and not established as anything whatsoever (just as the colors and shapes in a movie are nothing but the display of photons, which are ultimately unfindable). This aspect is "the ultimate lack of nature" per se. Note, however, that, while the Madhyamaka system greatly tends to speak only about the objective side of this "ultimate lack of nature," the Yogācāra tradition also emphasizes its subjective side. In other words, the lack of nature or emptiness is not just limited to being something like the bare fact of said photons being unfindable, but there is an awareness or experience of this very fact. Needless to say, for Yogācāras too, the true realization of the ultimate lack of nature also entails the emptiness or unfindability of that very experience, but any realization of this has to happen in the mind—it is not just an abstract fact like a mathematical equation at which no one looks. Fundamentally, all phenomena, including one's mind, have always been, are, and will be empty, but this fact alone makes nobody a buddha, unless it is made into an incontrovertible, all-pervasive, and personal experience of boundless freedom and compassion and is as natural an outlook informing all one's actions as it is for ordinary beings to experience themselves and the world as real, dualistic, and suffering.

Regarding emptiness understood in terms of the three natures, *Mahāyānasūtrālaṃkāra* XIV.34 says:

> If one knows the emptiness of the nonexistent,
> Likewise the emptiness of the existent,
> And also natural emptiness,
> Then this is expressed as "knowing emptiness."

On the level of seeming reality, the imaginary nature is just nominally existent, while the other-dependent nature is substantially existent in the sense of what conventionally performs functions. The perfect nature does not exist in any of these two ways, but is the ultimate incontrovertible state of mind experiencing its own true nature. Again, by definition, this personally experienced wisdom is in itself completely without any reference points, such as it existing or not existing. For these reasons, the imaginary nature is also called "the emptiness of the nonexistent"; the other-dependent nature, "the emptiness of the existent"; and the perfect nature, "the ultimate or natural emptiness." Thus, as mentioned above, the three natures not only accord with the prajñāpāramitā notions of emptiness and the lack of nature, but moreover serve as progressive stages of the transition from utter delusion to the undeluded wisdom of a buddha with all its qualities. Nguyen says:

> As an elaboration of the teaching of the Middle Path, the concept of the three identities may be compared to the Madhyamaka School's concept of Emptiness *(śūnyatā)*. *Śūnyatā* is a hermeneutic concept used to deconstruct the reification of all the constituent factors and processes that are thought to make up the reality of persons and phenomena. The three identities concept not only accomplishes a deconstruction of these factors, but also reveals a realization of their true nature *(tathatā)* replete with positive implications from the perspectives of both epistemology and soteriology.[104]

Thus, just as in the case of the notion of *cittamātra* above, the three natures are to be practically and progressively engaged as the bodhisattva path, with each one to be transcended by the following one. As the *Mahāyānasaṃgraha* says:

> How should one engage in [appearances as being mere cognizance]? . . . One engages in this just like in the case of a rope appearing as a snake in a dark house. Since a snake does not exist, [to see it] in the rope is mistaken. Those who realize [that the rope] is its referent have turned away from the cognition of [seeing] a snake where there is none and dwell in the cognition of [apprehending] a rope.

> [However,] when regarded in a subtle way, such is also mistaken, since [a rope] consists of [nothing but] the characteristics of color, smell, taste, and what can be touched. [Thus,] based on the cognition of [seeing color] and so on, the cognition of [apprehending] a rope has to be discarded too. Likewise, based on the cognition of [seeing] the perfect nature, . . . also the cognition of mere cognizance is to be dissolved. . . . Through engaging in mere cognizance, one engages in the other-dependent nature.
>
> How does one engage in the perfect nature? One engages in it by dissolving the notion of mere cognizance too. . . . Therefore, there is not even an appearance of [phenomena] as mere cognizance. When bodhisattvas . . . dwell in the dharmadhātu in an immediate way, what is observed and what observes are equal in these bodhisattvas. In consequence, what springs forth [in them] is equal nonconceptual wisdom. In this way, such bodhisattvas engage in the perfect nature.[105]

The path quality of the three natures is also taught in *Madhyāntavibhāga* III.9cd–10a:

> In full understanding, relinquishing,
> And attaining and revealing,
>
> The reality of the path is fully explained.

Mipham Rinpoche comments on this as follows.

> The imaginary [nature] is what is to be fully understood through the path, that is, it is to be understood that it does not exist as any entity. Therefore, it is taught [through the term "path" here] by way of designating the object through the name of the subject—the path. The other-dependent [nature] is what is to be relinquished through the path. This means that enlightenment is attained by virtue of false imagination, which entails dualistic appearances, becoming extinguished. Therefore, this corresponds to [line I.4d] in the chapter on the characteristics of afflicted phenomena above:
>
>> Its extinction is held to be liberation.

> Therefore, to designate [the other-dependent nature] through the name "path" is a designation of what is to be relinquished through the name of the remedy. The perfect [nature] is explained as the path, because it is that which is to be attained and revealed. [In this case,] the cause is designated through the name of the result.[106]

A similar statement is found in the opening lines of the *Dharmadharmatāvibhāga*:

> After having understood, something is to be relinquished
> And something else is to be revealed.

Also, the *Mahāyānasūtrālaṃkārabhāṣya* on XI.13 says:

> True reality is always free from duality, the basis of mistakenness,
> And inexpressible in every respect, having the nature of being free from reference points.
> It is held to be what is to be understood, relinquished, and purified, though it is naturally stainless.
> Its purity of afflictions is asserted to be like space, gold, or water.

> The true reality being always free from duality refers to the imaginary nature, because it absolutely never exists as the characteristics of apprehender and apprehended. [True reality serving as] the basis of mistakenness refers to the other-dependent [nature], because it is what imagines this [duality of apprehender and apprehended]. The inexpressible [true reality], having the nature of being free from reference points, is the perfect nature. Here, the first true reality is what is to be fully understood; the second one is what is to be relinquished; and the third one is both what is to be purified from adventitious stains and naturally pure. In its natural purity, like space, gold, or water, it is pure of afflictions. Space and so on are neither naturally impure, nor is their purity not asserted [as being revealed] by virtue of adventitious stains disappearing.[107]

Thus, one of the main reasons for speaking about the three natures and the other-dependent nature in particular is to account for the process of mind progressing from its mistaken state to freedom, which—as far as the Buddhist path is concerned—takes place within the dependently originating structure of the other-dependent nature, realizing the nonexistence of the imaginary nature and revealing or becoming immersed in the perfect nature instead. Thus, from the perspective of the path, the imaginary nature is to be known for what it is—utterly nonexistent; the other-dependent nature is to be relinquished in the sense of mind ceasing to create dualistic appearances; and the perfect nature is that which is to be manifested or realized, which is just the true nature of the first two natures, once the other-dependent nature ceases to project the imaginary nature. In other words, in terms of the Buddhist path, the delusive complexities of the ontologically and epistemologically more fragile structures of the imaginary nature and the other-dependent nature can be reduced to, or collapsed into, the underlying single ontologically and epistemologically stable structure of the perfect nature, which is simply uncovered. This is what is called "fundamental change of state" (see below). As should be clear, "stable" does not mean static or being established as some kind of intrinsically existing absolute entity, but refers to the basic unmistakenness and irreversibility of this change of state.

To conclude this discussion of the three natures and to get a glimpse of the variety of explanations on the three natures, let's look at the four models that are presented in Sthiramati's *Madhyāntavibhāgaṭīkā* on I.1.[108]

> False imagination exists.
> Duality is not present in it.
> But emptiness is present in it,
> And it is also present in this [emptiness].

> [Model 1] . . . Some think, "All phenomena are without nature in every respect, just like the horns of a rabbit." Therefore, in order to refute the denial of everything, [line I.1a] says, "False imagination exists." This is [to be] supplemented by the words, "by a nature of its own." "But in that case, since the sūtras state that all phenomena are empty, does this not contradict the sūtras?" There is no contradiction. For, [line I.1b] says, "Duality is not present in it." False imagination is said to be empty, because it is free from the nature of apprehender and apprehended, but it is not that it lacks a nature in every respect. Therefore, this does not contradict the sūtras. "But if duality does not exist in any respect, just as the horns of a rabbit, and false imagination exists ultimately by virtue of a nature of its own, then the nonexistence of emptiness would follow." It is not like that, because [line I.1c] says, "But emptiness is present

in it." Emptiness is the fact of false imagination being free from apprehender and apprehended. Thus, emptiness does not become nonexistent. You may think, "But if nonduality is emptiness and it exists in false imagination, why are we not liberated? Also, given that it is present [in false imagination], why is it not apprehended?" In order to remove such doubts, [line I.1d] says, "And it is also present in this [emptiness]." Since false imagination is present in emptiness, You, sir, are not liberated. By virtue of possessing stains, unlike clear water, it is not suitable to be realized.

[Model 2] Or, some may regard forms and so on to exist substantially as something other than mind and mental factors. So in order to refute them, [line I.1a], "False imagination exists" means that this very [false imagination] is what exists substantially, but form exists neither as something separate from it, nor substantially. "What is the reason [for that]?" For, [line I.1b] says, "Duality is not present in it." False imagination is neither the apprehender of anything, nor is it apprehended by anything. "So what is it?" It is just sheer being, free from apprehender and apprehended. Since no form and so on is apprehended outside of consciousness, just as in a dream, consciousness arises appearing as form and so on. "But if its cause does not exist, its arising is not tenable." Therefore, the lack of focal object is just as in a dream. You should understand that consciousness appearing as referents also arises in other cases, [such as the waking state,] by virtue of its seeds maturing. Since there is no apprehender without something to be apprehended, it is not tenable for an apprehender to exist if there is nothing to be apprehended. Therefore, form and so on do not exist apart from false imagination. "However, by virtue of there being nothing to be apprehended, there is no pure object (*viśuddhyālambana*) [either], and thus no liberation." This is not the case. For, [line I.1c] says, "But emptiness is present in it." Here, the word "but" means "because." That is, precisely because emptiness is the pure object—the freedom from apprehender and apprehended—that exists in false imagination, it is not that there is no liberation. "But if it exists in false imagination, given that it is present [there], why is it not apprehended?" It is [only] by virtue of its being obscured through false imagination that it is not suitable to be apprehended like the stainless sky, but not by virtue of its being nonexistent. In order to teach that, [line I.1d] says, "And it is also present in emptiness."

[Model 3] Or, in order to refute the denial of everything, [line I.1a] says, "False imagination exists." It is neither that all [phenomena] do not exist, nor is it that they have a real nature of their own—they exist as the nature of the modulations of consciousness. Some think, "Form and so on appear in just the way they appear, that is, through a nature of their own and as something separate from false imagination." In order to refute such superimpositions onto what is unreal, [Maitreya] retorts with [line I.1b], "Duality is not present in it." The intention here is that what is present is mere false imagination. Some apprehend the nonexistence of duality as having the nature of total extinction (*chedarūpa*), just as the son of a barren woman. Others say, "The freedom from an internal person as the agent (*antarvyāpārapuruṣa*) is the emptiness of phenomena." Therefore, in order to refute denials of emptiness and in order to teach true identitylessness (*bhūtanairātmya*), [line I.1c] says, "But emptiness is present in it." "But if emptiness exists in false imagination, it consequently follows that all living beings would be liberated without any effort." This is not so, for [line I.1d] says, "And it is also present in this [emptiness]." As long as emptiness is not purified, there is no liberation, and its being afflicted needs to be purified through great efforts. Thus, it is not that there is liberation without effort.

[Model 4] Or, in terms of characteristics,[109] there is nothing other than the description of what is afflicted and what is purified. Therefore, in order to investigate what is afflicted and what is purified, [line I.1a], "False imagination exists," represents the details [of what is afflicted]. The nature of false imagination is afflicted, because it has the characteristic of mistakenness. "How is this characteristic of mistakenness to be understood?" It is through [line I.1b], "Duality is not present in it." It is to be understood as the very nature of mistakenness, because it appears in the form of the aspects of apprehender and apprehended, which are not present in its own nature. Now, in order to investigate the very nature of what is purified, [line I.1c] says, "But emptiness is present in it." The nature of emptiness is what is purified, because it is the nature of the nonexistence of duality. You should know that also the path and cessation are included in this, because they are characterized by emptiness. The domain of what is purified is to be searched from right within the domain of what is afflicted—it does not exist as

> something separate from it. In order to teach this, [line I.1c] says "[emptiness is present] in it." You may ask, "If duality does not exist, given the presence of this [emptiness], why is the world mistaken?" Therefore, [line I.1d] says, "And it is also present in this [emptiness]." This refers to the imagination of apprehender and apprehended, just as an illusion is empty of the aspects of elephants and so on, yet the aspects of elephants appear.[110]

From Sthiramati's approach here, it is clear that he does not primarily speak about ontological models of the three natures, but treats them as pedagogical means to counteract particular wrong ideas. Thus, both false imagination and emptiness are described in several different ways. False imagination is said to be "existent by a nature of its own" (model 1); "substantially existent" (model 2); "of the nature of modulations of consciousness" (model 3); and "having the nature of being afflicted" (model 4). Emptiness is described as "the fact of false imagination being free from apprehender and apprehended" (models 1 and 2); "the pure object" (model 2); "true identitylessness" (model 3); and "having the nature of what is purified" and "being the nature of the nonexistence of duality" (model 4). The first two models sound rather realist and substantialist, but that does not necessarily mean that false imagination is held to be ultimately existent, which is in fact not affirmed anywhere.[111] Also, though Sthiramati describes the above four models, it does not mean that he fully subscribes to all of them. In fact, commenting on *Madhyāntavibhāga* I.5, Sthiramati explicitly states that false imagination is the other-dependent nature, which arises under the power of causes and conditions, but does not exist or come into being on its own. He also quotes two verses, which add that the other-dependent nature is the sphere of correct mundane cognition, while the perfect nature is the sphere of nonconceptual (supramundane) wisdom.[112]

Given the explicit objectives of Sthiramati's commentary to redress strong kinds of clinging to utter nonexistence or absolute existence and so on, from a pedagogical point of view, equally strong statements on relative existence (or relatively having a nature of its own) and emptiness, respectively, are suitable to counteract wrong ideas and guide disciples on the middle path between these two extremes, but this does not necessarily mean that those who make such statements accept everything in them as their own position. Such a middle path is clearly explained in Vasubandhu's and Sthiramati's commentaries on *Madhyāntavibhāga* I.2, following the statement in the prajñāpāramitā sūtras that all phenomena are neither absolutely empty nor absolutely nonempty. Sthiramati further clarifies that false imagination is conditioned, because it depends on causes and conditions, while emptiness is not. False imagination is present in emptiness in the form of phenomena, and emptiness is present in false imagination in the form of the nature of phenomena.[113] This is further clarified in Sthiramati's comments on I.13, where the being of the nonbeing of duality is described as the characteristic of emptiness, which is neither existent nor nonexistent. Emptiness is not existent because of the nonexistence of duality. Nor is it nonexistent, since the nonexistence of duality exists. In other words, emptiness is not just the sheer absence of apprehender and apprehended, but constitutes the true mode of being of all phenomena. Emptiness is also neither the same as, nor different from, false imagination. If it were different from false imagination, it would not be its nature, and if it were the same, it would not be the sole pure object that is conducive to liberation.[114]

To summarize, in the first two models, emptiness (or the perfect nature) is described more as an abstract property of false imagination (the other-dependent nature), which is said to not be without nature in every respect. Thus, duality (the imaginary nature) and emptiness are just the two poles of false imagination—the way it mistakenly appears and the way it actually is. Vasubandhu and Sthiramati both say that *Madhyāntavibhāga* I.5 is taught in order to include all three natures in false imagination, *if*—or as long as—mere false imagination exists. Since the immediately preceding line I.4d explicitly says that liberation is nothing but the extinction of false imagination, this can only mean that the three natures are only included in, and applicable to, false imagination as long as it exists as the display of saṃsāra. Within this saṃsāric framework, the imaginary nature is the mistakenly imagined duality of which false imagination is actually empty; the other-dependent nature is false imagination itself; and the perfect nature is the very absence of duality in false imagination. This seems to indicate that the first two models above revolve around false imagination as primarily describing the deluded saṃsāric mind. By contrast, the latter two models seem to discuss the three natures more from the perspective of the ultimate. Thus, false imagination is not said to have a nature of its own or to exist substantially, but to exist just as modulations of consciousness and as being afflicted. Emptiness is described as being more than just the mere absence of duality in false imagination—it is the very nature of the absence of duality, that is, true identitylessness, which is the pure object conducive to liberation and even includes the path that leads to this liberation (at the same time, it is not to be looked for outside of what appears as afflicted phenomena). Thus, emptiness (or the perfect nature) is only taken as the mere absence of duality in false imagination, when the latter is described in more ontological or saṃsāric terms (models 1 and 2). But in the more epistemological or path-oriented explanations of false imagination, emptiness is described in more encompassing, positive, and ultimate terms (models 3 and 4). In other words, in the former approach, emptiness is basically just a property of false imagination, but in the latter approach, it is the true ultimate nature of false imagination. The latter accords with *Madhyāntavibhāga* I.20, in which the last one of the sixteen emptinesses—the emptiness that is the nature of nonbeing—is said to be different from the other fifteen, which all refer to the nonexistence of persons and phenomena. Together, these emptinesses serve to remove all superimpositions and denials—if persons and phenomena were not empty and nonexistent, they would truly exist, but if emptiness itself were nonexistent too, persons and phenomena would not be empty and thus again be truly existent.[115] *Madhyāntavibhāga* I.21 is explained as "the establishing of emptiness," making it clear that this emptiness (and not false imagination) is the final word here—without it, there would be no path and no liberation.

> If this [emptiness] were not afflicted,
> All beings would be liberated.
> If it were not pure,
> Efforts would be fruitless.

From the ultimate perspective, verse I.22 says, emptiness is free from all dualistic pinpointing, such as existence, nonexistence, pure, impure, and so on.

> It is neither afflicted nor nonafflicted,
> Neither pure nor impure.

As for emptiness being neither afflicted nor impure, Sthiramati comments that what is described here is purity per se, and that the dual terminology just serves to emphasize this. He refers to Vasubandhu's quote from the scriptures, which says that it is pure "because of mind's natural luminosity," and says that "mind" here refers to the true nature of the mind (*cittadharmatā*). As for its being neither nonafflicted nor pure, this indicates that it is only afflicted through adventitious stains, but not afflicted by nature. The scriptural support is, "because of being afflicted by adventitious afflictions."[116] In this way, emptiness is far beyond being just the mere absence of duality in false imagination—it is the ultimate, luminous and pure nature of the mind.[117]

In brief, all these different models can be summarized in two, which Sponberg (1981, pp. 99ff) calls (a) the pivotal and (b) the progressive models. The "pivot" in (a) is the other-dependent nature (just as in models 1 and

2 above), with the imaginary and perfect natures just being its two "extreme" poles of how it mistakenly appears and actually is. Model (b) refers to the three natures as three levels of reality, progressing from dualistic delusion to nondual freedom from delusion, as well as the realizations of these levels as outlined in the four yogic practices above.

Mind's Fundamentally Different Outlook on Itself

As for the Sanskrit term *āśrayaparivṛtti* (change of state), there are a great number of Buddhist scriptures (from the Pāli canon up through the tantras) in which this term is used with reference to a variety of different states or processes (for an overview, see Davidson 1985). For some of these processes, the term "transformation," which is mostly used in translations, may be appropriate, but as far as the dharmadhātu, natural purity, buddha nature, or the luminous nature of the mind are concerned, the whole point of this notion of "change of state" is that there is absolutely no transformation of anything into anything else. Rather, the revelation of mind's primordially pure nature, which from the perspective of the path appears as fruitional enlightenment, only manifests as a change from the perspective of deluded mind—mind seeming to be obscured before and then unobscured later. But this does not refer to any change in nature, just as the sun first being covered by clouds and then being free from clouds would not be called a transformation of the clouds into the sun, or even any transformation of the sun itself. It is solely from the perspective of those who watch the sun that its state seems to have changed (being with and without clouds, respectively). Even children know that the presence or absence of clouds does not affect the sun itself in any way, but just our perception of it. In fact, for the sun itself, there is not even a question of whether it has changed, let alone how. *Mahāyānasūtrālaṃkāra* IX.22 says:

> Though without difference between before and after,
> It is immaculateness in terms of all obscurations.
> Being neither pure nor impure,
> Suchness is held to be buddhahood.

Sthiramati's commentary on this explains:

> "Purity" is said to mean having the nature of being afflicted before, and then the stains having become nonexistent later through having

cultivated the path, with "before" referring to the time of an ordinary being, and "later" to the time of full buddhahood. But the dharmakāya of a buddha is held to be of the nature of suchness, emptiness. Emptiness has the nature of being empty and naturally luminous even at the time of ordinary beings. Also later, at the time of full buddhahood, it has the nature of being empty and naturally luminous. Therefore, in its nature of purity, there is no difference.[118]

Mahāyānasūtrālaṃkāra XIII.18–19 says:

When murky water becomes clear,
[Its] transparency does not arise from elsewhere,
But is just its becoming free from pollution.
The same goes for the purity of your own mind.

It is held that mind, which is always naturally luminous,
Is [only] blemished by adventitious flaws.
It is stated that there is no other mind apart from
The naturally luminous mind of dharmatā.[119]

The most detailed presentation of the Yogācāra notion of change of state is given in the *Dharmadharmatāvibhāga* (covering two-thirds of its contents), which describes the nature of the change of state as follows.

As for apprehending its nature,
It is stainless suchness
In the sense of adventitious stains
Not appearing and
Suchness appearing.[120]

In the following, the text mainly speaks about the foundation of this change of state (lines 159–60), which is nonconceptual wisdom. In terms of the path, bodhisattvas cultivate and engage in this wisdom through (a) relinquishing the four progressively more subtle mistaken conceptions about factors to be relinquished, their remedies, suchness, and realization (lines 171–79);[121] (b) understanding that, by virtue of being ignorant about suchness, the delusive appearance of actually nonexistent false imagination and duality out of the ālaya-consciousness prevents the appearance of the nature of phenomena, and that the latter appears, once the former two cease to appear (lines

252–63); and (c) cultivating the above-mentioned four yogic practices (lines 180–85 and 264–75). The basic characteristics of nonconceptual wisdom are described as threefold (lines 186–204). Its characteristic of being grounded in the nature of phenomena means that it is nondual and inexpressible. Its characteristic of nonappearance means that duality, designations, sense faculties, objects, cognitions, and the outer world do not appear for it. Its characteristic of appearance means that, during meditative equipoise, all phenomena appear equal to space, while, during subsequent attainment, all conditioned phenomena appear like illusions. Nonconceptual wisdom is further characterized through excluding its being mistaken for five other states, such as its being nothing but the sheer absence of any mental engagement (such as deep sleep); its possessing five excellencies; and its five functions (223–46). Finally, the text presents four disadvantages, if there were no such change of state; four advantages, since it exists; and three examples of the fleeting nature of the adventitious stains and the unchanging basis of the change of state—the nature of phenomena (lines 293–307). The Third Karmapa's commentary on these examples explains:

> For example, space is nothing but pure by nature. Therefore, by virtue of certain conditions (such as fog or mist) in the world, one can observe statements such as, "The sky is not pure" and, "It is pure," [when] it is clear and free [from these conditions]. However, it is not suitable to claim such because of a change of the nature of space. Its own nature being pure, empty, and unconditioned, it is indeed not suitable that it either becomes pure by virtue of itself or becomes pure by virtue of something else. Still, mistaken minds that connect mere conventional terms to it cling to space as being pure and impure, [but] this is nothing but an error. Likewise, though it may appear as if the naturally pure nature of phenomena—the perfect [nature]—has become free from the fog and mist of conceptions, it is not asserted that this perfect [nature] has changed—it is absolutely without any arising or ceasing in terms of itself, others, both, or neither. In the same way, the fact of gold remaining in its excellent state is not changed by stains, and the fact of water remaining clear and moist is not changed in its nature, even if it becomes associated with sullying factors, such as silt. Likewise, all that happens to the unmistaken path and the pure dharmas is that they just become associated with stains and sullying factors through the conceptions of ignorance, but it is not asserted that these uncontaminated dharmas [—the path and the pure dharmas entailed by

> cessation—] change. Therefore, naturally luminous stainlessness is unconditioned and changeless. Thus, though the nature of phenomena is referred to by this term "fundamental change of state," it is also called "permanent."[122]

All of this underlines that there is no change of state in nature or substance, but only a revelation of the way things actually have always been, once the delusion of what is projected onto this is seen through. Also, nonconceptual wisdom as both the underlying basis and the result of this change of state is clearly described in terms of the dynamics of an enlightened mind, and not as sheer emptiness or an inert state. Thus, as far as the notion of "change of state" refers to this process of uncovering mind's fundamental nature, even when it is sometimes described in Buddhist texts as if there were a transformation of one "thing" into another "thing," or of something impure (such as the skandhas or mental afflictions) into something pure (such as the pure skandhas or wisdoms), this is just a conventional or expedient way of teaching. The Eighth Karmapa's commentary on the *Abhisamayālaṃkāra* says:

> Those present-day followers of [Mahā]mudrā whose confusion is even a hundred thousand times bigger than this exclaim, "Through refining the ālaya-consciousness into something pure, it turns into the result of mirrorlike wisdom." This is not justified for the following reasons. Something like this does not appear in any of the traditions of the mahāyāna, and what does not appear [there also] does not appear in the sense of something that is obtained through reasoning. A presentation of the ālaya-consciousness as the cause and mirrorlike wisdom as its result is not something that is obtained through reasoning. Rather, with respect to the mode of being of causes and results in terms of [such] causes and results in the abhidharma that actually fulfill these functions[123] (that is, what produces and what is produced), the ālaya-consciousness and mirrorlike wisdom are not adequate as a cause and a result that fully qualify as such. Also, since the very nature of the ālaya-consciousness is [nothing but] the adventitious stains, it is presented as impure. No matter how it may be refined by something else, it will not turn into something pure. It is not possible within the sphere of knowable objects that something impure turns into something pure, or that something pure turns into something impure.[124]

To highlight the different perspectives of the notion of change of state, Asaṅga's *Abhidharmasamucchaya*[125] speaks of three kinds of change of state—(1) the change of state of mind upon the attainment of the path of nonlearning; (2) the change of state of the path; and (3) the change of state of the impregnations of negative tendencies. Sthiramati's commentary[126] explains that (1) refers to the naturally luminous mind that is the nature of phenomena having become free from all adventitious afflictions without exception. This is also called "the change of state of suchness." (2) means that, once clear realization occurs on the mundane path, it has become the supramundane path. The latter is also called "the path of learning" because there still remain tasks to be accomplished. Once all antagonistic factors are eliminated through being free from attachment to the three realms, this is presented as the perfectly complete change of the state that is the nature of this path. (3) means the ālaya-consciousness being free from even the most subtle latent tendencies of all afflictions.

The tenth chapter of the *Mahāyānasaṃgraha* explains the change of state of the five skandhas as follows:

> Through how many kinds of masteries is the mastery of the dharmakāya attained? In brief, mastery is attained through five kinds: (1) Through the change of state of the skandha of form, mastery over [pure buddha] realms, kāyas, the excellent major and minor marks, infinite voices, and the invisible mark on the crown of the head [is attained]. (2) Through the change of state of the skandha of feeling, mastery over infinite and vast blissful states without wrongdoing [is attained]. (3) Through the change of state of the skandha of discrimination, mastery over the teachings [is attained] through all groups of words, groups of phrases, and groups of letters. (4) Through the change of state of the skandha of formation, mastery over creation, transformation, gathering retinues, and gathering the immaculate dharmas [is attained]. (5) Through the change of state of the skandha of consciousness, mastery over mirrorlike [wisdom], [the wisdom of] equality, discriminating [wisdom], and all-accomplishing [wisdom] is attained.[127]

In his commentary on *Mahāyānasūtrālaṃkāra* IX.12–17, Sthiramati[128] says that "state" in this context refers to the five skandhas, while "change" means that the dharmadhātu has become pure and has also become nonconceptual wisdom by virtue of the relinquishment of the afflictive and cognitive obscurations contained in these skandhas (for details, see below). In slightly different terms, *Mahāyānasūtrālaṃkāra* IX.41–47 also describes the various changes of state of the skandhas (primarily that of consciousness). Verse IX.48 concludes that the facets of such changes are in fact innumerable, but that all of them occur within the changeless and ever-pure dharmadhātu.

> Thus, infinite masteries are asserted
> In infinite changes of state
> By virtue of the inconceivable all-accomplishment
> Within the stainless foundation of the buddhas.

In sum, all these changes of state entail both a negative (relinquishment) and a positive aspect (attainment, purity), thus usually designating both a process and its result (cause and effect). By keeping in mind that the term "change of state" is used in Yogācāra texts sometimes to refer to the first and sometimes to the second aspect, seeming contradictions in differing ways of describing or applying this term are resolved. In other words, "state" may either refer to the ālaya-consciousness (or all eight consciousnesses, or adventitious stains) as that which changes from the perspective of the path. Or, it may be understood as nonconceptual wisdom, the Tathāgata heart, or the dharmadhātu as the very state within which any of the above "changes" take place, but which remains changeless itself.[129] As for "change," again, even in terms of the eight consciousnesses or adventitious stains, there is no real change, since all of them are always explained to be delusive and illusionlike, and thus actually nonexistent in the first place—the only "change" being the realization of exactly this fact. Thus, there is no change in terms of the object, but in terms of the realizing subject, which again happens only from the perspective of the (seemingly) evolving wisdom of the path, but not in terms of the fundamentally unchanging nature of nonconceptual wisdom. Thus, at any given time on the path, there is never any change in substance or nature (both on the side of what is to be relinquished and the side of what is to be attained)—all that happens is a cognitive change, or a change in one's outlook on oneself and the world.

These two aspects also represent the two reasons why, from the perspective of the path, any change of state is possible at all. First, what seems to "change" (the adventitious stains) can appear so precisely because it is merely an unreal and deceiving mental construct in the first place. Secondly, these fictitious mental projections are only superimposed onto, and occur nowhere else than within, the undeceiving ground of true reality, which is their actual nature, just to be revealed. In other words, though sentient beings' delusional seeming reality in the form of the imaginary and other-dependent natures has no beginning, for individual beings, it can end. On the other hand, ultimate reality—the perfect nature—has neither beginning nor end.

Thus, as said above, from a soteriological point of view, one of the primary purposes of speaking about the three natures and the other-dependent nature in particular is to highlight how mind is deluded about itself and how it can free itself from that self-delusion. The stage for the process of mind freeing itself—the Buddhist path—is the other-dependent nature, which starts by taking a thorough look at its own dramas (the imaginary nature) and thus first sees its own bare structure—the dependently originating acting of the mind (i.e, *cittamātra*). Next, taking a look at that very display of acting itself results in seeing, and becoming immersed in, its lucid yet empty true nature (the perfect nature). In other words, the more the complex, yet delusively quivering and fragile structures of the imaginary nature and the other-dependent natures collapse, the more their immovable and stable fundamental ground shines through, which is not simply yet another structure, but mind's natural state free from all reference points. Thus, it cannot be pinpointed as anything, but revealed and experienced as mind's most basic make-up, which is only possible through this very mind not entertaining any grasping at anything, including its own nongrasping. For example, upon seeing an ice sculpture of a dog, one may think of it as "a dog" with all its characteristics (the imaginary nature), but it is clear that it is just a particular configuration of ice (the other-dependent nature), which in turn is actually nothing but a particular state of water (the perfect nature). The "dog" is reducible to ice, which is in turn reducible to water. However, without ice, one cannot create the sculpture of "a dog"—such is not possible with water in its natural fluid state. Likewise, the dualistic sculptures of the imaginary nature are only possible through and within the other-dependent nature, but never in the perfect nature. At the same time, the former two natures can eventually "melt" into the natural and stable state of the perfect nature.

This natural state is nothing other than buddhahood, the dharmakāya, and so on. Yet again, "stable" does not mean static or being established as some kind of intrinsically existing absolute entity, but refers to the irreversibility of this change of state. Buddhahood (subject) and ultimate reality (object) themselves are no exceptions to being dynamic in nature, though it is impossible to fall back into delusion or duality from this particular dynamics. Of course, some people argue that there is no such state of permanent liberation or buddhahood without reversing into delusion, just as gold or water can only be heated up temporarily (or, as in the case of melted ice, can be refrozen again). When heated up, gold will become liquid, but eventually will always solidify again. Likewise, water may become hot and even boiling, but will inevitably cool down. The Buddhist reply is that these examples miss the point, because the nature of gold is precisely to be solid and cool—and not liquid and hot—to begin with, so it just reverts to its natural state (the same goes for water). As *Mahāyānasūtrālaṃkāra* IX.24ab and IX.25 say:

> Therefore, buddhahood is said to be
> Neither existent nor nonexistent.
>
> Just as with the subsiding of heat in iron
> And blurred vision in the eyes,
> The mind and wisdom of a buddha
> Are not said to be existent or nonexistent.

The *Bhāṣya* comments:

> Therefore, buddhahood is not said to be existent, because its characteristic is the nonexistence of persons and phenomena, and that is its nature. Nor is buddhahood said to be nonexistent, because its characteristic of being suchness exists.... The subsiding of heat and blurred vision is not existent, because its characteristic is the nonexistence of heat and blurred vision. Nor is it nonexistent, because it exists through the characteristic of having subsided. Likewise, the subsiding of attachment and ignorance (which resemble heat and blurred vision) in the mind and wisdom of buddhas is not said to be existent, since it consists of their nonexistence. Nor is it nonexistent, since the liberations of mind and prajñā exist through their respective characteristics of being liberated.[130]

In other words, heat and blurred vision do not exist any more, but the iron (characterized by its natural temperature and hardness) and clear eyesight still exist and function accordingly. Likewise, in buddhahood, ordinary states of mind (the eight collections of consciousness) have subsided, while the five wisdoms operate freely. Sthiramati adds that if the state of the visual disorder of blurred vision having subsided were absolutely nonexistent, then also the eye would not exist and could thus not perform the function of seeing clearly (the same goes for cool iron and a body free from illness functioning properly). Thus, the function of clear eyesight arises by virtue of blurred vision not existing. Likewise, in buddhahood, the afflictions and ignorance do not exist, but the liberation of mind (freedom from the afflictions—nirvāṇa) and prajñā (freedom from ignorance—omniscient wisdom) exist. The first liberation refers to being liberated from the afflictions to be relinquished through the paths of seeing and familiarization,[131] which arises from the lack of attachment. The liberation of prajñā means realizing, just as it is, that the liberation of mind actually *is* liberation, which arises from the lack of ignorance. In addition, the characteristic of the joy of being free from attachment and ignorance is not nonexistent either.[132] In brief, buddhahood is not just some indifferent state of lacking some things and seeing others, but it is the most fundamental freedom and insight that can possibly be experienced, which is naturally immensely joyful.

Thus, realizing buddhahood means nothing but to recognize the true nature of the mind, which can never be altered through its opposites, such as mistakenness and afflictions. Once the latter are seen through and recognized as adventitious illusory phenomena, mind will not revert to them. In other words, unlike water being reheatable over and again, once the nature of the mind is known for what it is, it is impossible to unknow it. As Dharmakīrti says in *Pramāṇavārttika* II.210cd–211ab:

> Having the nature of being free from harm
> And being actual reality, it is not reversed
>
> Through its opposites, even with effort,
> Since mind adheres to this side that is its [nature].[133]

Mind's Awakening

It should be noted at the outset that, fundamentally, both Yogācāras and Mādhyamikas agree that all descriptions of buddhahood (subject) or ultimate reality (object) are by definition incomplete, relative, and ultimately false, since it lies completely beyond the scope of words, thoughts, and dualistic perceptions. As *Mahāyānasūtrālaṃkāra* IX.36 says:

> The profundity of the buddhas
> In terms of their characteristics, state, and activity
> Within the stainless dharmadhātu
> Is said to be but a colorful painting in the sky.

Thus, Mādhyamikas usually refrain from saying much, if anything, about this topic. On the other hand, the Yogācāra approach is twofold. Just like the Mādhyamikas, the Yogācāras point out, as Vasubandhu and Sthiramati comment here, that the uncontaminated dharmadhātu is completely free from reference points, so that any teachings by the Buddha on the varieties of its profundity resemble painting space with colors.[134] However, the Yogācāras also acknowledge the pedagogical need for painting this colorful picture anyway, to be inspired by it, and also to inspire others, thus using it as an expedient means to facilitate progressing on the path, until what is painted in an illusory manner is nevertheless directly experienced. Accordingly, Sthiramati comments that, of course, it is difficult to paint space with colors, but if some very skilled person actually manages to do so, it is quite amazing. Similarly, the uncontaminated dhātu is the dharma that is to be personally experienced by the wisdom of the noble ones. As it is inexpressible in words, the Tathāgata's putting it in words by way of the threefold profundity in terms of characteristics, state, and activity is indeed a difficult task and something quite amazing to do. Still, it can be accomplished by virtue of the Buddha's skill and the dharmadhātu's existing in all beings. Thus, the next verse says:

> Though not being different in all of them,
> Suchness has become pure.
> Therefore, it is the Tathāgata,
> And all beings possess its Heart.

Sthiramati says that suchness refers to the nature of the two kinds of identitylessness in terms of persons and phenomena, which pervade all entities. The personal and phenomenal identitylessness that exists in ordinary beings and the personal and phenomenal identitylessness that exists in the noble ones are not different. It is only by virtue of this suchness having become pure that it is called "Tathāgata." Though suchness exists in everything, once the two kinds of identitylessness have become free from the adventitious afflictive and cognitive obstructions, they are pure, which is called "Tathāgata." Thus, because suchness exists in sentient beings, they are all said to have the Tathāgata heart.[135]

In general, buddhahood is described as both excellent relinquishment and realization (wisdom). Thus, in terms of the path, there is not only something to be relinquished (all reference points as per the Mādhyamikas, or the duality of apprehender and apprehended as per the Yogācāras),[136] but also something to be cultivated (the yogic valid perceptions of meditative equipoise and subsequent attainment), which eventually results in the culmination of the nondual nonconceptual wisdom of a buddha. It is precisely because this nonconceptual wisdom (or dharmadhātu, or buddha nature) is the fundamental ground for all activities on the Buddhist path toward its (re-)discovery that the sūtras, tantras, and the Yogācāras describe it not only in purely negative terms.

The classical Yogācāra "sky painting" of buddhahood (which greatly accords with the *Buddhabhūmisūtra*) is chapter 9 of the *Mahāyānasūtrālaṃkāra*, which begins with two verses on buddhahood being omniscience:

> Through hundreds of immeasurable hardships,
> Immeasurable accumulations of virtue,
> Immeasurable time,
> And the extinction of immeasurable obscurations,
>
> The knowledge of all aspects is attained—
> Immaculateness in terms of all obscurations.
> Buddhahood is illustrated
> By an opened jewel casket.

Sthiramati's commentary[136] says that it is the four wisdoms (such as mirrorlike wisdom) and the dharmadhātu that are called "buddhahood," and buddhahood is in turn referred to as "omniscience." Following Vasubandhu, Sthiramati continues by saying that buddhahood is taught here through three points: (1) Full realization is illustrated by the innumerable hardships undergone by bodhisattvas for the sake of other beings (such as giving away their possessions and even their bodies); their infinite accumulations of virtue (such as the six pāramitās, the ten bhūmis, and the thirty-seven dharmas concordant with enlightenment);[137] the innumerable eons (three or more) of practicing bodhisattva conduct; and the innumerable afflictive and cognitive obscurations that are overcome in this process. (2) The nature of buddhahood is the attainment of excellent relinquishment (being immaculate in terms of being free from all obscurations) and the attainment of excellent wisdom. The latter is called "knowledge of all aspects" by virtue of unmistakenly knowing [all phenomena] to be impermanent, suffering, empty, and identityless, just as they are. It is "omniscience" by virtue of knowing all phenomena, such as skandhas and dhātus, without exception.[138] (3) The example for buddhahood is an opened casket of very powerful and variegated wish-fulfilling jewels—once the covers of the afflictive and cognitive obscurations have been removed, the unique qualities of buddhahood (such as the ten powers and the four fearlessnesses) manifest. Thus, verses IX.4–5 speak about buddhahood being characterized by nonduality and power.

Buddhahood is all dharmas,
But itself is no dharma whatsoever.
It consists of pure dharmas,
But is not portrayed by them.

By virtue of its being the cause of the jewel of the dharma,
It resembles a jewel mine.
By virtue of being the cause of the harvest of virtue,
It is held to resemble a cloud.

Sthiramati comments that buddhahood is nondual in terms of apprehender and apprehended (any subject-object duality has been relinquished) as well as existence and nonexistence. As for the latter, at the time of buddhahood, what does not exist is the imaginary characteristic of imagined apprehender and apprehended, and what does exist is the characteristic of the existence of the perfect nature. What is called "buddhahood" is the dharma that consists of personal identitylessness, phenomenal identitylessness, nonarising, and nonceasing. There are no phenomena that are not pervaded by these two kinds of identitylessness and the fact of nonarising and nonceasing. The nature of twofold identitylessness, nonarising, and nonceasing of the dharmakāya of the buddhas and the nature of these in all phenomena is in no way different. But in buddhahood, no phenomena that are characterized as being imagined by childish beings (such as apprehender, apprehended, pots, or clothes) exist. Yet buddhahood consists of pure dharmas, because (a) it is accomplished through practicing virtues such as the pāramitās, the bhūmis, and the thirty-seven dharmas concordant with enlightenment, and (b) upon being accomplished, it abides as fully embodying these virtues as well as the unique buddha qualities of the ten powers and so on. Nevertheless, buddhahood is not portrayed by these pāramitās and so on, because the pāramitās that are characterized by being imagined and are observable as the three aspects of giver, recipient, and what is given do not exist by a nature of their own. These imaginary pāramitās and so on cannot be said to portray the nature of buddhahood, because buddhahood is not an imaginary phenomenon.[139] As for buddhahood's power, it resembles a jewel mine, because it is the cause, the condition, and the foundation for the innumerable jewels of the dharma (the teachings) as well as its qualities (such as the ten powers). It resembles a cloud, since its vast, wellspoken, and inexhaustible rain of dharma brings forth the harvests of the pāramitās and such in the fields of the mind streams of those to be guided.

Verses IX.7–11 explain how, based on all this, buddhahood is the supreme refuge for all beings, and the following six verses speak about buddhahood being the "fundamental change of state." Verse IX.12 says:

> Wherever the seeds of the afflictive and cognitive obscurations, ever present since primordial time,
> Are destroyed through all kinds of very extensive relinquishments,
> Buddhahood is attained as the change of state endowed with the supreme qualities of the pure dharmas,
> Which is obtained through the path of utterly pure wisdom that is nonconceptual and very vast in scope.

This describes the removal of the antagonistic factors of buddhahood and the remedies through which it is attained. The relinquishment of the latent tendencies of the two obscurations being "very extensive" refers to the path of supramundane wisdom from the first to the tenth bhūmi. "All kinds" means that the wisdoms on each one of these bhūmis have nine degrees in terms of lesser, medium, and great. "Wherever" refers to someone's mind in which the two obstructions have been purified through applying these remedial wisdoms, which is the meaning of "attaining the change of state." Once the two obstructions are relinquished in this way, this change of state consists of the attainment of the five dharmas (the four wisdoms and the pure dharmadhātu) as well as the unique qualities of a buddha (such as the ten powers), all of which are supreme, since śrāvakas and pratyekabuddhas do not possess them. The path of supramundane wisdom is twofold—utterly pure nonconceptual wisdom and the pure mundane wisdom of subsequent attainment, whose scope consists of all knowable objects. Utterly pure nonconceptual wisdom sees all phenomena to be empty, just as space. The pure mundane wisdom of subsequent attainment sees all entities of worldly realms in the three times as illusions and mirages.

Verse IX.14 plays on the word "change of state" by adding ten different prefixes to the Sanskrit word *vṛtti* in *āśrayaparivṛtti*,[141] most of which highlight the dynamic character of this change of state called "buddhahood." Thus, it is a "pro-change," because it is always engaged in the welfare of others—all sentient beings. It is a "super-change," since it is the best of all phenomena, superior to any mundane phenomena, and even superior to the change of state of supramundane śrāvakas. In the term "non-change-state," "state" refers to the state that is the result of change, which is a state of nonchange in the sense of the inactivity of the three causes of afflictions (that is, the presence of objects, improper mental engagement, and not having relinquished the latencies of both). It is a "counter-change," since it does not engage in afflictions or nonvirtue, and counteracts selfish actions. It is an "ongoing change," since it functions all the time (once this change of state has occurred, its operation will never decline until the end of saṃsāra) and engages in all the remedies for afflicted phenomena. It is a "dual change," because it first engages in demonstrating becoming fully enlightened and finally engages in demonstrating nirvāṇa. It is a "nondual change," because, ultimately, it neither engages in saṃsāra nor in nirvāṇā. For, by virtue of being endowed with prajñā, what is conditioned is relinquished, and by virtue of possessing compassion, what is unconditioned is relinquished. It is an "equal change," because as far as being liberated from all afflictions goes, it is equal in śrāvakas, pratyekabuddhas, and buddhas. It is a "special change," because it is superior to the change of state of the śrāvakas by virtue of the relinquishment of the cognitive obstructions and the qualities of the powers, the fearlessnesses, and so on. It is an "omnipresent change," because the three yānas engage all sentient beings in an omnipresent way. This change of state of the Tathāgata is endowed with all these supreme qualities, which are the uncontaminated dharmas, or the remedies for all afflictions. Therefore, it operates in a very vast manner. Verse IX.15 says:

> Just as space is held to be always omnipresent,
> Also this [buddhahood] is held to be always omnipresent.
> Just as space is omnipresent in what has form,
> Also this [buddhahood] is omnipresent in the hosts of beings.

Just as space is omnipresent in all entities in the three times, the uncontaminated dharmadhātu exists and is omnipresent in the mind streams of all sentient beings. This is to be understood here in terms of buddhas experiencing and accepting all beings as not being different from themselves in a perfect manner. Buddhahood has the nature of the dharmadhātu, and once the characteristic of the omnipresence of the dharmadhātu is realized on the first bhūmi, a state of mind of perceiving oneself and all beings as equal is attained. Through further cultivating this throughout the remaining bhūmis, at the time of buddhahood, this all-encompassing experience is perfected. This is what is called "being omnipresent in the hosts of beings."[142]

As for why sentient beings do not realize the dharmadhātu and do not see buddhas, though the dharmadhātu always exists and is omnipresent in them, verse IX.16 says:

> Just as a water container, when broken,
> Does not show the reflection of the moon,
> The image of the Buddha does not show
> In bad sentient beings.

Just as the moon is not seen in a vessel that is without water or broken, the mind streams of beings are either like an empty vessel through not being filled with the accumulations of merit and wisdom, or their mind streams are impaired through being full of afflictions and evil deeds. Despite such beings having the nature of a buddha, they do not see it. Of course, the reverse applies for beings whose mind streams are endowed with merit and wisdom.

This is followed by four verses (IX.17–21) with examples of buddha activity being effortless, spontaneous, and uninterrupted. The next sixteen verses (IX.22–37) explain the profundity of the uncontaminated dharmadhātu, which is free from all reference points of being pure, impure, existent, nonexistent, one, or many:

> Though without difference between before and after,
> It is immaculateness in terms of all obscurations.
> Being neither pure nor impure,
> Suchness is held to be buddhahood.

Verse IX.23 designates buddhahood as "the supreme self that is the lack of self":

> In pure emptiness, buddhas attain
> The supreme self of the lack of self.
> Through attaining the pure self,
> They have gone to the great self of the self.

To attain the supreme self means to attain the supreme lack of self. The supreme lack of self consists of personal identitylessness and phenomenal identitylessness. Since the buddhas have this twofold lack of a self as their self and nature within the uncontaminated dhātu, they are presented as being the supreme self. As for the word "self" (*ātman*), on the one hand, it means the imaginary self of the tīrthikas, referring to "self," "sentient being," "life-force," and so on. But on the other hand, it can also refer to the nature of a phenomenon, such as saying that the defining characteristic or nature of fire is to be hot. In these cases, the word "self" is used in the sense of "nature" (*svabhāva*). Thus, because the buddhas have the nature of the lack of self, it is said that they have attained the supreme self. So, what is the supreme lack of self? It means pure emptiness. Once the emptiness that is personal identitylessness and the emptiness that is phenomenal identitylessness have become pure of the stains of apprehender and apprehended, emptiness is pure. Having attained this purity is called "having attained the supreme lack of self." "The great self of the self" (*ātmamahātmatā*) designates the incomparable nature of this supreme self that is the supreme lack of self, which consists of the twofold identitylessness of persons and phenomena. In terms of exactly this being the very nature of buddhas, it is called "the self of the buddhas."[143] Consequently, verse IX.24 points out that buddhahood cannot be pinpointed.

> Therefore, buddhahood is said to be
> Neither existent nor nonexistent.
> So, upon such questions about the Buddha,
> The principle of being undecidable is held.

In the uncontaminated dharmadhātu, buddhahood is not existent, because buddhahood is the dharmakāya, and the dharmakāya is emptiness. In emptiness, there are neither any imaginary persons nor phenomena. Since the perfect nature does not exist in the way of imaginary persons and phenomena, which resemble the horns of a rabbit, it is not presented as existent at the time of budddhahood. However, buddhahood is not nonexistent either, because suchness—the perfect nature—exists at this time. The last two lines of this verse refer to, from a buddha's point of view, merely speculative and soteriologically pointless questions, such as the fourteen issues of whether buddhas still exist after their death or not and so on, which the Buddha did not answer in either an affirmative or a negative way.

The following verses of chapter 9 of the *Mahāyānasūtrālaṃkāra* speak about the masteries of śrāvakas, pratyekabuddhas, bodhisattvas, and buddhas being progressively more distinguished (38–40); the masteries of bodhisattvas and buddhas in terms of the changes of state of the five skandhas (41–48); buddhahood, by virtue of its masteries, being the cause for maturing beings (49–55); and the complete purity of the dharmadhātu (56–59). Verse IX.56 defines the nature of the uncontaminated dharmadhātu:

> It has the characteristic of the suchness of all phenomena
> Being pure of the two obscurations.
> It [also] has the characteristic of the inexhaustible mastery

> Over the wisdom of the real and [the wisdom] whose object
> that is.

The suchness of all conditioned, unconditioned, contaminated, and uncontaminated phenomena refers to emptiness. The suchness that is the emptiness of the buddhabhūmi has the characteristic and nature of being free from the afflictive and cognitive obstructions. This is the change of state of suchness. "The wisdom of the real" refers to the pure mundane wisdom that is attained subsequently to this change of state, while "the real" refers to the nonconceptual wisdom that is the characteristic of the change of state of the ālaya-consciousness, which is the other-dependent nature. This nonconceptual wisdom (of meditative equipoise) is known in an unmistaken manner through the pure mundane wisdom of subsequent attainment, but not through any other kind of wisdom. This describes the change of state of the ālaya-consciousness, which is the support for the impregnations of negative tendencies. The word "that" in the last line refers to the dharmadhātu, which means that nonconceptual wisdom focuses on the dharmadhātu. This describes the change of state of the path.[144] Through the pure mundane wisdom of subsequent attainment focusing on nonconceptual wisdom, inexhaustible mastery is attained, because this pure mundane wisdom realizes the nature of nonconceptual wisdom in an unmistaken manner. Also, nonconceptual wisdom attains inexhaustible mastery over suchness—the dharmadhātu—because nonconceptual wisdom settles one-pointedly on the dharmadhātu. This describes the nature of the dharmadhātu.[145]

As was said before, the realization of ultimate reality equals buddhahood—in fact buddhahood *is* nothing but ultimate reality, since there is no subject-object duality at that point. So to further highlight the close connection between the planes of ontology, epistemology, and soteriology, the above characteristics of buddhahood in Yogācāra (neither existent nor nonexistent, neither pure nor impure, being changeless suchness, like space, yet consisting of pure dharmas, and so on) may be compared with the characteristics of ultimate reality as presented in *Mahāyānasūtrālaṃkāra* VI.1:

> Neither existent nor nonexistent, neither such nor other,
> Neither arisen nor perished, neither decreasing nor increasing,
> Not purified and yet purified again—
> These are the characteristics of the ultimate.

Sthiramati[146] comments that the ultimate is twofold—suchness (the pure dharmadhātu) and nondual nonconceptual wisdom. Suchness is called the ultimate, since it is the fruition of having cultivated the path of the noble ones and represents all phenomena. Or, in terms of its being an object, it is the ultimate, because it is the object of ultimate nonconceptual wisdom.[147] Here, the above fivefold characteristic of the nonduality of the ultimate primarily refers to suchness (nonconceptual wisdom being explained later in chapter 9 and so on). (1) The ultimate—the perfect nature—is not existent, because it does not exist like the imaginary and the other-dependent natures. However, the essence of the ultimate—the perfect nature—is not nonexistent either. (2) The perfect nature is not the same as the imaginary nature, because the latter does not exist and appears in a mistaken way, while the former is the true reality and unmistaken. Nor is the perfect nature the same as the other-dependent nature, because the latter is the support for imaginary phenomena, with its nature being dependently originated and afflicted, while the former does not serve as a support for imaginary phenomena—it is not dependently originated and represents purified phenomenon. The perfect nature is also not different from the imaginary and the other-dependent natures, because what is referred to as "the perfect nature" is the fact of the other-dependent nature being free from the imaginary nature, but there is no extra perfect nature apart from that. (3) The perfect nature is not arisen, since it is not produced by karma and afflictions. It does not perish, since unarisen phenomena do not cease—it has the nature of being unconditioned. (4) The perfect nature is without decrease and increase, just as space. Even when clouds in space decrease, there is no decrease in space. Even when previously nonexistent clouds appear in it, space does not arise newly. Likewise, though saṃsāric afflictions decrease during the time of cultivating the path of the noble ones, there is no decrease in emptiness, and even though purified phenomena—the factors concordant with enlightenment—increase, there is no increase in emptiness. (5) The ultimate is emptiness. Just as space, gold, water, and a crystal are naturally pure, it is pure in that it is of the nature of emptiness. Just as the natural purity of space cannot be purified by washing it with water or the like, in the nature of emptiness, there are no stains to be purified. Therefore, it is said to be "not purified." Though there are no stains to be removed in this nature, it is not that the afflictive and cognitive obscurations that exist in emptiness in an adventitious manner are not to be removed—indeed they must be removed and purified, a process like removing adventitious clouds from space, or adventitious earth and stones from gold. This is called "the ultimate becoming pure." In brief, the ultimate refers to the emptiness that is personal identitylessness and the emptiness that is phenomenal identitylessness.

Mind's Three Enlightened Bodies and Four Wisdom Eyes

The nature and the functions of buddhahood as the realization of ultimate reality are described as the four wisdoms, which represent the cognitive processes within the all-encompassing dharmadhātu[148] that result in the two rūpakāyas performing enlightened activity within the dharmakāya. This description once again clearly highlights the fact that buddhahood is not an inactive or inert state. These processes are presented in the classical Yogācāra format of a change of state in terms of the eight consciousnesses on the one side and the four wisdoms and the three kāyas on the other side. As explained before, this does not mean any actual transformation of the former into the latter, such as miraculously transforming something really bad into something excellent. Still, conventionally speaking, it is taught that, upon being purified (or realized to be adventitious), the ālaya-consciousness manifests as mirrorlike wisdom, the afflicted mind as the wisdom of equality, the mental consciousness as discriminating wisdom, and the five sense consciousnesses as all-accomplishing wisdom. Most fundamentally, once the emptiness in these consciousnesses has become pure, the dharmadhātu is completely pure. In other words, these changes of state take place within the fundamental space of the dharmadhātu, while always being inseparable from it. The *Nighaṇṭa*[149] (a Sanskrit-Tibetan glossary of key Buddhist terms) describes the dharmadhātu and the four wisdoms as follows:

> *Dharmadhātuviśuddha* means the completely pure dharmadhātu. It serves as the cause and expanse for the arising and originating of the dharmas of the noble ones (such as the powers and fearlessnesses). Therefore, within the dharmadhātu (that is, suchness), the adventitious afflictive obscurations and cognitive obscurations (which are like clouds) are translucent and purified. Since it is similar to the pure expanse of the sky, it is called "the completely pure expanse of dharmas."
>
> *Ādarśajñāna* means mirrorlike wisdom. Since it focuses on the completely pure dharmadhātu, it is free from all conceptions of apprehender and apprehended. This refers to the change of state of the ālaya-consciousness, through which the reflections of all phenomena appear [as clearly in it] as anything whatsoever [can] appear in a polished mirror. Thus, it is called "mirrorlike wisdom."

> *Samatājñāna* means the wisdom of equality. When the utterly pure familiarization with the actuality of true reality is clearly realized for the first time on the first bhūmi, no distinction is made between oneself and others and they are realized to be an equality. Through purification on the following higher bhūmis, on the buddhabhūmi, this [eventually] becomes the nonabiding nirvāṇa. At this time, the afflicted mind has undergone a transition and changed state as wisdom. This is called "[the wisdom of] equality."
>
> *Pratyavekṣājñāna* means discriminating wisdom. Through the change of state of the mental consciousness, [this wisdom] serves as the basis for all dhāraṇīs, samādhis, dhyānas, and meditative absorptions. It represents the operating of the wisdom that is unobstructed with regard to all knowable objects, pours down the great rain of dharma, cuts through all kinds of doubt, and serves as the cause for [buddhas] displaying their kāyas in the colors of precious substances (such as blue beryll). This is called "discriminating wisdom."
>
> *Krityānuṣṭhānajñāna* means all-accomplishing wisdom. Through the change of state of the consciousnesses of the five sense faculties (such as the eye), [this wisdom] serves as the basis for promoting the welfare of many sentient beings in all worldly realms through various infinite means. This is called "all-discriminating wisdom."

To be sure, the set of the four wisdoms plus the pure dharmadhātu and the set of the three kāyas are absolutely equivalent—both describe the same thing, that is, complete buddhahood with all its qualities. Thus, when these two sets are matched, mirrorlike wisdom represents the dharmakāya, the wisdom of equality and discriminating wisdom make up the sambhogakāya, and all-accomplishing wisdom is the nirmāṇakāya.

As the quotes in the translations below show, these formats are already found in the *Buddhabhūmisūtra*, the *Trikāyanāmasūtra*, and the *Suvarṇaprabhāsottamasūtra*. However, the classical source on correlating the eight consciousnesses with the four wisdoms and the dharmadhātu in the Yogācāra tradition is the introduction in Sthiramati's commentary on verses IX.12–17 on the fundamental change of state in the *Mahāyānasūtrālaṃkāra*.

> Here, "state" refers to the five skandhas from the skandha of form up through the skandha of consciousness. After the afflictive and cognitive obscurations that exist in these skandhas have been relinquished, the dharmadhātu has become pure and has become nonconceptual wisdom. This is called "change of state into something else." In this regard, when the four skandhas of form, feeling, discrimination, and formation as well as [everything] in the skandha of consciousness from the eye consciousness up through the afflicted mind have become pure, the dharmadhātu becomes pure. When the ālaya-consciousness has become pure, it becomes nonconceptual wisdom.
>
> Or, when the emptiness that exists in form, feeling, discrimination, formation, and the eight consciousnesses has become pure, the dharmadhātu becomes pure. From among the eight consciousnesses, when the ālaya-consciousness has become pure, it becomes mirrorlike wisdom. When the afflicted mind has become pure, it becomes the wisdom of equality. When the mental consciousness has become pure, it becomes discriminating wisdom. When the five [sense] consciousnesses, from the eye [consciousness] up through the body [consciousness] have become pure, they become all-accomplishing wisdom. The attainment of these five—the four wisdoms and the pure dharmadhātu—are called "the five changes of state into something else."[150]

As for the three kāyas, *Mahāyānasūtrālaṃkāra* IX.59–60 highlights their not being static states, but different functions of the pure dharmadhātu.

> The purity of the dharmadhātu
> Of the buddhas is explained
> As its function varying in terms of
> Nature, enjoying the dharma, and emanating.
>
> The svābhāvika[kāya], the sāmbhogikakāya,
> And the other one, the nairmāṇikakāya,
> Are the divisions of the kāya of the buddhas.
> The first one is the foundation of the [other] two.[151]

Sthiramati comments that "nature" (*svābhāvika*) refers to the dharmakāya,[152] meaning that the nature of buddhahood as such is the pure dharmadhātu.

When the stains of apprehender and apprehended that exist in the ālaya-consciousness have been relinquished, and thus the dharmadhātu has become mirrorlike wisdom, this is called "dharmakāya." The sāmbhogikakāya refers to the afflicted mind having changed state, and thus having become the wisdom of equality, as well as the mental consciousness having changed state, and thus having become discriminating wisdom. It is called "enjoyment body," because it provides the great enjoyment of the dharma for bodhisattvas who have entered the bhūmis. The nairmāṇikakāya represents the change of state of the five sense consciousnesses and all-accomplishing wisdom. It demonstrates the twelve deeds of a buddha and brings sentient beings to maturity. Thus, the Tathāgatas are not limited to a single kāya, but there is a division into three, with the dharmakāya being the foundation or support of the other two.[153]

The different functions of the three kāyas and four wisdoms are described in detail in *Mahāyānasūtrālaṃkāra* IX.61–76.[154] Further treatises that deal with the eight consciousnesses, the three kāyas, the four wisdoms, and their changes of state include the *Mahāyānasaṃgraha* (chapter 10) and its commentaries. Also the explanations on the three kāyas in Śīlabhadra's *Buddhabhūmivyākhyāna* and Bandhuprabha's *Buddhabhūmyupadeśa* (which is largely based on the former) greatly rely on the *Mahāyānasūtrālaṃkārabhāṣya* on IX.60–66 and chapter 10 of the *Mahāyānasaṃgraha*. These texts also relate the four wisdoms to the three kāyas and explicitly say that the three kāyas are nothing but a division in terms of the functional aspects of buddhahood, which in itself is the single and indivisible purity of the dharmadhātu (of course, the same goes for the four wisdoms too). These functional aspects appear for different beings—the svābhāvikakāya or dharmakāya (which is equivalent to the pure dharmadhātu) is only realized by buddhas; the sambhogakāya is perceived by bodhisattvas; and the nirmāṇakāya is seen even by impure beings.[155] Both texts furthermore relate the dharmakāya and mirrorlike wisdom to the nonconceptual wisdom in meditative equipoise, and the two rūpakāyas and the remaining three wisdoms to the wisdom that is active during subsequent attainment. In particular, Śīlabhadra explains that all elements of the dualistic structure of the phenomenal world in terms of apprehender and apprehended (all consciousnesses and their objects) appear like reflections in mirrorlike wisdom and are discerned accordingly through the other three wisdoms, for which this mirrorlike wisdom serves as a foundation. Thus, it is primarily through mirrorlike wisdom that all aspects of phenomena appear for a buddha's mind, although without any dualistic discriminations. Rather, they are perceived "in their aspect of self-awareness," which is also referred to as buddha wisdom having the quality of total recall. Buddha is said to be omniscient by virtue of mirrorlike wisdom, which is ever present and ever clear.[156] The discussions of these topics in Nāgamitra's *Kāyatrayāvatāramukha* and its commentary by Jñānacandra also relate the three kāyas to the three natures. Buddhaśrījñāna's (eighth/ninth century) *Saṃcayagāthāpañjikā* discusses the last chapter of the *Abhisamayālaṃkāra* in terms of the change of state of the eight consciousnesses as the five wisdoms (adding dharmadhātu wisdom) and the four kāyas.

As mentioned before, the four wisdoms are not four different entities or static qualities of one entity, but just stand for the processes that represent the main functional activities of the single nonconceptual wisdom of a buddha, which cooperate with and supplement each other. Mirrorlike wisdom is like an all-encompassing TV screen that simply reflects what is there, thus providing the "raw data" to be processed and used. Discriminating wisdom means to intently look at this screen and clearly see all its distinct data without getting confused or mixing them up.[157] The wisdom of equality refers to being empathic, but lacking any kind of judgment, about the data seen on the screen, as well as making no difference between seer and seen. All-accomplishing wisdom represents the resultant impulse to altruistically act upon what is seen. Thus, nonconceptual buddha wisdom reflects all sentient beings and phenomena within a buddha's field of activity without any bias and personal concern (mirrorlike wisdom). At the same time, this nonconceptual wisdom perceives and discerns all these beings and phenomena in every minute detail, just as they are, with perfectly clear discernment and without any personal projections or superimpositions (discriminating wisdom). Nonconceptual wisdom is also completely nondual, which not only refers to its perceptual structure (no subject-object duality), but also to its "affective" structure—it neither takes saṃsāra as something bad to be avoided, nor nirvāṇa as something good to dwell in; lacks any attachment and aversion to anybody or anything; and instead sees the buddha nature of all beings, which is not different in essence from a buddha's very own state, thus naturally being loving and compassionate toward all those who do not see this (the wisdom of equality). By virtue of all these features, nonconceptual wisdom is the most efficient mental mode of operation possible, which underlies everything that, from the perspective of those to be benefited, appears as a buddha's helpful activity in an effortless, unpremeditated, and uninterrupted way (all-accomplishing wisdom).

As for the five wisdoms "in action" in realized beings during all situations, the Third Karmapa says that, when embraced by the correct yoga, sense perception, mental direct perception, and self-aware direct perception are all yogic valid perception, which is connate wisdom's own nature.[158] Through all aspects of knowing and what is to be known being embraced by the perfect view, in terms of its functions, this connate wisdom then manifests as the five wisdoms. These are the wisdom that discriminates all causes and results; the wisdom of being empty of a nature of its own (mirrorlike wisdom); the display of wisdom's power by virtue of having gained mastery over it (all-accomplishing wisdom); the wisdom of seeing the equality of all this; and the principle of not moving away from suchness, which pervades all of this (dharmadhātu wisdom).[159] Pawo Tsugla Trengwa, one of the main students of the Eighth Karmapa and a teacher of the Ninth, describes the complementary functions of these wisdoms as follows:

> [Buddhahood means] to know without exception how all the aspects of each phenomenon are, because it is endowed with discriminating wisdom. In this process, it is not endowed with a seeing [that entails] any subject or object to be seen, any higher or inferior, any same or different, and so on, because it is endowed with the wisdom of equality. This knowledge does not entail any efforts [either], because it is endowed with mirrorlike wisdom. Also, all of these are indescribable as being one or different and so on, and are neither a seeing nor a nonseeing, because they never move away from the dharmadhātu.[160]

The ninth chapter of the *Mahāyānasūtrālaṃkāra* concludes with a verse on buddhas being neither one nor many (IX.77), four verses on applying the means to attain buddhahood (IX.78–81), four verses on the unity of the activities of all buddhas (IX.82–85), and one verse on generating enthusiasm for buddhahood (IX.86). Sthiramati says that the means to attain buddhahood are the first five pāramitās. The pāramitā of prajñā is what renders these five pure, and it is taught in IX.78–81 (in themselves, these verses exhibit the typical style of the prajñāpāramitā sūtras).

> Precisely what does not exist
> Is the supreme existent.
> Nonobservation in every respect
> Is held to be the supreme observing.

On the first bhūmi, bodhisattvas realize that the imaginary nature—apprehender and apprehended—does not exist. The very fact of its nonexistence is designated as "the supreme existent," because the perfect nature—the freedom from apprehender and apprehended—exists. On this bhūmi, bodhisattvas neither observe nor see the imaginary nature, nor any conceptions of "me" and "mine," nor any conceptions of phenomena. This is called "the supreme observing," because they see the perfect nature—the freedom from apprehender and apprehended.

> The supreme meditation is held
> To be not seeing any meditation.
> The supreme attainment is held
> To be not seeing any attainment.

During the second up through the tenth bhūmis, bodhisattvas relinquish all conceptions of apprehender, apprehended, "me," and "mine." The very meditation in which neither a meditator nor something to be meditated on are seen is called "the supreme meditation," because bodhisattvas familiarize themselves with the characteristic that there is nothing to be observed. At the time of buddhahood, not seeing the sambhogakāya, the nirmāṇakāya, or the qualities such as the powers and fearlessnesses is called "the supreme attainment," because the supreme attainment consists of the dharmakāya—the supreme of all dharmas. Thus, to familiarize themselves with the characteristic of there being nothing to be observed is the means to become a buddha, while those who entertain any kind of focus or reference point will not become enlightened.

> For arrogant bodhisattvas who consider
> Their own grandeur, length [of practice],
> Characteristics, and vigor,
> Enlightenment is said to be far away

Some bodhisattvas may consider their own grandeur, since they see that enlightenment possesses magnificent qualities (such as the ten powers) and that it is difficult to attain. They may consider that attaining enlightenment takes a long time, since they must practice for three or more countless eons. They may see characteristics, since they see some objects to meditate on. They may think that enlightenment is to be attained through effort and feel superior, because they make such efforts, while others do not. When they are proud in this way and focused on real entities, enlightenment is distant for them.

> Nonconceptualizing bodhisattvas
> Who see all that has been mentioned

> To be mere imagination
> Are said to attain enlightenment.

On the contrary, those bodhisattvas who see all that has been explained above (one's own grandeur and so on) as being nothing but mere imagination and mere mind, and who do not even conceive of this mere mind have attained the poised readiness for the dharma of nonarising, with their nonconceptual wisdom thus being effortless and spontaneously present. Therefore, attaining this is called "attaining enlightenment."

For more details on buddhahood as the change of state of the eight consciousnesses to the four wisdoms as well as the descriptions, divisions, and relations of the kāyas (whether presented as two, three, four, or more), see the translations below and appendix 6.[161]

The Tibetan Tradition on the Five Maitreya Texts

WITH RESPECT TO THE five works by Maitreya, in Tibet, there is just about every possible interpretation in terms of which of them belong to "Mere Mentalism," Yogācāra, Yogācāra-Madhyamaka, Svātantrika-Madhyamaka, Prāsaṅgika-Madhyamaka, *Shentong* Madhyamaka, or "Great Madhyamaka." However, despite these differences, what is clear for most commentators is that, in terms of their contents, these five texts cover the entire range of the mahāyāna teachings. In particular, the Gelugpa School (and parts of the Sakya School) holds that the *Abhisamayālaṃkāra* teaches on the middle turning of the wheel of dharma (prajñāpāramitā) and represents the view of *Yogācāra-Svātantrika-Madhyamaka; the *Mahāyānasūtrālaṃkāra*, *Madhyāntavibhāga*, and *Dharmadharmatāvibhāga* teach on the third turning and represent nothing but Mere Mentalism (understood as asserting the ultimate existence of consciousness and being inferior to Madhyamaka); and the *Uttaratantra* represents *Prāsaṅgika-Madhyamaka.

By contrast, Dölpopa Sherab Gyaltsen[162] (1292–1361) says in his *Mountain Dharma* and elsewhere that all five Maitreya texts teach nothing but *shentong*, and that even the *Abhisamayālaṃkāra* does not contain what is known as *rangtong*. Tāranātha (1575–1635), in his *Essence of Other-Emptiness* and other works, agrees with this.[163]

Śākya Chogden's *Very Clear Definitive Meaning of the Five Maitreya Dharmas*[164] explains that what is explicitly taught by the *Abhisamayālaṃkāra* is the same as the explicit teaching in the sūtras of the second turning of the wheel of dharma—the nonimplicative negation of being empty of the duality of apprehender and apprehended. However, this alone is not suitable as the definitive meaning, since it does not go beyond being an isolate (an "elimination-of-other").[165] Therefore, it is definitely nothing but a direct object of conception, but not suitable as the experiential sphere of personally experienced wisdom.[166] Therefore, the ultimate definitive meaning is as identified in the *Mahāyānasūtrālaṃkāra* and the *Madhyāntavibhāga*, because the definitive meaning of the middle turning depends on what is identified as such in the final turning, which is the wisdom without the duality of apprehender and apprehended. This can be considered in terms of what bears the nature of phenomena and the nature of phenomena itself, but what is meant here is solely the latter. Thus, there is no difference whatosever in the way in which the ultimate view taught in these three texts is identified. However, they differ in the ways of teaching how to make this view a living experience through engaging in it, since the *Abhisamayālaṃkāra* explains this by combining the progression of the implicit teaching of the prajñāpāramitā sūtras (the clear realizations) with the progression of their explicit teaching (emptiness). Also, the nature of the definitive meaning taught in the *Uttaratantra* and the *Dharmadharmatāvibhāga* does not differ from the one taught in the other three Maitreya texts. However, this does not mean that the *Uttaratantra* and the *Dharmadharmatāvibhāga* just repeat what the *Mahāyānasūtrālaṃkāra* and the *Madhyāntavibhāga* say, because their ways of explanation differ. The *Mahāyānasūtrālaṃkāra* and the *Madhyāntavibhāga* indeed explain the final definitive meaning, but they do not dwell on its aspect of qualities. This aspect is explained in the *Uttaratantra* through the seven vajra points and through taking the nondual wisdom at the time of the ground as the basis of purification, which, by virtue of the purification of the adventitious stains to be purified during the time of the path, changes state as being buddha wisdom at the time of the fruition. In addition, the *Mahāyānasūtrālaṃkāra* and the *Madhyāntavibhāga* determine the view and then teach the manner of familiarizing with it through one's overall engagement in the six pāramitās, bodhicitta, and so on for countless eons, whereas the *Dharmadharmatāvibhāga* identifies the definitive meaning as "the nature of phenomena" and then teaches the familiarization with it from the perspective of mentally engaging in this nature of phenomena alone. In brief, in terms of determining the view in the works of Maitreya, whatever exists must be the dharmadhātu and emptiness, which must be what is called "the wisdom empty of the duality of apprehender and apprehended," also bearing the name "perfect nature." In his *Illuminating the Stages of the Path of the Five Maitreya Dharmas*,[167] Śākya Chogden explains that, in all five Maitreya works in general, at the time of studying and reflecting, the entirety of seeming reality is ascertained as self-empty. What is taught with regard to the time of meditating is to rest in equipoise in ultimate reality alone. Thus, in particular, also the *Abhisamayālaṃkāra* teaches both *rangtong* and *shentong*. In the context of studying and reflecting, the temporary definitive meaning in the *Abhisamayālaṃkāra* must be explained in accordance with how the Niḥsvabhāvavādins[168] comment on it, because what is to be experienced (later) through yogic valid perception needs to be identified first in the context of study and reflection. In the context of identifying what is to be experienced through having become familiar with it through meditation, this must be explained according to Asaṅga's and Vasubandhu's way of commenting, because what is to be experienced through yogic valid perception needs to be identified in the specific context of meditation.[169] In general, the *Abhisamayālaṃkāra*'s philosophical system is nothing other than what Asaṅga explains. Śākya Chogden's *Explanation of the Origin of Madhyamaka*[170] says that the main subject of both the *Abhisamayālaṃkāra* and the *Uttaratantra* is the Madhyamaka that represents the intention of the prajñāpāramita sūtras as commented on through the third turning of the wheel of dharma. In the *Abhisamayālaṃkāra*, the hidden meaning of these sūtras—the clear realizations—is identified from the perspective of the wisdom that is free from apprehender and apprehended, and the text's seventy points ascertain all phenomena as *rangtong* in accordance with the explicit teachings of said sūtras. Similarly, in the *Uttaratantra*, when emptiness and the Tathāgata heart are identified, both the way of negating the object of negation and the identification of the object that is to be made a living experience are clearly explained in the manner of *shentong*. Moreover, if the view of the three other Maitreya texts belonged to Mere Mentalism, all presentations of the five paths, the ten bhūmis, and the fruitional buddhabhūmi in them would have to be deprecated as not being in accord with how things actually are. Thus, all mahāyāna texts composed by Asaṅga and Vasubandhu, as well as all those by Dignāga and his spiritual heirs, represent nothing but the Madhyamaka of the definitive meaning, which is nothing but the intention of the prajñāpāramitā sūtras as commented on in the sūtras of the third turning.

Mipham Rinpoche's (1846–1912) introduction in his commentary on the *Dharmadharmatāvibhāga*[171] says that the five Maitreya works comment on the intentions of the entire teachings of the Buddha. Among them, the *Abhisamayālaṃkāra* comments on the intention of the middle turning of the wheel of dharma (prajñāpāramitā), and the *Uttaratantra* comments on the definitive meaning of the final turning (the intention of the sūtras that teach the Sugata heart). Both assert a final single disposition[172] and a final single yāna, and to that extent accord with the intention of Madhyamaka. The *Mahāyānasūtrālaṃkāra* is a synopsis that comments on the intentions of the majority of the remaining sūtras. Most of what is said in it, such as a single disposition and a single yāna not being definite, is mainly a commentary on the intention of the sūtras of Mere Mentalism.[173] The *Madhyāntavibhāga* and the *Dharmadharmatāvibhāga* teach the vast and the profound sides, respectively, of the general yāna. Though they extensively teach on the three natures and the nonexistence of outer objects, it is in no way definite for them to be exclusive Mere Mentalist texts merely by virtue of these features.

It is also not contradictory to present the intention of Madhyamaka through these terminologies, since the *Laṅkāvatārasūtra* teaches the five dharmas, the three natures, the eight consciousnesses, and the two kinds of identitylessness as the general dharma terminologies of the entire mahāyāna,[174] and since the three natures also appear in the Maitreya chapter of the prajñāpāramitā sūtras. However, there is no word or reasoning in any of those two texts by Maitreya that suggests a really established nondual consciousness as asserted by the Mere Mentalists. Thus, there is no flaw in explaining them to be unbiased commentaries on the intention of the general yāna. In particular, the *Madhyāntavibhāga* gives a detailed explanation of the paths of the three yānas, while the *Dharmadharmatāvibhāga* determines nonconceptual wisdom—the heart essence of the topics of all profound sūtras—in accordance with the Yogācāra-Madhyamaka principle of the two realities in union. In it, the manner of asserting the seeming (the bearers of the nature of phenomena) accords with Mere Mentalism, while the manner of asserting the ultimate (the nature of phenomena) accords with Madhyamaka. Thus, its final intention consists of Madhyamaka and can be understood as the manner of teaching the essential points of the mahāyāna view by way of the union of Mere Mentalism and Madhyamaka.

As for the Kagyü School, the Third Karmapa's introduction to his OED says:

> The *Abhisamayālaṃkāra* clearly teaches on prajñāpāramitā, the middle [cycle of the] Buddha's words, the dharma wheel of the lack of characteristics. The *Mahāyānasūtrālaṃkāra* illuminates the meaning of all teachings of the sūtras in the first and the middle [dharma wheel] and so on. The *Madhyāntavibhāga* teaches the meanings of the characteristics [of afflicted and purified phenomena] up through the unsurpassable yāna. The *Dharmadharmatāvibhāga* illuminates the meanings of saṃsāra and nirvāṇa. The *Uttaratantra* summarizes the meanings of the sūtras of the last [cycle of the] Buddha's words and of those that teach the buddhayāna . . .
>
> In particular, this *Dharmadharmatāvibhāga* illuminates the path including its fruition, which is the manner of engaging in the five dharmas[175] and the three natures (which elucidate the modes of the two realities) as well as in the true reality of the eight consciousnesses—nonconceptual wisdom that bears the name fundamental change of state, the buddha heart, the dharmakāya. Implicitly, it

> also teaches the liberations of all śrāvakas and pratyekabuddhas. Therefore, it is like a gate to enter all the words of the Buddha and the treatises [on them] . . .
>
> These five treatises are [Maitreya's] single continuous effort and, in order for these five to ascertain the meaning of the entire teachings, it is evident that homage is paid at the beginning of the *Abhisamayālaṃkāra*, while the completion part in the *Uttaratantra* teaches the dedication. [Through this,] one also realizes the order of these [five texts] as follows. [The *Abhisamayālaṃkāra*] was composed first, because prajñāpāramitā is like the mother of all texts that teach the paths (including their fruitions) of all wonderful yānas which give birth to all four noble ones. By saying that the diverse [other] sūtras of the three yānas accord with this meaning just mentioned, the *Mahāyānasūtrālaṃkāra* ascertains that they belong to the scope of what is to be understood and clearly realized. As a summary of this, the *Madhyāntavibhāga* explains merely how to engage in the characteristics of the factors to be relinquished and their remedies; the obscurations of these; true reality; abiding in the manner of cultivating the remedies, including their results; and the unsurpassable yāna.[176] If all of what is taught in this way is summarized further, everything is contained in this engagement in phenomena and their nature [as taught here in the *Dharmadharmatāvibhāga*]. The *Uttaratantra* teaches the actuality of the nature of phenomena, the basic nature of buddhahood, the final definitive meaning, which lies not within the sphere of any ordinary beings, śrāvakas, or pratyekabuddhas. [This nature is taught as] being endowed with [adventitious] stains, stainless enlightenment, its qualities, its enlightened activity, and the manner of engaging [in it].[177] Thus, one should know that all words of the Buddha's teaching and the treatises [on it] are summarized [in these five texts].[178]

The commentary on the *Madhyamakāvatāra* by the Eighth Karmapa, Mikyö Dorje, reports the position of his main teacher, the First Sangyé Nyenpa, Dashi Baljor (1457–1519)[179] on this:

> All these five dharma works by Maitreya are established as commentaries on the intentions of the entirety of the words of the Buddha in the causal and fruitional mahāyāna for the following

> reasons. As for the middle three treatises [*Mahāyānasūtrālaṃkāra*, *Madhyāntavibhāga*, and *Dharmadharmatāvibhāga*], it is not the case that they do not teach the principle of the Madhyamaka dharma in an ancillary way, but their explicit teaching is the distinct system of Yogācāra.[180] The first dharma work of Maitreya [*Abhisamayālaṃkāra*] is a treatise common to Madhyamaka and Yogācāra. The last dharma work of Maitreya [*Uttaratantra*] is a treatise common to sūtra and tantra.[181]

Jamgön Kongtrul Lodrö Tayé's (1813–1899) introduction to his commentary on the *Uttaratantra* states:

> First, [Maitreya] composed the *Abhisamayālaṃkāra*, which teaches the coarse dharma terminology of the Great Madhyamaka of definitive meaning in merely an abbreviated manner. Then, in the *Mahāyānasūtrālaṃkāra*, *Madhyāntavibhāga*, and *Dharmadharmatāvibhāga*, he explained it clearly and extensively. Finally, in the *Uttaratantra*, he ascertained the fine details of the philosophical system of the uncommon meaning of the sūtras on the [Tathāgata] heart.[182]

In brief, the texts by the Third Karmapa and others translated below are based on all five works by Maitreya in mainly the manners described by Rangjung Dorje and Sangyé Nyenpa Rinpoche, though—given their topics—they clearly emphasize the *Mahāyānasūtrālaṃkāra*, *Madhyāntavibhāga*, *Dharmadharmatāvibhāga*, and *Uttaratantra*.

The Third Karmapa's View

In the Tibetan tradition and Western scholarship alike, the Third Karmapa is often unequivocally identified as one of the main Kagyü exponents of "*Shentong* Madhyamaka." As discussed elsewhere, such categorizations depend entirely on what different people understand by this term, or by being a *shentongpa*, which can vary greatly.[183] As far as the Third Karmapa's own works are concerned, the fact is that not even the terms *shentong* or *rangtong* appear in them, let alone any definitions or further explanations. This is particularly noteworthy with respect to those of the Third Karmapa's texts that clearly present his view and in which one would expect to find these terms and their explanations if they had any significance for him. Therefore, the intention behind translating the texts below is to provide further substantial materials for the study of Rangjung Dorje's view through his own writings and not just through the filters of the later and significantly "loaded" labels *rangtong* and *shentong*.

As for the sources of the primary texts on the view by the Third Karmapa, his works are squarely based on the classical scriptures of both the Yogācāra and Madhyamaka traditions. He skillfully crafts a synthesis that consciously uses the elements of both systems, which—despite their sometimes differing hermeneutical approaches—are grounded in the same mahāyāna foundation, to supplement each other in furthering one's understanding of their common ground and to arrive at the same personally experienced wisdom of realizing the nature of one's own mind.

There are six main texts that present Rangjung Dorje's view in more or less great detail and show great consistency in this view's essential features. These six texts are:

(1) *The Profound Inner Reality* (ZMND; in particular, chapters 1, 6, and 9)
(2) the autocommentary (AC) on *The Profound Inner Reality*
(3) *Treatise on Pointing Out the Tathāgata Heart* (NT)
(4) *Treatise on the Distinction between Consciousness and Wisdom* (NY)
(5) *The Ornament That Explains the* Dharmadharmatāvibhāga (OED)
(6) the commentary on the *Dharmadhātustava* (DSC)

As for the chronology of these texts, OED's colophon says that it was written in a Tibetan Monkey Year at Upper Dechen, which can only be 1320.[184] The colophon of ZMND has a Tibetan Year of the Dog, which is 1322 according to Jamgön Kongtrul's commentary ("Water Male Dog Year"). AC's colophon gives 1325 as the year of composition. DSC was probably written in 1326 (possibly in 1327).[185] There is no date available for NT, while the colophon of NY says that it was authored at Upper Dechen in a Year of the Pig, which can only be 1323.[186] In any case, since both NY and NT are referred to by Rangjung Dorje in his AC, they were both composed before the latter and, given their overall context, after ZMND. Thus, Rangjung Dorje obviously set forth the cornerstones of his view by way of these closely interrelated texts between 1320 and 1326/27, starting with OED, followed by ZMND, NT, NY, AC, and finally DSC.

In addition, the following five shorter poetic works also exhibit many of the features found in the above texts:

(7) *The Aspiration Prayer of Mahāmudrā* (MM)

(8) *The Wisdom Lamp That Illuminates the Basic Nature*

(9) *Proclaiming Mind's Way of Being Mistaken*

(10) *Stanzas That Express Realization*

(11) *A Song on the Ālaya.*

The Third Karmapa's great interest in the texts by Maitreya and Asaṅga in particular is further demonstrated by his having composed summaries of the *Mahāyānasūtrālaṃkāra, Uttaratantra, Bodhisattvabhūmi,* and *Śrāvakabhūmi*; both summaries of, and commentaries on, the *Madhyāntavibhāga* and *Dharmadharmatāvibhāga*; and a synopsis and a table of contents of the *Abhisamayālaṃkāra.*[187]

From among the above eleven texts by Rangjung Dorje, (6) and (7) have been translated elsewhere;[188] (3), (4), (10), and (11) are translated below in full; and the remaining ones are translated below in their parts that focus on the view. In the Kagyü tradition, (1)–(4) are considered as a unity that is crucial in its elucidation of how the views and practices of vajrayāna and Mahāmudrā are based on the sūtrayāna teachings on buddha nature as the very ground, path, and fruition of these approaches and on mind's transition from being obscured in the form of dualistic consciousness to being free as nondual wisdom. These texts are not just mere philosophical or scholastic treatises, but inform and enhance meditation practice through their profound outlook and, occasionally, very alive and immediate diction. Among these four texts, the most famous one—ZMND together with its AC—is an extensive general commentary on the tantras. However, its first, sixth, and ninth chapters are, or include, discussions of general mahāyāna topics such as the eight consciousnesses or adventitious stains as the nature and the origin of saṃsāra; the nature of the mind (the Tathāgata heart or nonconceptual wisdom) as the basis of nirvāṇa; the transition from the one to the other; the two realities (ultimate and seeming); and the three natures. All of these explanations equally apply to sūtras and tantras and are supplemented by more details on buddha nature, consciousness, and wisdom in NT and NY. These elements are found in the same ways in the remaining six texts (5)–(10), which indeed indicates that they portray Rangjung Dorje's basic view as the common fundament of the mahāyāna in general and the vajrayāna in particular.

To highlight some essential features of the Third Karmapa's view, ZMND starts by stating the overarching theme that pervades all of the above texts—the purpose of its composition being the realization of our primordially pure buddha nature, which is only temporarily obscured by adventitious stains. This Tathāgata heart is ever present and unchanging throughout the three phases of its being impure (i.e., sentient beings or ground), being partially impure and partially pure (i.e., bodhisattvas or path), and being completely pure (i.e., buddhas or fruition). This theme is further elaborated at the end of the first chapter of ZMND and makes up all of DSC and NT. The first chapter of ZMND and AC (as well as NT) starts by describing the process of saṃsāric ignorance as mind being unaware of its own nature. Later in that chapter, AC (as well as NY) comments on the four conditions that make everything mind-made appear—the ālaya-consciousness as the causal condition; the sense faculties as the dominant conditions; forms, sounds, and so forth as the object-conditions; and the immediate mind as the immediate condition. Ultimately, these conditions may be asserted as nothing but dependent origination, but they are all simply expressions for particular events of mind's own imagination. The classical Yogācāra template of how these eight consciousnesses change state as the four wisdoms and the three kāyas is described and further refined in terms of the immediate mind in the sixth chapter of AC as well as in OED and NY (in greatest detail).

The extensive discussion of the two realities in chapter 9 of AC declares that, ultimately, all notions of ground, path, and fruition are just superimpositions. What exists ultimately, but free from all reference points, is naturally pure mind without any adventitious stains—the buddha heart endowed with the two realities. Commenting on a quote from the *Vajrajñānasamucchayatantra*, the two realities are primarily explained in classical Madhyamaka diction (using the *Akutobhayā*, commenting on *Mūlamadhyamakakārikā* XXV.8–10). The seeming is said to be dualistic appearance, with its reality being like a reflection of the moon in water, while the ultimate consists of the eighteen emptinesses, with its reality being nondual wisdom. DSC's even longer introduction on the two realities is based on the same quote but explains them in terms of both the Madhyamaka system and the Yogācāra framework of the three natures (supported by quotes from both traditions). Based on the *Ratnagotravibhāgavyākhyā*, those who do not see the inconceivable object of the buddhas (the Tathāgata heart) are identified as ordinary beings, tīrthikas who entertain views about a self, śrāvakas, pratyekabuddhas, and even beginner bodhisattvas whose minds are distracted from the correct realization of emptiness through conceptualizing suchness and the fruition. Thus, the path must be understood in terms of both the two realities and the three natures.

As for the two realities, it is the nature of dualistic appearances to appear like a reflection of the moon in water, which is seeming reality. Ultimate reality means that precisely these mere appearances are naturally free from all reference points. In this way, the two realities are completely free from being the same or different. At the same time, both are just conventional, and neither is independently real. The essential point of Madhyamaka is to put an end to every kind of clinging to reality, unreality, existence, and nonexistence. In this way, since the seeming is deceiving like an illusion, it is nothing but false imagination that appears as the abodes, objects, and bodies of sentient beings, all being just various aspects of the eight consciousnesses. Since these consciousnesses arise in dependence on false imagination, they are not real. But since they appear in a manner of being dependent on illusory causes and conditions, they are not utterly nonexistent either, thus being called "other-dependent." The labels and discriminations that are superimposed onto these other-dependent appearances are called "the imaginary nature," since what is nonexistent is wrongly imagined to be existent. The fundamental ground within this mistaken play is the stainless dharmadhātu being unaware of itself, but there is nothing on any level of ground, path, or fruition that is really established. When these teachings on the two realities are practiced as the path, they make up the two accumulations of merit and wisdom, and their fruition is the union of the two kāyas. DSC ends this topic by saying that Nāgārjuna's collection of reasoning negates the clinging to characteristics, but definitely not the teachings on the actual way of being of the Buddha, the dharma, wisdom, great compassion, and enlightened activity.

Further typical examples of combining Madhyamaka and Yogācāra explanations in Rangjung Dorje's texts are found in NY. Though this short text is largely based on the *Mahāyānasūtrālaṃkāra*, the *Mahāyānasaṃgraha*, and the *Uttaratantra*, it repeats three times (!) that all phenomena do not arise from themselves, from something other, from both, or without a cause. All phenomena are said to be nothing but dependent origination, with this very dependent origination being empty of a nature of its own, free from being one or different, and unaffected by being real or false, just as an illusion or the reflection of the moon in water. At the same time, all seemingly external objects are taught to be just appearances in one's own mind, while adding the typical Madhyamaka stance on the teachings on "mere mind," that is, their being given in order to eliminate ideas about any outer agent or creator.

The colophon of OED says:

> I commented on the profound by relying
> On the gist of the intentions of Asaṅga and Nāgārjuna.
> Through this virtue, may [all] enter the actuality free from
> extremes.[189]

Thus, in the context of a commentary on a Yogācāra text on the fundamental change of state of nondual nonconceptual wisdom, this change of state that is to be attained through studying this text and making it a living experience is identified as "the freedom from extremes"—the hallmark of the Madhyamaka teachings.

AC also provides a brief overview of the progressively remedial nature of the Buddha's teachings—replacing respectively coarser ideas by increasingly subtler ones. Notions such as minute material particles (as held by the Vaibhāṣikas and Sautrāntikas) are of course mistaken from the perspective that all seemingly external objects are just mental appearances emerging from the ālaya-consciousness. But the Buddha taught on particles and the like, since such teachings may serve as remedies for wrong views about an ātman or a creator. Next, the clinging to any external material entities is undermined through the instructions that all phenomena are nothing but appearances in the mind, which only emerge from the network of interrelated conditions represented by the eight consciousnesses. However, the ensuing clinging to all phenomena as being nothing but mind, or mind being the only real existent, also needs to be relinquished. Eventually letting go of it too makes one see true reality, which may either be described as mind—like everything else—being unborn (the identitylessness of all phenomena), or as the dharmadhātu free from the obscuring duality of apprehender and apprehended. Thus, all levels of the Buddha's teachings are justified and useful as expedient progressive means, which lead to the final realization of the one ultimate reality.

According to OED, the *Dharmadharmatāvibhāga* primarily teaches the manner of practically engaging in the Tathāgata heart. Among all of Rangjung Dorje's works, this text gives the most detailed presentations of nonconceptual wisdom, the notion of "change of state," and the three natures. It also connects the latter with the threefold lack of nature, explicitly states that both the imaginary and the other-dependent natures are not really established, and says that the fundamental change of state of the other-dependent is the perfect nature. It also extensively explains the four "yogic practices" found in many mahāyāna texts.

Just as do AC and NT, DSC describes the ground—the Tathāgata heart—as the dharmadhātu, which does not just refer to sheer emptiness—it is the twofold nondual and nonconceptual wisdom of knowing both how things truly are and the infinite variety of how they appear. This nonconceptual wisdom is revealed through becoming free from adventitious stains, which are the four characteristics of conceptualizing the factors to be relinquished, the remedies, suchness, and the fruition, as taught in the *Avikalpapraveśadhāraṇī* (see also OED, NTC, and NYC). The text explains how the dharmadhātu is endowed with the four pāramitās of genuine purity, self, bliss, and permanence and how these differ from the same set of four as the mistaken notions of ordinary beings. Similar to the *Uttaratantra's* nine examples on buddha nature, DSC matches the initial six examples in the *Dharmadhātustava* with the dharmadhātu, wisdom in general, and the four wisdoms such as mirrorlike wisdom, as well as with their corresponding kinds of obscurations. In terms of the path, DSC explains how the notions of cause and result with regard to the dharmadhātu (ground) and the dharmakāya (fruition) are just nominal—there is nothing to be newly attained and nothing to be removed. By virtue of the adventitious stains (the eight consciousnesses) being mere imaginations, mind's nature becomes aware of its own primordial state, once these stains are seen for what they are—illusions. The dharmadhātu is empty of both factors to be relinquished and their remedies and is never affected by either. Once both subside, mind's essence just displays its natural luminosity, similar to murky water becoming clear on its own when not being stirred. Thus, it is not empty of its own wisdom nature, which however cannot be pinpointed as being empty, not empty, both, or neither. Both factors to be relinquished and remedies (included in the imaginary and other-dependent natures) are unreal, not arising from themselves, something other, both, or without a cause. They are just the play of dependent origination, which is precisely what is called "emptiness." Through relinquishing all kinds of clinging to reference points or extremes, one enters the middle, as taught in both the *Madhyāntavibhāga* and the *Mūlamadhyamakakārikā*. Ultimate reality is the unity of appearance and emptiness, which is the unchanging and unmistaken perfect nature. The actual practice on the path consists of the two phases of meditative equipoise and subsequent attainment. The first is the union of nonconceptual wisdom and samādhi, being immersed in the suchness of the dharmadhātu (also expressed as Prajñāpāramitā and Mahāmudrā). During the phase of subsequent attainment, when sense perception, mental direct perception, and self-awareness are embraced by the correct yoga, they all become yogic direct cognition, which is nothing but the nature of dharmadhātu wisdom. Thus, the nature of the mind is discovered right within seemingly dualistic consciousnesses—gaining certainty that they are nothing but the dharmadhātu, all external and internal phenomena are seen to be just mind's own display, which is without any arising and ceasing. In brief, the difference between saṃsāra and nirvāṇa is whether the nature of mind is realized through prajñā or not. The fruition of the path is the dharmadhātu fully manifesting without obscurations, then being called "dharmakāya." In other words, it is the final fundamental change of state of the five skandhas into the five pure skandhas, with the skandha of the eight consciousnesses becoming the four wisdoms. DSC concludes by saying that all great masters (such as Nāgārjuna, Maitreya, Āryadeva, Asaṅga, Buddhapālita, Bhāvaviveka, and Candrakīrti), though they may sometimes give differing explanations, always agree on the vital point—the ultimate nature or dharmadhātu wisdom—and it is exactly this that is to be understood as the correct view and realization of all yānas.

NT is basically a synopsis of the *Uttaratantra*, while NY represents a digest of the Yogācāra presentations on the eight consciousnesses and the four wisdoms, both containing many of the above technical elements in more or less detail. In addition to these more scholarly explanations, the two texts often exhibit a distinctly experiential style, grounded in the Mahāmudrā approach, with some of their passages being more like direct meditation or pointing-out instructions.[190] As a pith instruction on this approach, MM is naturally more oriented toward meditative practice and does not give a systematic presentation of the view. Nevertheless, it still highlights some crucial points, such as the identification of what ground, path, and fruition are (verse 6); the basis of purification (mind as such, lucid and empty in union), the factors to be purified (adventitious stains), the means to purify them, and the fruition of purification—the stainless dharmakāya (verse 7);[191] appearances being mind; mind being empty (neither existent nor nonexistent), yet displaying in many unimpeded ways; and mind free from apprehender and apprehended being its natural luminosity to be realized, which is primordially present in sentient beings (verses 9–14, 18, and 22).

The Wisdom Lamp That Illuminates the Basic Nature gives a presentation of the three kāyas and five wisdoms related to mind's nature, the five buddha families, Madhyamaka, Mahāmudrā, and Dzogchen. The beginning of *Proclaiming Mind's Way of Being Mistaken* very much resembles what ZMND, AC, and NY say on mind's being deluded about itself. The *Stanzas That Express Realization* exhibits the already familiar synthesis of Yogācāra and Madhyamaka notions, joining it with an outline of the path in terms of the four realities of the noble ones, the thirty-seven dharmas concordant with enlightenment, and the six pāramitās. *A Song on the Ālaya* presents mind's own true nature as the single essence of everything that appears as saṃsāra and nirvāṇa—when not realized it seems to be dualistic delusion, and when realized, it is the mind of a buddha.

Karmapa Rangjung Dorje's synthesis of the two great mahāyāna traditions is further evidenced by the significant number of scriptural sources by major Indian Yogācāra and Mādhyamika masters that his above texts incorporate or quote.

AC (translated sections)
- *Mahāyānasaṃgraha* (eight extensive passages)
- *Mahāyānasūtrālaṃkāra* (twelve verses)
- *Bodhicittavivaraṇa* (eleven)
- *Dharmadhātustava* (eight)
- *Uttaratantra* (eight)
- *Triṃśikā* (seven)
- *Mahāyānaviṃśikā* (six)
- *Madhyāntavibhāga* (four)
- *Mūlamadhyamakakārikā* (three, plus the comments in the *Akutobhayā*).

Further texts include Jñānagarbha's *Satyadvayavibhāga*, Vasubandhu's *Pañcaskandhaprakaraṇa*, Dignāga's *Alambanaparīkṣa*, and Dharmakīrti's *Pramāṇaviniścaya* (two times each).[192]

DSC
- *Uttaratantra* (forty-two verses)
- *Mahāyānasūtrālaṃkāra* (twenty)
- *Madhyāntavibhāga* (seventeen)
- *Yuktiṣaṣṭikā* (eight)
- *Madhyamakāvatāra* (seven; implying another twenty-nine)
- *Abhisamayālaṃkāra* (seven)
- *Bodhicittavivaraṇa* (seven)
- *Mūlamadhyamakakārikā* (six)
- *Dharmadharmatāvibhāga* (eighteen lines).

Also quoted at length are Asaṅga's *Ratnagotravibhāgavyākhyā* and *Mahāyānasaṃgraha* (both four times), while Nāgārjuna's *Śūnyatāsaptati* and *Acintyastava* as well as the *Satyadvayavibhāga* are each represented with two verses. Nāgārjuna's *Ratnāvalī* is even quoted with forty-nine verses (twenty-nine of them are the elaboration on the causes of the thirty-two major marks of a buddha, while the presentation of each one of the ten bhūmis is supported by two verses).

OED (translated sections)
Mahāyānasūtrālaṃkāra (eight verses)
Mahāyānasaṃgraha (six passages)
Madhyāntavibhāga (six verses)
Yuktiṣaṣṭikā (six verses)

NT
Out of the 225 lines of this text, at least 67 are either literal quotes or passages closely resembling quoted material, almost in their entirety from among the above texts (for details, see the translations of NT and NTC).

NY
Almost half (at least 81) of its 179 lines are quotes or echo passages from some of the above texts.

That Rangjung Dorje was clearly aware of which sources his NT and NY are based on is evidenced by his own table of contents of NT,[193] which explicitly identifies a number of these sources. In addition, NTC and NYC identify most of them by quoting them from their originals.

NTC (cites or identifies)
Uttaratantra (twelve verses)
Mahāyānasūtrālaṃkāra (twelve)
Dharmadhātustava (eleven)
Mahāyānaviṃśikā (five)
Yuktiṣaṣṭikā (four)
Bodhicaryāvatāra (three)

The *Mūlamadhyamakakārikā*, *Bodhicittavivaraṇa*, *Madhyāntavibhāga*, and *Pramāṇavārttika* are all quoted two times. In addition, the text quotes ZMND (twelve lines) and AC (two extensive passages), and refers to *Abhisamayālaṃkāra* VIII.13–17 and VIII.21–32.

NYC (quotes or identifies)
Mahāyānasūtrālaṃkāra (twenty-one verses)
Uttaratantra (seven verses)
Triṃśikā (five verses)
Mahāyānasaṃgraha (four extensive passages)
Dharmadhātustava (three verses)
Madhyāntavibhāga (three)

In addition, there are three quotes from the prajñāpāramitā sūtras, while the *Satyadvayavibhāga*, *Abhisamayālaṃkāra*, and *Abhidharmakośa*, as well as Nāropa are all quoted two times.

In brief, all these texts by Rangjung Dorje share many of the same quotes or paraphrases from both Madhyamaka and Yogācāra works to support the same points (for details, see below). Throughout all his presentations, the Third Karmapa clearly sees not only no contradiction between Madhyamaka and Yogācāra, but explicitly states several times that they supplement each other and essentially come down to the same point. There can be no doubt that Rangjung Dorje's explanations are always equally based on the major Yogācāra texts by Maitreya, Asaṅga, and Vasubandhu as well as the Madhyamaka texts by Nāgārjuna, Candrakīrti, and others. In this regard, it is noteworthy that the Tibetan doxographical category "Mere Mentalist," otherwise so pervasively used, is only mentioned once (asserting buddha wisdom as really existent mere consciousness)[194] in all the above texts by Rangjung Dorje, but is clearly separated from the Yogācāra of Asaṅga and so on. Otherwise, the Karmapa's texts use the term Yogācāra or simply speak of individual masters.[195]

Rangjung Dorje's balanced approach not only has a number of Indian forerunners (such as Kambala, Śāntarakṣita, Kamalaśīla, Ratnākaraśānti, Jñānaśrīmitra, and Abhayākaragupta), but is also confirmed by several subsequent Kagyü masters. For example, Tülmo Dashi Öser opens his commentary on the *Uttaratantra* (which is based on Rangjung Dorje's lost summary of the text) as follows:

> I pay homage to the dharma lord Rangjung Dorje,
> Who commented on the intention of the Victor and his regent
> Maitreya
> By combining in a noncontradicory manner
> The essential points of the intentions of both Asaṅga and
> Nāgārjuna.[196]

Is Rangjung Dorje a *Shentongpa*?

That the Third Karmapa's view includes both the Yogācāra and the Madhyamaka systems is also stated by other Kagyü masters, but they often employ the categories of *rangtong* and *shentong* instead. Of course, such comparisons in terms of *rangtong* and *shentong* can only be made in hindsight, by employing certain terms, categories, and distinctions that Rangjung Dorje himself never used, since he does not speak about these two terms, let alone explain their differences, whether or how they exclude each other, and which one—if any at all—is superior. In addition, even if he uses certain terms, they do not necessarily—and in fact often don't—mean the same as when other people use them. To be sure, there is no problem if one wants to call the Third Karmapa's synthesis of Yogācāra, Madhyamaka, and buddha nature teachings *shentong*, as long as one does not simply use this as a generic or partisan label and is aware of what it means exactly in his case as distinct from other people who call themselves *shentongpas* and greatly elaborate on their version of what *shentong* means. As demonstrated elsewhere,[197] Rangjung Dorje's view neither matches *shentong* as understood by Dölpopa, Tāranātha, and other Jonangpas, nor Śākya Chogden's, or Jamgön Kongtrul Lodrö Tayé's presentations of it. Of course, one can find certain similarities, but there are also significant differences between the Third Karmapa's view and various brands of *shentong*. This is clearly acknowledged by several Kagyü masters, such as the First Karma Trinlépa, a close student of the Seventh Karmapa, Chötra Gyatso[198] (1454–1506) and an important teacher of the Eighth, who comments on lines 4–5 in the ninth chapter of AC as follows:

> The basic element of sentient beings is the stainless
> buddha heart endowed with the two realities.

> The meaning of this is that unconditioned and spontaneously present mind as such, the dharmakāya beyond the entire web of reference points, which has the nature of being all-pervading like space, exists as ultimate reality. However, this does not teach that the Sugata heart is really established, permanent, enduring, and totally unchanging. Also the [Seventh Karmapa's] statement in his *Ocean of Texts on Reasoning* that nondual wisdom is established as ultimate reality means that it is "established as *being* ultimate reality," but he does not assert that it is really established, permanent, enduring, and totally unchanging. Some think, "If something is established as ultimate reality, it must be really established," but

> they have not examined [this issue properly], since [their objection] comes down to nothing but being mistaken about the mere name "reality." For example, though something may be established as seeming reality, [that does not mean that] it needs to be really established. Therefore, most present-day proponents of *shentong* and the position of glorious Rangjung [Dorje] differ.
>
> Also the statement by my omniscient guru [the Seventh Karmapa] that "*rangtong* and *shentong* are not contradictory" is an excellent explanation, [which shows] that he has realized this meaning. Thus, [AC] says that what is to be expressed is the mode of being of the buddha heart that exists as the great freedom from extremes, the inseparability of appearance and emptiness, and the union of the two realities. The Sugata heart is nothing but the unmistaken own essence of the eight collections [of consciousness] explained in chapter 1. Here, the distinct and unmixed eight collections are the seeming, and their unmistaken own essence is the ultimate, the two realities thus being a union. However, those who do not realize the meaning of the two realities are ignorant about the dependent origination that is only satisfying when not examined, thus circling in saṃsāra through their views of clinging to extremes, such as permanence and extinction. By stating the shortcomings of not realizing the two realities, [Rangjung Dorje] teaches that one needs to train in the mode of being of the two realities in union.[199]

A poem by Karma Trinlépa, in which he answers questions by one of his students about *rangtong* and *shentong*,[200] starts by pointing out that this discussion involves a lot of rigid fixation on both sides.

> I will say a bit in reply to the competitive questions people ask me as to whether *rangtong* and *shentong* are contradictory or not, seeing that there is a good deal of clinging involved in this topic.

He continues by summarizing what the Seventh Karmapa says about how *rangtong* and *shentong* are understood wrongly and correctly, respectively. Out of attachment to a nihilistic view, he says, certain present-day conceited *rangtongpas* assert that emptiness as a nonimplicative negation is ultimate reality. But this is not the genuine *rangtong* asserted by the learned *rangtong* Mādhyamikas. Said people may well meditate by being attached to such a rabbit-hornlike nonexistence, but they will not experience the basic nature through this. Since nonexistence is not the sphere of valid cognition, how could it possibly be something that is realized by personally experienced wisdom? If one focuses on *rangtong* as a nihilistic view, forget about seeing true emptiness. The genuine *rangtong* explained by the previous learned ones is that all phenomena are empty of a nature of their own, but this is not a nonimplicative negation. Though it is empty of the appearances of apprehender and apprehended, the wisdom without the duality of apprehender and apprehended exists. "Empty" in the word "emptiness" does not mean "nothing whatsoever"—this is not the correct understanding of being empty, but just the extreme of being empty. Rather, one should consider that "-ness" is a suffix that indicates affirmation.

There are also some contemporary conceited *shentongpas* who claim that an ultimate which is permanent, enduring, eternal, immutable, and really established is the profound *shentong*, since it is empty of the adventitious stains of apprehender and apprehended. Such a claim amounts to nothing but faking one's clinging to such an eternalistic view as being profound emptiness, but is not the pure *shentong* taught in the sūtras. Through being mistaken about Maitreya's statement that "mind as such is not empty of unsurpassable qualities" (*Uttaratantra* I.155), they say that *shentong* refers to the sixty-four qualities that exist at the time of the ground in a manner of being empty of adventitious stains. However, this means nothing but deprecating the buddhas by implying that sentient beings are completely perfect buddhas in whom all obscurations are terminated and wisdom has unfolded, but who nevertheless circle in saṃsāra, because they experience the sufferings of the six types of beings in the hells and so forth.[201]

Finally, Karma Trinlépa reports what the Seventh Karmapa taught him about the correct view of *shentong* as explained by the Third Karmapa:

> The meaning that is taught in the tantras, the bodhisattva commentaries,[202]
> Many sūtras, and by those who follow the [five] dharmas of Maitreya
> Represents the *shentong* held by Rangjung Dorje,
> About which I heard the following from the mighty victor.
>
> He said that mind as such, unconfined, unbiased,
> Naturally luminous, expanse and awareness inseparable,
> The great sphere, ordinary mind,
> Whose essence does not change into anything,[203]
> Is known as "other-empty" from the point of view of

Having become buddhahood, once it is pure of adventitious
stains.

That this primordial ground is not tainted by any obscurations
Is the purport of "being empty of other."
This very mind as such being ignorant about itself
Is called "adventitious obscuration."
Since this is something suitable to be separated from mind,
The nature of phenomena is empty of it and thus "other-empty."

The sixty-four qualities that reside within the basic nature
Are indeed never separable from mind,
So speak about "obscured buddhahood" at the time of the ground
And "stainless buddhahood" at the time of the fruition!

The thirty-two qualities of freedom from all obscurations
And the thirty-two maturational [qualities] of enlightened
activity unfolding
Are the distinctive features of a perfect buddha alone—
We do not assert that these exist at [the time of] the ground.

The sixty-four qualities that exist at [the time] of the ground
Are obscured by obscurations—through eliminating these stains,
One becomes a stainless victor. Therefore, the basis of being
empty
In terms of other-emptiness is the Sugata heart—
The nature of the mind is primordially just this.
What it is to be emptied of[204] are the adventitious stains to be
relinquished,
Which are referred to as the imaginations of apprehender and
apprehended.

Therefore, ultimate reality is nothing but mind as such
Free from the imaginations of apprehender and apprehended,
Natural luminosity, the connate union,
The inseparability of expanse and awareness, ordinary mind—
This is the view of profound other-emptiness.
Therefore, "rangtong" and "shentong"
Are not held to be contradictory by my guru.

Thus, if phrased by way of a correct understanding of the categories *rangtong* and *shentong*, Rangjung Dorje's view can be said to regard these two as not being mutually exclusive and to combine them in a creative synthesis. As a song of realization by the Sixth Shamarpa, Chökyi Wangchug[205] (1584–1630) says:

> Indeed, the learned set up mere presentations
> Of "self-empty" and "other-empty,"
> But the great victor, glorious Rangjung [Dorje],
> Holds these two to be noncontradictory.[206]

Another song about the view by the Thirteenth Karmapa, Düdül Dorje[207] (1733–97) confirms this:

> Secondly, [the system of] Asaṅga and his brother who follow the final wheel [of dharma]
> Is known as "False Aspectarian Mere Mentalism" in the land of the noble ones
> And as "Shentong Madhyamaka" in Tibet.
> The meaning of these two names is the same.
>
> This is the completely pure system that,
> Through mainly teaching the luminous aspect of the mind,
> Holds that the fruitions—kāyas and wisdoms—exist on their own accord.
> As for its necessity, it is asserted that it is taught in order to
> Relinquish any arising of fear of emptiness and to awaken those with indefinite disposition.
>
> When commenting on its meaning, venerable Rangjung [Dorje] says
> That it is one with the system of Candrakīrti.
> Others assert that the ultimate is existent and really established
> And that emptiness is really established.
>
> As for the mahāyāna's sūtra portion, both the middle and the final wheel [of dharma]
> Have the purport of the Sugata heart, the unity of emptiness and luminosity.
> The middle [wheel] explains this mainly by teaching emptiness,

> While the final [wheel] elucidates it mainly by teaching
> luminosity.
> I understand that, in actuality, these are not contradictory.[208]

As illustrated above, Karma Trinlépa repeatedly states in his texts that the Seventh Karmapa follows the view of the Third Karmapa. The latter's approach toward both Yogācāra and Madhyamaka is also explicitly adopted by the Seventh Karmapa himself, as is evidenced by his *Ocean of Texts on Reasoning*:

> Therefore, the great Yogācāra-Mādhyamikas who follow noble Asaṅga and his brother, through ascertaining that the dualistic appearances of apprehender and apprehended, which obscure true reality, are not established in the way they [appear], mainly teach the wisdom that realizes self-aware self-luminous mind. Noble Nāgārjuna and his spiritual heirs, by thoroughly analyzing the clinging to real [existence] and its objects that obscure true reality through the great [Madhyamaka] arguments, mainly teach that the nature of luminous mind abides as emptiness. In this way, they ascertain that [any such clinging and its objects] are without nature. Both systems do not differ in teaching the final true reality, since this very nature of luminous mind is primordially emptiness, and this emptiness primordially abides as having the essential character of luminosity.[209]

Later, this text says that the ultimate reality of "Great Madhyamaka" is the naturally luminous dharmadhātu or Tathāgata heart, ever untainted by the stains of apprehender and apprehended. It is the natural prajñāpāramitā, which is the sphere of personally experienced wisdom and is taught as ultimate reality in the Madhyamaka scriptures. It is discussed in Nāgārjuna's Madhyamaka texts and his other works, such as the *Dharmadhātustava*, with the latter extensively speaking of mind as such, the inseparability of being lucid and empty, in which all reference points are at peace. This is also explained in the texts of Asaṅga, Vasubandhu, Dignāga, and Dharmakīrti.[210]

Pawo Tsugla Trengwa's *History of the Dharma* agrees:

> [The Seventh Karmapa] indeed commented on the view of both prajñāpāramitā and valid cognition mainly in terms of *shentong*, but this does not mean that he commented according to the assertions of some Tibetans who apply the name *shentong* to the view

> of Mere Mentalism. Rather, in general, this lord holds that the lineage of profound view teaches the basic nature of mind primarily as emptiness, while the lineage of vast activity teaches it primarily as natural luminosity. Thus, since mind's profundity and lucidity are not separable into two, the two charioteer traditions have the same basic intention.[211]

The Eighth Karmapa's commentary on the *Abhisamayālaṃkāra* contains several passages in which he in no unclear terms corrects misconceptions—even within the Kagyü School—about the Third Karmapa's view. For example, he denies that the latter "asserts the intention of the *Mahāyānottaratantra* to be that the Tathāgata heart exists in the dharmadhātu of the mind of sentient beings in an inseparable manner," or "that the Tathāgata heart that is not empty of qualities, such as the powers, exists in sentient beings." Rather, according to AC, he says, in sentient beings with obscured minds, the dharmadhātu does not exist—these very sentient beings *are* the adventitious stains produced by the false imagination that mistakenly strays away from the dharmadhātu. It is only the pure unobscured mind (i.e., what is known as "ordinary mind" and "original buddha") that is inseparable from the buddha qualities.[212] As mentioned above, the Eighth Karmapa also denies the claim of some very confused followers of Mahāmudrā that the ālaya-consciousness is actually transformed into mirrorlike wisdom.[213] As for the question of whether the classifications of the third turning of the wheel of dharma by Maitreya and Nāgārjuna come down to the same essential point, the Eighth Karmapa refers to the Third as saying the following. These two cycles share the same essential point in a general way in that they both teach the freedom from reference points. In particular though, Nāgārjuna speaks only about the sheer freedom from reference points, while Maitreya explains the personally experienced wisdom free from reference points. However, Nāgārjuna and his followers do not reject this wisdom, since it is taught in Nāgārjuna's collection of praises and Āryadeva's *Catuḥśataka*[214] (this passage about Maitreya and Nāgārjuna is also found in the same way in TOK).[215]

In his colophon to the Seventh Karmapa's *Ocean of Texts on Reasoning*, the Eighth Karmapa clarifies the following points about Rangjung Dorje's view:

> The proponents of Mere Mentalism only realize
> That outer referents lack real [existence], but cling to a really established
> Mind as such that is self-lucid and free from obscurations.

Therefore, through ascertaining one portion of knowable objects—the apprehended—
As lacking real [existence], they are able to progress only to the mahāyāna path of preparation,
But lack the relinquishment of the obscurations of clinging
To the real [existence of the] factor of the apprehender among knowable objects.[216]

Thus, since they have no chance to manifest
The emptiness of realizing the phenomenal identity's
Lack of nature that pervades all knowable objects,
It is appropriate to also refute this philosophical system of Vijñapti[vādins].

Nevertheless, the statement that lucid and aware mere mind,
Which is taught as being really established ultimately
In the sevenfold collection and the sūtra of Dignāga and [Dharma]kīrti,[217]
Abides as Madhyamaka was made by the victor Maitreya,

In order to guide Vasubandhu, by describing it
As Madhyamaka to the great noble master Asaṅga
In the three latter dharmas of Maitreya[218] and in the system
That extensively teaches the dharma principles of Vijñapti[vāda].

The Vijñapti[vādin]s who follow
The system of this trailblazer
Say that their own imperfect philosophical system
Represents the Mādhyamika system.

Here, when seeing no chance for [their system]
To be in accord with the system of the glorious protector Nāgārjuna,
Some Yogācāra masters explain
The scriptural system of Nāgārjuna as entailing a [certain] intention,
Because the system of Nāgārjuna amounts to the extreme of extinction.

Some Yogācāra masters, such as Dharmapāla
And [Ratnākara]śānti, comment on the Madhyamaka
That was asserted by Nāgārjuna as representing Vijñaptimātra.

Though many such systems of amending [Nāgārjuna's] position arose,
The mighty victor by name Rangjung [Dorje] said,
"Though cognizance is indeed devoid of being established ultimately,
As a mere illusion and from the perspective of undeceiving conventionalities,
It is real as the foundation of what is called saṃsāra and nirvāṇa.

On the basis of this as a mere common worldly consensus,
Within the unimpeded aspect of mind's being lucid,
All of saṃsāra and nirvāṇa is suitable to occur—
This is what the great master Asaṅga emphasized in his explanations.

Within the aspect of mind's being empty that is without arising and ceasing,
There is freedom from all reference points of saṃsāra and nirvāṇa—
This is what the great glorious protector Nāgārjuna emphasized in his explanations.
[However,] the intention in both [explanations] is without contradiction."

Some who do not fathom the intention of this [statement]
Say that the position of the mighty victor Karmapa
In terms of the definitive meaning represents a mixture of Vijñapti[vāda] and Madhyamaka,
[But] I have no patience with these [people].

Rather, the intention of the great mighty victor is as follows.
He said that dependent origination is justified within being empty is the principle of Madhyamaka,
While the Vijñaptivādins assert dependent origination as an entity.

Also, dependent origination being free from reference points is said to be Madhyamaka.

[However,] in terms of both systems, to merely speak of dependent origination
As an entity is the position of master Asaṅga,
Which is established as being very much noncontradictory
As the very door and stepping stone for mind progressively [engaging]
In the dependent origination free from reference points that is asserted by Nāgārjuna.

As for the manner of such being established, the Buddhist Vaibhāṣikas and Sautrāntikas,
In order to refute permanent entities without momentary change,
Extensively prove impermanent entities that entail momentary change
As representing dependent origination.

Through such [proofs], as the pith instructions on mind gradually engaging
In dependent origination free from reference points,
Most learned ones, such as Dignāga and [Dharma]kīrti,
Who know the constitutions and faculties of those to be guided
Employ all kinds of means to progressively lead [the latter's] insight
From the lower philosophical systems to the higher ones.[219]

Thus, it is with this intention that [Rangjung Dorje] declared said two systems to be noncontradictory.
[However, some] who do not fathom the intention of this say,
"The statement that even Nāgārjuna has no Madhyamaka
That is superior than [the one of] the False Aspectarians
Is the intention of the mighty victor Karmapa."

But if this were the case,
How could such idle and self-contradictory talk
Of saying that mere cognizance is both real and unreal
Be appropriate for the noble Karmapa,
Who has cast far away false words?[220]

In brief, the main points in these verses are as follows. Asaṅga is not considered as a Mere Mentalist or Vijñaptivādin in the above sense of only realizing the lack of nature of the apprehended, but follows what Maitreya taught as Madhyamaka (lucid and aware mere mind). According to the Third Karmapa, Asaṅga emphasized mind's aspect of being lucid, which can mainfest as anything in saṃsāra and nirvāṇa, while Nāgārjuna highlighted mind's aspect of being empty, which refers to anything that appears in the mind being free from all reference points. Rangjung Dorje's position of these two explanations not being contradictory does not just represent some plain mixture of Vijñaptivāda and Madhyamaka, but the subjective and objective sides of the very same cognitive process toward buddhahood. This means that Asaṅga's system outlines the progression and refinement of mundane and supramundane states of mind (the subject) in terms of first conceptually and then directly realizing the ultimate reality of dependent origination free from reference points (the final object) as emphasized by Nāgārjuna.

In terms of any meaningful discussion on *rangtong* and *shentong*, the most crucial point was unfortunately often overlooked by later *shentongpas* as well as their opponents (whether deliberately or not). This point lies in Dölpopa's original presentation of these terms (such as in his *Mountain Dharma*) clearly differentiating a "philosophical system" (Skt. siddhānta, Tib. grub mtha') based on certain explanations and arguments from a "point of view," in the sense of a more encompassing and experiential outlook (Skt. darśana, Tib. lta ba). He understands the latter not as being primarily focused on, or limited to, what can be determined through scholarly analyses, all such intellectual approaches representing only a preliminary part of a worldview that is primarily grounded in direct meditative experiences and realizations (often in the context of advanced vajrayāna practices). It is the entirety of this that Dölpopa calls "Great Madhyamaka" and *shentong*—the outlook of noble beings who have directly realized the nature of their minds, just as it is. In this sense, *shentong* is clearly contrasted with Madhyamaka or *rangtong* as a mere philosophical system. Consequently, on these two levels, one's entire perspective of what ultimate reality or the nature of phenomena is, how it is perceived, and any style of discourse about this must be very different. Therefore, despite the claims of his later opponents, Dölpopa's own use of the *rangtong-shentong* distinction is epistemological in nature and not ontological or reifying (also, he never spoke about people or schools who propound *rangtong* as opposed to those who propound *shentong*). He portrays *rangtong* as a philosophical system that he accepts himself as far as it can take one on the conceptual level of philosophical analysis, but not as adequately portraying the experiential level of direct insight into the ultimate nature of phenomena. Essentially the same distinction is made by the Eighth Karmapa in his JNS,[221] which says that the fully qualified view or outlook is the one that is associated with mind being immersed in yogic meditation, after one has progressed through the preceding inferential valid cognitions of refuting any real existence and understanding all phenomena to be unborn. Having arrived at this meditative outlook, there are no claims of any philosophical positions, such as "being unborn," since all objects of negation have ceased on their own and there is nothing whatsoever to be proved or affirmed either.

However, many *shentongpas* after Dölpopa felt compelled to defend their views within the context of philosophical investigation in a classical Madhyamaka framework, because they were criticized by others as being people who hold reifying non-Buddhist views about an eternal ātman like the Indian tīrthikas. However, within the limits of conceptual analysis through Madhyamaka reasoning, the overall paradigm shifts from epistemology and meditative experience to ontology and mere logic, with notions such as an ultimately existing buddha nature, wisdom, and enlightened qualities being by definition untenable. Thus, in the later *rangtong-shentong* controversies, often the discourse on the level of philosophical systems became conflated with the discourse on the level of the direct vision of true reality, which resulted in attempts to either invalidate or support primarily experiential statements through conceptual reasoning, which in turn eliminated or obscured any common ground for a genuine exchange. At best, such controversies resemble disputes about which restaurants in New York City have the best food between someone who has eaten at restaurants in New York City and someone else who has only read about these restaurants in a guide book, but who has never eaten at one. At worst, they are like two people, neither having been to New York, arguing about its restaurants, with the one conducting a thorough logical analysis of all guide books and the other just speculating about what they heard from people who have actually been to these restaurants. Though both Dölpopa and many later *shentongpas* say that *shentong* includes, and is based on, *rangtong* as a form of analytical rigor, but supersedes this level of discourse, a significant number of later *shentongpas* argued for the supremacy of *shentong* even on the level of philosophical analysis (which is vehemently denied by their opponents).

In brief, all disputes about *rangtong* and *shentong* are rather pointless as long as these notions are regarded as belonging to the same level of discourse, experience, and realization, and to be mutually exclusive on that same level. Instead, any fruitful conversation about *rangtong* and *shentong* can start only from acknowledging that they pertain to different levels. As Ruegg says:

> [O]ne could assume an incompatibility, at one and the same level of reference, between two philosophical propositions, both of which cannot be true in accordance with the principle of contradiction. Alternatively, one might perhaps suppose a complementarity — perhaps even an incommensurability — between two doctrines that relate to different levels of reference or discourse, and which are accordingly not mutually exclusive or contradictory.[222]

That is why, following Śākya Chogden, many (also contemporary) so-called "nonexclusive" *shentongpas* say that *rangtong* is supreme for cutting through all wrong views, reifications, and reference points, while *shentong* is more amenable to, and beneficial for, describing and enhancing meditative experience and realization. They teach that the views of *rangtong* and *shentong* are not only not contradictory, but—when properly understood—they supplement each other and are one in terms of the definitive meaning. In particular, Śākya Chogden highlights the indispensability of both approaches in practicing vajrayāna:

> If there were not these texts of what Asaṅga maintains—
> The dharma system of the ālaya and the presentation of the three emptinesses—
> Through what could you explain the basis of purification, the means for purification,
> And the presentation of "outer," "inner," and "other" in the texts of the great way of being?[223]
>
> If there were not the manner in which nondual wisdom is empty of a nature,
> As elucidated by the texts of Prāsaṅgikas and Svātantrikas,
> What would [enable us to] relinquish our clinging to the reality of profound luminous wisdom
> And our conceptions of being attached to magnificent deities?[224]

On the question of what is the most important difference between *rangtong* and *shentong*, the contemporary Kagyü scholar and yogi Khenpo Tsultrim Gyamtso Rinpoche answered that, according to *shentong*, the dharmakāya and the buddha qualities are not created newly (through the path), but just become manifest or revealed once what obscures them is removed or seen through. From an experiential point of view, he phrased this as follows:

> [The nature of the mind] is the inseparability of [mind's] open expanse and awareness (*dbyings rig dbyer med*) and is lucid-empty. Therefore, from its creative display, its inconceivable companions (*grogs po*)—the kāyas and wisdoms—can dawn. For example, if there is bright light in a clear cloud-free sky, rainbows appear. . . . Thus, in the *shentong* system, the dharmakāya exists in the basic nature at the time of the ground. At the time of the fruition—buddhahood—this dharmakāya is neither just a mere nonimplicative negation, nor the mere peace of all reference points, nor nothing whatsoever, once the skandhas have ceased. It consists of the inconceivable and inexpressible qualities of the kāyas and wisdoms that are grounded in the inseparability of [mind's] open expanse and awareness.[225]

As mentioned before, among Tibetan masters, there are a great number of differing presentations of what exactly *shentong* means and how this differs from *rangtong*. Some use the term *shentong* to refer to a doctrine with set positions (which can also differ greatly); some speak about it in the sense of an experiential outlook; some refer to it as an approach to practicing meditation (*sgom lugs*); and others take it to be a synthesis of both view and meditation. Obviously, these approaches are more or less overlapping, and their "borderlines" are fluid and often keep shifting when they are taught or disputed. As for the Kagyü School, it makes a standard distinction between "luminosity *shentong*" (*gsal ba gzhan stong*) and "expanse (dhātu) *shentong*" (*dbyings gzhan stong*). Briefly speaking, the first refers to buddha nature's wisdom being empty of adventitious stains (the "other"), and this wisdom itself not being empty, but existing as the ultimate nature of luminosity. Thus, the ultimate existence of the luminous nature of mind and its innate buddha qualities are emphasized. Typical proponents are Dölpopa, Tāranātha, and Jamgön Kongtrul Lodrö Tayé, who base their explanations mainly on the *Uttaratantra* and combine them with Yogācāra templates, such as the three natures. "Expanse *shentong*" means that, in and of itself, the nondual and nonconceptual, personally experienced wisdom that realizes the fundamental space of the dharmadhātu as mind's true nature is free from reference points. Though not denying the ultimate validity of realizing one's primordial Tathāgata heart with all its qualities, this view accords much more with a classical Madhyamaka approach. Its most typical presentation (which one is tempted to call "*shentong* lite") is found in the Eighth Karmapa's massive commentary on the *Abhisamayālaṃkāra*[226] and in some of the works of the Sixth Shamarpa. Also certain aspects of Mipham Rinpoche's presentations of *shentong* (who states that his own system is *rangtong* and that he does not have the burden of feeling compelled to establish the *shentong* view),[227] such as his constant emphasis on understanding the Madhyamaka approach to emptiness and the inseparability of appearance and emptiness, seem to tend more toward an "expanse *shentong*" approach.

As should be clear from the above and Rangjung Dorje's own writings, his "*shentong*," if anything, could be described as a combination of "luminosity *shentong*" and "expanse *shentong*," steering clear of the pitfalls of reification and nihilism. Yet again, rather than trying to find the "right" doxographical box to stash away the Third Karmapa's view, as with any accomplished and original philosopher or spiritual master, it seems more fruitful and refreshing to understand the full scope of Rangjung Dorje's distinct approach—persistently pointing out the essential points of the Buddha's teachings on mind's true nature in both traditions of the mahāyāna—in its own terms.

Rangjung Dorje's Unique Explanation of the Seventh Consciousness

The close relationship between the afflicted mind, the immediate mind, the mental consciousness, and the mental-sense faculty are described in great detail in AC, DSC, and NY. The basic position of Rangjung Dorje is that the seventh consciousness (mentation) consists of two aspects, the afflicted mind and the immediate mind (also referred to as "stainless mentation"), with the latter being the primary aspect. These two aspects are mixed until the fundamental change of state of the seventh consciousness occurs. In other words, mentation has two faces—the actual immediate or stainless mind is nothing but consciousness's own essence,[228] while it is presented as the afflicted mind from the perspective of its being mistaken about itself, just as a small child who, not recognizing himself or herself in a mirror, then searches for, and tries to interact with, this other person he or she seems to see. Thus, the seventh consciousness is presented as the afflicted mind from the perspective of its distorting aspect—misconceiving the ālaya-consciousness as a self and being associated with the four afflictions (ignorance, the views about a real personality, self-conceit, and attachment to the self). It is called "immediate mind" in its dynamic aspect of being the continuum of triggering the arising and ceasing of the other six consciousnesses from, and back into, the ālaya-consciousness. It is expressed as "stainless mentation," once it is embraced by the immaculate dharmas that are grounded in the enlightenment of a buddha.

AC explains the immediate mind explicitly within the mahāyāna presentation of eight consciousnesses, while rejecting other explanations, such as that the immediate mind is just a part of the sixth consciousness; that it does not exist at all; or that it is a ninth consciousness. In general, the immediate mind can be explained in many different ways, such as its being the seventh consciousness, which usually refers to a moment of any one of the six consciousnesses having just ceased, and thus triggering the following one (i.e., the immediate condition). Thus, in the framework of the eight consciousnesses, it is the mental energy that momentarily facilitates the emerging of the other six consciousnesses from the ālaya and their merging back down into it. This may also be equated with the mental-sense faculty, which represents the dominant condition of the mental consciousness. The immediate mind can furthermore be described as a particular one among the potentials of the ālaya. In the context of the twelve āyatanas, this means that the very potential that functions as the gateway for the arising of the mental consciousness is the āyatana of mentation, because it is related to the āyatana of phenomena as subject and object, respectively. Since this is without affliction, it is also called "stainless mentation." In the context of the eighteen dhātus, it may be presented as the dhātu of mentation (any one of the six consciousnesses having just ceased), in the sense of its bearing the nature of being without a real agent, and even as the dhātu of the mental consciousness.

As for "having just ceased," though some people (such as the Vaibhāṣikas) assert that the immediate condition is the very cessation of a preceding moment of the six consciousnesses, cessation itself is not suitable as a cause.[229] Rather, according to the *Saṃdhinirmocanasūtra*, when any one of the six consciousnesses has ceased, the consciousness that is explained to be the same as the dhātu of mentation transports them into the ālaya. Right after that, just as with waves emerging from water, the immediate mind (mixed with the afflicted mind) again stirs from the ālaya-consciousness. Consequently, as many instances of the six collections arise and cease, just that many instances of the immediate mind too arise and cease. The latter are what immediately trigger the subsequent instances of the six consciousnesses, once the preceding ones have ceased. Thus, the immediate mind represents the immediate condition—the support and "locus" of the arising and ceasing of consciousness. In other words, the immediate mind is the dynamic impulsion of the mind that "pushes" the latent tendencies of the six consciousnesses from their dormant existence within the ālaya into clearly manifesting and perceiving their respective objects, thus triggering a seamless stream of subject-object interactions. At the same time, this immediate mind provides the energy to redirect and plant the traces and potentials of these interactions back into the ālaya, just to "revive" them at a later point. In terms of the dynamic nature of this process, the immediate mind cannot really be said to be a "locus" or something separate from the other six consciousnesses. It is just a term for the propelling impulse that is intrinsic to each moment of consciousness and makes it arise from and sink down into the ālaya-consciousness—similar to the force through which waves move, which cannot be separated from the water of the waves. In itself, this endless circular movement of latent tendencies arising from and merging back into the ālaya is neutral, but represents the actual driving force or "propeller" of saṃsāra, while the afflicted mind decides on the pleasant or unpleasant places to which we are propelled. In other words, the immediate mind is treated as an undeceiving aspect or function of the mind, clearly set off from the afflicted mind, which is essentially mistaken, deceiving, and distorting.

From the perspective of the six consciousnesses being results, it is fine to say that they arise from their respective dominant conditions, object conditions, and immediate conditions. In general, the four conditions in Yogācāra texts simply stand for the entirety of causes and conditions that are produced by the mind. Though these conditions can be understood as sheer dependent origination, they in fact refer to nothing but particular cases of mind's imaginative play. Being just nominal pedagogic devices, these conditions do not refer to any really existing entities, let alone external material ones. Dependent origination is understood as the infinite web of all the different facets (be they labeled as the four conditions, false imagination, or something else) of the incessant constructive activity of the mind interacting with each other, just as waves keep criss-crossing and interfering with each other, constantly forming new ones. Through the power of mutual dependence, object, sense faculty, and the immediate mind appear as if they were causes and conditions, but, ultimately, there is no arising or ceasing in all of this. It may appear that a magician causes many illusory beings to be born, some to die, some to come, and some to leave, but nothing of this really happens, because these very "beings" do not exist in the first place. Just as the illusory beings in this example depend on the necessary conditions to produce their appearance, what appear as the above conditions are nothing but the products of sheer imagination whose own nature is not realized. However, through knowing and realizing their luminous nature as being without arising and ceasing, they are seen for what they truly are—the dharmadhātu.

From a slightly different point of view, DSC (fols. 24b–25a) presents mentation in terms of three aspects—the afflicted mind, the mental consciousness, and the immediate mind—being closely interconnected. In due order, these three represent (a) the aspect of stains, which is produced through the afflicted mind; (b) the sixth consciousness, which specifically focuses on phenomena as its objects; and (c) the immediate mind that serves as the momentary locus of the arising and ceasing of all consciousnesses. The first one is the imaginary nature, which is absolutely nonexistent. The second one appears in accordance with the five sense doors, but is empty of nature. The third one is the sheer aspect of the stirring of consciousnesses, which can be either factors to be relinquished or their remedies.[230] The relationships between these three aspects of mentation as well as between the sixth and the seventh consciousness are also described in NY (lines 75–81; 87–91; and 122–26) and NYC (pp. 90–97). The latter adds that, when the immediate mind produces a purified instance of consciousness, such as giving rise to confidence in the dharma or a genuine spiritual friend, the afflicted mind does not stir. Therefore, the immediate mind is also called "stainless mentation" in the sūtras.[231]

In terms of the change of state of the sixth and seventh consciousnesses into the corresponding wisdoms and kāyas, due to Rangjung Dorje's detailed treatment of the immediate mind as the primary aspect of the seventh consciousness, his presentation slightly varies from, and elaborates on, the classical Yogācāra format (see the charts in appendix 6). The latter says that it is the sixth consciousness plain and simple which changes state as discriminating wisdom and (together with the afflicted mind) the sambhogakāya. AC agrees with this in a general sense, but explains that the two changes of state of those aspects of the mental consciousness that are the thinking mind and mental perception[232] represent two aspects of the nirmāṇakāya. Usually, the sixth consciousness is taught to consist of nothing but the thinking mind and mental perception, so one may wonder what is left of it to change state. NY explicitly identifies the immediate mind as that which changes state into discriminating wisdom and (together with the afflicted mind) the sambhogakāya. Thus, as NYC clarifies, strictly speaking, it is neither the conceptual nor the perceptual parts of the sixth consciousness that change state as discriminating wisdom, but the immediate mind as its underlying dynamic aspect that triggers both perceptual and conceptual processes.[233] In this vein, NY says that the immediate mind is also referred to as conception, since it produces conceptions. This explanation is not as surprising as it may seem at first. For, as explained above, the immediate mind (depending on the context) is either subsumed under the sixth or the seventh consciousness, or, together with the afflicted mind and the sixth consciousness, taken to make up mentation. Thus, not only is the close relationship of the immediate mind with the sixth consciousness repeatedly emphasized throughout Rangjung Dorje's works, but also its dynamic nature (rather than its being something that "remains in one place"). As a logical consequence of this (again differing from the classical Yogācāra format), both AC and NY agree that it is not only the five sense consciousnesses, but these five plus the sixth consciousness's aspect of mental perception that change state as all-accomplishing wisdom. In general though, when the sixth consciousness is not explicitly divided into the above three aspects (conceptual, perceptual, and immediate mind), it is simply explained that it changes state as discriminating wisdom and (together with the afflicted mind) the sambhogakāya, while the five sense consciousnesses do so as all-accomplishing wisdom and the nirmāṇakāya.

ZDKT (pp. 65–67) summarizes these explanations on mentation in the context of how mind is ignorant about itself in AC's first chapter. In terms of identifying innate ignorance, it is the lucid aspect of mind as such that is referred to by the term "seventh consciousness," while "ignorance" means not recognizing its own essence. This also means that the formation of immaculate karma through the movement of the seventh consciousness is correct imagination, and that what abides as its own stainless essence is "stainless mentation." Since the latter is included in a particular aspect of the Sugata heart—the unfolding disposition—it is the wisdom of equality at the time of the ground. Hence, it is the wisdom that entails the purity of the seventh consciousness. This means the same as the explanation in the sixth chapter of ZMND that the wisdom of equality is the change of state of the afflicted mind and the internally oriented part of the sixth consciousness. Therefore, the seventh consciousness that is explained here in the first chapter as that which causes mind to form objects refers to mentation in general, without differentiating between the afflicted mind and pure mentation. Since it is the mentation that is the immediate condition for the six consciousnesses, AC says again and again that its synonym is the "immediate mind." Accordingly, the Seventh Karmapa holds that mentation has three parts—from the perspective of immediacy, it is presented as the seventh consciousness of mentation; from the perspective of being embraced by the set of four afflictions, it is the afflicted mind; and from the perspective of being embraced by the immaculate dharmas, it is stainless mentation. These days, ZDKT says, many Tibetans who discuss the abhidharma only include the afflicted mind as the seventh of the eight consciousnesses, without ever presenting the immediate mind as the seventh consciousness. This approach is even followed in some commentaries on ZMND, but Rangjung Dorje himself holds that the seventh consciousness is the immediate mind. He takes it as the afflicted mind from the perspective of being ignorant about the immediate mind's own essence and thus conceiving of it as a self, therefore functioning as the root of all mistakenness in saṃsāra.

Some Differences between Rangjung Dorje and Dölpopa

This is not the place for a detailed study of all the differences—or the definitely existing similarities—between the views of Rangjung Dorje and Dölpopa, but a few major diverging positions shall be mentioned here. Dölpopa is clearly the first one to use the terms *rangtong* and *shentong* (starting between 1330 and 1333). His first two works in which he discusses them are his *General Commentary on the Teachings* (*Bstan pa spyi 'grel*) and *Mountain Dharma*, both of which he finished in 1333 (or just shortly before). In contrast, as mentioned above, Rangjung Dorje's main texts on the view were finished by 1327 at the latest. Also, Rangjung Dorje and Dölpopa met briefly only once between 1320 and 1324, if at all.[234] These facts make it very unlikely that Dölpopa's view was greatly influenced by Rangjung Dorje's, and they certainly don't lend any credibility to claims—still held today by some—that the Karmapa "invented" the *shentong* view, that Dölpopa may have received his terminology of *rangtong* and *shentong* from the Karmapa, or even that Rangjung Dorje was very much influenced by Dölpopa and his *shentong* view.[235] Such claims are further invalidated when one looks at some of the major differences between the views of these two great masters (note that the following is by no means an exhaustive list).

1) Rangjung Dorje never uses the terms *rangtong* and *shentong*, let alone giving any explanations on what they mean or their relationship, while they can rightly be said to be *the* cornerstones of Dölpopa's view, who employs and discusses them in great detail.

2) Dölpopa typically describes both buddha nature and the dharmakāya as being really established (*bden grub*), enduring (*brtan pa*), immutable (*ther zug*), and eternal (*g.yung drung*), while Rangjung Dorje never uses these terms.[236]

3) Dölpopa is the first one to use the term "ālaya-wisdom" (*kun gzhi ye shes*) as opposed to "ālaya-consciousness." This term and the ensuing distinction appear frequently in Dölpopa's works, such as his *Mountain Dharma*,[237] but are absent in Rangjung Dorje's texts.[238]

4) Though both Dölpopa and Rangjung Dorje say that the two realities are inexpressible as the same or different, Dölpopa concludes from this that they are "different in the sense of negating sameness" (*gcig pa bkag pa'i tha dad*), while Rangjung Dorje always emphasizes the unity of the two realities or appearance and emptiness (see especially the sections on the two realities in DSC on verse 2 of the *Dharmadhātustava* and the ninth chapter of AC).

5) In the same vein, Dölpopa makes a sharp distinction between the spheres of ordinary consciousness and nondual wisdom as being two separate

kingdoms, because consciousness is merely seeming and empty of itself, while nondual wisdom is really established and only empty of other seeming phenomena. The object of consciousness is exclusively saṃsāra and the object of wisdom is exclusively nirvāṇa. Rangjung Dorje makes no such distinctions, but constantly refers to wisdom as the actual nature of consciousness, as highlighted by the eight consciousnesses eventually being revealed as the four wisdoms, which would not be possible if they were totally separate.

6) Dölpopa explicitly declares that nondual wisdom and ultimate reality withstand analysis. In other words, self-emptiness—phenomena being empty of a nature of their own—pertains only to conventional reality, but not to ultimate reality, which is not empty of itself. Consequently, the views of the Svātantrikas and Prāsaṅgikas—who assert the opposite—are impure. Rangjung Dorje never says any of this, but instead explains in the ninth chapter of AC that buddha nature is endowed with the two realities, with ultimate reality being explained extensively as natural emptiness (or the eighteen emptinesses) free from reference points. Also, OED (pp. 526–28) says that the nature of phenomena is suchness and the perfect nature, which—among the three kinds of lack of nature—is the ultimate lack of nature. It is to be understood that all kinds of emptiness are divisions derived from this. The text also quotes Nāropa as saying that this very being empty is the Tathāgata heart.

7) Dölpopa often states that buddha nature or ultimate reality is not, or is beyond, dependent origination, while Rangjung Dorje says that mind's own essence—be it with stains or stainless—is free from being the same as, or other than, dependent origination (see AC, p. 36).

8) In terms of the three natures, Rangjung Dorje does not speak about a "pure other-dependent nature," while Dölpopa—though acknowledging that it is not found in Indian texts—frequently uses and explains the term in detail.

9) In this vein, Dölpopa says that the unmistaken perfect nature actually belongs to the "pure other-dependent nature" and is only included in the perfect nature in a nominal sense—the perfect nature being the unchanging perfect nature alone. Rangjung Dorje clearly describes the perfect nature as actually consisting of both its unmistaken and its unchanging aspect.

10) Dölpopa's *Mountain Dharma* says that ultimate buddhahood is taught to be unconditioned, which is also intended to mean that it is free from moments.[239] This applies equally to nondual wisdom, while Rangjung Dorje's NT (lines 142–47) says that buddhahood's discriminating wisdom entails momentary arising and ceasing.

11) As evidenced by AC and NT as well as by Karma Trinlépa's ZDKT (pp. 396–97) and his above reports on the Seventh Karmapa's describing the view

of the Third, Rangjung Dorje does not hold that the sixty-four qualities of a completely perfect buddha exist in a complete and unobscured manner at the time of the ground, that is, in ordinary sentient beings. In other words, he does not hold that the fruition is present right now in these beings, while Dölpopa does. This is also highlighted by the Eighth Karmapa's JNS:

> Nowadays some people say, "The intention of the Omniscient Rangjung Dorje is that the Tathāgata heart that is not empty of qualities, such as the [ten] powers, exists in sentient beings. This is clearly explained by the mighty victor, [the Seventh Karmapa] Chötra Gyatso." This is [just] putting to melody what others say, but it is not our own [Kagyü] system.[240] You may wonder, "Which other great ones assert such a system?" In Tibet, the land of snows, there are indeed also many others who assert something like that, but the one who explains it by excessively promoting it is Dölpopa Sherab Gyaltsen. He declares that "such a Heart, which is free of all flaws and endowed with all qualities, exists in sentient beings. Through its *existing* in sentient beings, sentient beings do not have to *be* it. Therefore, one must make a difference between existing and being [something], without mixing them."[241]

12) According to Dölpopa, the thirty-two qualities of the dharmakāya also pertain to the rūpakāyas and the major and minor marks pertain to the dharmakāya too. As most everybody else, Rangjung Dorje clearly separates the qualities of the dharmakāya from those of the rūpakāyas.

13) Throughout his texts, Rangjung Dorje several times says that not realizing the nature of one's mind or buddha nature is saṃsāra and realizing it is liberation,[242] while Dölpopa explicitly rejects this at length.[243]

14) As mentioned above, Dölpopa says that the five Maitreya works do not represent different tenets, but all teach nothing but *shentong*, with even the *Abhisamayālaṃkāra* containing nothing that is *rangtong*. Rangjung Dorje says that the *Abhisamayālaṃkāra* clearly teaches on the middle cycle of the Buddha's teachings (the lack of characteristics), while the *Mahāyānasūtrālaṃkāra* explains all sūtras in the first and the middle cycle, and the *Uttaratantra* comments on the sūtras of the last cycle.

15) Dölpopa, followed by almost all later *shentongpas*, consistently asserts that, just as are Nāgārjuna and other Mādhyamikas, so also Maitreya, Asaṅga, and Vasubandhu are "Great Mādhyamikas" and he explicitly includes templates such as the three natures under Madhyamaka. Rangjung Dorje makes

no such claims, but clearly distinguishes the traditions of Yogācāra and Madhyamaka.[244]

Of course, there are also agreements to be found in Rangjung Dorje's and Dölpopa's positions, such as denying that the ultimate is a nonimplicative negation; asserting that the essence of buddha nature during ground, path, and fruition is the same; asserting that the fruition of buddhahood is not something newly produced through the path; and asserting that the foremost masters from both the Madhyamaka and the Yogācāra traditions agree on the ultimate view.

Some Remarks on Rangjung Dorje's Commentators

As for commentaries by other Kagyü masters on Rangjung Dorje's above works, there are many on his ZMND, including those by Trimkang Lotsāwa[245] (1424–1482), his student Chatral Rinchen Sangpo[246] (born late fifteenth century), Tagbo Rabjampa Chögyal Denba[247] (1449–1524), Karma Trinlépa, Ngotro Rabjampa Wangchug Bal[248] (born sixteenth century), the Fifth Shamarpa, Göncho Yenla[249] (1525–1583) (three commentaries), Jamgön Kongtrul Lodrö Tayé, and the Fifteenth Karmapa, Kakyab Dorje[250] (1870/71–1921/22).[251] Each one of the last three also wrote commentaries on NT and NY. Finally, there are Dashi Öser's *Uttaratantra* commentary (which basically represents Rangjung Dorje's own lost summary of the text with a few additional clarifications) and a commentary by the Eighth Situpa, Chökyi Jungné[252] (1699–1774) on MM.

Among the commentaries on ZMND, Jamgön Kongtrul's ZDC is the one that is most commonly used at present. It is a kind of reader's digest of most of the preceding commentaries and greatly relies on those by Tagbo Rabjampa and Karma Trinlépa (in fact, many passages in ZDC are literally copied from ZDKT). In the translation of AC below, I mainly relied on these three commentaries as well as Trimkang Lotsāwa's. Karma Trinlépa's excellent ZDKT is the commentary that most closely follows, and also comments on, Rangjung Dorje's own AC. Included in the translations below is an excerpt from the first chapter of ZDKT on buddha nature, which is based on Rangjung Dorje's explanations in his ZMND, AC, DSC, and NT. In this excerpt, ZDKT also refers to the *Dharmadharmatāvibhāga*, thus acknowledging the underlying unity of all these texts. The excerpt explains the meanings of dhātu, wisdom, and ordinary mind in detail, elaborates on the naturally abiding and the unfolding dispositions, and addresses some qualms by others about these topics.

As for the commentaries on NT and NY, the Fifth Shamarpa's annotations are just very brief glosses, while the Fifteenth Karmapa's commentaries on these two texts consist almost entirely of excerpts from Jamgön Kongtrul's NTC and NYC, omitting its citations from other texts and showing a few variants here and there. Though Jamgön Kongtrul's own presentations of the view in his other texts often differ significantly from Rangjung Dorje's, I decided to translate his NTC and NYC for the following reasons:

1) They are the only available actual commentaries on NT and NY.

2) Many passages in both NTC and NYC are either literally from AC, or based on it and/or ZDKT (the clearest commentary on AC).

3) NTC and NYC identify many of the passages from Indian texts that NT and NY incorporate or rely on.

4) The entire outline of NTC is identical to Rangjung Dorje's own outline of NT (Rang byung rdo rje 2006c).

5) Throughout Jamgön Kongtrul's commentaries on ZMND, NT, and NY, he never even mentions the terms *rangtong* or *shentong*, obviously strictly following Rangjung Dorje's own approach, which is quite remarkable for several reasons. First, elsewhere (such as in his TOK), Jamgön Kongtrul identifies Rangjung Dorje repeatedly as a *shentongpa*.[253] Secondly, ZMND, NT, and NY could be readily interpreted in terms of *shentong*. Thirdly, Jamgön Kongtrul indeed never hesitates to give such an interpretation of the same topics in his own works, usually clearly identifying himself as a *shentongpa* (frequently relying on Tāranātha as one of the most outspoken *shentongpas*). However, in his commentaries on the above three texts, Jamgön Kongtrul follows Rangjung Dorje's synthesis of classical Yogācāra and Madhyamaka in a very faithful manner, not only identifying the texts on which Rangjung Dorje's works rely, but often supporting them with further quotations from both traditions.

The Eighth Situpa's commentary on the Third Karmapa's MM quotes and refers to ZMND several times, and many of its explanations closely follow those of Rangjung Dorje. For example, the commentary on verse 6 of MM presents the two realities in a way that is very similar to the one in AC's ninth chapter and quotes the same passage from the *Akutobhayā*.[254] On verse 7, the text follows the division into, and explanation of, pure mind (Tathāgata heart as the basis of purification) and impure mind (adventitious stains as what is to be purified) in AC's first chapter. The result of purification is described as the eight consciousnesses having changed state as the four wisdoms and the three kāyas, following AC's sixth chapter in explaining discriminating wisdom as belonging to both the nirmāṇakāya and the sambhogakāya, and referring to this text for details.[255] The commentary on verse 10 quotes the first sixteen lines of the first chapter of ZMND and follows AC in explaining the manner in which mind is ignorant of itself, the interdependent play of the eight consciousnesses, how beings circle in saṃsāra through this, and how all phenomena in saṃsāra and nirvāṇa are nothing but the display of mind.[256] The commentary also refers to ZMND and AC saying that nāḍī, vāyu, and tilaka[257] are the dependent origination that appears from mind's radiance and serves as the support for connate wisdom, thus being the basic nature of the vajra body. In addition, both the Third and the Seventh Karmapas are said to hold that the unfolding disposition is the very own stainless essence of the eight consciousnesses existing as the nature of the four kāyas (almost literally corresponding to AC, p. 35). Furthermore, the commentary quotes ZMND (chapter 10, lines 16–27) on the five paths.[258]

As for Pawo Tsugla Trengwa's presentation of buddhahood, kāyas, wisdoms, and enlightened activity in his commentary on the *Bodhicaryāvatāra*, excerpts from it are included here as an appendix, since it discusses these subjects from the points of view of both the Yogācāra and Madhyamaka traditions. In addition, it is largely based on, extensively quotes, and comments on the two main sūtra sources for these topics—the *Buddhabhūmisūtra* and the *Trikāyanāmasūtra*.

To conclude, in his oral commentary on NT, the contemporary Kagyü master Thrangu Rinpoche says the following about the reasons for studying NT and NY (needless to say, this applies equally to the other texts by the Third Karmapa presented here):

> The fact that we are beings within saṃsāra means that we have to experience various kinds of sufferings. . . . so what we need to do is to ultimately attain complete freedom from all these different sufferings. The way to achieve that is to eliminate the faults or defects that we have within our own mind. . . . [T]he buddhas and bodhisattvas have been able to . . . reach the level of perfect bliss, and so we need to do the same. . . . Can we do that? Yes, we can do it because we ourselves possess . . . buddha nature . . . and the way to achieve that result is to meditate. In order to meditate within the Buddhist tradition, there are the instructions of Mahāmudrā and Dzogchen. . . . Then to do those meditations, if one knows clearly how one meditates and what the result of the meditation is, if one knows what needs to be known for this meditation, then there will be no difficulty in doing the practice, whereas it will be difficult just to start directly on the meditation without a clear understanding.

For this reason, there is this text which gives the teachings on the buddha nature.

Jamgön Kongtrül said that when one meditates, one needs to know the reasons for the meditation, which means that . . . one has to have the meditation accompanied by the possession of the view. If one has meditation without . . . the view, it is said that one is like a man without any hands who is trying to climb the side of a cliff. . . . Whereas if someone has the view but doesn't meditate, . . . that is like being a rich person who is also a miser. . . . If one both understands and meditates, then Jamgön Kongtrül says that is like a bird flying through the sky. This bird has the right wing of meditation and the left wing of understanding.

. . . [I]n order to help in one's meditation of Mahāmudrā, it would be helpful to be able to distinguish between what are the consciousnesses and what are the wisdoms, and in order to get the benefit of that understanding, there is Rangjung Dorje's short text *The Distinction between Consciousness and Wisdom* . There is also the wisdom that arises in Mahāmudrā, the root of which is the buddha nature, and so in order to understand that, there is the other short text by Rangjung Dorje, *The Treatise That Teaches the Buddha Nature*. . . So these two texts are branch texts to aid one in one's practice.[259]

Elsewhere, Thrangu Rinpoche describes the relationships of the different kinds of consciousness (both among each other and with the nature of the mind) in more detail and how an understanding of this benefits meditation:

As longs as sentient beings dwell within conditioned existence, known as the impure phase, mind expresses itself in the form of the eight collections of consciousness. As a result of dharma practice and meditative concentration (Skt. *samādhi*), the eight kinds of consciousness will be purified. At that point they will transform and thus reveal themselves to be the five kinds of primordial awareness. In order to understand the essence of these five kinds of awareness, we first have to look at the eight collections of consciousness. Understanding how consciousness transforms itself into primordial awareness also helps us to understand the way the paths to buddhahood are traversed and which kinds of result can be attained by each path. Furthermore, it contains a temporary benefit for our meditation practice, which is to know how meditation functions. This is valid for meditation on the body of a deity as well as for other kinds of meditative concentration, such as calm abiding or deep insight. For those times when we just let our mind rest in itself, it is very beneficial to know about the characteristics and divisions of the eight kinds of consciousness.

For the meditation on the nature of your own mind it is customary to ask your teacher for pointing-out instructions. Some practitioners are lucky enough to realize their true nature of mind straight away, whereas others merely perceive a sensation of it, a certain experience of the true nature of mind. But if they don't know exactly how mind and the consciousnesses function, their experience will dissolve after a few days. The understanding of mind and the eight kinds of consciousness is obtained through the highest understanding (Skt. *prajñā*) of listening and reflecting. When we really meditate on this basis and glimpse the true nature of mind, we will be able to steadily increase our experience of it through all subsequent meditation. That's why it is extremely useful to know about the eight kinds of consciousness.

A beginner who visualizes the body of a deity and does not know the distinctive characteristics of the different aspects of consciousness would think that the deity must be seen as clearly during the mental meditation as if seen directly with the eyes. The eyes, however, have a much coarser way of perceiving concrete forms. Beginners do indeed meditate in the hope of attaining such clarity. Nevertheless, it will not arise, because the meditation on a deity does not happen through the medium of the eye consciousness, but through the medium of the mind consciousness. The objects of the mind consciousness are much less clear. The mind consciousness most definitely does not work like the eye consciousness. That's why some meditators who perceive a vague mental image think they are not capable of meditating correctly on a deity. The result is that they develop an aversion for their meditation. Those, however, who understand that each consciousness perceives in a different way know that mental images aren't as clear as the forms perceived with the eyes, and therefore they are content with their meditation.

They know how to meditate, do indeed so meditate, and thus their meditation works well.

. . . The eye consciousness is thought-free. It is not in the least able to meditate on a deity. It merely perceives what is in its sight, but it cannot "visualize" as such. It is the mind consciousness that visualizes the deity. While the mind consciousness is meditating, there is no real external object, as is the case when the eye perceives forms. Nevertheless, there is a kind of image of the object that appears to the mind consciousness. This image is created by the mind itself. As soon as the mind wavers, the object that it has created will change as well and at once be unstable. That's why we cannot visualize clearly while the mind is unstable. When the mind becomes more stable it is able to keep the self-created appearances longer. . . . Whether the visualization of the deity in our meditation is clear or not depends solely on the stability of our mind. And this is exactly what we are training in when we meditate on a deity.

In the meditation on calm abiding also, it is not the five sense consciousnesses that meditate, but the mind consciousness. Some practitioners believe that when they constantly see objects with their eyes while meditating on calm abiding, their meditation is impaired, or that when they perceive sounds with their ears, their meditation will not be that beneficial. However, the five sense consciousnesses . . . cannot distract our mind either. The eyes indeed see forms, but . . . . this does not disturb the meditation in the least, because the sense perception does not involve any thoughts. It is only a matter of mere appearances. This is the reason why we don't have to stop them. We would not even be able to stop them, nor do we have to modify anything in any way.

. . . [T]he most important consciousness by far is the mind consciousness. It acts as the root for all attachment and aversion, all happiness and suffering. Thus it is as important for our daily life as it is for our meditation. For, it is only the mind consciousness that can meditate. In the context of the three activities of Buddhist practice—namely listening, reflecting, and meditating—the mind consciousness plays the largest part. "Listening" happens immediately after the arising of an ear consciousness which itself merely perceives the sounds of the words but which cannot itself connect the sounds to any meaning. "Reflecting" about the meaning of the words is undertaken solely by the mind consciousness, which is also responsible for "meditating."

. . . There are the five sense consciousnesses that clearly perceive and have direct contact with the object. And then there is the mind consciousness that merely perceives its own self-created images of these objects, and therefore these objects appear as vague, wavering, or unclear.

Another difference between the five sense consciousnesses and the mind consciousness concerns time. The sense consciousnesses can only perceive in the very present moment, whereas the mind consciousness can think about the past, the present, and the future. . . . "The five sense consciousnesses are like a mute with good eyes." They perceive clearly, but are not able to express themselves . . . " The thoughts are like blind persons who are gifted speakers." The mental consciousness does not perceive what the sense consciousnesses perceive, but chatters about its own vague images.

While meditating with a focus, the mind consciousness necessarily entertains a certain conceptual activity. While meditating without a focus, on the other hand, you simply let your mind relax, . . . so that it is not possible for either positive or negative thoughts to arise. In this case, the clarity aspect of mind is not interrupted. Because of its continuous clarity aspect, the mind indeed perceives everything; it is just that the rough thoughts, such as, "I went here" or "I remember this," dissolve. . . .

Whereas the mind consciousness is involved in each meditation, the seventh consciousness, the klesha-mind, is not. From within the eight collections of consciousness, the klesha-mind is the only consciousness for which there is no meditation method at all.

The all-base consciousness plays its role in the meditation as well. When the mind rests calmly within equipoise and meditates, when it relaxes and becomes stable, and when there arise barely any thoughts, then the mind consciousness rests within the mere clarity aspect of the all-base. Through relaxing the mind, mind consciousness and the all-base consciousness rest together in the

> mere continuous clarity aspect of mind. The clarity aspect of mind is an unfabricated cognition, a mere perception (sheer cognition)—the true nature of mind. . . . When the coarse thoughts of the mind consciousness are pacified, it comes to rest in the all-base, and both abide within the true nature of mind.[260]

In sum, the above texts by the Third Karmapa not only provide the general view that underlies all Buddhist meditation practices, but also serve to directly inform the very process of being engaged in such practices.

TRANSLATIONS

The Autocommentary on *The Profound Inner Reality*[261]

Introduction

1. Presenting the body of the treatise

...

1.1. Presenting the essence, including the purpose

> **The stainless Heart of the victors**
> **Being impure, impure and pure,**
> **And utterly pure, in due order,**
> **Is expressed as sentient beings, those who dwell on the path,** [20]
> **And Tathāgatas, respectively.**[262]
> **Therefore, the actuality of this is to be realized.**

This is the vajrayāna's subject that is very difficult to realize, is embraced by the [four] "inconceivable points," and rests upon buddha enlightenment.[263] Here, "vajra" refers to unchanging buddhahood, and traveling on the path toward it means "yāna," which makes the children of the victors proceed there. Alternatively, because the indestructible buddha heart is the basis from which all of saṃsāra and nirvāṇa never move away, it is the "vajrayāna." Since this matrix is not tainted by any stains at all, it is **stainless.**[264] Because it is the nature of buddhahood, it is called "buddha **heart.**" It has three phases—the phase of **sentient beings** with **impurity**; the phase of bodhisattvas **on the path,** which is by virtue of their being endowed with [certain degrees of] both **impurity and purity**; and the phase of the **utterly pure Tathāgatas.** These three aspects [in which the buddha heart appears] **are expressed** by earlier scholars and siddhas **as** [many] synonymous conventional terms, such as ground, path, and fruition; ground-tantra, means-tantra, [21] and fruition-tantra; the basic nature of entities as the ground, the stages of the path, and the stages of the arising of the fruition.

You may wonder, "What is the manner of being inconceivable here?" The [inconceivable] point of the "basic element" is that the buddha heart is [primordially] not tainted by any stains, but does not become buddhahood until all afflictive and cognitive stains have been relinquished. The [inconceivable] point of enlightenment is that [the basic element] is associated with these stains since beginningless time, but because these stains are adventitious, they are not established as any real substance. The [inconceivable] point of the qualities [of enlightenment] is that the sixty-four qualities of buddhahood exist in all sentient beings right now in a complete way, but if they are not triggered[265] through the condition of the immaculate dharmas (the natural outflow of the utterly stainless dharmadhātu), their power does not come forth. [The inconceivable point of enlightened activity is that] there is no difference in enlightened activity's [effortless, spontaneous, and nonconceptual] operation in terms of all sentient beings and buddhas being either the same or different. Thus, its inconceivability is its being free from all expressions, yet serving as the basis for all expressions.[266] In brief, the *Uttaratantra* says:

> Since it is pure and yet [22] endowed with afflictions,
> Since it is not afflicted and yet purified,
> Since its qualities are inseparable,
> And since [its activity] is spontaneous and nonconceptual . . .[267]

Though it is said that this mode of being is difficult to realize by śrāvakas, pratyekabuddhas, and even bodhisattvas who have newly entered the [mahā] yāna,[268] for the time being, it shall be taught by way of an example. When a big precious gem of blue beryl is encrusted, despite its being associated with encrustations, the encrustations do not mix with the gem inside. Likewise, at the time of sentient beings, the buddha heart is obscured by stains, but not mixed [with them]. Therefore, it is pure and yet associated with afflictions. Also, though this gem may be encrusted from the very beginning, the encrustations neither arise from the gem, nor do they arise from something other than this gem. Thus, through purifying these encrustations that do not arise from anywhere, [the gem] becomes pure. Likewise, buddhahood, which is [nothing but] the obscurations of mind—the buddha heart—having become pure, is exactly like this. Again, there is no difference in the qualities of that gem at first and in the end. Nevertheless, these qualities did not shine forth earlier, but later, when [the gem] has become free from stains, [23] is tied onto the pinnacle of a victory banner, and is supplicated, its qualities come forth.[269]

Likewise, all buddha qualities exist right now, but if not triggered by flawless immaculate [deeds], their power does not come forth. Therefore, these qualities are the inseparable true nature [of the buddha heart]. Said gem does not think, "I am encrusted," "I am without encrustations," "I grant qualities to those who supplicate me," or "I do not grant [them to others]," and it is spontaneous [in granting these qualities]. Since enlightened activity operates just like that, the buddha heart too is spontaneous and nonconceptual. This is how its mode of being **is to be realized.**

Not understanding these reasons, [others] explain that the fruition exists [already] right now, that the afflictions are not to be relinquished, that new remedial wisdom cannot be produced, and that natural purity is the partial aspect of nothing but a nonimplicative negation.[270] Such explanations are a far cry from the vajrayāna. Therefore, one should know that this inconceivable matrix—the very essence of what dependently originates (such as the ultimate and seeming [realities], buddhas and sentient beings, appearance and emptiness)—is contained in the three phases [of sentient beings, those on the path, and buddhas]. [24] Its essence is expressed as follows:

> Though beginningless, it entails an end—
> What is naturally pure and consists of permanent dharmas
> Is not seen, since it is obscured by a beginningless cocoon,
> Just as in the example of a golden statue being obscured.[271]

In detail, I have already explained this in my *Treatise Determining the Buddha Heart.* . . Now follows the detailed explanation of the treatise in eleven sections.

1. General instruction on causes and conditions[272]

This has four parts:

1) Explaining mind as the essence of purity and impurity
2) The manner of being mistaken
3) The division of causes and conditions
4) The division of the three phases [25]

1.1. Explaining mind as the essence of purity and impurity

This has two parts:

1) Essence
2) Way of appearing

1.1.1. Essence

> **The cause is beginningless mind as such.**
> **Though it is neither confined nor biased, . . .**

The general terminology of all yānas speaks of "**mind as such**." However, [this mind] should be understood as being twofold—pure and impure. As for teaching the pure [aspect of "mind as such"] as "mind," the *Uttaratantra* states:

> Earth rests on water, water on wind,
> And wind on space,
> [But] space does not rest on the elements
> Of earth, water, and wind.
>
> Likewise, skandhas, dhātus, and faculties
> Rest on karma and afflictions,
> Karma and afflictions always rest on
> Improper mental engagement,
>
> And improper mental engagement
> Rests on the purity of mind,
> [But] the nature of mind does not rest
> On any of these phenomena.[273]

This expresses the buddha heart as "mind," which means that it is the basis of everything in saṃsāra and nirvāṇa. [Saraha's] *Dohā[kośagīti* ("*People Dohā*")*]* declares:

> Mind as such alone is the seed of everything,
> From which [saṃsāric] existence and nirvāṇa bloom.
> I pay homage to mind, which grants the fruitions we wish for,
> Just like a wish-fulfilling jewel.[274] [26]

The *[Aṣṭasāhasrikā]prajñāpāramitāsūtra* says:

> The mind is no-mind. The nature of the mind is luminosity."[275]

This is also stated many times in the tantras and treatises, thus expressing that [mind as such] is endowed with purity.

To express the impure [aspect of mind as such] as "mind" refers to what is taught as the "ālaya-consciousness." The *Abhidharmasamucchaya* says:

> Mind being impregnated by all the latent tendencies of skandhas, āyatanas, and dhātus is the ālaya-consciousness with all seeds.[276]

This [ālaya-consciousness] is embraced by false imagination, consists of the minds and mental factors in the three realms, is the root of all obscurations, and is to be overcome by buddha wisdom. With this in mind, the *Laṅkāvatārasūtra* says:

> O children of the victors, these three realms are merely mind.[277]

Also the *Madhyāntavibhāga* states:

> False imagination consists of
> The minds and mental factors in the three realms.[278] [27]

Therefore, this ālaya shall be explained briefly. Master Vasubandhu says the following about it in his *Triṃśikā[kārikā]*:

> Here, maturation is the "ālaya-consciousness,"
> Which contains all the seeds.
>
> Its appropriation, state,
> And cognizance are unconscious,
> Yet it is always endowed with contact, mental engagement,
> Feeling, discrimination, and impulse.
>
> Its feeling is indifference.
> It is unobscured and neutral.
> The same goes for its contact and so on.[279]
> It flows like a river stream.
>
> In arhathood, it becomes extinguished.[280]

As for what is called "ālaya," if the term "consciousness" is not [explicitly] stated, it is suitable [in certain contexts] to express suchness as "ālaya" too.[281] Therefore, [the term] "consciousness" is used [here]. You may wonder, "If 'consciousness' expresses that which sees an object, how is this [ālaya] presented as [having] an object?" It is called "consciousness," because it represents the entity of mutual causes and conditions by virtue of the other seven collections of consciousness[282] [serving] as its objects in terms of maturing and being its seeds. Since everything is gathered within it, it represents maturation, just as the ocean [exists] due to rain water. From the point of view of it serving as the cause that produces all manifest conditions, it is what consists of all seeds. [28] Because [the ālaya-consciousness] is accompanied by the group of the five omnipresent [mental factors] contact, mental engagement, feeling, discrimination, and impulse at all times, these mental factors also represent features of [it being considered as] a consciousness. The feeling [that accompanies] the ālaya is indifference, and it is unobscured and neutral, resembling the clarity of a mirror. That it is "flowing like a river stream" refers to the uninterrupted flux of all seeds of objects, subjects, and sense faculties. [In the above quote, when Vasubandhu] says, "In arhathood, it becomes extinguished," what he has in mind is buddhahood—in śrāvaka arhats, the ālaya definitely [still] exists. However, it is fine to explain that the extinction of the support that is the afflicted [mind], which clings to a personal self, represents the extinction of one part [of the ālaya-consciousness].[283] A very detailed explanation of this [ālaya] is given in the *Mahāyānasaṃgraha*:

> The Bhagavat taught a verse in the *Abhidharmasūtra*:
>
> . . .
>
> The alaya is the consciousness
> With all the seeds of all phenomena.
> Therefore, I explained the ālaya-consciousness
> To the excellent ones.
>
> This is the scriptural support. Why is it called "ālaya-consciousness?" [29] All afflicted phenomena that entail arising adhere[284] to it as [its] resultant entities, or, it adheres to them as [their] causal entity. Therefore, it is the ālaya-consciousness. Or, it is the ālaya-consciousness, since sentient beings adhere to it as being their identity.
>
> It is also called "appropriating consciousness." The scriptural support for this corresponds to what the *Saṃdhinirmocanasūtra* says:
>
> The appropriating consciousness is profound and subtle.
> All [its] seeds flow like the stream of a river.
> It is inappropriate to conceive of it as a self.
> I did not teach it to childish beings.[285]

> Why is it called "appropriating consciousness?" Because it is the cause of all physical sense faculties and serves as the locus of appropriating all [kinds of] bodies. Thus, it seizes the five physical sense faculties, without them perishing, for as long as one's life lasts, and it also seizes their full manifestion when the link with a [new] body is established. Therefore, it is that which seizes the body, thus being called "appropriating consciousness."[286]
>
> . . . How are its characteristics presented? In brief, there are three: . . . [30] The intrinsic characteristic of the ālaya-consciousness is that it, by virtue of the latent tendencies of all afflicted phenomena, has the feature of holding their seeds, thus being the cause for their arising. Its characteristic of being a cause is that the ālaya-consciousness, which constitutes all seeds, abides as the cause for these afflicted phenomena at all times. To present it as a result means that the ālaya-consciousness arises by virtue of the beginningless latent tendencies of these afflicted phenomena.[287]

[The *Mahāyānasaṃgraha* continues that] these latent tendencies arise and cease simultaneously with pure and impure phenomena. However, it is the mind [—the ālaya-consciousness—] that arises as the continuum of these [tendencies], and the cause for the afflicted phenomena [arising] from that is the ālaya-consciousness. Likewise, these afflicted phenomena in turn are presented as serving as the causal condition for the ālaya-consciousness, since no other causal condition is observable. Variegated latent tendencies dwell [in the ālaya] in a way of not being observable as variegated, [31] but appear as different [phenomena] later, once they arise as distinct karmic [results], just as a [piece of] cotton conditioned by kernel [extracts][288] is dyed and thus will [appear] to be variegated. This is the highly profound "dependent origination of differentiating the nature."[289] The other [seven] operating consciousnesses and the ālaya-consciousness are to be regarded as [bearing] the characteristic of being mutual causes and conditions. As the *Madhyāntavibhāga* says:

> A single one is the conditioning consciousness.
> The remaining entail experience.
> Experience, delimitation,
> And setting in motion are the mental factors.[290]

For this reason, the ālaya is said to be the special matrix of sentient beings, but it is stated that it is not the cause for the wisdom of great nirvāṇa. Nevertheless, some may wonder, "As for saying that the ālaya is the cause of everything, but not the cause of purified phenomena, how is this [to be understood], since there are also [instances when it] is taught as being the cause of purified phenomena?" It is fine to use the conventional term "purified phenomena" by virtue of the ālaya-consciousness having become pure, [32] but it is not suitable to expain the ālaya-consciousness as being the cause for the buddha wisdom of nirvāṇa. "But isn't it the case that also the conceptuality that is based on the correct view of the immaculate dharmas being inseparable from buddha enlightenment is input into the ālaya-consciousness? [Otherwise,] how are these purified phenomena produced?" They are grounded in the above-mentioned dharmakāya that is the purity of mind, the Tathāgata heart. The *Uttaratantra* says:

> Like a treasure and a fruit tree,
> The disposition is to be known as twofold—
> Naturally abiding without beginning
> And the supreme of what is accomplished.[291]
>
> It is held that the three buddhakāyas
> Are attained by virtue of these two dispositions—
> The first kāya through the first one,
> And the latter two through the second one.[292]

This is also explained in detail in the *Mahāyānasaṃgraha*:

> "How could the maturational consciousness with all the seeds, which is the cause of afflicted phenomena, be the seed of its remedy, that is, supramundane mind? Since supramundane mind is not contained in [the minds of ordinary beings], the latent tendencies of this [supramundane mind] [33] do not exist [in them]. But if these latent tendencies do not exist [in them], it must be stated from which seeds they arise." [Supramundane mind] originates from the natural outflow of the pure dharmadhātu, that is, the seeds which are the latent tendencies for listening. You may wonder, "What are these latent tendencies for listening anyway? Are they of the nature of the ālaya-consciousness or are they not? If they were of the nature of the ālaya-consciousness, how could they be suitable as the seeds of its remedy? And if they are not of its nature, then look what the matrix of these seeds of latent tendencies for listening is." What these latent tendencies for listening

> in dependence on the enlightenment of a buddha are, which matrix they enter, and that they enter the maturational consciousness in a manner of coexisting with it—all this is like [a mixture of] milk and water. They are not the ālaya-consciousness, because they are the very seeds of its remedy.[293]
>
> Small latent tendencies turn into medium latent tendencies, and these medium latent tendencies then turn into great latent tendencies, all this by virtue of being associated with listening, reflection, and meditation that are performed many times. The small, medium, and great latent tendencies for listening are to be regarded as the seeds of the dharmakāya. Since they are the remedy for the ālaya-consciousness, [34] they are not of the nature of the ālaya-consciousness. [In the sense of being a remedy,] they are something mundane, but since they are the natural outflow of the supramundane—the utterly pure dharmadhātu—they are the seeds of supramundane mind. Although this supramundane mind has not originated yet, they are the remedy for being entangled [in saṃsāra] through the afflictions, the remedy for migrating in the lower realms, and the remedy that makes all wrongdoing vanish. They are what is in complete concordance with meeting buddhas and bodhisattvas.
>
> Though beginner bodhisattvas are mundane, [these latent tendencies] should be regarded as being included in the dharmakāya and [those of] śrāvakas and pratyekabuddhas as being included in the vimuktikāya.[294] They are not the ālaya-consciousness, but included in the dharmakāya and vimuktikāya, respectively. To the extent that they gradually shine forth in a small, medium, and great way, to that same extent the consciousness of complete maturation wanes and changes state too. If it has changed state in all aspects, the consciousness becomes devoid of seeds and is also relinquished in all aspects.[295]

Some may think that the unfolding disposition arises newly, but this is not the case. To present the naturally abiding disposition—the dharmadhātu—as the eight consciousnesses, such as the ālaya-consciousness, is a presentation and classification in terms of false imagination. Likewise, [the unfolding disposition]—the very own stainless essence of these eight collections [of consciousness]—exists as the nature of the four wisdoms, which is the presentation in terms of correct imagination. By virtue of previous stains having been overcome through the immaculate dharmas that are grounded in buddha enlightenment, the mistakenness of the eight collections does not exist [anymore later]. Therefore, this is expressed [using] the phrase "the wisdom of the fundamental change of state." For this reason, the *Madhyāntavibhāga* says:

> Purity is asserted to be like the purity
> Of the element of water, gold, and space.[296]

Accordingly, [mind] without stains should be regarded as wisdom and [mind] with stains as consciousness. The *Mañjuśrīnāmasaṃgīti* states:

> Beyond the nature of consciousness,
> Wisdom bears a nondual nature.[297]

In detail, I explained this in the *Treatise of Examining Consciousness and Wisdom*, [36] and will also instruct [more on it] below in the chapter that teaches the connection of consciousness [and wisdom in the four states].[298]

Having explained pure and impure mind in this way, [the meaning of] "**beginningless**" is as follows. Since a beginning and an end in time are conceptual superimpositions, here, [mind's] own essence—be it with stains or stainless—is free from being the same as or other than dependent origination. Since there is no other beginning than that, this is called "beginningless time." In the very instant of [mind] itself being aware (*rig pa*) of or realizing its own essence, it is liberated, whereas its not being aware (*ma rig pa*) of this [essence] is the beginning of mistaken mind, which is called "ignorance." Therefore, the *Abhidharmasūtra* says:

> The dhātu of beginningless time
> Is the matrix of all phenomena.
> Since it exists, all beings
> And also nirvāṇa are obtained.

Also the *Saṃdhinirmocanasūtra* states:

> The defining characteristic of the realm of formations and the ultimate
> Is the defining characteristic that they are free from being one or different.[299]

[37] [Moreover,] there have been infinite [moments in] past times apart from just this [present] moment [of not realizing mind's nature], which are connected as a continuum [all the way up to this moment]. Therefore, to express this [infinite continuum of ignorance] through the term "beginningless" is fine too. However, thoughts about mind with stains existing as something permanent from the beginning, or, about its arising out of nothing are nothing but instances of the views about a true personality. If [mind] were permanently connected with its stains, they would simply be impossible to relinquish. [Arising out of nothing means that] mind would arise without a cause. Since [thinking in such ways] entails these flaws, it also contradicts reasoning. Nāgārjuna says [in his *Yuktiśaśṭikā*]:

> How could what is dependent origination
> Have a beginning or an end?
>
> How could what has arisen earlier
> Come to an end later on?
> Free from the extremes of earlier and later,
> The world appears like an illusion.[300]

In all buddhas and sentient beings, this mind cannot be expressed as being either the same or different. Therefore, **it is not confined.** Since it does not fall into any bias, such as permanence or extinction, it is **not biased.** This teaches the very nature of mind.

1.1.2. Mind's way of appearing

> **Due to the unimpeded play of that very [mind],**
> **Empty in essence, lucid in nature,**
> **And unimpeded in manifestation, it appears as everything.** [38]

Due to the unimpeded play of that very mind's own essence through momentary consciousnesses, [while] its nature abides as **emptiness** and it is **lucidity** by **nature** (which represents the basis for everything), the individual **manifestations** of the collections of mental factors and the seven collections of consciousness **appear** in an **unimpeded** and momentary way from that [empty and lucid ground]. Therefore, during the phase of [mind] being impure, [these three aspects of mind's empty essence, lucid nature, and unimpeded display] are called "mind," "mentation," and "consciousness" [respectively]. Once they have become pure, they are expressed through the names of the three kāyas and the wisdoms. This is also stated by noble Nāgārjuna in his *Dharmadhātustava*:

> Covered by the web of the afflictions,
> It is called a "sentient being."
> Once it's free from the afflictions,
> It should be expressed as "buddha."[301]

1.2. Explaining the manner of being mistaken

[This has two parts:]

1) Instruction on the ālaya and the afflicted mind that rests on it
2) Instruction on the six collections and the order of the five skandhas

1.2.1. Instruction on the ālaya and the afflicted mind that rests on it

> **That very [mind], being ignorant of itself,**
> **Is stirred by formational mentation.**
> **Due to being stirred like waves on water, . . .** [39]

As for **that very** mind **being ignorant of itself**, of what is it ignorant, through what is it ignorant, and in which way is it ignorant? Firstly, it is ignorant of its own naturally pure essence. Through what [is it ignorant]? It is ignorant of its own essence through [its own] unimpeded creative display appearing as if it were [distinct] subjects and objects. In which way is it ignorant? Due to being **stirred by formational mentation**, it appears as if it were causes and conditions, based on which it is rendered afflicted. Therefore, ignorance is produced and, through false imagination, it serves as both the basis [—the ālaya-consciousness—] and the condition [—mentation—] of saṃsāra. Since this [mentation] and the ālaya[-consciousness] manifest in the form of mutual causes and conditions, just **like water and waves**, they are incessantly **stirring** and forming [each other]. Hence, this is ignorance. Its being explained as "mentation" is also discussed in the *Triṃśikā[kārikā]*:

> What operates by resting on the [ālaya-consciousness]
> Is the consciousness called "mentation,"
> Which has it as its focal object, its nature being self-centeredness.
>
> It is always associated with the four afflictions,
> And is obscured yet neutral.[302]

As for this [mentation] that rests on the [ālaya-consciousness], it operates by resting on the ālaya, and [40] when the other six collections of consciousness arise and cease, it inputs their potentials into the ālaya. Therefore, it is called "mental consciousness." [In his *Pramāṇaviniścaya*,] Dharmakīrti states that the own essence of this [consciousness] is valid cognition:

> The mentation that is produced by its immediate condition—the sense consciousness that cooperates with the immediately following object of its own specific object—is [valid] perception.[303]

Secondly, the "mentation that has it as its focal object" has the character of regarding the ālaya as "me," and is called "afflicted mind." Since [this aspect of] mentation conceives the ālaya as a self and is always tainted by a set of four afflictions, it is the locus of the afflictedness of consciousness. Therefore, it lacks any valid cognition and gives rise to all minds that are nonvalid cognitions.[304] This ["mentation" in general has] both [aspects]: the one [—the immediate mind—] is said to be consciousness's own essence, and the other [—the afflicted mind—] is described from the perspective that, based on it, mistakenness is caused. Thus, they are said to be like a rope and taking that [rope] to be a snake [respectively].

Here, others explain the immediate [mind] as a part of the sixth—the mental—[consciousness], and some explain that, ultimately, it does not exist. However, those [people], [41] by clinging to the presentation of the śrāvakas who assert that there are only six collections [of consciousness], do not understand the mahāyāna's presentation of the eight collections [of consciousnesses], which is given in detail in the *Mahāyānasaṃgraha*:

> Among those, mentation is twofold. Since it is the support that acts as the immediate condition, the "mentation which is [any] consciousness that has just ceased" is the support for [the arising of] consciousness. The second is the afflicted mind, which is always congruently associated with the four afflictions of the views about a real personality, self-conceit, attachment to the self, and ignorance. This is the support for the afflictedness of consciousness. [Thus,] consciousness is produced by virtue of the first [aspect of mentation] as its support, while the second one makes it afflicted. [Mentation] is a consciousness, because it cognizes objects. Since it is [both] immediately preceding and self-centered, mentation has two aspects."[305]

"Afflicted" is a possessive term. For this reason, this [afflicted mind] is the root of all mistakenness of circling in the three realms. Therefore, [42] it neither exists in the meditative absorption of cessation that transcends the three realms, nor in the meditative equipoises of the paths of arhats and supramundane bodhisattvas. [However,] in the meditative absorption without discrimination, which is the cause for being born as a long-living [god] without discrimination, the afflicted mind exists. Thus, one will understand the difference [between these meditative absorptions].[306]

Furthermore, if one takes the immediacy of the arising and ceasing of the consciousnesses that dwells in the ālaya to be a part of the sixth—the mental—[consciousness], then at the time of being able to dwell in the meditative absorption of cessation, since there would be no [seventh consciousness] separate from the ālaya and the six [other] collections [of consciousness], there would be only seven collections [altogether at that time]. For, [the immediate mind is claimed to be included in the sixth consciousness and] the afflicted mind does not exist [in said meditative absorption]. [On the other hand,] if [some people] thus come to think] that the "stainless mentation" taught by the Bhagavat must be presented as a ninth collection [of consciousness],[307] this is not justified either.

You may wonder then, "Due to what is this seventh consciousness (mentation), which is [also] explained as the immediate [mind], presented as the afflicted mind, and due to what is it presented as stainless?" It is good [to say that] it becomes afflicted, once it is embraced by the four afflictions [mentioned above], but [43] to express it as stainless mentation, once it is embraced by the immaculate dharmas that are grounded in the enlightenment of a buddha. It is said that, as long as these two have not undergone the change of state of having become completely pure, they will remain blended together.[308] The *Mahāyānasaṃgraha* discusses this in detail:

> "What is the evidence for the existence of the afflicted mind?" If it did not exist, there would be the flaw of the nonexistence of isolated ignorance.[309] Also, there would be the flaw of [the mental consciousness] being dissimilar to the five [sense consciousnesses; for, just as the dominant conditions of] the eyes and so on are the [respective] simultaneous supports for the collections of these five [consciousnesses, mentation is the dominant condition that supports the sixth consciousness]. There would furthermore be the flaws of the lack of a hermeneutical etymology [for mentation][310] and of there being no difference between the meditative absorption without discrimination and [the meditative absorption of]

> cessation. In fact, the meditative absorption without discrimination is characterized by [the presence of] the afflicted mind, while the meditative absorption of cessation is not. Otherwise, these two would be without difference. Moreover, if there were no clinging to a self and self-conceit in said [state] without discrimination, there would be the flaw of being without afflictions throughout one's entire rebirth as [a god in such a state] without discrimination. [44] A further reason is that the occurrence of clinging to a self is observable in virtuous, nonvirtuous, and neutral states of mind at all times. Otherwise, [if it were] congruently associated solely with nonvirtuous states of mind, the affliction of self-conceit would therefore [only] occur [in these], but not in virtuous or neutral ones. Therefore, by virtue of the simultaneous occurrence [of afflicted mentation with all virtuous, nonvirtuous, and neutral states of mind] and occurrence in terms of being congruently associated together,[311] these flaws will not accrue. . . . Since mentation is afflicted, it is obscured yet neutral. It is always congruently associated with the four obscuring afflictions.[312]

Furthermore, [in the context of] the explanation of the eighteen dhātus, when the aspects of the [three] dhātus of mentation, dharmas, and mental consciousness are presented, to express [the immediate mind] as the dhātu of the sixth—the mental—consciousness is just one particular [way to present this]. But when it is taught as the seventh [consciousness], it is described as [any one of] the six [consciousnesses] having just ceased. The *Pañcaskandhaprakaraṇa* says:

> The six dhātus of consciousness depend on the eyes and so on, [45] cognizing [their respective] focal objects, such as form. The dhātu of mentation is [any one of] these [consciousnesses] having just ceased, because the locus of the sixth consciousness is stable. In this way, the dhātus are presented as eighteen.[313]

1.2.2. Instruction on the six collections and the order of the five skandhas

[This is taught by] two verses. First, I shall explain the six consciousnesses. The *Triṃśikā[kārikā]* says:

> The third [modulation] is the observation
> Of the six kinds of objects, . . .[314]

Accordingly, "mind" refers to the ālaya[-consciousness], "mentation" to the two [aspects] explained above, and the third [—"consciousness"—] refers to the six collections of consciousness. It is said that the [latter] are the ones that focus on the six objects (forms, sounds, smells, tastes, tangible objects, and phenomena) and that they are congruently associated with what follows [in the above text], that is, they are congruently associated with the fifty-one mental factors.

> . . . Which is virtuous, nonvirtuous, or neither.
>
> It is congruently associated with
> The omnipresent, delimiting,
> And virtuous mental events, as well as with
> Afflictions and secondary afflictions, its feelings being threefold.[315]

[46] Now, I shall teach on my text proper. You may wonder, "What happens **due to** the stirring of mind and mentation, which is like waves on water, as it was explained above?"

> **Referents and apprehenders appear as two.**
> **[Mind] itself projects onto itself and grasps [at that].**

Referents (the six objects) **and** the six consciousnesses that **apprehend** [them], though not really existing as something different ultimately, will arise in a way that they **appear as two.** Such appearances arise by virtue of the dependent origination of the triad of object, sense faculty, and consciousness coming together. Through appearances [further] expanding based on that, they become linked to the conceptual mind, which is called, "Through making one see referents, appearances are obtained." Therefore, it is taught that,

> **Due to the appearance aspect of mind moving outward,**
> **The consciousnesses that apprehend objects as referents arise.**

Those who do not know that all phenomena are mind, despite these consciousnesses being their own minds, entertain the thoughts that objects—outer referents—are produced by subtle particles or hidden entities. In order to demonstrate that this is not the case, the manner in which [mind] **itself projects** [the aspects of subject and object] **onto itself and grasps** [at them as self and other] is to be taught. This is [47] the inconceivable force of the incessant flux of the seeds of objects, sense faculties, and consciousnesses—the mutually dependent origination of the power of causes and results—within the essence of the ālaya, which constitutes all seeds. This is stated in the *Vajraśikharamahāguhyayogatantra*:

> The ālaya, which possesses all seeds,
> Is held to be the nature of [everything] internal and external.[316]

The reasoning for this is given by Dignāga in his *Ālambanaparīkṣā* [and its autocommentary]:

> The essence of knowable objects, which is internal,
> Is what appears as if it were external.
> This is its referent, since it has the nature of consciousness
> And also is its condition.
>
> While there are no outer referents, what appears as if it were external definitely exists inside—this is the object condition. Because it is internal consciousness that appears as [outer] referents, and [in turn] arises from these [projected referents], it has these two natures [of being both subject and object]. Therefore, the object condition is nothing but what exists inside.[317]

[Consciousness appearing as an object] is justified as a condition [for that very consciousness appearing as that object's subject], though it arises simultaneously [with this subject]; by virtue of [the object's] potential being input, a sequential [relation between object and subject] is not contradictory either; and it is not contradictory for a potential to even be a sense faculty—in order to instruct on [these three points, the *Ālambanaparīkṣā* continues]:

> Even if being one, it is the condition because of being
>   unmistaken.
> It [may also] be sequential, since its potential is input. [48]
> The essence of the potential of the concomitant
> Sense faculty is that very sense faculty.[318]

In this way, based on the dependent origination of differentiating the nature, there occurs the twelvefold dependent origination of differentiating what is desired and undesired. Therefore, by virtue of the condition of ignorance, karmic formations [arise], and through this condition, **the consciousnesses that** see the six **objects as referents arise.** [Being appearances of one's own mind,] these [objects] are neither to be adopted nor to be rejected, [but] they are conceived as objects that are something other [than mind]. Through [some of them] being conceived as something to be **adopted**, pleasant [feelings arise]; through [some] being conceived as something to be **rejected**, [feelings of] suffering [arise]; and [for some] in between, **feelings** of indifference **arise**. Under the sway of that, **discrimination** comes about through **apprehending the characteristics of those** objects. Through [further] apprehending characteristics [through formation], the latent tendencies of **conceiving of objects as something other** [than one's own mind] are solidified. Due to that, **through clinging** to the essence of form as shape, color, and so on, **the skandha of form** will **be established.**[317] These [five skandhas] appear by virtue of the dependent origination that is the coming together of numerous appearances in the form of causes and conditions in terms of impure mind. This is why they are called "skandhas" [lit. heap], similar to heaps of grain. [49] Therefore, I say:

> **[From] adopting and rejecting, feelings arise.**
> **To apprehend the characteristics of those is discrimination.**
> **Formation conceives of appearances of objects as something other,**
> **And through clinging, the skandha of form is established.**

Since [all of] this is the inconceivable power within the mind (the ālaya-consciousness), as taught above, it is discussed under many classifications, such as skandhas, dhātus, and āyatanas. One should be aware that these are presented for the sake of relinquishing the bad views of conceiving of [mind] as being single, the experiencer, and a creator [respectively. This is to be understood] through the meaning of [the skandhas] being assemblies of many [phenomena]; through the meaning of [the dhātus] bearing the characteristics of their own specific essences [—the six objects, six sense faculties, and six consciousnesses—] without there being any agent [extrinsic to them]; and through the meaning of [the āyatanas] functioning as the gates for the arising of consciousness, whereas there is no other creator. Since this is discussed in detail in the *Pañcaskandhaprakaraṇa*, I will not elaborate on it here.[320]

Thus, to summarize this instruction on all phenomena of saṃsāra being mistaken, one speaks of "mistakenness" because of not realizing the two realities' own essence, just like the mistakenness of not realizing a dream or an illusion [for what they are]. This [50] is expressed by noble Nāgārjuna in his *Bodhicittavivaraṇa*:[321]

From ignorance up through aging and death,
I hold the twelve links
Of dependent origination
To be like dreams and illusions.

This wheel of the twelve links
Rolls on the path of [saṃsāric] existence.
I do not hold that any sentient beings
Engage in actions and their results in any other way.[322]

Accordingly, the same is stated in many sūtras, tantras, and treatises. Having explained the manner of being mistaken in this way, there follows:

1.3. The division of causes and conditions

This has two parts:

1) [Instruction on] the six causes
2) Instruction on the four conditions

1.3.1. Instruction on the six causes

"The five elements and consciousness as the sixth are the causes,"
Is a conventional statement made by thinking.

In the terminology of the general yāna, the **conventional statement** is made that "**the five elements** (earth, water, fire, wind, and space) **and** the element of **consciousness as the sixth are the causes** of everything internal and external." As for the definitions of these, in due order, the five elements are being hard and solid, wet and moistening, hot and burning, light and moving, and empty and providing room. Consciousness was already explained above.[323] [51]

1.3.2. Instruction on the four conditions

1.3.2.1. The causal condition

Since the latent tendencies of these [causes]
Are accumulated in the ālaya, it is called the "causal condition."

This [ālaya-consciousness], which constitutes all seeds and was taught above, **is called the "causal condition."** For, without it, no other cause of sentient beings is observable. Together with examples, this is frequently stated in the *Mahāyānasaṃgraha*:

> Or, it is characterized by way of likeness, since the ālaya-consciousness is like an illusion, a mirage, a dream, and blurred vision. If it did not have this [characteristic], as the seed of false imagination, it would not be suitable as the cause of mistakenness. Therefore, it must exist.[324]

1.3.2.2. The dominant condition

> **The dominant conditions are the sense faculties,**
> **Such as the eyes, that appear in between.**

The dominant conditions of the six consciousnesses **are** said to be **the** five **sense faculties that appear in between** [these consciousnesses and their objects] as well as the [sixth] sense faculty of consciousness. It is taught that **the eye** sense faculty looks like a flax flower, possessing translucent form; the ear sense faculty resembles a twisted birch gnarl; the nose sense faculty resembles aligned copper needles; the tongue sense faculty looks like [two aligned] half-moons; and the body sense faculty is similar to the skin of the "bird that is soft to the touch."[325] [52] All of them possess translucent form. You may wonder, "Why do they possess form?" They arise from the four elements as their causes. "Translucent" refers to lucidity, since they are connected to consciousness. These [faculties] are also referred to as inner seeds or potentials in [Dharmakīrti's] *Sambandhaparīkṣā*, while the *Mahāyānasaṃgraha* holds that it is the apprehended aspect of the ālaya that appears as the five sense faculties. However, all [of these explanations] are not contradictory.

As for the mental faculty, it is explained [in several ways], such as being the immediate [mind] (arising from and ceasing into the ālaya), the dhātu of mentation ([any one of] the six [consciousnesses] having just ceased), or a particular one among the potentials of the ālaya. However, the meaning [of all this] is that the very potential that functions as the gateway for the arising of the mental consciousness is suitable as the āyatana of mentation,[326] because it and the āyatana of conditioned and unconditioned phenomena dependently originate as subject and [its related] object.[327]

1.3.2.3. Instruction on the object condition

> **The object conditions are what are cognized,**
> **Which appear as objects, such as forms.**

These are **forms**, sounds, smells, tastes, tangible objects, as well as conditioned and unconditioned phenomena. [53] Form refers to the referents that are the experiential sphere of the eyes, that is, the four great elements or that for which these four serve as causes, or, [in other words,] colors, shapes, and perceptible [form].[328] Sounds—both those conjoined and not conjoined [with the actions of beings]—are the **objects** of the ears and [also] arise from the elements. Smells are the objects of the nose, [which include] pleasant smells, bad smells, and [smells] other than those. Tastes are the objects of the tongue, that is, the six [kinds of taste]. Tangible objects are the objects of some part of the body, that is, softness, roughness, lightness, heaviness, cold, warmth, hunger, and thirst. As for phenomena, there are [eight] conditioned ones: (1) aggregational [form], (2) circumstantial [form], (3) [form] originating from correct commitment and symbols, (4) mastered [form], (5) imputed [form],[329] (6) feeling, (7) discrimination, and (8) formation. Unconditioned [phenomena] are the two cessations,[330] space, and suchness, [but] if they are divided into [further] enumerations, they are explained to be eight.[331] In brief, [the object conditions] **are what are cognized.**

1.3.2.4. The immediate condition

> **The "immediate condition"**
> **Is whatever has just ceased,**
> **Associated with the sixth, mentation.**[332]

About this, the Vaibhāṣikas [54] assert that the very cessation of each [moment] of the six collections [of consciousness] is the immediate [condition] for the next [moment]. However, because of the reasoning of cessation being unsuitable as a cause,[333] here, [I follow] what is said in the *Saṃdhinirmocana[sūtra]*. Accordingly, when [any one of] the six collections [of consciousness] has ceased, the consciousness that is explained to be the same as the dhātu of mentation transports them into the ālaya. Immediately upon that, just as with the condition of waves [emerging] from water, from [the ālaya] that consists of all seeds, the mentation that dwells in the ālaya stirs again and comes forth, that is, the immediate mind arises as explained above.[334] When a single conditional [instance] of the six collections arises, also a single [instance of the] immediate [mind] arises, but no second one. If triggered by the condition of many such [instances] arising, then just that many [instances of the immediate mind] will arise. Therefore, as for [the phrase,] "**whatever has just ceased**," once the earlier [instances of] the six collections have ceased, the following **conditional** [instances] are triggered[335] **immediately**. Thus, this is the immediate [condition]. Consequently, it is not contradictory to even explain this [phrase] as, "whatever is just arising." The reason is given in the *Triṃśikā[kārikā]*:

> In the root consciousness,
> The five consciousnesses arise according to conditions,
> Either together or not,
> Just like waves in water.[336]

Accordingly, [55] the "root consciousness" is the ālaya. "The five consciousnesses arise according to conditions" means that they arise together with the three conditions.[337] Or, by having in mind that consciousness itself is the dominant condition, [Vasubandhu takes] the sense faculty, the object, and the consciousness to be produced in such a way that they are generated by the immediate [mind alone]. With this in mind, [Vasubandhu] said, "either together or not." The way in which the sixth—the mental—consciousness arises is also stated in this text:

> The mental consciousness occurs always,
> Except for in those without discrimination,
> In the two kinds of meditative absorption,
> [Deep] sleep, fainting, and also the state without mind.[338]

Since the sixth—the mental—[consciousness] is temporarily withdrawn into the ālaya during these five[339] states, its aspect of being directed toward phenomena is not clear. Therefore, it is explained that it does not occur in these states. In all other states, it is held to be present.

Here, "**associated with the sixth, mentation**" refers to the assertion that the immediate mind exists in the sixth [consciousness]—mentation—as well. Therefore, the immediate [mind] is a particular instance of the mentation that rests in the ālaya.[340] [However,] since there are assertions by others that the immediate [mind] is a particular instance of the sixth [consciousness]—mentation—[alone], [56] these [above] words teach that all six consciousnesses equally arise [in this] immediate [way]. When the six consciousnesses are referred to as results, it is tenable [to say] that they arise from the three conditions [mentioned just above]. The four conditions in Yogācāra texts, [as explained here, simply] stand for the entirety of causes and conditions that are produced by the mind. Ultimately, though these conditions are tenable as sheer dependent origination, they refer to nothing but particular cases of imagination.

Though there are indeed many reasonings and scriptural elaborations [for this], that much elaboration shall suffice. Having thus explained the divisions of causes and conditions, there follows:

1.4. The division of the three phases

This has three parts:

1) The impure [phase]
2) The [phase] of being endowed with both [purity and impurity]
3) The completely pure [phase]

1.4.1. The impure phase

This is [taught by] three verses, starting with the general statement.

> **In this way, by virtue of the dependent origination of causes and conditions,**
> **All phenomena of saṃsāra and nirvāṇa appear.**

In dependence on **causes and conditions, dependent origination** in progressive order [arises] as **saṃsāra and**, through realizing this as well as realizing its reverse order, **nirvāṇa** comes about. If this is expressed in more detail, [57] as taught above, through ignorance, karmic formations [arise], and through this condition, consciousness, name and form, the six āyatanas, contact, and feelings arise. Therefore,

> **Craving and grasping form the link to establish existence.**[341]

Since this [saṃsāric] existence is threefold, I say:

> **The formless [realm], the form realm, and the desire realm,**
> **In due order, represent apprehending the characteristics of objects**
> **To a lesser, middling, and great degree.**

The four **formless** [states] **represent apprehending the characteristics of objects to a lesser degree**, because the appearances of the desire and form [realms] as well as their obstructiveness have ceased. Since **the form realm** is free from the desire of the desire [realm] and arises through the force of its four samādhis, it represents the **middling** degree [of apprehending characteristics]. By virtue of being endowed with all [types] of imagination [and attachment to sense pleasures], **the desire realm** involves the **great** degree of apprehending the characteristics of its [objects].

All [these realms] are produced **through** improper **thoughts of adopting and rejecting** because of not realizing the basic nature of one's own mind, thus **being formed through the triad of virtuous, nonvirtuous, and neutral** [actions]. Therefore, I say:

> **Through thoughts of adopting and rejecting all this,** [58]
> **And by virtue of the conditions of being formed through**
> **the triad**
> **Of virtuous, nonvirtuous, and neutral [actions], . . .**

Having thus stated the features of the causes, you may wonder what their results are. The answer is:

> **The results of happiness, suffering, and meditative absorptions**
> **Are produced, [all of which] entail afflictions.**

Through the lesser, middling, and greater forces of the ten virtues, lesser, middling, and greater **results of happiness** are produced, which represent the [three] happy realms within the desire realm. Those [of its states] that entail **suffering**, which is produced by nonvirtue, are the three lower realms. The form and formless [realms] **are produced** through the **meditative absorptions** of the four dhyānas and the four formless [absorptions, respectively], which [all] lack prajñā. All [of these states] are not free from the **afflicted** mind. Therefore, [the following line] expresses [the phase during which mind's nature] is endowed with stains:

> **This is the impure phase of mind as such.**

1.4.2. The phase of being both pure and impure

> **As for those who know these stains to be adventitious**
> **And then purify them with the methods,**
> **The victor declared them to be "those on the path."**

As taught above, **those who know** the obscurations **to be adventitious and then** engage in **purifying** these obscurations through relying on the [dharmas] concordant with enlightenment and through the distinctive features of **the methods** of the creation and completion [stages], [59] are said **to be**

those on the path.[342] [This refers to] the phase of being both pure and impure, starting from the path of accumulation until the end of the continuum of the ten bhūmis.

1.4.3. The completely pure [phase]

> **Stainless and purified, it is buddhahood.**
> **Therefore, all beings are buddhas indeed.**

Being free from all afflictive and cognitive **stains** as well as from those of meditative absorption **is buddhahood**, and since the minds of **all** sentient **beings** are not separated from this [freedom], they **are** said to be **buddhas**. The *Hevajra[tantra]* says:

> Sentient beings are buddhas indeed.
> However, they are obscured by adventitious stains.
> If these are removed, they are buddhas.[343]

[The sūtras] declare:

> The Sugata heart pervades all beings.
> There is no sentient being here who is not its vessel.[344]

[Thus, the above two lines] teach the meaning that is [expressed in these scriptures].

Chapter Six: Explaining the Manner in Which Consciousness and Wisdom Are Connected in the Four States[345]

The detailed explanation of the ordinary waking state

This has three parts:

1) Its nature
2) Its purity
3) The factors to be relinquished, the remedies, and the results

1. Its nature

[This is taught by] two and a half verses.

> **As for consciousness during the ordinary [state],**
> **Through the ālaya being formed by the afflicted mind**
> **As explained above, triggered by the four conditions,**
> **The six consciousnesses, such as the visual one,**
>
> **Are connected with the six sense faculties,**
> **And it appears as the six objects, such as form.**
> **The three feelings—happiness, suffering, and indifference—**
> **Produce attachment, aversion, and dullness.**
>
> **Transported by the immediate mind,**
> **They are input into the ālaya and reformed again.**

This states from where **consciousness during the ordinary** waking state arises, and what, **through the ālaya being formed by the afflicted mind as explained above,** is **triggered by the four conditions.** Through the four conditions explained above (the causal, dominant, immediate, and object conditions), **the six consciousnesses, such as the visual one, are connected with the six sense faculties.** Through not knowing that what externally **appears as the six objects, such as form,** is one's own mind, toward **the three** kinds of **feelings—happiness, suffering, and indifference—attachment** (toward happiness), [199] **aversion** (toward suffering), **and dullness** (through not realizing indifference) are **produced.** Through being **transported by the immediate mind, they are input into the ālaya and reformed again** [later in dependence on these latent tendencies]. Thus, this becomes the wheel of afflictions and saṃsāric suffering. This is also stated by the great scholar Vimala[mitra] in the context of summarizing the meaning of the Dzogchen tantras:

Within unmistaken alpha purity from the beginning,
Indeterminate spontaneous presence,
Warped by [variegated] mistaken wisdom,[346]
Due to threefold ignorance,[347]
[Present] consciousness so vividly lucid and aware,
By virtue of the aspect of it appearing to shift outside for just an instant,
[Turns into] mind apprehending objects as [having a real] identity,
And through its impure focus of the four conditions,
The appearances of the six objects emerge.
Through the six afflictions, they are fettered as [having a real] identity.
In this way, objects are taken to [have a real] identity.
Then, gradually, the forms of the many appearances
Of container and contents[348] mingle.
Childish beings, ignorant of this [kind of dependent origination],
Remain in it continuously, like in a water wheel,
Assuming their individual bodies and characters.

Having thus explained the nature of the ordinary [waking] state, there follows:

2. Its purity

The purity of this consists of threefold wisdom— [200]
Mentation is unmoving, [the wisdom of] equality;
Pure imagination is discriminating [wisdom];[349]
And the five doors and their objects are all-accomplishing [wisdom].

You wonder, "How can we be certain that these five wisdoms—these **three** as well as the mirrorlike [wisdom] and the dharmadhātu **wisdom**, which were taught above [in the section on deep sleep]—arise from the mistakenness of the four states having becoming pure?" This is stated in the mantra scriptures, such as the *Guhyasamāja[tantra]*, and the change of state of the five skandas is also taught in the *Mahāyānasaṃgraha*:

> Through how many kinds of masteries is the mastery of the dharmakāya attained? In brief, mastery is attained through five

> kinds. (1) Through the change of state of the skandha of form, mastery over [pure buddha] realms, kāyas, the excellent major and minor marks, infinite voices, and the invisible mark on the crown of the head [is attained]. (2) Through the change of state of the skandha of feeling, mastery over infinite and vast blissful states without wrongdoing [is attained]. (3) Through the change of state of the skandha of discrimination, mastery over the teachings [is attained] through all groups of words, groups of phrases, and groups of letters. [201] (4) Through the change of state of the skandha of formation, mastery over creation, transformation, gathering retinues, and gathering the immaculate dharmas [is attained]. (5) Through the change of state of the skandha of consciousness, mastery over mirrorlike [wisdom], [the wisdom of] equality, discriminating [wisdom], and all-accomplishing [wisdom] is attained.[350]

The change of state of the ālaya is mirrorlike [wisdom].[351] The change of state of the **mentation** that rests in the ālaya **is** [the wisdom of] **equality**.[352] The change of state of the sixth—the mental—[consciousness] **is discriminating** [wisdom]. The change of state of [the consciousnesses] that engage entities **is all-accomplishing** [wisdom]. Dharmadhātu wisdom is what abides as the nature that is the utterly pure essence of these wisdoms.[353] As for the natures of these [wisdoms], the *[Mahāyāna]sūtrālaṃkāra* says:

> Mirrorlike wisdom is without "me" or "mine,"
> Unconfined, ever present,
> Not ignorant about the entirety of knowable objects,
> Yet never directed toward them.
>
> Since it is the cause of all wisdoms,
> It is like a great jewel mine of wisdom.
> It is the sambhoga-buddhahood,
> Since the reflection of wisdom arises.[354]

Thus, [mirrorlike wisdom] is unmoving, [202] without "mine," unconfined, ever present, and not ignorant about all knowable objects, but not directed toward them.[355] Since it is the cause of all wisdoms, it is also [the cause] of sambhoga-buddhahood, thus being presented as their causal condition. As for its hermeneutical etymology, since the reflections of all wisdoms arise from it,[356] from among the three kāyas of a buddha, it is the dharmakāya. The *Mahāyānasaṃgraha* says:

> [The dharmakāya is constituted] by the buddhadharma of purity, since the dharmakāya is attained by the ālaya-consciousness having changed state.[357]

Also the *Suvarṇaprabhāsottama[sūtra]* discusses this extensively:

> Through relinquishing the ālaya-consciousness, the dharmakāya is displayed. Through mentation, which rests in it, having become pure, the sambhogakāya is displayed. Through the consciousnesses that engage entities having become pure, the nirmāṇakāya is displayed . . .

This is furthermore explained in [the *Buddhabhūmisūtra* and] the *Āryabuddhabhūmivyākhyāna*. Also the *Śrīḍākārṇava[mahā]yoginītantra* treats it in detail, such as saying:

> The ālaya is mirrorlike wisdom—
> This is the dharmakāya.[358]

[203] There is the assertion by some that this *is* sambhoga-buddhahood, but they just did not grasp the intention of master Vasubandhu's commentary [on the above line IX.69c in the *Mahāyānasūtrālaṃkāra]*, which says:

> It is *also* sambhoga-buddhahood.

Adding the term "also" [serves as] a word that links dharmakāya and mirrorlike wisdom to sambhoga-buddhahood as the latter's causal condition, just as linking the ālaya to the seven collections of consciousness as their causal condition. If it were not like this, [that is, if mirrorlike wisdom were the sambhogakāya,] there would indeed be numerous flaws in terms of scriptures, [such as contradicting the above and other sources,] and reasoning, [such as messing up the basis of purification and the means of purification], but that much elaboration shall suffice.[359]

[As for the wisdom of equality, the *Mahāyānasūtrālaṃkāra* continues:]

> The wisdom of equality toward sentient beings
> Is held to be stainless by virtue of pure cultivation.

Residing in nonabiding peace
Is asserted to be the wisdom of equality.

Said to be endowed at all times
With great love and compassion,
The image of the Buddha displays,
Just as sentient beings aspire.[360]

Because it [arises from] the pure cultivation of nonconceptual samādhi, is unbiased in any way, is the peace of not abiding in either [saṃsāric] existence or peace, engages in great compassion, and [204] displays [in various physical forms with] the major and minor marks to sentient beings according to their inclinations, this wisdom of equality is the change of state of the mentation that rests in the ālaya. The change of state of this and one part of the sixth—the mental—[consciousness (that is, the immediate mind)][361] represents the sambhogakāya.

[As for discriminating wisdom, the *Mahāyānasūtrālaṃkāra* says:]

Discriminating wisdom
Is always unimpeded toward all knowable objects.
It is just like a treasury
Of dhāraṇīs[362] and samādhis.

In the maṇḍala of retinues,
It displays all masteries,
Cuts through all doubts,
And rains down the great dharma.[363]

Since it resembles a treasury of dhāraṇīs and samādhis, and manifests as the conch shell of the spoken dharma, the change of state of the sixth—the mental—consciousness [in general, together with the just-mentioned change of state of the afflicted mind,] represents the sambhogakāya. However, each one of its following two aspects belongs to the nirmāṇakāya—(a) the display of [pure] realms and such by virtue of the change of state of [the part of the sixth consciousness that] apprehends [outer] referents[364] and (b) wisdom and enlightened activity being unimpeded at all times by virtue of the change of state of the conceptual [part of the sixth consciousness].[365]

[As for all-accomplishing wisdom, the *Mahāyānasūtrālaṃkāra* states:]

All-accomplishing wisdom
Accomplishes the welfare of all sentient beings
In all realms through various
Immeasurable and inconceivable emanations. [205]

Through the differences in accomplishing their deeds,
In terms of number, and in terms of realms,
Always and in all respects,
Buddha emanations should be known to be inconceivable.[366]

Since it engages all worldly realms in various forms, the change of state of [all] the consciousnesses that engage [outer] entities—the five doors [of the sense consciousnesses] and the one [perceptual] part of the mental [consciousness]—represents all-accomplishing [wisdom]. This is the nirmāṇakāya.[367]

Thus, the terms for the four wisdoms bear their [respective] meanings by virtue of retaining all wisdoms, being mind's equality, teaching the dharma, and accomplishing all deeds. [In the *Mahāyānasūtrālaṃkāra*,] we find:

Due to retaining, due to equanimity,
Due to elucidating the perfect dharma,
And due to accomplishing activities,
The four wisdoms arise.[368]

You may wonder, "How about the fifth, dharmadhātu wisdom?" It is the essence in which the disposition and the purpose are not different,[369] in which saṃsāra and nirvāṇa are complete, which has neither beginning nor end, is neither single nor multiple, and, by virtue of these features, is free from all characteristics of reference points. Therefore, this is evidently what is taught by [the *Mahāyānasūtrālaṃkāra*]:

In view of different dispositions, in view of uselessness,
In view of completeness, and in view of no beginning,
Buddhahood is not single; [206] nor is it multiple,
Since there is no difference in the stainless ground.[370]

There is [a way to] match the wisdoms with the five skandhas, but this will be explained below.[371]

3. The factors to be relinquished, the remedies, and the results

[This is taught by] two verses and one line.

> **The obscurations are what are relinquished through seeing and familiarization.**
> **The four kinds of remedies are aspiration,**
> **Identitylessness, samādhi, and compassion.**

The obscurations of the wisdoms that pertain to mentation and the five doors [in particular] **are** the [coarse imputed and subtle innate] afflictions **that are** [respectively] **relinquished through** [the paths of] **seeing and familiarization**. The obscurations of all eight collections [of consciousness in general] are the [entirety of] afflictive and cognitive obscurations. **The remedies are** to greatly cultivate **aspiration** for the dharma of the mahāyāna; [the prajñā that realizes] personal and phenomenal **identitylessness**; **samādhis**, such as the sky treasure; **and** great **compassion** that engages all sentient beings. This is stated in the *Uttaratantra*:

> Those who possess the seed of aspiration for the supreme yāna,
> Prajñā as the mother who gives birth to the buddhadharmas,
> The abode of the womb of blissful samādhi, and the nanny of compassion
> Are the children born to follow the sages.[372]

This is just as explained in the above section on wisdom.

> **Purified through them, the nirmāṇakāya—which promotes the welfare of beings—**
> **And, since mentation and dreams are the same,**
> **The sambhogakāya [207] are said to be the fruitions.**
> **Because this is discussed extensively in all dharmas,**
> **Here, I just gave a summary.**
> **Therefore, bind with the dharmamudrā.**[373]

Chapter Nine: Instruction on the Basis of Purification and the Means of Purification of All Phenomena

2. Detailed explanation

This has six parts:

1) Explaining the correct two realities
2) Relinquishing wrong and mistaken ideas due to not realizing their mode of being [232]

. . .

2.1. Explaining the correct two realities

[This is taught by] two and a half verses. In the great vajrayāna, the following are inseparable—wisdom as the perfect fruition; the generation of a remedial consciousness that is approximately concordant with this; and the immaculate dharma of the Buddha as the cause for the arising of the correct view. Therefore, one speaks of "making the fruition the path." Ultimately, what are labeled, regarded, and conceived of as ground, path, and fruition are merely conceptual superimpositions. Actually, they do not exist. You may wonder, "So what does exist ultimately?" What exists is naturally pure mind beyond the entire web of imagination, that is, **the basic element of sentient beings**, their buddha heart.[374] Therefore, I express its mode of being by saying:

> **The basic element of sentient beings is the stainless**
> **Buddha heart endowed with the two realities.**[375]

This **buddha heart** is indeed nothing but **the stainless**ness [in terms of] the mistakenness of the eight collections [of consciousness] mentioned above. But [233] since those who have not revealed the actuality of **the two realities** are ignorant about the mode of being of dependent origination and thus fixate on different views, they circle [in saṃsāra].[376] They are mistaken just as noble Nāgārjuna describes in his *Mahāyānaviṃśikā*:

> How sentient beings experience objects
> Is exactly like in the case of illusions.
> Beings have the nature of illusions—
> Just like them, they originate dependently.

Just as a painter may paint
The form of a terrifying yakṣa
And then becomes frightened by it himself,
The saṃsāra of the stupid is like that.

Just as, through their own struggling in a swamp,
Some childish beings sink down [in it],
Through being swamped in the mire of imagination,
Sentient beings are unable to emerge.

Those who view nonentities as entities
Experience feelings of suffering,
Fettered through the poison of conceiving
Of objects and consciousnesses.[377]

Relative to this [mistakenness], one may speak of "attaining buddhahood," [but such can only] be said in terms of seeming reality. How is this [to be understood]? [Nāgārjuna] continues:

Through them seeing the lack of essence, [234]
And through a mind of prajñā and compassion,
In order to benefit sentient beings,
They are to be linked to perfect buddhahood.

Having gathered the accumulations through that,
Seemingly, they attain unsurpassable enlightenment,
Being free from the fetters of imagination.[378]

You may wonder, "If what are labeled as sentient beings and buddhas, and whatever appears are seeming reality, how is ultimate reality?" The *Guhyasamāja[tantra]* says:

Free from all entities,
With skandhas, dhātus, āyatanas,
Apprehender, and apprehended relinquished,
Due to the equality of phenomenal identitylessness,
Your own mind is primordially unborn,
Being of the nature of emptiness.

Wishing to teach this, noble Nāgārjuna, the great being, declares in his *Bodhicittavivaraṇa*:[379]

> The mind of enlightenment of the buddhas
> Is held to be unobscured by conceptions
> That cognize a self, skandhas, and so forth,
> While always being characterized by emptiness.[380]

As for these two realities, here, I summarize a passage **in the *Vajrajñāna-*** *samucchaya[tantra]* as follows: [235]

> **It is said that the seeming is the appearance of apprehender and apprehended.**
> **[Its] reality is like a [reflection of] the moon in water.**
> **The ultimate consists of the eighteen emptinesses.**
> **[Its] reality is nondual wisdom.**[381]

"**Seeming**" is a term that stands for "totally unreal." Therefore, what is imagined as the duality **of apprehender and apprehended** is nonexistent in every respect. Also noble Maitreya states that all imaginary apprehenders and apprehended [objects] are simply nonexistent in every respect. [His *Madhyāntavibhāga* says]:

> Consciousness arises as the appearance of referents,
> Sentient beings, a self, and cognizance,
> [But] it does not have an [external] referent.
> Since that does not exist, it does not exist either.[382]

You may wonder, "But how are [these appearances] then presented as a reality?" What merely **appears** while not existing is called "seeming **reality**," since [precisely this feature] is its undeceiving own essence. "But isn't just this [—to be undeceiving—] ultimate reality? What is undeceiving is what is able to perform a function and is connected to valid cognition. So isn't it for this reason that the texts on reasoning say:

> What is able to perform a function
> Is what exists ultimately."[383]

This [236] is indeed a presentation of the nominal ultimate, but for those who follow the reasonings pertaining to the [ultimate] nature of phenomena,

the ultimate reality **consists of** nothing but the natural emptiness mentioned above, whose aspects are explained as **the eighteen emptinesses**. This is also stated by master Jñānagarbha [in his *Satyadvayavibhāga*]:

> Just these very appearances, as they [appear],
> Are the seeming. The other is its counterpart.[384]

Wishing to divide these seeming [appearances] into the mere seeming and what is [seemingly] real, he says:

> Although [phenomena] are similar in appearance,
> Since they are able to perform functions or not,
> Due to being correct or false,
> The division of the seeming was made.[385]

Just as phenomena and the nature of phenomena, the two realities as explained [above] are free from being exactly alike or other, [thus] being inexpressible as either being the same or different. This principle is also the purport of all the dharmas that are realized and taught by the buddhas, the Bhagavats. [Nāgārjuna's] commentary on the *Mūlamadhyamakakārikā* [XXV.8–10], the *Akutobhayā*,[386] says:

> The dharma taught by the buddhas [237]
> Is perfectly based on the two realities—
> Worldly seeming reality
> And ultimate reality.
>
> Those who do not understand
> The division of these two realities
> Do not understand the profound true reality
> Of the Buddha's teaching.
>
> *The dharma taught by the buddhas*, the Bhagavats, came about *based on these two realities*. This so-called "*worldly seeming reality*" is the seeing that all phenomena arise, since the mistakenness of worldly [beings] does not realize that all phenomena are empty of nature. Seemingly, this is the very reality for just these [beings]. Hence, it is seeming reality. As for *ultimate reality*, since the unmistakenness of the noble ones realizes it, it is the seeing that all phenomena do not arise. Ultimately, this is the very reality for precisely these [noble

ones]. Therefore, it is ultimate reality. *Those who do not understand the division of* seeming reality and ultimate *reality* in this way [238] are the ones who *do not understand the profound true reality of the Buddha's teachings.* You may think here: "If this ultimate reality is that 'all phenomena are without arising,' for what do you need this second, conventional reality?"

Without relying on the conventional,
The ultimate cannot be taught.
Without realizing[387] the ultimate,
Nirvāṇa will not be attained.

Since *without relying on the conventional, the ultimate cannot be taught*, and since *without* relying on *the ultimate, nirvāṇa will not be attained*, both realities need to be designated.[388]

Therefore, since correct imagination and view arise based on this mode of being, I say:

What is produced by the conceptions that examine[389] this
Is explained to be the remedial means of purification.[390]

[Some people] may think, "This is justified in the texts of mantra and the texts of Yogācāra, which [both] explain the meaning of the two realities as the buddha heart in this way, but in the Madhyamaka texts it is taught that all phenomena are without nature. Therefore, [239] there is no teaching [in them] that the Tathāgata heart and the basic element exist." You should not be confused by [just] the words of the Mādhyamikas. [For, Nāgārjuna's] *Dharmadhātustava* discusses this extensively in passages such as the following:

Likewise, from all seeds there are,
Fruits are born that match their cause.
By which person could it then be proved
That there is a fruit without a seed?

This basic element, which is the seed,
Is held to be the basis of all dharmas.
Through its purification step by step,
The state of buddhahood we will attain.

Spotless are the sun and moon,
But obscured by fivefold stains:
These are clouds and smoke and mist,[391]
Rahu's face[392] and dust as well.

Similarly, mind so luminous
Is obscured by fivefold stains.
They're desire, malice, laziness,
Agitation, and doubt too.[393]

A garment that was purged by fire
May be soiled by various stains.
When it's put into a blaze again,
The stains are burned, the garment not.

Likewise, mind that is so luminous
Is soiled by stains of craving and so forth.
The afflictions burn in wisdom's fire,
But its luminosity does not. [240]

The sūtras that teach emptiness,
However many spoken by the victors,
They all remove afflictions,
But never ruin this dhātu.[394]

The synonyms of this [dhātu] are taught in great detail in the *Uttaratantra*, such as [in the following lines]:

As for the basic element of completely pure mind,
. . .
Its nature is the dharmakāya,
Suchness, and the disposition too.[395]

Through nine examples, [this text] summarizes all the afflictions there are into sixty-four [main types of afflictions], with their purification making the stainless sixty-four qualities of buddhahood appear. [Thus,] **the basis of purification** and the complete purification through the means of purification, including their justification, have been described. In this vein, I say:

All phenomena are taught to correspond in number to the bases of purification.

In this way, what is called "the correct view of the mantra principle"—the mode of being of the two realities that are the great union free from extremes—has been explained.

2.2. Instruction on relinquishing the cherished belief systems of those who do not realize the mode of being of the [two realities]

This has two parts:

1) Non-Buddhist philosophical systems

2) Philosophical systems of the hīnayāna [241]

. . .

[243] 2.2.2. Philosophical systems of the hīnayāna

[This is taught by] two verses and three lines. First, the aspect of being mistaken about outer objects is discussed.

> **[The notions of] external minute particles and hidden [entities]**
> **[Flourish] under the influence of not realizing that the potential**
> **For the appearance of objects [lies in] the ālaya and mentation.**

The Vaibhāṣikas of our own [Buddhist] faction [244] assert directly perceptible outer referents, that is, **external** referents that are **minute particles** other than mind, which either have parts or not, and either involve space [between them and] those [particles] that surround them or not, and so forth, while the Sautrāntikas [speak of] **hidden** [external matter]. But since they do **not realize that the potentials** of **the ālaya and mentation** [represent or trigger] the factors that **appear** as **objects**, the mistakenness of conceiving [these potentials] as something else arises [in them]. However, there is nothing that is real as being different from, and other than, consciousness. **Nevertheless, the teachings** on the dhātus, [which contain explanations on matter consisting of] minute particles, and so on, are remedies for the thoughts that [things] **such as a self**, or **an agent** exist. Therefore, I say:

> **Nevertheless, in order to refute an agent, such as a self,**
> **There are these teachings by the Victor.**

[Nāgārjuna's] *Bodhicittavivaraṇa* says:

> As the entities of apprehender and apprehended,
> The appearances of consciousness

Do not exist as outer objects
That are different from consciousness.

Therefore, in the sense of having the nature of entities,
Outer objects do not exist in any way.
It is these distinct appearances of consciousness
That appear as the aspects of forms.

Just as people with deluded mind
See illusions, mirages,
Cities of gandharvas and so forth, [245]
The appearance of forms and such is just like that.

The skandhas, dhātus, and so on were taught
In order to put an end to clinging to a self.[396]

Self and person are stated as imputations,
Lacking even an atom's worth of being established as real substances.

Also the statements by some of our śrāvakas that a **self** and so on exist[397] **are** mere **imputations** by names. But if a **real** and **substantially established person** existed, **there would be flaws** in terms of reasoning. If this substance pertained to saṃsāra itself, nirvāṇa would not be tenable, and if this substance pertained to nirvāṇa, one would be **liberated effortlessly**. Therefore, I say:

It is taught that if they existed, there would be the flaws
Of effortless liberation or no liberation.

This is the meaning that is discussed in detail in the *Mahāyānasūtrālaṃkāra*:

It should be said that the person exists
By imputation, but not in terms of substance . . .[398]

Factors to be relinquished and their remedies (such as these),
Which appear to the mind, accord with what the learned teach.

[246] Through understanding the above-mentioned causes and results, **which appear to the mind**, and also that everything [in general] is mind, bad views

are relinquished. But it is through also **relinquishing** one's taking [phenomena] to be mind that true reality will be seen. The *Bodhicittavivaraṇa* declares:

> By abiding in [the view of] mere mind,
> Those with good fortune relinquish them too.
>
> For the Vijñānavādins,
> All this variety is established as mind.
> If you wonder what the nature of consciousness is,
> This shall be explained now.
>
> The teaching of the sage that
> "All of these are mere mind"
> Is for the sake of removing the fear of childish beings
> And not [meant] in terms of true reality.
>
> As for the imaginary, the other-dependent,
> And the perfect [natures],
> Their nature is the single character of emptiness.
> They are imputations onto mind.
>
> For those whose character is delight in the mahāyāna,
> The Buddha's teaching is in brief:
> Phenomena are identityless and equality,
> And mind is primordially unborn.[399]

Also the *Mahāyānasūtrālaṃkāra* states:

> The mind is aware that nothing other than mind exists.
> Then, it is realized that mind does not exist either. [247]
> The intelligent ones are aware that both do not exist
> And abide in the dharmadhātu, in which these are absent.[400]

Accordingly, also the relinquishment of [assertions] **such as** [some form of] real cognizance is **taught** extensively. Therefore, one should realize the way to engage in the entire mahāyāna, that is, the basic nature of the two realities.[401]

The Ornament That Explains the *Dharmadharmatāvibhāga*

Brief Introduction to Phenomena and Their Nature[402]

[Vasubandhu's] commentary [on the *Dharmadharmatāvibhāga*][403] says that all knowable objects are contained in phenomena and their nature, so this is a division in terms of their characteristics, but it is neither a division in terms of them being different objects, nor a division in terms of singling out these two from among a great number.

The nature [of phenomena and their nature] consists of the three natures, with saṃsāra consisting of the imaginary and the other-dependent [natures], and the perfect [nature]—suchness and perfect wisdom—being nirvāṇa. Therefore, this is a division in terms of characteristics. For example, just as when a rope is mistaken for being a snake, the imaginary nature is [like the snake for which the rope is mistaken, that is,] a nonexistent that [seems to] appear. The other-dependent [nature is like] the rope—it appears, but it is not real in the way [it appears], since all that appears is a mere collection of threads with [certain] colors and shape. The perfect nature is (a) the snake's and the rope's very own nature of lacking reality and (b) unmistaken self-awareness, since [such awareness] is without mistakenness about what appears [to it]. Therefore, [phenomena and their nature] do not exist as different objects. This very meaning is also expressed by noble Nāgārjuna:

> Between saṃsāra and nirvāṇa,
> There is not the slightest difference.
> Between nirvāṇa and saṃsāra,
> There is not the slightest difference.[404]

Furthermore, the domain of all [phenomena of] saṃsāra and nirvāṇa is the dharmadhātu, which is their general characteristic. As the *Madhyāntavibhāga* says:

> Except for the dharmadhātu,
> There is thus no phenomenon.
> Therefore, it is the general characteristic,
> And this is the unmistakenness about it.[405]

As for not singling out these two [—phenomena and their nature—] from among a great number, [Vasubandhu's] commentary says that the entirety of the Bhagavat's presentations of skandhas, dhātus, āyatanas and so on, when summarized, is twofold, that is, phenomena and their nature.

The division of [phenomena and their nature][406]

Here, based on their defining characteristics, both the imaginary and the other-dependent [natures] are explained to be obscurations and phenomena, while the perfect [nature]—the fundamental change of state—is said to be the nature of phenomena. Therefore, this includes all ten topics [of the *Mahāyānasaṃgraha*]. Another enumeration of these is stated in the *Laṅkāvatārasūtra*:

> In the five dharmas, the [three] natures,
> The eight consciousnesses,
> And the two kinds of identitylessness,
> The entire mahāyāna is included.[407]

As for [the relationship between the] five dharmas and the three natures, . . . names and causal features are the imaginary [nature], and imagination is the other-dependent [nature]. These two [natures] make up phenomena. Perfect wisdom refers to the uncontaminated phenomena that consist of [the realities of] cessation and the path. Suchness is the nature of the two realities that abides in all knowable objects, that is, the lack of nature of all phenomena. Among the latter two, the former is the unmistaken perfect [nature] and the latter is the unchanging perfect [nature].[408] In a general way, these three [natures] are referred to as "ālaya," while the first two [natures] are called "ālaya-consciousness." Since the other consciousnesses—the afflicted mind and the six collections—are in [502] a mutual [relationship of] dependent origination with [the ālaya-consciousness], the eight consciousnesses are explained to be the obscurations. The four wisdoms are taught to be the stainlessness of these consciousnesses, thus being the perfect nature, with dharmadhātu wisdom being like the matrix of all of these. Therefore, [these consciousnesses and wisdoms] are the factors to be relinquished and the remedies [respectively].

For this reason, the assertion by some people who present the unfolding disposition based on the ālaya-consciousness, and thus say that the dharmas during subsequent attainment, which accomplish the two kāyas, arise from the ālaya-consciousness is wrong.[409] Also, since the sūtras and tantras explain that this [unfolding disposition] relinquishes the ālaya-consciousness by destroying it like a vajra, a philosophical system with the assertion that buddhas do not possess wisdom came about, but this is wrong [too]. This is also said in the *Mahāyānasaṃgraha*, which identifies [the ālaya-consciousness in terms] of afflicted phenomena, but does not include any purified phenomena in it.

> All afflicted phenomena that entail arising adhere to it as [its] resultant entities, or, it adheres to them as [their] causal entity. Therefore, it is the ālaya-consciousness.[410]

Furthermore, in the context of explaining the dominant condition, [the *Mahāyānasaṃgraha*] says:

> Just as the ālaya-consciousness is the cause of afflicted phenomena, these afflicted phenomena in turn are presented as the causal condition for the ālaya-consciousness, since no other causal condition is observable.[411]

This [503] is the basis of saṃsāric dependent origination, the "dependent origination of differentiating the nature." Based on it, the twelve [links] of "the dependent origination of differentiating what is desired and undesired" come about. The dependent origination of nirvāṇa consists of the two [aspects of the perfect nature]—the unchanging and the unmistaken. [Respectively, these latter two] should be understood as the two realities in terms of the nature of knowable objects, and the two realities in terms of the convention of the pure minds that are the knowers [of these objects]. These are explained as the two dharmakāyas,[412] and represent the remedy for the ālaya-consciousness. The *Mahāyānasaṃgraha* states:

> "How could the maturational consciousness with all the seeds, which is the cause of afflicted phenomena, be the seed of its

> remedy, that is, supramundane mind? Since supramundane mind is not contained in [the minds of ordinary beings], the latent tendencies of this [supramundane mind] do not exist [in them]. But if these latent tendencies do not exist [in them], it must be stated from which seeds they arise." [Supramundane mind] originates from the natural outflow of the pure dharmadhātu, that is, the seeds which are the latent tendencies for listening.[413]

Because these [latent tendencies] and the stains exist right now as a mixture, [the text continues]:

> What these latent tendencies for listening in dependence on the enlightenment of a buddha are, which matrix they enter, and that they enter the maturational consciousness in a manner of coexisting with it—all this is like [a mixture of] milk and water. They are not the ālaya-consciousness, because they are the very seeds of its remedy.[414]

[504] Therefore, as taught below, the dharmakāya originates from uncontaminated dharmas, but since the basic element of the stainless dharmakāya exists right now, the dharmas that are its natural outflow arise. Look at this in detail in the *Mahāyānasaṃgraha* and the *Yogācārabhūmi*. [I summarize] what is taught here in all seriousness in some intermediate verses:

> In the sky of the great dharmadhātu,
> The characteristics of saṃsāra and nirvāṇa are like illusions.
> The perfect [nature as] the dependent origination of the nature of phenomena
> [Consists of] the dharmakāya and the dharmas that are its natural outflow.
>
> The dependent origination of what does not exist yet appears
> Consists of the causes and results of nonrealization, conception, imagination,
> And the ālaya-consciousness that is based on them.
> When you understand these two in an unmistaken way,
> This is the prajñā that distinguishes saṃsāra and nirvāṇa,
> Which is praised by the victors.

Nowadays, most scholars and siddhas
Are like blind people speaking about grabbing an elephant.
Therefore, take seriously what is elucidated here
In this [treatise on] phenomena and their nature.

This [completes] the instruction on the division [of phenomena and their nature].

The defining characteristics of phenomena
This is taught through three parts:
1) Actual defining characteristics
2) Hermeneutical etymology
3) The meaning of imagination

1) Defining characteristics

[The *Dharmadharmatāvibhāga*] says, "What appears as duality and how it is designated is false imagination, which is the defining characteristic of phenomena."[415] What appear as duality are the six apprehended objects (which appear as forms, sounds, smells, tastes, tangible objects, and phenomena) and [505] the six apprehending consciousnesses (of the eyes, ears, nose, tongue, body, and mind). As for how these are designated, based on conceptions, [names are imputed, such as,] "This is form." Based on the distinct features of color and shape that derive from such [form], for example, the name "moon" is imputed on something white and round in the sky. Based on such imputations, characteristics of this white and round referent are apprehended and so on. What appears to be designated in these ways is [also] false imagination. Thus, based on the twelve āyatanas, [what appears as] duality and how it is designated represents phenomena. This is the instruction on the complete and unmistaken characteristics [of phenomena].

2) Hermeneutical etymology of this [false imagination]

[The *Dharmadharmatāvibhāga*] says, "Since what does not exist appears, it is unreal." Since these phenomena are not existent, yet appearing, they are unreal. You may wonder how it is that they do not exist? Though childish beings think that something like a [visible] form is really existent, it is [actually] without real existence. Thus, something like a vase is not real as something singular, as it consists of many minute particles. The śrāvakas indeed cling to these particles as being real, but if these particles are divided into ten or six sides by virtue of their parts, it is established that they are not real. Thus, if the object is not real, how could it be reasonable that the consciousness which apprehends the [apprehended] aspect that [appears as] a vase be unmistaken? [506] This is [obvious] from the words of the great being [Maitreya]:

> If there is nothing apprehended, there is no apprehender of it.
> Without this, consciousness does not exist either.[416]

Therefore, it is established that referents do not really exist. [At the same time,] they also appear, that is, by virtue of the dependent origination of object, sense faculty, and consciousness, they appear as mere cognizance in the form of the aspects of color and shape, [such as] the aspect that is a vase. Master Dignāga says [in his *Ālambanaparīkṣāvṛtti*]:

> The nature of inner knowable objects is that which appears as if it were external—this is [what appears as] a referent. While there are no outer referents, that which appears as if it were external definitely exists inside—this is the object condition.[417]

Inner knowable objects are nothing but mere cognizance. Since nothing but this appears as the aspects of object, sense faculty, and consciousness, these seem to function as object condition, dominant condition, and immediate condition, [respectively,] for each other. Therefore, this cognizance is called "other-dependent." The *Mahāyānasūtrālaṃkāra* says:

> What appear as three aspects each
> Are the characteristics of apprehender and apprehended,
> Which are false imagination,
> The defining characteristic of the other-dependent.[418]

What appear as [the three aspects of] places, referents, and bodies are not at all established as having the natures of such [places and so on]. Being nothing but mere conception, appearances exist as mere mistakenness. For these reasons, one speaks of "false imagination" and "the imaginary." This is twofold—the nominal imaginary and the imaginary without any characteristics.[419] In brief, it consists of names [507] and causal features. The [above] three [aspects of] what is apprehended as well as the three [aspects of] the apprehender—the afflicted mind, apprehension through the five [sense] doors, and the sixth (mentation including the conceptual [consciousness])—appear like that, but are not real. Therefore, they are false imagination.

3) Teaching yet another meaning of imagination

[The *Dharmadharmatāvibhāga*] says, "There are no referents in any case and they are mere conception. Therefore, they are imagination." They do not really exist as referents, but they appear. Thus,[420] by virtue of beginningless latent tendencies, such as those of forms and feelings, the causal features of referents appear at present, they appear as if they were referents, and [there are] discriminations [of them. All these] make up the nominal imaginary [nature]. [The *Mahāyānasūtrālaṃkāra*] says:

> The causal features of referents
> As designated, their latent tendencies,
> And the appearance of referents through them
> Are the defining characteristics of the imaginary.[421]

By virtue of having labeled something white and round in the sky as "moon," when its name is pronounced, even if this referent is not [visible], a white and round aspect comes to mind. [Likewise,] with regard to the aspect that is a certain shape, having a round belly, and so on, one may think, "This is a vase."[422] These are [instances of] the imaginary [nature]. [The *Mahāyānasūtrālaṃkāra*] says:

> That referents appear like [their] names [508]
> And names [like their] referents
> Is the cause of false conception,
> Which is the defining characteristic of the imaginary.[423]

These two kinds of the imaginary are nothing but conceptions and expressions that are based on conceptions, thus not existing as [actual] referents. Therefore, they are called "imagination." Those who cling to them, just as deers chasing after a mirage, create nothing but suffering. Therefore, this is pointless. This completes the explanation of the characteristics of phenomena.

The defining characteristic of the nature of phenomena

[The *Dharmadharmatāvibhāga*] says, "The defining characteristic of the nature of phenomena is suchness, which is without a difference between apprehender and apprehended, or objects of designation and what designates them." The appearance of the duality of apprehender and apprehended is not real. Therefore, the fact that this duality actually does not exist is the basic nature that is the nature of phenomena. As for [this nature] being without a difference between objects of designation and what designates them, nonduality cannot be expressed, just as when Mañjuśrī rejoiced in Vimalakīrti not saying anything. This is the basic nature that is the perfect [nature]. The imaginary is absolutely nonexistent. If that nonexistence is realized to be nonexistence, this is unmistakenness, which consequently exists. However, on the level of seeming reality, both existence and nonexistence are equal in being nothing but mere cognizance. Ultimately, both saṃsāra (the lack of peace) and nirvāṇa (peace) [509] cannot be discriminated as different within nonconceptual wisdom. Therefore, this is the perfect [nature]. As the *Mahāyānasūtrālaṃkāra* states:

> Being nonexistent, existent,
> And the equality of existence and nonexistence;
> The lack of peace and peace; and nonconceptuality
> Are the defining characteristics of the perfect.[424]

How is the perfect [nature] to be understood as twofold here? The unchanging [perfect nature] is expressed through the name "emptiness," because it is empty of the characteristics of both the imaginary and the other-dependent. Since this is never other, it is called "suchness." Because it is the unmistaken actuality to be realized, it is "the true end." Because it is the cessation of the characteristics of the [above] two, it is "signlessness." Because it is the sphere of the noble ones, it is "the ultimate." Because it is the cause of the dharmas of the noble ones, it is the "dharmadhātu." These are its synonyms. As the *Madhyāntavibhāga* says:

> If emptiness is summarized,
> Suchness, the true end,
> Singlessness, the ultimate,
> And dharmadhātu are its synonyms.
>
> By virtue of not being other, not being mistaken,
> Putting an end to [signs], being the sphere of noble ones,
> And being the cause of the dharmas of the noble ones,
> The meanings of these synonyms match the [above] order.[425]

Here, the unmistaken perfect nature is the nature of the wisdom of the noble ones, produced by perfect prajñā. Its enumerations are said to be the ten [kinds of] unmistakenness, [510] that is, being unmistaken about letters, their meaning, mental engagement, not straying away, the specific characteristic, the general characteristic, impurity and purity, what is adventitious, nonaversion, and lack of arrogance. This is taught in detail [in the *Madhyāntavibhāga*]:

> Letters, meaning, mental engagement,
> Not straying away, the two characteristics,
> Impurity and purity, what is adventitious,
> Nonaversion, and lack of arrogance.[426]

In brief, [the two aspects of the perfect nature] are to be understood through the following division. The former is the dharmakāya that is the stainless dharmadhātu, and the latter is the very profound dharmakāya, which is the natural outflow [of this stainless dharmadhātu]. Through these, the characteristics of the nature of phenomena are taught in a complete and unmistaken way.

You may wonder, "If there is no mistakenness in the nature of phenomena, while mistakenness itself does not really exist, how does one become mistaken?"

The way of being mistaken

This is discussed through three [topics]:

1) Appearance of what does not exist
2) Example
3) The way in which what exists does not appear

1) [The *Dharmadharmatāvibhāga*] says, "The appearance of what does not exist is mistakenness. Therefore, it is the cause of afflictedness." While not existing, based on the other-dependent [nature], the threefold afflictedness [of afflictions, karma, and birth][427] arises. This is mistakenness. How does it arise? In dependence on the seeds that are the latent tendencies of expression, cognizance arises [in the form] of (1) bodies, (2) possessors of bodies, (3) experiencers, (4) what is experienced by them, (5) experience, (6) time, (7) enumeration, (8) lands, and (9) conventions. [511] From the seeds that are the latent tendencies of views, cognizance arises [in the form] of (10) the distinctions between oneself and others. From the seeds of the branches of existence, cognizance arises [in the form] of (11) the deaths and transitions of the happy realms and the miserable realms. In these [eleven kinds of]

cognizance, all realms, beings, and birthplaces are included. They constitute false imagination, which is the other-dependent characteristic. The fact that, based on this, nothing but this mere cognizance appears as referents, though there are no referents, is the imaginary.[428] Then, the threefold afflictedness of afflictions, karma, and birth makes one suffer. Since these are nothing but mere conception, it is taught that, "there are no referents." One should know that glorious Dharmakīrti too had this in mind, when he said:

> What is connected with conception
> Does not entail the clear appearance of referents.[429]

Thus, one should not entertain views that assert outer referents. Also the *Yuktiṣaṣṭikā* says:

> Since the buddhas said
> That the world entails the condition of ignorance,
> Why should it not be justified
> That this world is conception?
>
> Once ignorance has ceased,
> Why should it not be clear
> That that which will cease
> Was imagined by ignorance?[430]

2) The example [for false imagination in the *Dharmadharmatāvibhāga*] says, "It is like the appearance of an elephant in a magical illusion." Elephants, horses, riches, and so on that are produced by an illusionist appear, [512] but they do not exist in the way [they appear]. Likewise, false imagination does not exist, yet still appears. Noble Nāgārjuna's *Mahāyānaviṃśikā* states:

> How sentient beings experience objects
> Is exactly like in the case of illusions.
> Beings have the nature of illusions—
> Just like them, they originate dependently.[431]

3) As for the nonappearance of what exists, [the *Dharmadharmatāvibhāga*] says, "and furthermore, because what exists does not appear either." Thus, it is mistakenness, because what is to be realized through the three yānas—the existence of twofold identitylessness—does not appear. As the *Mahāyānasūtrālaṃkāra* says:

> Therefore, what is this particular kind of darkness
> Of not seeing what exists and seeing what does not exist?[432]

Though the two [aspects of] the perfect [nature] exist, they are not seen. Consequently, this is mistakenness. Also the *Yuktiṣaṣṭikā* states:

> The victors have declared
> That nirvāṇa alone is real,
> So which wise one would think
> That the rest is not delusive?[433]

Since the [ultimate] reality is not realized, this is mistakenness. It is just as, in a mundane context, the thought of mistaking a cairn for a human being. In these ways, the reasons for being mistaken are understood.

Without the one, they are not justified as two

[The *Dharmadharmatāvibhāga*] says, "If any one of these two—nonexistence and appearance—did not exist, mistakenness, unmistakenness, afflicted phenomena, and purified phenomena would not be justified." Through [mistakenly using] the reasons of appearance and nonexistence [respectively], [513] one either conceives of appearances as existent (such as being real, a creator, or a self), or one thinks that these appearances—despite being established [as mere appearances]—are [utterly] nonexistent. This is called "mistakenness" for two reasons. As far as utter nonexistence goes, it is not possible to be mistaken about what does not exist per se, and if there indeed existed the slightest real [entity], this existent would be without mistakenness. Furthermore, if there were no mistaken consciousness, the existence of an unmistaken consciousness would be unreasonable too, because it depends on the [former]. If both did not exist, neither being afflicted in mistaken saṃsāra, nor nirvāṇa as its purified state would be justified. If one accepts that these are not justified either, everything would simply be meaningless. Therefore, what would be the point of presenting saṃsāra and nirvāṇa? And if [one thinks that] either an absolutely [unchanging] saṃsāra or effortless liberation are reasonable, [both of these notions] contradict direct perception. Through realizing the reasons for being mistaken by virtue of nonexistence and appearance, one also sees dependent origination. Through realizing that appearances are empty of reality, just as illusions, the correct consciousness of directly realizing that they are free from arising and ceasing [appears].

Based on this, yogic valid perception occurs, which gives rise to liberation. This meaning accords with what noble Nāgārjuna says [in his *Yuktiṣaṣṭikā*]:

> You are neither liberated through being
> Nor through nonbeing from this [saṃsāric] existence.
> Great beings are liberated
> Through fully understanding being and nonbeing.[434] [514]

Not accepting [phenomena and their nature] as one or different

You may wonder, "In this case, should phenomena and their nature be accepted as the same or as something different?" [The *Dharmadharmatāvibhāga*] says, "These two are neither one nor are they distinct, because there is a difference as well as no difference in terms of existence and nonexistence." It is not suitable, if phenomena and the nature of phenomena are accepted to be one. If the nature of phenomena—the perfect [nature]—is definitely existent, whereas phenomena, just as mirages, do not really exist at all, how could they be accepted as one? Furthermore, the nature of phenomena would be seen through merely seeing the bearers of this nature, and any efforts [on the path] would be pointless. Therefore, in the light of such differences, they cannot be accepted as one. You may wonder then how it cannot be suitable to accept them as different. This is [because] the direct appearance of the nature of phenomena is nothing but [the fact of] mere dualistic cognizance—the imaginary and the other-dependent natures—appearing without the characteristics of such cognizance, and because the nature of phenomena is characterized by nothing but the lack of phenomena. In the inseparability of appearing and being empty, phenomena and their nature are not established as different. Thus, it is not reasonable that they are two. [515] So, if you wonder how they are—they are free from being the same or other. The *Mahāyānasūtrālaṃkāra* says:

> Mind is what appears as twofold:
> It appears as desire and such, and likewise,
> It appears as confidence and so on.
> There is no other phenomenon that is affliction and virtue.[435]

Through seeing in this way that phenomena and their nature are taught as the three natures and are not suitable to be the same or different, the unmistaken characteristics of all knowable objects will be realized. This meaning is also expressed in the *Triṃśikā*:

Whichever entity is imagined
By whichever imagination
Is the imaginary nature,
Which is unfindable.[436]

Thus, the imaginary is the appearance of what does absolutely not exist.

The other-dependent nature, on the other hand,
Is conception that arises from conditions.[437]

Through the potentials of object, sense faculty, and consciousness, [the other-dependent nature] arises as if it were cognizance that entails apprehender and apprehended.

The perfect [nature] is its state
Of always being free from the former.

Therefore, it is said to be neither other
Nor not other than the other-dependent,
Just like impermanence and such—
It is not that the one is seen, if the other one is not seen.[438]

The perfect [nature] is said to be the lack of the characteristics of the former two [natures]. Therefore, cognizance that appears [dualistically] but does not exist [that way] is called "other-dependent." If it is free from these characteristics, it is the perfect [nature]. By virtue of cognizance being mistaken, there arises the imaginary [nature] of thinking that it—despite not existing [that way]—is real. Therefore, cognizance [516] and the other-dependent [nature] are not accepted to be one or different.

Thus, the imaginary lacks any reality and the other-dependent exists as mere cognizance. However, through seeing that [the latter] lacks the duality of apprehender and apprehended, the perfect [nature] will be seen. This is taught in detail below. Also noble Nāgārjuna says in his *Bodhicittavivaraṇa*:

As for the imaginary, the other-dependent,
And the perfect [natures],
Their nature is the single character of emptiness.
They are imputations onto mind.[439]

The *Mahāyānasaṃgraha* discusses this in very great detail. [This concludes] the brief introduction of the treatise.

Detailed Explanation

This has two parts:

1) Engaging in phenomena
2) Engaging in the nature of phenomena

1) Engaging in phenomena[440]

Along the lines of the well-known four yogic practices of the mahāyāna, the presentation of phenomena mainly consists of an extensive discussion of there being no apprehender if there is nothing apprehended. Consequently, one eventually enters the lack of any appearances of apprehender and apprehended.[441] This section concludes as follows.[442]

By virtue of realizing that both the imaginary and the other-dependent [natures] are not at all established as real, it is said that "the dependent origination of the nature of phenomena is seen in dependence on phenomena." This is also said in the *Madhyāntavibhāga*:

> If it were not defiled,
> All beings would be liberated.
> If it did not become pure,
> Efforts would be fruitless.
>
> It is neither defiled nor undefiled,
> Neither pure nor impure.[443]

Noble Nāgārjuna states [in his *Yuktiṣaṣṭikā*]:

> In dependent origination,
> What could beginning and end be?
>
> How could what has arisen earlier
> Be put to an end later?
> Devoid of any end in terms of earlier and later,
> The world appears like an illusion.[444]

In detail, this is discussed in the *Saṃdhinirmocana[sūtra]* and the *Yogācārabhūmi*.

2) Engaging in the nature of phenomena

Defining characteristics[445]

As mentioned before [in the *Dharmadharmatāvibhāga*], "the defining characteristic of the nature of phenomena is suchness, which is without a difference between apprehender and apprehended, or objects of designation and what designates them." This is the perfect nature, for which numerous synonyms are given in the sūtras and tantras. Glorious Nāropa says:

> This very being empty is awareness, mind.
> Also bodhicitta is just this.
> The Tathāgata heart is nothing but this.
> Great bliss is precisely this.
>
> What is called "secret mantra" is just this.
> The reality of valid cognition is exactly this.
> The fourth empowerment is this.
> Connate joy is nothing but this.
>
> The pāramitās are precisely this.
> Unity is simply this.
> Great Madhyamaka is solely this.
> Vairocana is this.
>
> Vajrasattva is simply this.
> The sixth family is only this.
> The buddha disposition is just this.
> Many enumerations, such as these,
> Which are stated in the sūtras and tantras,
> Are for the most part based on this.

As for the meaning of noble Nāgārjuna's statement that all phenomena lack a nature, the nature of all phenomena is that they neither arise through any essence, nor cease through any essence. For this reason, since they are not real as being permanent or extinct, coming or going, or one or different, they are free from reference points. Therefore, they are both referred to as "all phenomena" and "the lack of a nature." The enumerations [of this lack of nature] are "the lack of nature in terms of characteristics," "the lack of nature in terms of arising," and "the ultimate lack of nature," which are taught in relation to the imaginary, other-dependent, and perfect [natures, respectively]. One should understand that all [kinds of] emptiness are divisions derived from this.

The matrix of the nature of phenomena[446]

[The *Dharmadharmatāvibhāga*] says, "Its matrix are all phenomena and all sūtras included in the twelve branches of the Buddha's words." As for all phenomena, all the phenomena as taught above are the matrix of the nature of phenomena, because the nature of phenomena is just these phenomena being empty of specific and general characteristics. The *Mahāyānasaṃgraha* says:

> In the other-dependent, the imaginary does not exist.
> The perfect exists in it.
> Therefore, as for these two, in it,
> Nonobservation and observation occur together.[447]

Once it is liberated from afflicted phenomena, the other-dependent—as mere cognizance—comes to be without the imaginary. Therefore, once cognizance embraced by purified phenomena changes state, it becomes the perfect [nature]. Consequently, nonobservation of both the imaginary and the other-dependent as well as observation of the nature of phenomena occur together.[448] Therefore, all saṃsāric phenomena are the matrix of the nature of phenomena. Purified phenomena are the twelve kinds of the Buddha's words, . . . which are the pure dharmas of a buddha (the uncontaminated dharmas). They are the natural outflow of the dharmakāya and thus [also] the matrix of the nature of phenomena. This explanation that both [phenomena and the dharma] are the matrix of the nature of phenomena in these ways is given in terms of that which is to be personally experienced [through nonconceptual wisdom].

Fundamental change of state

Once mind, mentation, and consciousness have changed state, they are perfect as the nature of the five wisdoms . . .[449]

That which changes state is the ālaya-consciousness. That through which it changes state is the dharmakāya that is the natural outflow [of the stainless dharmadhātu]. That into which it changes state is the stainless dharmakāya. The way in which it changes state is that the two nonexistent phenomena [—the imaginary and other-dependent natures—] become pure and the existent nature of phenomena appears. The times during which it changes state are the four [phases] of aspiration, contact, recollection, and instantaneous [realization].[450]

The nature of the fundamental change of state[451]

[The *Dharmadharmatāvibhāga* says:] "As for engaging in its nature, in the sense of adventitious stains not appearing and suchness appearing, suchness is stainless." Adventitious stains are one's own stainless and naturally luminous mind as such, but by virtue of this very [mind's] being ignorant of itself, cognizance appears in a dualistic way as if it were [a separate] apprehender and apprehended. Miragelike mental conceptions arise, and these false imaginations obscure luminous suchness. If these obscurations do not appear, suchness will appear, just as water appears clear and transparent, once it has become pure of silt. This is the essence of the change of state. The *Mahāyānasūtrālaṃkāra* says:

> When murky water becomes clear,
> [Its] transparency does not arise from elsewhere,
> But is just its becoming free from pollution.
> The same goes for the purity of your own mind.
>
> It is held that mind, which is always naturally luminous,
> Is [only] blemished by adventitious flaws.
> It is stated that there is no other mind apart from
> The naturally luminous mind of dharmatā.[452]

Luminosity and natural emptiness are not tainted by the nature of conceptions, since conceptions are [nothing but] nonexistents that appear. This is stated many times, such as in the *Dharmadhātustava*:

> About water at the time of spring,
> What we say is that it's "warm."
> Of the very same [thing], when it's chilly,
> We just say that it is "cold."
>
> Covered by the web of the afflictions,
> It is called a "sentient being."
> Once it's free from the afflictions,
> It should be expressed as "buddha."[453]

Also the *[Hevajra]tantra* says:

> Sentient beings are buddhas indeed.
> However, they are obscured by adventitious stains.
> If these are removed, they are buddhas.[454]

This is the nature of the change of state. To understand it in this way is explained as "engaging in it."

The object of focus for this change of state[455]

In the *Uttaratantra*, this is taught through the term "basic element." Here, it is discussed through the term "nonconceptual wisdom." In the prajñāpāramitā [texts], it is treated through the term "prajñāpāramitā." The *Mahāyānasaṃgraha* states:

> There is no difference between prajñāpāramitā and nonconceptual wisdom.[456]

Engaging in it through relinquishing characteristics[457]

This refers to relinquishing the four characteristics of conceptualizing (1) adverse factors, (2) their remedies, (3) suchness, and (4) realization, which are said to correspond to the four characteristics in the *Avikalpapraveśadhāraṇī*[458] (quoted on p. 566.3). [In more detail,] (1) adverse factors are the four mistaken kinds of clinging to impermanent sentient beings as being permanent; to empty conditioned phenomena, as being real entities; to saṃsāric existence, whose nature is threefold suffering, as being real; and to identityless phenomena, as having an identity. (2) The remedies are their opposites. (3) Suchness means that both the factors to be relinquished and their remedies are mere cognizance. If one clings to them as having characteristics, one will not be liberated from the imaginary and the other-dependent natures. Also, the cognizance that is produced through the conceptions of factors to be relinquished and their remedies is without arising and ceasing. Therefore, it is unconditioned by nature. This is the nature of phenomena that is the perfect [nature]. Those who see the buddha heart as [consisting of the pāramitās of] purity, self, bliss, and permanence are the children of the victors. (4) Realization refers to qualities such as fourfold mastery[459] and enlightened activity. (1) and (2) are relinquished on the paths of accumulation and preparation, (3) on the seven impure bhūmis, (4) on the three pure bhūmis, and the very last remainders of the latter, through the vajralike samādhi.

Defining characteristics of nonconceptual wisdom[460]

First, nonconceptual wisdom is explained through three characteristics. (1) The characteristic of how it abides means that nonconceptual wisdom abides as the nature of phenomena that is nondual and inexpressible. (2) The characteristic of nonappearance refers to what does not appear in nonconceptual wisdom, that is, all forms of the imaginary and other-dependent natures, because these are the obscurations of nonconceptual wisdom and it never appears as them. The nonappearance of names, characteristics, and imagination is what it means to be without obscurations. (3) The characteristic of appearance is as follows. Since meditative equipoise is free from all clinging to any characteristics of any phenomena, these phenomena appear like the center of space, because the unchanging perfect nature is seen. During subsequent attainment, all conditioned phenomena appear as mere appearances, just as illusions, mirages, echoes, and dreams, because the nature of saṃsāra is seen. In brief, because the imaginary and the other-dependent natures do not appear, suchness and the unmistaken perfect nature that engages it appear. This is called "nonconceptual wisdom," which—despite no dualistic phenomena appearing for it—obviously does not mean not cognizing anything at all. . . .

The defining characteristics of nonconceptual wisdom are also explained by way of excluding the following five aspects:[461]

1) a complete lack of mental engagement
2) states that are beyond the levels that entail examination and analysis
3) the peaceful state in which discrimination and feeling have ceased
4) the nature of matter
5) pinpointing.[462]

Four shortcomings if there were no change of state[463]

Without the fundamental change of state of dualistic consciousness into nonconceptual wisdom, there would be four flaws:

1) no basis for afflictions not operating again
2) no basis for engaging in the path
3) no basis for designating persons who have passed into nirvāṇa
4) no basis for designating the differences between the three types of enlightenment (śrāvaka [arhats], pratyekabuddha arhats, and buddhas)

Three examples for the change of state[464]

For example, space is nothing but pure by nature. Therefore, by virtue of certain conditions (such as fog or mist) in the world, one can observe statements such as, "The sky is not pure," and "It is pure," [when] it is clear and free [from these conditions]. However, it is not suitable to claim such because of a change of the nature of space. Its own nature being pure, empty, and unconditioned, it is indeed not suitable that it either becomes pure by virtue of itself or becomes pure by virtue of something else. Still, mistaken minds that connect mere conventional terms to it cling to space as being pure and impure, [but] this is nothing but an error. Likewise, though it may appear as if the naturally pure nature of phenomena—the perfect [nature]—has become free from the fog and mist of conceptions, it is not asserted that this perfect [nature] has changed—it is absolutely without any arising or ceasing in terms of itself, others, both, or neither.

In the same way, the fact of gold remaining in its excellent state is not changed by stains, and the fact of water remaining clear and moist is not changed in its nature, even if it becomes associated with sullying factors, such as silt. Likewise, all that happens to the unmistaken path and the pure dharmas is that they just become associated with stains and sullying factors through the conceptions of ignorance, but it is not asserted that these uncontaminated dharmas [—the path and the pure dharmas entailed by cessation—] change. Therefore, naturally luminous stainlessness is unconditioned and changeless. Thus, though the nature of phenomena is referred to by this term "fundamental change of state," it is also called "permanent."[465]

> There is nothing to be removed from it
> And not the slightest to be added.
> Actual reality is to be seen as it really is—
> Who sees actual reality is released.
>
> The basic element is empty of what is adventitious,
> Which has the characteristic of being separable.
> It is not empty of the unsurpassable dharmas,
> Which have the characteristic of being inseparable.[466]

This teaches the defining characteristics of the emptiness endowed with the supreme of all aspects, free from the extremes of superimposition and denial.[467]

Colophon[468]

Though [this text] is not within the sphere of fools like me,
I commented on the profound by relying
On the gist of the intentions of Asaṅga and Nāgārjuna.
Through this virtue, may [all] enter the actuality free from
extremes.

Four Poems by the Third Karmapa

The Wisdom Lamp That Illuminates the Basic Nature[469]

The view of being free from extremes,
The meditation that is a continuous flow,
The conduct of being without do's and don'ts,
And the fruition of being without hope and fear—
All yogins who realize these to be one
[Embody] the three kāyas and five wisdoms.[470]

The three kāyas are threefold—
Mind's primordial purity is the dharmakāya,
Speech's unrestrained empty resounding is the sambhogakāya,
And the body's various ways of conduct are the nirmāṇakāya.

What are their divisions?
Mind's great luminosity is the dharmakāya,
Its being without meeting or parting is the sambhogakāya,
And unobstructed thought-activity is the nirmānakāya—
These are the three kāyas of mind, the dharmakāya.

Speech beyond words, thought, and expression is the dharmakāya,
Sound resounding yet empty and free from clinging is the
sambhogakāya,
And breath's many ways of coming and going are the
nirmāṇakāya—
These are the three kāyas of pure speech, the sambhogakāya.

The body in activity-free equipoise is the dharmakāya,
Its unconstrained ways of conduct are the sambhogakāya,
And its various movements are the nirmāṇakāya—
These are the three kāyas of pure body, the nirmāṇakāya.

Great meditators who cultivate the basic nature,
Point out the three kāyas in this way!

What are the pure realms of the three kāyas?
The ālaya free from extremes, the actuality of the middle,
Is the pure realm of the dharmakāya.
Mind's great unchanging bliss
Is the pure realm of the sambhogakāya.
Mind's unceasing flow of luminosity
Is the pure realm of the nirmāṇakāya.

You great meditators traveling through mountain retreats,
If you are headed for the pure realms, do so for these!

Yogins who realize basic nature's reality,
The skandha of form being pure in its own place,
The supreme abode of Akaniṣṭha being spontaneously present,
And resting in unchanging dharmadhātu wisdom
Are the family of the sambhogakāyas, such as Vairocana,
Of all buddhas in the three times—
If you're looking for a place to practice, go for this!

The skandha of consciousness being pure in its own place,
The pure realm of Abhirati being spontaneously present,
And resting in mind being lucid-empty, mirrorlike wisdom,
Are the family of enlightened mind, such as Akṣobhya—
If you're looking for a place to practice, go for this!

The skandha of feeling being pure in its own place,
The supreme abode of Śrīmat being spontaneously present,
And resting in the wisdom of inseparable equality
Are the family of qualities, such as Ratnasambhava—
If you're looking for a place to practice, go for this!

The skandha of discrimination being pure in its own place,
Sukhāvatī being spontaneously present,
And resting in blissful-empty mind, discriminating wisdom,
Are the entire assembly of the deities of enlightened speech—
If you're looking for a place to practice, go for this!

The skandha of formation being pure in its own place,
The pure realm [of Karmaprapūraṇā] being spontaneously present,
And resting in inseparable mind, all-accomplishing wisdom,
Are the place to practice enlightened activity, so go for it!

Great meditators headed for solitary places,
If you wish for places to practice, go for these!

Manifest realization is [the wisdom of] suchness,
And knowing the mind streams of others is the one of variety—
Not realizing that these two knowledges,
As well as the three kāyas and the five wisdoms, are your own mind,
Wishing to search for them somewhere else is just wishful thinking.
Not realizing that the three kāyas and the pure realms
Of the victors are complete within yourself,
To wish for them outside is just wishful thinking.

Within the ground, uncontrived spontaneously present Samantabhadra,
The essence of the buddhas of the three times is perfectly complete.[471]
In the state of the ālaya, the great being,
Saṃsāra and nirvāṇa are perfectly complete without exception.
Within unchanging great bliss,
All efforts, accomplishing, flaws, and qualities are perfectly complete.
Within the unborn inconceivable[472] mind, the dharmakāya,
The qualities of all buddhas of the three times
Are perfectly complete without exception—
Effortless, spontaneously present, and amazing,
Make this great perfection a living experience!

Proclaiming Mind's Way of Being Mistaken[473]

I pay homage to all buddhas and bodhisattvas.
This is a proclamation of mind's way of being mistaken.

Mind, mentation, and consciousness
Are what engage naturally pure and unconstrained luminosity,
Free from reference points, through all kinds of clinging to
reference points.
You [mind], who conceives them as one, two, three, or six,
Do not rest in anything but intrinsic lucidity.

Completely ensnaring yourself by saying "me,"
Conceiving of forms, sounds, smells, tastes, and tangible objects,
Objects and subjects are imagined as being two.
Through adopting and rejecting them, you deceive yourself.

Your ways are as fickle as those of a dancer,
Being an object of ridicule in [all] places in the three realms.
I will discuss the ways you act a bit, so listen!

Through name and form, you produce characteristics,
Which make attachment, aversion, and dullness flourish greatly
in saṃsāra.
Thus, you are born in its six sectors and dance through saṃsāra,
Serving as a ludicrous performance for the wise.

Stanzas That Express Realization[474]

I pay homage to noble Mañjuśrī Kumārabhūta.

I pay homage to the Tathāgata
Who taught dependent origination
To be free from the extremes
Of existence, nonexistence, and both existence and nonexistence.[475]

Once the vivid arising
Of all phenomena is completely pure,
Cessation is not observable,
Just as in an entity that never arose.

Once mind and mental factors
Have become unobservable,
How could it be tenable that the natures
Of form and so on appear?

Nonappearing and unseen,
Where do phenomena arise?
If the primordially pure nature of phenomena
Is conceived as arising and ceasing,
It is like tying a knot into space.

Childish beings are mistaken
About the actuality that is like this,
Just as being happy and suffering while dreaming,
Thus clinging to self and mine.

The world is imagined by your own imagination
Imagination is not real as imagination.
Imagination is not what is past, nor is it what is in the future,
And in which middle could there be imagination?
What could be the place of an imagination
Arising outside of the three times?

The victorious Buddha said,
"Temporarily, from name and form,[476]

The āyatanas arise, and from these, contact,
Craving, grasping, and becoming."

Ultimately, they are pure.[477]
If you wonder why, this is because
The Omniscient One did not see arising and ceasing.
Once there is no stirring
Of false imagination's formations,
What becomes of consciousness?
This omnipresent formation,
From where does it arise?
What is its creator?
This is very profound indeed.

This ālaya-consciousness,
Including its appropriating part,
Just as water, gold, and space,
Is primordially pure and luminous.[478]

Since it is without coming [and going],[477] being different, or one,
It is the actuality of dependent origination.
Through not realizing precisely this,
Suffering and its origin are produced.

In order to realize cessation and the path,
Correctly rely on the two realities.
Starting with the application of mindfulness
All the way up through buddhahood,
This is very profound indeed.

Since sentient beings are unobservable,
How could compassion observe them?
Therefore, since this [compassion] is boundless,
The children of the victors give rise to bodhicitta.

Since the body is devoid of the body,
Form is like foam spraying up.
Because feelings are void,
Understand them to be like bubbles.

Since they are like a mirage, a banana tree, and an illusion,
Discrimination, formation, and consciousness
Are primordially pure.[480]
Therefore, mind and phenomena will be realized.[481]

By virtue of this, the dharmas of the [four]
Correct efforts are manifested.
Based on them, the very profound [four]
Limbs of miraculous powers are attained.[482]

Confidence, mindfulness, vigor,
Samādhi, and prajñā are the five faculties,
Which are the support for turning into the five powers.
Through realizing that the apprehended is void,

Where could the apprehender abide?[483]
This is just like seeing the horns of a rabbit.
Nevertheless, in an illusory manner,
They are to abide in sentient beings.

Through the seven branches of enlightenment,
And all phenomena to be relinquished through seeing
Being viewed as utterly void, one is liberated.[484]
Therefore, one should train in this through the correct view.

Through realizing this view of the freedom from extremes,
Excellent right thought,
Speech, livelihood, aims of actions,
Effort, mindfulness, and samādhi [come about].

What make you attain these supreme [aspects] of the path of the
noble ones[485]
Are emptiness, signlessness, and wishlessness,[486]
Which are the doors to samādhi.

Generosity, ethics, patience,
Vigor, and dhyāna, these five,
Through practicing by abiding in this actuality,
Will receive the name pāramitā.

This is prajñāpāramitā—
Being nonreferential and skilled in means.
Being infinite, just as space,
This is the supreme powerful armor.

Just like the sky, aspiration prayers become limitless.
Based on that, wisdom is boundless [too],
And from this arise all buddhadharmas,
Such as samādhis, dhāraṇīs, fearlessnesses,
Perfectly discriminating awarenesses,[487]
And the eighteen unique [qualities].

This is the mahāyāna—
The relinquishment of [saṃsāric] existence and peace.
It is not [taught] in order to be afraid of it.
Whoever does not engage in it,
Through what would [their practice] become pāramitā?

These words that manifested through confidence
In the sons of the victors,
Mañjughoṣa, Avalokita, and Ajita,
Were written by the one called "Rangjung Dorje"
In the place [named] Lhadeng.[488]

It may well be that this contains mistakes—
May they not turn into flaws that obscure.
[But] if there is a little bit of virtue in it,
May it become the basis for the liberation of all beings.

A Song on the Ālaya[489]

Namo Guru

I supplicate the supreme guru,
Who shows me that my own mind is dharmakāya.

Please take a seat here and listen to these words.
Realize their significance and make them your living experience.

The ālaya is the basis of all of saṃsāra and nirvāṇa.
When not realized, it is saṃsāra,
And when realized, it is the Tathāgata mind.
This describes the essence of the ālaya.

For example, in a mirror pure of tarnish,
Reflections may appear. Likewise,
In the open expanse of your own stainless mind,
Various consciousnesses rise and perish.

Since this clinging to the duality of subject and object
Rises and appears within this open expanse all by itself,
The single essence of saṃsāra and nirvāṇa being nondual
Not realized is delusion and, if realized, is liberation.

Though the thinker and what it thinks of are not two,
Taking them to be two is the ground of saṃsāra.
Once you see the nondual essence,
The Heart of the victors is revealed.

This song on determining the ālaya
Arose in a solitary place.
Through dispelling all that obscures the ālaya,
May you realize your own stainless mind.

This song was sung in the lower [valley of Tsurpu] Dölung Gyal
During the waxing ninth moon in the year of the sheep
By the dharma lord Rangjung Dorje
To the great meditator, master Ngarma, and his servant.

Jamgön Kongtrul Lodrö Tayé's Commentary on *The Treatise on Pointing Out the Tathāgata Heart*

A Commentary on *The Treatise on Pointing Out the Tathāgata Heart*, Illuminating the Intention of Rangjung [Dorje]

I pay homage to the guru, the Victor, and his children.

Supreme Heart of everything in saṃsāra and nirvāṇa,
Changeless throughout the three phases
And endowed with inseparable qualities—
I pay homage to the dharmadhātu.

Protectors of beings with infinite knowledge and loving care,
Self-arisen victor and your children,
Who point out the profound reality of this Heart,
I bow to you with a mind full of undivided devotion.

The sphere of the sole all-seeing one
Is the Heart of the victors—
Its way of being is illuminated by the second Omniscient One's
Excellent text, which I shall expound a little.

The Omniscient Victor spoke about [this Heart] in the collection of the sūtras of the final definitive meaning and in the very profound collection of tantras in an unconcealed and clear way. The illustrious sons of this victor, such as the mighty lords of the tenth bhūmi, the regent Ajita and Avalokiteśvara, [131] as well as the mahāsiddha Saraha and his heirs, noble Nāgārjuna, venerable Asaṅga, and others commented on it as being [the Buddha's] direct and straightforward intention. The way of being of the very profound actuality of this Heart does not fit within the scope of the minds of those who roam the [sphere of] dialectics. It was extensively illuminated by the second mighty sage, Rangjung Dorje, the charioteer who was the first in the land of snow mountains to utter the unassailable great lion's roar of the Heart that is the definitive meaning. The quintessence of all his excellent words is this *Treatise on Pointing Out the Tathāgata Heart.*

Its explanation has five parts:[490]

1) Instruction on the title
2) Paying homage
3) Brief introduction by means of scriptures
4) Detailed explanation of their meaning
5) Conclusion through [indicating] the manner of receiving [this text]

1. Instruction on the title

The Treatise on Pointing Out the Tathāgata Heart

[In general,] "that" [Skt. **tat**; Tib. de] is a word that is linked with other conventional terms, but here it applies to the basic nature, the dharmadhātu. The word "gone" [Skt. **gata**; Tib. gshegs pa] indicates the realization of this [nature] as it is [Skt. **tathā**; Tib. bzhin], because of having arrived at the end of this actuality.[491] Since it is the matrix or body of all dharmas, it is also said to be the dharmakāya. Since it is the suchness of all entities, it is indicated by the term "**Heart.**" In general, the word "heart" applies to being undeceiving, enduring, indivisible, pervasive, or the innermost essence [of something]. Thus, here too, [132] it is taken to have these meanings. Since "Tathāgata" and "Heart" are connected by having the same nature, they are linked through the connective term.[492] Since [this treatise] properly points out the meaning of this [Heart], it is called "**Pointing Out** the Heart." The nature of [a treatise as] the means to express [Buddhist topics, such as this,] is to be a discourse through which its author, with a mind free from the distractions of the afflictions, comments on the intention of the Buddha's words and teaches the path to liberation. The hermeneutical etymology of the term *śāstra* indicates that the afflicted mind streams of those to be guided are mended and protected from lower forms of existence as the results [of these afflictions]. Therefore, it is a **treatise.**[493] In terms of [treatises] being classified as superior or inferior, it is said that there are nine [types], such as meaningless ones, those with wrong meanings, and meaningful ones.[494] In terms of function, there are three—those that bring scattered [materials] together, those that comment on what is profound, and those that restore corrupted or deteriorated [scriptural traditions]. From among these [types of treatises], this one here is included in [the categories of] the three superior treatises. [In terms of its function, it belongs] to those that bring scattered [materials] together and comment on what is profound. There are many ways to give [a text] a name, such as giving it a title deriving from an example. From among these, this [treatise] here is given its title due to the profound meaning to be expressed [by it].

2. Paying homage

> **I pay homage to all buddhas and bodhisattvas.**[495]

In terms of the expedient meaning, **buddhas** are endowed with consummate relinquishment and realization—the relinquishment of having awakened from the sleep of ignorance and the wisdom of mind having unfolded toward [all] knowable objects.[496] [Bodhisattvas] are the courageous ones who one-pointedly have in mind the attainment of **bodhi**—the naturally pure [dharma]dhātu—for the welfare of [all] beings.[497] [133] **To all** of these noble beings, **I** [—Rangjung Dorje—] **pay homage** with my three gates, full of great respect. Or, in terms of the definitive meaning, [a buddha] is the entity in which, primordially, the afflictions are not established and are purified, while the [enlightened] qualities are spontaneously present and unfolded. This means it is the connate basic state of the fundamental nature, bodhicitta,[498] or the mahāsukhakāya. If this is classified through the aspects [in which it manifests], it appears starting with the five kāyas and the five wisdoms up through infinite kinds [of kāyas and wisdoms], while bodhisattvas, such as Maitreya and Kṣitigarbha, appear as the essences of the pure six object-related consciousnesses.[499] So, the term "paying homage" may also be applied to [Rangjung Dorje's bowing to buddhas and bodhisattvas] in the manner of encountering the view of the basic nature. Thus, through the special action of paying homage to special objects (buddhas and bodhisattvas), special purposes will be [accomplished]—the fundamental disposition of the audience is awakened; natural freedom from obstacles is established; the principles of dharma are spread for a long time; and, through having generated [bodhi]citta, obstacles will be prevented.

3. Brief introduction by means of scriptures

This has two parts:

1) A quotation from the *Abhidharmasūtra*
2) A quotation from the *Hevajra[tantra]*

3.1. A quotation from the *Abhidharmasūtra*

It is said: "Though beginningless, it entails an end—
What is naturally pure and consists of permanent dharmas
Is not seen, since it is obscured by a beginningless cocoon,
Just as in the example of a golden statue which is obscured.

The dhātu of time without beginning
Is the matrix of all phenomena.
Because it exists, all beings
And also nirvāṇa are obtained."[500] [1–8][501]

The Sugata heart (mind as such, free from all reference points, such as beginning, end, arising, and ceasing) and the obscurations are not established as being one or different. [134] Therefore, the stains neither have a beginning in terms of some temporal continuum, nor a beginning in terms of some real substance. Consequently, **though** saṃsāra is **beginningless**, once the reality that is free from stains and dwells within ourselves becomes manifest, buddhahood with its two excellent welfares is accomplished. In this sense, [saṃsāra] **entails an end.**[502] In the essence of the [Sugata] heart, the stains are **naturally pure and**, since [this heart] is changeless throughout its three phases [of being called and appearing as a sentient being, a bodhisattva, and a buddha], it **consists of permanent dharmas.** It naturally resides within the mind streams of sentient beings, but **since it is obscured by a cocoon**[503] that coexists with it since **beginningless** saṃsāra, **it is not seen** as it is until these stains are eliminated through the conditions of studying and so on. This is **just as in the example of a** buddha **statue** made of the element of **gold being obscured** by [things] such as a lotus or mud, thus not being seen. This corresponds to the meaning that is clearly taught through the nine examples in the *Tathāgatagarbhasūtra* and is explained in the *Uttaratantra.* The first line of this [first] verse [above] is stated in terms of both mistakenness and liberation, the second in terms of the basic nature, and the third and fourth [lines] solely in terms of the manner of being mistaken.

The latter verse [above] gives a brief introduction to the ālaya. **The basic element of time without** any previous **beginning** such that it could be said, "It originated at just this point," which is the disposition or cause of buddhahood (the Sugata heart), **is the matrix** or support **of all** afflicted and purified **phenomena.** Therefore, as a general name, it is called "ālaya." [135] Just as with murky [water], in which water and earth are mixed, wisdom and consciousness dwell [together] as a mix. **Because the** ālaya **exists,** through ignorant imagination, that is, improper mental engagement, karma, afflictions, skandhas, dhātus, and āyatanas arise. Thus, **all beings** of saṃsāra **and**, once this basic element is liberated from the fetters of apprehender and apprehended, **also** the great **nirvāṇa**—the ultimate one of the three kinds of enlightenment,[504] called "perfect buddhahood"—**are obtained.** This corresponds to the *Uttaratantra*'s and noble Nāgārjuna's clearly expressing the ways of being mistaken and liberated as being based on the basic element:

> Earth rests on water, water on wind, . . .[505]

[The *Dharmadhātustava* says]:

> This basic element, which is the seed,
> Is held to be the basis of all dharmas.
> Through its purification step by step,
> The state of buddhahood we will attain.[506]

3.2. A quotation from the *Hevajratantra*

> **A passage in the tantras says:**
> **"Sentient beings are buddhas indeed.**
> **However, they are obscured by adventitious stains.**
> **If these are removed, they are buddhas."**[507] [9–12]

Thus, primordially, **sentient beings are buddhas indeed**, [in terms of] the nature [of their minds'] being spontaneously present and free from reference points. **However, they are obscured by** the **adventitious stains** of apprehender and apprehended. **If these** obscurations **are removed** through the [proper] means, in terms of the fundamental ground being revealed, **they are** labeled as "**buddhas.**" The manner in which the essence [of mind] is completely pure and yet obscured by adventitious stains is comparable to the murkiness of water, a film on gold, or clouds in the sky. The *Madhyāntavibhāga* says:

> Afflicted and purified phenomena [136]
> Represent its being with stains and without stains.
> Being pure is asserted to be like the purity
> Of the water element, gold, and space.[508]

Likewise, noble Nāgārjuna says [in his *Dharmadhātustava*]:

Spotless are the sun and moon,
But obscured by fivefold stains:
These are clouds and smoke and mist,
Rahu's face and dust as well. [18]

Similarly, mind so luminous
Is obscured by fivefold stains.
They're desire, malice, laziness,
Agitation and doubt too.[509]

In this example, it is said that mind as such—the Sugata heart—is endowed with the quality of natural luminosity and so on, just like the sun and the moon. However, temporarily, it is [covered by] adventitious obscurations—cloudlike covetous desire, which moistens [saṃsāric] existence; smokelike maliciousness, which is created by a mind full of hatred; mistlike laziness, which is [mind's] being made hazy through ignorance; a mind agitated with pride, which is like Rahu's face; and doubt produced by all kinds of [mistaken] views, which is like swirling dust. These five obscurations do not taint the nature [of the mind], but from the perspective of mistaken appearances, it seems as if it is obscured [by them], thus becoming unclear.[510]

4. Detailed explanation

This has five parts:

1) Detailed explanation of the meaning of the quote from the *Abhidharma[sūtra]*
2) Explaining false and correct imagination
3) Explaining the buddha heart [137]
4) Determining it through answers to objections
5) Gaining certainty about the explanation of the essence through scriptures

4.1. Detailed explanation of the meaning of the quote from the *Abhidharmasūtra*

This has six parts, which explain

1) The manner of being beginningless
2) The meaning of the basic element
3) The dharmas that dwell in it
4) The matrix itself
5) The manner of existing in that way
6) The meaning of end

4.1.1. Explaining the manner of being beginningless

> **Here, "beginningless"** [means that]
> **There is absolutely nothing before that.**
> **The time is this very moment,**
> **How could it come via somewhere else?** [13–16]

Here, in the passage quoted above, the meaning of **"beginningless"** is as follows. **Before that** essence (the pure nature [of the mind]), there is nothing that could be called "buddhahood," and before the latent tendencies of ignorant mistakenness, **there is absolutely nothing** that could be called a "sentient being." **The time** of saṃsāra and nirvāṇa appearing and being mistaken as two **is this very moment,**[511] **it** does not **come via some** place **else,** because all phenomena are dependent origination. The *Yuktiṣaṣṭikā* says:

> From dependent origination
> [Stem] the causes and results of all beings—
> Apart from this, there are no sentient beings at all.
> From phenomena that are solely empty,
> Nothing but emptiness arises.[512]

4.1.2. The meaning of the basic element

> **The basic element is without creator,**
> **But since it bears its own characteristic, it is labeled in that way.**
> [17–18]

In **the basic element**—the buddha heart—all buddha qualities are complete. Because they exist [in this way], it **is without** any other **creator** of something new that did not exist before. **But since it bears its own characteristic** [138]—its essence being changeless[513]—**it is labeled in that way,** that is, "basic element"[514] or "disposition" in the sense of a cause.

4.1.3. The dharmas that dwell in it

> **The dharmas are explained as appearing**
> **As both saṃsāra and nirvāṇa,**
> **Which is called "the ground of the latent tendencies of**
> **ignorance."**

> **The movement of the formations of correct and false**
> **imagination**
> **Is the producing cause.**
> **This causal condition is explained as the ālaya.** [19–24]

The dharmas that dwell in the basic element **are explained as appearing as both** the existence of **saṃsāra and** the peace of [personal] **nirvāṇa.** The collection of the latent tendencies of these two **is** also **called "the ground of the latent tendencies of ignorance."**[515] Due to **the movements of the formations of** both **correct** imagination (the remedies) **and false imagination** (saṃsāra), it is **the causal condition** that **produces** both saṃsāra and nirvāṇa through black and white latent tendencies, respectively. **This** is known **as the ālaya,** which **is explained** with this meaning in mind.

4.1.4. The matrix itself

> **The matrix is the Heart of the victors.**
> **False imagination**
> **Rests on the purity of mind.** [25–27]

Thus, **the matrix,** or support, of all phenomena of saṃsāra and nirvāṇa **is** mind as such, **the Heart of the victors. False imagination** and all the karmas, afflictions, and sufferings produced by it **rest on the** natural complete **purity of mind** as such. However, since the natural luminosity of mind as such has the nature of being unconditioned (being free from arising, abiding, and ceasing), it is neither based on any of these [phenomena], nor tainted by their arising and ceasing. As the *Uttaratantra* says:

> And improper mental engagement
> Rests on the purity of mind, [139]
>
> [But] the nature of mind does not rest
> On any of all these phenomena.[516]

4.1.5. The manner of existing in that way

> **This purity exists in that way.**[517]
> **Though it exists, through ignorant imagination,**
> **It is not seen, and therefore is saṃsāra.**[518] [28–30]

This mind as such, the Heart of the victors, natural complete **purity** (with its essence being empty, its nature being lucid, and its way of appearance being unimpeded), **exists in that way**, that is, as the nature of the three kāyas residing in all sentient beings. **Though it exists** like that, being obscured **through ignorant imagination,** its own essence **is not seen** or realized. **Therefore**, this **is saṃsāra** in the form of the realms of the six [kinds of] beings, who are drowning in the ocean of mistaken imagination. The *Bodhicittavivaraṇa* says:

> Through their ignorant minds,
> People see illusions, mirages,
> The city of gandharvas and so on—
> The appearance of form and such is just like that.[519]

4.1.6. The meaning of end

> **When that is eliminated, it is nirvāṇa,**
> **Which is conventionally called "end."** [31–32]

In this way, through understanding that **those** adventitious stains—the factors to be relinquished—were never established from the very beginning, the conceptions of apprehender and apprehended and of something to be adopted or rejected **are eliminated**. Therefore, **when** the actuality of saṃsāra's and nirvāṇa's inseparability is revealed, due to having passed into **nirvāṇa** beyond existence, it is [just] the aspect of being free from stains—being pure of what is adventitious—**which is conventionally called**, "saṃsāra has an **end.**" However, because mind as such, the Heart of the victors, is primordially pure by nature and its qualities [140] dwell [within it] in an intrinsic fashion, in its essence, there is nothing to be improved. The glorious *[Cakra]-saṃvara[tantra]* says:

> No matter whether buddhas have arrived
> Or not arrived, in every respect,
> The unceasing nature of phenomena
> Remains devoid of increase and decrease.

Therefore, it is [only] due to realizing or not realizing mind as such that distinct aspects [of it manifesting]—such as buddhas or sentient beings, the ultimate or the seeming, saṃsāra or nirvāṇa—appear and are expressed in these ways. Noble Nāgārjuna's [*Dharmadhātustava*] says:

Mind as such is seen as two:
Worldly and beyond the world.
By clinging [to it] as a self, it is saṃsāra—
In your very own awareness, true reality.[520]

4.2. Explaining false and correct imagination

This has three parts:

1) The way in which saṃsāra is based on false imagination
2) The root of saṃsāra originates from adopting and rejecting
3) The meaning of remedial thoughts

4.2.1. The way in which saṃsāra is based on false imagination

Beginning and end depend on nothing but imagination.
Through windlike formation,
Karma and afflictions are created.
Through these, skandhas, dhātus, and āyatanas—
All dualistically appearing phenomena—are displayed. [33–37]

Though mind as such, the Heart of the victors, which is naturally pure, lacks the particular characteristics of beginning and end, a temporal **beginning and end depend on nothing but** superimpositions through false **imagination**. This refers to the rising of **windlike** imagination by virtue of spacelike mind as such being unaware of itself, [141] that is, the **formation** of the afflicted mind stirring, which entails clinging to mind as such as being "me" and a "self." [This stirring of the afflicted mind] **creates karma and afflictions**, which are like water. **Through these** karmas and afflictions, the five **skandhas** (such as form); the eighteen **dhātus** (the six dhātus that are the focal objects, the six dhātus that are the sense faculties as the supports [for consciousness], and the six dhātus of consciousness as what are supported); the twelve **āyatanas** (the six inner āyatanas, such as the eye [sense faculty], and the six outer āyatanas, such as form), and so forth—which [all together] resemble the orb of the earth—are produced. Just as beings are supported by the earth, **all dualistically appearing phenomena**, while not being really established, from the perspective of mistakenness, **are displayed** as if they were real. The *Uttaratantra* says:

Improper mental engagement
Rests on the nature of mind

And improper mental engagement
Produces karma and afflictions.

From the water of karma and afflictions,
Skandhas, dhātus, and āyatanas arise.[521]

4.2.2. The root of saṃsāra originates from adopting and rejecting

The one who adopts and rejects these is mistakenness.
Through rejecting [mind's] own appearances, where should they cease?
Through adopting [mind's] own appearances, what should come about?
Is clinging to duality not delusive? [38–41]

Thus, since appearances are mind's own appearances, they are not established as the duality of apprehender and apprehended. However, consciousness is **the one who adopts and rejects these** imaginary objects—the nonexistents that originate from mistaken imagination and are imputed as existents, thus appearing as the duality of apprehender and apprehended. Through adopting the desirable and rejecting the undesirable [among these objects, consciousness] [142] **is mistakenness.** If you wonder why, [the reasons are as follows]. Since outer objects are superimpositions by the mistaken mind, but do not exist ultimately, there is nothing apprehended. Because this [what is apprehended] does not exist, there is definitely no apprehender that depends on it either. Still, due to the power of beginningless latent tendencies unfolding, [both apprehender and apprehended] appear. For example, just as there is nothing to be adopted or rejected in naturally empty space, inasmuch as objects are the **appearances** of your **own** mind, there is neither anything undesirable, nor anything to be **rejected.**[522] On the other hand, **what should come about through adopting** these very **appearances** of your **own** mind? There is nothing to be adopted. Therefore, **is** false imagination—the one who **clings to** nothing but [mind's] own appearances as being the **duality** of something to adopt and to reject—**not delusive?** Most certainly, it is not real, but delusive.

4.2.3. The meaning of remedial thoughts

Understanding this is indeed said to be the remedy,
But the thought of nonduality is not real [either],

> **For the lack of thought [just] turns into a thought.**
> **You thought about emptiness, dissecting form and so on into parts,**
> **Are you not mistaken yourself?**
> **Nevertheless, this was taught in order to stop the clinging to reality.** [42–47]

Understanding it in **this** way, thinking, "There is no duality of apprehender and apprehended," **is indeed said to be the remedy** for these [dualistic appearances].[523] **But the thought**, "There is **no duality** of apprehender and apprehended, and they are empty" **is not real** or ultimate either. **For**, just as you may think, "[My] son is no more" after you have dreamt that he died, though there is no son who could [really] die in a dream, this consciousness about **the lack of thought** that thinks, "Apprehender and apprehended are not established as two" [just] **turns into a** great **thought**, with which you boast to yourself. Śāntideva['s *Bodhicaryāvatāra*] says:

> Therefore, the lack of a delusive entity
> Is clearly delusive [too].
>
> Thus, when one's son dies in a dream, [143]
> The conception "He does not exist"
> Removes the thought that he does exist,
> But it is also delusive.[524]

It is taught that emptiness is the remedy for reification, but if one fixates on emptiness, this is an incurable view. The *Ratnakūṭa* states:

> Kāśyapa, those who have views about the person that are as big as Mount Meru are better off than those who proudly entertain views about emptiness. Why is this? Kāśyapa, as emptiness means to emerge from all views, I declare that those who have views about this very emptiness are incurable.[525]

The *Mūlamadhyamakakārikā* says:

> By the flaw of having views about emptiness,
> Those of little understanding are ruined, . . .[526]

and

> The victors taught that emptiness
> Means to eradicate all views,
> While those who have views about emptiness
> Will not accomplish anything.[527]

Therefore, the very state of mind that fixates on emptiness must be relinquished too. The *Mahāyānasūtrālaṃkāra* declares:

> The mind is aware that nothing other than mind exists.
> Then, it is realized that mind does not exist either.
> The intelligent ones are aware that both do not exist
> And abide in the dharmadhātu in which these are absent.[528]

Śāntideva['s *Bodhicaryāvatāra*] says:

> Through familiarity with the latent tendencies of emptiness,
> The latent tendencies of entities will be relinquished.
> Through familiarity with "utter nonexistence,"
> Later on, these too will be relinquished.[529]

By **dissecting form and so on**—which are nothing but appearances of your own mind, just like objects in a dream—**into** [144] distinct **parts** of being one or many, [there arises] the **thought about emptiness** in the sense that, just as with space, there is nothing whatsoever as an object of mind. **You**—this consciousness who is the one doing this dissecting into parts—**are you not mistaken yourself** too about actual reality**?** All appearances are the mind's own light—appearance and emptiness inseparable, like [the reflection of] the moon [in] water. Therefore, if you dissect what is not established as something to be dissected into parts, this is mistaken. Through not understanding this inseparability of appearance and emptiness, by [thinking that] something that existed as an entity before is destroyed through emptiness later, one clings to nonexistence. This is said to be a great mistake. Saraha states:

> Whoever clings to entities is like cattle,
> But whoever clings to the lack of entities is even more stupid.[530]

Nevertheless, in order to stop the clinging to reality, such as taking the five skandhas to be a single unit, **this** way of dissecting them into distinct parts and thus determining them to be empty **was taught** in the Buddha's words and the treatises [on them, all of which are authentic sources of] valid cognition.

4.3. Explaining the buddha heart

This has three parts:

1) Pointing out its own essence
2) Explaining its qualities
3) Explaining this by matching an example and its meaning

4.3.1. Pointing out its own essence

> **All is neither real nor delusive—**
> **Held to be like [a reflection of] the moon in water by the learned.**[531]
> **Just this ordinary mind**
> **Is called "dharmadhātu" and "Heart of the victors."**
> **Neither is it to be improved by the noble ones**
> **Nor made worse by sentient beings.**
> **Without doubt, it may be expressed through many conventional terms,**
> **But its actual reality is not understood through expressions.** [48–55]

Since **all** phenomena that appear in this way are primordially unborn and not really established ultimately, they **are not real**. But since mind's own unimpeded creative display appears in distinct ways, from the perspective of mistakenness, they are **not delusive** either. For example, [145] when a reflection of the moon appears in clear water, from the very time of its appearing as the moon, it never exists as the moon. At the same time, while there is no moon [in the water], the mere appearance of the form and the color of the moon is unimpeded. To appear as a moon and actually being nonexistent are inseparable, and the characteristic of [this reflection of] **the moon in water** is being empty. If one understands this, the clinging to a [real] moon is liberated in its own place. **Like**wise, from the very time of the appearances of objects appearing, they never existed as something real. While they do not really exist, their mere appearance appears in an unimpeded way. Therefore, through understanding appearance and emptiness to be inseparable and their characteristic as being empty, the clinging to appearances is liberated in its own place. This is what **the** Victor and his children, who are **learned** in all objects of knowledge, maintain and **hold**. The *Hevajra[tantra]* says:

> Just as the nature is primordially unborn,
> Neither delusive nor real, everything is held

To be like [a reflection of] the moon in water.
Therefore, yoginī, understand this![532]

Thus, the nature of the union of appearance and emptiness—**just this ordinary mind** in its natural state, uncontrived by philosophical systems and remedies—**is called** by many names, such as **"dharmadhātu,"** "dharmakāya," "great bliss," "prajñāpāramitā," **and "Heart of the victors,"** but their meaning is just a single one, that is, mind as such, mind in its natural state. Except for the mere difference of whether one is aware of this or not, it is the nature of phenomena whose essence is unchanging. Therefore, [146] **it is neither to be improved by the noble ones**, such as this fundamental ground being revealed at the time of fruition, or previously nonexistent qualities being produced, once bodhisattvas realize [this ground] on the path. **Nor** is it **made worse by sentient beings**, such as them not being endowed with the qualities of its essence, when they do not realize it during the phase of the ground. For, the nature of phenomena is free from something to be added or removed. As the *Uttaratantra* says:

It is the same before as after—
This is the changeless nature of phenomena.[533]

This actuality is inconceivable even for bodhisattvas on the ten bhūmis. Therefore, until perfect buddhahood is attained, the actual reality of the basic nature **may no doubt be expressed through many** words and **conventional terms, but** the **actual reality of the** nature of phenomena, just as it is, **is not understood through expressing** it by conventional terms, because the nature of phenomena is inconceivable and not an object of dialectics.

You may wonder, "Granted, but why is it then that what is the sphere of buddhas alone is taught to ordinary beings?" The victor Maitreya said [in his *Uttaratantra*]:

They taught this in order to eliminate
The five faults in those in whom they exist.
These are faintheartedness, contempt for inferior sentient beings,
Clinging to what is not actual, deprecating the actual dharma, and
excessive attachment to oneself.[534]

Accordingly, this is taught in order to relinquish the following five faults. Through not knowing that the buddha heart, which is endowed with all qualities, pervades all sentient beings, one remains fainthearted and thinks, "I will not attain buddhahood," thus not generating [bodhi]citta. Through not knowing that inferior sentient beings possess the basic element [as well], one will have contempt for them. [Furthermore,] one clings to the stains, which obscure the basic element [147] and do not exist in actual fact, as being real and superimposes existence [onto them]. One deprecates the primordially existent actual qualities of buddhahood, such as the powers, [by saying] that they do not exist. Through not knowing that all sentient beings are alike in that the basic element exists in them, once the slightest qualities have come forth [in one's mind], one becomes proud, thinking, "I am superior."

Some explain that, due to this instruction on their purpose, the teachings on the actuality of the Tathāgata heart are of expedient meaning. However, if that were the case, then all teachings on emptiness would also be of expedient meaning, since they were spoken for the purpose of putting an end to the clinging to identity, singularity, and single units.[535] [Said people] may think that this is not the same, since emptiness is the basic nature of all phenomena, but if even the sheer emptiness that [they maintain, which still] belongs to the sphere of [ordinary] mental states, were the basic nature, why would the nature of phenomena that is beyond mind—the nature of luminosity—not be this basic nature?[536] Therefore, everything that is said in the middle [turning of the] wheel [of dharma] in the many scriptures on emptiness free from reference points is a teaching that this inconceivable dhātu is devoid of the characteristics of being conditioned (such as arising, abiding, and ceasing). But it is not a teaching that this basic element does not exist. Noble Nāgārjuna's [*Dharmadhātustava*] says:

> The sūtras that teach emptiness,
> However many spoken by the victors,
> They all remove afflictions, [148]
> But never ruin this dhātu.[537]

4.3.2. Explaining its qualities

This has two parts:

1) Brief introduction
2) Detailed explanation

4.3.2.1. Brief introduction

> **As for the unimpeded play of this,**
> **The sixty-four qualities**

Are a coarse [classification]—each one
Is said to [consist of] tens of millions. [56–59]

This buddha heart is empty in essence, lucid in nature, and its way of appearing is an **unimpeded play. As for** the [latter] aspect, the explanation that **the sixty-four qualities**—the thirty-two qualities of the dharmakāya and the thirty-two of the rūpakāyas—exist in it in a complete way **is a** classification that refers to the main ones [among its qualities]. If treated in detail, **each one** of them **is said to** consist of **tens of millions**, or countless, [qualities].

4.3.2.2. Detailed explanation

This has two parts:

1) Explaining the qualities of the dharmakāya
2) Explaining the qualities of the rūpakāyas

4.3.2.2.1. Explaining the qualities of the dharmakāya

This has five parts:

1) The ten powers
2) The four fearlessnesses
3) The eighteen unique [qualities]
4) The manner of [them] not appearing despite their present existence
5) The manner in which this is to be realized, including scriptural support

4.3.2.2.1.1. The ten powers

Knowing what is the case and what is not the case, karma
And maturation, knowing constitutions, faculties,
And inclinations, the paths that lead everywhere,
The dhyānas, the divine eye,
Recollecting places [of rebirth], and peace—these are the ten powers.[538] [60–64]

Due to having generated [bodhi]citta before and having a firm commitment to their vows, all buddhas [possess] **the ten** kinds of **powers**, which represent the unrivaled force of their capacity. (1) The first power is to **know what is the case** (that pleasant [karmic] maturations are obtained through virtue) **and what is not the case** (that unpleasant maturations could be obtained [through virtue]) as well as their opposites.[539] (2) The second power is to know the **maturation** of karmas through knowing **karma** and its results. (3) The third power is to **know** the various [mental] **constitutions** of sentient beings through having engaged them in accordance with these constitutions. [149] (4) The fourth power is to know the higher and lower **faculties** [of these beings] through having taught the dharma in accordance with these faculties. (5) The fifth power is to know the various **inclinations** of beings through having dealt with them in accordance with these inclinations. (6) The sixth power is to know, through having become familiar with all yānas, the three yānas, or **the** various **paths that lead everywhere** in saṃsāra and nirvāṇa. (7) The seventh power is to know, through having mainly focused on samādhi, what is free from stains and afflictions, such as **the dhyānas.** (8) The eighth power is to know, by virtue of one's superior intention[540] and so forth toward sentient beings, their [future] deaths, transitions, and rebirths through **the divine eye.** (9) The ninth power is to **recollect**, due to [the buddhas'] virtues not becoming lost, the former **places** [of rebirth] of themselves and others. (10) The tenth power is to know the termination of what is contaminated.[541]

4.3.2.2.1.2. The four fearlessnesses[542]

> **The four fearlessnesses based on these**
> **Are enlightened realization of all phenomena, teaching**
> **the obstacles,**
> **Teaching the path and cessation, [all] being**
> **indisputable.**[543] [65–67]

The four fearlessnesses that are **based on these** ten powers **are** as follows. (1) The fearlessness about asserting [the aspect of] one's own welfare that consists of excellent realization means to declare amidst the people that surround one, "I have **realized** completely perfect **enlightenment** within the dhātu **of all phenomena,**" and there being no opponents [able to prove] that one has not realized enlightenment. (2) The fearlessness about teaching the phenomena that are hindrances for the welfare of others means **teaching**, "Since desire and so on are **the obstacles** for liberation, [150] they are put to an end," and there being no opponents [able to prove] that these are not obstacles. (3) The fearlessness about **teaching the path** that brings forth the welfare of others means teaching, "The thirty-seven factors oriented toward enlightenment are the path to bring you out of saṃsāra," and there being no opponents [able to prove] that these are not the path. (4) The fearlessness about demonstrating [the aspect of] one's own welfare that consists of consummate relinquishment means teaching, "I have attained the **cessation** in which [all] contaminations including their latent tendencies have been put to an end," and there being no opponents [able to prove] that one has not attained this. In brief, whether directly or indirectly, these [four statements] are **indisputable** by anyone who [argues] in accord with the dharma.

4.3.2.2.1.3. The eighteen unique qualities

> **Due to that cause, the eighteen [unique qualities] are unmistakenness, lack of chatter,**
> **Undeclining awareness, constant meditative equipoise,**
> **Lacking the plethora of discriminating notions,**
> **Lacking unexamining indifference;**
> **Undeclining striving, vigor, recollection,**
> **Samādhi, prajñā,**
> **And the vision of the wisdom of liberation;**
> **Activities being preceded by wisdom,**
> **And being unobscured with regard to time.**
> **Being endowed with these thirty-two is the dharmakāya.**[544]
> [68–77]

Due to the cause of having obtained the four fearlessnesses, [buddhas] have **eighteen** dharmas that are unique to them when compared to śrāvakas, pratyekabuddhas, and bodhisattvas. The six that consist of conduct are (1) **unmistakenness**, since their physical conduct lacks being mistaken; (2) the expressions of their speech **lack chatter**; (3) lacking forgetfulness, since their minds' **awareness** of all knowable objects is **undeclining**; (4) being in **constant meditative equipoise** during the four kinds of conduct;[545] (5) **lacking the plethora of discriminating notions** about differences between saṃsāra and nirvāṇa; (6) **lacking indifference** that does **not examine** [everything] in a distinct manner.[546]

The six [qualities] that consist of realization are to lack any decline in (7) their **striving** to teach the dharma [no matter what difficulties there may be]; [151] (8) likewise, **vigor** toward this goal;[547] (9) the **recollection** of those to be guided and so on;[548] (10) the **samādhi** that realizes equality; (11) the **prajñā** that knows all of saṃsāra and nirvāṇa; (12) **the vision of the wisdom of liberation** that is liberated from [all] contaminations including their seeds. These six are completely **undeclining**.

The three [qualities] that consist of enlightened activity are (13) the enlightened activity of the body, for which there are no sentient beings that could not be guided through [any one among] all its ways of conduct; (14) the enlightened activity of speech by virtue of being endowed with the sixty branches;[549] and (15) the enlightened activity of mind through knowing those to be guided and caring for them with loving-kindness.[550] Thus, [buddhas] manage that all these three enlightened **activities are preceded by wisdom** and followed by wisdom.

The three [qualities] that consist of wisdom are (16–18) the **unobscured** vision of wisdom that is unattached and unhindered[551] **with regard to** the three **times**, that is, whatever happens in the past, present, and future.

Being endowed with these thirty-two qualities **is the** naturally pure **dharmakāya.** Once the adventitious stains have become pure, the power of these qualities becomes manifest.[552]

4.3.2.2.1.4. The manner of them not appearing despite their present existence

> **At present, we oppose them.**
> **Since we lack certainty about what is, just as it is,**
> **We produce the imaginary, construing what is nonexistent as existent.**
> **The conceptuality produced by this is the other-dependent.**
> **Through not knowing the perfect,**
> **We are agitated by our own doing.**
> **Alas, in those who realize these qualities of the dharmakāya**
> **To be what is real, this is the knowledge of reality.**
> **[Even] their present little power is reality—**
> **Casting away this knowledge, we fabricate what is unreal**
> **And are carried away by the agitation of pursuing it.** [78–88]

Though the qualities of the dharmakāya exist in a complete way in mind as such, the Tathāgata heart, **at** the **present** time of the ground, as sentient beings, **we oppose these** qualities through ignorance. How do we do this? In this mind as such, the inseparability of dhātu and awareness, all buddha qualities are complete and, at the same time, not established as any essence whatsoever. **Since we** do not know and **lack certainty about what is** [like this], **just as it is, we produce the imaginary** [nature],[553] that is, our conceptuality is **construing nonexistent** objects **as existent. The** mistaken **conceptuality produced by these** objects **is the other-dependent** [nature]. The *Mahāyānasūtrālaṃkāra* says:

> Therefore, what is this particular kind of darkness
> Of not seeing what exists and seeing what does not exist?[554]

Under the influence of apprehender and apprehended, **the perfect** [nature]—the ultimate reality that is the unchanging nature of phenomena, or, the nature of mind as such beyond apprehender and apprehended—is not aware of and does **not know** itself. **Through** this, **our** very **own doing**—clinging to the reality of the appearances of our own mistakenness—turns into the latent tendencies that perpetuate saṃsāra, and **we are agitated by** many sufferings.[555] Noble Nāgārjuna says [in his *Mahāyānaviṃśikā*]:

> Just as, through their own struggling in a swamp,
> Some childish beings sink into it,
> Through being mired in the swamp of conceptuality,
> Sentient beings are unable to emerge.
>
> Those who view nonentities as entities
> Experience feelings of suffering.[556]

"**Alas**" has the meaning of being amazed. Why? **In those who realize** that the unchanging perfect [nature] (**these qualities of the dharmakāya** that have the characteristic of being inseparable [from it]) exists in the mind streams of sentient beings as the essence of ultimate reality, just as it is, [153] [and who realize this] **to be what is real** in a trustworthy way, **this is** the prajñā that is **the knowledge of** ultimate **reality**—the unmistaken perfect [nature]. Though these qualities exist at the **present** time of being ignorant, **their power** is **little**. [Nevertheless, even their present limited power should be] understood [as an indication] that these qualities exist as ultimate **reality. Casting away this knowledge, we fabricate** the many mistaken appearances of saṃsāra and nirvāṇa through contriving a split in terms of apprehender and apprehended (which are nonexistent and **unreal** ultimately), **and are carried away by the** wavelike **agitation** of the many formational consciousnesses that **pursue them.**

4.3.2.2.1.5. The manner in which this is to be realized, including scriptural support

> **Understand now what is, just as it is,**
> **And you attain power in it.**
> **In this, there is nothing to be removed**
> **And not the slightest to be added.**
> **Actual reality is to be seen as it really is—**
> **Whoever sees actual reality is released.**

> **The basic element is empty of what is adventitious,**
> **Which has the characteristic of being separable.**
> **But it is not empty of the unsurpassable dharmas,**
> **Which have the characteristic of being inseparable.**[557] [89–98]

Since the presence of the dharmakāya in ourselves is realized through study and reflection, **understand what is, just as it is**—that all [enlightened] qualities exist right **now** in a complete way in this mind as such, the buddha heart. Through becoming familiar with **this** understanding, refreshing it again and again, you will realize this, just as it is, which is sufficient—**you** will directly **attain** the **power** of these qualities. Why is that? **In this** mind as such, the Sugata heart, **there are no** separate stains **to be removed** that are established as any real entities other than [just] your being fettered through your own discriminating notions of mistaken appearances. Since [this Sugata heart] is naturally endowed with its qualities, there is **not the slightest to be added** or produced newly that did not exist before. Therefore, **actual reality**—mind as such free from something to be removed or added—**is to be seen as it really is**, that is, in the manner of it being unable to look at itself. [154] Through looking in this way [of not looking], it is seen that mind as such—the inseparability of dhātu and wisdom—actually *is* [this inseparability]. Hence, the adventitious stains are [nothing but your] discriminating notions, and these lack any essence of their own, just like mirages. If this lack [of any essence] is **actually seen** for what it is, you **are released** from being fettered by these discriminating notions. The *Śrīmahābalatantra* says:

> In this, there is nothing to be removed
> And not the slightest to be added.
> Whoever sees true reality is released.[558]

Since mind as such totally lacks any activity of relinquishing and attaining, the stains are not the nature of the mind. Hence, **the basic element**—the Sugata heart—**is** not tainted by **the adventitious** stains, **which have the characteristic of being separable** from mind as such, thus being **empty of** them and naturally pure. **But** there is no object of purification[559] to be added newly, and the [enlightened] qualities are the nature of mind as such. Therefore, the basic element **is not empty of the unsurpassable** buddha**dharmas, which have the characteristic of being inseparable** and indivisible from mind as such. This is the meaning that is explained in the *Śrīmālādevīsūtra*, and the [passages in the above text of NT that are] quotations are from the *Uttaratantra*.

4.3.2.2.2. Explaining the qualities of the rūpakāyas

This has three parts:

1) The essence of the qualities
2) Justification that they dwell in the body
3) The manner of purity and impurity

4.3.2.2.2.1. The essence of the qualities

> **In this, the nature of the two rūpakāyas**
> **Consists of the thirty-two major and the minor marks. [99–100]**

[155] The aspect of appearance **in the** dharmakāya is taught to be the play of sambhoga[kāya] and nirmāṇa[kāya], that is, **the nature** or qualities **of the two rūpakāyas**, which **consists of the thirty-two** excellent **major** marks and **the** eighty **minor marks.** Without elaborating [any of them] here, the major marks are as taught in the *Uttaratantra* by "Well-planted [feet], marked with wheels, . . .,"[560] an by "It is marked with wheels on hands and feet, and has tortoiselike feet."[561] These slightly different ways of enumerating [the major marks] in these two [texts] represent the intentions of distinct sūtras.[562] The minor marks are as taught in the *Abhisamayālaṃkāra* by "The sage's nails are copper-colored, glossy and prominent."[563]

4.3.2.2.2.2. Justification that they dwell in the body

> **The attained qualities are your own body.**
> **This body is not created by a self, Cha, Īśvara,**
> **Brahmā, real external particles,**
> **Or hidden [objects].**[564]
> **Through the refinement of the impure transmutations**
> **Of apprehender and apprehended of the five gates,**
> **At that point, the conventional term "attainment" is applied.**
> [101–107]

Since the cause that leads to the **attainment** of the qualities of the two rūpakāyas (the major and minor marks) is just this body of your own (which is made up of nāḍīs, vāyus, and tilakas), these **qualities** come from **your own** completely pure **body**. You may wonder where **this body** comes from. According to the assertion of the Tibetan [followers of Bön], it is created **by Cha**; or, as maintained by the tīrthikas, by a permanent, single, and independent **self, Īśvara, Brahmā**, and so on; or, as held by the śrāvakas who are

Vaibhāṣikas, by partless **really** established **external particles**; **or**, according to the Sautrāntikas, [156] by the real objects that exist **hidden** or concealed [from consciousness] and are able to cast an aspect toward the sense faculties, although what appears [as this aspect] is not real. [However,] this body **is not created** by [any of the factors] in these and other such assertions.

So [then through] what is [it created]? The mind appears as if it were a mind, and the mind [also] appears as if it were a body, thus existing as two aspects. From among these, the body is what [appears] subsequently, hence appearing from the aspect that [seems] to be a mind. *The Profound Inner Reality* says:

> Thus, the triad of nāḍī, vāyu, and tilaka
> Appears from the aspect that is mind.[565]

Therefore, until the mind has become pure, also throughout the three intermediate states,[566] the continuity of the body is uninterrupted. Even in the formless [realm], there is a mental body. [*The Profound Inner Reality*] states:

> What is called "formless" is a mental body.[567]

Thus, the aspect that is mind, when pure, becomes the qualities of the dharmakāya as taught above. The aspect that is the body—**the impure transmutations of apprehender and apprehended of** the consciousnesses of **the five** sense **gates**—is **refined** and becomes pure through realization on the path. **Through** this, **at that point** when the nature of the basic state becomes manifest, **the conventional** expression and **term** "having **attained** the rūpakāyas" **is applied.** As for that [attainment], once the first bhūmi is attained, the five sense faculties undergo a change of state, or, attain mastery. This means that each one of them, such as the eye sense faculty, [is able to] perceive all five [sense] objects (forms, sounds, smells, tastes, and tangible objects). Through this, all five senses attain mastery over the arising of hundred times twelve specific qualities. The *Mahāyānasūtrālaṃkāra* [157] says:

> In the change of state of the five sense faculties,
> Supreme mastery is attained
> Over the perception of all their objects
> And the arising of twelve hundred qualities in all of them.[568]

These qualities increase accordingly on the second bhūmi and so on. Once they have reached their culmination, on the buddhabhūmi, the number of these qualities is infinite and inconceivable.[569] The *Mahāyānasūtrālaṃkāra* states:

> Through the differences in accomplishing their deeds,
> In terms of number, and in terms of realms,
> Always and in all respects,
> Buddha emanations should be known to be inconceivable.[570]

Here, some may think, "It is reasonable for the stains of mind to become buddhahood, once they have become pure. However, since the body has arisen from the conditions of one's father and mother, it has the nature of being impure and perishable. Therefore, it is not reasonable for unconditioned qualities to arise from something conditioned." Nāgārjuna declares [in his *Dharmadhātustava*]:

> Due to realization and its lack,
> All is in this very body.
> Through our own conceptions, we are bound,
> But when knowing our nature, we are free.[571]

Noble Asaṅga's [*Mahāyānasaṃgraha*] states:

> Through the change of state of the skandha of form, mastery over [pure buddha] realms, kāyas, the excellent major and minor marks, infinite voices, and the invisible mark on the crown of the head [is attained].[572]

[158] Thus, as exemplified by [these quotes], even in the dharma systems that accord with the common yāna, there are statements about the major and minor marks that are the change of state of the body. The two-part *[Hevajratantra]* says:

> In the lady's bhaga of great bliss,
> The teacher with the thirty-two major marks,
> The principal one with the eighty minor marks,
> Dwells in the form of what is called purity.[573]

As in this [passage], in the uncommon yānas, it is said again and again that this very body has the nature of the rūpakāyas. Therefore, in this body that appears as the creative display of the mind, all the qualities of the two rūpakāyas exist in a complete way, but since we are fettered by our own mistaken conceptuality, they are invisible. Once we become free from this bondage, [the body] will appear as the qualities of the two rūpakāyas.

For these sixty-four qualities [of the dharmakāya and the rūpakāyas], there are both direct and conditional causes. From among these, the direct cause of the dharmakāya is mind as such with its nature of luminosity, while the direct cause of the rūpakāyas is the very fact that the mind appears as if it were a body. The conditional causes that purify and eliminate the stains are the causes of each of the sixty-four qualities being accomplished. These are as discussed in the *Ratnādārikāparipṛcchasūtra*, such as the knowledge about what is or is not the case through having generated [bodhi]citta before, and hands and feet being marked with wheels through having escorted the gurus.[574]

4.3.2.2.2.3. The manner of purity and impurity

> **Therefore, the nāḍīs, vāyus, and tilakas,**
> **When pure, are the pure rūpakāyas.**
> **Unpurified, they are the impure rūpakāyas.** [108–110]

[159] **Therefore**, according to the just explained manner in which the two kinds of rūpakāya abide in the body, through **nāḍīs, vāyus, and tilakas** (the basis of purification) becoming completely **pure** of adventitious stains (what is to be purified), they undergo a change of state as **the pure rūpakāyas**. This means that nāḍīs, vāyus, and tilakas are purified as the maṇḍalas of enlightened body, speech, and mind [respectively]. During the phase of sentient beings with **unpurified** stains, [nāḍīs, vāyus, and tilakas] abide as **the impure** or stained **rūpakāyas.** These [points] are clearly discussed in the omniscient and venerable Rangjung [Dorje]'s *Profound Inner Reality*. With the phase of purity in mind, it says:

> The three kāyas with nāḍīs, vāyus, and tilakas, . . .[575]

With the impure phase in mind, it states:

> Thus, the skandhas, dhātus, āyatanas,
> And what consist of nāḍīs, vāyus, and tilakas

Originate from the stained mind as such.
This is said to be the stained nimāṇakāya.[576]

The [auto]commentary on this [passage] says:

> Here, the meaning of the statement in the mantrayāna that birth is the nirmāṇakāya of a buddha is as follows. During the time when the skandhas, dhātus, and āyatanas are gradually completed, this is the supreme emanation, the stained rūpakāya of a buddha. Once purified, being without stains, the bhaga is the dharmadhātu; the [ten] months [in the womb] are the ten bhūmis; natural full ordination[577] is wisdom; the mother is the preceptor; the placenta is the dharma robes; the mantra[578] of speech [160] is A HAṂ; to cleanse this body and so on is the manner of bestowing empowerment, great light rays; and the completion of the four states abides as the buddha endowed with the four kāyas. However, through not realizing this, it shows as an [ordinary] saṃsāric body.[579]

Thus, this is as [Rangjung Dorje] explains it here in detail, including quotes from the two-part *[Hevajratantra]* and others.

4.3.3. Explaining this by matching an example and its meaning

This has four parts:

1) Giving the example proper
2) Matching it with its meaning
3) The manner of overcoming [the obscurations] through the two imaginations, including their order
4) The manner of attaining unchanging reality, including scriptural support

4.3.3.1. Giving the example proper

For example, in an encrusted blue beryl,
Its qualities do not shine forth.
Through cleansing it with a woven cloth and an alkaline solution,
Cleansing it with acid and a towel,
And cleansing it with pure water and [cotton] from Kāśī,
It becomes pure—the gem that is the source [fulfilling all] needs and desires. [111–116]

To illustrate this mind as such—the Heart of the victors—through an **example, in an encrusted** gem of **blue beryl, its qualities** that are the source [which fulfills all] needs and desires **do not shine forth**, since they are obscured by its encrustations. In order to make these qualities shine forth, first, it is **cleansed** through alternately scrubbing **it with a woven cloth and** soaking it in **an alkaline solution**, thus being freed of coarse stains. Next, its more subtle stains are **cleansed** through soaking it in an **acid** solution **and** [wiping it] **with a** woolen **towel**. Finally, its most subtle stains are **cleansed** through soaking it in **pure water and** [polishing it] **with** fine cotton **from Kāśī**.[580] **Through** that, all stains of the encrustations that obscure [this gem] **become pure**, it thus being the supreme of all jewels, **the gem that is the source** [fulfilling all] **needs and desires.**[581]

4.3.3.2. Matching it with its meaning

> **Likewise, in order to cleanse the blue beryl of mind**
> **From the three encrustations—**
> **Afflictive and cognitive [obscurations], and those of meditative absorption—**
> **It is purified on [the paths of] accumulation and preparation,**
> **The seven impure bhūmis, and the three pure bhūmis.**
> [117–121]

[161] **Likewise**, as in this example, in **the beryl**like nature **of mind**—luminosity, the buddha heart—all buddha qualities exist in a complete way. However, they are not clearly manifest, being obscured by **the three** obscuring **encrustations. Afflictive** obscurations, such as avarice, are the antagonistic factors of the six pāramitās. **Cognitive** obscurations are the clinging to the three spheres[582] as being real. The obscurations **of meditative absorption** are agitation and dullness. **In order to cleanse** that [luminous buddha heart], in the beginning, the coarse stains—the afflictive obscurations—**are** what is to be **purified on** the twelve (three times four) [stages of the] path of **accumulation**[583] **and** through the four factors conducive to penetration [on] the path of **preparation.**[584] On **the seven impure bhūmis**, the more subtle [stains]—the cognitive obscurations—are to be purified, **and** on **the three pure bhūmis**, the most subtle ones—[the obscurations of] meditative absorption, or the fourfold clinging to characteristics[585]—are to be purified. Noble Nāgārjuna says [in his *Dharmadhātustava*]:

A blue beryl, that precious gem,
Is luminous at any time,
But if confined within its ore,
Its shimmer does not gleam.

Just so, the dharmadhātu free of stain,
While it's obscured by the afflictions,
In saṃsāra doesn't shine its light,
But in nirvāṇa, it will beam.[586]

The detailed meaning of these [points] is found in the autocommentary on *The [Profound] Inner Reality* by lord [Rangjung Dorje], which states the following.

> The *Uttaratantra* says:
>
> > Since it is pure and yet endowed with afflictions,
> > Since it is not afflicted [162] and yet purified,
> > Since its qualities are inseparable,
> > And since [its activity] is spontaneous and nonconceptual,
> > . . .[587]
>
> Though it is said that this mode of being is difficult to realize by śrāvakas, pratyekabuddhas, and even bodhisattvas who have newly entered the [mahā]yāna, for the time being, it shall be taught by way of an example. When a big precious gem of blue beryl is encrusted, despite its being associated with encrustations, the encrustations do not mix with the gem inside. Likewise, at the time of sentient beings, the buddha heart is obscured by stains, but not mixed [with them]. Therefore, it is pure and yet associated with afflictions. Also, though this gem may be encrusted from the very beginning, the encrustations neither arise from the gem, nor do they arise from something other than this gem. Thus, through purifying these encrustations that do not arise from anywhere, [the gem] becomes pure. Likewise, buddhahood, which is [nothing but] the obscurations of mind—the buddha heart—having become pure, is exactly like this. Again, there is no difference in the qualities of that gem at first and in the end. Nevertheless, these qualities did not shine forth earlier, but later, when [the gem] has become free from stains, is tied onto the pinnacle of a victory banner, and is supplicated, its

qualities come forth. Likewise, all buddha qualities exist right now, but if not triggered by flawless immaculate [deeds], their power does not come forth. Therefore, these qualities are the inseparable true nature [of the buddha heart]. Said gem does not think, "I am encrusted," "I am without encrustations," "I grant qualities to those who supplicate me," or "I do not grant [them to others]," and it is spontaneous [in granting these qualities]. Since enlightened activity operates just like that, the buddha heart too is spontaneous and nonconceptual. This is how its mode of being is to be realized.[588]

4.3.3.3. The manner of overcoming the obscurations through the two imaginations, including their order

Through false imagination
Meeting pure imagination,
There is freedom from imagination, just like two wooden sticks being burned.
This is the freedom from the fourfold clinging to characteristics—
The conceptions about what is to be relinquished, remedies, suchness, and fruition. [122–126]

The conceptions about what is to be relinquished and remedies exist on [the paths of] accumulation and preparation. As for the nature [of these two], **false imagination** has the characteristic of being what is to be relinquished—clinging to what is impermanent as being permanent; clinging to what is conditioned as being [real independent] entities; clinging to [saṃsāric] existence, which has the nature of the three sufferings, as being happiness; and clinging to entities that have no identity as having, [or being,] an identity. **Pure imagination**, which has the characteristic of being the remedy [for false imagination], is to understand that what is conditioned is impermanent, that what is contaminated is suffering, that all phenomena are empty and identityless, and that nirvāṇa is peace. **Through** [the factors to be relinquished and their remedies] **meeting** each other [as] in battle, what happens [is illustrated by the following] example. Through rubbing a wooden stick on a piece of wood (neither of which have the characteristics of fire), a fire comes forth from them and **burns** these very **two wooden sticks**, upon which also the fire disappears on its own. **Just like** that, since the remedies depend on the factors to be relinquished, [164] simultaneously with the extinction of what is to be relinquished, the conceptions that are its remedies become extinguished too.

At that point, through the power of the nonconceptual prajñā of the noble ones arising, **there is freedom from** the **imaginations** of what is to be relinquished and its remedies. The *Kāśyapaparivarta* says:

> From rubbing two sticks, fire comes forth.
> Once arisen, this [fire] burns those very [sticks].
> Likewise, once the power of prajñā has arisen,
> This arisen [prajñā] burns those very [conceptions].

The fourfold clinging to characteristics consists of (1)–(2) the just-mentioned two [kinds of] **conceptions about what is to be relinquished** and its **remedies**, (3) conceptions about **suchness**, which are like knowing that the water in a dream is a dream [appearance], yet still making efforts to cross it, **and** (4) the clinging to characteristics of the **fruition**. The conceptions of clinging to both what is to be relinquished and its remedies—which exist on [the paths of] accumulation and preparation—are eliminated through focusing on suchness. Through being free from the conceptions of clinging to these two, the nature of phenomena is seen directly, which is the path of seeing. The conceptions of taking suchness as a reference point refer to the nonconceptual wisdom [of bodhisattvas] during the meditative equipoise [on the first seven bhūmis] and their merely taking [saṃsāric] existence and peace to be equal (in that [both] are illusionlike) during subsequent attainment. Since there is a remainder of the afflicted mind during this phase, [one speaks of] abiding on the seven "impure bhūmis" of the path of familiarization. Through becoming free from the waves of the [afflicted] mind as well as clinging and conceptions [about suchness], the eighth bhūmi is attained. Right upon that, only characteristics in terms of the fruition emerge [in the minds of bodhisattvas]. Then, through as many buddhas as there are sand grains in the Ganges [River] showing their faces [to these bodhisattvas], they cause them to rise from their nonconceptual [meditative equipoise]. Thus, since [these bodhisattvas] engage in buddha realms and the heart of enlightenment, both of which are completely purified, these are the pure bhūmis. [Finally,] by relinquishing the still [remaining] portion of the stains of the [ālaya-consciousness], which contains all seeds, through the three pure bhūmis, the clinging to characteristics of the fruition subsides too. Thus, **the freedom from the fourfold clinging to characteristics** is called "the nonconceptual wisdom of buddhahood."

4.3.3.4. The manner of attaining purity despite [the buddha heart] being unchanging, including scriptural support

> **At that point, in those who have the kāya of space,**
> **The flowers of the major marks will blossom.**
> **Impure, impure and pure,**
> **And utterly pure, in due order,**
> **Are expressed as the three phases**
> **Of sentient beings, bodhisattvas, and Tathāgatas.**[589]
> **But buddhahood is nothing newly arisen—**
> **Being the same before as after,**
> **It is the changeless buddha heart.**[590]
> **It is the freedom from stains that is expressed as change.**
> [127–136]

At that point when there is freedom from the stains of the fourfold clinging to characteristics (as just explained), [buddhas] abide in the state of great peace—the dharmakāya—and are free from all reference points. **In those who have** found **the kāya of space,** the light rays of knowledge, loving-kindness, and power[591] **will** make **the flowers of the major** and minor **marks blossom,** with the two rūpakāyas promoting the welfare of sentient beings. *The Profound Inner Meaning* says:

> The victor endowed with the kāya of space, through the orb of the sun of wisdom,
> Displays the rūpakāyas in all the worlds in the ten directions for as long as saṃsāra lasts.[592]

As for this buddhahood, [there are] the phase of **not** being **pure** of stains, the phase of possessing both **impure and pure** [aspects], **and** the phase of being **utterly pure. In due order,** these three **are expressed** or taught **as the three phases of sentient beings** in saṃsāra, **bodhisattvas** who have entered the path, and buddhas, that is, **Tathāgatas. But buddhahood** [166] **is nothing newly arisen** that did not exist before. Existing as **the same before as after, it is changeless,** because **the buddha heart** is suchness, whose essence is without change. Nevertheless, **it is the** very aspect of being **free** and liberated **from** adventitious **stains** (the fetters of apprehender and apprehended) **that is expressed as** the factor which is the "**change** of state." The *Mahāyānasūtrālaṃkāra* states:

> Though without difference between before and after,
> It is immaculateness in terms of all obscurations.

Being neither pure nor impure,
Suchness is held to be buddhahood.[593]

4.4. Determining this through answers to objections

This has seven parts:

1) Brief instruction on causelessness and outer causes being untenable
2) Explaining the certainty[594] about pure and impure mentation
3) The essence of all-accomplishing wisdom
4) The enlightened activity of all-accomplishing [wisdom]
5) The meaning of the wisdom of equality
6) The manner in which the three kāyas are permanent
7) Dispelling uncertainty about that

4.4.1. Brief instruction on causelessness and outer causes being untenable

Those who engage in poor views
Think that buddha qualities are without cause
Or not [in] ourselves, but produced
Through external causes and conditions.
How are these different from non-Buddhist [views on]
permanence and extinction? [137–141]

Those persons **who** have not arrived at the intention of the Buddha's words and the treatises [on them], thus **engaging in poor views** in their minds through a flawed understanding of the teachings, assert **that** the **buddha qualities** arise from the nature of phenomena, which is nothing but empty, and [thus] **are without cause.** Such a philosophical system neither accords with scriptures and reasoning, nor is it the intention of the sūtras und tantras. A dohā declares: [167]

Since there is no result other than the cause,
The means is not emptiness.

Nāgārjuna says [in his *Dharmadhātustava*]:

Likewise, from all seeds there are,
Fruits are born that match their cause.
By which person could it then be proved
That there is a fruit without a seed?[595]

Or, some assert that the buddha qualities **are not** primordially existing in **ourselves**. Rather, [they say,] we newly plant latent tendencies of **external** studying and reflecting, reflect again and again about the meaning of what we have studied, and meditate on that meaning and so forth. Since we do this many times, **through** all these **causes and conditions**, those latent tendencies increase and expand, which produces previously nonexistent buddha qualities. Such **thinking** is not reasonable. Since the kāyas and wisdoms of the Buddha Bhagavats are unconditioned, they are not produced through conditioned causes and conditions. The *Cakrasaṃvara[tantra]* says:

> The spontaneously present nature
> Is mistaken as being produced by causes and conditions.

The protector Maitreya states [in his *Mahāyānasūtrālaṃkāra*]:

> Though not being different in all of them,
> Suchness has become pure.
> Therefore, it is the Tathāgata,
> And all beings possess its Heart.[596]

[Take] the **non-Buddhist** tīrthikas' views on **permanence** (illustrated by the assertion of the followers of Īśvara that all inner and outer entities are created by Īśvara and other such [views]) [168] **and** their view on **extinction** (the assertion by the followers of Bṛhaspati[597] that all entities arise without a cause, just by their own nature). **How are these** [above wrong views by Buddhists] **different from** these bad views here? They are not in the slightest!

4.4.2. Certainty about pure and impure mentation

> **The appearing of momentarily arising and ceasing formations**
> **Is comparable to impure formations.**
> **If it were not like this,**
> **The continuum of the enlightened activity of the rūpakāyas**
> **would be interrupted.**
> **However, this is not expressed by the name "formations,"**
> **[But] by "discriminating wisdom."** [142–47]

With their discriminating wisdom, the victors view all worlds six times per day and night, thus knowing the different mind streams of sentient beings simultaneously and so on. These **formations**[598] of their [all-]knowing and loving wisdom, which surge or radiate for the welfare of others, **appear** as if they were **arising and ceasing momentarily**. In terms of merely the factor of causing arising and ceasing without depending on any effort, they **are comparable to the impure formations** that are the movements of mentation.[599] **If it were not like this**—buddha wisdom appearing on the level of seeming [reality] as if it arises and ceases—**the continuum of the enlightened activity of the rūpakāyas** (both sambhogakāya and nirmāṇakāya) **would be interrupted.** The reason for this is that it would not be justified for the continuum of nirmāṇakāyas to arise in an uninterrupted manner, since the wisdom of the victors would neither know nor see those to be guided.[600] Therefore, this is not reasonable. **However, this** wisdom **is not expressed by the name "formations."** Rather, it is expressed **by** the name **"discriminating wisdom,"** since it does not exist as something really established as it is imputed by the mind, and is beyond being one or different.[601] *The Profound Inner Reality* says:

> Purified imagination is discriminating wisdom, [169]
> And the objects of the five gates are all-accomplishing
> [wisdom].[602]

The *Trikāyanāmasūtra* says:

> The purified state of the ālaya-consciousness is mirrorlike wisdom, the dharmakāya. The purified state of the afflicted mind is the wisdom of equality, [and] the purified state of the mental consciousness is discriminating wisdom, [both being] the sambhogakāya. The purified state of the consciousnesses of the five [sense] gates is all-accomplishing wisdom, the nirmāṇakāya.[603]

4.4.3. The essence of all-accomplishing wisdom

This has two parts:

1) The manner in which the subjects and objects of the five gates appear
2) The difference [between beings and buddhas] and the reason [for that]

4.4.3.1. The manner in which the subjects and objects of the five gates appear

> **What has the nature of the great elements and so on,**
> **And is associated with apprehension, displays its powerful**
> **essence.**

> **As for both mistakenness and unmistakenness,**
> **There is no difference as far as appearance goes.** [148–151]

As for **what has the nature of** causal form (**the great elements** of earth, water, fire, and wind) **and so on** (the elementary derivatives of [visible] forms, sounds, smells, tastes, and tangible objects), at the time of sentient beings, it **is** tainted by the adventitious stains of being **associated with** the **apprehension** of names and characteristics and so on, because [at that time] the mind appears as external objects. Once what [has this nature of the elements] has become pure and has changed state, on the buddhabhūmi, it becomes the **powerful essence** of each [of the elements and their derivatives],[604] which is the completion of the great creative display of wisdom. Through this, [buddhas] attain mastery over pure realms and extensively **display** enjoyments just as they please. The *Mahāyānasūtrālaṃkāra* says:

> In the change of state of the apprehender and its referents,
> Supreme mastery is attained
> Over pure realms in order to display
> Enjoyments just as one pleases.[605]

[170] Therefore, **both** from the perspective of what appears for **mistaken** sentient beings **and** from the perspective of what the **unmistaken** noble ones see, **there is no difference as far as** the mere appearing of **appearances goes.** This is just as in the example of an illusionist and those who watch the illusion [that is created]. For both, there is no difference as far as the mere appearing of illusory horses, cows, [beautiful] women, and so on goes.

4.4.3.2. The difference [between beings and buddhas] and the reason [for that]

> **The difference is whether there is clinging to duality or not.**
> **If it were not like this,**
> **How could the enlightened activity of the victors engage**
> **[anything]?** [152–154]

You may wonder, "If there is no difference between sentient beings and buddhas as far as mere appearances go, then what distinguishes mistakenness and unmistakenness?" Though there is no difference as far as mere appearances go, there is a difference in the way of apprehending [these appearances]. In those who are mistaken, **there is** the **clinging to** the **duality** of apprehender and apprehended [in the sense of them] being different, while in those who are unmistaken, there is **no** such clinging to duality. Therefore, this **is the difference**. Since sentient beings do not know that appearances are mind's own appearances—appearance and emptiness inseparable—they take them to be real. Then, they engage in adopting or rejecting them, through which they become fettered. This is just as in the example of people who watch an illusion, taking illusory horses, cows, and so on to be real. Nāgārjuna says [in his *Mahāyānaviṃśikā*]:

> It is exactly like illusions
> How sentient beings experience objects.
> Beings have the nature of illusions—
> Just like them, they originate dependently.[606]

Since the noble ones know that objects are appearance and emptiness inseparable [171] and do not cling to them as being real, they will not be mistaken, just as illusionists do not cling to the horses, cows, and so on that they themselves have created. [Nāgārjuna's] *Yuktiṣaṣṭikā* says:

> With their eyes of wisdom,
> Great beings see entities
> As being like reflections
> And do not get stuck in the mire of so-called "objects."[607]

Therefore, just as with [a reflection of] the moon in water, buddhas do not apprehend appearances as any kind of entities or nonentities whatsoever, but see them as appearance and emptiness inseparable, and also establish others in this [realization]. The *Samādhirājasūtra* says:

> Since the victors who are in nirvāṇa
> See everything like [a reflection of] the moon in water . . .[608]

If it were not like this—the difference [between ordinary beings and buddhas] lying in whether there is clinging to duality or not—and if the [outer] container [of this world] and its contents were thus not appearing as the objects of the Buddha's wisdom like [a reflection of] the moon in water, then in what manner **could the enlightened activity** of the two rūpakāyas **of the victors engage** which object? Since this would amount to the fault that enlightened activity lacks any engagement, it is not reasonable.

4.4.4. The enlightened activity of all-accomplishing wisdom

This has five parts:

1) Presenting[609] the purpose of explaining examples [for it]
2) Addressing the fault of asserting that [enlightened activity] is solely [something in] the mind streams of others
3) Stating that there is no certainty as to appearances entailing mistakenness by giving a counterexample
4) Explaining the example and the meaning of the wisdom of variety not being mistaken
5) The meaning of being connected with enlightened activity

4.4.4.1. Presenting the purpose of explaining examples for it

> **Giving the examples of a wish-fulfilling jewel and such**
> **Explains the display of thoughtfree power, but . . .** [155–156]

[172] The buddhas manifest the dharmakāya as their own welfare, and, for the welfare of others, they are endowed with the boundless wisdom that consists of knowledge, loving-kindness, and power. Through this, they know simultaneously all entities that are to be known as well as all mind streams of sentient beings without exception, and display the enlightened activities of body, speech, and mind that guide whomever is suitable in whatever suitable ways. The sūtras say:

> The Tathāgatas do not give up their bodies, which have the nature of space, displaying in all buddha realms. They do not give up their speech, whose true nature is inexpressibility, teaching the dharma in words that accord with the cognitions [of individual sentient beings]. Their minds are free from all reference points, fully knowing the conduct and thinking of the minds of all sentient beings.

The reason for this happening lies in the coming together of three [factors]—the blessing influence of the victors, the power of their [former] aspiration prayers, and the pure karma of those to be guided. The *Uttaratantra* says:

> Just as on a pristine ground of blue beryl
> The reflection of the body of the lord of gods appears,
> In the pristine ground of the minds of beings,
> The reflection of the body of the mighty sage displays.[610]

Therefore, the *Uttaratantra* [173] **gives** nine **examples** for the enlightened activity of the Tathāgatas (Indra, the drum [of the gods], clouds, and so on),[611] and other [texts speak of] **a wish-fulfilling jewel and such** (a wish-fulfilling tree). [However,] these are not examples for [buddhahood] being without wisdom [like these inanimate things]—buddhahood *is* wisdom per se. The *[Prajñāpāramitāsaṃcayagāthā]* says:

> Without wisdom, there is no increase in qualities,
> No enlightenment, and no oceanlike buddhadharmas.[612]

However, [buddhas] **display** the **power** of their knowing and loving wisdom in a way that is **free** from clinging to characteristics, **thoughts**, and effort, thus cutting through the suffering and afflictions of sentient beings. The *Uttaratantra* says:

> Since power, wisdom, and compassion
> Overcome suffering and afflictions.[613]

In brief, while enlightened activity is without thoughts, it occurs in a spontaneous way. Nāgārjuna says [in his *Dharmadhatustava*]:

> In the stainless dharmakāya,
> The sea of wisdom finds its place.
> As with variegated jewels,
> Beings' welfares are fulfilled from it.[614]

The enlightened activities of the dharmakāya—the two rūpakāyas—are the display of the wisdom, loving-kindness, and power of the buddhas. They are **explained** as arising for those with pure karmic appearances, **but** it is not explained that they are nothing but the pure appearances of those to be guided. [174]

4.4.4.2. Addressing the fault of asserting that enlightened activity is solely something in the mind streams of others

> **not that this is solely [an appearance in] the mind streams of others.**
> **If it were, wisdom would become the mind streams of others,**
> **[But] if that is accepted, wisdom would be mistakenness.**
> [157–159]

As just pointed out, such explanations of the kāyas and wisdoms of the victors are **not** explanations **that they are solely** some pure appearances in **the mind streams of others**, that is, those to be guided. Otherwise, **if** the buddhas had no wisdom and the rūpakāyas **were** solely the pure appearances in the mind streams of others to be guided, the **wisdom** of the buddhas **would become** a wisdom in **the mind streams of** those **others** to be guided, because this wisdom is solely [something in] the mind streams of those others. **If** such **is accepted**, this very **wisdom would be mistakenness**, since it would be the mistakenness of the mind streams of those others that appears as being wisdom. Furthermore, if this wisdom were [just] an appearance [in the minds] of those others [and not in the minds of buddhas], it would be unable to take care of others, since rūpakāyas that themselves lack wisdom are nothing but a name, just as there is no food to be given by a beggar.[615]

4.4.4.3. Stating that there is no certainty as to appearances entailing mistakenness by giving a counterexample

> **If it is asserted that [wisdom] grasps at its own appearances,**
> **Then also a mirror would possess conceptions**
> **Of grasping at what appears [in it].** [160–162]

[Someone may object,] "If the Buddha has a wisdom that entails appearances, and the mistakenness of sentient beings appears for this wisdom, there is a fault. It lies in **asserting** that this wisdom **grasps at its own appearances**, therefore being something that possesses grasping conceptuality." **If** such **is** [claimed], **then** [the following absurd consequence ensues]. When a reflection **appears** in **a mirror, also** the mirror at the time of such an appearance [in it] **would possess conceptions of grasping at** [175] [this appearance], because a reflection appears [in it]. Therefore, though those to be guided appear to a buddha's wisdom of variety, [this wisdom] is not something that possesses grasping conceptuality, just as in this example of a mirror, which lacks grasping and conceptuality with regard to the forms that appear in it.[616]

4.4.4.4. Explaining the example for the wisdom of variety not being mistaken and its meaning

> **The variety of the mistakenness of sentient beings**
> **Appears as the object of wisdom,**
> **But wisdom is not tainted by mistakenness.**
> **For example, in space, the arising and ceasing**

> **Of the great elements appears, but space**
> **Is not tainted and is without arising and ceasing.**[617] [163–168]

Thus, in just the way **the variety** of the appearances **of the mistakenness of sentient beings** is, it **appears as the object of wisdom,**[618] **but** what appears [to this buddha wisdom] does not entail mistakenness [on the side of the Buddha]. The [world, which consists of the outer] container and its contents, being just like [a reflection of] the moon in water, is beheld as appearance and emptiness inseparable, but not apprehended as either real or delusive in any way whatsoever. Therefore, at any time, **wisdom** and enlightened activity **are not tainted by** sentient beings' **mistakenness** of clinging to some reality. The *Yuktiṣaṣṭikā* says:

> Whoever holds that dependent things
> Are like [the reflection of] the moon in water,
> Neither real nor delusive,
> Is not carried away by views.[619]

For example, in empty **space, the great elements appear** to be **arising and ceasing, but space is not tainted** by creation or perishing **and is without arising and ceasing.** Likewise, wisdom is not tainted by mistakenness. Āryadeva says:

> For example, [the reflection of] the moon in water
> Is not at all tainted by the water.
> The [world's] variety is like a reflection—
> [Simply] through seeing it, you will not be tainted by its flaws.[620]
> [176]

4.4.4.5. The meaning of being connected with enlightened activity

> **Likewise, the wisdom of the victors**
> **Engages sentient beings, but is untainted.**
> **This is not expressed by the name "mistakenness"—**
> **It is called "all-accomplishing [wisdom]."** [169–172]

Similar to what was just explained, **the** [all-]knowing **wisdom** and the loving compassion **of the victors engage** and know the realms of **sentient beings** by being in the company of the variety of [their] afflictions, **but** it **is untainted** by this host of afflictions even in the slightest, just **like** space is not tainted by arising and perishing. For example, the rays of the sun touch unclean places, such as mountains, earth, and forests without any [sense of] being near or far, and illuminate, dry, or burn them, but the sunlight is not tainted by these [places]. The *Mahāyānasūtrālaṃkāra* states:

> Just as there is no sense of ownership
> In sun rays radiating,
> There is no sense of ownership
> In the wisdom of buddhas.[621]

Since it is a buddha's wisdom for the welfare of others, **this** wisdom **is not expressed by the name "mistakenness."** Among the four wisdoms, **it is called "all-accomplishing** [wisdom]**."** In the phase of impurity, the consciousnesses of the five senses engage their objects without needing any effort. Likewise, all-accomplishing wisdom, which comes from the change of state of these [consciousnesses], engages all worldly realms through various immeasurable [177] and inconceivable forms of emanations, without needing any effort, thus accomplishing the welfare of all sentient beings. The *Mahāyānasūtrālaṃkāra* says:

> All-accomplishing wisdom
> Accomplishes the welfare of all sentient beings
> In all realms through various
> Immeasurable and inconceivable emanations.[622]

You may wonder what the way of this change of state is. It is just as in the example of the sky being pure by nature [at all times]. But once it has become pure of conditions such as mist and haze, it is said that it "has changed its state" or that "the sky has become pure." However, there is nothing to be attained newly that is other than its own essence and did not exist before. As [the *Madhyāntavibhāga*] says:

> Purity is asserted to be like the purity
> Of the water element, gold, and space.[623]

4.4.5. Stating the meaning of the wisdom of equality

> **Mentation resting pure of the three obscurations**
> **Is equality, which is peace.**
> **Because it is endowed with great love and compassion,**

The sambhoga[kāya] and so forth appear for those
[to be guided].
This is stated in order to refute some [people's claim]
Of becoming like [arhats of] the hīnayāna, once buddhahood
is attained. [173–178]

Once **the three obscurations**—afflictive and cognitive [obscurations] as well as those of meditative absorption—have become **pure** through their remedies, afflicted **mentation** (the clinging to I and me), which is **resting** in the ālaya, **is** liberated from clinging to oneself and others as being different, and thus has changed state as the wisdom of **equality**. This [wisdom] means to not abide in the extreme of [saṃsāric] existence, but to dwell in the state of great **peace**, which is the nonabiding nirvāṇa. On the other hand, [this wisdom] does not abide in the extreme of [personal] peace either. **Because it is endowed with great love and compassion**, [178] in precise accordance with the inclinations of sentient beings, the **appearances** of the rūpakāyas (**the sambhoga**[kāya] **and so forth**) are displayed **for those** to be guided individually. The *Mahāyānasūtrālaṃkāra* says:

Dwelling in nonabiding peace
Is asserted to be the wisdom of equality.

Said to be endowed at all times
With great love and compassion,
The image of the Buddha displays,
Just as sentient beings aspire.[624]

In the thinking of **some** [people], **once** perfect **buddhahood is attained**, the continuum of consciousness is interrupted, just as a butter lamp goes out, and one dwells in the extreme of peace alone. If such is asserted, [buddhahood] would mean to **become like** śrāvaka and pratyekabuddha arhats of **the hīnayāna**, having entered their nirvāṇa without remainder, with the continuum of enlightened activity thus being interrupted. Therefore, this way of being [of buddha wisdom] **was** clearly **stated in order to refute** such wrong ideas.

4.4.6. Explaining the manner in which the three kāyas are permanent

This has three parts:

1) The meaning of the three ways of being permanent
2) The meaning of threefold impermanence
3) Explaining these as wisdoms and stains [respectively]

4.4.6.1. The meaning of the three ways of being permanent

> **Wisdom is permanent in three ways—**
> **Being permanent by nature is the dharmakāya,**
> **Being permanent in terms of continuity is the sambhogakāya,**
> **And being so in terms of an uninterrupted series is**
> **the nirmāṇakāya.**[625] [179–182]

Since the **wisdom** of the buddhas never changes, it **is permanent in three ways. Being permanent by nature is** the dharmadhātu (one's own welfare, which is the inseparability of dhātu and wisdom), because [179] **the dharmakāya** is without change. **Being permanent in terms of continuity is the sambhogakāya**, because it is endowed with the five certainties.[626] **Being** permanent in the sense of **an uninterrupted series is the nirmāṇakāya**, because the deeds of enlightened activity are uninterrupted until saṃsāra is empty.[627] The *Mahāyānasūtrālaṃkāra* says:

> By nature, in terms of continuity,
> And in terms of an uninterrupted series, they are permanent.[628]

4.4.6.2. The meaning of threefold impermanence

> **Related to these, there are three impermanent phenomena—**
> **Mentally fabricated emptiness is not permanent,**
> **The moving conceptual mind is not permanent,**
> **And the conditioned six collections are not permanent.**
> [183–186]

Related to these three wisdoms [of equality, discrimination, and all-accomplishment] as explained [above], **there are three impermanent phenomena** which obscure [them]. An **emptiness** that is **mentally fabricated** and contrived through not understanding that the five skandhas (such as form) are by nature the ultimate—the wisdom of emptiness—**is** a limited kind of emptiness. Therefore, it is **not permanent**. Since the afflicted mind and **the moving conceptual mind** that is produced by it **are** mistakenness, they are **not permanent** [either]. Since the consciousnesses that consist of **the six collections** of consciousness are **conditioned** by the four conditions,[629] they **are not permanent.**

4.4.6.3. Explaining these as wisdoms and stains, respectively

> **However, in these, there is threefold permanence.**
> **The three impermanent phenomena are the stains,**
> **While threefold permanence is wisdom as such.** [187–189]

However, in the cocoon of **these** three impermanent phenomena just explained, **there is** the **threefold permanence** of wisdom in an intrinsic way, because stains and wisdom are mixed during the phase of sentient beings. **The three impermanent phenomena** related to [threefold permanence] [180] **are the** adventitious **stains** to be purified (mistakenness), **while threefold permanence is** the basic state—the **wisdom** that is the perfect [nature] and the result of purification.

4.4.7. Dispelling uncertainty

This has six parts:

1) The meaning of being unlike the self of the tīrthikas
2) The meaning of not being comparable to the peace of śrāvakas and pratyekabuddhas
3) The meaning of not being comparable to sentient beings
4) The meaning of not regressing
5) The meaning of the stains never rising [again]
6) Summary of all [these points]

4.4.7.1. The meaning of being unlike the self of the tīrthikas

> **It is not comparable to the self of the tīrthikas,**
> **Since that is imputed by mind, while [the buddha heart] is not.**
> [190–191]

You may wonder, "If the dharmadhātu—natural luminosity, the buddha heart—existed in this way in an unchanging and permanent manner as the nature of the three kāyas, it would be comparable to the self of the tīrthikas." **The** personal **self** imputed by **the tīrthikas** is mentally designated as permanent, since it is [held to be] unchanging; as singular, since it is not multiple; and as independent, since it does not depend on causes and conditions. [But the buddha heart] **is not comparable to** this mistakenness of imputing a self onto the five skandhas, which [actually] lack a self. The reason is that mind as such—the dharmakāya— is taught as being "ultimately permanent," since it is free from the entire web of reference points (such as arising and ceasing), thus having the nature of being unconditioned, spontaneously present, and all-pervading like space. Therefore, [the self] is a superimposition **imputed by** the tīrthikas through their **minds** that entertain mental fabrications. [181] The Tathāgata is the ultimate, that is, the wisdom of emptiness, free from being one or different, which has the nature of lacking a self. Therefore, **since** it is not something that is superimposed as a self and mine and **is not** imputed by conceptuality, it is not comparable to the self imputed by the tīrthikas. Nāgārjuna says [in his *Dharmadhātustava*]:

> Since dharmadhātu's not a self,
> Neither woman, nor a man,
> Free from all that could be grasped,
> How could it be labeled "self"?[630]

4.4.7.2. The meaning of not being comparable to the peace of śrāvakas and pratyekabuddhas

> **It is not comparable to the peace of śrāvakas and**
> **pratyekabuddhas,**
> **For it displays all the qualities of the rūpakāyas.** [192–193]

As for the peace of śrāvakas and pratyekabuddhas, it is taught that they dwell in a state of nothing but [personal mental] peace until they are exhorted by the buddhas [to proceed onto the path of the mahāyāna]. As Nāgārjuna says [in his *Bodhicittavivaraṇa*]:

> For as long as they are not exhorted by the buddhas,
> Existing in a wisdom body,
> The śrāvakas stay in a swoon,
> Intoxicated by samādhi.[631]

Thus, buddhas (who dwell in the dhātu of not abiding in the two extremes [of saṃsāra and nirvāṇa]) **are not comparable to śrāvakas and pratyekabuddhas**, who dwell in the state of one-sided **peace. For**, due to the power of nonreferential compassion, they **display all** the many aspects of **the qualities of the rūpakāyas** (the sambhogakāya and the nirmāṇakāya), which guide whomever among the infinite [number of] beings to be guided in whatever ways suitable.[632] [182] The same is also stated in a hundred thousand Yogācāra texts:

Through skill in means, they do not abide in peace,
And through prajñā, not in saṃsāra.
Having abandoned the two extremes,
They engage in beings' welfare free from thoughts.[633]

4.4.7.3. The meaning of not being comparable to sentient beings

These are not comparable to the bodies of sentient beings,
Since they are not produced by contaminated conditions.
[194–195]

You may wonder whether such "rūpakāyas" are comparable to the bodies of sentient beings, [since both possess form]. **They are not comparable to the bodies of sentient beings** (which have the nature of skandhas, dhātus, and āyatanas, that is, conditioned phenomena propelled by karma and afflictions), **since** the two rūpakāyas **are not produced by contaminated conditions** (karma and afflictions). Additionally, in the phase of utter purity (buddhahood), if there is not even the birth of a body that has a mental nature and is produced by uncontaminated karma, what is there to say about the [kind of] birth in which the [contaminated] skandhas become manifest? If there is not even aging in terms of various transmutations, forget about aging that is the maturing of [psychophysical] formations. If there is not even the sickness of subtle latent tendencies, forget about the sickness of the afflictions. If there are not even the death and the transition that are inconceivable transformations, forget about the death and the transition of having reached the end of one's lifetime.[634] The *Uttaratantra* says:

It is not born with a body
Of mental nature, [183] since it is permanent.
It does not die through the death and transition
That are inconceivable transformations, since it is steadfast.

It is not harmed by the sicknesses
Of latent tendencies, since it is peace as such.
Since it is immutable, it is without the aging
Through uncontaminated formations.[635]

4.4.7.4. The meaning of not regressing

> **[Buddhas] will not regress,**
> **Since what is has become manifest, just as it is.** [196–197]

You may wonder, "As for these buddhas who possessed stains before, though these stains are eliminated through[636] the path, will they not go back into saṃsāra again?" Buddhas, in whom the basic nature has become manifest through their realization, **will not regress** and become afflicted again, **since what is**—primordially present mind as such, the basic nature as it is—**has become manifest, just as** its way of being **is**, through personally experienced wisdom. Glorious Dharmakīrti says [in his *Pramāṇavārttika*]:

> Having the nature of being harmless
> And actual reality, it is not reversed
> Through its opposites, even with effort,
> Since mind adheres to this side that is its [nature].[637]

4.4.7.5. The meaning of the stains never rising again

> **The stains never rise [again],**
> **Since there is freedom from any imagination of difference.**
> [198–199]

You may wonder, "Though [buddhas] have reached the end of the path, will the stains of mistaken mind not rise again?" Once [true reality] has become manifest [in buddhas], **the stains never rise** again, **since there is freedom from** stains. For, these stains are the mistaken **imagination** that clings to apprehender and apprehended being **different**, and [184] the cause of this [imagination] is ignorance. Dharmakīrti says:

> Since they have relinquished the seeds of the views about a self,
> These definitely do not return.[638]

4.4.7.6. Summary

> **Therefore, this mind as such—buddhahood—**
> **Exists right now, but we don't know it.** [200–201]

For these reasons, **this mind as such**—natural luminosity, **buddhahood** endowed with the sixty-four qualities—**exists** in a complete fashion **right now** at the time of sentient beings (the ground), **but** by virtue of its being obscured by the stains of apprehender and apprehended, **we don't know it**. This is like in the example of poor persons who do not know that there is a treasure in their home and thus suffer from being destitute. The *Uttaratantra* says:

> In the earth beneath a poor person's home,
> There may be an inexhaustible treasure,
> But that person does not know of it,
> And the treasure does not exclaim, "I am here!"
>
> Likewise, with the stainless treasure contained within the mind—
> The dharma that is inconceivable and without decay—
> Not being realized, the suffering of being destitute
> Is continuously experienced by all beings in many ways.[639]

4.5. Gaining certainty about the explanation of the essence through scriptures

This has four parts:

1) A quote from the *Mahāyānasūtrālaṃkāra*
2) A quote from noble Nāgārjuna's *Mahāyānaviṃśikā*
3) A quote from the *Uttaratantra*
4) Summary of the meaning taught in sūtras and tantras [185]

4.5.1. A quote from the *Mahāyānasūtrālaṃkāra*

> **At the time of realization,**
> **Just as with the subsiding of heat in iron**
> **And blurred vision in the eyes,**
> **The mind and wisdom of a buddha**
> **Are not said to be existent or nonexistent.**[640] [202–206]

In general, through the prajñā arising from study, reflection, and meditation, and, in particular, the dependently originating blessings of the guru and the disciple's devotion coming together, mind as such—the basic nature of the Sugata heart—is directly **realized. That time** is **just as** in the examples of **the** [eventual] **subsiding of heat in** burning **iron** ([meaning] no more painful torment) **and** the subsiding of painful **blurred vision in the eyes**, ([meaning] no more blurred vision). Therefore, [at that point,] it is neither the case that the entities of heat and blurred vision exist, nor that the iron and clear eye[sight] (which are characterized by the [former] two having subsided) do not exist, since they are [still] existent. Likewise, when [**buddhas**] have [awoken from or] cleared away ignorance and unfolded wisdom,[641] **mind** (the eight collections of consciousness) is cleared away **and** the five **wisdoms** have unfolded. As for [this state of buddhahood], the stains of the mistakenness of seeming [reality] (just as heat and blurred vision) **are not said to be existent**, while [buddhahood itself] is not said to be **nonexistent** [either] (just as iron and clear eye[sight]).

4.5.2. A quote from noble Nāgārjuna's *Mahāyānaviṃśikā*

> **Since there is no arising ultimately,**
> **In terms of true reality, there is no liberation either.**
> **Buddhas are just as space,**
> **And sentient beings have the same characteristic.**
> **Since the here and the hereafter are unarisen,**
> **There is no natural nirvāṇa either.**
> **Therefore, conditioned formations are empty,**
> **The sphere of omniscient wisdom.**[642] [207–214]

Ultimately (that is, in the definitive sense), **since** all phenomena **are** primordially **not arising, in terms of** this ultimate **true reality, there is no**thing to be **liberated** from saṃsāra **either. Just as space** is without arising and ceasing and is changeless, **buddhas are** unchanging throughout all phases. Hence, [186] apart from merely realizing this or not, both **sentient beings** and buddhas **have the same characteristic** and are inseparable in essence. **Since the here** (saṃsāra) **and the hereafter** (nirvāṇa) **are** both **unarisen, there is no natural nirvāṇa either. For that** reason, all phenomena that are **conditioned formations are empty** and identityless. Consequently, this inconceivable point is **the sphere of omniscient** buddha **wisdom** alone, but inconceivable for everybody else.

4.5.3. A quote from the *Uttaratantra*

> **Since it is subtle, it is not an object of study.**
> **Since it is the ultimate, it is not one of reflection.**
> **Since it is the profound nature of phenomena,**
> **It is not one of mundane meditations and so forth.**[643] [215–218]

Since the true nature of all phenomena—this buddha heart—**is** hard to fathom and very **subtle**, and thus beyond being an object of speech, thought, and expression, **it is not an object of** the prajñā [arising from] **study. Since it is the ultimate** reality, **it is** also **not** an object **of** the prajñā [arising from] **reflection** through examination and analysis. As [the latter] is [a part of] seeming [reality], it is not able to evaluate the ultimate, just as it is. **Since it is the** true **nature of** all **phenomena**, whose **profound** ground is hard to fathom and thus beyond the sphere of characteristics, **it** can**not** be realized by making it the object **of mundane meditations** (the [four] samādhis [of the form realm] and the four formless [meditative absorptions]) **and so forth** either, which includes the [four] applications of mindfulness, the [meditation on] dependent origination in progressive and reverse [order], the eight liberations,[644] and the meditative absorption [of cessation] of śrāvakas and pratyekabuddhas. [187]

4.5.4. Summary of the meaning taught in the sūtras and tantras

> **It is the sphere of personally experienced wisdom.**[645]
> **Confidence in the self-arisen gives rise to the ultimate.**[646]
> **Alas, since they do not realize this way of being,**
> **Childish beings roam the ocean of saṃsāra.** [219–222]

You may wonder, "If mind as such—the luminous Sugata heart—is not an object that is realized by any of those [factors just mentioned], then what is the means to realize it?" **It is the sphere of** the **personally experienced wisdom** of yogins. As for the means to manifest it, the dharmadhātu is awakened through the power of the virtue of the previous familiarization with **the self-arisen** Heart that is the basic ground of being, and it is this very [dharmadhātu] that appears as the gurus who are endowed with all [supreme] aspects. Through the power of our trust in, and certainty about, [its being like that], unbearable intense longing [wells up]. By virtue of that, the inexpressible experience of all possible appearances appearing as the guru, which leaves its stamp on all phenomena, [triggers] **confidence** beyond time. This [leads to] all that obscures **the ultimate** being cleared away on its own, and thus **gives rise to** the wisdom of directly realizing the final culmination of wisdom. Maitreya says [in his *Uttaratantra*]:

> The ultimate of the self-arisen ones
> Is to be realized through confidence.

Then, unbearable great compassion wells up naturally for those who are in the three realms and do not realize this in accordance with the stages of realizing the basic nature. Not only that, to practice meditation for the sake [of these beings] is the great alley of the children of the victors. Therefore, in order to instruct those who follow [this path] in such a manner, with his loving mind, [188] this victor [Rangjung Dorje] summarized the meaning of his text in a concluding dedication. Since this needs to be done through a phrase that is easily accessible, he combined [all that is said] here as follows. **Alas, since they do not realize this way of being** of the profound basic nature, **childish beings**, in whom the prajñā regarding the points to be adopted and rejected has not arisen, **roam the ocean of saṃsāra** through engaging in what is mistaken—they [truly] are objects of compassion.

5. Conclusion through the manner of obtaining [this text]

This has two parts:

1) The actual manner of obtaining[647]
2) An aspiration prayer

5.1. The actual manner of obtaining

> **Through the power of the great sage,**
> **Mañjuśrīghoṣa, Maitreya, and Avalokiteśvara,**
> **This was written by Rangjung Dorje.** [223–225]

For countless eons, [the Third Karmapa] familiarized himself with the stainless words of our guide, **the great sage** [Śākyamuni] and the liberating life examples of **Mañjuśrīghoṣa**, the embodiment of supreme knowledge; the regent **Maitreya**, the source of happiness and excellence for all sentient beings; **and** the supreme noble **Avalokiteśvara**, who stirs the depths of saṃsāra through his compassion. By the power of that, and through revealing without error the intention of the words of the Victor and his children as well as the treatises [on them] in his present [life as Rangjung Dorje], he lovingly instructed future beings to be guided. **Through** having attained **the** great **power** and might **of** that, this [treatise on the] actuality of the Sugata heart **was written** in a clear manner for the welfare of others **by** the glorious Third Karmapa, **Rangjung Dorje.**

5.2. An aspiration prayer

> **May all beings know this buddha heart**
> **Perfectly and without error!**
> **This completes the determination of the buddha heart,**
> **The essence of the vajrayāna.** [226–229]
>
> **Śubhaṃ (auspiciousness).**

[189] Thus, though this final actuality of the mahāyāna has [already] been proclaimed by countless buddhas, the virtue of illuminating it is associated with infinitely great benefit. Therefore, [Rangjung Dorje] passes on this virtue to **all beings**, the objects to whom he dedicates it. By the power of that, **may** all these sentient beings, through **perfectly** studying, reflecting, and meditating on this profound instruction on the essential point—**this** very **buddha heart** that exists in themselves—**know** and realize the basic nature pure of all adventitious stains **without error!** This **determination of the buddha heart**, which is clearly and extensively taught in the causal yāna, is [also] **the** quint**essence** of the view **of the vajrayāna** of secret mantra. Therefore, **this completes** the explanation of the final view.

It is profound and not realized by all,
But when realized, it is the actuality of becoming a buddha.
Understanding just a fraction will pierce
The thick cocoon of adventitious stains.

Even the dawning of mere trust in the existence of this Heart,
Is said to make you a successor of the victors.
This excellent text that summarizes the meaning so that it is easy
to understand,
Please perfect it through understanding, experience, and realization!

With a mind [set on] benefiting those of equal fortune,
I commented merely on the words, by following the supreme ones. [190]
Through this virtue, may all beings
Meet the Sugata heart face to face.

For this text that determines the Heart, there exist some earlier and later commentaries and interlinear annotations. However, [among these,] the words of Jamyang Töndrub Öser[648] are especially eminent and their meaning is summarized in the interlinear annotations written by the omniscient Fifth Shamarpa [Göncho Yenla]. Taking the essence of these [texts], I, Karma Ngawang Yönten Gyatso Lodrö Tayébé Dé,[649] clarified the excellent explanations of earlier commentaries, which are [authentic sources of] valid cognition, at the temple of Palpung Tubden Chökor Ling,[650] the great Kagyü seat in Dokam.[651]

May virtue increase!

Jamgön Kongtrul Lodrö Tayé's Commentary on *The Treatise on the Distinction between Consciousness and Wisdom*

A Commentary That Clarifies the Meaning of the Words of *The Treatise on the Distinction between Consciousness and Wisdom,* An Ornament for the Intention of Rangjung [Dorje]

I pay homage to the Omniscient One.

I pay homage to the one known as the victor Rangjung,
The mighty sage who shows the path to liberation
Through voicing from his glorious throat
The melody of excellent speech endowed with threefold valid cognition.

All phenomena of saṃsāra and nirvāṇa
Have the form of either consciousness or wisdom.
The teaching on these principles is the essence of the eighty-four
thousand collections of dharma.
Whoever realizes this puts an end to [saṃsāric] existence.

Even through understanding and experiencing just a fraction [of this],
The quintessential nectar in the vase of one's heart will overflow.
In order for the youth[652] of peace to blossom,
I shall comment on this distinguished text.

Since you have seen the true reality of all phenomena as being free from obscurations, you have mastery over the wisdom of a buddha. Appearing as Avalokiteśvara in the form of a nirmāṇakāya, your enlightened activity, which illuminates the Buddha's teachings, is unrivaled on the three planes.[653] This treatise which was composed by the mighty victor, omniscient Rangjung Dorje, has few words and profound meaning.

It is explained in three main parts:

1) The introduction of engaging in the composition [64]
2) The meaning of the text that is to be engaged in
3) The conclusion subsequent to such engagement

1. The introduction of engaging in the composition

This has three parts:

1) Teaching the title of the treatise
2) Paying homage
3) Commitment to compose [the text]

1.1. Teaching the title of the treatise

> **The Treatise on the Distinction between Consciousness and Wisdom**

[The text] **distinguishes** the way in which the eight collections of **consciousness** (the root of saṃsāra) exist in sentient beings, who are full of mistakenness; the way in which **wisdom** (the nature of nirvāṇa) appears in buddhas, who are free from mistakenness; and the way in which these [two] appear as different aspects within the same ground. It is called a "**treatise**" because of having the two qualities of mending the flaws of mistaken consciousness and protecting the nature of stainless wisdom.[654] [The Karmapa] chose this title because of its meaning and function, with the idea that it is easy [to see] what the text covers from beginning to end, and that it points out its meaning in a concise way. [The *Cittavajrastava*)] by Nāgārjuna says:

> Saṃsāra is nothing but imagination—
> The lack of imagination is liberation.[655]

Accordingly, the superimpositions of saṃsāra and nirvāṇa are a mere division in terms of mind being endowed with the stains of imagination, or lacking these stains. Therefore, if one realizes this principle, the natural state of all phenomena will be realized.

1.2. Paying homage

I pay homage to all buddhas and bodhisattvas.

[Here,] to **pay homage** is taken as the basis for the [following] explanation. [65] So, who pays homage? It is the author of the treatise, Rangjung Dorje. When does he pay homage? It is at the beginning of composing this [treatise]. To what object does he pay homage? It is **to all buddhas and bodhisattvas** who arrive and dwell in the three times. [Buddhas][656] are those who have purified what is to be relinquished (the two adventitious obscurations)[657] and have unfolded what is to be realized (the stainless twofold knowledge).[658] [Bodhisattvas] are those who give rise to the mind directed toward enlightenment and have the courageous motivation to benefit others. In what manner [does Rangjung Dorje pay homage]? [He pays homage] with his three gates, in a respectful and devoted manner. For what purpose [does he pay homage]? It is in order to complete the task of composing [the text] through increasing the accumulation of merit in the mind stream and pacifying obstacles, as well as to attain temporal and lasting happiness—the excellencies of both the higher realms and definite excellence.[659] [The prajñāpāramitā sūtras—] the *Mother of the Victors*—say:

> If any sons of good family or daughters of good family say, "I pay homage to the Tathāgata," they will all reach the end of suffering.

1.3. Commitment to compose the text

Having relied on study and reflection,
In order to immerse myself in the ways of meditation,
While dwelling in seclusion,
I will express how this principle appears. [1–4]

In terms of the definitive meaning, this Lord [Rangjung Dorje] led the life of a buddha, but for the purpose of taking care of childish beings to be guided, he appeared like an ordinary person. Taking the training in stainless ethics as his foundation, in the beginning, he **studied** without bias in the presence of many spiritual friends who were learned and had attained siddhis. [66] In the middle, he penetrated the meaning of what he had studied through the precise examination and analysis in his **reflection. Having relied on** that, in the end, he practiced by internally **meditating** on the meaning of what he had studied and reflected on in a proper **way**, thus becoming perfectly **immersed in** the fruition. **In order to** [do so, he says], **I**, Rangjung Dorje, **dwell** in the meditative equipoise of many doors of samādhi **in seclusion** from outer, inner, and secret distractions (being busy, afflictions, and mistaken conceptions, respectively). Having realized, just as it is, **this** profound **principle** of mistakenness and liberation, it **appears** clearly for [all-]knowing wisdom. During subsequent attainment, with nonreferential compassion, [I, Rangjung Dorje,] **will** explicitly **express** this very [principle] for the implicit purpose of others—the fortunate ones to be guided—realizing it. [Through this introductory verse, Rangjung Dorje] gives an instruction by way of the example of his life. This is also expressed by the second buddha Vasubandhu [in his *Abhidharmakośa*]:

> Resting in [proper] conduct and equipped with study and reflection,
> One then engages in meditation.[660]

Persons who wish to attain liberation and omniscience and are the support [for the path leading to such attainment] must first keep stainless ethics, the basis for [all] qualities. [Nāgārjuna's] *Suhṛllekha* says:

> The sage said that ethics is the foundation of qualities,
> Just like the earth is for what moves and is immovable.[661]

Those endowed with ethics must then engage extensively in study. You may wonder why that is. In order to attain buddhahood, you must realize the actuality of twofold identitylessness. [67] In order to realize that, you need to understand the scriptures and reasonings [that allow you] to understand the meaning of the Buddha's words and the treatises [on it]. To understand those [scriptures and reasonings], you need to study. If you don't, you will not understand the actuality of twofold identitylessness, and if you do not understand that, you will not know how to familiarize with identitylessness. If you do not know how to familiarize with identitylessness, even if you practice meditation, the prajñā which arises from meditation will not arise. If that [prajñā] does not arise, it is impossible for the path of seeing of the noble ones to arise. If that [path] does not arise, it is impossible to attain buddhahood, which is the culmination of [said] familiarization. This is said many times, such as in [Asaṅga's] *Mahāyānasaṃgraha*:

> Since, without the latent tendencies for listening and so on,
> It is not suitable that their result arises.[662]

Therefore, if you lack the prajñā of studying, by virtue of not discriminating what to adopt and reject, whatever you do will have little impact. In all your births, your faculties will be dull. Even if you practice meditation, the root of the clinging to identity will not be severed. [Thus,] there are many such and other shortcomings.

[On the other hand,] if you engage in studying, your mind will not be ignorant, since you will be learned in all that can be known. Through your insight expanding, you will attain the self-confidence of not fearing anything. Since your mind stream is completely liberated, your mind is happy. You will join the ranks of those called "learned ones." In all lifetimes, you will have excellent prajñā, sharp faculties, and retain what you have studied. You will meet with buddhas and bodhisattvas and be able to teach eloquently on the meaning of the dharma. Your own cognitive obscurations will be purified, and you will unmistakenly turn the wheel of dharma for others. [68] [Thus,] there are many such and other qualities. This is proclaimed extensively, such as in the *Prajñāpāramitāsaṃcayagāthā*:

> Having fully realized the nature of phenomena through prajñā,
> He perfectly transcended the three realms without exception.
> Through turning the precious wheel, the supreme leader of
> humans,
> In order to extinguish suffering, also taught the dharma for the
> world.[663]

and the *Ratnakūṭa*:

> Through studying, the dharma is understood.
> Through studying, what is worthless is relinquished.
> Through studying, evil is abandoned.
> Through studying, nirvāṇa is attained.

If you engage in the meditation of fools, lacking the prajñā of studying and reflection and not understanding the actuality of twofold identitylessness, even if you attain a little bit of samādhi, due to being unable to relinquish the root of the afflictions, you will fall into saṃsāra [again and again]. An example for this is Udraka, the son of the tīrthika Rāma, who gave rise to the ultimate resting in meditative equipoise within a samādhi of emptiness for twelve years. As the *Samādhirājasūtra* says:

> You may cultivate any samādhi in the world
> And the notion of a self may not appear through that,
> [But] afflictions will stir up again in you,
> Just as with Udraka's cultivation of samādhi here.[664]

Having attained the eye of the profound prajñā of studying and reflecting, you need to intensely exert yourself in pursuing meditation. The *Samādhisambhāraparivarta* states:

> What expands prajñā is studying. [69]
> Once both it and reflecting are present,
> Then you apply yourself to meditation.
> From this, you attain unsurpassable siddhi.[665]

Also, the *Bodhisattvadaśabhūmikasūtra* says:

> O children of the victors, beginner bodhisattvas should first be enjoined to do recitations. After they have studied a lot, they should be seen off into solitude.

You may wonder what fault there is in not being endowed with meditation. Through mere studying and reflecting that is not endowed with meditation, you will not directly realize ultimate reality. The *Buddhāvataṃsakasūtra*[666] states:

> The sweet flavor of sugar cane
> Is not tasted through explaining it,
> But when you eat the sugar cane,
> Its sweet flavor is tasted.
>
> Likewise, the actuality of emptiness
> Is not tasted through explanations,
> But if you devotedly meditate,
> It will spring forth in self-awareness.

Therefore, persons who strive for liberation first purify their three gates [of body, speech, and mind] through the ethics of renunciation. Then, they cut through doubts with the prajñā of studying. Through the prajñā which arises from reflection, by means of reasoning, they should contemplate again and again whether they are mistaken regarding the meaning of what they have studied or not, and familiarize [themselves with what is unmistaken]. Next, if they meditate on the unmistaken meaning in a way of being endowed with the three stages of preparation, main part, and conclusion,[667] through the prajñā which arises from the mundane states of [Buddhist] meditation, they will attain the clear appearance of identitylessness on the path of preparation. [70] Through the prajñā which arises from supramundane meditation, on the path of seeing, they will see identitylessness directly. On the path of familiarization, they familiarize with [what they saw on the path of seeing], and through the culmination of that familiarization, they will attain liberation and omniscience. The *Ratnakūṭa* says:

> Dwelling in ethics, samādhi is attained.
> Having attained samādhi, prajñā is cultivated.
> Through prajñā, pure wisdom is attained.
> Pure wisdom is perfect ethics.

For example, when a field, seeds, water, fertilizer, and heat come together, the fruition—a harvest—will arise. If even one [of these conditions] is lacking, the result will not arise. In the same way, when the ground of ethics, the seeds of studying, and the water, fertilizer, heat, and moisture of reflecting and meditating are all complete, the fruition—buddhahood—will easily ripen.

2. The meaning of the text

This has three parts:

1) Explaining the aspect of consciousness
2) Explaining the aspect of wisdom
3) Summary of the meaning of those

2.1. Explaining the aspect of consciousness

This has four parts:

1) Explaining that the root of mistakenness and nonmistakenness is mind as such
2) Establishing that appearances are mind
3) Teaching that mind is unborn
4) Explaining that the causes and conditions of mistakenness are the eight collections [of consciousness]

2.1.1. Explaining that the root of mistakenness and nonmistakenness is mind as such

This has three parts: [71]

1) Wrong ideas of others [about this]
2) How this was taught by the Victor
3) The manner of it being taught through [Rangjung Dorje's] own realization

2.1.1.1. Wrong ideas of others about this

> **[People] think that all sentient beings in the three realms**
> **Arise either from themselves, from something other,**
> **From both or without a cause.**[668]
> **They say: "A creator (such as Cha, Īśvara,**
> **Brahmā, or Viṣṇu), outer particles,**
> **Or a real hidden substance**
> **Creates myself and the world."**[669] [5–11]

All these **sentient beings**, who circle **in the three realms** of desire, form, and formlessness, consist of consciousness and have the nature of being mistaken. As for the ways [to explain] from which causes they arise, childish beings who do not adhere to a philosophical system have no ideas about this at all, because they do not know how to examine and analyze. The tīrthikas who adhere to philosophical systems have wrong ideas about causes and conditions. Among Buddhists, the śrāvakas realize just a fraction of actual reality, just as it is, but do not realize the ways in which appearances are mind, mind is emptiness, and emptiness arises as dependent origination. Therefore, they proclaim a great deal of superimposition and denial.

[In more detail,] as for the tīrthikas, the Sāṃkhyas refer to the cause that consists of the equilibrium of motility, darkness, and lightness[670] as the "primal cosmic substance,"[671] which is permanent, singular, immaterial, hidden, and has the unobstructed power to emanate [all kinds of] manifestions. Since it exists by being endowed with these five characteristics, within the cause (the primal substance), the result (its perturbations) arises. Thus, [the Sāṃkhyas] assert that [phenomena] **arise from themselves**. The followers of Īśvara [72] say that "Īśvara" is singular, permanent, dynamic, divine, worthy to be honored, pure, a creator, and independent. This single [godhead] who possesses [these] eight characteristics exists as the cause of all outer and inner entities. Thus, [his followers] hold that results arise **from** a cause that is **something other** [than these results]. The followers of Viṣṇu and others maintain that inner and outer entities arise **from both** the self, which is endowed with five characteristics,[672] and the power of a creator, who is something other. The Lokāyatas[673] assert that the entire world and its inhabitants arise **without a cause**, that is, just by nature. As [their scriptures] say:

> The rising of the sun, and the downhill flow of rivers,
> The roundness of peas, the long sharp tips of thorns,
> And the colorful patterns of the feathers of a peacock's wings—
> All these were created by nobody. They came about through their very nature.

From among all the proponents of philosophical systems, these [latter] are the worst, because they completely deny even the ways in which the world directly appears.

As for those who assert **a creator**, in Tibet, [the followers of Bön] assert that everything good and bad in the [world, which consists of the outer] container and its contents, is created by the so-called "Unfathomable **Cha**."[674] The tīrthikas **say** that [everything] is created by **Īśvara, Brahmā, or Viṣṇu**, with oneself and the world thus being produced [by them]. Since all of these [views] are nothing but the mistakenness of wrong ideas, one should cast them far away. [73]

The first among the four Buddhist philosophical systems is the one of those śrāvakas who are Vaibhāṣikas. They [assert] that the entities which appear as **outer** objects are unreal, but the substantial partless **particles**, which are not the sphere of the sense faculties, are ultimate [reality]. The partless moments of inner consciousness are [said to be] "mental particles." The former of these two [particles] cannot be destroyed by other entities, while mental particles cannot be [further broken down by] mental analysis. Therefore, both [substantial and mental particles] are permanent. Once such [particles] come together, conglomerated particles are established, which are the entities of seeming [reality], being the objects of the sense consciousnesses and having the characteristic of impermanence. The individual particles of outer objects (forms, sounds, smells, tastes, tangible objects, and phenomena) are asserted to be real. [However,] if, through prajñā, substantial particles are divided into six or ten sides, and mental particles are split up into the three times, none of them are established and are therefore untenable. [Furthermore,] if there are no parts, coarse [entities] cannot be built up [by these particles] either.

Those śrāvakas who are Sautrāntikas say, "Since manifest outer objects, such as forms, are seeming [reality], they do not appear directly to consciousness. Rather, when object and sense faculty meet, what appears is something like an image [drawn] in the ashes of incense.[675] Outer objects—the specifically characterized objects[676] that cast [their aspects] toward consciousness—exist as **real hidden** or concealed **substances**. Through that, **myself**—the inner person—**and the** realms, or objective phenomena of the outer **world** are **created.**" This too is untenable. If the hidden [object] appears to consciousness, this contradicts its being hidden, and [74] if it does not so appear, it would not be able to cast its aspect [toward consciousness].

2.1.1.2. How this was taught by the Victor

> **The sole all-knowing one**
> **Taught sentient beings from his realization**
> **That these three realms are merely mind—**[677]
> **They neither arise from themselves, nor from something other,**
> **Nor from both, nor without a cause.**
> **Phenomena are [nothing but] dependent origination,**
> **While this very [dependent origination] is empty of a nature of its own,**
> **Free from being one or different,**
> **Devoid of being real or delusive,**
> **And just like illusions, the moon in water, and so on.**[678] [12–21]

The perfect buddha is liberated from the two obscurations, including their latent tendencies, and therefore directly **knows** the suchness of **all** knowable objects as well as their entire variety. This **sole one** who is unrivaled in the world **taught that these three realms are merely** the embodiment of the imagining **mind** that is impaired by ignorance, but that they are not established ultimately. The *Daśabhūmikasūtra* says:

> O children of the victors, those three realms are mere mind.[679]

The *Laṅkāvatārasūtra* states:

> Just as forms in a mirror
> Appear, but do not exist,
> In the mirror of latent tendencies,
> Childish beings see two aspects of mind.
>
> Through not knowing [that they are] appearances of mind,
> Two kinds of conception arise.[680]

. . .
Through conceptions connected to latent tendencies,
Great variety springs from the mind.
To human beings, external [things] appear—
They are merely the minds of worldly beings.[681]

In the mantra [system], it is said:

Outside of this jewel[like] mind,
There are no buddhas and no sentient beings.
There are not the slightest outer referents
On which consciousness could dwell.

Therefore, these entities [75] do **not arise from themselves** as in the assertions of the tīrthikas. If something is already established as itself, there is no need for it to arise again. **Nor** do [entities] arise **from something other**. If something "other" has to depend on "self," since there is no "self" as the basis on which [that "other"] could depend, as whose "other" would it be justified? However, if something were produced by something other, then the sun would [absurdly] have to produce darkness and [a piece of] felt a vase and so on, but such [things] are impossible. **Nor** are [entities] produced **from both** [the just-mentioned possibilities] together—there will just be the [added] faults of both these previous [possibilities]. Also, it is untenable for some simultaneously existing "self" and "other"—like the left and right horns [of a bull]—to serve as mutual causes and conditions. **Nor** is [arising] **without a cause** justified, as long as [everybody's] direct sense perceptions see that a sprout arises from a seed and so on.

You may wonder, "Well, how is it then?" Ultimately, the **phenomena** contained in saṃsāra and nirvāṇa are emptiness beyond [all] extremes of reference points. Within that [emptiness], as seeming appearances, they **are the dependent origination** of mutual causes and results. **This very** dependent origination **is empty of** any real entity established by **a nature of its own.** Dependent origination's own nature consists of the appearances of the duality of apprehender and apprehended, **just like** [the reflection of] **the moon in water**. These [appearances] are seeming reality, that is, the phenomena that bear the nature [of emptiness]. These very mere appearances are naturally free from all reference points, and their own essence abides as emptiness. This is the nature of phenomena, ultimate reality. [76] Jñānagarbha's [*Satyadvayavibhāga*] says:

> Just these very appearances, as they [appear],
> Are the seeming. The other is its counterpart.[682]

The *[Vajra]jñānasamucchaya[tantra]*[683] states:

> The seeming is dualistic appearance. [Its] reality is like [a reflection of] the moon [in] water. Ultimate reality is free from all characteristics, and its locus consists of the eighteen emptinesses.

You may wonder, "Is this seeming appearance of duality the same as or different from its nature, the ultimate reality that is emptiness?" They are not the same. Seeming reality is established as mistaken appearances, but not ultimately, whereas ultimate reality is established as the nature of phenomena, but not as seeming [reality]. This is just as in the example of the appearance of the moon in water not being established as the actual moon, and the actual moon not being established as a [reflection of the] moon in water. The *Saṃdhinirmocanasūtra* states four flaws, if [the two realities] were the same, such as that those who see seeming reality would see ultimate reality [too].

The two realities are also not different. For example, when a rope is mistaken for a snake, what is actually there is a rope, but there is no snake. However, in the mistaken appearance, both what exists and what does not exist come together in the same basis, therefore not being different. Likewise, since whatever appears as seeming [reality] is inseparable from the ultimate (emptiness), they are not established as being different. The *Saṃdhinirmocanasūtra* states four flaws, if [the two realities] were different, such as that ultimate reality would not be the nature of seeming reality. [77]

Therefore, the two realities are **free from being one or different** and abide as the inseparability of appearance and emptiness. The *Saṃdhinirmocanasūtra* states:

> The defining characteristic of the conditioned realms and the ultimate
> Is their defining characteristic of freedom from being one and different.
> Those who think of them in terms of oneness and difference
> Have not mentally engaged them in a proper way.[684]

[The two realities] are also not **delusive** in the sense of being neither the same nor different. For, from the viewpoint of mistakenness, the seeming is the undeceiving [display of] causes and results, while the ultimate is **real** as the basic nature. So one may just conclude, "Well then, both [realities] are real." [However,] though the seeming appears, it is empty in that it is not established as any nature, while the ultimate is beyond the sphere of the mind. Therefore, they are **devoid of** any presentations of them being really established, and unable to be made into a thesis [that one could defend]. [The two realities] are similar to the example of **illusions**, which are not real as the entities of horses and cows, but still may appear as such. [The words] **"and so on"** [in line 21 of NY] include mirages, echoes, optical illusions, reflections, rainbows, clouds, and lightning, [all of] which [are similar in] appearing while not existing. [Nāgārjuna's] Madhyamaka [text called] *Bodhicittavivaraṇa* declares:

> Starting with ignorance up through aging [and death],
> The twelve links
> Of what originates in dependence
> I hold to be like dreams and illusions.[685]

Nāropa's *Summary of the View* says [78]:

> As for this nonreferential self-awareness,
> It appears while being empty, and is empty while appearing.
> Therefore, it is the inseparability of appearing and being empty,
> Just as [a reflection of] the moon in water.[686]

Therefore, the Blessed One, **realizing** that all three realms are **like** this, taught **sentient beings** the means for realizing this principle.

2.1.1.3. The manner of this being taught through [Rangjung Dorje's] own realization

> **"From where arises the root**
> **Of mistakenness and unmistakenness?"**
> **Just as [recognizing] one's own form due to a mirror**
> **And fire due to smoke,**
> **Through teaching the principle**[687] **of dependent origination,**
> **I will clearly express this realization here.** [22–27]

Mistakenness (saṃsāra) is the aspect of consciousness, **and unmistakenness** (nirvāṇa) is the aspect of wisdom. **"From where arises the root of** both, and how [does it arise]**?"** That [Rangjung Dorje] himself realizes this and is able to teach it to others has its basis in the profound dependent origination of causes and conditions. For example, **due to a** clear **mirror** free from corrosion, the reflected **form** of **one's own** face is realized to be beautiful or ugly. Likewise, through the development of the prajñā of studying and reflecting, which is based on the stainless sūtras, tantras, treatises, and instructions of the guru, the basic nature of the two realities is understood. **Just as** the existence of **fire** is inferred **due to** the rising of **smoke**, the wisdom of the change of state is pointed out due to developing the clear realization of meditation in the mind stream. In brief, all phenomena of saṃsāra and nirvāṇa are primordially beyond [all] extremes of reference points, yet **the principle of dependent origination** appears as anything whatsoever. **Through** having relied on [his] profound innate prajñā as well as the one he cultivated [during his present life], [Rangjung Dorje realized] this very [principle], just as it is, in an unerring way, and **will clearly express this realization** [in this] treatise **here**, not hiding anything and with a loving heart for [his] followers.

2.1.2. Establishing that appearances are mind

This has four parts:

1) Explaining the interdependent origination of the five operating consciousnesses and establishing it as mind
2) Dispelling wrong ideas that this is not mind
3) Presenting evidence that another agent does not exist
4) Explaining interdependence in terms of the sixth [consciousness], mentation[688]

2.1.2.1. Explaining the dependent origination of the five operating consciousnesses and establishing it as mind

> **The consciousnesses of the five [sense] gates**
> **Appropriate form, sound, smell, taste, and tangible objects**
> **Or reject them, which produces the afflictions.**
> **When those with prajñā examine carefully**
> **What these objects are,**
> **They are not established as something external**
> **(such as particles)**
> **That is other than the cognizing consciousness.**[689] [28–34]

Out of the causal condition (the ālaya-consciousness together with the afflicted mind), the dominant conditions (**the five gates** of the eye, ear, nose, tongue, and body [sense faculties], together with **the consciousnesses** connected with them—[the latter being] the immediate mind) meet with their object conditions (the five respective objects of **form, sound, smell, taste, and tangible objects**). Based on the contacts due to [these conditions] coming together, [mentally] **appropriating** desirable and attractive objects (such as what is beautiful [to the eye] or pleasant to hear) **produces the affliction** of desire. **Rejecting** undesirable repugnant things (such as what is visually unpleasant or unpleasant to hear) produces aversion. Not realizing the nature of what is [experienced as] neutral and indifferent produces ignorance. Through this, karma is accumulated.

If you ask how we come to take up roaming about in saṃsāra through that, this happens by clinging to mistaken appearances[690] as being real. You may wonder from **what** causes and conditions such appearances of the five apprehended **objects are** arising. **When those with** the eye of **prajñā** (which comes from study, reflection, and meditation) [80] **examine carefully**, it is nothing but the consciousnesses of the five gates, which arise from the creative potential of the **cognizing** mind, that arise as their respective five objects. **They are not established as** the slightest **external** causes and conditions **that are other than** [consciousness appearing as objects], **such as** the **particles** or hidden [outer] objects asserted by the śrāvakas who are Vaibhāṣikas or Sautrāntikas, or any self or agent asserted by the tīrthikas. Thus, Āryadeva's *Jñānasārasamucchaya* states:

> "Something that has parts" does not exist,
> And minute particles do not exist [either].
> What [seems to] appear distinctly is [actually] unobservable—
> Experiences are like a dream.[691]

2.1.2.2. Dispelling wrong ideas that this is not mind

> **If the substance of objects were other than consciousness,**
> **They would not have the same nature.**
> **[Also,] from cognizance that cannot be pinpointed and**
> **obstructed,**
> **Material substance does not arise.**
> **Because of that, they have no causal connection.**
> **If this is accepted, it is untenable that objects**
> **Appear to consciousness, since they have no connection.** [35–41]

If the substance of outer **objects** (such as form) **were** to exist as real referents **other than consciousness** (such as the eye [consciousness]), it **would** follow that consciousness and object do **not have** either a connection of the

same nature or a causal connection.[692] **Cognizance cannot be pinpointed** through the interaction between consciousness and object, **and** it cannot be **obstructed** due to not being established as a tangible form. **From** [such cognizance,] **material substance**—which appears to the contrary (as what can be pinpointed and obstructed)—**does not arise**, since it is contradictory in terms of substance for a result that is an entity to arise from a cause that is not an entity. **Because of that** argument, it needs to be accepted that consciousness and object **have no causal connection. If this is accepted** by realists,[693] [81] then it would follow that **objects**, such as form, do not appear [at all]. For, **it is untenable that** they **appear to consciousness**, such as the eye [consciousness], **since these** two [—object and consciousness—] **have no connection.** [In general,] whatever appears as such [seemingly outer objects] is necessarily something that is [connected either in terms of] identity or causality. [On the reverse side,] whatever does not have either connection does not appear [as such objects], just as in the examples of [illusory appearances] in a dream, invisible entities, or the eye consciousness not hearing sound and the tongue consciousness not seeing form. It is because of this point that Nāropa's *Summary of the View* says:

> All these appearing and possible phenomena
> Do not exist apart from self-aware mind,
> Since they are appearing and lucid,
> Just as the experience of self-awareness.
> If they were not mind,
> It would follow that they do not appear, since there is no
> connection.
> In this way, the seeming is determined.[694]

2.1.2.3. Presenting evidence that another agent does not exist

> **Hence, these appearances, however they may [manifest],**
> **Do not exist as objects that are other than consciousness.**[695]
> **[Their] arising [from] it is like an experience of one's own awareness.**
> **Whether partless particles or a plateau—**
> **Appearances are mind. The purport of this is**
> **To realize that Brahmā and such are not creating agents,**
> **Since nothing is established as something external to or other [than mind].**[696] [42–48]

Hence, due to the arguments just explained, **these** outer **appearances, however they may** [manifest], **do not exist as** really established **objects that are other than** inner **consciousness.** As for the certainty about this, the **awareness** that discriminates, [for example,] an utpala flower as the object of **one's own** thoughts **arises** from the mind with its latent tendencies, to which one has been habituated since beginningless [time]. That [awareness] manifests as **a** vivid **experience** within one's mind. However, something like a vase [appearing] within the mind of someone else, which lacks any connection to [one's own mind], [82] does not appear to one's own [mind]. Since it is **like** that, however **appearances** manifest (**whether** as subtle **partless particles or** vast [forms], such as the Tibetan **plateau**), they **are** just one's own **mind** appearing as if it were an object. Through **the purport of these** arguments and reasonings, **since** there is **no** real entity that **is established as something external to or other** than mind, it is **realized that Brahmā and such** (Īśvara, Viṣṇu, a self, minute particles, or hidden [objects]) **are not** established as **creating agents**, all of them being just mere appearances of mind, but not involving any real entities. The *Mañjuśrīvikrīḍitasūtra* states this extensively:

> The son of the gods, Padmavikrīḍita, questioned Mañjuśrī, "Are outer objects created by a creator or how should one view them?" Mañjuśrī answered, "Son of the gods, these outer objects have not been created by a creator. Rather, they appear by virtue of the unfolding power of the latent tendencies of the imagining mind." The son of the gods asked, "No matter how these latent tendencies may unfold, how could it be suitable for them to appear as these kinds of hard and solid [things] that mountains, oceans, the sun and so forth are?" Mañjuśrī replied, "It is suitable for them to appear like that due to the unfolding of our imagination. In the great city of Vārāṇasī, an old woman, by virtue of having constantly meditated on her body as being a tiger, was seen by all the people in that city as a tiger. [83] Thus, all these people ran away and the city became empty. It also happened that some monks, by virtue of having meditated on their bodies being impure, were seen as some foul and rotten sentient beings. If they can appear like that even by virtue of [having familiarized in these ways] for only a short while, why could [mountains and such] not appear by virtue of beginningless latent tendencies unfolding?"

2.1.2.4. Explaining interdependence in terms of the sixth [consciousness], mentation

> **As for the connection between mentation and phenomena,**
> **Just like in an experience in a dream,**
> **This is nothing but one's clinging to focusing on that,**
> **Whereas real entities do not exist.**[697] [49–52]

You may wonder how **the connection between mentation** (the sixth collection [of consciousness]) **and** the **phenomena** which appear as its objects is asserted. **In a dream** while being overcome by sleep, the latent tendencies of what you think and feel during the day become unmistaken **experiences** of sight and hearing as if they were directly perceived sense objects. **Just like** that, though the earlier latent tendencies of mind that have arisen as the thought of a vase have ceased [to appear] as **this** [vase], the next thoughts further prolong **focusing on that** [prior image of a vase]. Such **is nothing but clinging to** apprehended phenomena as real, thinking from the perspective of no examination, "This is a vase," **whereas** separate **real**ly established **entities** that are phenomena other than mind **do not exist.** The reason for this is as follows. In a dream, with not even a tiny particle being established, the various things that appear [in it] are appearances of utter nonexistents. Likewise, the latent tendencies of a vase, its characteristics, and the arising of thoughts about its being real have the nature of [possessing] many [different] moments.

2.1.3. Teaching that mind is unborn

This has two parts:

1) The actual [explanation] [84]
2) Adducing scriptural evidence

2.1.3.1. The actual explanation

> **Thus, this consciousness in its six collections**
> **Arises as the appearances of referents and sentient beings,**
> **Clinging to identity, cognizance,**
> **And whatever forms of appearances.**[698]
> **What are they? If not produced by something other,**
> **They are not produced by themselves [either],**
> **Nor are they produced by both or neither of the two.** [53–59]

You may wonder [now], "Granted, external objects are not really established, but is inner consciousness [really] established or not?" It is not so established. Just as what is called "the mountain over there" depends on "the mountain here," consciousness depends on an object to be known [by it]. Therefore, if the apprehended object does not exist, it is established that the apprehending consciousness does not exist either. The *Abhisamayālaṃkāra* says:

> If apprehended referents do not exist like that,
> Can these two be asserted as the apprehenders of anything?
> Thus, their characteristic is the emptiness
> Of a nature of an apprehender.[699]

Also master Nāgārjuna['s *Lokātītastava*] states:

> Without being cognized, there is nothing cognizable,
> But consciousness does not [exist] without that.[700]

Thus, because of that, for **this consciousness in its six collections**, [consciousness itself] appears as **referents**, that is, external objects that consist of forms and so on. [It also] **appears** as **sentient beings**, consisting of the supports [for perceiving these objects], such as the eye sense faculty. [It further appears as] **clinging to identity** (the apprehending consciousness) and **cognizance** of objcets (the mental factors). Through that, [mind] is engaged in adopting and rejecting. In brief, [all] **these** [phenomena] that **arise as whatever forms of appearances** are merely mind, but you may [still] wonder whether they are **not produced by some other** cause. **They are not produced by themselves** because, primordially, something that can be called "real" is not established. **Nor are they produced by both**, because both a [self] and something other do not exist. For, something other is not tenable, given that a self does not exist. [85] **Nor** are they produced without a cause, which would be from **neither** themselves nor something other. The *Prajñānāmamūlamadhyamakakārikā* says:

> Not from themselves, not from something other,
> Not from both, and not without a cause—
> At any place and any time,
> All entities lack arising.[701]

2.1.3.2. Adducing scriptural evidence

> **Therefore, according to the words of the Victor,**
> **Everything in saṃsāra and nirvāṇa is merely mind.** [60–61]

For the reasons explained above, **the words of the Victor** say in infinite ways in the sūtra collections of the mahāyāna in general and the *Buddhāvataṃsakasūtra* in particular:

> Mind is like a painter.
> The skandhas are created by the mind.
> All the many worldly realms there are
> Are painted by the mind.

Every phenomenon **in saṃsāra** is the mistaken mind's own form, **and** every phenomenon in **nirvāṇa is** the appearance of the basic state—mind free from the stains of apprehended and apprehender. Therefore, all sūtras, tantras, and treatises say that phenomena are **merely mind**. As the great Brahman [Saraha] states [in his *Dohākośagīti* ("*People Dohā*")]:

> Mind as such alone is the seed of everything.
> I pay homage to that mind, which is like a wish-fulfilling jewel,
> Granting anyone their desired results
> In existence and nirvāṇa.[702]

As for the gradual stages of realizing this actuality during the phases of the path, [86] first, [in] dependence on observing [objects] as mere cognizance, one realizes that outer objects other than mind do not exist. Thus, what arises [in the mind] is the nonobservation of [outer] objects. If there is nothing apprehended, there is no apprehender either. Therefore, in dependence on the nonobservation[703] of objects, there also arises nonobservation of the apprehender as being mere cognizance. The *Madhyāntavibhāga* states:

> In dependence on observation,
> Nonobservation arises.
> In dependence on nonobservation,
> Nonobservation arises.
>
> Therefore, observation is established
> As the nature of nonobservation.[704]

In this way, if one realizes the basic state, just as it is, in which apprehended and apprehender do not exist, then one realizes the dharmadhātu. The *Mahāyānasūtrālaṃkāra* says:

> The mind is aware that nothing other than mind exists.
> Then, it is realized that mind does not exist either.
> The intelligent ones are aware that both do not exist
> And abide in the dharmadhātu in which these are absent.[705]

2.1.4. Explaining the causes and conditions of mistakenness, the eight collections [of consciousness]

This has two parts:

1) Brief introduction
2) Detailed explanation

2.1.4.1 Brief introduction

> **He says that the dependent origination of the causes and conditions of this**
> **Lies in the six collections, mentation, and the ālaya.** [62–63]

You may wonder, "If everything in saṃsāra and nirvāṇa is explained as mind, how is this the case?" First, it is essential to know **the causes and conditions of this** saṃsāra as well as the mode in which these two arise by virtue of **dependent origination**. Therefore, the stainless sūtras, tantras, and treatises **say that** this principle [of mental causes and conditions] **lies in the six collections** of consciousness, [87] afflicted **mentation, and the ālaya.** The ālaya functions as the causal condition, its result being the seven collections [of consciousness]. From that, all karmas and sufferings of the three realms ripen individually. The latent tendencies of these, remaining in the ālaya, produce the [further] potentials of the ālaya. Therefore, the ālaya is also called "the result of the seven collections [of consciousness]." The *Vajraśikhara[mahāguhya]yogatantra* says:

> The ālaya, from which all seeds rise,
> Is held to be the nature of [everything] internal and external.

As a matter of course, one should know the dependent origination of nirvāṇa. We study the buddhadharma (a seemingly external condition) by virtue of the power of the basic element that is the stainless dharmakāya. Through that, the prajñā of knowing that the basic element of the dharmakāya exists within ourselves, that it can be attained by ourselves, and that it is endowed with great qualities will arise, and we will have confidence in that fact. Based on [such] confidence, aspiration arises; based on aspiration, the vigor of engagement arises; and by relying on that, we gather the two accumulations. Consequently, we become liberated from the defilements, while the completely pure dharmakāya manifests. As the *Uttaratantra* states:

> With devotion, they aspire:
> "This inconceivable object exists,
> People like me are able to attain it,
> And such attainment [entails excellent] qualities." [88]
>
> Therefore, being vessels of [all] qualities, such as striving,
> Vigor, mindfulness, dhyāna, and prajñā,
> The mind of enlightenment
> Will be ever present in them.
>
> Since that [mind] is present all the time,
> The children of the Victor do not fall back
> And reach the utter purity
> Of the complete pāramitā of merit.[706]

2.1.4.2. Detailed explanation

This has three parts:

1) Explaining the six collections
2) Explaining the immediate condition together with the afflicted mind
3) Explaining the causal condition—the ālaya

2.1.4.2.1. Explaining the six collections

This has four parts:

1) Identifying the six collections
2) Identifying the object condition
3) Identifying the dominant condition
4) Explaining from what those arose

2.1.4.2.1.1. Identifying the six collections

> **The consciousnesses of the six collections** [64]

First, if you wonder what **the consciousnesses of the six collections** that appropriate apprehender and apprehended are, they are the following six: (1) the eye consciousness apprehending form, (2) the ear consciousness apprehending sound, (3) the nose consciousness apprehending smell, (4) the tongue consciousness apprehending taste, (5) the body consciousness apprehending touch, and (6) the mental consciousness apprehending phenomena.

2.1.4.2.1.2. Identifying the object condition

> **Depend on their object conditions.**
> **These are the six objects of form and so on.** [65–66]

It is impossible that these six consciousnesses are naturally [89] established by their own nature. Rather, they arise in dependence on the four conditions. First, they **depend on their object conditions**, and since there are six objects as the factors on which they depend, the consciousnesses as the factors that depend [on these] are also six [in number]. What are **these** [objects]? They **are the** list of **six** that are known as the **objects** or referents **of form and so on** (sounds, smells, tastes, tangible objects, and phenomena). Generally, in terms of the five skandhas, the sense faculties and their objects are included in the skandha of form; [within that,] causal form consists of the four elements of earth, water, fire, and wind. Resulting forms, which derive from these four elements, are taught as eleven [in number]—the ten that are the five sense faculties and the five objects plus imperceptible form. Here, [in NY, the object conditions] are explained as the five [sense] objects (such as form as the object of the eyes) [and phenomena as the object of the mental consciousness]. The presentation of their subdivisions appears in detail in the *Abhidharmakośa*:

> Form is twofold and twentyfold.
> Sound has eight kinds.
> Taste is sixfold, smell fourfold,
> And tangible objects are of eleven types.

and

> Also, the virtuous or nonvirtuous continuities
> In those distracted or without mind,
> Which are outcomes of the great elements,
> Are called imperceptible.[707]

As for phenomena, one should know that they are twofold (conditioned and unconditioned), each having eight [subcategories]. There is also a presentation of three unconditioned phenomena and so on. [All of] these should be known from other [sources].[708]

2.1.4.2.1.3. Identifying the dominant condition

> **The dominant conditions are the six sense faculties,**
> **Which possess form and are translucent.** [67–68]

[90] **The dominant conditions** of the six consciousnesses **are the** unimpaired **six sense faculties.** The eye sense faculty is like a flax flower, the ear sense faculty is like a knot in birch bark, the nose sense faculty is like parallel copper needles, and the tongue sense faculty is like the [two] halves of a split moon. It is explained that these [four] faculties exist within [their corresponding] sense organs, while the body sense faculty (which is like the skin of the "bird that is soft to the touch") pervades the entire body. All of the five sense faculties **possess form and are translucent**, giving rise to consciousness that is able to apprehend an object. "Possessing [physical] form" refers to being made up of minute particles, or arising from the four elements as their causes. "Translucent" means that, just like a clear reflection in a mirror, [the sense faculties] are clear vivid objects, due to their own particular locations being occupied by other particles, while [at the same time appearing as something] that is connected to consciousness.[709] This [connection] is explained as one of being connected by virtue of internal [mental] seeds or potentials. In the *Mahāyānasaṃgraha*, it is held that the apprehended part of the ālaya is what appears as the five sense faculties. However, all of these [explanations] are not contradictory.

As for the mental faculty, it is explained as the immediate [mind] (which is the arising and ceasing within the ālaya) and as the dhātu of mentation[710] (which is [either one of] all six [consciousnesses] having just ceased). It is also explained as a particular one among the potentials of the ālaya and so on. However, the meaning [of this] is that what functions as the gateway for the arising of the mental consciousness is suitable as the āyatana of mentation,[711] [91] because it and the āyatana of (conditioned and unconditioned) phenomena dependently originate as [interrelated] subject and object.

2.1.4.2.1.4. Explaining what those arise from

> **Both arise from the mind.**
> **What vividly appears as objects and sense faculties**
> **Is based on beginningless potentials.**[712]
> **Consciousness is what perceives objects,**
> **While the formations of mental factors [perceive their]**
> **features,**[713]
> **Which is based on the mental consciousness.** [69–74]

In this way, the six sense faculties and the six objects (apprehender and apprehended) **both** only **arise from the mind**, but are not established ultimately. You may wonder, "Well, then what are these appearances?" **What vividly appears as** external **objects and** inner **sense faculties is** as follows. Under the sway of ignorance since **beginningless** time, we think that the nonexistence of the duality of apprehender and apprehended exists [as such a duality]. The seeds of the latent tendencies of such [mistaken thinking] are then input into the ālaya, and [sense faculties and objects] appear **based on** the awakening of these **potentials**. For the five **consciousness**es (such as the eye [consciousness]) **that perceive** external **objects**, forms, sounds, smells, tastes, and tangible objects appear, but [these consciousnesses] do not cognize the distinctive features [of these objects], [such as] thinking, "This is a pillar," "This is a vase." For, the scriptures say:

> The eye consciousness cognizes blue,
> But it does not think, "This is blue."

Consequently, first, objects appear to the sense consciousnesses, while what cognizes their **features** is the **mental factor** of discrimination.[714] Therefore, among mental factors, it is discrimination ([defined as] what apprehends the characteristics of objects) that thinks, "This form is beautiful," "This one is ugly," "This sound is pleasant," and "This one is unpleasant." Discriminations such as these [92] arise **based on the mental consciousness**. The *Madhyāntavibhāga* states:

> Here, consciousness is the seeing of an object,
> While mental factors [refer to seeing] its distinctive features.[715]

Regarding the circumstances in which this mental consciousness does not arise, master Vasubandhu says in his *Triṃśikākārikā*:

The mental consciousness occurs always,
Except in those without discrimination,
In the two kinds of meditative absorption,
[Deep] sleep, fainting, and also the state without mind.[716]

One should know that these are said to be the circumstances in which the mental consciousness does not arise, since in those five circumstances, the mental consciousness merges temporarily into the ālaya, so that there is no clear focus on phenomena.

2.1.4.2.2. Explaining the immediate condition together with the afflicted mind

This has two parts:

1) Brief introduction by way of their names
2) Detailed explanation of their defining characteristics

2.1.4.2.2.1. Brief introduction by way of their names

> **[Mentation] is twofold—the immediate and the afflicted mind.** [75]

You may wonder what the immediate condition is, which is explained [as one] among the four conditions for the arising and ceasing of the six collections [of consciousness]. Some assert it to be a part of the sixth [consciousness] (mentation), and some assert that it does not exist actually. However, these [people] base themselves just on the presentation of the śrāvakas, who assert only six collections [of consciousness], but simply have no idea about the mahāyāna's system of asserting eight collections [of consciousnesses]. For that reason, the mentation that rests in the ālaya is taken to have two facets, existing as the **two** that are the so-called "**immediate** mind" **and the afflicted mind.** [93]

2.1.4.2.2.2. Detailed explanation of their defining characteristics

This has three parts:

1) Explaining the immediate mind
2) Explaining the afflicted mind
3) Summarizing the characteristics of both

2.1.4.2.2.2.1. Explaining the immediate mind

> **Due to being the condition for the arising and ceasing of the six [consciousnesses],**
> **It is the immediate [condition].**[717]
> **Matching the number of the arising and ceasing of the moments**
> **Of the six collections, [the immediate mind] is connected with them.**
> **By virtue of a mind immersed in yoga**
> **And the words of the Victor, this is realized.** [76–81]

As for what is called "immediate mind," whenever **the six** collections of consciousnesses **arise**, it functions as **the condition for** their immediate arising, and whenever the six collections **cease**, it functions as the condition for immediately planting the seeds that are the potentials of these six collections into the ālaya. **Due to** this, **it is the immediate** condition for both the arising and ceasing [of the six consciousnesses]. When the six collections cease, this immediate consciousness (which is explained to be the same as the dhātu of mentation) transports them into the ālaya. Immediately upon that, just like the condition of waves [emerging] from water, from the ālaya that consists of all seeds, the mentation that rests in the ālaya stirs again and operates. Through this, the immediate mind comes about. When a single conditional [instance] of the six collections arises, a single [instance of the] immediate [mind] arises too, but not a second one. If there are many such conditional [instances], then the same number of [instances of the immediate mind] will arise. Therefore, once the earlier [instances of] the six collections have ceased, the following conditional [instances] are triggered immediately, thus being immediate. Consequently, by **matching the number of** [moments of] the immediate [mind] causing **the arising and ceasing of the moments of the six collections**, it arises in a way that it **is connected with them** by equaling their number. [94]

If you wonder from which [sources] such a principle is known, **this** [immediate] mind **is realized by virtue of** the direct perception of **a mind immersed in** the **yoga** of the unity of calm abiding and superior insight, **and** through inference [based on] the principles [presented in] **the** profound and vast **words of the Victor**.

2.1.4.2.2.2.2. Explaining the afflicted mind

> **The [other] part of this, with regard to mind as such,**
> **Entails self-centeredness, holding on to pride,**
> **Attachment to "me," and ignorance.**
> **Since it produces all [views about] the perishing collection,**
> **It is called "the afflicted mind."**[718] [82–86]

The part of this immediate mind that is known as the "afflicted mind" operates by being based on the ālaya. Through not realizing **mind as such** free from stains and [instead] focusing on the ālaya (mind as such with stains), it **entails self-centeredness; holding on to pride**, thinking, "I am superior"; clinging and **attachment to "me,"** cherishing [oneself] more than others; **and ignorance** due to not understanding that this very "I" lacks any reality. Thus, [the afflicted mind] is always tainted with these four afflictions. Therefore, it clings to the basis [that consists of] the five skandhas (**the collection** that, when analyzed, cannot stand its ground, but **perishes**)[719] as being "mine"; to the self as possessing the skandhas; to the self as abiding in the five skandhas; and to the five skandhas as arising from the self. Therefore, [by applying each of these four assumptions to each of the five skandhas,] there are twenty [mistaken views about a real personality]. Through wrongly engaging in each one of these [twenty views] in the three times (past, present, and future), [they sum up to] sixty, and by [adding] the general clinging [to this self] as being permanent or becoming extinct [after death], [one arrives at] sixty-two. **Since it produces all** [these views], **it is called the "afflicted mind."** Master Vasubandhu's [95] *Triṃśikākārikā* says:

> What operates based on the [ālaya-consciousness]
> Is the consciousness called "mentation,"
> Which has it as its focal object, its nature being self-centeredness.
>
> It is always associated with the four afflictions,
> And obscured yet neutral.[720]

Since this is the locus of the afflictedness of consciousness, this [afflicted mind] lacks any valid cognition and gives rise to all minds that are nonvalid cognitions. Because it obscures the ālaya through latent tendencies, while its nature is neutral,[721] it is the root of the entirety of the imaginary [nature] and the afflictions. Consequently, it is also explained as "false imagination." From this, the internally oriented afflictions (the factors to be relinquished through familiarization) arise.[722] By virtue of this condition also staining the six collections [of consciousness], the externally oriented afflictions (the factors to be relinquished through seeing) arise.

2.1.4.2.2.2.3. Summarizing the characteristics of both

> **The mentation immediately after the ceasing of the six [consciousnesses]**
> **Is the locus of the arising of consciousness.**
> **The afflicted mind is the locus of affliction.**
> **Since it has the capacity to produce and to obscure,**
> **This mentation has two aspects.**[723] [87–91]

Summarizing the characteristics of those two [types of mentation], **the mentation immediately after the ceasing of the six** [consciousnesses by their merging] into the ālaya **is the locus** or connector that causes **the arising of** the following six collections of **consciousness. The afflicted mind is the locus of** the six collections being made **afflicted. Since** the immediate mind **has the capacity to produce** the six collections, while the afflicted mind [96] has the capacity **to obscure** [them], **this mentation** [in general], which rests in the ālaya, is classified into **two aspects**.

When the immediate mind produces a purified [instance of] consciousness, such as confidence [in the dharma or a spiritual friend], the afflicted [mind] does not stir. Therefore, the [immediate mind] is called the "stainless mentation" in the sūtras. The meaning of [what] these [say] is taught in the *Mahāyānasaṃgraha*:

> Among those, mentation is twofold. Since it is the support that acts as the immediate condition, the "mentation which is [any] consciousness that has just ceased" is the support for [the arising of] consciousness. The second is the afflicted mind, which is always congruently associated with the four afflictions of the views about a real personality, self-conceit, attachment to the self, and ignorance. This is the support for the afflictedness of consciousness. [Thus,] consciousness is produced by virtue of the first [aspect of mentation] as its support, while the second one makes it afflicted. [Mentation] is a consciousness, because it cognizes objects. Since it is [both] immediately preceding and self-centered, mentation has two aspects."[724]

As for "afflicted" [in "afflicted mind"], it is a word for grasping at "me." For this reason, it is the root of all the mistakenness of circling in the three realms. Therefore, this [afflicted mind] neither exists in the meditative absorption of cessation that transcends the three realms, [97] nor in the meditative equipoises of noble arhats and bodhisattvas. You should also know the distinctive feature of [the afflicted mind still] existing in the meditative absorption without discrimination.

2.1.4.2.3 Explaining the causal condition—the ālaya[-consciousness]

This has two parts:

1) Brief introduction by means of its name
2) Detailed explanation of its specific characteristics

2.1.4.2.3.1 Brief introduction by means of its name

> **For those with special insight,**
> **[The buddha] taught the ālaya-consciousness.**[725] [92–93]

The followers of the mahāyāna are endowed **with** the **insight** that is more **special** than the insight that realizes the [kinds of] identitylessness of the hīnayāna and is capable of realizing the profound basic state of the nature of phenomena, just as it is. **For those**, the omniscient victor clearly **taught "the ālaya-consciousness,"** which serves as the causal condition of the six collections [of consciousness]. The *Abhidharmasūtra* says:

> The ālaya is the consciousness
> Of all seeds of all phenomena.
> Therefore, I explained this ālaya-consciousness
> To the genuine ones.

As for its summarized characteristics, master Vasubandhu's *Triṃśikākārikā* says:

> Here, maturation is the "ālaya-consciousness,"
> Which contains all the seeds.
>
> Its appropriation, state,
> And cognizance are unconscious,
> Yet it is always endowed with contact, mental engagement,
> Feeling, discrimination, and impulse.

Its feeling is indifference.
It is unobscured and neutral.
The same goes for its contact and so on.
It flows like a river stream.

In arhathood, it becomes extinguished.[726]

[98] Accordingly, because it is the basis for the arising of all phenomena of imagination, it is called "ālaya." If you wonder how it comes that the term "consciousness" is added to it, this is in order to discriminate [it properly], since there are contexts in which suchness, or the Tathāgata heart are also called "ālaya." You may [also] wonder, "If it is said that consciousness is what sees an object, what is posited as [its] object here?" It is called "consciousness," since it is the entity of mutual causes and conditions by virtue of the appropriation of the seven collections of consciousness, in which [process] it seems as if the ālaya's being endowed with all maturations and seeds is the object and its aspect of lucidity is the [perceiving] subject. Since everything is collected in it, it is maturation, like an ocean [resulting] from rain water. Because it produces all that is produced by conditions, it serves as a cause. From that point of view, it is that which contains all seeds. At all times, it is accompanied by the five omnipresent [mental factors] contact, mental engagement, feeling, discrimination, and impulse. Therefore, these mental factors serve as distinct features of [its being a] consciousness, with the [specific] feeling associated with the ālaya being indifference.

The nature of the ālaya is to be unobscured and neutral, just like the clarity of a mirror. Similar to a flowing river, it is the continuous flow of seeds of subject, object, and sense faculties. [99] As for "in arhathood, it becomes extinguished" [in the above quote by Vasubandhu], he refers to a buddha; in śrāvaka arhats, the ālaya exists. However, it is fine to explain that the extinction of the support that is the afflicted mind, which clings to a personal self, represents the extinction of one part [of the ālaya]. Such an ālaya was not taught to the followers of the hīnayāna out of the concern that they [might] mistake it as being equivalent to the self of the tīrthikas. The *Saṃdhinirmocanasūtra* says:

The appropriating consciousness is profound and subtle.
All [its] seeds flow like the stream of a river.
It is inappropriate to conceive of it as a self.
I did not teach it to childish beings.[727]

2.1.4.2.3.2 Detailed explanation of its specific characteristics

> **It is also taught as support, matrix,**
> **Or appropriating consciousness.**
> **Since all karmas produced by the seven collections are gathered**
> **In an unmixed and neutral way,**
> **It is called "maturational,"**
> **Just as rain water [flows] into the ocean.**
> **Since it produces everything,**
> **It is the ground from which all seeds rise,**
> **Thus being designated "the causal condition."**
> **Because it dissolves, when the seven collections dissolve,**
> **It is also called "conditioned consciousness."**[728] [94–104]

This "ālaya-consciousness" is the ground of mistakenness in the three realms. **It is also** called "**support**ing consciousness," since it is the cause of all physical sense faculties. It is called "**matrix** consciousness," because it is the matrix that appropriates all seeds of latent tendencies and physical bodies. Furthermore, it is taught as "**appropriating consciousness,**" since, through appropriating a self, skandhas, desire, and views, the link with a [new] body is established and their full manifestation is seized. [100] **It is called "maturational** consciousness" too, **since all** the individual seeds of the positive and negative **karmas produced by the seven collections** of consciousness and their objects and sense faculties **are gathered in an unmixed and neutral way** (with their nature being neither virtuous nor unvirtuous) in this ālaya, **just as rain** falls into rivers, and the rivers flow and are gathered **into the ocean.** Here, the six collections are like the rain, the karmas accumulated by mentation like the rivers, and the ālaya like the ocean.

One should understand that any karma for which preparation, main part, and conclusion are complete is called "accumulated karma," which has the capacity to bring forth its results. From the point when an action has ceased until its result has matured, it is called "maturing [karma]." Just as waves immediately arise from the ocean and move if the [proper] conditions meet, the afflicted mind arises from the ālaya, which constitutes all seeds, and moves. Therefore, the "immediate mind" arises, which is what produces the individual results of the seeds that exist within the ālaya in an unmixed way. The *Abhidharmasūtra* says:

> Consciousness arises from mentation,
> And mentation arises from the ālaya.

In the ālaya, all phenomena
Are moving just like waves.

Another sūtra says:

Just as waves arising from the great ocean [101]
That is stirred up by the wind,
From the "ālaya with all seeds,"
Its own potential—a mere consciousness—arises.

Since it produces everything internal and external, **it is the ground from which all seeds rise, thus being designated "the causal condition"** of the six collections [of consciousness]. **When**, through the force of studying and meditating, **the seven collections dissolve** inside, there are no newly accumulated latent tendencies. Hence, just like an ocean runs dry [due to a lack] of rain water, through there being no more causes for producing the ālaya, the ālaya **dissolves. Because** of that, **it is also called "conditioned consciousness,"** since it depends on the conditions of the seven collections. Furthermore, just as the ālaya-consciousness is the cause of afflicted phenomena, afflicted phenomena too are presented as the causal condition of the ālaya-consciousness, because other causal conditions [for it] are not observable. As for the way these [topics] are, you need to understand that this is a condensed ancillary teaching in accordance with the detailed [presentation] in the *Mahāyānasaṃgraha*. [In this context,] it is appropriate to refer to the pure aspect of the ālaya, as it was explained, through the conventional term "cause for purified [phenomena]." But it is not appropriate to explain that the ālaya-consciousness is the cause of the buddha wisdom of nirvāṇa. *The Tantra of Complete Nonabiding*[729] declares:

Though the ālaya is the ground of all, [102]
It is not the ground for purified [phenomena].

However, there are numerous ways to explain this. You may wonder, "As for the realization that is based on the correct view that the pure qualities are inseparable from buddha enlightenment, isn't it too presented on the basis of the ālaya? How are these purified phenomena produced?" They are based on the suchness of all phenomena, the dharmakāya of the naturally pure mind, the Tathāgata heart. This principle should be known in detail from the omniscient Rangjung Dorje's text *Pointing Out the Tathāgata Heart* and its commentaries.

2.2. Explaining the wisdoms and the kāyas that are the change of state of the eight collections [of consciousness]

This has two parts:

1) Brief introduction of the general meaning
2) Detailed explanation of the meaning of the text

2.2.1 Brief introduction of the general meaning

Being unaware of the ālaya's own essence, the movement of apprehender and apprehended functions as the cause of mistakenness. From that, this great ocean of suffering in [saṃsāric] existence arises, which is hard to cross by those who are called sentient beings and circle in the three realms. Once free from the adventitious stains of grasping at sentient beings' five skandhas, the change of state appears as the five wisdoms, which have the nature of the four kāyas. In brief, the basis for the label "sentient being" is the five skandhas, and the substantial causes of these [skandhas] are mind, mentation, and [103] consciousness. The cause of buddhahood stems from the change of state of the five skandhas of sentient beings. The *Mahāyānasaṃgraha* states:

> Through how many kinds of masteries is the mastery of the dharmakāya attained? In brief, mastery is attained through five kinds. (1) Through the change of state of the skandha of form, mastery over [pure buddha] realms, kāyas, the excellent major and minor marks, infinite voices, and the invisible mark on the crown of the head [is attained]. (2) Through the change of state of the skandha of feeling, mastery over infinite and vast blissful states without wrongdoing [is attained]. (3) Through the change of state of the skandha of discrimination, mastery over the teachings [is attained] through all groups of words, groups of phrases, and groups of letters. (4) Through the change of state of the skandha of formation, mastery over creation, transformation, gathering retinues, and gathering the immaculate dharmas [is attained]. (5) Through the change of state of the skandha of consciousness, mastery over mirrorlike [wisdom], [the wisdom of] equality, discriminating [wisdom], and all-accomplishing [wisdom] is attained.[730]

The manner of the change of state of the [first] four skandhas is understood through that quote itself. Here, as for the change of state of consciousness [(the fifth skandha)], [104] the manner of its changing into the four buddha wisdoms is explained briefly. Firstly, this is taught as the four causes for attaining wisdom, and [secondly,] as the four causes for the change of state.

First, the cause of mirrorlike [wisdom] is the prajñā of studying and retaining the dharma of the three piṭakas. The cause of the wisdom of equality is to cultivate a mind-set of [regarding] all sentient beings as equal. The cause of discriminating wisdom is to teach the dharma to others. The cause of all-accomplishing wisdom is to accomplish [beneficial] activities for others. The *Mahāyānasūtrālaṃkāra* says:

> Due to retaining, due to equanimity,
> Due to elucidating the perfect dharma,
> And due to accomplishing activities,
> The four wisdoms arise.[731]

The second [four causes] are as the *Trikāyanāmasūtra* says:

> The purified state of the ālaya-consciousness is mirrorlike wisdom, the dharmakāya. The purified state of the afflicted mind is the wisdom of equality, [and] the purified state of the mental consciousness is discriminating wisdom, [both being] the sambhogakāya. The purified state of the consciousnesses of the five [sense] gates is all-accomplishing wisdom, the nirmāṇakāya.[732]

These wisdoms can be summarized in the two categories of knowing suchness and knowing variety. As for the first, the nature of all phenomena—the ultimate lack of appearance—refers to the wisdom of knowing suchness in meditative equipoise. [105] As the *Satyadvayavibhāga* says:

> When there is no seeing of a nature
> Of cognition and what is cognized,
> Since characteristics do not come about,
> Dwelling [in samādhi] is stable, so there is no rising [from it].[733]

The wisdom of knowing variety during subsequent attainment is the direct realization that all possible types of substances of all phenomena within the three times are illusionlike. The *Satyadvayavibhāga* says:

> A single instant of [your] knowing
> Encompasses the entire maṇḍala of knowable objects.[734]

Although there are no distinctions between meditative equipoise and subsequent attainment in buddha wisdom, [the above two wisdoms] are labeled [in this way] merely due to [this buddha wisdom's two] ways of knowing.

2.2.2 Explaining the actual meaning of the text

This has six parts:

1) Explaining mirrorlike wisdom as the dharmakāya
2) Explaining the wisdom of equality
3) Explaining discriminating wisdom
4) Explaining the [latter] two [wisdoms] as the sambhogakāya
5) Explaining all-accomplishing wisdom as the nirmāṇakāya
6) Explaining the dharmadhātu

2.2.2.1. Explaining mirrorlike wisdom as the dharmakāya

This has two parts:

1) [Explaining] what is to be purified and what purifies it
2) Explaining the result of purification—the kāya and the wisdom

2.2.2.1.1. Explaining what is to be purified and what purifies it

> **The nature of the external and internal,**
> **This very ālaya-consciousness,**
> **Is the root of everything to be relinquished.**
> **It is said that it is to be overcome**
> **Through the vajralike samādhi.** [105–109]

As was just explained, **the nature of internal** consciousness **and external** objects is **this very ālaya-consciousness.** It is the ground or root of the entirety of apprehender and apprehended—actual ignorance as such. Since it obscures the buddhabhūmi, [106] it **is the root of everything to be relinquished.** As for the remedy to relinquish it, let alone mundane samādhis, it cannot even be relinquished through the ultimate prajñā of śrāvakas and pratyekabuddhas that realizes identitylessness. **It is said that it is to be overcome through the vajralike samādhi.**

2.2.2.1.2. Explaining the result of purification—the kāya and the wisdom

> **Once the ālaya including the obscurations is extinguished,**
> **It becomes mirror[like] wisdom.**
> **All wisdoms appear [in it] without any "mine."**

> **It is unconfined and ever present.**
> **It realizes all knowable objects, yet is never directed toward them.**
> **Since it is the cause of all wisdoms,**[735]
> **It is called the "dharmakāya."** [110–116]

By virtue of neither being attached to anything nor obstructed with regard to anything, the vajralike samādhi is the antidote to the most subtle obscurations. Through it, **the ālaya**—the two **obscurations including** [their] latent tendencies—is overcome. **Once** the ālaya **is extinguished** in that way, **it becomes** the **mirror**[like] **wisdom** of a buddha. As for the meaning of this term, as in the example of a clear mirror, a reflection is suitable to arise in dependence on it. Likewise, from mirrorlike wisdom, the three other wisdoms and the sambhogakāya appear in the manner of reflections. The *Mahāyānasūtrālaṃkāra* says:

> Since the reflection of wisdom arises.[736]

In that mirrorlike wisdom, **all** other **wisdoms** and all knowable objects **appear**, but **without** being grasped as "**mine.**" Since **it is unconfined**, [mirrorlike wisdom] is **ever present**. Since it is free from all obscurations and not ignorant about the entirety of knowable objects, it is not directed toward the consciousnesses that are triggered by objects [107] and is free from not knowing. Hence, **it realizes all knowable objects, yet is never** apprehending them through being **directed** outward **toward them**. The *Mahāyānasūtrālaṃkāra* says:

> Mirrorlike wisdom is without "me" or "mine,"
> Unconfined, ever present,
> Not ignorant about the entirety of knowable objects,
> Yet never directed toward them.[737]

Furthermore, during the phase of impurity, the ālaya-consciousness functions as the support of the other [seven consciousnesses, such as] "mentation". Accordingly, on the buddhabhūmi, mirrorlike wisdom functions as the support of the three other wisdoms. The *Mahāyānasūtrālaṃkāra* says:

> Mirrorlike wisdom is unmoving.
> The three [other] wisdoms have it as their foundation—
> Equality, discriminating,
> And all-accomplishing as well.[738]

Therefore, **since it is the cause of all** three **wisdoms**, and since it produces the other three wisdoms and the sambhogakāya, the *Mahāyānasūtrālaṃkāra* says:

> Since it is the cause of all wisdoms,
> It is like a great jewel mine of wisdom.
> It is the sambhoga-buddhahood,
> Since the reflection of wisdom arises.[739]

This mirrorlike wisdom **is called the "dharmakāya."** As for the reason for this, the *Mahāyānasaṃgraha* states:

> [The dharmakāya is constituted] by the buddhadharma of purity, since the dharmakāya is attained by the ālaya-consciousness having changed state.[740]

[108] The *Śrīḍākārṇava[mahāyoginī]tantra* says:

> The ālaya is mirrorlike wisdom—
> This is the dharmakāya.

The dharmakāya is the final wisdom that is the knowledge of a buddha, the attainment of supreme wisdom in which all reference points have come to rest and in which there are no appearances. It is the nonduality of dhātu and wisdom. The *[Sarvabuddhaviṣayāvatāra]jñānālokālaṃkārasūtra* says:

> Genuine wisdom, identityless
> And without appearance, is not seen.

As it is said:

> Prajñāpāramitā, beyond speech, thought, and expression,
> Unborn and unceasing, the very nature of space,
> The sphere of personally experienced wisdom,
> Mother of the victors of the three times, I pay homage to You.[741]

2.2.2.2. Explaining the wisdom of equality

This has two parts:

1) [Explaining] what is to be purified and what purifies it
2) Explaining the wisdom that is the result of purification

2.2.2.2.1. Explaining what is to be purified and what purifies it

> **The afflicted mind is overcome**
> **Through the "heroic stride."** [117–118]

Focusing on the ālaya-consciousness, [the afflicted mind] operates in the form of constantly imputing an "I." Therefore, it is always associated with the four afflictions—views about a self, ignorance about a self, attachment to a self, and pride about a self. Hence, its nature is to have the characteristics of obscuring the attainment of liberation and being neutral. This is known as **the afflicted mind,** which **is overcome through the** "samādhi of the lion-like **heroic stride,**" [which bears this name,] since it can never be taken away through the afflictions.[742] [109] Then, the stains of mistakenness do not rise up [anymore], due to which the wisdom of equality is attained. As for the meaning of this term, it is the wisdom which, through having familiarized with the equality of self and others on the path of training, realizes the equality of [saṃsāric] existence and peace upon attaining buddhahood.

2.2.2.2.2 Explaining the wisdom that is the result of purification

> **Once the afflictions are relinquished through seeing and familiarization,**
> **There are no afflictions, no existence, and no peace.**
> **This is designated as the "wisdom of equality."**[743] [119–121]

The imputed **afflictions** (which are coarse and externally oriented) **are relinquished through** the path of **seeing, and** the innate afflictions (which are subtle and inwardly oriented) are relinquished through the path of **familiarization.** Therefore, **there are no afflictions** [left]. At the time of [practicing] the path, one cultivates nonconceptual samādhi in a pure manner and [also] cultivates the peace of not falling into the sides of either saṃsāra or nirvāṇa, thus not abiding in either existence or peace. Through that, on the buddhabhūmi, there is **no existence and no peace,** and the nirvāṇa that does not abide in the two extremes is attained. Therefore, **this is designated as the "wisdom of equality."** The *Mahāyānasūtrālaṃkāra* says:

> The wisdom of equality toward sentient beings
> Is held to be stainless by virtue of pure cultivation.
> Residing in nonabiding peace
> Is asserted to be the wisdom of equality.[744]

In this context, the factors to be relinquished through seeing and familiarization are classified as follows. The factors to be relinquished through seeing are the ten imputed afflictions—the five [views] (views about a real personality, views about extremes, wrong views, holding views as paramount, and holding ethics and spiritual disciplines as paramount) and the five [nonviews] (desire, anger, pride, [110] ignorance, and doubt). Through wrongly engaging [by these ten] in the [four] realities of suffering, the origin [of suffering], cessation, and the path, there are forty [factors to be relinquished] in the desire realm. In the two higher realms, since there is no anger, there are nine [such imputed afflictions, which, when multiplied by the] four [realities as above, make] two sets of thirty-six. Thus, there is a total of one hundred and twelve [factors to be relinquished through seeing].

As for the factors to be relinquished through familiarization, in the desire realm, they are the six innate afflictions of desire, anger, pride, ignorance, views about a real personality, and views about extremes. In the two higher realms, since anger has been relinquished [already], there are the [remaining] five in each [realm]. Through [these realms'] being classified by the four dhyānas [of the form realm] and the four formless [meditative absorptions], in these eight higher [states, there are] eight [times] five [innate afflictions], which equals forty. Through adding the six of the desire realm, there are forty-six. [Since] each of these is [again] multiplied by nine [degrees, ranging] from the smallest of the small to the largest of the large, it is explained that there are four hundred and fourteen [factors to be relinquished through familiarization in total]. In detail, these should be known from other texts.[745]

2.2.2.3 Explaining discriminating wisdom

This has two parts:

1) [Explaining] what is to be purified and what purifies it
2) Explaining the wisdom that is the result of purification

2.2.2.3.1 Explaining what is to be purified and what purifies it

> **The immediate mind**
> **Is seizing, since it seizes the six [consciousnesses].**
> **[Since] it causes conceptions, it is conception.**
> **It is overcome through perfect prajñā**
> **And the illusionlike samādhi.** [122–126]

The continuum that represents the place of the arising and ceasing of the six collections of consciousness, that is, the locus that causes their arising and ceasing, is called **the immediate mind. Since it** produces and **seizes the six** consciousnesses, it **is** called **seizing.** Since **it** produces **conceptions, it is** also given the name **conception.** In any case, this conception [111] **is overcome through** the **perfect prajñā** of realizing that all phenomena are impermanent, suffering, empty, and identityless, **and** [through] **the samādhi** of knowing that all imaginations of objects and mind are **illusionlike**. Through that, [the immediate mind] becomes discriminating wisdom. As for the meaning of this term, it is the wisdom of unimpededly knowing all phenomena in their entire variety in a distinct, instantaneous, and unmixed way. The *Mahāyānasūtrālaṃkāra* says:

> Discriminating wisdom
> Is always unimpeded toward all knowable objects.[746]

2.2.2.3.2. **Explaining the wisdom that is the result of purification**

> **Through this, when great poised readiness is attained,**
> **The apprehender and its referents change state.**
> **Thus, the change of state of conception,**
> **Which represents the display of pure realms,**
> **Wisdom in all times,**
> **And being unimpeded in all activities,**[747]
> **Is discriminating wisdom.** [127–133]

On the eighth bhūmi, **when great poised readiness** for the dharma of nonarising[748] **is attained,** one attains mastery over nonconceptual wisdom through the change of state of the afflicted mind. The *Mahāyānasūtrālaṃkāra* says:

> In the change of state of mentation,
> Supreme mastery is attained
> Over utterly stainless nonconceptual
> Wisdom ensuing from mastery.[749]

Also, on the eighth bhūmi, **the apprehender and its referents change state. Thus,** through gaining mastery over pure realms, [bodhisattvas] attain the mastery over the **display** of the enjoyments of **pure realms** (such as Sukhāvatī and Abhirati), just as they please, for others to be guided. The *Mahāyānasūtrālaṃkāra* [112] continues:

In the change of state of the apprehender and its referents,
Supreme mastery is attained
Over pure realms in order to display
Enjoyments just as one pleases.

Furthermore, by virtue of the conceptual mental consciousness having changed state on this eighth bhūmi, on the ninth bhūmi, one gains mastery over the unattached and unimpeded operation of **wisdom in all times** (past, present, and future). On the tenth bhūmi, one gains mastery over engaging **in** various enlightened **activities** of guiding whomever in whichever suitable ways, which are **unimpeded** with regard to **all** those to be guided. The *Mahāyānasūtrālaṃkāra* says:

In the change of state of conception,
Supreme mastery is attained
Over wisdom and activities
Unimpeded at all times.

As for all of this arising in a complete way on the three pure bhūmis, the *Mahāyānasūtrālaṃkāra* concludes:

By virtue of the change of mentation, perception,
And conception, there is fourfold command
Over nonconceptuality, [pure] realms,
Wisdom and activity.

It is held that there is fourfold mastery
On the three bhūmis, such as the Immovable—
Two masteries on one [bhūmi]
And one on each of the others.[750]

Such is the manner of **the** final **change of state of conception**, which, on the buddhabhūmi, **is** called "**discriminating wisdom.**"

2.2.2.4. Explaining the [latter] two [wisdoms] as the sambhogakāya

Thus, these two wisdoms,
Through pure cultivation, are the peace
Of not abiding in either existence or peace,
Endowed with love and compassion,

And display all kinds of kāyas and speech for their retinues.
In this way, the maṇḍala of the melody of the great dharma manifests.
This treasury of all samādhis and dhāraṇīs[751]
Is called the "sambhogakāya." [134–141]

[113] **Thus**, as for **these two wisdoms** of equality and discrimination just explained, during the path, they arise from the **pure cultivation** of nonconceptual samādhi and the pure cultivation of the prajñā that does not abide **in either existence or peace**. The nature of the wisdom of equality is to dwell in the state of **the** great **peace of not abiding** in the two extremes. Its aids refer to being **endowed with** great **love and** great **compassion** for all sentient beings at all times. Its function is to **display all kinds of** forms of buddha nirmāṇa**kāyas** for those to be guided precisely in accord with their individual inclinations. The *Mahāyānasūtrālaṃkāra* says:

Said to be endowed at all times
With great love and compassion,
The image of the Buddha displays,
Just as sentient beings aspire.[752]

The nature of discriminating wisdom is to know the entire variety of knowable objects without exception in an unmixed way. Its function is to display riches for the maṇḍalas of retinues, just as they wish, and, in order to sever all doubts, to display the dharma as their **speech**. Therefore, [this wisdom] **manifests the great melody of the dharma** of the mahāyāna, which descends upon **the maṇḍala of retinues**. The *Mahāyānasūtrālaṃkāra* says:

In the maṇḍala of retinues, [114]
It displays all masteries,
Cuts through all doubts,
And rains down the great dharma.[753]

As for the fruition, since one is endowed with immeasurable gates of **samādhis and dhāraṇīs** and also gives rise to them in others, this is like a great **treasury of all** these [samādhis and dhāraṇīs]. The *Mahāyānasūtrālaṃkāra* says:

It is just like a treasury
Of dhāraṇīs and samādhis.[754]

Because the two wisdoms of equality and discrimination are endowed with such qualities, they **are called the "sambhogakāya** of the buddhas." The sambhogakāya is endowed with the five certainties: (1) the certainty of place is to dwell in the pure realm of Richly Adorned Akaniṣṭha, (2) the certainty of retinue is to be accompanied [solely] by bodhisattvas who dwell on the [ten] bhūmis, (3) the certainty of body is to be adorned with the major and minor marks, (4) the certainty of dharma is to teach only the mahāyāna, and (5) the certainty of time is to remain until saṃsāra is emptied.[755] The *Mahāyānasūtrālaṃkāra* says:

> In all the realms, the sambhoga[kāya]
> Differs in terms of attracting retinues,
> [buddha] realms, names, bodies,
> Dharma, enjoyments, and activities.[756]

2.2.2.5. Explaining all-accomplishing wisdom as the nirmāṇakāya

This has two parts:

1) Explaining what is to be purified and what purifies it
2) Explaining the kāyas that are the result of purification

2.2.2.5.1. Explaining what is to be purified and what purifies it

> **As for the five [sense] gates and a part of mentation,**
> **True actuality is seen and realized as reality**
> **Through the sixteen [wisdoms], such as poised readiness for cognition,**
> **Which arise from correct imagination**
> **And entail the aspects of the principles of the four realities.**
> [142–146]

[115] The path of seeing, **which arises from** the **correct imagination** of the path of preparation, relinquishes the consciousnesses of **the five gates** of the sense faculties (such as the eye) **and a part of mentation** (the sixth [consciousness]). [In other words, it relinquishes] the consciousnesses of the five [sense] gates together with the one part [of the mental consciousness] that is outwardly oriented.[757]

As for the path of seeing, each one of all the realities that exist as **the principles of the four realities** (suffering, the origin [of suffering], the cessation [of suffering], and the path) **entails the aspects of** the four wisdoms. [This refers to] fourfold dharma cognition: (1) poised readiness [for dharma cognition], (2) dharma cognition, (3) poised readiness for subsequent cognition, and (4) subsequent cognition. (1) The **poised readiness for** the dharma **cognition** [of suffering] is the uncontaminated wisdom that directly sees the true nature of the reality of suffering and relinquishes the factors to be relinquished through seeing with regard to suffering. ([The words] "**such as**" [in NY] include [the following three wisdoms].) (2) The dharma cognition of suffering is the liberation right after the poised readiness [for dharma cognition], that is, manifesting the cognition that suffering is unarisen. (3) The readiness for the subsequent cognition of suffering is the uncontaminated prajñā that manifests in oneself as [the insight that] the two preceding wisdoms are the causes of the qualities of the noble ones. (4) The subsequent cognition of suffering is the prajñā of [fully] realizing and retaining that preceding readiness for subsequent [cognition]. The same [pattern] applies to [the other] three [realities], such as the origin [of suffering]. **Through the sixteen** wisdoms,[758] [116] the previously unseen **true actuality** of the nature of phenomena **is** directly and freshly **seen and realized as** ultimate **reality**, which becomes all-accomplishing wisdom. As for the meaning of this term, it is the wisdom of spontaneously accomplishing actions for the benefit of sentient beings in infinite worldly realms through all kinds of effortless means.

2.2.2.5.2. Explaining the kāyas that are the result of purification

> **Through this, the five sense faculties change state,**
> **Mastering engagement in all objects**
> **And the twelve hundred qualities of all [bhūmis].**
> **The culmination of such [mastery]**
> **Is all-accomplishing wisdom.**
> **It accomplishes the welfare of all sentient beings**
> **In all realms through various**
> **Immeasurable and inconceivable emanations.**[759]
> **This is the great nirmāṇakāya.** [147–155]

Thus, at the time of realizing reality on the path of seeing and attaining the first bhūmi, the mistakenness of the consciousnesses of **the five sense faculties** (such as the eye) becomes pure and **changes state**. Since each sense faculty engages in each one of the five [sense] objects (forms, sounds, smells, tastes, and tangible objects), each faculty **masters engagement in all objects and** [bodhisattvas master] the beginning of **all** the qualities of the bhūmis—**the twelve hundred qualities** that are present on [the first bhūmi, called] Supreme Joy. On that first bhūmi, one gains mastery over, in one moment:

(1) beholding the faces of a hundred buddhas, (2) listening to the dharma of a hundred buddhas, (3) issuing forth a hundred emanations, (4) displaying them for a hundred eons, (5) one's wisdom engaging in a hundred past and future lifetimes, (6) resting in a hundred samādhis, (7) emerging from these hundred [samādhis], (8) shaking a hundred realms, (9) illuminating a hundred realms with light, (10) opening a hundred gates of dharma, [117] (11) displaying a hundred of one's own bodies, and (12) displaying each of these bodies as being surrounded by a hundred perfect retinues.[760] The *Mahāyānasūtrālaṃkāra* says:

> In the change of state of the five sense faculties,
> Supreme mastery is attained
> Over the perception of all their objects
> And the arising of twelve hundred qualities in all of them.[761]

Furthermore, as an ancillary, one should know that, according to the *Daśabhūmikasūtra*, on the second bhūmi, one gains mastery over a thousand times the above-mentioned twelve qualities, thus beholding the faces of [a thousand] buddhas and so on; on the third bhūmi, [one gains] 1,200,000 [such qualities]; on the fourth bhūmi, 120,000,000; on the fifth bhūmi, 12,000,000,000; on the sixth bhūmi, 120,000,000,000; on the seventh bhūmi, 12,000,000,000,000; on the eighth bhūmi, their number equals twelve times the atoms in a million buddha realms; on the ninth bhūmi, their number equals twelve times the atoms in a million innumerable buddha realms; on the tenth bhūmi, their number equals twelve times the atoms in a hundred million innumerable buddha realms.[762] Through **the culmination of such** mastery, on the buddhabhūmi, it **is** called "**all-accomplishing wisdom**." The function of this wisdom is to **accomplish the welfare of all sentient beings in all** worldly **realms through** the manifestation of **various immeasurable and inconceivable emanations** beyond limit. [118] This is also said in the *Mahāyānasūtrālaṃkāra*:

> All-accomplishing wisdom
> Accomplishes the welfare of all sentient beings
> In all realms through various
> Immeasurable and inconceivable emanations.[763]

From among the three kāyas, **this** all-accomplishing wisdom **is the** great **nirmāṇakāyas**. The nirmāṇakāyas of the buddhas are various kinds of indefinite emanations that promote the welfare of others. They are classified as (1) supreme emanations who display the twelve deeds [of a buddha], such as [Buddha Śākya]muni; (2) artistic emanations, such as the emanation of a skillful singer in order to tame Pramuditā, the king of the gandharvas; and (3) incarnate emanations, such as emanating as a deer. The *Mahāyānasūtrālaṃkāra* says:

> Through artistry, incarnation, and great enlightenment
> And always demonstrating nirvāṇa,
> The nirmāṇakāya of the Buddha
> Is the great means for liberation.[764]

This manner in which the three kāyas derive from the purity of mind, mentation, and consciousness is stated in the *Suvarṇaprabhāsottamasūtra*:

> Through relinquishing the ālaya-consciousness, the dharmakāya is displayed. Through mentation, which rests in it, having become pure, the sambhogakāya is displayed. Through the consciousnesses that engage entities having become pure, the nirmāṇakāya is displayed.

2.2.2.6. Explaining dharmadhātu wisdom as the svābhāvikakāya

This has two parts:

1) The actual explanation [119]
2) Critical analysis of the kāyas

2.2.2.6.1. The actual explanation

> **The three kāyas including their activities,**
> **Which are the changes of state of mind, mentation, and consciousness,**
> **Are perfected as the maṇḍala of the dharmadhātu free from reference points.**
> **That everything in saṃsāra and nirvāṇa without beginning**
> **Abides free from being one or different**[765]
> **Is held to be the svābhāvikakāya.** [156–161]

The three kāyas including their activities are the freedom from stains and **the changes of state** of **mind, mentation** (afflicted mind), **and** the six collections of **consciousness,** [respectively]. They **are perfected** in an inseparable way **as** one in **the maṇḍala of the dhātu** of all **dharmas free from** all **reference points**

of apprehender and apprehended. They cannot be designated as **saṃsāra** or **nirvāṇa.** They are not different in type or actuality, **without beginning** and end, and neither **one nor different.** To **abide free from** all reference points of such kinds of characteristics **is held to be** dharmadhātu wisdom and **the svābhāvikakāya.** The *Mahāyānasūtrālaṃkāra* says:

> In view of different dispositions, in view of uselessness,
> In view of completeness, and in view of no beginning,
> Buddhahood is not single; nor is it multiple,
> Since there is no difference in the stainless ground.[766]

As for the meaning of the term [dharmadhātu] wisdom, it is the completely pure dharmadhātu, which is like a pure sky, free from the clouds of the two obscurations, that is, the locus of the qualities of the noble ones and the wisdoms arising from suchness. A sūtra says:

> The suchness of all phenomena has the characteristic
> Of being endowed with, or being pure of, the two obscurations,
> [respectively]. [120]

2.2.2.6.2. Critical analysis of the kāyas

> **In some other texts, the Victor**
> **Taught this as the "dharmakāya."**
> **In this case, mirrorlike [wisdom] is called the "wisdom kāya,"**
> **And the others, the "two rūpakāyas."** [162–165]

In some other mahāyāna **texts, the** omniscient **Victor taught this** present explanation [of the svābhāvikakāya] **as the "dharmakāya." In this case, mirrorlike** wisdom (as taught above) **is called** the svābhāvikakāya or **the "wisdom kāya," and the** three **other** wisdoms of equality, discrimination, and all-accomplishment are called **the "two rūpakāyas"** (the sambhogakāya and the nirmāṇakāya). In this context, in the general system of the mahāyāna teachings, the kāyas of a buddha are definitely three in number—the dharmakāya as one's own welfare and the two rūpakāyas as the welfare of others. As the *Mahāyānasūtrālaṃkāra* says:

> One should know that the kāyas of the Buddhas
> Consist of the three kāyas.

> Through those three kāyas, the welfares of oneself and others
> Including their foundation are shown.[767]

There are also some texts, in which what is called "svābhāvikakāya" is held to be equivalent to, and a synonym for, the dharmakāya. The *Mahāyānasaṃgraha* states:

> First, the svābhāvikakāya is the dharmakāya of the Tathāgatas, since it is the basis of mastery over all dharmas.[768]

Moreover, in terms of differentiating these two [kāyas] through the isolates of dhātu and wisdom, they are classified as the "svābhāvikakāya" (the buddhadharmas free from the adventitious stains that have to be relinquished within the naturally pure dhātu) [121] and the "dharmakāya of realization" (the twenty-one sets of [uncontaminated] qualities[769] that are realized by it), while their essence comes down to the same. The *Abhisamayālaṃkāra* states:

> Those who have attained purity in every respect
> And the uncontaminated dharmas,
> Theirs is the svābhāvikakāya of the sage,
> Which bears the characteristic of the nature of these.[770]

In brief, since the aspect of twofold purity is classified as the svābhāvikakāya and the aspect of ultimate wisdom as the dharmakāya, they are contained in [the presentation of] the three kāyas. In addition, [one speaks of] the two kāyas, that is, one's own welfare being the ultimate dharmakāya and the welfare of others being the seeming rūpakāyas. [Also,] since there are no other dharmas apart from the all-pervading dharmadhātu, when divided in terms of isolates, [these kāyas] are different, but their essence is indivisible. With this in mind, [the Buddha said in the *Vajracchedikāprajñāpāramitāsūtra*]:

> The buddhas are seen by way of the dharma—
> The guides are dharmakāya indeed.[771]

This means that [all kāyas] are included in the dharmakāya alone. [Thus,] these and many other divisions and summaries [of the kāyas] are taught.

One may wonder whether the three buddhakāyas are one or different. Just as space is indivisible from the nature of space, in the undefiled dhātu, the buddhas are not different. Still, since buddhas arise from the preceding practice of bodhisattva conduct of each individual sentient being [who is to become a buddha], they are not one either. [122] The *Mahāyānasūtrālaṃkāra* says:

> In the undefiled dhātu,
> Buddhas are neither one nor many,
> Since they have no body, just like space,
> And yet accord with their previous bodies.[772]

Nevertheless, there also appears the explanation that the dharmakāyas and sambhogakāyas of [all] buddhas are one, but that the manners of promoting the welfare of beings through their nirmāṇakāyas are different, since [these manners] follow their former aspiration prayers. The enlightened activities of body, speech, and mind of the three buddhakāyas operate spontaneously in an inconceivable, effortless, and nonconceptual way, and in accordance with the thinking of those to be guided for as long as there are worldly realms. Even if infinite orbs of suns were to appear, the function of all of them is to dry up swamps, eliminate darkness, and ripen seedlings. Likewise, the enlightened activities of all buddhas dry up the swamp of saṃsāra, eliminate the darkness of ignorance, and ripen the seedlings of enlightenment. Therefore, the enlightened activities of all buddhas operate as one. When the time to guide those to be guided has come, the enlightened activities of the buddhas never fail to be timely, and these activities take place in a way of guiding whomever [is to be guided] by whatever [means suitable]. Though the enlightened activities of buddhas benefit infinite sentient beings, they are inexhaustible, and the extent of their actions of body, speech, and mind equals the sky, [123] manifesting uninterruptedly until saṃsāra is emptied. The extensive manner of their [enlightened activities] should be known from the *Mahāyānasūtrālaṃkāra*, the *Uttaratantra*, and other [texts].[773]

2.3. Summary of the meaning of [consciousness and wisdom]

> **Buddhahood is the manifestation of the nature**
> **Of the five wisdoms and the four kāyas.**
> **The ālaya is what possesses the stains**
> **Of mind, mentation, and consciousness.**
> **Its stainlessness is called the Heart of the victors.**
> **What overcomes impure imagination**
> **Is pure imagination, from which**
> **The power of the prajñā of the noble ones arises—**
> **Seizing it is taught to be the reality of the path.** [166–174]

To summarize the meaning of the above explanations, once all sentient beings are free from what is imaginary (all the adventitious stains of the mistakenness of apprehender and apprehended), they **manifest** as **the** unchanging **nature of the** primordially and naturally present **five wisdoms and the four kāyas**. This **is** called "**buddhahood**." The *[Hevajra]tantra* says:

Sentient beings are buddhas indeed.
However, they are obscured by adventitious stains.
If these are removed, they are buddhas.[774]

Noble Nāgārjuna's [*Dharmadhātustava*] says:

Due to just that being purified
What is such circling's cause,
This very purity is then nirvāṇa.
Likewise, dharmakāya is just this.[775]

The ālaya is what possesses the stains of mind, afflicted **mentation, and** the six collections of **consciousness**, [all of] which appear as apprehender and apprehended. It is the root of mistakenness, called "ālaya with stains" or "ālaya-consciousness." While possessing the stains of these eight collections [of consciousness], its own nature abides as the nature of **stainlessness**, which [124] **is** called **the Heart of the victors** (the buddhas), and is present in an unchanging way during all the phases of ground, path, and fruition.[776] The *Uttaratantra* says:

Since it is associated with flaws that are adventitious
And endowed with qualities that are its very nature,
It is the same before as after.
This is the changeless nature of phenomena.[777]

What obscures this buddha heart is impure imagination. Noble Nāgārjuna's [*Dharmadhātustava*] says:

Spotless are the sun and moon,
But obscured by fivefold stains:
These are clouds and smoke and mist,
Rahu's face and dust as well.

Similarly, mind so luminous
Is obscured by fivefold stains.
They're desire, malice, laziness,
Agitation and doubt too.[778]

The victor Maitreya states [in his *Uttaratantra*]:

Hostility toward the dharma, views about a self,
Fear of saṃsāra's suffering,
And not considering the welfare of sentient beings—
These are the four obscurations

Of those with great desire, tīrthikas,
Śrāvakas, and pratyekabuddhas.[779]

As for the remedies **that overcome** these four types of obscuring **impure imagination** in the mind streams of these four (worldly beings, tīrthikas, śrāvakas, and pratyekabuddhas), [the *Uttaratantra*] says:

The causes of purification are the four properties
Of aspiring and so forth.[780]

[125] Accordingly, [through] the seed of aspiration for, and confidence in, the mahāyāna, as well as through the [motherlike] prajñā that realizes identitylessness, **which arises from pure** correct **imagination**, one comes to be endowed with womb[like blissful] dhyānas and samādhis as well as compassion, which is like a nurturing nanny. Consequently, one becomes a child of the victors who has entered the path and is gradually **seizing the power of the prajñā of the noble ones** more and more, which **is taught to be the reality of the path.**

In this context, [Rangjung Dorje] holds, "What arises from correct imagination is the object of the noble ones—the power of prajñā. What bears the meaning of seizing this very [power] is taught to be the reality of the path." Accordingly, the position of the omniscient [Fifth Shamarpa,] Göncho Yenla, is to explain that the term "dharma," in addition to applying to nine [other] meanings, [also] has the sense of seizing everything. Due to that, here, [it means that], when applying oneself to the dharma of the path, one is seized through the path of the mahāyāna so as to not fall into the two extremes. Alternatively, what is found in the stream of the guiding instructions of the mighty learned masters is as follows. On the path of accumulation, by virtue of engagement through aspiration, there is the seizing of something to be relinquished; on the path of preparation, there is the seizing of remedies; on the impure bhūmis, there is the seizing of the nonduality of what is to be relinquished and remedy; and on the three pure bhūmis, there is the seizing of the result of buddhahood. Therefore, these are taught to be the reality of the path.

To summarize the meaning of these [points], the nature of phenomena (the Sugata heart's) being obscured by the adventitious stains of mistakenness (the triad of mind, mentation, and consciousness) [126] is a "sentient being." Making efforts through purifying these stains through their remedies is called "a person who has entered the path." Being completely liberated from the cocoon of stains, that is, the manifestation of the primordially present kāyas and wisdoms, is a "buddha." As the *Uttaratantra* says:

> [Its] being impure, both impure and pure,
> And completely pure, in due order,
> Are expressed as sentient beings,
> Bodhisattvas, and buddhas.[781]

3. Conclusion

This has three parts:

1) Purpose of explaining this text
2) Aspiration for realizing it
3) Stating how the text was composed

3.1. Purpose of explaining this text

> **Because they do not realize the way of being of the ultimate,**
> **The oblivious roam the ocean of saṃsāra.**
> **They will not reach the other shore through anything**
> **Except for this ship of the mahāyāna.** [175–178]

Childish beings who are obscured by the adventitious stains of mistakenness, ordinary beings, and those who have entered the hīnayāna **do not realize the way of being of the ultimate** basic state that is clearly taught in the texts of the profound and vast mahāyāna—the nature of consciousness (the phenomena of saṃsāra) and of wisdom (nirvāṇa). **Because** of that, **those** who are **oblivious** by virtue of the obscurations of ignorance (such as clinging to me and mine), driven fiercely by the wind of karma, helplessly **roam the** great **ocean of** the suffering of **saṃsāra** since beginningless [time]. [127] Those who possess the insight to desire liberation from this [misery] rely on **this** great **ship of the mahāyāna**, which is superior to the hīnayāna through the seven greatnesses.[782] **Except for** that, can **they reach the other shore** of that ocean of suffering **through any** other means? They can**not** reach it! Therefore, for those who desire to attain the great nonabiding nirvāṇa, nothing but the realization of this mahāyāna principle [of the nature of consciousness and wisdom] is important. As the *[Prajñāpāramitā]saṃcayagāthā* says:

> Whoever mounts it leads all sentient beings to nirvāṇa—
> This yāna is like space, a greatly immense palace.
> It is the supreme yāna for attaining delight, ease, and happiness.[783]

3.2. Aspiration for realizing it

> **May all realize this true actuality!** [179]

[Sentient beings] are, in general, those who have been our fathers and mothers from beginningless [time], and, in particular, the fortunate ones to be guided. **May all** [of them], first, through the prajñā of studying, understand **this** dharma principle which embodies the heart of the mahāyāna (the distinction between consciousness and wisdom); in the middle, experience it through contemplation; and at the end, **realize** the natural state, just as it is, through meditation. May they truly attain the great enlightenment of not abiding in the extremes of saṃsāra and nirvāṇa!

3.3. Stating how the text was composed

> **This *Treatise on the Distinction between Consciousness and Wisdom* was composed by Rangjung Dorje in the mountain retreat of Upper Dechen on the first day of the tenth month in the year of the pig** [1335 CE].

The basis of the arising of the phenomena of saṃsāra that entails mistakenness [128] consists of the eight collections of **consciousness**, which exist in sentient beings. The nature of nirvāṇa that is free from mistakenness is the principle of **wisdom**, which appears in buddhas. **The distinction between** [these two] lies in **this** stainless **treatise** that clarifies this meaning properly. It **was** excellently **composed by** the vajra (**Dorje**) of emptiness (prajñā), self-arisen (**Rangjung**) from nonreferential compassion (the means), who liberates [beings] from all the shackles of existence and peace. [This was accomplished]

in the mountain retreat free from hustle and bustle, called **Upper Dechen**, in Tsurphu (Kecarī, the [maṇḍala] wheel of enlightened mind),[784] **on the** auspicious **first day of the tenth month in the** [first] **year of the pig** within the sixth [Tibetan] sixty-year cycle [1335 CE]. [It was written] in a manner of summarizing the meaning so that it may be understood easily.

For this text, we have [a number of commentarial materials], such as its outline by Venerable Rangjung [Dorje]; an extensive commentary by his spiritual son, Sherab Rinchen;[785] notes by the Fifth Shamarpa that summarize the meaning; and an interlinear commentary by the powerful learned one, Lhalungpa,[786] which is [the result of] his own independent analysis. However, cherishing the very words of the victor, Rangjung [Dorje],[787] I wrote a small commentary that is easy to understand and clear in meaning, without elaborating a detailed explanation.

From among all the words of the buddha, the most marvelous,
The innermost quintessence of the mahāyāna,
Few in words but vast in meaning,
Was illuminated by the second victor.

Since its meaning is profound and vast,
My mind cannot fathom it, just as it is.
[With] the eye of insight that sees just a fraction,
I wrote [this down], so that others of equal fortune may attain
[this Heart]. [129]

Liberated from the cocoon of mistaken consciousness
The radiance of wisdoms and kāyas spreads.
Through everlasting and [all-]pervasive enlightened activity,
May the welfare of beings, whose number equals the sky, be
accomplished.

Up to this day, the reading transmissions for the one major and the two minor texts[788] of Venerable Rangjung [Dorje] as well as the continuity of explanations on these source texts have remained in an uninterrupted way. Therefore, with my mind set only on being of service to the excellent speech of the second omniscient victor, and not for the sake of competing through the ambition to be a famous scholar, but motivated by the superior intention of thinking, "Wouldn't it be good if this pure lineage doesn't become interrupted?" I, Karma Ngawang Yönten Gyatso, alias Lodrö Tayé, a reflection of someone erudite and trained in virtue, composed this in Palpung's most secluded place, Künsang Déchen Ösel Ling.[789]

May virtue increase!

Karma Trinlépa's Explanation of the Sugata Heart[790]

The glorious guru Rangjung Dorje holds that the Sugata heart is the nature of dhātu and wisdom being inseparable, just ordinary mind, which is free from being real or delusive, like [a reflection of] the moon in water, and beyond identification and characteristics. For, *The Treatise Called Pointing Out the Tathāgata Heart*, composed by this lord, says:

> All is neither real nor delusive—
> Held to be like [a reflection of] the moon in water by the learned.
> Just this ordinary mind
> Is called "dharmadhātu" and "Heart of the victors."[791]

Here, "dhātu" refers to the naturally luminous dharmadhātu. Therefore, the meaning of "dharmadhātu" is understood as follows. Since both saṃsāra and nirvāṇa are not really established as something different from their own side, the entirety of what appears as dualistic phenomena, such as saṃsāra and nirvāṇa, factors to be relinquished and remedies, apprehender and apprehended, or objects of expression and means of expression, is of equal taste with the essence of nonduality, the great primordial indestructible sphere.[792] This is called "dharmadhātu," which is stated in the commentary on the *Dharmadhātustava* composed by this lord [Rangjung Dorje]:

> As for dharmas, there are the two modes of being of factors to be relinquished and remedies. As for the dhātu of these, it is the suchness that cannot be analyzed as something different and in which there is no distinction between apprehender and apprehended, or objects of expression and means of expression. What is this nature is the essence of buddhahood.[793]

This passage appears based on its scriptural source, which is the following statement in the *Dharmadharmatāvibhāga*:

> The defining characteristic of the nature of phenomena is suchness, which is without a difference between apprehender and apprehended, or objects of designation and what designates them.[794]

As for the meaning of "natural luminosity," I have already explained elsewhere that nature, essence, actual mode of being, and so on are synonyms. "Luminosity" is [the dharmadhātu's] own light, which is beyond identification and characteristics. Therefore, the gist of this is that, within this actual mode of being [of mind's nature], various creative displays of its own unimpeded radiance appear, but that this is free from [all] reference points of being "this" and not "that." The [term] "dhātu" in "the nature of dhātu and wisdom being inseparable" has already been explained [above]. As for "wisdom," since [the Sanskrit word] *jñāna* refers to wisdom, consciousness, and realization, in this context, the meaning of wisdom is understood as personally experienced awareness. Therefore, it is expressed as wisdom in terms of lucidity, illumination, and awareness. Thus, the meaning of "the nature of dhātu and wisdom being inseparable" is understood as the personally experienced awareness of [mind] being profound and lucid in a nondual way. As the *Commentary on the Two-Part [Hevajratantra]* composed by this lord [Rangjung Dorje] says:

> As for wisdom, all phenomena are mind, mind is self-awareness, self-awareness is bliss, and bliss is freedom from reference points. If sealed in this way, there are the threefold sealing, the threefold consolation, and the four kāyas. This is the wisdom that realizes the true reality of entities.

and

> When all phenomena are realized to be the mind's manifestations,[795] thoughts about outer referents are relinquished. When the mind is realized to be self-awareness, thoughts about red and white are relinquished. When self-awareness is realized to be bliss, thoughts of suffering and indifference are relinquished. When bliss is realized as freedom from reference points, thoughts of clinging to entities are relinquished.

The meaning of "free from being real or delusive, like [a reflection of] the moon in water, and beyond identification and characteristics" is easy to understand.

"Ordinary mind" is natural consciousness—this very present [moment of] mind unaltered by contrivance, scheming, and so on. . . . Though this [buddha] heart is neither confined nor biased, its remedial side may well be expressed through the term "virtue." From [the state of] sentient beings up through buddhahood, it lacks any distinctions of good and bad, and is beyond conventional terms, speech, and expression, but it represents a continuous stream since [time] without beginning. Its essence is unchanging, and it bears the nature of being a cause, but [at the same time] it abounds with many qualities. Though ground and fruition are inseparable, it appears as being pure or impure, respectively.

Now, to explain the meaning of this a bit further, the essence of dhātu and wisdom being inseparable lacks any confinement (such as permanence or extinction) and bias (such as factors to be relinquished and remedies). Therefore, it is established as the all-pervading sovereign. For, [Rangjung Dorje's] text says:

> The cause is beginningless mind as such.
> Though it is neither confined nor biased, . . .

It is referred to as "virtue," because it is beyond the characteristics of nonvirtue. But since it is not of the nature of karma, it is not a [real] entity that is virtuous. It is said to be the remedy that purifies the ālaya-consciousness, because it is the seed of the dharmakāya of all buddhas. Though it pervades all mundane states, it is the outflow of the pure dharmadhātu. Therefore, it is asserted that it has the nature of being the cause for realizing the dharmas of the noble ones. The *Mahāyānasaṃgraha*, which is quoted in [Rangjung Dorje's] autocommentary, says:

> The small, medium, and great latent tendencies for listening are to be regarded as the seeds of the dharmakāya. Since they are the remedy for the ālaya-consciousness, they are not of the nature of the ālaya-consciousness. [In the sense of being a remedy,] they are something mundane, but since they are the natural outflow of the supramundane—the utterly pure dharmadhātu—they are the seeds of supramundane mind.[796]

Though these [seeds] have not become manifest [in sentient beings], just as they are, through merely focusing on them, saṃsāra is relinquished and they are united with enlightenment. [The *Mahāyānasaṃgraha* continues:]

> Although this supramundane mind has not originated yet, they are the remedy for being entangled [in saṃsāra] through the afflictions, the remedy for migrating in the lower realms, and the remedy that makes all wrongdoing vanish. They are what is in complete concordance with meeting buddhas and bodhisattvas.

The *Ratnāvalī* says:

> In those of little merit, not even doubt
> About this dharma arises.
> Even the arising of doubt about this,
> Will tear [saṃsāric] existence into shreds.[797]

Since the essence of naturally luminous mind as such—the dharmadhātu—is emptiness, it is unchanging throughout all states. Therefore, the ground (the suchness of sentient beings), the path (the suchness of bodhisattvas), and the fruition (the suchness of buddhas) cannot be divided as different things by virtue of being better or worse, higher or lower, and so on. As *Pointing Out the [Tathāgata] Heart* says:

> It is neither to be improved by the noble ones
> Nor made worse by sentient beings.[798]

As for realizing this, just as it is, it is solely an object of buddha wisdom—it is inconceivable even for bodhisattvas on the ten bhūmis. Therefore, it is beyond terms and thinking, and though it may be expressed through many words and conventional terms, it is inexpressible. The [same] text says:

> It may no doubt be expressed through many conventional terms,
> But its actual reality is not understood through expressions.[799]

Before this natural purity, there are absolutely no buddhas or sentient beings who did not arise from it. Since it is not established as any real substance and is of the nature of dependent origination, there is no beginning in terms of a first arising or in terms of any real substance. The [text] says:

> Here, "beginningless" [means that]
> There is absolutely nothing before that.[800]

In the basic element (the Sugata heart), there is no other creator of previously nonexistent new buddha qualities, but it primordially abides in a way of being inseparable from all these qualities, thus bearing the defining characteristic of its essence not changing into anything else. Therefore, it is presented in the sense of basic element or cause. The [text] says:

> The basic element is without creator,
> But since it bears its own characteristic, it is called that way.[801]

Within the creative display of the unimpeded radiance of this [buddha] heart, being indivisible [from it], there dwell the tens of millions times sixty-four inseparable qualities (summarized as [the qualities of] freedom and maturation). The [text] says:

> As for the unimpeded play of this,
> The sixty-four qualities
> Are a coarse [classification]—each one
> Is said to [consist of] tens of millions.[802]

The dharmas that are these qualities are called "stainless qualities" at the time of buddhahood, and "stained qualities" during the phase of sentient beings. The [text] says:

> Therefore, nāḍīs, vāyus, and tilakas,
> When pure, are the pure rūpakāyas.
> Unpurified, they are the impure rūpakāyas.[803]

Throughout, the autocommentary also says many times that [these qualities] are obscured during the phase of sentient beings and unobscured during the phase of buddhas.

Once this naturally pure ground is purified through being skilled in the means to purify the stains, at the time of being liberated from characteristics, the samādhi of the dharmakāya that pervades [all of] space is manifested. Thus, while not moving away from this spacelike kāya that is free from being identifiable, the welfare of beings is spontaneously promoted through the rūpakāyas, which are ornamented with the major and minor marks. Therefore, the phase of its not being pure of even a fraction of stains is [called] "sentient being." The phase of just some parts of these stains having become pure, but not all of them without exception, though one is in the process of purifying them, is [called] "bodhisattva." The phase of [these stains] having become utterly pure is called "buddhahood." The [text] says:

> At that point, in those who have the kāya of space,
> The flowers of the major marks will blossom.
> Impure, impure and pure,
> And utterly pure, in due order,
> Are expressed as the three phases
> Of sentient beings, bodhisattvas, and Tathāgatas.[804]

When this buddha heart is enveloped by the cocoon of ignorance, from the perspective of being a cause, it is called "disposition," which is twofold—the naturally abiding disposition and the unfolding disposition. The first is naturally pure mind as such, inseparable from the sixty-four buddha qualities, that is, the dharmadhātu whose nature is luminous emptiness. Though its essence is indifferentiable, [the *Abhisamayālaṃkāra*] states:

> But by virtue of the divisions of the phenomena founded on it,
> Its divisions are expressed.[805]

Accordingly, the classification of noble persons (śrāvakas, pratyekabuddhas, and bodhisattvas) is made by virtue of the gradual process of how, right within the disposition (which is the cause for [itself] becoming pure of stains), [certain] parts of its complete purity are realized. Though naturally pure mind is not tainted by the stains of consciousness, the presentation of eight consciousnesses is given by individually distinguishing them through false imagination.

The second [disposition] is the stainless own essence of the eight collections of consciousness, which abides as the nature of the four wisdoms and is inseparable from naturally luminous mind as such (the dharmadhātu, emptiness), because this is the disposition that is the cause for unfolding the two rūpakāyas. This means that, through accomplishing the immaculate dharmas, the stains of not recognizing the eight consciousnesses' own essence are overcome, due to which all eight collections are liberated as self-awareness. Once this happens, it is designated by the expression, "the eight collections of consciousness have changed state into the four wisdoms." As an appearance for others, these [wisdoms] appear as the rūpakāyas. In brief, these two dispositions are [just] the divisions of their unity. Lord Daö Shönnu says:

> Connate mind as such is the dharmakāya.
> Connate appearances are the light of the dharmakāya.

Accordingly, the unborn fundamental nature of mind as such with stains is the naturally abiding disposition, and its unimpeded radiance is the unfolding disposition. Therefore, this is called the "stained unity of the two kāyas." Completely pure of stains, the unborn fundamental nature of mind as such appears as the dharmakāya (one's own welfare) and its unimpeded radiance as the rūpakāyas (the welfare of others). Therefore, this is expressed as the "stainfree unity of the two kāyas." For, the autocommentary says:

> Some may think that the unfolding disposition arises newly, but this is not the case. To present the naturally abiding disposition—the dharmadhātu—as the eight consciousnesses, such as the ālaya-consciousness, is a presentation and classification in terms of false imagination. Likewise, [the unfolding disposition]—the very own stainless essence of these eight collections [of consciousness]—exists as the nature of the four wisdoms, which is the presentation in terms of correct imagination. By virtue of previous stains having been overcome through the immaculate dharmas that are grounded in buddha enlightenment, the mistakenness of the eight collections does not exist [anymore later]. Therefore, this is coined as the phrase "the wisdom of the fundamental change of state." For this reason, the *Madhyāntavibhāga* says:
>
> > Purity is asserted to be like the purity
> > Of the element of water, gold, and space.[806]
>
> Accordingly, [mind] without stains should be regarded as being wisdom and [mind] with stains to be consciousness.[807]

Also Lord Rölbé Dorje states:

> The light rays of this Heart
> Exist as what is called "the unfolding disposition."

and

> It is held that these four [wisdoms] are the nature
> With stains and the unfolding disposition,

> And that these two [dispositions]
> Dwell in all beings primordially.

Now, [certain] qualms shall be eliminated. Some say, "Mind[808] is presented from the perspective of its being lucid and aware of objects. Matter, mind, and nonassociated formations are all three subdivisions of conditioned phenomena. Mind is what evaluates its specific objects to be evaluated. For all these reasons, ordinary mind is not the Sugata heart, because this Heart is explained to be unconditioned and spontaneously present." It is established through scripture that there is a common locus between awareness and the basic element, since the *Uttaratantra* says:

> The great sage with his omniscient eye,
> Seeing this honeylike basic element of awareness, . . .[809]

and

> Likewise, this honeylike uncontaminated consciousness that exists in living creatures . . .[810]

This basic element of awareness is not produced by a cause in the beginning, not established as any nature whatsoever in the middle, and not changed through any condition in the end. Therefore, it is unconditioned, since [the *Uttaratantra*] says [on buddhahood:]

> It is unconditioned, since its nature
> Is to be without beginning, middle, or end.[811]

Furthermore, do you people assert buddha wisdom to be conditioned, or do you assert that it is not lucid and aware of objects? In the first case, you claim that the dharmakāya is conditioned, which is the talk of those who have not learned the terms of the definitive meaning. In the second case, omniscient wisdom is deprecated. Also, the statement "Matter, mind, and nonassociated formations are subdivisions of conditioned phenomena" just means to follow the talk of the proponents of [real] entities, but you would have to come up with a source within the scriptures of definitive meaning, such as the vajrayāna, that explains things in this way. Saying, "[Mind] is conditioned, because it evaluates its specific objects to be evaluated" means to be ignorant about the connection between the reason and the subject—completely perfect buddhahood directly knows all phenomena, but it is not asserted to be conditioned.

Some people came up with the conventional term "conditioned naturally abiding disposition" for this naturally luminous mind. But "naturally abiding" and "being conditioned by causes and conditions" are nothing but contradictory. Therefore, a naturally abiding disposition that entails arising and ceasing is an object of ridicule. Some others say, "The dhātu is unconditioned, but wisdom is conditioned, so a nature of these two being inseparable is impossible." In that case, they should be asked whether they assert that primordial wisdom and connate wisdom are conditioned too. Yet others say, "If this Heart had the sixty-four qualities from the very beginning, the qualities of perfect buddhahood would exist in the mind streams of sentient beings, and in that case, does the buddha wisdom in the mind stream of a hell being experience the sufferings of hell?" Such is indeed said, but it is precisely for this reason that we speak about [wisdom or luminous mind] by making the distinction that it is stained during the phase of sentient beings and stainless in the state of a buddha. In other words, perfect buddhahood and its powers and so on do not exist in the mind streams of sentient beings. This is definitely how it is, but it will be understood through saying again and again, "*Stained* buddhahood and its powers and so on exist [in their mind streams]."

Again, some say, "The naturally abiding disposition being a continuous stream since beginningless [time] is the intention of all the words [of the buddha]. Therefore, it is tenable, but this statement that the unfolding disposition is not newly arisen is not something one should listen to. If you wonder why, it is because this [disposition] is explained as the new accomplishment of roots of virtue, as in [*Uttaratantra* I.149c] 'the supreme of what is accomplished.' Furthermore, if the fact that the unfolding disposition abides as a continuum since beginningless [time] applies to all sentient beings, how could [the following verse in] the *Mahāyānasūtrālaṃkāra* be adduced:

> Some are solely devoted to wrongdoing,
> Some have completely destroyed the immaculate dharmas,
> Some lack the virtue conducive to liberation,
> Some have inferior immaculate [dharmas], and [some] lack the cause."[812]

Therefore, this shall be explained a bit. In a treasure below the earth, the qualities of all one may wish or need exist right from the start. Likewise, the naturally abiding disposition is the naturally luminous dharmadhātu (mind as such), in which all buddha qualities dwell primordially in an inseparable way. Its having become pure of stains is called "having attained one's own welfare, the dharmakāya." From the very time of the fruit of a palm tree or a mango fruit dwelling inside their respective skins, they have the disposition that is the cause for the unfolding of the leaves of a palm tree and the core of a mango, which will then [actually] unfold through [additional conditions,] such as water, manure, warmth, and moisture. Likewise, the unfolding disposition is the essence of the eight collections [of consciousness], which abides as the nature of the four wisdoms and is inseparable from naturally luminous mind as such, the empty dharmadhātu. Through accomplishing the roots of virtue, it seems as if it increases and then enlightened activity unfolds. This is called "having attained the welfare of others, the two rūpakāyas," since the *Mahāyānottaratantra* says:

> Like a treasure and a fruit tree,
> The disposition is to be known as twofold—
> Naturally abiding without beginning
> And the supreme of what is accomplished.
>
> It is held that the three buddhakāyas
> Are attained by virtue of these two dispositions—
> The first kāya through the first one,
> And the latter two through the second one.[813]

Therefore, though the naturally abiding disposition exists right from the beginning, without its essence ever changing, the dharmakāya will be attained through purifying the stains. Likewise, also the unfolding disposition exists indeed right from the beginning, but through accomplishing the roots of virtue, the supreme of enlightened activities—the twofold rūpakāya—will unfold. This is why [the *Uttaratantra*] speaks of "the supreme of what is accomplished."

In brief, from the perspective of its looking as if enlightened activity unfolds through accomplishing the roots of virtue, [the Buddha] spoke of "the unfolding disposition." However, the accomplishing of the roots of virtue itself is not the unfolding disposition. The equivalent [Sanskrit] term for "disposition" is "dhātu,"[814] which refers to disposition, basic element, cause, nature, expanse, and so on. Therefore, since the accomplishing of the roots of virtue itself is not this expanse (dhātu), it is not the unfolding expanse. But if [some people] assert that the accomplishing of the roots of virtue is the unfolding disposition, then, by the same token, it would follow that the gathering of the accumulation of wisdom is the naturally abiding disposition. If they accept this, they thereby also claim a common locus between the naturally abiding disposition and the unfolding disposition. Consequently, they cannot steer clear of the three circles.[815] Also, in the context of the nine examples and their nine meanings [in the *Uttaratantra*], what is taught in the example of a fruit is the unfolding disposition:

> Just as seeds and sprouts that exist in fruits, such as mangos and palm fruits,
> And have this indestructible property [of growing into a tree],
> Through coming together with ploughed earth, water and so on,
> Gradually become the entity of a majestic tree, . . .[816]

Here, one needs to examine [and thus understand] that the seed of a palm tree and the unfolding disposition are correlated as being the example and its meaning. In terms of being correlated as example and meaning, the same goes for [the seed's] unfolding through ploughed earth, water, and so on, and the unfolding of enlightened activity through accomplishing the roots of virtue. With this meaning in mind, the *Dharmadhātustava* says that confidence and so forth are what unfold the basic element, but it does not say that these are the actual basic element.[817] The intention of this must be understood. Also the *Mahāyānasūtrālaṃkāra* does not speak about a cut-off unfolding disposition, since it is not a text of the Vijñapti[vādins]. Therefore, having in mind that [some beings] may temporarily lack the conditions that awaken the unfolding disposition, [this text] says [above], "Some lack the virtue conducive to liberation." Having in mind that [some] may lack the conditions that awaken the naturally abiding disposition, it says, "Some have inferior immaculate [dharmas]." Thus, the claim of a common locus between the disposition and what is conditioned at the time of the ground, as well as the claim of a common locus between buddhahood and what is conditioned at the time of the fruition should be known to arise from the eyes that look at the definitive meaning by being blinded through the blurred vision of clinging to dialectics.

Appendix I: Pawo Tsugla Trengwa's Presentation of Kāyas, Wisdoms, and Enlightened Activity

The Nature of Buddhahood[818]

By virtue of having relinquished the two obscurations including their latent tendencies and having mastered the four wisdoms, the kāya that is not different from the dharmadhātu is perfect buddhahood for the following reasons. If the two obscurations including their latencies have not been relinquished, [the dharmadhātu] is not established as buddhahood. The four wisdoms have the nature of the three kāyas. What is primordially present as the nature of the dharmadhātu is fully realized as the dharmadhātu, just as it is, just as the space within a vase and the space outside are not different, when this vase has been destroyed. The *Uttaratantra* says:

> Buddhahood is indivisible,
> Yet consists of pure dharmas—
> The two characteristics of wisdom and relinquishment,
> Which are similar to the sun and space.[819]

In addition, also the lineage of profound view presents both [aspects of] purification (*sangs*) and unfolding (*rgyas*). [684] As for relinquishment, it means having relinquished the afflictive obscurations and the cognitive obscurations. On this, the scriptures [of the lineage] of vast activity say:

> Conceptions in terms of the three spheres
> Are asserted as the cognitive obscurations.
> Conceptions such as miserliness
> Are asserted as the afflictive obscurations.[820]

In the scriptures [of the lineage] of profound view, the factor of being ignorant about knowable objects is explained as the cognitive obscurations, and the obscurations of meditative absorption that function as obstacles to certain samādhis are included in the two obscurations as appropriate. The manifest forms of these two [obscurations] are relinquished on the paths and bhūmis, and, finally, their most subtle latencies are eradicated through the vajralike samādhi, so that they do not rise [again]. This is excellent relinquishment. When one has arrived at this culmination of having relinquished everything that was to be relinquished, everything to be realized is fully known. This is [simply] the nature of phenomena, because knowing is well known as the opposite of not knowing (or ignorance) even in the world. Thus, the culmination of unmistakenly knowing all ultimate and seeming phenomena (suchness and variety, [respectively]) is excellent realization, which has the character of the four wisdoms. Since both this relinquishment and this realization are inseparable as the nature of the dharmadhātu itself, they are beyond being objects of speech, thought, and expression—they are indeed not even objects seen by the Tathāgatas. Nevertheless, they are endowed with the function of all beings being benefited and becoming happy through the effortless enlightened activity of body and speech, which equals space [in its extent] and is uninterrupted. This is expressed by the conventional term "perfect buddhahood."

Even when a precious gem is covered by layers of dross, the gem does not mix with these layers and exists as the source of all qualities. Still, until these layers are purified, the shine and the qualities [of this gem] are not clearly manifest. Once the layers have been purified, its shine dispels darkness and all that is needed and desired arises. [685] Likewise, even at the time when the gem of mind appears to be associated with the layers of obscurations, its nature is not tainted by these obscurations. This aspect is relinquishment—the naturally abiding disposition. Just as the qualities of this gem, the power of all qualities (such as the ten powers) being suitable to arise is primordially spontaneously present, which is like the power of the arising of countless fruits existing in a single seed or grain. This aspect is realization—the unfolding disposition. This inseparable presence of the two dispositions is purified through the path, which resembles the three [steps of] washing and the three [steps of] polishing [an encrusted gem]).[821] Through this, the culmination of relinquishment and realization is manifested.

As for all phenomena always abiding as nothing but the dharmadhātu (which is unconditioned like space), this is just like the space within a vase and the space outside not being different, even when the vase has not been destroyed. Once the vase has been destroyed, the indivisibility of this inner and outer space becomes manifest as this very indivisibility. Likewise, the nature of the mind, which is primordially present as the dharmadhātu, resembles the space within the vase. Similar to the indivisibility of inner and outer space [becoming manifest], once the vase has been destroyed, when the vaselike stream of formational conceptions and mind has come to an end, the nondifference of this dharmadhātu is manifested. Just as the extent of space [cannot] be gauged by anybody, the nature of the Tathāgata cannot be conceived by anybody. Just as space provides room for all entities, [the Tathāgata] serves as the support of all sentient beings. Just as space appears in [all entities], from a trichiliocosm down to the husks of a mustard seed, in a respectively matching extent, [the Tathāgata] appears for all those to be guided as [respectively suitable] kāyas that guide them. However, just as all these spaces cannot be designated as one or different, all buddhakāyas [686] cannot be designated as one or different either. Though a single person who is endowed with a Tathāgata's miraculous manner of moving may move only in the east with as many [physical appearances] as there are atoms in all eons and realms, one still cannot say that [this person] has moved through this many fractions of just the eastern space, while that many were left behind as [untraversed] remainders [of this space]. Likewise, each single part of [all] the qualities of a Tathāgata is as vast as space.

As for the layers of obscurations, just as strands of hair may appear to those with blurred vision, they never existed through a nature of their own, but are nothing but appearances from the perspective of mistakenness, because [assumptions] such as something previously existing ceasing later and something previously nonexisting arising later are taught as the views of permanence and extinction. Therefore, all phenomena are not different in that their not being present as any forms of superimposition or denial (such as existence and nonexistence) whatsoever cannot be altered by anybody, be it at the time of being or not being a buddha. However, to engage in superimposition and denial by virtue of not realizing this is "the state of saṃsāra," while understanding this fact for what it is is indeed labeled by the conventional expression "the attainment of buddhahood." However, in this ["attainment"], there is nothing that is real as any conditioned or unconditioned substance or entity that is attained, nor is there anybody or anything that is an attainer and so on. Therefore, it is the mere exhaustion of error that is taught to be liberation. The sūtras say that, if a person wishes to search for space or be liberated from space, they will neither find nor be liberated from space. Similarly, all phenomena being not other than the dharmadhātu is just like that.

Therefore, the attainment of buddhahood is also referred to as, "attaining nothing whatsoever," or "attaining the supreme among [all] states"; "all phenomena being completely and perfectly realized in all aspects," [687] or "realization is a mere name, no phenomenon has been realized, is realized, or will be realized"; "having gone beyond all phenomena," or "not having moved away in the slightest from any phenomenon"; "being empty in not being established as anything whatosever," or "the permanent, enduring, immutable, and eternal kāya"; "not seeing any phenomena whatsoever as anything whatsoever at any time," or "knowing and seeing all aspects."[822] . . . [692] The *Mahāyānasūtrālaṃkāra* says:

> Buddhahood is endowed with all dharmas, or devoid of all
> dharmas.
> . . .
> Just as space is held to be always omnipresent,
> Also this [buddhahood] is held to be always omnipresent.
> Just as space is omnipresent in what has form,
> Also this [buddhahood] is omnipresent in the hosts of beings.
> . . .
> Though without difference between before and after,
> It is immaculateness in terms of all obscurations.
> Being neither pure nor impure,
> Suchness is held to be buddhahood.
> . . .
> Therefore, buddhahood is said to be
> Neither existent nor nonexistent.
> So, upon such questions about the Buddha,
> The principle of being undecidable is held.
> . . .
> Those who do not see attainment
> Are held to have the supreme attainment.[823]

Thus, this is explained in detail in all sūtras and treatises. Furthermore, in the *Bodhisattvabhūmi*, enlightenment is explained as (1) twofold relinquishment and twofold wisdom, (2) pure wisdom, omniscience, wisdom without attachment, the annihilation of the afflictions, and the relinquishment of nonafflicted ignorance, (3) being endowed with the 140 unique buddhadharmas,[824] dispassion, knowledge through aspiration, and the [four] discriminating awarenesses, and (4) being endowed with the seven [kinds of] genuineness—genuine kāyas, accomplishment, excellence, wisdom, power, relinquishment, and abiding. Thus, [so far, there are] five systems of explaining [buddhahood]. The *Mahāyānasūtrālaṃkārabhāṣya* explains the attainment of the threefold change of state as enlightenment. [693] Following the *Buddhabhūmisūtra*, enlightenment is explained as the inseparability of dhātu and wisdom. In these and many other such [explanations], the term "enlightenment" describes nothing but the state of buddhahood.

The Divisions[825]

Since space is omnipresent and without distinction, space is called "single," which means indivisible. Likewise, perfect buddhahood is beyond all phenomena, or does not move away from all phenomena, or is present as the nature of all phenomena. But since it is not observable as anything whatsoever, perfect buddhahood is also said to be single and not divisible into anything, because [any of its] divisions depend on the minds [of individual beings], while buddhahood [itself] is not an object of anybody's mind. This is one specification of the definitive meaning. The *Madhyamakāvatāra* says:

> Just as there are no divisions in space through the divisions of vessels,
> There are no divisions produced by entities in true reality.
> Therefore, once they are fully realized as being of equal taste, [695]
> You, excellent knower, realize [all] knowable objects in a single instant.[826]

The *Bodhisattvabhūmi* says:

> Furthermore, since it is beyond all paths of conception, it is to be known as inconceivable.

The *Mahāyānasūtrālaṃkāra* states:

> Buddhahood is all dharmas,
> But itself is no dharma whatsoever.
> It consists of pure dharmas,
> But is not portrayed by them.[827]

Still, just as space is divided through conceptions into "the space of the east" and so on and [such labels] are superimposed onto it, distinctions within buddhahood are made by way of [individual people] taking it as a referent [in different ways]. Thus, it is divided into two, three, four, and five up through infinite kāyas. Therefore, it [can be said to] be twofold as the ultimate kāya (one's own welfare) and the seeming symbolic kāya (the welfare of others) that is supported by the [former]. As the *Uttaratantra* says:

> One's own welfare and the welfare of others are the ultimate kāya
> And the seeming kāya that is supported by it, [respectively].[828]

Or, it is twofold as the dharmakāya that is one's own excellent welfare and the dharmakāya that is the welfare of others and the natural outflow of the [former]:

> The dharmakāya is to be known as twofold . . .[829]

Or, it is twofold as the vimuktikāya (one's own welfare, excellent relinquishment) and the dharmakāya (the welfare of others, excellent realization):

> In brief, this is to be understood
> As the functions of the two wisdoms—
> The vimuktikāya being completion
> And the dharmakāya being refinement.
> . . .
>
> The vimuktikāya and the dharmakāya
> Indicate the welfare of oneself and others.[830]

Or, as for the kāyas being threefold, the *Suvarṇaprabhāsottama[sūtra]* says:

> All Tathāgatas possess three kāyas—the dharmakāya, the sambhogakāya, and the nirmāṇakāya.[831]

. . . [696] Or, [the scriptures speak of] the svābhāvikakāya (or svabhāvakāya) plus the sambhogakāya and the nirmāṇakāya. The *Mahāyānasūtrālaṃkāra* states:

> The svābhāvika[kāya], the sāmbhogikakāya,
> And the other one, the nairmāṇikakāya,
> Are the divisions of the kāyas of the buddhas.
> The first one is the foundation of the [other] two.
> . . .

One should know that the buddhakāyas
Consist of the three kāyas.[832]

Or, when divided by taking the dharmakāya as the basis of division, the three kāyas are the svābhāvikakāya, the sāmbhogikakāya, and the nairmāṇikakāya. In [line I.4d] . . . in the brief introduction of the *Abhisamayālaṃkāra*, all kāyas are included in the dharmakāya. Later, [this text] says:

As svābhāvika[kāya], sambhoga[kāya],
And also as nairmāṇika[kāya], which is other . . .[833]

On this [verse], [Ratnākara]śānti's *Śuddhimatī* . . . [explicitly] comments that the dharmakāya represents the three kāyas (with enlightened activity [being the fourth point]). This manner of [commenting] is an [other] specification of explaining [the three kāyas].[834]

Or, [the kāyas] are three as the profound svābhāvikakāya, the vast sambhogakāya, and the magnanimous nirmāṇakāya. The *Uttaratantra* says:

When divided, this pertains to the three kāyas,
Such as the svābhāvika[kāya],
Which are characterized by the qualitative properties
Of profoundness, vastness, and magnanimity.[835]

Or, they are twofold as the natural dharmakāya that is the utterly stainless dharmadhātu and the dharmakāya that is its natural outflow:

The dharmakāya is to be known as twofold—
[697] The utterly stainless dharmadhātu
And its natural outflow, which displays
In profound and various ways.[836]

If the dharmakāya that is the natural outflow is divided, it is twofold—the profound dharmakāya (the sambhogakāya) and the dharmakāya that displays in various ways (the nirmāṇakāya). In brief, there are three—the natural dharmakāya and the two dharmakāyas that are its natural outflow.

Or, through adding the dharmakāya and its enlightened activity to the triad of the svābhāvikakāya and so on, master Haribhadra and others assert four kāyas as being the intention of [*Abhisamayālaṃkāra* I.17] . . . [The concluding verse of] the *Buddhabhūmisūtra* states:

This pure dharmadhātu of the buddhas
Is proclaimed as entailing
The svabhāva-, dharma-, sambhoga-,
And nirmāṇa[kāyas] as different modes.[837]

Thus, having explicitly taught four wisdoms and four kāyas, [this sūtra] explains that they all are inseparable from dharmadhātu wisdom. In its brief summary, it explains five wisdoms:

> the buddhabhūmi consists of five dharmas . . . dharmadhātu wisdom, . . .[838]

Thus, implicitly, it also teaches five kāyas, including the dharmadhātukāya.

In brief, the *Samādhirājasūtra* explains that one is not able to gauge the physical size and so on of the rūpakāyas of the buddhas:

If one were to find any size
Of the buddhakāyas being that much,
The teacher would be no different
From gods and humans.

Accordingly, the buddhakāyas appear in as many numbers as the conceptions of those to be guided. However, just as space can be divided in any way whatsoever, whereas the extent of space is not found by anybody, the buddhakāyas are simply inconceivable. [698] For, its manner of being inconceivable is explained repeatedly and in detail, such as in the *Samādhirājasūtra*:

Just as space is,
Also my body is taught
To be inexpressible and hard to understand.

The *[Tathāgata]jñānamudrā[samādhisūtra]* states:

> Or, in terms of its nature, it is like space.

As for the meaning of *Uttaratantra* [I.145 above], "The dharmakāya is to be known as twofold," most Tibetans indeed take it to be the dharmakāya that is realization (the actual dharmakāya) and the [twofold] dharmakāya that is the vast dharma of the mahāyāna and the dharma of various yānas. In brief, they refer to the dharma spoken by the Buddha as the dharmakāya that is the teachings.[839] However, this is not the intention of the *Uttaratantra*. What it teaches are the dharmakāya ("Since the perfect buddhakāya radiates"), suchness ("Since suchness is undifferentiable"), and the disposition ("And because of the disposition").[840] The inseparability of these three is the Sugata heart:

> Its nature is the dharmakāya,
> Suchness, and the disposition.[841]

The dharmakāya is taught through the first three [among the *Uttaratantra*'s nine] examples—a buddha [statue], honey, and a kernel . . . From among [the two dharmakāyas as taught above in I.145], for the utterly stainless dharmakāya, no other example can be found. Also, for the Buddha, no other example is findable. Consequently, these two are matched, saying:

> By virtue of being beyond the world, for it, [699]
> No example is observable in the world.
> The dhātu is demonstrated
> As resembling the Tathāgata.[842]

Since the profound and subtle sambhogakāya is endowed with the five certainties and is not the sphere of others than noble bodhisattvas, it is like honey. For, just as all [kinds of] honey are of a single taste in their being sweet, all dharmas taught by this [sambhogakāya] are of a single taste in their being the inconceivable mahāyāna:

> The display of the subtle and profound way
> Is to be known as a single taste, just as honey, . . .[843]

The nirmāṇakāya, which teaches the dharma in various forms that, respectively, guide certain [beings] is like a kernel. For, just as various kernels exist within the husks of various seeds, the dharmas taught by this [nirmāṇakāya] are taught in various ways in reaction to [various] beings to be guided:

> And the display of the way of various forms,
> Like kernels in various husks.[844]

[In terms of] causes, by virtue of the naturally abiding disposition having become pure, the first dharmakāya is attained, and, by virtue of the unfolding disposition having become pure, the two latter dharmakāyas are:

> It is held that the three kāyas are attained
> By virtue of these two dispositions—
> The first kāya, through the first one,
> And the latter two, through the second one.[845]

It may be said, "But since the three kāyas are then taught through both the first three and the last three examples . . . it follow that this is repetitive." However, then it would equally follow that all nine examples are repetitious, since they all teach the single Sugata heart, and that the last three examples [alone are so too, because] they teach nothing but buddhahood. [700] If it is said that these are not repetitive by virtue of different purposes, just the same applies here. The first three examples are taught in order to understand that the natural dharmakāya is without example, and that the profound dharmakāya and the vast dharmakāya [have] the functions of teaching the dharmas that are of a single taste and of teaching various dharmas, respectively. The last three [examples] are presented in order to realize these kāyas' own natures. Otherwise, [that is, according to the above position of those Tibetans who speak about the twofold dharmakāya that is the mahāyāna dharma and the dharma of various yānas, respectively], since the nine examples are [all] means to explain the Sugata heart, it would follow that the dharma of the mahāyāna and the various dharmas are the Sugata heart. Also, this would contradict both the [*Uttaratantra*'s] explanation [in I.103–104] . . . that the honey is the basic element and that the bees are the latencies of hatred, and its explanation [in I.107] . . . that the kernel is the dharmakāya with obscurations and that the husks are the latencies of ignorance [I.107]. For, it is impossible for both the dharma of the mahāyāna and the dharmas of various [yānas] to be obscured by these stains. . . .

[701] Therefore, there are many different [ways to explain the kāyas], such as the *Abhisamayālaṃkāra*'s manner of explanation by taking the dharmakāya as the basis of division and then dividing it into three—the svābhāvikakāya and so on; the assertion of the *Trikāyanāmasūtra* and others of presenting three kāyas by taking the dharmakāya as the nature of the division; the presentation of four kāyas by taking the dharmakāya as the nature of the division, which is explained in the *Buddhabhūmisūtra*; the sections in the *Uttaratantra* that present the dharmakāya itself as threefold; and the phrase, "the dharmakāya being refinement" in *Uttaratantra* [II.21d] that presents solely the rūpakāyas as dharmakāya. Therefore, each one of the presentations of the kāyas by way of what is asserted by those present-day bibliophiles who boast about being proclaimers of the pāramitā[yāna] appear to be like scooping a drop from the ocean and then shouting, "The ocean is exactly this!"

Kāyas and Wisdoms in the Lineages of Profound View and Vast Activity[846]

[According to] the scholars of the lineage of profound view, through having trained on the paths of familiarizing with the entire collection of the firewood of knowable objects' being without nature, also the mere very dry rest of this [collection] that is free from the moisture of reification is burned without remainder through the flame of the instantaneous prajñā at the end of the continuum of the ten bhūmis—the vajralike samādhi—in a singe instant. Then, with no firewood, there is no fire either. Therefore, also wisdom itself (which is like a burning fire) comes to rest within the dhātu, through which the dharmadhātu, just as it is, is revealed. This is the dharmakāya. As the *Madhyamakāvatāra* says:

> With the dry firewood of knowable objects' being incinerated
> without remainder,
> This peace is the dharmakāya of the victors.
> At this point, there is neither arising nor ceasing.
> The cessation of mind is revealed through this kāya.[847]

[As *Madhyamakāvatāra* XI.14–16] says, . . . a wheel that has been turned by a potter with effort before keeps turning even without effort later, and [the result of] pottery is accomplished by virtue of that. Or, a garuḍa pillar retains its capacity to pacify poison even if a long time has elapsed after its builder has passed away. Likewise, though the dharmakāya itself is without any effort and thinking, by virtue of previous aspiration prayers and great compassion, its appearance as the sambhogakāyas and the nirmāṇakāyas that respectively guide those to be guided is permament and uninterrupted and it appears to teach the dharma. Through hearing the [dharma], the people in the world will realize true reality. This represents the rūpakāya. [758] [*Madhyamakāvatāra* XI.18 says]:

> This kāya of peace is lucidly manifest like a wish-fulfilling tree
> And nonconceptual like a wish-fulfilling jewel.
> For the sake of the world's affluence and until beings are liberated,
> It appears permanently within the freedom from reference points.

[*Bodhicaryāvatāra* IX.36] says:

> For example, when a worshipper of Garuḍa . . .[848]

Here, by virtue of both fire and firewood having ceased, there is nothing whatsoever [left]. Unlike that, the dharmakāya should not be understood as nothing whatsoever. For, the very [notions of] existence and nonexistence represent reifications, and these are the firewood of wisdom. Thus, just as a fire whose firewood is exhausted, also this very wisdom of the samādhi at the end of the continuum comes to rest on its own, through which the uncontrived dharmadhātu is just as it is. This is called "having found the dharmakāya." [The *Madhyamakāvatāra*] says:

> The cessation of mind is revealed through this kāya.
>
> . . .
>
> In Akaniṣṭha, you attain supreme peace—the state for which you made efforts,
> The incomparable culmination of all qualities.
>
> . . .
>
> You, excellent knower, realize [all] knowable objects in a single instant.[849]

This also eliminates the assertion that, just as the nirvāṇa without remainder of śrāvakas and pratyekabuddhas, buddhahood in the Madhyamaka system [is held] to be the extinction of a continuum (as in the case of a fire having died out). For, such an assertion directly contradicts these [above quotes], with "revealed through this kāya" and "supreme peace . . . " indicating that which is to be attained, and "you attain" explaining the manifesting of enlightenment.

[759] As for the explanation in the scriptures of the lineage of profound view that buddhas do not possess wisdom, the reasons for it are as follows. The very wisdom of the vajralike samādhi at the end of the continuum comes to rest within the dhātu. Also, in general, though subject and object are never different within the nature of phenomena, through not knowing this, [sentient beings] superimpose them [onto this nature] and thus simply cling to them as being different. However, in order to realize the dhātu of subject and object being primordially nondual, [buddhas] do not possess any wisdom that operates as something which realizes an object to be realized. Since all reifications must be put to an end, the clinging to wisdom being established is relinquished. Just as the nature of all phenomena is not observable as anything whatsoever, upon analysis, also the nature of wisdom is nothing but this. Therefore, it is explained that [buddhas] do not possess wisdom, but it is not categorically explained that, in general, the four wisdoms and so on do absolutely not exist, because the only difference lies in their being explained

through the names of "kāyas" or through the names of "wisdoms," with the three kinds of kāyas being accepted in this [lineage of profound view] too.

In brief, [in this lineage,] it is not the case that, after having refuted arising, the lack of arising is asserted. Likewise, the clinging to wisdom being established [as anything] is put to an end, but it is not that [wisdom] is presented as "nonestablished." The same goes for the kāyas, because existence, nonexistence, and so on are nothing but the reifications of childish beings. In particular, Atiśa explained that the great master Śāntideva asserts the view as being the inseparability of dhātu and wisdom. In general, when Mādhyamikas refute the arising of a sprout, this means putting an end to the clinging to arising being real, but not putting an end to farming as a whole. The same should be understood here [in the context of kāyas and wisdom].

The explanation [of the kāyas] through the scriptures [of the lineage] of vast activity shall be given together with the presentation of wisdom. The *Trikāyanāmasūtra* says:

> [760] The purified state of the ālaya-consciousness is mirrorlike wisdom, the dharmakāya. The purified state of the afflicted mind is the wisdom of equality, [and] the purified state of the mental consciousness is discriminating wisdom, [both being] the sambhogakāya. The purified state of the consciousnesses of the five [sense] gates is all-accomplishing wisdom, the nirmāṇakāya.[850]

The *Buddhabhūmisūtra* states:

> In a very condensed form, the buddhabhūmi consists of five dharmas. What are these five? They are the pure dharmadhātu, mirrorlike wisdom, the wisdom of equality, discriminating wisdom, and all-accomplishing wisdom.[851]

The natures of these wisdoms shall be explained according to the intentions of these two sūtras. In the [*Buddhabhūmisūtra*], the pure dharmadhātu is indicated by the example of space. Space provides room for all forms, but it is in no way the same as, or different from, all forms. It is untainted by forms, makes no effort to provide room, and provides the room for arising and ceasing, but is without arising and ceasing. Though all increase and decrease, middle and ends, formation and cessation appear in space, [space] itself lacks all of these, is completely unchanging, and has no characteristics of [any one among] all forms. Though all realms appear in it, [space] itself lacks formation. In just the same ways, the dharmadhātu abides as what provides room for all of saṃsāra and nirvāṇa, but is in no way the same as, or different from, all of this and so on, up through lacking formation. It is not different from the dhātu of the minds of all sentient beings, but also not tainted by the flaws of sentient beings. As [the *Buddhabhūmisūtra*] continues:

> Space is present as not being different from all forms, but it is not tainted by the flaws of forms. Likewise, [761] the pure dharmadhātu of the Tathāgatas is present as not being different from all sentient beings in that it is perfect as the equality of mind, but it is not tainted by the flaws of sentient beings.[852]

In general, the secret mantra[yāna] explains five wisdoms, but in the yāna of characteristics, there are many explanations of four wisdoms, without applying the conventional term "wisdom" to the dharmadhātu. However, though the *Buddhabhūmisūtra* does not apply the conventional term "wisdom" to the dharmadhātu in its brief introduction, in its detailed explanation, it explains five wisdoms, speaking of "the first wisdom . . ."[853]

The meaning of "change of state" [here] is that the state of [the dharmadhātu] having stains before has later changed into a state other than that—its being pure of stains. However, since this dharmadhātu itself is primordially pure in all respects, there is no change of state [of the dharmadhātu itself].

When the ālaya-consciousness has become pure of stains, it is called "mirrorlike wisdom," or "dharmkāya." In a clear mirror, one's face appears, and it demonstrates one's flaws and qualities. It is lucidly clear, and it is the cause for reflections. It does not dwell in these reflections, nor does it possess or not possess these reflections. They appear in a complete manner, and everything is suitable to appear in it. Therefore, [a mirror] is complelety unbiased, but the blind and those without the proper fate do not see [it or its reflections]. Likewise, as for this kāya, the rūpakāyas appear [in it] and demonstrate the dharma. It is lucidly clear by nature, and it is the cause for the reflections of wisdom. This kāya does not dwell in the rūpakāyas, nor does it possess or not possess the two rūpakāyas. The [latter] appear [in it] in a complete manner, and they appear as whatever guides [those to be guided]. Therefore, [the dharmakāya] is without bias, but does not appear to those who are not [proper] vessels, and is not seen by those with the karma of being destitute of the dharma. Therefore, it matches the example of a mirror. This very dharmakāya [762] is the actual nonabiding nirvāṇa, because the *Mahāyānasūtrālaṃkāra* explains the change of state of the foundation—the ālaya[-consciousness]—as the nonabiding nirvāṇa:

> In the change of state of the foundation,
> Supreme mastery is attained
> Over the nonabiding nirvāṇa
> In the stainless state of the buddhas.[854]

The change of state of the afflicted mind is the wisdom of realizing the equality of all phenomena. [The *Buddhabhūmisūtra*] explains this as the ten perfections of equality: (1) the perfection of the equality of name, sovereign, and joy, (2) the equality of experiencing dependent origination, [the ones of] (3) signlessness, (4) great love, (5) great compassion, (6) the display of rūpakāyas, (7) words worthy to adopt, (8) being of one taste with peace, (9) suffering and happiness being of one taste, and (10) the perfection of the equality of greatly giving rise to qualities.[855]

The change of state of the sixth—the mental—consciousness is the wisdom of knowing all phenomena in an unmixed distinct manner, just as they are. This [discriminating wisdom] and the wisdom of equality are expressed as the sambhogakāya. Or, the sambhogakāya is presented as just the wisdom of equality by referring to it as the common cause of the two rūpakāyas. As [*Mahāyānasūtrālaṃkāra* IX.71cd] says:

> The image of the Buddha displays,
> Just as sentient beings aspire.

[In the *Buddhabhūmisūtra*,] this [wisdom] is referred to in detail as being the abode of the dharmas of the victor, the cause of the wisdom of knowing variety, full of qualities, and highly differentiated. All beings appear [to it], the three realms appear [to it], the dharmas of nirvāṇa appear [to it], and it is undisturbed and encircled by nonignorance.[856] Through these [features], it knows the situations of beings and [everything else] up through the great circumferential wall.[857] It does not see these objects by virtue of their existing by a nature of their own, nor does it appear as a seeing under the sway of the latent tendencies of subject and object. [763] Nevertheless, when one sees clear water, one also sees the form of [the reflection of] the moon [in it], its ripples, and so on, which are all not different from it. Likewise, once the dharmadhātu is known, also all the collections of dependent origination (the bearers of this nature), which are not different from it, are known without exception. In this sense, [the sūtras] say:

> The entirety of the particular causes
> Of a single peacock's eye

> Cannot be known by those who are not omniscient—
> By virtue of knowing such, it is omniscience.

And

> A single instant of [your] knowing
> Encompasses the entire maṇḍala of knowable objects.

[*Madhyamakāvatāra* XI.11d] says:

> You, excellent knower, realize [all] knowable objects in a single instant.

In this way, from the point of view of omniscience being unobscured, it is explained that objects appear [to it]. As [the *Buddhabhūmisūtra*] says:

> For the discriminating wisdom of the buddhas, the five [kinds of] beings appear, which entail infinite divisions of manifesting, including their causes and results.[858]

Therefore, this [wisdom] refers to the [detailed] knowledge about something like a blue utpala [lotus]—the different causes and conditions for its color, anthers, and so on; through which [phases] it went in which ways from the beginning of its seed; and how the continuum of this seed develops in the future and where it ceases at the end. For example, it is said:

> [Imagine that] a person scoops a single drop of water with a fraction of a split tip of a hair, goes to the Bhagavat, and entrusts it to him, saying, "O Gautama, I entrust my water here to you. I entrust it to you so that it does not get wasted, but do not pour it out for sentient beings or let it dry out." The teacher will fling it into the great ocean, and then the ocean will be struck and churned by winds, so that this drop of water bcomes scattered in many ways. Then, after infinite years, or many eons, have passed, if this person comes [again], saying, "O Gautama, please give me my water back," [764] [the Buddha] knows exactly in which directions of the ocean the minute particles of this drop of water are. He collects them into one, without even a single one of the minute particles of this drop of water remaining in the ocean and without even a single one of

> the minute particles of the water of the ocean being mixed with the [drop], and gives it back to that person.

Therefore, [buddhahood means] to know without exception how all the aspects of each phenomenon are, because it is endowed with discriminating wisdom. In this process, it is not endowed with a seeing [that entails] any subject or object to be seen, any higher or inferior, any same or different, and so on, because it is endowed with the wisdom of equality. This knowledge does not entail any efforts [either], because it is endowed with mirrorlike wisdom. Also, all of these are indescribable as being one or different and so on, and are neither a seeing nor a nonseeing, because they never move away from the dharmadhātu.

Therefore, the explanation in the scriptures of [the lineage of] profound view that buddhas are not even endowed with wisdom as such is given in order to destroy the clinging to cognizance being established as wisdom, but it is not a teaching on buddhahood being matter, or emptiness in the sense of extinction. In general, the [Indian and Tibetan] paṇḍitas and translators gave out the decree that the term *jñāna*, when it expresses the cognitions of sentient beings, [must be translated into Tibetan] as "cognition" (*shes pa*) or "consciousness" (*rnam shes*), and when it expresses the cognition of buddhas, it must be translated as "wisdom" (*ye shes*). However, there are no [different] linguistic equivalents for these [two Tibetan terms in Sanskrit]. When distinguishing consciousness and wisdom, the mind to be purified—the mind of apprehender and apprehended—[is explained through the term] "consciousness," and the naturally luminous nature of phenomena is explained through the term "wisdom." [However, in itself,] this [term] does not represent any aspects of superimposition or denial (such as existence or nonexistence) whatsoever. Therefore, the debate about whether buddhas are or are not endowed with wisdom [just reflects] biased minds—from the point of view of discriminating wisdom, they cannot be described as not being endowed [with wisdom], while [765] from the point of view of the dharmadhātu, they cannot be described as being endowed [with wisdom]. In general, if the sheer unceasing manifestations of what appears at present, such as form, are examined through one's personally experienced cognition, they cannot be designated in any way as appearing, not appearing, existent, or nonexistent. Understand this and you will be close to the way things actually are. Otherwise, it seems to be nothing but a bad denigration of buddhahood to cling to the thoughts that apprehend by mixing terms and referents in terms of one or different, existent or nonexistent, and so on in just the manner in which the discriminations of lay people operate, and then to make statements about buddhahood, such as, "It exists" or "It does not exist." Therefore, existence, nonexistence, and so on are superimpositions by conceptions, but you should understand that buddhahood is not an object of conceptions.

As for the change of state of the consciousnesses of the five [sense] gates (such as the eyes), together with their appearing as if there were subjects and objects, [it happens] through the culmination of one's previous generation of bodhicitta and the efforts in order to accomplish the welfare of all sentient beings since beginningless time. It is the uninterrupted manifestation of the welfare of others, which equals [the extent of] space, yet is without effort and is nonconceptual. This is called "all-accomplishing wisdom," or "nirmāṇakāya." It is the functional activity of all other kāyas and wisdoms. Thus, [the *Buddhabhūmisūtra*] says that its activity lies in artistic emanations, incarnate emanations, the formations of enlightened speech, sustaining the trainings, dispelling doubts, knowing the minds [of beings], perfectly establishing [them in maturation and liberation], describing the characteristics [of phenomena], and giving answers.[859] In the *Mahāyānasūtrālaṃkāra*, the changes of state and the four wisdoms are explained separately:

> In the change of state of the five sense faculties,
> Supreme mastery is attained
> Over the perception of all their objects
> And the arising of twelve hundred qualities in all of them.[860]

[766] This [verse] refers to the change of state of the skandha of form. The four [changes of state of] the afflicted mind, the sense consciousnesses, conception, and the ālaya[-consciousness] within the skandha of consciousness are explained by the following [four] verses, respectively:

> In the change of state of mentation,
> Supreme mastery is attained
> Over utterly stainless nonconceptual
> Wisdom ensuing from mastery.
>
> In the change of state of the apprehender and its referents,
> Supreme mastery is attained
> Over pure realms in order to display
> Enjoyments just as one pleases.
>
> In the change of state of conception,
> Supreme mastery is attained

Over wisdom and activities
Unimpeded at all times.

In the change of state of the foundation,
Supreme mastery is attained
Over the nonabiding nirvāṇa
In the stainless state of the buddhas.[861]

[There follows] the change of state of [the skandha of] feeling:

In the change of state of sexual union,
Supreme mastery is attained
Over the blissful state of a buddha
And being unafflicted upon seeing spouses.[862]

[Next is] the change of state of [the skandha of] discrimination:

Turning away from discriminating space,
Supreme mastery is attained
Over a wealth of desired objects
And the evolutions of movement and form.[863]

Thus, explicitly, eleven [kinds of] change of state[864] are explained, while [IX.48 speaks of] infinite ones:

Thus, infinite masteries are asserted
In infinite changes of state
By virtue of the inconceivable all-accomplishment
Within the stainless foundation of the buddhas.

As for mirrorlike wisdom, [*Mahāyānasūtrālaṃkāra* IX.67 says that] it is the foundation for the other three wisdoms:

Mirrorlike wisdom is unmoving.
The three [other] wisdoms have it as their foundation—
Equality, discriminating,
And all-accomplishing as well.

This mirrorlike wisdom is endowed with eight characteristics:

> Mirrorlike wisdom is without "me or mine,"
> Unconfined, ever present, [767]
> Not ignorant about the entirety of knowable objects,
> Yet never directed toward them.
>
> Since it is the cause of all wisdoms,
> It is like a great jewel mine of wisdom.
> It is the sambhoga-buddhahood,
> Since the reflection of wisdom arises.[865]

(1) [Mirrorlike wisdom] is without mine, because the clinging to a self has come to an end. (2) It engages objects fully without any limitations, because it engages the dharmadhātu just as the dharmadhātu is, and because it is nondual with this dhātu. (3) It is described as ever present, because it is always without decline. (4) It is not ignorant about the entirety of knowable objects, because the cognitive obscurations have been relinquished. (5) It is never directed toward knowable objects, because it lacks any discriminations in terms of being one or different. (6) Since the other three wisdoms arise from this [wisdom], it is like a jewel mine. *The Sūtra of the Arising of Buddhas*[866] says:

> Since the Buddha Bhagavat is endowed with the wisdom that is the foundation of the knowledge of all aspects, this wisdom is like a great jewel mine.

(7) Since the nature of this wisdom is indeed the dharmakāya, but the sambhogakāya appears from it, [*Mahāyānasūtrālaṃkāra* IX.69c above] says, "It is the sambhoga-buddhahood." This is presented from the point of view of its being the foundation [of the latter], or from the point of view of their natures not being different. (8) In brief, it is called "mirrorlike wisdom," because it is the cause for the arising of the other three wisdoms or the two rūpakāyas, which are [all] like reflections.

The wisdom of equality is endowed with six qualities. [*Mahāyānasūtrālaṃkāra* IX.70–71] says:

> The wisdom of equality toward sentient beings
> Is held to be stainless by virtue of pure cultivation.
> Residing in nonabiding peace
> Is asserted to be the wisdom of equality.

Said to be endowed at all times
With great love and compassion, [768]
The image of the Buddha displays,
Just as sentient beings aspire.

(1) As for the cause [of the wisdom of equality], it is attained by virtue of having cultivated the mindset of oneself and others being equal on the [paths of] accumulation and preparation, and this [cultivation] having become utterly pure on the paths of the noble ones. (2) The object [of this wisdom] consists of focusing on all sentient beings. (3) Its nature is to always reside in the peace of not abiding in anything whatsoever, thus not seeing any phenomena that are not equal. (4) Its aids consist of always being endowed with great love and compassion. (5)–(6) [The sūtras] say:

> When they see the Buddha Bhagavat, all sentient beings are always delighted. Therefore, wisdom is like a great moon.

Thus, it functions as the foundation for the appearing of the rūpakāyas, just as sentient beings aspire.

[According to *Mahāyānasūtrālaṃkāra* IX.72–73,] discriminating wisdom is endowed with four characteristics:

Discriminating wisdom
Is always unimpeded toward all knowable objects.
It is just like a treasury
Of dhāraṇīs and samādhis.

In the maṇḍala of retinues,
It displays all masteries,
Cuts through all doubts,
And rains down the great dharma.

(1) It is omniscient, (2) a treasury of all dhāraṇīs and samādhis, (3) displays the sambhogakāya for noble bodhisattvas, and (4) teaches the dharma in an uninterrupted manner.

[According to *Mahāyānasūtrālaṃkāra* IX.74, all-accomplishing wisdom] is the display of the nirmāṇakāya:

All-accomplishing wisdom
Accomplishes the welfare of all sentient beings

In all realms through various
Immeasurable and inconceivable emanations.[867]

As for why four wisdoms are presented, [*Mahāyānasūtrālaṃkāra* IX.76] says:

Due to retaining, due to equanimity,
Due to elucidating the perfect dharma,
And due to accomplishing activities,
The four wisdoms arise.

In this way, in the [above sūtras] and the *Mahāyānasūtrālaṃkāra*, the four wisdoms are taught as the three kāyas. The commentators [769] explain that the wisdoms are the supports and the kāyas the supported, but either way this is not contradictory.

Enlightened Activity[868]

According to *Abhisamayālaṃkāra* [VIII.34cd–40], the nature of enlightened activity consists of twenty-seven uninterrupted activities of guiding those to be guided as long as saṃsāra lasts . . . Thus, it is described as a fixed number of [such activities that range] from pacifying the states of nonleisure [of beings] and establishing them in the freedoms and riches [of a precious human birth] up through establishing them in the nonabiding nirvāṇa. [Enlightened activity] not being fixed in number means that it is infinite, because even the activities of māras serve as the enlightened activity of buddhas. For, the *Sāgaramatiparipṛcchasūtra* says:

In just the ways that māras inflict their activities on bodhisattvas who perfectly engage in the superior intention, [770] these bodhisattvas accordingly muster vigor with great power. Venerable Śāradvatīputra, through this specification, you should understand that this very māra activity is described as the enlightened activity of the buddhas—it is not māra activity.

[The sūtra also] says that there is no phenomenon that does not serve as the enlightened activity of the buddhas. According to the *Uttaratantra*, [enlightened activity] consists of [promoting] the immeasurable welfare of others that entails being spontaneously present and uninterrupted:

> An all-embracing sovereign engages always and spontaneously
> In the constitutions of those to be guided, the means to guide them,
> The activities of guidance [that suit] the constitutions of those to be guided,
> And in proceeding to their whereabouts at the [right] time.[869]

Thus, [enlightened activity] is suitable to [be described as] either entailing [the features of] being all-pervading and permanent, or entailing [the features of] being profound and vast. As the *Madhyamakāvatāra* remarks in passing:

> The profound [quality] is emptiness.
> The other qualities are vast.[870]

Other Tibetans proclaim an "enlightened activity that exists in the recipient (the object)" and an "enlightened activity that exists in the agent." However, enlightened activity is not something that those to be guided are endowed with, just as sun rays are possessed [only] by the sun itself, whereas it is not reasonable to present them as being possessed by both the sun and lotuses.

As for the manner in which enlightened activity is performed, it operates without effort or toil in a spontaneously present and uninterrupted manner. Summarizing the points described in the *Jñānālokālaṃkārasūtra*, the *Uttaratantra* teaches [enlightened activity] through nine examples. In this regard, the following probative argument is to be formulated—"the enlightened activity of the buddhas" is the subject; "its operating in an effortless and spontaneously present way" is the thesis; "because they are endowed with the enlightened mind of nonconceptual dhātu and wisdom" [771] is the reason; and "just as in the nine cases of the physical form of Indra and so on" are the examples. [As *Uttaratantra* IV.83] says:

> In establishing the meaning of its nature,
> The thesis is efforts having subsided,
> The reason is nonconceptual mind,
> And the examples are such as the physical form of Indra.

. . . [772] As explained before, the rūpakāyas appear by virtue of the triad of the power of the dharmakāya, the force of previous aspiration prayers, and the pure mind streams of those to be guided. Thus, they are explained as the kāyas of dependent origination, but not taught to be [just] the eye-consciousnesses of those to be guided. For, if the seeing of the physical form of Indra were nothing but the eye-consciousness of an individual [being who sees it], it would follow that it has to appear even if the dominant condition of Indra [himself] is absent, and that it has to appear even if the object condition is an impure ground [in which his form cannot be reflected]. [773] Therefore, what appear under the influence of these [three factors] coming together, while not existing [in actuality], are the kāyas of dependent origination. All phenomena should be understood just like that.

The nature of the mind, which is primordially empty of stains and luminous with qualities, does not abide as any entity in terms of superimposition and denial, such as existent, nonexistent, real, or delusive. Thus, it is not an object of mind, unconfined with regard to everything, and not biased in any way whatsoever. This is called "dharmadhātu."

> The past is suchness, what has not arrived is suchness,
> The present is suchness, what is arhathood is suchness,
> All phenomena are suchness—all these are not different.

Accordingly, the dhātu of the minds of all buddhas, bodhisattvas, śrāvakas, pratyekabuddhas, and sentient beings is not different, just as the element of space is omnipresent in all forms. Therefore, it is also said that [buddhas] see no phenomenon other than the dharmadhātu. Also, all the places in which all buddhas become fully perfect buddhas; the means through which, when they realize them, they become buddhas; and the nature that represents the essence of their becoming buddhas are nothing but this [dharmadhātu]. Not moving away from it is the abode of the buddhas—they always abide by virtue of this [dharmadhātu], and it is not observable as abiding or not abiding. Therefore, it is described as "the nonabiding abiding." Though [the dharmadhātu] is not connected to sentient beings, the stream of the basic element of sentient beings is nothing other than this.[871] Therefore, it is also said that all buddhas always abide in the stream of the basic element of sentient beings. Through the power of this basic element in [beings'] own mind streams, a mind of virtue [can] arise [in them], they [are able to] see spiritual friends and rūpakāyas, and, through having purified their mind streams through that, they are able to see the dharmakāya of their own mind streams, just as it is. Therefore, [*Uttaratantra* I.40] speaks about the power of the basic element:

> If the basic buddha element did not exist, [774]
> One would not be weary with suffering,
> Not wish for nirvāṇa,
> And lack striving and aspiring [for it].

[*Uttaratantra* IV.25ab] says that [what appears as the enlightened activity of the rūpakāyas] is a reflection [by virtue] of the dhātu of one's own mind stream and the force of virtues coming together:

> Indeed, ordinary beings do not understand
> That this is an appearance in their own minds.

[*Uttaratantra* IV.26cd] says that, based on that, the dharmakāya of one's own mind stream will be seen, just as it is:

> The inner genuine dharmakāya
> Will be seen through the eye of wisdom.

Therefore, buddhahood is neither regarded to be fully complete through just the rūpakāyas, nor is it regarded as being other than the dharmakāya. Likewise, it is neither regarded as solely the minds of those who see [the rūpakāyas], nor is it regarded as being other than their minds. Hence, all phenomena are taught to be mere dependent origination. Since the dharmakāya is emptiness, the rūpakāyas are suitable to appear as dependent origination, and one cannot observe any dharmakāya that is other than the very dependent origination of the rūpakāyas. Consequently, [*Mūlamadhyamakakārikā* XXIV.19] says:

> Since there is no phenomenon whatsoever
> That is not dependent origination,
> There is no phenomenon whatsoever
> That is not emptiness.

Exactly this should also be understood in the context of fruitional Madhyamaka—the unity of the two kāyas. Thus, the position of some who claim to be *rangtongpas* that buddhahood is nonexistent as anything and the assertion by some who claim to be *shentongpas* that buddhahood is a permanent substance represent destructions of the Buddha's teachings. For, it has been taught again and again:

> For those who even speak about the Buddha as being either permanent or extinct, what other dharma could there be about which they do not speak in terms of the extremes of permanence and extinction? Those who speak about the extremes of permanence and extinction are not his followers and he is not their teacher.

[775] It is also explained:

> The permanent kāya of the Tathāgata
> [Bears] the excellency of permanent characteristics.

This is not a statement like the assertion of the tīrthikas that Īśvara is a permanent self-arisen source of valid cognition. For, the *Aṅgulimālīyasūtra* says that [this kāya] is solely a fruition of virtue:

> Through having given away my body again and again in order to establish those with nonvirtue in virtue, my body is the unborn kāya . . . Through having established those who speak what is not true in the truth, I attained the permanent kāya. Through having given away my body in order to protect the dharma, I attained the unconditioned kāya . . . Through having taught the dhātu of the permanent Sugata heart in an unconcealed manner, I attained the permanent kāya.

Also, it is not good to assert that the sambhogakāya is actual buddhahood (like an illusionist) and that the nirmāṇakāya is its miraculous creation (like an illusory person). [*Uttaratantra* III.39cd] says:

> Just as with the form of the moon in water and in the sky,
> Seeing these [two] is also of two kinds.

Thus, the sambhogakāya is explained like the form of the moon in the sky, and the nirmāṇakāya like the form of the moon [that is reflected] in water. However, this is not like the assertion in the systems of Vaibhāṣikas and Sautrāntikas that the form of the moon in water, though it appears like the form of the moon, is not the form of the moon. The form of the moon in water and the form of the moon in the sky are neither the same nor different. For, if they were [both] the actual form of the moon (that is, one), the moon would have to be in the water. If they were not [both] the actual form of the moon (that is, different), the form of the moon [in the water] would have to be unable to point out the moon in the sky's being released or not released from Rahu. Therefore, these two are neither one (the same) nor different (other), and inexpressible as either being real or not being real as the form of the moon—the reasons for how they appear are not understood by ordinary beings. [You may think,] "Granted, but [776] according to this position, the action without interval[872] that consists of causing blood to flow from a buddha with a bad intention would be impossible altogether, because nobody is able to do that to a sambhogakāya, and the nirmāṇakāya is an illusory person. Thus, there is no evil in the killing and so on of an illusory person, since it has no mind." It is taught that a "nirmāṇakāya" is a miraculous manifestation, but not that it is not buddha. This is to be understood as explaining it to be "the kāya that resembles a miraculous manifestation" and "the kāya that resembles an illusion." Furthermore, those people who do not assert that the lords of the teachings—the supreme nirmāṇakāyas—are buddhakāyas would not only be unable to give any response to the statements by the tīrthikas that, "The śrāmaṇa Gautama is an illusion and does not exist as a real entity" and "Omniscience is impossible in the world, and the śrāmaṇa Gautama is neither a buddha, nor an omniscient one." In addition, [those people] would [even] have to agree, "Excellent, excellent, it is just like that." Also, they would have to accept that all the statements by the compilers [of the sūtras], such as, "Thus have I heard at one time—the Bhagavat was dwelling in Rājagṛha . . . ," are lies, because the one who dwelled in Rājagṛha was not the Buddha. They equally would have to accept that the twelve deeds are not the deeds of the Buddha, and that these teachings here are not the teachings of the Buddha. Therefore, [Gampopa's] *Ornament of Liberation* explains:

> One should understand that the two rūpakāyas arise from the coming together of the triad of the blessing influence of the dharmakāya, the appearances of those to be guided, and previous aspiration prayers. If they arose from the blessing influence of the dharmadhātu alone, since the dharmadhātu pervades all sentient beings, it would be reasonable for all of them to be liberated without effort. Or, it would be reasonable for all sentient beings to meet buddhas face to face. . . . In the hypothetical case of [the rūpakāyas] being solely the appearances of those to be guided, [777] any appearance of nonexistents represents wrong cognition, and if one were to become a buddha based on wrong cognition, it would be reasonable that all sentient beings have already become buddhas within merely that [mindset of wrong cognition], because they all have engaged in wrong cognition since beginningless [time]. . . . In the hypothetical case of [the rūpakāyas] arising from aspiration prayers alone, if the perfect buddhas have not gained mastery over aspiration prayers, nobody will become a buddha. If they have gained mastery, since they make aspiration prayers for the sake of all sentient beings, it would be reasonable for all of them to become liberated through these [prayers] without effort. . . . Since each one

> of these [possibilities] is not the case, [the rūpakāyas] arise [only] from the coming together of these three [factors].[873]

Therefore, in order to dispel the clinging to a buddha being conditioned and a person who is a collection of both matter and consciousness (the mind-set of the hīnayāna), it is also taught that a buddha does not abide as form. In general, these appearances of rūpakāyas are not included in the skandha of form. For, the skandha of form has already undergone its change of state; [through statements] such as "they are untainted by desires," it is taught that they are beyond the three realms; and they are not included in [saṃsāric] existence or [nirvāṇic] peace. Thus, it is taught that they do not consist of anything in existence or peace. Therefore, though they are beyond form, they display as assuming all forms. Though they are not included in sounds, they are endowed with the melodious voice that has all aspects [of qualities]. Though they are beyond the three realms, they do not move away from the three realms. Though they are not the objects of sentient beings, they appear as infinite kāyas that respectively guide each one of these sentient beings. Though they are free from any extent in that they are free from any middle and extremes and cannot even be exemplified by the element of space, they are the sole foundation of the benefit and happiness of all sentient beings. We should have confidence in the [Buddha], go for refuge, and wish [to attain] this state. But we who are even ignorant about the depth of just Lake Manasarovar should not gauge the extent of this great water reservoir of the Buddha, which is not even matched by as many great oceans as there are sand grains in the Ganges river.

Appendix II: The Treatise on Pointing Out the Tathāgata Heart

I pay homage to all buddhas and bodhisattvas.

It is said: "Though beginningless, it entails an end—
What is naturally pure and consists of permanent dharmas
Is not seen, since it is obscured by a beginningless cocoon,
Just as in the example of a golden statue being obscured.

The dhātu of time without beginning
Is the matrix of all phenomena.
Because it exists, all beings
And also nirvāṇa are obtained."

A passage in the tantras says:
"Sentient beings are buddhas indeed.
However, they are obscured by adventitious stains.
If these are removed, they are buddhas."

Here, "beginningless" [means that]
There is absolutely nothing before that.
The time is this very moment,
How could it come via somewhere else?
The basic element is without creator,
But since it bears its own characteristic, it is called that way.

The dharmas are explained as appearing
As both saṃsāra and nirvāṇa,
Which is called "the ground of the latent tendencies of
ignorance."
The movement of the formations of correct and false imagination

Is the producing cause.
This causal condition is explained as the ālaya.

The matrix is the Heart of the victors.
False imagination
Rests on the purity of mind.
This purity exists in that way.
Though it exists, through ignorant imagination,
It is not seen, and therefore is saṃsāra.
When that is eliminated, it is nirvāṇa,
Which is conventionally called "end."

Beginning and end depend on nothing but imagination.
Through windlike formation,
Karma and afflictions are created.
Through these, skandhas, dhātus, and āyatanas–
All dualistically appearing phenomena–are displayed.

The one who adopts and rejects these is mistakenness.
Through rejecting [mind's] own appearances, where should they cease?
Through adopting [mind's] own appearances, what should come about?
Is clinging to duality not delusive?

Understanding this is indeed said to be the remedy,
But the thought of nonduality is not real [either],
For the lack of thought [just] turns into a thought.
You thought about emptiness, dissecting form and so on into parts,
Are you not mistaken yourself?
Nevertheless, this was taught in order to stop the clinging to reality.

All is neither real nor delusive–
Held to be like [a reflection of] the moon in water by the learned.
Just this ordinary mind
Is called "dharmadhātu" and "Heart of the victors."
It is neither to be improved by the noble ones
Nor made worse by sentient beings.

It may no doubt be expressed through many conventional terms,
But its actual reality is not understood through expressions.

As for the unimpeded play of this,
The sixty-four qualities
Are a coarse [classification]–each one
Is said to [consist of] tens of millions.

Knowing what is the case and what is not the case, karma
And maturation, knowing constitutions, faculties,
And inclinations, the paths that lead everywhere,
The dhyānas, the divine eye,
Recollecting places [of rebirth], and peace–these are the ten powers.

The four fearlessnesses based on these
Are enlightened realization of all phenomena, teaching the obstacles,
Teaching the path and cessation, [all] being indisputable.

Due to that cause, the eighteen [unique qualities] are unmistakenness, lack of chatter,
Undeclining awareness, constant meditative equipoise,
Lacking the plethora of discriminating notions,
Lacking unexamining indifference;
No decline in striving, vigor, recollection,
Samādhi, prajñā,
And the vision of the wisdom of liberation;
Activities being preceded by wisdom,
And being unobscured with regard to time.
Being endowed with these thirty-two is the dharmakāya.

At present, we oppose them.
Since we lack certainty about what is, just as it is,
We produce the imaginary, construing what is nonexistent as existent.
The conceptuality produced by this is the other-dependent.
Through not knowing the perfect,
We are agitated by our own doing.
Alas, in those who realize these qualities of the dharmakāya

To be what is real, this is the knowledge of reality.
[Even] their present little power is reality–
Casting away this knowledge, we fabricate what is unreal
And are carried away by the agitation of pursuing it.

Understand now what is, just as it is,
And you attain power in it.
In this, there is nothing to be removed
And not the slightest to be added.
Actual reality is to be seen as it really is–
Whoever sees actual reality is released.
The basic element is empty of what is adventitious,
Which has the characteristic of being separable.
But it is not empty of the unsurpassable dharmas,
Which have the characteristic of being inseparable.

In this, the nature of the two rūpakāyas
Is the thirty-two major and the minor marks.
The attained qualities are your own body.
This body is not created by a self, Cha, Īśvara,
Brahmā, real external particles,
Or hidden [objects].
Through the refinement of the impure transmutations
Of apprehender and apprehended of the five gates,
At that point, the conventional term "attainment" is applied.

Therefore, nāḍīs, vāyus, and tilakas,
When pure, are the pure rūpakāyas.
Unpurified, they are the impure rūpakāyas.

For example, in an encrusted blue beryl,
Its qualities do not shine forth.
Through cleansing it with a woven cloth and an alkaline solution,
Cleansing it with acid and a towel,
And cleansing it with pure water and [cotton] from Kāśī,
It becomes pure–the gem that is the source [fulfilling all] needs
and desires.

Likewise, in order to cleanse the blue beryl of mind
From the three encrustations–

Afflictive and cognitive [obscurations], and those of meditative
absorption–
It is purified on [the paths of] accumulation and preparation,
The seven impure bhūmis, and the three pure bhūmis.

Through false imagination
Meeting pure imagination,
There is freedom from imagination, just like two wooden sticks
are burned.
This is the freedom from the fourfold clinging to characteristics–
The conceptions about what is to be relinquished, remedies,
suchness, and fruition.

At that point, in those who have the kāya of space,
The flowers of the major marks will blossom.
Impure, impure and pure,
And utterly pure, in due order,
Are expressed as the three phases
Of sentient beings, bodhisattvas, and Tathāgatas.
But buddhahood is nothing newly arisen–
Being the same before as after,
It is the changeless buddha heart.
It is the freedom from stains that is expressed as change.

Those who engage in poor views
Think that the buddha qualities are without cause
Or not [in] ourselves, but produced
Through external causes and conditions.
How are these different from non-Buddhist [views on]
permanence and extinction?

The appearing of momentarily arising and ceasing formations
Is comparable to impure formations.
If it were not like this,
The continuum of the enlightened activity of the rūpakāyas
would be interrupted.
However, this is not expressed by the name "formations,"
[But] by "discriminating wisdom."

What has the nature of the great elements and so on,
And is associated with apprehension, displays its powerful
essence.
As for both mistakenness and unmistakenness,
There is no difference as far as appearance goes.
The difference is whether there is clinging to duality or not.
If it were not like this,
How could the enlightened activity of the victors engage
[anything]?

Giving the examples of a wish-fulfilling jewel and such
Explains the display of thoughtfree power,
But not that this is solely [an appearance in] the mind streams of
others.
If it were, wisdom would become the mind streams of others,
[But] if that is accepted, wisdom would be mistakenness.

If it is asserted that [wisdom] grasps at its own appearances,
Then also a mirror would possess conceptions
Of grasping at what appears [in it].

The variety of the mistakenness of sentient beings
Appears as the object of wisdom,
But wisdom is not tainted by mistakenness.
For example, in space, the arising and ceasing
Of the great elements appears, but space
Is not tainted and is without arising and ceasing.

Likewise, the wisdom of the victors
Engages sentient beings, but is untainted.
This is not expressed by the name "mistakenness"–
It is called "all-accomplishing [wisdom]."

Mentation resting pure of the three obscurations
Is equality, which is peace.
Because it is endowed with great love and compassion,
The sambhoga[kāya] and so forth appear for those [to be guided].
This is stated in order to refute some [people's claim]
Of becoming like [arhats of] the hīnayāna, once buddhahood is
attained.

Wisdom is permanent in three ways–
Being permanent by nature is the dharmakāya,
Being permanent in terms of continuity is the sambhogakāya,
And being so in terms of an uninterrupted series is the
nirmāṇakāya.

Related to these, there are three impermanent phenomena–
Mentally fabricated emptiness is not permanent,
The moving conceptual mind is not permanent,
And the conditioned six collections are not permanent.
However, in these, there is threefold permanence.
The three impermanent phenomena are the stains,
While threefold permanence is wisdom as such.

It is not comparable to the self of the tīrthikas,
Since that is imputed by mind, while [the buddha heart] is not.
It is not comparable to the peace of śrāvakas and
pratyekabuddhas,
For it displays all the qualities of the rūpakāyas.
These are not comparable to the bodies of sentient beings,
Since they are not produced by contaminated conditions.

[Buddhas] will not regress,
Since what is has become manifest, just as it is.
The stains never rise [again],
Since there is freedom from any imagination of difference.
Therefore, this mind as such–buddhahood–
Exists right now, but we don't know it.
At the time of realization,
Just as with the subsiding of heat in iron
And blurred vision in the eyes,
The mind and wisdom of a buddha
Are not said to be existent or nonexistent.

Since there is no arising ultimately,
In terms of true reality, there is no liberation either.
Buddhas are just as space,
And sentient beings have the same characteristic.
Since the here and the hereafter are unarisen,
There is no natural nirvāṇa either.

Therefore, conditioned formations are empty,
The sphere of omniscient wisdom.

Since it is subtle, it is not an object of study.
Since it is the ultimate, it is not one of reflection.
Since it is the profound nature of phenomena,
It is not one of mundane meditations and so forth.

It is the sphere of personally experienced wisdom.
Confidence in the self-arisen gives rise to the ultimate.
Alas, since they do not realize this way of being,
Childish beings roam the ocean of saṃsāra.

Through the power of the great sage,
Mañjuśrīghoṣa, Maitreya, and Avalokiteśvara,
This was written by Rangjung Dorje.

May all beings know this buddha heart
Perfectly and without error!
This completes the determination of the buddha heart,
The essence of the vajrayāna.

Śubhaṃ (auspiciousness).

Appendix III: The Treatise on the Distinction between Consciousness and Wisdom

I pay homage to all buddhas und bodhisattvas.

Having relied on study and reflection,
In order to immerse myself in the ways of meditation,
While dwelling in seclusion,
I will express how this principle appears.

[People] think that all sentient beings of the three realms
Arise either from themselves, from something other,
From both or without a cause.
They say: "A creator (such as Cha, Īśvara,
Brahmā, Viṣṇu), outer particles,
Or a real hidden substance
Creates myself and the world."

The sole all-knowing one
Taught sentient beings from his realization
That these three realms are merely mind:
They neither arise from themselves, nor from something other,
Nor from both, nor without a cause.
Phenomena are [nothing but] dependent origination,
While this very [dependent origination] is empty of a nature of its own,
Free from being one or different,
Devoid of being real or delusive,
And just like illusions, the moon in water, and so on.

"From where arises the root
Of mistakenness and unmistakenness?"

Just as [recognizing] one's own form due to a mirror
And fire due to smoke,
Through teaching the principle of dependent origination,
I will clearly express this realization here.

The consciousnesses of the five [sense] gates
Appropriate form, sound, smell, taste, and tangible objects
Or reject them, which produces the afflictions.
When those with prajñā examine carefully
What these objects are,
They are not established as something external (such as particles)
That is other than the cognizing consciousness.

If the substance of objects were other than consciousness,
They would not have the same nature.
[Also,] from cognizance that cannot be pinpointed and
obstructed,
Material substance does not arise.
Because of that, they have no causal connection.
If this is accepted, it is untenable that objects
Appear to consciousness, since they have no connection.

Hence, these appearances, however they may [manifest],
Do not exist as objects that are other than consciousness.
[Their] arising [from] it is like an experience of one's own
awareness.
Whether partless particles or a plateau—
Appearances are mind. The purport of this is
To realize that Brahmā and such are not creating agents,
Since nothing is established as something external to or other
[than mind].

As for the connection between mentation and phenomena,
Just like in an experience in a dream,
This is nothing but one's clinging to focusing on that,
Whereas real entities do not exist.

Thus, this consciousness in its six collections
Arises as the appearances of referents and sentient beings,
Clinging to identity, cognizance,

And whatever forms of appearances.
What are they? If not produced by something other,
They are not produced by themselves [either],
Nor are they produced by both or neither of the two.

Therefore, according to the words of the Victor,
Everything in saṃsāra and nirvāṇa is merely mind.

He says that the dependent origination of the causes and conditions of this
Lies in the six collections, mentation, and the ālaya.

The consciousnesses of the six collections
Depend on their object conditions.
These are the six objects of form and so on.

The dominant conditions are the six sense faculties,
Which possess form and are translucent.

Both arise from the mind.
What vividly appears as objects and sense faculties
Is based on beginningless potentials.
Consciousness is what perceives objects,
While the formations of mental factors [perceive their] features,
Which is based on the mental consciousness.

[Mentation] is twofold—the immediate and the afflicted mind.
Due to being the condition for the arising and ceasing of the six [consciousnesses],
It is the immediate [condition].
Matching the number of the arising and ceasing of the moments
Of the six collections, [the immediate mind] is connected with them.
By virtue of a mind immersed in yoga
And the words of the Victor, this is realized.

The [other] part of this, with regard to mind as such,
Entails self-centeredness, holding on to pride,
Attachment to "me," and ignorance.

Since it produces all [views about] the perishing collection,
It is called "the afflicted mind."

The mentation immediately after the ceasing of the six
[consciousnesses]
Is the locus of the arising of consciousness.
The afflicted mind is the locus of affliction.
Since it has the capacity to produce and to obscure,
This mentation has two aspects.

For those with special insight,
[The Buddha] taught the ālaya-consciousness.

It is also taught as support, matrix,
Or appropriating consciousness.
Since all karmas produced by the seven collections are gathered
In an unmixed and neutral way,
It is called "maturational,"
Just as rain water [flows] into the ocean.
Since it produces everything,
It is the ground from which all seeds rise,
Thus being designated "the causal condition."
Because it dissolves, when the seven collections dissolve,
It is also called "conditioned consciousness."

The nature of the external and internal,
This very ālaya-consciousness,
Is the root of everything to be relinquished.
It is said that it is to be overcome
Through the vajralike samādhi.

Once the ālaya including the obscurations is extinguished,
It becomes mirror[like] wisdom.
All wisdoms appear [in it] without any "mine."
It is unconfined and ever present.
It realizes all knowable objects, yet is never directed toward them.
Since it is the cause of all wisdoms,
It is called the "dharmakāya."

The afflicted mind is overcome
Through "the heroic stride."

Once the afflictions are relinquished through seeing and familiarization,
There are no afflictions, no existence, and no peace.
This is designated as the "wisdom of equality."

The immediate mind
Is seizing, since it seizes the six [consciousnesses].
[Since] it causes conceptions, it is conception.
It is overcome through perfect prajñā
And the illusionlike samādhi.

Through this, when great poised readiness is attained,
The apprehender and its referents change state.
Thus, the change of state of conception,
Which represents the display of pure realms,
Wisdom in all times,
And being unimpeded in all activities,
Is discriminating wisdom.

Thus, these two wisdoms,
Through pure cultivation, are the peace
Of not abiding in either existence or peace,
Endowed with love and compassion,
And display all kinds of kāyas and speech for their retinues.
In this way, the maṇḍala of the melody of the great dharma manifests.
This treasury of all samādhis and dhāraṇīs
Is called the "sambhogakāya."

As for the five [sense] gates and a part of mentation,
True actuality is seen and realized as reality
Through the sixteen [wisdoms], such as poised readiness for cognition,
Which arise from correct imagination
And entail the aspects of the principles of the four realities.

Through this, the five sense faculties change state,
Mastering engagement in all objects
And the twelve hundred qualities of all [bhūmis].
The culmination of such [mastery]

Is all-accomplishing wisdom.
It accomplishes the welfare of all sentient beings
In all realms through various
Immeasurable and inconceivable emanations.
This is the great nirmāṇakāya.

The three kāyas including their activities,
Which are the changes of state of mind, mentation, and consciousness,
Are perfected as the maṇḍala of the dharmadhātu free from reference points.
That everything in saṃsāra and nirvāṇa without beginning
Abides free from being one or different
Is held to be the svābhāvikakāya.

In some other texts, the Victor
Taught this as the "dharmakāya."
In this case, mirrorlike [wisdom] is called "the wisdom kāya,"
And the others, the "two rūpakāyas."

Buddhahood is the manifestation of the nature
Of the five wisdoms and the four kāyas.
The ālaya is what possesses the stains
Of mind, mentation, and consciousness.
Its stainlessness is called the Heart of the victors.
What overcomes impure imagination
Is pure imagination, from which
The power of the prajñā of the noble ones arises—
Seizing it is taught to be the reality of the path.

Because they do not realize the way of being of the ultimate,
The oblivious roam the ocean of saṃsāra.
They will not reach the other shore through anything
Except for this ship of the mahāyāna.

May all realize this true actuality!

This *Treatise on the Distinction between Consciousness and Wisdom* was composed by Rangjung Dorje in the mountain retreat of Upper Dechen on the first day of the tenth month of the year of the pig [1335].

Appendix IV: Outline of NTC

1. Instruction on the title
2. Paying homage
3. Brief introduction by means of scriptures
3.1. A quotation from the *Abhidharmasūtra*
3.2. A quotation from the *Hevajratantra*
4. Detailed explanation
4.1. Detailed explanation of the meaning of the quote from the *Abhidharmasūtra*
4.1.1. Explaining the manner of being beginningless
4.1.2. The meaning of the basic element
4.1.3. The dharmas that dwell in it
4.1.4. The matrix itself
4.1.5. The manner of existing in that way
4.1.6. The meaning of end
4.2. Explaining false and correct imagination
4.2.1. The way in which saṃsāra is based on false imagination
4.2.2. The root of saṃsāra originates from adopting and rejecting
4.2.3. The meaning of remedial thoughts
4.3. Explaining the buddha heart
4.3.1. Pointing out its own essence
4.3.2. Explaining its qualities
4.3.2.1. Brief introduction
4.3.2.2. Detailed explanation
4.3.2.2.1. Explaining the qualities of the dharmakāya
4.3.2.2.1.1. The ten powers
4.3.2.2.1.2. The four fearlessnesses
4.3.2.2.1.3. The eighteen unique qualities
4.3.2.2.1.4. The manner of them not appearing despite their present existence

4.3.2.2.1.5. The manner in which this is to be realized, including scriptural support
4.3.2.2.2. Explaining the qualities of the rūpakāyas
4.3.2.2.2.1. The essence of the qualities
4.3.2.2.2.2. Justification that they dwell in the body
4.3.2.2.2.3. The manner of purity and impurity
4.3.3. Explaining this by matching an example and its meaning
4.3.3.1. Giving the example proper
4.3.3.2. Matching it with its meaning
4.3.3.3. The manner of overcoming the obscurations through the two imaginations, including their order
4.3.3.4. The manner of attaining purity despite [the buddha heart] being unchanging, including scriptural support
4.4. Determining this through answers to objections
4.4.1. Brief instruction on causelessness and outer causes being untenable
4.4.2. Certainty about pure and impure mentation
4.4.3. The essence of all-accomplishing wisdom
4.4.3.1. The manner in which the subjects and objects of the five gates appear
4.4.3.2. The difference [between beings and buddhas] and the reason [for that]
4.4.4. The enlightened activity of all-accomplishing wisdom
4.4.4.1. Presenting the purpose of explaining examples for it
4.4.4.2. Addressing the fault of asserting that enlightened activity is solely something in the mind streams of others
4.4.4.3. Stating that there is no certainty as to appearances entailing mistakenness by giving a counterexample
4.4.4.4. Explaining the example for the wisdom of variety not being mistaken and its meaning
4.4.4.5. The meaning of being connected with enlightened activity
4.4.5. Stating the meaning of the wisdom of equality
4.4.6. Explaining the manner in which the three kāyas are permanent
4.4.6.1. The meaning of the three ways of being permanent
4.4.6.2. The meaning of threefold impermanence
4.4.6.3. Explaining these as wisdoms and stains, respectively
4.4.7. Dispelling uncertainty
4.4.7.1. The meaning of being unlike the self of the tīrthikas
4.4.7.2. The meaning of not being comparable to the peace of śrāvakas and pratyekabuddhas
4.4.7.3. The meaning of not being comparable to sentient beings

4.4.7.4. The meaning of not regressing
4.4.7.5. The meaning of the stains never rising again
4.4.7.6. Summary
4.5. Gaining certainty about the explanation of the essence through scriptures
4.5.1. A quote from the *Mahāyānasūtrālaṃkāra*
4.5.2. A quote from noble Nāgārjuna's *Mahāyānaviṃśikā*
4.5.3. A quote from the *Uttaratantra*
4.5.4. Summary of the meaning taught in the sūtras and tantras
5. Conclusion through the manner of obtaining [this text]
5.1. The actual manner of obtaining
5.2. An aspiration prayer

Appendix V: Outline of NYC

1. The introduction of engaging in the composition
1.1. Teaching the title of the treatise
1.2. Paying homage
1.3. Commitment to compose the text
2. The meaning of the text
2.1. Explaining the aspect of consciousness
2.1.1. Explaining that the root of mistakenness and nonmistakenness is mind as such
2.1.1.1. Wrong ideas of others about this
2.1.1.2. How this was taught by the victor
2.1.1.3. The manner of this being taught through [Rangjung Dorje's] own realization
2.1.2. Establishing that appearances are mind
2.1.2.1. Explaining the dependent origination of the five operating consciousnesses and establishing it as mind
2.1.2.2. Dispelling wrong ideas that this is not mind
2.1.2.3. Presenting evidence that another agent does not exist
2.1.2.4. Explaining interdependence in terms of the sixth [consciousness], mentation
2.1.3. Teaching that mind is unborn
2.1.3.1. The actual explanation
2.1.3.2. Adducing scriptural evidence
2.1.4. Explaining the causes and conditions of mistakenness, the eight collections [of consciousness]
2.1.4.1 Brief introduction
2.1.4.2. Detailed explanation
2.1.4.2.1. Explaining the six collections
2.1.4.2.1.1. Identifying the six collections
2.1.4.2.1.2. Identifying the object condition
2.1.4.2.1.3. Identifying the dominant condition

2.1.4.2.1.4. Explaining what those arise from
2.1.4.2.2. Explaining the immediate condition together with the afflicted mind
2.1.4.2.2.1. Brief introduction by way of their names
2.1.4.2.2.2. Detailed explanation of their defining characteristics
2.1.4.2.2.2.1. Explaining the immediate mind
2.1.4.2.2.2.2. Explaining the afflicted mind
2.1.4.2.2.2.3. Summarizing the characteristics of both
2.1.4.2.3 Explaining the causal condition—the ālaya[-consciousness]
2.1.4.2.3.1 Brief introduction by means of its name
2.1.4.2.3.2 Detailed explanation of its specific characteristics
2.2. Explaining the wisdoms and the kāyas that are the change of state of the eight collections [of consciousness]
2.2.1 Brief introduction of the general meaning
2.2.2 Explaining the actual meaning of the text
2.2.2.1. Explaining mirrorlike wisdom as the dharmakāya
2.2.2.1.1. Explaining what is to be purified and what purifies it
2.2.2.1.2. Explaining the result of purification—the kāya and the wisdom
2.2.2.2. Explaining the wisdom of equality
2.2.2.2.1. Explaining what is to be purified and what purifies it
2.2.2.2.2 Explaining the wisdom that is the result of purification
2.2.2.3 Explaining discriminating wisdom
2.2.2.3.1 Explaining what is to be purified and what purifies it
2.2.2.3.2. Explaining the wisdom that is the result of purification
2.2.2.4. Explaining the [latter] two [wisdoms] as the sambhogakāya
2.2.2.5. Explaining all-accomplishing wisdom as the nirmāṇakāya
2.2.2.5.1. Explaining what is to be purified and what purifies it
2.2.2.5.2. Explaining the kāyas that are the result of purification
2.2.2.6. Explaining dharmadhātu wisdom as the svābhāvikakāya
2.2.2.6.1. The actual explanation
2.2.2.6.2. Critical analysis of the kāyas
2.3. Summary of the meaning of [consciousness and wisdom]
3. Conclusion
3.1. Purpose of explaining this text
3.2. Aspiration for realizing it
3.3. Stating how the text was composed

Appendix VI: The Change of State of the Eight Consciousnesses into the Four(Five) Wisdoms and the Three (Four) Kāyas

According to Yogācāra

	Consciousness	*Wisdom*	*Kāya*	*Bhūmi of change of state*
1	eye consciousness	all-accomplishing wisdom	nirmāṇakāya	1
2	ear consciousness			
3	nose consciousness			
4	tongue consciousness			
5	body consciousness			
6	mental consciousness	discriminating wisdom	samboghakāya	8
7	afflicted mind	wisdom of equality		8
8	ālaya-consciousness	mirrorlike wisdom	dharmakāya	10
			D H A R M A D H Ā T U	

According to the Third Karmapa

1	eye consciousness	all-accomplishing wisdom	nirmāṇakāya	1
2	ear consciousness			
3	nose consciousness			
4	tongue consciousness			
5	body consciousness			
6a	nonconceptual mental consciousness			
6b	conceptual mental consciousness	discriminating wisdom		8
7a	immediate mind		samboghakāya	
7b	afflicted mind	wisdom of equality		8
8	ālaya-consciousness	mirrorlike wisdom	dharmakāya	10
		dharmadhātu (wisdom)	svābhāvikakāya	

Glossary: English–Sanskrit–Tibetan

English	Sanskrit	Tibetan
adventitious stain	āgantukamala	glo bur gyi dri ma
afflicted phenomena	saṃkleśa	kun nas nyon mongs pa
afflictive obscuration	kleśāvaraṇa	nyon mongs pa'i sgrib pa
basic element	dhātu	khams
causal condition	hetupratyaya	rgyu rkyen
(fundamental) change of state	āśrayaparivṛtti	gnas yongs su gyur pa
clinging to reality/real existence	*satyagrahaṇa	bden 'dzin
cognitive obscuration	jñeyāvaraṇa	shes bya'i sgrib pa
correct imagination	bhūtaparikalpa	yang dag kun rtog
dependent origination of differentiating the nature	*svabhāvavibhāgaḥ pratītyasamutpādaḥ	ngo bo nyid rnam par 'byed pa can gyi rten 'brel
dependent origination of differentiating what is desired and undesired	*prīyāprīyavibhāgaḥ pratītyasamutpādaḥ	sdug pa dang mi sdug pa rnam par 'byed pa can gyi rten 'brel
dependent origination of experience	*upabhogaḥ pratītyasamutpādaḥ	nyer spyod can gyi rten 'brel
disposition	gotra	rigs
dominant condition	adhipatipratyaya	bdag rkyen
emptiness endowed with the supreme of all aspects	sarvākāravaropetāśūnyatā	rnam kun mchog ldan gyi stong pa nyid
entity	bhāva/vastu	dngos po
factors conducive to liberation	mokṣabhāgīya	thar pa cha mthun
factors conducive to penetration	nirvedhabhāgīya	nges 'byed cha mthun

false imagination	abhūtaparikalpa	yang dag ma yin kun rtog
freedom from reference points	niṣprapañca	spros bral
ground of the latent tendencies of ignorance	avidyāvāsanābhūmi	ma rig bag chags kyi sa
identitylessness	nairātmya	bdag med
imaginary (nature)	parikalpita(svabhāva)	kun brtags (kyi rang bzhin)
immediate condition	samanantarapratyaya	de ma thag rkyen
immediate mind	*samanantaramanas	de ma thag yid
impregnations of negative tendencies	dauṣṭhulya	gnas ngan len pa
innate	sahaja	lhan skyes
isolate	vyatireka	ldog pa
lack of nature	niḥsvabhāva	ngo bo nyid/ rang bzhin med pa
latent tendencies for listening	śrutavāsanā	thos pa'i bag chags
latent tendency	vāsanā	bag chags
lineage of profound view	—	zab mo lta rgyud
lineage of vast activity	—	rgya chen spyod rgyud
meditative absorption of cessation	nirodhasamāpatti	'gog pa'i snyoms 'jug
meditative absorption without discrimination	asaṃjñisamāpatti	'du shes med pa'i snyoms 'jug
mental consciousness	manovijñāna	yid kyi rnam shes
mentation	manas	yid
mere cognizance	vijñaptimātra	rnam rig tsam
Mere Mentalist	—	sems tsam pa
mere mind/Mere Mentalism	cittamātra	sems tsam
mind as such	cittatvam, cittam eva	sems nyid
modulation	pariṇāma	rnam 'gyur
natural outflow	niṣyanda	rgyu mthun pa
naturally abiding disposition	prakṛtisthagotra	rang bzhin gnas rigs
nominal ultimate	paryāyaparamārtha	rnam grangs pa'i don dam
nonconceptual wisdom	nirvikalpajñāna	rnam par mi rtog pa'i ye shes
nondual wisdom	advayajñāna	gnyis med ye shes

nonentity	abhāva/avastu	dngos med
nonimplicative negation	prasajyapratiṣedha	med dgag
nonobservation	anupalabdhi, anupalambha	mi dmigs pa
nonreferential	anupalambha, anālambana	mi dmigs pa, dmigs med
object condition	ālambanapratyaya	dmigs rkyen
other-dependent (nature)	paratantra(svabhāva)	gzhan dbang (gi rang bzhin)
perfect (nature)	pariniṣpanna(svabhāva)	yongs grub (kyi rang bzhin)
personal identitylessness	pudgalanairātmya	gang zag gi bdag med
personally experienced (wisdom)	pratyātmavedanīya(jñāna) (svapratyātmāryajñāna)	so so rang rig (pa'i ye shes)
phenomenal identitylessness	dharmanairātmya	chos kyi bdag med
philosophical system	siddhānta	grub mtha'
purified phenomenon	vyavadāna	rnam par byang ba
reference point	prapañca	spros pa
reification	bhāvagrāha	dngos 'dzin
result of freedom	visaṃyogaphala	bral ba'i 'bras bu
seeming (reality)	saṃvṛti(satya)	kun rdzob (bden pa)
self-aware(ness)	svasaṃvedana, svasaṃvitti	rang rig
sphere	gocara	spyod yul
stainless mentation	—	dri ma med pa'i yid
subsequent attainment	pṛṣṭhalabdha	rjes thob
three natures	trisvabhāva	ngo bo nyid/ rang bzhin gsum
three spheres	trimaṇḍala	'khor gsum
true end	bhūtakoṭi	yang dag pa'i mtha'
true reality	tattva	de (kho na) nyid
ultimate (reality)	paramārtha(satya)	don dam (bden pa)
unconditioned (phenomenon)	asaṃskṛta	'dus ma byas
unfolding disposition	paripuṣṭagotra	rgyas 'gyur gyi rigs
valid cognition	pramāṇa	tshad ma
views about a real personality	satkāyadṛṣṭi	'jig tshogs la lta ba
wisdom of knowing suchness	yathāvatjñāna	ji lta ba mkhyen pa'i ye shes

wisdom of knowing variety	yāvatjñāna	ji snyed mkhyen pa'i ye shes
yogic valid perception	yogipratyakṣapramāṇa	rnal 'byor mngon sum tshad ma

Glossary: Tibetan–Sanskrit–English

Tibetan	***Sanskrit***	***English***
kun brtags (kyi rang bzhin)	parikalpita(svabhāva)	imaginary (nature)
kun nas nyon mongs pa	saṃkleśa	afflicted phenomenon
kun rdzob (bden pa)	saṃvṛti(satya)	seeming (reality)
khams	dhātu	basic element
'khor gsum	trimaṇḍala	three spheres
gang zag gi bdag med	pudgalanairātmya	personal identitylessness
glo bur gyi dri ma	āgantukamala	adventitious stains
'gog pa'i snyoms 'jug	nirodhasamāpatti	meditative absorption of cessation
rgya chen spyod rgyud	—	lineage of vast activity
rgyas 'gyur gyi rigs	paripuṣṭagotra	unfolding disposition
rgyu rkyen	hetupratyaya	causal condition
rgyu mthun	niṣyanda	natural outflow
nges 'byed cha mthun	nirvedhabhāgīya	factors conducive to penetration
ngo bo nyid rnam par 'byed pa can gyi rten 'brel	*svabhāvavibhāgaḥ pratītyasamutpādaḥ	dependent origination of differentiating the nature
ngo bo nyid med pa	niḥsvabhāva	lack of nature
dngos po	bhāva/vastu	entity
dngos med	abhāva/avastu	nonentity
dngos 'dzin	bhāvagrāha	reification
chos kyi bdag med	dharmanairātmya	phenomenal identitylessness
chos nyid	dharmatā	nature of phenomena

ji snyed mkhyen pa'i ye shes	yāvatjñāna	wisdom of knowing variety
ji lta ba mkhyen pa'i ye shes	yathāvatjñāna	wisdom of knowing suchness
'jig tshogs la lta ba	satkāyadṛṣṭi	views about a real personality
rjes thob	pṛṣṭhalabdha	subsequent attainment
nyer spyod can gyi rten 'brel	*upabhogaḥ pratītyasamutpādaḥ	dependent origination of experience
nyon mongs pa'i sgrib pa	kleśāvaraṇa	afflictive obscuration
gnyis med ye shes	advayajñāna	nondual wisdom
thar pa cha mthun	mokṣabhāgīya	factors conducive to liberation
thos pa'i bag chags	śrutavāsanā	latent tendencies for listening
de (kho na) nyid	tattva	true reality
de ma thag rkyen	samanantarapratyaya	immediate condition
de ma thag yid	*samanantaramanas	immediate mind
don dam (bden pa)	paramārtha(satya)	ultimate (reality)
dri ma med pa'i yid	—	stainless mentation
bdag rkyen	adhipatipratyaya	dominant condition
bden 'dzin	*satyagrahaṇa	clinging to reality/ real existence
'du shes med pa'i snyoms 'jug	asaṃjñisamāpatti	meditative absorption without discrimination
'dus byas	saṃskṛta	conditioned (phenomenon)
'dus ma byas	asaṃskṛta	unconditioned (phenomenon)
ldog pa	vyatireka	isolate
sdug pa dang mi sdug pa rnam par 'byed pa can gyi rten 'brel	*prīyāprīyavibhāgaḥ pratītyasamutpādaḥ	dependent origination of differentiating what is desired and undesired
gnas ngan len pa	dauṣṭhulya	impregnations of negative tendencies
gnas yongs su gyur pa	āśrayaparivṛtti	(fundamental) change of state

rnam kun mchog ldan gyi stong pa nyid	sarvākāravaropetāśūnyatā	emptiness endowed with the supreme of all aspects
rnam grangs pa'i don dam	paryāyaparamārtha	nominal ultimate
rnam 'gyur	pariṇāma	modulation
rnam par byang ba	vyavadāna	purified phenomenon
rnam par mi rtog pa'i ye shes	nirvikalpajñāna	nonconceptual wisdom
rnam rig tsam	vijñaptimātra	mere cognizance
rnal 'byor mngon sum tshad ma	yogipratyakṣapramāṇa	yogic valid perception
spyod yul	gocara	sphere
spros pa	prapañca	reference point
spros bral	niṣprapañca	freedom from reference points
bag chags	vāsanā	latent tendency
bral ba'i 'bras bu	visaṃyogaphala	result of freedom
ma rig bag chags kyi sa	avidyāvāsanābhūmi	ground of the latent tendencies of ignorance
mi dmigs pa	anupalabdhi, anupalambha	nonobservation, nonreferential
med dgag	prasajyapratiṣedha	nonimplicative negation
dmigs rkyen	ālambanapratyaya	object condition
dmigs med	anupalambha, anupalabdhi	nonreferential, nonobservation
tshad ma	pramāṇa	valid cognition
gzhan dbang (gi rang bzhin)	paratantra(svabhāva)	other-dependent (nature)
zab mo lta rgyud	—	lineage of profound view
yang dag kun rtog	bhūtaparikalpa	correct imagination
yang dag pa'i mtha'	bhūtakoṭi	true end
yang dag ma yin kun rtog	abhūtaparikalpa	false imagination
yid	manas	mentation
yongs grub (kyi rang bzhin)	pariniṣpanna(svabhāva)	perfect (nature)
rang bzhin gnas rigs	prakṛtisthagotra	naturally abiding disposition
rang bzhin med pa	niḥsvabhāva	lack of nature
rang bzhin gsum	trisvabhāva	three natures

rang rig	svasaṃvedana, svasaṃvitti	self-aware(ness)
rigs	gotra	disposition
shes bya'i sgrib pa	jñeyāvaraṇa	cognitive obscuration
sems nyid	cittatvam, cittam eva	mind as such
sems tsam	cittamātra	mere mind, Mere Mentalism
sems tsam pa	—	Mere Mentalist
so so rang rig (pa'i ye shes)	pratyātmavedanīya(jñāna) (svapratyātmāryajñāna)	personally experienced (wisdom)
lhan skyes	sahaja	innate

Selected Bibliography

Canonical Works[874]

Āryadeva. *Jñānasārasamucchaya* (Ye shes snying po kun las btus pa). D3851.

Asaṅga. *Abhidharmasamucchaya* (Chos mngon pa kun las btus pa). D4049. English translations by S. Boin-Webb, Fremont: Asian Humanities Press, 2000; and Migme Chodron (from the French by W. Rāhula), Pleasant Bay: Gampo Abbey (Canada) 2001.

——. *Bodhisattvabhūmi* (Byang chub sems dpa'i sa). D4037.

——. *Mahāyānasaṃgraha* (Theg chen bsdus pa). D4049.

——. *Ratnagotravibhāgavyākhyā* or *Mahāyānottaratantraśāstravyākhyā* (Theg pa chen po'i rgyud bla ma'i bstan bcos rnam par bshad pa). D4025. Sanskrit edition by E. H. Johnston. Patna, India: Bihar Research Society, 1950.

——. *Saṃdhinirmocanabhāṣya* (Dgongs pa nges par 'grel pa'i rnam par bshad pa). P5481. D3981.

——. *Viniścayasaṃgrahaṇī* (Rnam par gtan la dbab pa bsdu ba). D4038.

——. *Yogācārabhūmi* (Rnal 'byor spyod pa'i sa). D4035.

Asvabhāva. Ālokamālāṭīkāhṛdānandajananī (Snang ba'i phreng ba'i 'grel pa yid dga' ba bskyed pa). D3896.

——. *Mahāyānasaṃgrahopanibandhana* (Theg pa chen po bsdus pa'i bshad sbyar). D4051.

——. *Mahāyānasūtrālaṃkāraṭīkā* (Theg pa chen po mdo sde'i rgyan gyi rgya cher bshad pa). D4029.

Bodhibhadra. *Samādhisambhāraparivarta* (Ting nge 'dzin gyi tshogs kyi le'u). D3924.

Dignāga. *Ālambanaparīkṣā* (Dmigs pa brtag pa). D4205.

——. *Ālambanaparīkṣāvṛtti* (Dmigs pa brtag pa'i 'grel pa). D4026.

Dharmakīrti. *Pramāṇavārttika* (Tshad ma rnam 'grel). D4210.

——. *Pramāṇaviniścaya* (Tshad ma rnam nges). D4211.

Guṇaprabha. *Pañcaskandhavivaraṇa* (Phung po lnga'i rnam par 'grel pa). D4067.

Jñānacandra. *Kāyatrayavṛtti* (Sku gsum 'grel pa). D3891.

——. *Yogacaryābhāvanātātparyārthanirdeśa* (Rnal 'byor spyod pa'i sgom pa'i don mdor bsdus te bstan pa). D4077/4546.

Jñānagarbha. Satyadvayavibhāga (Bden gnyis rnam 'byed). T3881. Not in D or P.

Kambala. *Ālokamālāprakaraṇanāma* (Snang ba'i phreng ba zhes bya ba'i rab tu byed pa). D3895.

——. *Bhagavatīprajñāpāramitānavaślokapiṇḍārtha* (Bcom ldan 'das ma shes rab kyi pha rol tu phyin pa don bsdus pa'i tshigs su bcad pa dgu pa). D3812 [14 stanzas]. *Navaślokī* (Tshigs su bcad pa dgu pa). D4462 [15 stanzas].

——. *Bhagavatīprajñāpāramitānavaślokapiṇḍārthaṭīkā* (Bcom ldan 'das ma shes rab kyi pha rol tu phyin pa don bsdus pa'i tshigs su bcad pa dgu pa'i rgya cher bshad pa). D3813.

Maitreya. *Abhisamayālaṃkāra* (Mngon rtogs rgyan). D3786. Sanskrit edition by T. Stcherbatsky and E. Obermiller. Bibliotheca Buddhica 23. Leningrad, 1929; G. Tucci, Baroda, 1932; U. Wogihara, Tokyo, 1932–35; K. Kajiyoshi in *Hannya-kyō no kenkyu*, 1944, pp. 275–320.

——. *Dharmadharmatāvibhāga* (Chos dang chos nyid rnam par byed pa). D4022.

——. *Madhyāntavibhāga* (Dbus dang mtha' rnam par 'byed pa). D4021.

——. *Mahāyānasūtrālaṃkāra* (Theg pa chen po'i mdo sde rgyan). D4020.

——. *Ratnagotravibhāgamahāyānottaratantraśāstra* (Theg pa chen po'i rgyud bla ma). D4024. Sanskrit edition by E. H. Johnston. Patna, India: The Bihar Research Society, 1950 (includes the Ratnagotravibhāgavyākhyā).

Nāgamitra. *Kāyatrayāvatāramukha* (Sku gsum la 'jug pa'i sgo). D3890.

Nāgārjuna. *Bodhicittavivaraṇa* (Byang chub sems kyi 'grel pa). D4556.

——. *Cittavajrastava* (Sems kyi rdo rje bstod pa). D1121.

——. *Dharmadhātustava* (Chos dbyings bstod pa). D1118.

——. *Lokātītastava*. ('Jig rten las 'das pa'i bstod pa). D1120.

——. *Mūlamadhyamakavṛttyakutobhayā* (Dbu ma rtsa ba'i 'grel pa ga las 'jigs med). D3829.

——. *Prajñānāmamūlamadhyamakakārikā* (Dbu ma rtsa ba'i tshig le'ur byas pa shes rab ces bya ba). D3824.

——. *Suhṛllekha* (Bshes pa'i springs yig). D4182.

Nāropa. *Summary of the View* (Lta ba mdor bsdus pa).

Saraha. *Dohākośagīti* (Do hā mdzod kyi glu; "People Dohā"). D2224.

Śīlabhadra. *Buddhabhūmivyākhyāna* (Sangs rgyas kyi sa'i rnam par bshad pa). D3997.

Sthiramati. *Abhidharmasamucchayavyākhyā* (Mngon pa chos kun nas btus pa'i rnam par bshad pa). D4054.

——. *Madhyāntavibhāgaṭīkā* (Dbus dang mtha' rnam par 'byed pa'i 'grel bshad). D4032. Sanskrit editions: S. Lévi, ed. Paris: Bibliothèque de l'École des Hautes Études, 1932; S. Yamaguchi, ed. Tokyo: Suzuki Research Foundation, 1966.

——. *Pañcaskandhaprakaraṇavaibhāṣa* (Phung po lnga'i rab tu byed pa bye brag tu bshad pa). D4066.

——. *Sūtrālaṃkāravṛttibhāṣya* (Mdo sde rgyan gyi 'grel bshad). D4034.

——. *Triṃśikābhāṣya* (Sum cu pa'i bshad pa). D4064.

Vasubandhu. *Abhidharmakośa* (Chos mngon pa mdzod). D4089.

——. *Abhidharmakośabhāṣya* (Chos mngon pa mdzod kyi bshad pa). D4090.

——. *Āryaśatasāhasrikāpañcaviṃśatisāhasrikāṣṭādaśasāhasrikāprajñāpāramitābṛhaṭṭīkā* (Sher phyin 'bum pa dang nyi khri lnga stong pa dang khri brgyad stong pa'i rgya cher 'grel pa; abbreviated as Yum gsum gnod 'joms). D3808.

——. *Dharmadharmatāvibhāgabhāṣya* (Chos dang chos nyid rnam par 'byed pa'i 'grel pa). D4028.

——. *Madhyāntavibhāgabhāṣya* (Dbus mtha' rnam 'byed kyi 'grel pa). D4027.

——. *Mahāyānasūtrālaṃkārabhāṣya* (Theg pa chen po'i mdo sde rgyan gyi 'grel pa). D4026.

——. *Vyākhyāyukti.* (Rnam bshad rigs pa) D4061.

Tibetan Works

Bdud 'joms 'jigs bral ye shes rdo rje. 1991. *The Nyingma School of Tibetan Buddhism.* Translated by Gyurme Dorje and M. Kapstein. 2 vols. Boston: Wisdom Publications.

Blo gros grags pa, 'dzam thang mkhan po. 1993. *Fearless Lion's Roar* (Rgyu dang 'bras bu'i theg pa mchog gi gnas lugs zab mo'i don rnam par nges pa rje jo nang pa chen po'i ring lugs 'jigs med gdong lnga'i nga ro). Dharamsala: LTWA.

Bu ston rin chen grub. 1931. *History of Buddhism.* Translated by E. Obermiller. Heidelberg: Otto Harrassowitz.

Chos grags rgya mtsho (Karmapa VII). 1985. *The Ocean of Texts on Reasoning* (Tshad ma legs par bshad pa thams cad kyi chu bo yongs su 'du ba rigs pa'i gzhung lugs kyi rgya mtsho). 4 vols. Rumtek (Sikkim), India: Karma Thupten Chosphel and Phuntsok.

Chos kyi 'byung gnas (Situpa VIII). n.d. *Nges don phyag rgya chen po'i smon lam gyi 'grel pa grub pa chog gi zhal lung.* Sikkim, India: Rumtek Monastery. Translated by Lama Sherab Dorje, as *Mahāmudrā Teachings of the Supreme Siddhas.* Ithaca, N.Y.: Snow Lion Publications, 1995.

Chos kyi 'byung gnas (Situpa VIII) and 'Be lo tshe dbang kun khyab. 1972. *Sgrub brgyud karma ka¦ tshang brgyud pa rin po che'i rnam par thar pa rab 'byams nor bu zla ba chu shel gyi phreng ba.* 2 vols. New Delhi: Gyaltsan and Kesang Legshay.

Dbu ma gzhan stong skor bstan bcos phyogs bsdus deb dang po. 1990. Rumtek (Sikkim), India: Acharya (the senior-most class of Karma Shri Nalanda Institute).

Dkon mchog yan lag (Shamarpa V). 2006. *De bzhin gshegs pa'i snying po gtan la dbab pa'i bstan bcos mchan can.* In *Collected Works* of Rangjung Dorje, vol. ja: 291–307.

Dngul chu thogs med bzang po dpal. 1979. *Theg pa chen po mdo sde rgyan gyi 'grel pa rin po che'i phreng ba*. Bir, India: Dzongsar Institute Library.

Dol po pa shes rab rgyal mtshan. 1998. *The Mountain Dharma Called the Ocean of Definitive Meaning* (Ri chos nges don rgya mtsho). Beijing: Mi rigs dpe skrun khang.

Dpa' bo gtsug lag phreng ba. 2003. *History of the Dharma, A Feast for the Learned* (Dam pa'i chos kyi 'khor lo bsgyur ba rnams kyi byung ba gsal bar byed pa mkhas pa'i dga' ston). 2 vols. Sarnath: Vajra Vidya Library.

———. n.d. *Byang chub sems dpa'i spyod pa la 'jug pa'i rnam bshad theg chen chos kyi rgya mtsho zab rgyas mtha' yas pa'i snying po*. Rouffignac, France: Nehsang Samten Chöling.

Dpal sprul 'jigs med chos kyi dbang po. 1997. *Shes rab kyi pha rol tu phyin pa'i man ngag gi bstan bcos mngon par rtogs pa'i rgyan ces bya ba'i spyi don dang 'bru 'grel*. Beijing: Mi rigs dpe skrun khang.

Dvags po rab 'byams pa mkhas grub chos rgyal bstan pa. 2005. *Dpal rdo rje'i tshig zab mo nang gi don gyi 'grel bshad sems kyi rnam par thar pa gsal bar byed pa'i rgyan*. Seattle: Nitartha *international* Publications.

'Gos lo tsā ba gzhon nu dpal. 1996. *The Blue Annals*. Translated by G. N. Roerich. Delhi: Motilal Banarsidass.

———. 2003a. *Deb ther sngon po*. 2 vols. Sarnath: Vajra Vidya Library.

———. 2003b. *Theg pa chen po'i rgyud bla ma'i bstan bcos kyi 'grel bshad de kho na nyid rab tu gsal ba'i me long*. Nepal Research Centre Publications 24. Edited by Klaus-Dieter Mathes. Stuttgart: Franz Steiner Verlag.

'Ju mi pham rgya mtsho. 1975. *Bde gshegs snying po stong thun chen mo seng ge'i nga ro. In Collected Writings of 'Jam-mgon 'Ju Mi-pham-rgya-mtsho*. Vol. pa. Edited by Sonam T. Kazi. Gangtok: fols. 282–304.

———. c. 1990a. *Collected Works* (gsungs 'bum). Sde dge dgon chen edition. Edited by Dilgo Khyentse Rinpoche. Kathmandu.

———. c. 1990b. *Chos dang chos nyid rnam par 'byed pa'i tshig le'ur byas pa'i 'grel pa ye shes snang ba rnam 'byed*. In *Collected Works*. Vol. pa: 1–51.

———. c. 1990c. *Dbus dang mtha' rnam par 'byed pa'i 'grel pa od zer 'phreng ba*. In *Collected Works*. Vol. pa: 660–784.

———. c. 1990d. *Gzhan stong khas len seng ge'i nga ro*. In *Collected Works*. Vol. ga: 359–99.

———. 1992. *Dbu ma rgyan rtsa 'grel*. Chengdu, China: Si khron mi rigs dpe skrun khang.

Karma 'phrin las pa. 1975. *Dri lan yid kyi mun sel zhes bya ba lcags mo'i dris lan*. In *The Songs of Esoteric Practice (Mgur) and Replies to Doctrinal Questions (Dri lan) of Karma-'phrin-las-pa*. Containing a reproduction of Volume GA *Chos kyi rje karma phrin las pa'i gsung 'bum las rdo rje mgur kyi 'phren ba rnams* (Songs of esoteric practice given on various occasions) and volume CHA *Chos kyi rje Karma phrin las pa'i gsung 'bum las thun mong ba'i dri lan gyi phreng ba rnams* (Replies to various doctrinal questions and polemics). New Delhi: Ngawang Tobgay.

———. 2006. *Zab mo nang don gyi rnam bshad snying po gsal bar byed pa'i nyin byed 'od kyi phreng ba*. In *Collected Works* of Rangjung Dorje. Vol. tram: 1–553.

Khrims khang lo tsā ba. 2006. *Zab mo nang don gyi yang snying gsang ba gsum gyi gnad rnam par phye ba zhes bya'i zin bris*. In *Collected Works* of Rangjung Dorje. Vol. hrīḥ: 443–578.

Kong sprul blo gros mtha' yas. 1982. *Theg pa'i sgo kun las btus pa gsung rab rin po che'i mdzod bslab pa gsum legs par ston pa'i bstan bcos shes bya kun khyab*; includes its autocommentary, *Shes bya kun la khyab pa'i gzhung lugs nyung ngu'i tshig gis rnam par 'grol ba legs bshad yongs 'du shes bya mhta' yas pa'i rgya mtsho* (abbreviated as Shes bya kun kyab mdzod). 3 vols. Beijing: Mi rigs dpe skrun khang.

———. 1990a. *Rnam par shes pa dang ye shes 'byed pa'i bstan bcos kyi tshig don go gsal du 'grel pa rang byung dgongs pa'i rgyan*. In *Dbu ma gzhan stong skor bstan bcos phyogs bsdus deb dang po*, 63–129. Rumtek (Sikkim), India): Karma Shri Nalanda Institute. Also as Rumtek blockprint, n.d.

———. 1990b. *De bzhin gshegs pa'i snying po bstan pa'i bstan bcos kyi rnam 'grel rang byung dgongs gsal*. In *Dbu ma gzhan stong skor bstan bcos phyogs bsdus deb dang po*, 130–90. Rumtek (Sikkim), India: Karma Shri Nalanda Institute. Also as Rumtek blockprint, n.d.

———. 2005a. *Rnal 'byor bla na med pa'i rgyud sde rgya mtsho'i snying po bsdus pa zab mo nang don nyung ngu'i tshig gis rnam par 'grol ba zab don snang byed*. Seattle: Nitartha *international* Publications. Also as Rumtek blockprint, n.d.

———. 2005b. *Theg pa chen po rgyud bla ma'i bstan bcos snying po'i don mngon sum lam gyi bshad srol dang sbyar ba'i rnam par 'grel ba phyir mi ldog pa seng ge nga ro*. Seattle: Nitartha *international*. Also as Rumtek blockprint, n.d.

Krang dbyi sun et al. 1993. *Bod rgya tshig mdzod chen mo*. 2 vols. Beijing: Mi rigs dpe skrun khang.

Mi bskyod rdo rje (Karmapa VIII). 1990. *Dbu ma gzhan stong smra ba'i srol legs par phye ba'i sgron me. In Dbu ma gzhan stong skor bstan bcos phyogs bsdus deb dang po*, 13–48. Rumtek (Sikkim), India: Karma Shri Nalanda Institute.

———. 1996. *The Chariot of the Tagbo Siddhas* (Dbu ma la 'jug pa'i rnam bshad dpal ldan dus gsum mkhyen pa'i zhal lung dvags brgyud grub pa'i shing rta). Seattle: Nitartha *international*.

———. 2003. *The Noble One Resting at Ease* (Shes rab kyi pha rol tu phyin pa'i lung chos mtha' dag gi bdud rtsi'i snying por gyur pa gang la ldan pa'i gzhi rje btsun mchog tu dgyes par ngal gso'i yongs 'dus brtol gyi ljon pa rgyas pa). 2 vols. Seattle: Nitartha *international*.

Mkha' khyab rdo rje (Karmapa XV). 1976. *De bzhin gshegs pa'i snying po bstan pa'i bstan bcos kyi mchan 'grel byams mgon dgyes pa'i zhal lung nor bu dbang po dri ma med pa'i 'od*. In *Three important verse treatises on aspects of Mahayana and Vajrayana Buddhism by the 3rd Karma-pa Raṅ-byuṅ-rdo-rje: with annotations expanding the text (mchan) by the 15th Karma-pa Mkha'-khyab-rdo-rje*, 1–37. New Delhi: Karmapae Chodhey Gyalwae Sungrab Partun Khang.

———. 1993a. *Rnam par shes pa dang ye shes 'byed pa'i bstan bcos kyi mchan 'grel rje btsun 'jam pa'i dbyangs kyi zhal lung nor bu ke ta ka dri ma med pa'i 'od*. In *Rgyal dbang mkha' khyab rdo rje'i bka' 'bum*. Vol. 9: 415–36. Delhi: Konchog Lhadrepa.

———. 1993b. *Zab mo nang gi don gsal bar ston pa'i gzhung bde blag tu rtogs par byed pa'i mchan 'grel rdo rje sems dpa'i zhal lung nor bu rnam par snang ba dri ma med pa'i 'od*. In *Rgyal dbang mkha' khyab rdo rje'i bka' 'bum*. Vol. 9: 269–413. Delhi: Konchog Lhadrepa.

Ngag dbang yon tan bzang po. 2000. *Jo nang chos 'byung dang rje jo nang chen po'i ring lugs.* Beijing: Mi rigs dpe skrun khang.

Rang byung rdo rje (Karmapa III). 1983. *Rang byung rdo rje'i mgur rnam.* Bidung, Tashigang, Bhutan: Kunchhap.

———. 1990a. *Rnam par shes pa dang ye shes 'byed pa'i bstan bcos.* In *Dbu ma gzhan stong skor bstan bcos phyogs bsdus deb dang po*, 49–54. Also as Rumtek blockprint, n.d.

———. 1990b. *De bzhin gshegs pa'i snying po bstan pa zhes bya ba'i bstan bcos.* In *Dbu ma gzhan stong skor bstan bcos phyogs bsdus deb dang po*, 55–62. Also as Rumtek blockprint, n.d.

———. 2006a. *Collected Works* (Dpal rgyal dbang ka rma pa sku phreng gsum pa rang byung rdo rje'i gsung 'bum). 11 vols. Lhasa: Dpal brtsegs bod yig dpe rnying zhib 'jug khang.

———. 2006b. *Chos dang chos nyid rnam par 'byed pa'i bstan bcos kyi rnam par bshad pa'i rgyan.* In *Collected Works*, vol. cha: 488–613.

———. 2006c. *De bzhin gshegs pa'i snying po bstan pa'i sa bcad.* In *Collected Works*, vol. ja: 277–81.

———. 2006d. *Sems kyi khrul tshul brjod pa.* In *Collected Works*, vol. ca: 101–6.

———. 2006e. *Rtogs pa brjod pa'i tshig bcad.* In *Collected Works*, vol. ca: 89–92.

———. 2006f. *Gnas lugs gsal byed ye shes sgron me.* In *Collected Works*, vol. A: 21–44.

———. n.d.[a] *Zab mo nang gi don gsal bar byed pa'i 'grel pa.* Rumtek (Sikkim), India.

———. n.d.[b] *Zab mo nang gi don zhes bya ba'i gzhung.* Rumtek (Sikkim), India.

Śākya mchog ldan. 1975. *Dbu ma'i 'byung tshul rnam par bshad pa'i gtam yid bzhin lhun po. In The Complete Works (gsuṅ 'bum) of gSer-mdog Paṇ-chen Śākya-mchog-ldan.* Vol. 4, ed. Kunzang Tobgey, 209–48. Thimpu, Bhutan.

———. 1988a. *'Dzam gling sangs rgyas bstan pa'i rgyan mchog yongs rdzogs gnas lngar mkhyen pa'i paṇḍita chen po gser mdog paṇ chen shākya mchog ldan gyi gsung 'bum legs bshad gser gyi bdud rtsi* (Collected Works). 24 vols. Delhi: Nagwang Tobgyal.

———. 1988b. *Byams chos lnga'i nges don rab tu gsal ba zhes bya ba'i bstan bcos.* In *Collected Works*, vol. da: 1–38.

———. 1988c. *Byams chos lnga'i lam gyi rim pa gsal bar byed pa'i bstan bcos rin chen sgrom gyi sgo 'byed.* In Collected Works, vol. da: 39–156.

———. 2000. *Three Texts on Madhyamaka.* Translated by Iaroslav Komarovski. Dharamsala, India: Library of Tibetan Works and Archives.

Sgam po pa. 1990. *The Jewel Ornament of Liberation* (Thar pa rin po che'i rgyan). Chengdu, China: Si khron mi rigs dpe skrun khang.

Tāranātha. 1980. *History of Buddhism in India.* Translated by Lama Chimpa and Alaka Chattopadhyaya. Calcutta: Bagchi.

———. n.d. *Collected Works.* 'Dzam thang edition. TBRC no. W22276.

Tshal pa kun dga' rdo rje. 1981. *Deb ther dmar po.* Beijing: Mi rigs dpe skrun khang.

Zur mang padma rnam rgyal. n.d. *Full Moon of Questions and Answers* (Dri lan tshes pa'i zla ba). n.p.

Modern Works

Anacker, Stefan. 1978. "The Meditational Therapy of the *Madhyāntavibhāgabhāṣya*." In *Mahāyāna Buddhist Meditation: Theory and Practice*, edited by Minoru Kiyota, 83–113. Honolulu: University of Hawai'i Press.

———. 1986. *Seven Works of Vasubandhu*. Delhi: Motilal Banarsidass.

———. 1992. "An Unravelling of the *Dharma-Dharmatā-Vibhāga-Vṛtti* of Vasubandhu." AS 46 (1): 26–36.

Arnold, Dan. 2003. "Verses on Nonconceptual Awareness: A Close Reading of *Mahāyānasaṃgraha* 8.2–13." *Indian International Journal of Buddhist Studies* 4: 19–49.

———. 2005. "Is Svasaṃvitti Transcendental?" *Asian Philosophy* 15 (1): 77–111.

Arya Maitreya. 2000. *Buddha Nature: The Mahayana Uttaratantra Shastra with Commentary. Commentary* by Jamgön Kongtrül Lodrö Thayé and Khenpo Tsultrim Gyamtso Rinpoche. Translated by Rosemarie Fuchs. Ithaca, N.Y.: Snow Lion Publications.

Asaṅga. 2004. *The Universal Vehicle Discourse Literature (Mahāyānasūtrālaṁkāra)*. Translated by L. Jamspal, et al. Treasury of the Buddhist Sciences, editor-in-chief Robert A. F. Thurman. New York: American Institute of Buddhist Studies, Columbia University.

Bareau, André. 1955. *Les sectes bouddhiques du Petit Véhicule*. Saigon: École française d'Extrême-Orient.

Boquist, Åke. 1993. *Trisvabhāva: A Study of the Development of the Three-Nature-Theory in Yogācāra Buddhism*. Lund Studies in African and Asian Religions 8. Lund: Dept. of History of Religions, University of Lund.

Broido, Michael. 1989. "The Jo-nang-pas on Madhyamaka: A Sketch." *Tibet Journal* 14 (1): 86–91.

Brown, Brian E. 1991. *The Buddha Nature*. Delhi: Motilal Banarsidass.

Brunnhölzl, Karl. 2004. *The Center of the Sunlit Sky*. Ithaca, N.Y.: Snow Lion Publications.

———. trans. and introd. 2007a. *Straight from the Heart: Buddhist Pith Instructions*. Ithaca, N.Y.: Snow Lion Publications.

———. trans. and introd. 2007b. *In Praise of Dharmadhātu*. Ithaca, N.Y.: Snow Lion Publications.

Burchardi, Anne. 2002. "Toward an Understanding of Tathāgatagarbha Interpretation in Tibet with Special Reference to the '*Ratnagotravibhāga*.'" In *Religion and Secular Culture in Tibet*, Tibetan Studies 2: Proceedings of the Ninth Seminar of the International Association for Tibetan Studies, edited by Henk Blezer, 59–77. Leiden: Brill, 2000.

———. 2007. "The Diversity of the *gzhan stong* Madhyamaka Tradition." *Journal of the International Association for Tibetan Studies* 3. www.thdl.org.

Cha, John Younghan. 1996. "A Study of the *Dharmadharmatāvibhāga*: An Analysis of the Religious Philosophy of the Yogācāra, together with an Annotated Translation of Vasubandhu's Commentary." PhD diss., Northwestern University.

Conze, Edward. 1975. *The Large Sutra on Perfect Wisdom*. Berkeley: University of California Press.

Conze, Edward, and Iida Shotaro. 1968. "'Maitreya's Questions in the Prajñāpāramitā." In *Mélanges d'Indianisme à la mémoire de Louis Renou*, Publications de l'Institut de Civilisation Indienne, Fasc. 28, 229–42. Paris: Institut de Civilisation Indienne.

D'Amato, Mario. 2003. "Can All Beings Potentially Attain Awakening? *Gotra*-Theory in the *Mahāyānasūtrālaṃkāra*." *JIABS* 26 (1): 115–38.

——. 2007. "Trisvabhāva in the *Mahāyānasūtrālaṃkāra*." www.empty-universe.com/yogacara/trisvabhava_in_msa.pdf.

Dargyay, Lobsang. 1990. "What is Non-Existent and What is Remanent in *Śūnyatā*." *JIP* 18: 81–91.

Davidson, Ronald M. 1985. "Buddhist Systems of Transformation: Asraya-parivrtti/-paravrtti among the Yogacara." PhD diss., University of California.

——. 1989. "*Āśrayaparāvṛtti* and *Mahāyānābhidharma*: Some Problems and Perspectives." In *Amalā Prajñā: Aspects of Buddhist Studies*, edited by N. H. Samtani, 253–62. Delhi: Sri Satguru Publications.

Dragonetti, Carmen. 1979. "Some Notes on the *Pratītyasamutpādahṛdayakārikā* and the *Pratītyasamutpādahṛdayavyākhyāna* Attributed to Nāgārjuna." *Buddhist Studies* 6 (Delhi): 70–73.

——. 1986. "On Śuddhamati's *Pratītyasamutpādahṛdaya* and on *Bodhicittavivaraṇa*." *WZKS* 30: 115–22.

——. 2000. "Marginal Note on the Idealistic Conception of *citta-mātra*." *JIABS* 23 (2): 165–75.

Dreyfus, Georges B. J. 2005. "Where Do Commentarial Schools Come From? Reflections on the History of Tibetan Scholasticism." *JIABS* 28 (2): 273–98.

Dreyfus, Georges, and Christian Lindtner. 1989. "The Yogācāra Philosophy of Dignāga and Dharmakīrti." *Studies in Central and East Asian Religions* 2: 27–52.

Duckworth, Douglas S. 2005. "Buddha-Nature and a Dialectic of Presence and Absence in the Works of Mi-pham." PhD diss., University of Virginia.

Eckel, Malcolm D. 1985. "Bhāvaviveka's Critique of Yogācāra Philosophy in Chapter XXV of the *Prajñāpradīpa*." In *Miscellanea Buddhica*, Indiske Studier 5, edited by Christian Lindtner, 24–75. Copenhagen: Akademisk Forlag.

Forman, Robert. 1989. "Paramārtha and Modern Constructivists." *PEW* 39: 398–418.

Frauwallner, Erich. 1951. "Amalavijñāna und Ālayavijñāna." *Beiträge zur indischen Philosophie und Altertumskunde: Walter Schubring zum 70. Geburtstag dargebracht*. Alt- und Neu-Indische Studien 7, 148–59. Hamburg.

Freeman, Ch. E. 1991. "*Saṃvrtti, Vyavahāra* and *Paramārtha* in the *Akṣayamatinirdeśa* and Its Commentary by Vasubandhu." In *Buddhist Forum* 2, edited by Tadeusz Skorupski, 97–114. London: University of London, School of Oriental and African Studies.

Friedmann, David. L. 1937. *Sthiramati*: Madhyāntavibhāgaṭīkā: *Analysis of the Middle Path and Extremes*. Utrecht: Utrecht University.

Fujita, Kōtatsu. 1975. "One Vehicle or Three?" *JIP* 3: 79–166.

Garfield, Jay L. 2002. *Empty Words.* New York and Oxford: Oxford University Press.

Galloway, Brian. 1980. "A Yogācāra Analysis of the Mind, Based on the Vijñāna Section of Vasubandhu's *Pañcaskandhaprakaraṇa* with Guṇaprabha's Commentary." *JIABS* 3: 7–20.

Gimello, Robert. 1976. "Apophatic and Kataphatic Discourse in Mahāyāna: A Chinese View." *PEW* 26 (2): 117–36.

Griffiths, Paul J. 1986. *On Being Mindless.* La Salle, Ill.: Open Court.

——. 1990a. "Painting Space with Colors: Tathāgatagarbha in the *Mahāyānasūtrālaṃkāra*-Corpus IX.22–37." In *Buddha Nature*, edited by P. Griffiths and J. Keenan, 41–63. Tokyo: Kenkyusha.

——. 1990b. "Omniscience in the *Mahāyānasūtrālaṃkāra* and Its Commentaries." *Indo-Iranian Journal* 31: 85–120.

——. 1994a. *On Being Buddha.* Albany: State University of New York Press.

——. 1994b. "What Else Remains in Śūnyatā? An Investigation of Terms for Mental Imagery in the *Madhyāntavibhāga*-Corpus."*JIABS* 17 (1): 1–25.

Griffiths, Paul J., et al. 1989. *The Realm of Awakening.* Oxford: Oxford University Press.

Grosnick, William. 1981. "Nonorigination and Nirvāṇa in the Early Tathāgatagarbha Literature." *JIABS* 4 (2): 33–43.

Gyamtso Rinpoche, Khenpo Tsultrim. 1988. *Progressive Stages of Meditation on Emptiness.* Translated by Shenpen Hookham. Oxford: Longchen Foundation.

Habito, Ruben L. F. 1986. "The Notion of Dharmakāya: A Study in the Buddhist Absolute." *Journal of Dharma* 11 (4): 348–78.

Hakamaya, Noriaki. 1971. "Asvabhāva's Commentary on the *Mahāyānasūtrālaṃkāra* IX. 56–76." *JIBS* 20 (1): 473–65.

——. 1980. "The Realm of Enlightenment in *Vijñaptimātratā*: The Formulation of the 'Four Kinds of Pure Dharmas.'" *JIABS* 3: 22–41.

——. 1992. "Some Doubts about the Evaluation of the Ten sNying po'i mdos and Tathāgatagarbha Thought." In *Proceedings of the 5th Seminar of the International Association of Buddhist Studies, Narita 1989*, edited by S. Ihara and Z. Yamaguchi, 67–75. Narita: Naritasan Shinshoji.

Hall, Bruce C. 1986. "The Meaning of Vijñapti in Vasubandhu's Concept of Mind." *JIABS* 9 (1): 7–23.

Harris, Ian Charles. 1991. *The Continuity of Madhyamaka and Yogācāra in Indian Mahāyāna Buddhism.* Leiden, Netherlands: E. J. Brill.

Harrison, Paul. 1997. "Is the *Dharma-kāya* the Real 'Phantom Body' of the Buddha?" *JIABS* 15 (1): 44–95.

Hattori, Masaaki. 1982. "The Dream Example in Vijñānavāda Treatises." In *Indological and Buddhist Studies: Volume in Honour of Professor J. W. de Jong on His Sixtieth Birthday,* edited by L. A. Hercus et al., 235–41. Canberra: Australian National University, Faculty of Asian Studies.

Hirabayashi, Jay, and Shotaro Iida. 1977. "Another Look at the Mādhyamika versus Yogācāra Controversy Concerning Existence and Non-existence." In *Prajñāpāramitā and Related Systems*, edited by Lewis Lancaster, 341–60. Berkeley: Published under the auspices of the Group in Buddhist Studies and the Center for South and Southeast Asian Studies at the University of California and the Institute of Buddhist Studies.

Hookham, Shenphen. 1991a. *The Buddha Within*. Albany: State University of New York Press.

——. 1991b. "The Practical Implications of the Doctrine on Buddha-Nature." In *Buddhist Forum* II, edited by Tadeusz Skorupski, 149–61. London: University of London, School of Oriental and African Studies.

Hopkins, Jeffrey. 2002. *Reflections on Reality*. Berkeley: University of California Press.

——. trans. and introd. 2006. *Mountain Doctrine*. Ithaca, N.Y.: Snow Lion Publications.

——. trans. and ann. 2007. *The Essence of Other-Emptiness by Tāranātha*. Ithaca, N.Y.: Snow Lion Publications.

Huntington, C.W., Jr. 1986. "The Akutobhayā and Early Indian Madhyamaka." PhD diss., University of Michigan.

——. 1995. "A Lost Text of Early Indian Madhyamaka." *AS* 49 (4): 693–767.

Iwata, Takashi. 1984. "One Interpretation of the Saṃvedana Inference of Dharmakīrti." *JIBS* 33 (1): 397–94.

Jackson, David P. 1987. *The Entrance Gate for the Wise (Section III)*. 2 vols. Vienna: Arbeitskreis für Tibetische und Buddhistische Studien Universität Wien.

Jackson, Roger R. 1990. "Luminous Mind among the Logicians—An Analysis of *Pramāṇavarttika* II.205–211." In Buddha Nature, edited by P. Griffiths and J. Keenan, 95–123. Tokyo: Kenkyusha.

Jampa Thaye (David Stott). 1994. *An Introduction to the Cycle of Texts Belonging to the Madhyamaka Empty-of-Other System*. Bristol: Ganesha Press.

Kajiyama, Yuichi. 1968. "Bhāvaviveka, Sthiramati, and Dharmapāla." *WZKS* 12: 193–203.

Kano, Kazuo. 2006. "rNgog Blo-ldan Shes-rab's Summary of the Ratnagotravibhāga." PhD diss., University of Hamburg.

Kaplan, Stephen. 1990. "A Holographic Alternative to a Traditional Yogācāra Simile: An Analysis of Vasubandhu's Trisvabhāva Doctrine." *Eastern Buddhist* 23: 56–78.

Kapstein, Matthew T. 1989. "The Purificatory Gem and Its Cleansing: A Late Tibetan Polemical Discussion of Apocryphal Texts." *History of Religions* 28 (3): 217–24.

——. 2000. "We Are All Gzhan stong pas." *Journal of Buddhist Ethics* 7: 105–25.

Karma Thinley. 1980. *The History of the Sixteen Karmapas of Tibet*. Boulder, Colo.: Prajñā Press.

Kawamura, Leslie S. 1993. "Āśrayaparivṛtti in the *Dharma-dharmatā-vibhāga*." In *Studies in Original Buddhism and Mahayana Buddhism in Commemoration of Late Professsor Dr. Fumimaro Watanabe*, vol. 1, edited by E. Mayeda, 73–90. Kyoto: Nagata Bunshodo.

Keenan, John P. 1980. "A Study of the *Buddhabhūmyupadeśa*: The Doctrinal Development of the Notion of Wisdom in Yogācāra Thought." PhD diss., University of Wisconsin.

——. 1982. "Original Purity and the Focus of Early Yogacara." *JIABS* 5 (1): 7–18.

——. 1989. "Asaṅga's Understanding of Mādhyamika." *JIABS* 12: 93–107.

——. 1997. *Dharmapāla's Yogācāra Critique of Bhāvaviveka's Mādhyamika Explanation of Emptiness*. Studies in Asian Thought and Religion 20. Lewiston: The Edwin Mellen Press.

——. 2002. *The Interpretation of the Buddha Land*. Berkeley: Numata Center for Buddhist Translation and Research.

King, Richard. 1994. "Early Yogācāra and Its Relationship with the Madhyamaka School." *PEW* 44 (4): 659–83.

——. 1998. "Vijñaptimātratā and the Abhidharma Context of Early Yogācāra." *Asian Philosophy* 8 (1): 5–18.

King, Sallie B. 1992. *Buddha Nature*. New Delhi: Sri Satguru Publications.

Krang dbyi sun, ed. 1985. *Bod rgya tshig mdzod chen mo*. Beijing: Mi rigs dpe skrun khang.

Kritzer, Robert. 1999. *Rebirth and Causation in Yogācāra Abhidharma*. Wiener Studien zur Tibetologie und Buddhismuskunde, Heft 44. Wien: Arbeitskreis für Tibetische und Buddhistische Studien , Universität Wien.

——. 2005. *Vasubandhu and the* Yogācārabhūmi: Yogācāra Elements in the Abhidharmakośabhāṣya. Tokyo: The International Institute for Buddhist Studies.

Kunst, Arnold. 1977. "Some Aspects of the Ekayāna." In *Prajñāpāramitā and Related Systems*, edited by Lewis Lancaster, 313–26. Berkeley: Published under the auspices of the Group in Buddhist Studies and the Center for South and Southeast Asian Studies at the University of California and the Institute of Buddhist Studies.

Lamotte, Étienne, trans. 1998. *Śūraṃgamasamādhisūtra: The Concentration of Heroic Progress*. English translation by S. Boin-Webb. London: Curzon Press.

Lancaster, Lewis, ed. 1977. *Prajñāpāramitā and Related Systems*. Berkeley: Published under the auspices of the Group in Buddhist Studies and the Center for South and Southeast Asian Studies at the University of California and the Institute of Buddhist Studies.

La Vallée Poussin, Louis de. 1928–1948. *Vijñaptimātratāsiddhi: La Siddhi de Hiuan-tsang*. Paris: P. Geuthner.

Lévi, Sylvain. 1932. *Un système de philosophie bouddhique: Matériaux pour l'étude du système Vijñaptimātra*. Paris: H. Champion.

Limaye, Surekha Vijay, trans. 1992. *Mahāyānasūtrālaṃkāra*. Delhi: Sri Satguru Publications.

Lindtner, Christian. 1982. *Nāgārjuniana*. Indiske Studier 4. Copenhagen: Akademisk Forlag.

——. 1985. "A Treatise on Buddhist Idealism." In *Miscellanea Buddhica*, 109-220. Indiske Studier 5. Copenhagen: Akademisk Forlag.

———. 1986. "Bhavya's Critique of Yogācāra in the *Madhyamakaratnapradīpa*, Chapter IV." In *Buddhist Logic and Epistemology*, edited by B. K. Matilal and R. D. Evans, 239–63. Dordrecht: D. Reidel.

———. 1992. "The *Laṅkāvatārasūtra* in Early Indian Madhyamaka Literature." *AS* 46 (1): 244–79.

———. 1997. "*Cittamātra* in Indian Mahāyāna until Kamalaśīla." *WZKS* 41: 159–206.

Lipman, Kennard. 1980. "Nītārtha, Neyārtha, and Tathāgatagarbha in Tibet." *JIP* 8: 87–95.

———. 1982. "Cittamātra and Its Madhyamaka Critique." *PEW* 32: 295–308.

Lopez, Donald S., Jr. 1992. "Paths Terminable and Interminable." In *Paths to Liberation: The Mārga and Its Transformations in Buddhist Thought*, edited by Robert Buswell and Robert Gimello, 147–92. Honolulu: University of Hawai'i Press.

Lusthaus, Dan. 2002. *Buddhist Phenomenology: A Philosophical Investigation of Yogācāra Buddhism and the Ch'eng Wei-shih lun*. London: RoutledgeCurzon.

Makransky, John J. 1997. *Buddhahood Embodied*. Albany: State University of New York Press.

Mano, Ryūkai. 1967. "Gotra in Haribhadra's Theory." *JIBS* 40 (2): 22–28.

Mathes, Klaus-Dieter. 1996. *Unterscheidung der Gegebenheiten von ihrem wahren Wesen (Dharmadharmatāvibhāga)*. Swisttal-Odendorf, Germany: Indica et Tibetica Verlag.

———. 1998. "Vordergründige und höchste Wahrheit im *gZhan stong*-Madhyamaka." *Annäherung an das Fremde*: XXVI. Deutscher Orientalistentag vom 25. bis 29. 9. 1995 in Leipzig. Zeitschrift der Deutschen Morgenländischen Gesellschaft 11, edited by H. Preissler and H. Stein, 457–68.

———. 2000. "Tāranātha's Presentation of trisvabhāva in the *gŹan stoṅ sñiṅ po*." *JIABS* 23: 195–223.

———. 2002. "'Gos Lo tsâ ba gZhon nu dpal's Extensive Commentary on and Study of the *Ratnagotravibhāgavyākhyā*." In *Religion and Secular Culture in Tibet*, 79–96. Proceedings of the International Association of Tibetan Studies 2000, Brill's Tibetan Studies Library, vol. 2/2, edited by H. Blezer with the assistance of A. Zadoks.. Leiden, Netherlands: E. J. Brill.

———. 2004. "Tāranātha's 'Twenty-one Differences with regard to the Profound Meaning'—Comparing the Views of the Two gzhan stoṅ Masters Dol po pa and Śākya mchog ldan." *JIABS* 27 (2): 285–328.

———. 2006. "Blending the Sūtras with the Tantras: The Influence of Maitrīpa and His Circle on the Foundation of Sūtra Mahāmudrā in the Kagyü Schools." In *Buddhist Literature and Praxis: Studies in Its Formative Period 900–1400*. Proceedings of the 10th Seminar of the International Association of Tibetan Studies, Oxford 2003, vol. 4, edited by Ronald M. Davidson and Christian K. Wedemeyer, 201–27. Leiden: Brill.

———. 2007. "The Ontological Status of the Dependent (*paratantra*) in the *Saṃdhinirmocanasūtra* and the *Vyākhyāyukti*." In *Indica and Tibetica: Festschrift für Michael Hahn. Zum 65. Geburtstag Űberreicht von Freunden und Schülern*. Wiener Studien zur Tibetologie und Buddhismuskunde 66, edited by Konrad Klaus and Jens-Uwe Hartmann, 323–40. Wien: Arbeitskreis für tibetische und buddhistische Studien, Universität Wien.

———. 2008. *A Direct Path to the Buddha Within: Gö Lotsāwa's Mahāmudrā Interpretation of the* Ratnagotravibhāga. Boston: Wisdom Publications.

May, Jacques. 1971. "La Philosophie Bouddhique Idéaliste." *AS* 25: 265–323.

Meinert, Carmen. 2003. "Structural Analysis of the *Bsam gtan mig sgron*: A Comparison of the Fourfold Correct Practice in the *Āryāvikalpapraveśanāmadhāraṇī* and the Contents of the Four Main Chapters of the *Bsam gtan mig sgron*." *JIABS* 26 (1): 175–95.

Nagao, Gadjin M. 1964. *Madhyāntavibhāga-bhāṣya*. Tokyo: Suzuki Research Foundation.

———. 1991. *Mādhyamika and Yogācāra. A Study of Mahāyāna Philosophy*. Translated by L. Kawamura. Albany: State University of New York Press.

———. 1994. *An Index to Asaṅga's Mahāyānasaṃgraha*. 2 vols. Tokyo: International Institute for Buddhist Studies.

Matsumoto, Shirō. 1997. "A Critical Exchange on the Idea of *Dhātu-vāda*." In *Pruning the Bodhi Tree*, edited by J. Hubbard and P. L. Swanson, 205–19. Honolulu: University of Hawai'i Press.

Nagasawa, Jitsudo. 1962. "Kamalaśīla's Theory of the Yogācāra." *JIBS* 10 (1): 364–71.

Narima, J. K. 1992. *Literary History of Sanskrit Buddhism*. Delhi: Motilal Banarsidass. Orig. publ. 1919.

Nguyen, Cuong Tu. 1990. "Sthiramati's Interpretation of Buddhology and Soteriology." PhD diss., Harvard University.

Nishio, Kyōo, ed. 1982. *The* Buddhabhūmi-Sūtra *and the* Buddhabhūmi-Vyākhyāna *of Śīlabhadra*. Tokyo: Kokusho Kankokai.

Olson, Robert F. 1974. "Candrakīrti's Critique of Vijñānavāda." *PEW* 24 (1): 405–11.

Pandeya, Ramchandra. 1999. *Madhyānta-vibhāga-śāstra: Containing the Kārikā-s of Maitreya, Bhāṣya of Vasubandhu and Ṭīkā by Sthiramati*. Delhi: Motilal Banarsidass.

Paul, Diana. 1979. "The Concept of Tathāgatagarbha in the *Śrīmālādevī Sūtra* (Sheng-man Ching)." *JAOS* 99 (2): 191–203.

———. 1982. "The Life and Times of Paramārtha." *JIABS* 5 (1): 37–69.

———. 1984. *Philosophy of Mind in Sixth-Century China: Paramārtha's "Evolution of Consciousness."* Stanford: Stanford University Press.

Pettit, J. W. 1999. *Mipham's Beacon of Certainty*. Boston: Wisdom Publications.

Potter, Karl H., ed. 1999. *Encyclopedia of Indian Philosophies*. Vol. 8, *Buddhist Philosophy from 100 to 350 A.D.* Delhi: Motilal Banarsidass.

———. ed. 2003. *Encyclopedia of Indian Philosophies*. Vol. 9, *Buddhist Philosophy from 350 to 600 A.D.* Delhi: Motilal Banarsidass.

Powell, James K. 1998. "The Great Debate in Mahāyāna Buddhism: The Nature of Consciousness." PhD diss., University of Wisconsin.

Powers, John. 1992. *Two Commentaries on the* Saṃdhinirmocana-Sūtra *by Asaṅga and Jñānagarbha*. Lewiston: The Edwin Mellen Press.

Prasad, H. S., ed. 1991. *The* Uttaratantra *of Maitreya: E. H. Johnston's Sanskrit Text and E. Obermiller's English Translation.* Delhi: Sri Satguru Publications.

Rawlinson, Andrew. 1983. "The Ambiguity of the Buddha-Nature Concept in India and China." In *Early Ch'an in China and Tibet*, edited by Whalen Lai and Lewis Lancaster, 259–79. Berkeley, Calif.: Asian Humanities Press.

Ruegg, David Seyfort. 1963. "The Jo naṅ pas: A School of Buddhist Ontologists according to the *Grub tha' śel gyi me loṅ.*" *JAOS* 83: 73–91.

——. 1968/69. "Ārya and Bhadant Vimuktisena on the Gotra Theory of the Prajñāpāramitā." In *Festschrift für E. Frauwallner.* WZKS 12–13: 303–17.

——. 1969. *La théorie du tathāgatagarbha et du gotra.* Paris: École Française d'Extrême-Orient 70.

——. 1971a. "Le *Dharmadhâtustava* de Nâgârjuna." In *Études Tibetaines: Dediées à la mémoire de Marcelle Lalou* (1890-1967), 448–71. Paris: Librairie d'Amérique et d'Orient.

——. 1971b. "On the Knowability and Expressibility of Absolute Reality in Buddhism." *JIBS* 20 (1): 489–95.

——. 1976. "The Meanings of the Term Gotra and the Textual History of the *Ratnagotravibhāga.*" *Bulletin of the School of Oriental and African Studies* 39: 341–63.

——. 1977. "The Gotra, Ekayāna and Tathāgatagarbha Theories of the Prajñāpāramitā according to Dharmamitra and Abhayākaragupta." In *Prajñāpāramitā and Related Systems*, edited by Lewis Lancaster, 283–312. Berkeley: Published under the auspices of the Group in Buddhist Studies and the Center for South and Southeast Asian Studies at the University of California and the Institute of Buddhist Studies.

——. 1989. *Buddha-Nature, Mind and the Problem of Gradualism in a Comparative Perspective.* London: School of African and Oriental Studies.

——. 2000. *Three Studies in the History of Indian and Tibetan Madhyamaka Philosophy: Studies in Indian and Tibetan Madhyamaka Thought, Part 1.* Wiener Studien zur Tibetologie und Buddhismuskunde 50. Wien: Arbeitskreis für Tibetische und Buddhistische Studien, Universität Wien.

Saito, Akira. 1998. "Bhāvaviveka and the *Madhya(anta)vibhāga/-bhāṣya.*" *JIBS* 46 (2): 1038–32.

Samtani, Narayan H. 2002. *Gathering the Meanings: The* Arthaviniścaya Sūtra *and Its Commentary Nibandhana.* Berkeley: Dharma Publishing.

Schaeffer, Kurtis R. 1995. "The Enlightened Heart of Buddhahood: A Study and Translation of the Third Karma pa Rang byung rdo rje's Work on Tathagatagarbha, the *De bzhin gshegs pa'i snying po gtan la dbab pa.*" MA thesis, University of Washington.

Schmithausen, Lambert. 1967. "Sautrāntika-Voraussetzungen in *Viṃśatikā* und *Triṃśikā.*" *WZKS* 11: 109–36.

——. 1969a. "Zur Literaturgeschichte der älteren Yogācāra-Schule." *Zeitschrift der Deutschen Morgenländischen Gesellschaft, Supplement* 1: 811–23.

——. 1969b. *Der Nirvāṇa-Abschnitt in der* Viniścaya-saṃgrahaṇī *der* Yogācārabhūmiḥ. Österreichische Akademie der Wissenschaften, Philosophische-Historische Klasse, Sitzungsberichte, 264, Band 2. Wien: Hermann Böhlaus.

——. 1971. "Philologische Bemerkungen zum *Ratnagotravibhāga*." *WZKS* 15: 123–77.

——. 1973a. "Spirituelle Praxis und Philosophische Theorie im Buddhismus." *Zeitschrift für Missionswissenschaft und Religionswissenschaft* 57 (3): 161–86.

——. 1973b. "Zu D. Seyfort Rueggs Buch 'La théorie du tathāgatagarbha et du gotra' (Besprechungsaufsatz)." *WZKS* 22: 123–60.

——. 1981. "On Some Aspects of Descriptions of Theories of 'Liberating Insight' and 'Enlightenment.'" In *Studien zum Jainismus und Buddhismus: Gedenkschrift für L. Alsdorf*, edited by K. Bruhn and A. Wezler, 199–250. Wiesbaden: Franz Steiner Verlag.

——. 1984. "On the Vijñaptimātra Passage in *Saṃdhinirmocanasūtra* VIII.7." *Acta Indologica* 7: 433–55.

——. 1987. *Ālayavijñāna: On the Origin and the Early Development of a Central Concept of Yogācāra Philosophy*. 2 vols. Tokyo: International Buddhist Institute for Buddhist Studies.

——. 1992. "A Note on Vasubandhu and the *Laṅkāvatārasūtra*." *AS* 46 (1): 392–97.

——. 2000. "On Three *Yogācārabhūmi* Passages Mentioning the Three *Svabhāvas* or *Lakṣaṇas*." In *Wisdom, Compassion, and the Search for Understanding*, edited by J. Silk, 245–63. Honolulu: University of Hawai'i Press.

——. 2001. "Zwei charakteristische Lehren der Yogācāras." In *Buddhismus in Geschichte und Gegenwart*. Bd. 5, 5–14. Hamburg: Universität Hamburg.

Sharma, Ramesh Kumar. 1985. "Dharmakīrti on the Existence of Other Minds." *JIP* 13: 55–71.

Shastri, Yajneshwar S. 1989. Mahāyānasūtrālaṃkāra *of Asaṅga: A Study in Vijñānavāda Buddhism*. Delhi: Sri Satguru Publications.

Shih, Heng-Ching. 1988. "The Significance of Tathāgatagarbha: A Positive Expression of Śūnyatā." *Philosophical Revue* (Taiwan) 11: 227–46.

Sparham, Gareth. 1993. *Ocean of Eloquence: Tsong kha pa's Commentary on the Yogācāra Doctrine of Mind*. Albany: State University of New York Press.

Sponberg, Alan. 1979. "Dynamic Liberation in Yogacara Buddhism." *JIABS* 2 (1): 44–64.

——. 1981. "The Trisvabhāva Doctrine in India and China." *Bukkyō Bunka Kenkyujo Kiyo* 21: 97–119.

Stanley, Richard. 1988. "A Study of the *Madhyāntavibhāga-bhāṣya-ṭīkā*." PhD diss., Australian National University, Canberra.

Stcherbatsky, Theodore. 1978. *Madhyānta-Vibhaṅga: Discourse on Discrimination between Middle and Extremes*. Delhi: Oriental Books Reprint Corporation. Originally published as Vol. 30 of Bibliotheca Buddhica, 1936.

Stearns, Cyrus. 1995. "Dol-po-pa Shes-rab rgyal-mtshan and the Genesis of the *gzhan stong* Position in Tibet." *AS* 49 (4): 829–52.

——. 1999. *The Buddha from Dolpo*. Albany: State University of New York Press.

Sutton, Florin Giripescu. 1991. *Existence and Enlightenment in the* Laṅkāvatāra-sūtra: *A Study in the Ontology and Epistemology of the Yogācāra-School of Mahāyāna-Buddhism*. Albany: State University of New York Press.

Suzuki, Daisetz Teitaro. 1979. *The Laṅkāvatārasūtra*. Boulder: Prajñā Press.

——. 1998. *Studies in the* Lankavatara Sutra. Delhi: Munshiram Manoharlal Publishers. Originally published in 1930.

Takasaki, Jikido. 1966. *A Study on the* Ratnagotravibhāga (Uttaratantra). Serie Orientale Roma 33. Rome: Istituto Italiano per il Medio ed Estremo Oriente.

Takeuchi, Shoko. 1977. "Phenomena and Reality in Vijñaptimātra Thought: On the Usages of the Suffix 'tā' in Maitreya's Treatises." In *Buddhist Thought and Asian Civilization: Essays in Honor of Herbert V. Guenther on His Sixtieth Birthday*, edited by Leslie Kawamura and Keith Scott, 254–67. Emeryville: Dharma Publishing.

Thrangu Rinpoche. 1990. *Commentary on* A Teaching on the Essence of the Tathāgatas. Pleasant Bay, Canada: Gampo Abbey.

——. 2001. *Transcending Ego: Distinguishing Consciousness from Wisdom*. Boulder: Namo Buddha Publications.

——. 2002. *Everyday Consciousness and Buddha-Awakening*. Ithaca, N.Y.: Snow Lion Publications.

——. 2006. *On Buddha Essence*. Boulder, Colo.: Namo Buddha Publications.

Thurman, Robert A. F., trans. 1997. *The Holy Teaching of Vimalakīrti*. University Park: Pennsylvania State University Press.

Tillemans, Tom J. F. 1990. *Materials for the Study of Āryadeva, Dharmapāla, and Candrakīrti*. 2 vols. Wiener Studien zur Tibetologie und Buddhismuskunde 36. Wien: Arbeitskreis für Tibetische und Buddhistische Studien, Universität Wien.

Tillemans, Tom J. F., and Toru Tomabechi. 1995. "Le *Dbu ma'i byuṅ tshul* de Śākya mchog ldan." *AS* 49 (4): 891–918.

Tola, Fernando, and Carmen Dragonetti. 1982. "Dignāga's *Ālambanaparīkṣāvṛtti*." *JIP* 10: 105–34.

——. 1983. "The *Trisvabhāvakārikā* of Vasubandhu." *JIP* 11: 225–66.

——. 2004. *Being as Consciousness: Yogācāra Philosophy of Buddhism*. Delhi: Motilal Banarsidass.

Tucci, Giuseppe. 1971. "Ratnākaraśānti on *Āśraya-Parāvṛtti*." In *Opera Minora*, vol. 2: 529–32. Rome: Rome University.

——. 1986. *Minor Buddhist Texts*. Delhi: Motilal Banarsidass. Originally published in Serie Orientale Roma 1956/58.

Ueda, Yoshifumi. 1967. "Two Main Streams of Thought in Yogācāra Philosophy." *PEW* 17: 155–65.

Waldron, William. 1994–95. "How Innovative Is the Ālayavijñāna?" *JIP* 22 (3) and 23 (1): 199–258 and 9–51.

———. 2003. *The "Buddhist Unconscious": The Ālaya-vijñāna in the Context of Indian Buddhist Thought.* Surrey: Curzon Press.

Wangchuk, Dorji. 2004. "The rÑiṅ-ma Interpretations of the Tathāgatagarbha Theory." *WZKS* 48: 171–213.

Wayman, Alex. 1961. "The Mirror-Like Knowledge in Mahāyāna Buddhist Literature." *AS* 25: 353–63.

———. 1979. "Yogācāra and the Buddhist Logicians." *JIABS* 2 (1): 65–78.

———. 1989. "Doctrinal Affiliations of the Buddhist Master Asaṅga." In *Amalā Prajñā: Aspects of Buddhist Studies,* edited by N. H. Samtani, 201–21. Delhi: Sri Satguru Publications.

Wayman, Alex, and Hideko Wayman. 1974. *The Lion's Roar of Queen Śrīmālā.* New York: Columbia University Press.

Williams, Paul. 1983. "On Rang Rig." In *Contributions on Tibetan Buddhist Religion and Philosophy.* Proceedings of the Csoma de Körös Symposium held at Velm-Vienna, Austria, 13–19 September 1981, edited by E. Steinkellner and H. Tauscher, 321–32. Wiener Studien zur Tibetologie und Buddhismuskunde 11. Vienna: Arbeitskreis für Tibetische und Buddhistische Studien, University of Vienna.

———. 1998. *The Reflexive Nature of Awareness.* Surrey: Curzon Press.

Willis, Janice D. 1979. *On Knowing Reality: The* Tattvārtha *Chapter of Asaṅga's* Bodhisattvabhūmi. New York: Columbia University Press.

Wilson, Joe B. 2001. "Gung thang and Sa bzang Ma ti Paṇ chen on the Meaning of 'Foundational Consciousness' (ālaya, kun gzhi)." In *Changing Minds,* edited by Guy Newland, 215–30. Ithaca, N.Y.: Snow Lion Publications.

Xing, Guang. 2002. "The Evolution of the Concept of the Buddha from Early Buddhism to the Formulation of the Trikāya Theory." PhD diss., University of London.

Yamabe, Nobuyoshi. 1997. "The Idea of *Dhātu-vāda* in Yogācāra and *Tathāgata-garbha* Texts." In *Pruning the Bodhi Tree,* edited by J. Hubbard and P. L. Swanson, 193–204. Honolulu: University of Hawai'i Press.

Yao, Zhihua. 2003. "Knowing That One Knows: The Buddhist Doctrine of Self-Cognition." PhD diss., Boston University.

Zimmermann, Michael. 2000. "Tathāgatabarbha." In *Buddhismus in Geschichte und Gegenwart* Bd. 4, 235–47. Hamburg: Universität Hamburg.

———. 2002. *A Buddha Within: The* Tathāgatagarbhasūtra: *The Earliest Exposition of the Buddha-nature Teaching in India.* Bibliotheca Philologica et Philosophica Buddhica 6. Tokyo: International Research Institute for Advanced Buddhology, Soka University.

Endnotes

1 The image here alludes to this river being considered as very holy by Hindus—even its mere sight is said to wash away all one's negative deeds. (It rises on the summit of Mount Amarakaṇṭaka in Madhya Pradesh in central India, and after a westerly course of about eight hundred miles ends in the Gulf of Cambay below the city of Bharuch.)

2 Tib. rang byung rdo rje.

3 Tib. 'jam mgon kong sprul blo gros mtha' yas.

4 Tib. karma phrin las pa phyogs las rnam rgyal.

5 Tib. dpa' bo gtsug lag phreng ba.

6 Tib. mi bskyod rdo rje.

7 Nguyen 1990, 317 and 336.

8 Hall 1986, 18–19.

9 The only Yogācāras who could be—and often are—read as asserting such a consciousness are Paramārtha and Dharmapāla. However, without going into the details here, Paramārtha explains that what he calls "stainless consciousness" (*amalavijñāna*) is nothing other than the stainless nondual dharmadhātu, or mind's ultimate nature of luminosity, which is the same as buddha nature. He also says that "mere cognizance" (*vijñaptimātra*) means that both objects and consciousness do not exist (see below). As evidenced by Dharmapāla's commentaries on Āryadeva's *Catuḥśataka* and *Śataśāstra*, his position is rather complex and subtle. He indeed says that the other-dependent nature really exists (in the sense of not being totally nonexistent like the horns of a rabbit), but he adds that it is not itself the ultimate. Furthermore, he says, "One should be convinced of the voidness of all dharmas"; "The principle of voidness is free from all characters of dharmas, such as existence, [nonexistence,] etc." (Tillemans 1990, 93); and "Thus all dharmas are likened to illusions: in them not the slightest substance whatsoever can be found. . . . Thus, dharmas are produced by causes and conditions; their natures are all void, like an illusion" (ibid., 171). Indeed, though Dharmapāla uses Yogācāra templates, many passages of his commentary could as well have been written by a Mādhyamika. In general, he emphasizes the framework of the two realities, with existence and nonexistence pertaining only to seeming reality, while ultimate reality lies beyond these as well as any other kinds of duality.

10 King 1994, 663.

11 Lusthaus 2002, 178.

12 King 1994, 662.

13 Note that, in pre-Christian Greek etymology, *soter* means "healer"—which matches well with the frequent description of the Buddha as the great physician for mental afflictions.

14 "The invincible" (an epithet of Maitreya).

15 Tāranātha 1980, 203.

16 King 1994, 670.

17 *Tshad ma'i bstan bcos kyi shing rta'i srol rnams ji ltar 'byung ba'i tshul gtam du bya ba nyin mor byed pa'i snang bas dpyod ldan mtha' dag dga' bar byed pa* (Śākya mchog ldan 1988a, vol. dza, p. 95).

18 *Sngags la 'jug pa'i mun pa sel bar byed pa'i chos kyi sgron me gzhung tshan bcu bdun* pa (ibid., vol. pa, p. 230).

19 Nguyen 1990, 320.

20 In the following, I will not deal with all the many questions of whether the authors listed here were actual historical persons, whether they actually authored these texts, and when exactly they lived. Also, the texts listed include only the typical Yogācāra works by these authors, though many of them also wrote on other Buddhist topics or composed commentaries on several sūtras (such as the prajñāpāramitā sūtras). The main point here is to roughly identify the basic scriptural corpus of Yogācāra treatises, no matter by whom they were composed or when.

21 Though this text is primarily a summary of the prajñāpāramitā sūtras, as has been pointed out repeatedly by modern scholars, it does so by mapping a number of classical Yogācāra templates onto these sūtras (see my forthcoming translation of the *Abhisamayālaṃkāra* and several of its Tibetan commentaries).

22 Note that the structure (though not always the contents) of the *Mahāyānasūtrālaṃkāra* corresponds to the *Bodhisattvabhūmi* in the *Yogācārabhūmi* and that its ninth chapter on buddhahood is largely based on the *Buddhabhūmisūtra* (verses IX.56–59 and 82–85 are directly from this sūtra). Both Sthiramati's and Asvabhāva's commentaries on the *Mahāyānasūtrālaṃkāra* extensively quote and refer to the *Buddhabhūmisūtra* (also Pawo Rinpoché's discussion of buddhahood in appendix 1 relies primarily on these two texts).

23 Certain Western and Japanese scholars attempt to draw a sharp distinction between the Yogācāra tradition and any scriptures on buddha nature, such as the *Uttaratantra*, even speaking of different schools. Indeed, the *Uttaratantra* is exclusively devoted to, and gives the most detailed presentation of, buddha nature, while not mentioning typical Yogācāra notions such as the three natures or the eight consciousnesses. On the other hand, there is only one verse in the other four works attributed to Maitreya (*Mahāyānasūtrālaṃkāra* IX.37) that mentions *tathāgatagarbha*, and it is absent in most of the works of Asaṅga (except for the *Ratnagotravibhāgavyākhyā*), Vasubandhu, and other major Yogācāras (for the consistent comments of Vasubandhu, Sthiramati, and Asvabhāva on *tathāgatagarbha* as suchness or identitylessness being the same in all phenomena/beings, see below). However, the equivalent notions such as mind's natural luminosity being obscured only by adventitious stains are rather common themes in Yogācāra texts (for the related topic of *agotraka*—"those who lack the disposition"—see below). As Keenan (1982, 15) remarks, "This does not mean that *tathāgatagarbha* is to be reckoned as a defined academic school in contrast to Mādhyamika and Yogācāra. As Takasaki has pointed out, such an evaluation was a peculiarity of Chinese Buddhism and is not found in either India or Tibet. This is further borne out by the complete

lack of polemic against *tathāgatagarbha* teachings in Yogācāra works. . . . The foregoing textual data seem to suggest that the initial pre-Asaṅgan Yogācāra thinkers represent a theoretical development from within the same circles that produced the *tathāgatagarbha* teachings. They appear to have taken their initial insights from the notion of the pure mind, as in the *Mahāyānasūtrālaṃkāra*" (see its verses IX.37 and XIII.18–19 below).

24 Besides this text, the only other two known Indian "commentaries" on the *Uttaratantra* are Vairocanarakṣita's (eleventh century) very brief *Mahāyānottaratantraṭippaṇī* (eight folios) and Sajjana's (eleventh/twelfth century) *Mahāyānottaratantraśāstropadeśa* (a summary in thirty-seven verses).

25 The *Tengyur* also contains an anonymous commentary on the first chapter of the *Mahāyānasaṃgraha*, called *Vivṛtagūḍhārthapiṇḍavyākhyā* (attributed by some to Vasubandhu).

26 As for the meaning of the Sanskrit compound *tathāgatagarbha*, its first part (*tathā*) can be taken as either the adverb "thus" or the noun "thusness/suchness" (as a term for ultimate reality; several texts gloss *tathāgatagarbha* as "suchness"). The second part can be read either as *gata* ("gone"), or *āgata* ("come, arrived"; the Tibetan *gshegs pa* can also mean both). However, in the term *tathāgata*, both meanings more or less come down to the same. Thus, the main difference lies in whether one understands a *Tathāgata* as (a) a "Thus-Gone/Thus-Come One" or (b) "One Gone/Come to Thusness," with the former emphasizing the aspect of the path and the latter the result. The final part of the compound—*garbha*—literally and originally means embryo, germ, womb, the interior or middle of anything, any interior chamber or sanctuary of a temple, calyx (as of a lotus), having in the interior, containing, or being filled with. At some point, the term also assumed the meaning of "core," "heart," and "pith" (which is also the meaning of its usual Tibetan translation *snying po*). Technically speaking, the compound *tathāgatagarbha* can be understood as either a *bahuvrīhi* or a *tatpuruṣa* compound, meaning "containing a Tathāgata (as core)" or "the core of a Tathāgata," respectively. The first is the most natural reading and is also supported by numerous passages in the scriptures. As for the term *sugata*, it means "one who has fared well," "one who goes well," or "one who lives in bliss." The compound *sugatagarbha* is to be understood in an analogous way as above.

27 The *Tengyur* attributes the *Hastavālanāmaprakaraṇa* and its *Vṛtti* to Āryadeva, while the Chinese canon has Dignāga as its author. Given the use of typical Yogācāra terms and notions in these texts, the latter seems more likely.

28 D4054 (attributed to Jinaputra in the *Tengyur*). The attribution to Sthiramati stems from the Chinese tradition and is supported by many Western scholars.

29 In due order, Taishō 1584, 1593, 1599, 1595, 1589, and 1587.

30 Taishō 1666.

31 Taishō 1610. The Chinese canon attributes the text to Vasubandhu (which is highly unlikely) and gives Paramārtha as the translator.

32 Taishō 1587.

33 Further sources of the *amalavijñāna* are his *Shih pa k'ung lun* (Taishō 1616) and *San wu-hsing lun* (Taishō 1617).

34 Other Indians involved in transmitting and translating mahāyāna and Yogācāra materials in China include Guṇavarman (367–431), Dharmarakṣa (385–433), Dharmagupta, and Prabhākaramitra (both sixth/seventh century).

35 The *Buddhabhūmyupadeśa* is only extant in Chinese (Taishō 1530). It is attributed to Bandhuprabha and others, and translated by Hsüan-tsang. As Keenan 1980 and 2002 points out, about half of the text is identical to Śīlabhadra's commentary and the other half is almost exclusively added from Hsüan-tsang's *Vijñaptimātratāsiddhi*. Thus, the text was obviously compiled in the seventh century, either by Hsüan-tsang himself, or, much more unlikely, by Bandhuprabha in India, drawing from no-longer-extant Sanskrit materials used in the *Vijñaptimātratāsiddhi*. Interestingly, the text contains a passage about mind being self-illuminating that refutes precisely the arguments that *Bodhicaryāvatāra* IX.18–19ab adduces against self-illuminating mind. It also explains all four buddha wisdoms (such as mirrorlike wisdom) to be self-awareness and gives a detailed presentation of the relationships between the four aspects of consciousness that manifest as the apprehended, the apprehender, the self-awareness of the apprehending of the apprehended, and the self-awareness of the very act of being self-aware (see Keenan 2002, 86–89).

36 See *The Life of Hsüan-tsang* (Taishō 2053.244a–246b), translated by Li Yung-hsi, 149–65. Peking: The Chinese Buddhist Association, 1959.

37 Both Bu ston rin chen grub 1931, II.133 and Tāranātha 1980, 207 attribute a *Kāyatrayāvatāra* to Candragomī.

38 The attribution of the *Durbodhālokā* commentary on the *Abhisamayālaṃkāra* to him is even disputed within the Tibetan tradition.

39 As for the developments of Yogācāra after Vasubandhu, there are several ways to distinguish various schools or lineages. In *The Essentials of Buddhist Philosophy* (Honolulu: University of Hawaii Press, 1947), 83–84, Junjirō Takakusu identifies three main streams—(1) the line of Dignāga, Agotra, and Dharmapāla at Nālandā; (2) the line of Guṇamati and Sthiramati at Valabhi; and (3) the line of Nanda, whose tenets were later followed by Paramārtha. Not much is known of further Yogācāras such as Guṇaśrī, Nanda, Śrīsena, Candrapāla (he is referred to as an early commentator on the *Madhyāntavibhāga*), Śuddhacandra, Citrabhānu, and Bandhuśrī (except for Guṇaśrī, the others and some of their positions are mentioned throughout the *Vijñaptimātratāsiddhi*). There are also a number of later commentators on Dharmakīrti's texts, primarily on his *Pramāṇavārttika*, whose primary focus is, of course, on valid cognition, but who also sometimes discuss the more specific Yogācāra topics in this context (these commentators include Dharmottara, Prajñākaragupta, Devendrabuddhi, Śākyabuddhi, Yāmāri, Ravigupta, and Jina). In general, except for most of the works by Maitreya, Asaṅga, and Vasubandhu, the majority of the above texts (in both the Tibetan and Chinese canons) still remain to be studied in detail.

40 Limaye 1992, 69 and D4034, fol. 75b.1ff.

41 *Webster's Third New International Dictionary* says that "concept" comes from Latin *conceptus* (collection, gathering, fetus) and is "something conceived in the mind : THOUGHT, IDEA, NOTION: as a *philos* : a general or abstract idea : a universal notion: (1) : the resultant of a generalizing mental operation : a generic mental image abstracted from percepts; *also* : a directly intuited object of thought (2) : a theoretical construct . . ." About "conceive," *Webster's* says, "to take into one's mind . . . to form in the mind . . . evolve mentally . . . IMAGINE, VISUALIZE . . ." Thus, somewhat differing from "concept," when "conceive" is understood in these latter senses in a very general way, it comes closer to the above meanings of *kalpana* and its related terms.

42 In the following translations, depending on the context, I use either "conception" or "imagination" for the above terms.

43 When I speak of "classical Yogācāra terms," this refers to these terms being predominantly used by Yogācāra masters, but does not mean that they invented them, since almost all of them are to be found in the sūtras (a notable exception is Vasubandhu's notion of "modulations" of consciousness [*pariṇāma*]). Even the term "false imagination," which is primarily known from the texts by Maitreya, is already found in early mahāyāna sūtras such as the *Vimalakīrtinirdeśasūtra* and the *Bodhisattvapiṭakasūtra*.

44 Pandeya 1999, 9.13.

45 Ibid., 11.30–12.3 (D4032, fol. 135b.1–3).

46 Tib. rong ston shes bya kun gzigs.

47 *Shes rab kyi pha rol tu phyin pa'i man ngag gi bstan bcos mngon par rtogs pa'i rgyan gyi 'grel pa'i rnam bshad tshig don rab tu gsal ba*, edited by by David P. Jackson and S. Onoda, 1988, fol. 40b.3–5.

48 Skt. asatkalpa, Tib. yod min rtog pa. This term is equivalent to "false imagination."

49 When used in terms of ultimate reality, *dharmadhātu*—or just *dhātu*—is understood in two main ways, which are reflected by two different Tibetan words that translate the latter term. In its most general way, *dhātu* in *dharmadhātu* refers to the ultimate nature of all phenomena—being equivalent to emptiness—which is usually translated into Tibetan as *dbyings* ("open expanse," "space," or "vastness"). If *dhātu* signifies specifically the nature of the mind of sentient beings in the sense of buddha nature as the most basic element of their entire being, it is typically rendered as *khams* (lit. "element"). To be sure, these two meanings and their Tibetan renderings are not necessarily regarded or employed in a mutually exclusive way. Still, generally speaking, they represent the understanding of (dharma)dhātu in Madhyamaka texts and the texts on buddha nature, respectively. In Yogācāra texts, the term is used and understood in both ways, depending on the context, but it is always clear that the direct realization of the dharmadhātu by nonconceptual wisdom does not just refer to a nonimplicative negation or blank voidness, but to mind's ultimate nature.

50 For more details on the characteristics of nonconceptual wisdom, see also the translation of OED below.

51 For "the supreme self that is the lack of self" realized by the buddhas, see *Mahāyānasūtrālaṃkāra* IX.23 below.

52 Sanskrit in Anacker 1986, 416. For mere cognizance being by definition without a referent, see also verse 27 of the *Triṃśikā* below.

53 Hall 1986, 13–18.

54 D4051, fol. 221a.4–221b.2.

55 These four steps are also found in *Laṅkāvatārasūtra* X.256–57, *Mahāyānasūtrālaṃkāra* XIV.23–28, *Dharmadharmatāvibhāga* (lines 182–185, 264–275), *Madhyāntavibhāga* I.6–7ab, as well as in *Triṃśikākārikā* 28–30 and *Trisvabhāvanirdeśa* 36–37ab. Śāntarakṣita's autocommentary on his *Madhyamakālaṃkāra* (D3885, fol. 79a–b) as well as Kamalaśīla's *Madhyamakālaṃkārapañjikā* (P5286, fols. 137a–138a) and first *Bhāvanākrama* (D3915, fol. 33a–b) also quote *Laṅkāvatārasūtra* X.256–257 and refer to these four stages, commenting on the last one from a Madhyamaka perspective (see Brunnhölzl 2004, 300–302). See also AC (p. 246) and NYC on NY lines 60–61.

56 Limaye 1992, 73.

57 III.13 (P5549, fol. 29b.2).

58 III.12 (ibid., fol. 29a.3–7; the phrases in "[ ]" are from the commentaries by Vasubandhu and Asvabhāva).

59 Pandeya 1999, 23.11ff. (P5534, fols. 35b–36b).

60 Lines 264–275. The same is also expressed in lines 182–185, which treat "the four yogic practices."

61 This refers to the mastery over a wealth of qualities that result from the change of state of the five skandhas, particularly from the eight consciousnesses becoming the four wisdoms (see below).

62 Sthiramati (*Madhyāntavibhāgaṭīkā*, Sanskrit edition by Lévi, p. 43) comments that this is equivalent to supramundane nonconceptual wisdom without subject and object (*anālambyālambakaṃ*). With the propensities of the clinging to apprehender and apprehended being eliminated, mind as such is resting in its own true nature (*svacittadharmatāyāṃ ca cittam eva sthitaṃ bhavati*).

63 Ibid., 15ff.

64 This term refers to mental factors, such as feeling and discrimination.

65 Quoted and translated in Lusthaus 2002, 465 (Taisho 1585.6c; chap.2:4B).

66 As translated in Paul 1984, 159–60.

67 Ibid., 163–64 and 167. The *Yogācārabhūmi*, one of the major Yogācāra texts (and definitely the longest one), only mentions the term *cittamātra* twice (P5536–8, zi, fols. 70b.2 and 80b.2f), but both times explicitly not as a denial of outer objects (for details, see Schmithausen 1973a, 165–66 and addendum after p. 186). However, given the consistent abhidharmic foundation of this text, this is not as surprising as one may think at first.

68 Paul 1984, 166.

69 I.9ab.

70 Verses 1–2, 5bd, 6ab, and 8ac.

71 Note that, unlike the works by Asaṅga, Vasubandhu, and so on, the five Maitreya works do not mention the terms ālaya-consciousness and afflicted mind.

72 *Manas* has a wide semantic range, primarily being one of the many Sanskrit words for "mind" in general, also meaning "conceptual mind," "thought," and "imagination" (it can also refer to "intellect," "intelligence," "perception," "spirit," "opinion," "intention," "inclination," and more). There is a definite lack of proper equivalents for most of the rich Sanskrit and Tibetan terminologies used for mind and its many facets, but there is also a need for distinctive terms when going into the subtleties of mapping out mind in Buddhist texts, especially in the context of the eight consciousnesses. This is why *manas* is rendered throughout by the English technical term "mentation" (coming from the Latin *mens* ["mind," "thinking"] and *mentare* [to "think"], which are cognate with Skt. *manas*). The *Oxford English Dictionary* defines "mentation" as "mental action or a mental state," with the former suggesting mind being in some kind of operational mode, which is also one of the primary meanings of the Sanskrit and Tibetan terms (its other meanings referring specifically to the sixth consciousness or the afflicted mind).

73 To wit, when just the term *ālaya* appears, depending on the context, it can either refer to the ālaya-consciousness or, especially in the tantras, to the fundamental ground of all being, equivalent to the luminous nature of mind or the Tathāgata heart.

74 Literally, *kliṣṭamanas* means "defiled mind," but here I rather follow the Tibetan (lit. "plagued or plaguing mind"), since it is not just a question of mind being defiled like a dusty but insentient mirror. Rather, as the above process shows, mind experiences mental and physical suffering through such defilement.

75 In general, the eight consciousnesses (primary minds) and their accompanying mental factors are said to be always congruent in five respects. They are congruent in terms of (1) the support, in that they depend on the same sense faculty; (2) the focal object, in that they observe the same object; (3) the aspect, in that they have the same apprehended aspect triggered by the object; (4) time, in that they occur at the same time; and (5) substance, in that at any given time, each primary mind is only accompanied by one single kind within each of its accompanying mental factors (for example, one cannot have a pleasant and unpleasant feeling at the same moment).

76 I.6 (D4048, fols. 3b.5–4a.1). Mentation being associated with the above four afflictions is also mentioned in Vasubandhu's *Triṃśikā* (verse 6) and his *Pañcaskandhaprakaraṇa* (D4059, fol. 15b.5).

77 In general, there are two neutral actions—those that obscure liberation and those that do not (such as walking or sitting).

78 D4066, fols. 231b.5 and 232b.2.

79 D4067, fol. 25a.2–4. The beginning of chapter 5 of Hsüan-tsang's *Vijñaptimātratāsiddhi* (La Vallée Poussin 1928–1948, 289–90) explains that the six collections of consciousnesses all rely on mentation as their immediate condition. However, it is only the sixth one that receives the name of "mentation consciousness" (*manovijñāna*), because it is named after its specific support—the seventh consciousness or mentation—just as the five sense consciousnesses, despite also relying on mentation, are named after their specific supports, such as the eye sense faculty. Or, the mental consciousness is so called, because it depends only on mentation, whereas the other five depend in addition on their respective material sense factulties. The six consciousnesses are therefore named in this way because of their supports and in relation to one another—"eye consciousness" up through "mentation consciousness." This is unlike the case of the seventh and eighth consciousnesses, which are named in accordance with their natures—mentation (*manas*) by virtue of the activity of egoistic thinking/conceit (*manyanā*), and mind (*citta*) due to "accumulating/variety" (*citra*).

80 Note though that the explicit term "immediate mind" seems to be a later Tibetan term—it does not appear in any of the texts by Maitreya, Asaṅga, or Vasubandhu (or any other Yogācāra texts I have consulted). For more details on this specific topic, see the introduction to the Third Karmapa's view below; he further divides "mentation" into the afflicted mind, the immediate mind, and "pure or stainless mentation."

81 D4066, fol. 239a.7–239b.3.

82 This meditative absorption represents the cessation of all primary minds and mental factors with an unstable continuum (the first six consciousnesses) as well as one of the two consciousnesses with a stable continuum (the afflicted mind with its mental factors, but not the ālaya-consciousness). This absorption is used as the culminating meditative absorption in the process of "ninefold progressive abiding" (which includes various alternating ways of

training in entering and rising from the four samādhis of the form realm and the four formless absorptions).

83 D4049, fol. 53a.7–b.1.

84 Guṇaprabha's *Pañcaskandhavivaraṇa* (D4067, fol. 27a.1–2) explains that, during the meditative absorption of cessation and the path of the noble ones, the afflicted mind ceases insofar as its latent tendencies do not manifest. However, once one rises from these states, it rearises from its seeds.

85 Note that, as Paul (1984, 139) remarks, "this consciousness is never enumerated specifically as a ninth consciousness, though this is the implication from the assertion that the *amala-vijñāna* is separate from all defilement and emerges only after the cessation of the *ālaya*."

86 Taishō 1584, 1616 (esp. pp. 863b20f and 864a28), 1617 (esp. p. 872a1f). Apparently, there are no Indian, but only Chinese scriptural sources for this ninth consciousness, so the Tibetan tradition seems to have obtained its information on it from the latter, including the Chinese commentary on the *Saṃdhinirmocanasūtra* (translated into Tibetan as P5517) by the Korean master Wonch'uk (aka Yüan-ts'e; 613–96). According to Hsüan-tsang's *Vijñāptimātratāsiddhi* (La Vallée Poussin 1928–1948, 109–11), the notion of *amalavijñāna* was originally a teaching of the Vibhajyavādins (more precisely, the Mahāsāṃghika-Ekavyāvahārika-Lokottaravādin-Kaukkuṭikas), who speak about the natural purity of the mind being merely obscured by adventitious stains. Paul (1984, 240–41) points out the following: "The Tunhuang manuscript, *She ta-sheng lun chang* {a text on the *Mahāyānasaṃgraha*}, attributes the following to the WHL {a *Mahāyānasaṃgraha*-related threefold anthology attributed to Paramārtha}: 'The characterless and unproduced state is the *amala*[*-vijñāna*], the ultimately pure consciousness' (T.2807.85.1013c20–21). 'The nature of discrimination (*parikalpita-svabhāva*) is forever nonexistent. The nature of dependence (*paratantra-svabhāva*) also does not exist. As for these two, they have no existence and this is identical to the *amala-vijñāna*. Thus, it is ultimately the only pure consciousness. Furthermore, it is a foreign tradition that states in the *Shih-ch'i ti-lun*, "Chapter on the Bodhisattva," {another text by *Paramārtha*} that the *amala-vijñāna* is explained as the ninth consciousness' (T.2807.85.1016c19-22)."

87 As for the last term, most translations that come purely from the Tibetan *yongs grub* (instead of the Sanskrit *pariniṣpanna*) say "thoroughly established nature" or the like. This is usually based on too literal an understanding of the Tibetan (while disregarding its underlying Sanskrit, which simply means "perfect" or "perfected") and on certain Tibetan doxographical hierarchies, which consider this term as an exclusive feature of so-called "Mere Mentalism" with its alleged assertion of some ultimately existing or "thoroughly established" consciousness. However, neither the Sanskrit term nor its understanding by all major Yogācāra masters justify any such wrongly reifying rendering. Also, it seems somewhat misleading to say "perfected nature," since there is nothing to be changed, let alone perfected, in this nature, its whole point being rather to signify primordial perfection and completeness.

88 A detailed study of all these different models would cover a large volume on its own (for an overview, see Boquist 1993).

89 II.17 (P5549, fol. 18b.5–8).

90 II.28 (ibid., fol. 22a.6–7).

91 II.26 (P5549, fol. 21a.5–21b.4). Note that Vasubandhu (P5551, fol. 180b.4–5) comments on the pure object (4) that, if it were the imaginary nature, it would have arisen from the cause

of afflicted phenomena; and if it were the other-dependent nature, it would be something that is unreal.

92 See also below for Sthiramati's comments on verses 23–24 of Vasubandhu's *Triṃśikā* and his equating the other-dependent nature with the ālaya-consciousness, which is eventually eliminated in its fundamental change of state.

93 II.27 (ibid., fols. 21b.5–22a.4).

94 Nguyen 1990, 84–85.

95 II. 132 (verse 198; D107, fol. 172a.5–6).

96 P5481, fols. 8b.7–9a.3.

97 For example, P5562, fols. 116b.7–117b.7 and 122a.7–123a.1.

98 Ibid., fol. 123b.2–6 (from D106, fol. 34a.7–34b.3).

99 This quote is also found in the *Abhidharmakośabhāṣya* (Pradhan ed., p. 468.20–21).

100 This is the second from among three ways to understand *paramārtha* (for details, see below). In Yogācāra, usually, "mundane" and "supramundane" cognition or wisdom are understood as the perceptive modes during a bodhisattva's subsequent attainment and meditative equipoise, respectively.

101 This is *Samādhirājasūtra* IX.23.

102 P5562, fols. 127b.6–128a.5. That the general characteristic of all phenomena is suchness is explained by both Vasubandhu and Asvabhāva in their commentaries on *Mahāyānasaṃgraha* II.26 (P5551, fol. 180a.6–7 and D4051, fols. 230b.7–231a.1; for details, see below).

103 Sanskrit edition by Lévi, p. 41.

104 Ibid., 110–11.

105 III. 8–9, fols. 28a.5–29a.7.

106 'Ju mi pham rgya mtsho c. 1990c, 705–6.

107 Limaye 1992, 172.

108 Following the words of I.1, Sthiramati does not explicitly state the names of the three natures here, but only speaks about false imagination, duality, and emptiness. However, as his commentary on I.5 (which introduces the three natures by name) makes clear, in due order, these correspond to the other-dependent, imaginary, and perfect natures.

109 The topic of the first chapter of the *Madhyāntavibhāga* is the characteristics of afflicted and purified phenomena, or false imagination and emptiness.

110 Pandeya ed., pp. 9.25–11.30.

111 Neither Vasubandhu's nor Sthiramati's commentaries state anywhere that false imagination exists ultimately. They do say several times that both false imagination and emptiness exist, but it is very obvious that this does not refer to the same level of existence.

112 Ibid., 19.

113 Ibid., 13.16–21.

114 Ibid., 36–38.

115 Ibid., 46.

116 Such statements are not only found in the mahāyāna scriptures, but also in the Pāli canon (from which Vasubandhu most probably quotes), such as *Aṅguttara Nikāya* I.10, "O monks, the mind is luminosity, and yet it is afflicted by adventitious afflictions." Also the *Saṃyutta Nikāya* (III.151.22–23; 31–32; and 152.8–9) states, "O monks, sentient beings are afflicted because of the afflictions of the mind. Because of the purity of the mind, sentient beings are purified." The Tibetan tradition considers the two lines, "because of mind's natural luminosity" and "because of being afflicted by adventitious afflictions" not as parts of Vasubandhu's commentary, but as two additional lines in *Madhyāntavibhāga* I.22.

117 The above four models also show that quite different interpretations of the three natures obviously existed already at the time of Sthiramati, and that at least some of them may have been interpreted in more or less reifying ways by certain people.

118 P5531, fol. 138b.2–4.

119 XIII.18–19.

120 Mathes 1996, lines 128–132.

121 These four are found in the *Avikalpapraveśadhāraṇī* (D142), which says that bodhisattvas have to gradually relinquish all four of these conceptions in order to enter the sphere of nonconceptuality. Rangjung Dorje seemed to consider the *Avikalpapraveśadhāraṇī* as important, since he composed a (now lost) synopsis of it and also refers to these four conceptions in his OED and DSC (for details, see there as well as NTC and NYC).

122 OED, pp. 610–11. For more details, see the translation of the excerpts from OED below.

123 That means being actual effective causes and results, and not just nominal ones.

124 JNS, vol. 1, p. 210.

125 D4049, fol. 100a.7–100b.1.

126 D4054, fol. 231a.6–231b.2. See also Sthiramati's comments on *Mahāyānasūtrālaṃkāra* IX.56 below.

127 X.5 (D4048, fol. 38a.4–8).

128 D4034, fol. 113b.1–2.

129 Note that the Yogācāra literature in fact sometimes employs two terms—*āśrayapāravṛtti* (lit. "change of state into something else") versus *āṣrayaparivṛtti*—as referring to the former and the latter aspects above, respectively. However, the use of these two terms in the texts is not consistent in this way. Ultimately, both come down to the same, basically indicating two sides of the same process.

130 Limaye 1992, 116–17.

131 Throughout, the reason for using "familiarization" instead of the—at least in popular western Buddhist literature—more familiar word "meditation" is that, in Buddhism, both the Sanskrit *bhāvanā* and the Tibetan *sgom pa* mostly mean "familiarizing with," mentally "cultivating," or "enhancing" something, either some certainty gained through prior reflection or a direct insight into true reality. Thus, this process can be either conceptual or nonconceptual. However, it should be noted that the original meaning of "meditation" is just "reflection" (Lat. meditatio, meditare), which is clearly conceptual, while the original meaning of the term "contemplation" (Lat. contemplatio, contemplare) is "viewing" or "looking" at something in

a settled state of mind (possibly being either conceptual or nonconceptual). Also, as for compassion and other virtuous mental states, the point is not really to meditate *on* them as some more or less abstract object or in a conceptual way, but to cultivate and familiarize with them as integral constituents of one's mind. Of course, this is even more obvious in the case of mind's ultimate true nature (of which it is invariably said that it cannot be meditated on anyway, but one can definitely familiarize oneself with it). Likewise, the texts often speak about cultivating or familiarizing with a path, *śamatha*, or *vipaśyanā*, and it obviously makes no sense to say "meditating on a path," and even less to say "meditating on *śamatha* or *vipaśyanā*." As for the Sanskrit term *bhāvanā*, it generally refers to an act of producing, manifesting, or promoting. Specifically, it means imagining, forming in the mind, occupying one's imagination with or directing one's thoughts to something. In this sense, the word *can* also refer to reflection, meditation, or contemplation (thus, depending on the context and to follow common consensus, I sometimes use "meditation" too). The term can also mean the application of perfumes and the like, or saturating or steeping any powder with fluid. Thus, similar to the process of a scent fully pervading a cloth or the like and actually becoming inseparable from it, "cultivation" or "familiarization" in this sense may be seen as "perfuming" the mind stream with liberating insights.

132 D4034, fol. 120b.1–121a.1

133 For more details on "change of state," see the translation of OED below.

134 Limaye ed. p. 121; D4034, fol. 124a.2–5.

135 D4034, fol. 124a.5–124b.2. Vasubandhu's very brief comment on this agrees, saying that, since suchness is the same in all beings and a Tathāgata has the nature of pure suchness, all beings are said to have the Tathāgata heart (Limaye 1992, 122). This conforms to his *Mahāyānasaṃgrahabhāṣya* (P5551, fol. 180a.6–7) on "natural purity" in *Mahāyānasaṃgraha* II.26 above, which says that, inasmuch as this natural purity exists as suchness, it exists in all sentient beings as their general characteristic. Therefore, it is said that all phenomena (!) are endowed with the Tathāgata heart. Asvabhāva's *Ṭīkā* is silent on *Mahāyānasūtrālaṃkāra* IX.37, but his *Mahāyānasaṃgrahopanibandhana* (D4051, fols. 230b.7–231a.1) on II.26 follows Vasubandhu, saying that natural purity is the actual true nature of ordinary beings, which means that suchness never changes into anything else, and therefore is the general characteristic of all phenomena. Thus, it is said that all sentient beings possess the Tathāgata heart. Later (D4051, fol. 246b.4), Asvabhāva's text comments on bodhisattvas on the first bhūmi attaining an equal mind with regard to all beings (III.11) by saying that they see all beings as equality in the sense of their identitylessness, which is why the scriptures say that all beings have the Tathāgata heart. Also, Bandhuprabha's *Buddhabhūmyupadeśa* (Keenan 2002, 48 and 103) says that the teachings on buddha nature refer to the pure dharmadhātu being present in the mind streams of all sentient beings. However, these teachings only refer to those beings who (among the five kinds of disposition) possess the buddha disposition. They were given only as skillful means, referring only to a small part of sentient beings, and in order to guide those of indeterminate disposition to swiftly enter the mahāyāna. Note that most of this is remarkably identical with certain Madhyamaka explanations (particularly the one found in the Tibetan Gelugpa school) of what buddha nature is. Coming from several Yogācāras, this evidences that at least some followers of this tradition did not explain *tathāgatagarbha* as the *Uttaratantra* and its commentaries do, but simply as "natural purity" in the sense of suchness being the same in all beings. One reason may be that the above commentators, in line with the *Mahāyānasūtrālaṃkāra*'s many verses on buddhahood, dharmadhātu, and suchness being free from reference points (such as IX.36 above; for more, see below), did not want to provide any ground for reification on the level of ultimate reality. Another reason may lie in

certain Yogācāras explaining that being "one who lacks the disposition" (*agotraka*) means to absolutely never attain nirvāṇa (see below). However, as evidenced in some of the passages quoted earlier, the same masters also refer to mind's luminous nature being obscured only by adventitious stains, and emptiness being both empty and naturally luminous at the time of sentient beings as well as at the time of the noble ones. Also, later in his commentary (D4034, fol. 196a.5–196b.1), Sthiramati states that it is untenable to say that only one among all the innumerable sentient beings who are endowed with the disposition to become a buddha will become a buddha, while the others will not. In fact, everybody who has gathered the two accumulations of merit and wisdom will become a buddha. Interestingly, *Mahāyānasūtrālaṃkāra* IX.37 is also quoted in Asaṅga's *Ratnagotravibhāgavyākhyā* (J 71.16–17) in the context of saying that the suchness of the Tathāgatas is the *tathāgatagarbha* of sentient beings, which is typically and explicitly equated with the natural purity and luminosity of mind being obscured only by adventitious stains.

136 Some people say that the freedom from apprehender and apprehended is less encompassing and profound than twofold identitylessness. However, the freedom from apprehender and apprehended corresponds exactly to twofold identitylessness, since all possible objects and subjects in terms of both persons and phenomena are included in the former as well. Moreover, the relinquishment of obscurations in terms of apprehender and apprehended is also extensively discussed in both the prajñāpāramitā sūtras and the *Abhisamayālaṃkāra*. Technically speaking, in the latter's detailed descriptions of many different levels of progressively more subtle mistaken conceptions about apprehender and apprehended to be relinquished on the paths of preparation, seeing, and familiarization, respectively, these levels comprise all cognitive obscurations, but implicitly include the afflictive obscurations too.

137 If not noted otherwise, the following comments on the select verses from the ninth chapter of the *Mahāyānasūtrālaṃkāra* are all excerpts from Sthiramati's commentary (D4034, fols. 106a.6–144b.7), which usually follows, but often greatly elaborates on, Vasubandhu's *Bhāṣya*.

138 These consist of seven sets of practices: (1) the four applications of mindfulness (Skt. catuḥ smṛtyupasthāna, Tib. dran pa nye bar bzhag pa bzhi), (2) the four correct exertions (Skt. catvāri samyakprahāṇāni, Tib. yang dag spong ba bzhi), (3) the four limbs of miraculous powers (Skt. catvāra ṛddhipādāḥ, Tib. rdzu 'phrul gyi rkang pa bzhi), (4) the five faculties (Skt. pañcendriyāṇi, Tib. dbang po lnga), (5) the five powers (Skt. pañcabalāni, Tib. stobs lnga), (6) the seven branches of enlightenment (Skt. saptasaṃbodhyaṅgāni, Tib. byang chub kyi yan lag bdun), and (7) the eightfold path of the noble ones (Skt. āryāṣṭāṅgamārga, Tib. 'phags pa'i lam yan lag brgyad). In the mahāyāna, sets (1)–(3) make up the lesser, medium, and greater levels of the path of accumulation; (4)–(5) respectively correspond to the first two (heat and peak) and the second two (poised readiness and supreme dharma) of the four levels of the path of preparation; (6) is equivalent to the path of seeing; and (7) represents the path of familiarization.

139 These two kinds of knowing represent the two buddha wisdoms of knowing suchness and variety. Elsewhere (D4034, tsi, fol. 231a.7–231b.2), Sthiramati comments that "omniscience" refers to knowing the imaginary nature, that is, knowing that all phenomena that are imagined as apprehender and apprehended are like horns of a rabbit and lack characteristics. "Knowing all referents without exception" means to know the entire seeming reality—knowable objects such as skandhas, dhātus, āyatanas, contaminated phenomena, and uncontaminated phenomena.

140 The *Bhāṣya* says that the pāramitās and so on are not perfect (*aparinispanna*) in the sense of there being any intrinsic being of them.

141 Besides "change," *vṛtti* in itself has many meanings (such as "operation," "activity," "function," "mode of life or conduct," "nature," "state," "practice," and "mood") which are modulated here by the ten prefixes *pra-*, *ud-*, *a-*, *ni-*, *ā-*, *dvaya-*, *advaya-*, *samā-*, *viśiṣṭā-*, and *sarvagā-*.

142 Note that *Uttaratantra* I.27a gives the fact that "buddha wisdom enters into the hosts of beings" as one of the three reasons why all sentient beings are said to have the Tathāgata heart. For a detailed discussion of these three reasons in *Uttaratantra* I.27–28, see Brunnhölzl 2007b, n. 280.

143 Note that this is similar to "the pāramitā of ultimate self" in *Uttaratantra* I.37cd. Also, the use of "self" in the double sense of what is to be relinquished and the ultimate nature of phenomena resembles the use of "nature" (*svabhāva*) in Madhyamaka, which says that phenomena lack any nature and that precisely this is the nature of phenomena.

144 This corresponds to the above-mentioned threefold change of state as in the *Abhidharmasamucchaya*.

145 Vasubandhu's *Bhāṣya* does not comment on the last two lines of this verse, while Asvabhāva's *Ṭīkā* (D4029, fol. 72b.5–73a.1) agrees in identifying "the wisdom of the real" (*vastujñāna*) as the wisdom of subsequent attainment, and "that" in the last line as the dharmadhātu. However, it says that "the real" (*vastu*) refers to the ālaya-consciousness—the other-dependent nature. Still, this describes the change of state of the impregnations of negative tendencies—when the other-dependent nature has changed state, it becomes the sphere of the wisdom that is attained subsequently to nonconceptual wisdom, but not the sphere of other wisdoms. Nonconceptual wisdom attains mastery over suchness, because it rests in meditative equipoise at will, while the wisdom that is attained subsequently to this meditative equipoise attains mastery over the other-dependent nature in the sense of being unmistaken about it. Sthiramati's comments are literally confirmed by Ngülchu Togmé's commentary on this verse (Dngul chu thogs med 1979, 174–75), which concludes, "Thus, the nature of phenomena is realized through meditative equipoise, and meditative equipoise is realized through subsequent attainment. Since this is uninterrupted, it is the characteristic of inexhaustible mastery." Note that in Asaṅga 2004, 93–94, the translators Jamspal et al. present a greatly abbreviated, but partly mistaken form of Sthiramati's above explanation (misidentifying "the real" as the ālaya-consciousness). Against Sthiramati and Asvabhāva, Jamspal et al. also prefer to follow the Gelugpa scholar dBal Mang, who takes "the wisdom of the real" as referring to the wisdom of meditative equipoise, thus, as Jamspal et al. put it, "tacitly correcting Sthiramati's (or the translator's) equation of *vastujñāna* with mundane, aftermath intuition."

146 D4034, fols. 74a.3–75b.1.

147 That even the Madhyamaka understanding of the ultimate is not limited to its being solely an object is shown by Bhāvaviveka's *Tarkajvālā* (D3856, fol. 59a.7–59b.2). He explains that, in *paramārtha*, *artha* ("object," "purpose," or "actuality") refers to what is to be understood, realized, or examined. *Parama* means "supreme." Thus, (1) since *paramārtha* is an object and ultimate (or supreme), it is the ultimate object. (2) Or, it may be read as "the object of the ultimate." Since it is the object of ultimate nonconceptual wisdom, it is the object of the ultimate. (3) Or, it can be understood as "that which is in accordance with the ultimate object." Since the ultimate object exists in the prajñā that is in approximate accordance with the realization of this ultimate object, it is what is in accordance with the ultimate object. In other words, in (1), both *parama* and *artha* refer only to the object as opposed to the subject that realizes it, (2) means that *parama* refers to the subject (wisdom) and *artha* to the object (emp-

tiness), and (3) indicates a reasoning consciousness that cognizes ultimate reality not directly but inferentially.

148 The Yogācāra system does not present the dharmadhātu as a fifth wisdom (dharmadhātu wisdom), which has its origin in the Buddhist tantras. Later however, especially in Tibet, listing five wisdoms became the predominant general presentation (see also Pawo Rinpoché's discussion of the *Buddhabhūmisūtra* in appendix 1). When the dharmadhātu wisdom is added, it is usually matched with the svābhāvikakāya. Some explanations (for example, TOK vol. 3, p. 607) also say that dharmadhātu wisdom is the change of state of the empty aspect of the ālaya-consciousness, while mirrorlike wisdom is the change of state of its lucid aspect.

149 P5833, fol. 6a–b.

150 D4034, fol. 113b.1–5.

151 As mentioned before, verses IX.56–59 are literally found in the *Buddhabhūmisūtra*.

152 Vasubandhu's *Bhāṣya* agrees, adding that the dharmakāya's characteristic is the fundamental change of state. The dharmakāya is often referred to as "svābhāvika-dharmatākāya" or "dharmatākaya," with dharmakāya being explained as an abbreviation of these two terms. For example, see *Mahāyānasaṃgrāhabhāṣya* on X.1, *Buddhabhūmyupadeśa* (Taishō 1530, 325c5–7), *Buddhabhūmivyākhyāna* (D3997, fol. 272b.5), Jñānacandra's *Kāyatrayavṛtti* (D3891, fol. 8b.2), and Ārya Vimuktisena's *Abhisamayālaṃkāravṛtti* (D3787, fol. 192a.7–8).

153 Note that the Sanskrit grammatical forms svābhāvikakāya, sāmbhogikakāya, and nairmāṇikakāya (as opposed to svabhāvakāya, sambhogakāya, and nirmāṇakāya) are quite standard (being not only used in the *Mahāyānasūtrālaṃkāra* and its commentaries, but also throughout the *Abhisamayālaṃkāra*, the *Uttaratantra*, their commentaries, and other texts). These forms indicate these kāyas are related to the dharmakāya as its features and not as three separate entities on their own. Thus, in terms of its nature, the dharmakāya is referred to as svābhāvikakāya (this is why these two are usually said to be equivalent); in terms of its bringing the enjoyment of the mahāyāna dharma to bodhisattvas, it is the sāmbhogikakāya; and in terms of its manifesting in all kinds of forms for all kinds of beings, it is the nairmāṇikakāya.

154 Most of these verses as well as the related IX.41–48 are quoted and explained in the translations below.

155 Note that Haribhadra's commentaries on the *Abhisamayālaṃkāra* say the same.

156 Nishio 1982, esp. 59, 84–92, 125–26.

157 Literally, Skt. *pratyavekṣā* is "looking back" and also means "paying attention," "looking after," or "care."

158 On this, compare DSC on *Dharmadhātustava* verses 38–45 on Mahāmudrā meditation related to sense perceptions and the mental consciousness (see Brunnhölzl 2007b, 245–51).

159 AC, fol. 163b.

160 Dpa' bo gtsug lag phreng ba n.d., 764.

161 For further details on the Yogācāra system in general as well as the notions of naturally luminous mind and the Tathāgata heart, see the bibliography in general as well as Brunnhölzl 2004, 457–95 and 2007b, 57–109.

162 Tib. dol po pa shes rab rgyal mtshan.

163 Tāranātha even wrote two commentaries on the *Heart Sūtra* from the perspective of *shentong*. Tāranātha n.d., vol. 17, pp. 571–759 and 759–83.

164 Śākya mchog ldan 1988b, 13–15.

165 Tib. ldog pa gzhan sel gyi cha. An "elimination-of-other" is a conceptual phenomenon arrived at through excluding everything it is not.

166 The same is said by Karma Trinlépa below.

167 Śākya mchog ldan 1988c, 40ff.

168 Lit. "proponents of the lack of a nature." This is another term for the Mādhyamikas.

169 This accords with Śākya Chogden's repeated statements that the view of *rangtong* is the best one for cutting through all reference points, while the view of *shentong* is more helpful for describing and facilitating meditative experience and realization.

170 Śākya mchog ldan 1975, 225–27.

171 'Ju mi pham rgya mtsho c. 1990b, 3–6.

172 Skt. *gotra* is sometimes still translated as "family" or "lineage" (two of the word's ordinary literal meanings), when it refers to buddha nature. Of course, by virtue of having buddha nature, all beings could be said to *belong* to the family or lineage of the buddhas, but one cannot help but wonder what it should mean that buddha nature itself *is* a "family" or "lineage."

173 In Tibet, there have been long-standing and complex debates about the questions of whether the *Mahāyānasūtrālaṃkāra*—as well as the *Madhyāntavibhāga* and *Dharmadharmatāvibhāga*—belongs to what Tibetans call "Mere Mentalism" (thus being inferior to Madhyamaka); whether it and the Yogācāra School teach that some beings have no disposition to attain enlightenment at all (and what exactly "disposition" means in this context); and whether they assert three yānas ultimately, and so forth. The Gelugpa School in particular answers these questions in the affirmative and many modern scholars do so too. There is no room here to address these issues in detail (such as the complex treatment of *gotra* in different Yogācāra texts), but as can be seen from the above, there are Tibetan teachers (as well as some modern scholars) who disagree with the Gelugpa answers. In particular, as for the term "disposition" (*gotra*), it should first be noted that, differing from this term's primary meaning in the *Uttaratantra*, in the *Mahāyānasūtrālaṃkāra*, it is not synonymous with buddha nature. Like the *Laṅkāvatārasūtra*, the text speaks about five categories of *gotra* (those of bodhisattvas, pratyekabuddhas, śrāvakas, those with uncertain *gotra*, and those without *gotra*). The *Laṅkāvatārasūtra* identifies the last category with those who just follow their great desire (*icchantika*) and reject the dharma, thus having eliminated all their roots of virtue and not attaining parinirvāṇa. The *Mahāyānasūtrālaṃkāra* follows this very common definition of *gotra* in general, which is "roots of virtue" (see also Sthiramati's *Madhyāntavibhāgaṭīkā*, ed. Yamaguchi, 188). The *Bhāṣyā* on *Mahāyānasūtrālaṃkāra* III.4 explains that *gotra* is that from which qualities arise and increase. Also the distinction between the naturally abiding (*prakṛtistha*) and the accomplished (*samudānīta*) or unfolding dispositions in this verse differs from how these terms are understood in the *Uttaratantra*, with the former defined as what has the nature of being a support for further virtue (*prakṛti* can also mean "cause") and the latter as what is thus supported. On *Mahāyānasūtrālaṃkāra* III.9 and III.11, the *Bhāṣya* comments that accumulating roots of virtue is indispensable for acquiring a disposition, but once the bodhisattva disposition is acquired, it serves as the source of an infinite number of further roots of virtue. Thus, *gotra* in this sense refers to conditioned and multiple phenomena,

whereas *gotra* in the sense of buddha nature is clearly unconditioned and single. The former sense is also evident from Sthiramati's commentary (D4034, fols. 41b.6–43a.2), which says that beings have infinite *gotras*, all of which refer to some (conventional) nature of theirs, such as being an angry or passionate person, or liking sweet versus other tastes. Just as the possession of the *gotra* of desire functions as the cause for giving rise to desire, but not for hatred, the three different *gotras* of the three yānas are indispensable for there being three yānas. As for *Mahāyānasūtrālaṃkāra* III.11, the *Bhāṣya* explains that to be without disposition means to possess the property of not attaining parinirvāṇa—either for a certain time (the first four kinds of beings in the verse) or forever (the last one). According to Sthiramati's commentary (D4034, fols. 48a.4–49b.1) this refers to those with the property of not attaining parinirvāṇa (that is, buddhahood) for a certain time and those who have the property of not attaining *any* kind of nirvāṇa for a certain time. He says that the first four pertain to those who *do* possess the bodhisattva disposition, but, by virtue of certain conditions, will temporarily (for many eons) not attain parinirvāṇa (that is, buddhahood). Among these, "those who are solely devoted to wrongdoing" are engaged in the five negative actions without interval. "Those who have completely destroyed the immaculate dharmas" are those who, under the influence of wrong spiritual teachers, have fallen into the wrong view of nihilism, thus denying karma, the three jewels, and so on. "Those who lack the virtue conducive to liberation" have not gathered the complete accumulations of merit and virtue necessary to attain parinirvāṇa, but only the virtues for higher rebirths as gods and humans within saṃsāra. "Those who have inferior immaculate dharmas" have only gathered a fraction of the merit and wisdom necessary to attain parinirvāṇa. Thus, as long as these four do not fully remove their negative actions and wrong views, and accumulate the complete accumulations of merit and virtue necessary to attain parinirvāṇa, they will not attain this state. As for those who will not attain any nirvāṇā, "lacking the cause" refers to lacking the virtuous roots and the disposition for any of the nirvāṇas of the three yānas, because without such a disposition, they do not attain any of these three nirvāṇas. They do lack the property of attaining nirvāṇa, just as the natures of stones and trees do not turn into something that has the nature of consciousness, such as minds and mental factors. Thus, in the first four cases, Sthiramati says, "lack of disposition" has only a pejorative sense, while "lacking the cause" means utter nonexistence, because they absolutely do not attain nirvāṇa. However, considering the text's (and the commentators') understanding of "disposition" (virtuous roots), its explicit stance that all beings possess *tathāgatagarbha* (IX.37), and its statement that mind is natural luminosity, which is merely obscured by adventitious stains (XIII.18–19), being without *gotra* (*agotraka*; the text does not use *icchantika*) forever is not equivalent to saying that some beings have no buddha nature or absolutely can never attain enlightenment. Rather, there are some beings who simply never acquire a "disposition" for any of the yānas in the sense of never acquiring any—or at least a significant—amount of virtue that qualifies as such a disposition. In other words, all beings have the potential for buddhahood, but some just never actualize this potential even remotely, which is exactly why saṃsāra in general is said to be endless. This is basically also what Asaṅga's *Ratnagotravibhāgavyākhyā* on I.40–41 (J 36–37; P5526, fols. 96b.8–97b.6) explains, using the term *gotra* in both the above way and also for buddha nature. Without *tathāgatagarbha*, the text says, beings would neither be weary of suffering nor wish and strive for being free of it (nirvāṇa). These are the two functions that the pure buddha disposition exhibits, which dwells even in beings who are fixated on their wrong ways. However, to be aware of the shortcomings of saṃsāric suffering and the advantages of nirvāṇic happiness is not without any cause or condition, but due to the existence of the *gotra* of persons with virtuous dharmas. If this kind of *gotra* were without any cause or condition and not brought about through terminating wrongdoing, it would also have to exist in those who just follow their great desire, having the *gotra* of not passing into parinirvāṇa (*icchantikānām apy aparinirvāṇagotrānām*; clearly, here, *gotra* does not refer to buddha nature, but to virtuous roots as above). The *gotra* being pure of adventitious stains does not happen as long as one does not aspire for the dharma of one of the three yānas through connecting with the four conditions of relying on a genuine spiritual friend and so on (that is, dwelling in a conducive place, accumulating merit, and making aspiration prayers). The *Jñānālokālaṃkārasūtra* says that the light rays of sunlike buddha wisdom touch even those who are fixated on wrongdoing, thus benefiting them and enhancing the arising of future causes for happiness through virtuous dharmas. In other sūtras, we find the statement that those who just follow their great desire possess the property of not attaining parinirvāṇa forever. But this refers to having aversion toward the mahāyāna dharma as being the cause for not attaining parinirvāṇa. Therefore, this statement was made for the sake of turning such people away from their aversion, with the intention of referring to another time (that is, their actually attaining nirvāṇa at some point in the future). By virtue of the existence of the naturally pure *gotra*, it is impossible for there to be any beings who can never become pure, which is said with the intention that, by virtue of essentially not being different from the Bhagavat, it is possible for all sentient beings to become pure. Sthiramati's *Madhyāntavibhāgaṭīkā* (ed. Yamaguchi, 55.19–56.6) on I.19a ("the emptiness of the primordial nature" among the sixteen emptinesses) juxtaposes the positions on there being three versus a single *gotra*, but takes all of them to be primordial: "As for [I.19a] 'In order to purify the gotra,' its emptiness is the emptiness of the primordial nature. The reason for this is that, [according to the *Bhāṣya*,] '*gotra* is the primordial nature.' How so? 'Because of having a nature of its own,' which means to have a nature of its own from beginningless time that is not adventitious. Just as some [phenomena] in beginningless saṃsāra are sentient and some are insentient, here too, some [sets of] the six āyatanas represent the *buddhagotra* and some the *śrāvakagotra* and so on. The *gotra* is not accidental, because it has been continuing since beginningless time [up through the present], just as the distinction between what is sentient and insentient. Others say that, since all sentient beings are endowed with the *tathāgatagotra*, *gotra* should be understood here in this way" (depending on how the Sanskrit here is reconstructed, "in this way" could also be read as "as suchness," which would conform to the above-mentioned comments by Vasubandhu, Sthiramati, and Asvabhāva on *Mahāyānasūtrālaṃkāra* IX.37). As for the issue of there being only a single yāna, *Mahāyānasūtrālaṃkāra* XI.53–54 gives seven reasons for why the Buddha spoke about there being only one yāna. The commentaries by Vasubandhu (Limaye 1992, 199–200), Sthiramati (D4034, fols. 196a.5–199b.2), and Asvabhāva (D4029, fols. 93b.6–95a.2) elaborate on these reasons as (1) the dharmadhātu not being different in śrāvakas, pratyekabuddhas, and bodhisattvas; (2) all those who progress through the yānas up through a buddha equally lacking a self; (3) the state of being liberated from the afflictions being the same in all of them; (4) śrāvakas with uncertain disposition being led into and liberated through the mahāyāna; (5) a buddha's mind of equality toward all beings and the attainment by certain śrāvakas who remember that they have been bodhisattvas before being partially similar; (6) the Buddha having emanated as śrāvakas and attained parinirvāṇa through the śrāvakayāna; and (7) there being nothing more supreme to go to than the buddhahood to be reached through the mahāyāna. With buddhahood having only a single yāna, the respective statements in various sūtras that there is a single yāna should be understood through these seven intentions (*abhiprāya*). However, it is not the case that the three yānas do not exist. The reason why the buddhas teach a single yāna is to attract śrāvakas with uncertain disposition to the mahāyāna and to prevent bodhisattvas with uncertain disposition from falling away from this yāna. Sthiramati says explicitly that those sūtras that speak of a single yāna and three yānas are of expedient and definitive meaning, respectively. *Mahāyānasaṃgraha* X.32 quotes the very same two verses from the *Mahāyānasūtrālaṃkāra* as the answer to the question, "If this dharmakāya of the buddhas, which is endowed with such excellent qualities, is not in common with śrāvakas and pratyekabuddhas, with what intention was a single yāna taught?" The commentaries by Vasubandhu (D4050, fol. 187a.1–187b.6) and Asvabhāva (D4051, fol. 292b.6–293b.3) repeat that the teachings on the single yāna entail the above seven intentions (however, Asvabhāva also says that there is a single yāna because, ultimately, the yānas of śrāvakas and pratyekabuddhas are the mahāyāna). Many Tibetan and most Western scholars follow this, holding that the Yogācāras in general, as in the *Mahāyānasūtrālaṃkāra*, assert the ultimate existence of three yānas. In large part, this is due to the common hermeneutical approach of taking the Sanskrit *abhiprāya* (Tib. dgongs pa) by default to mean "intention," and this by default meaning that anything with an intention is necessarily of expedient meaning. However, it is very hard to defend the position that the Yogācāras in general assert three yānas, let alone ultimately, and said hermeneutical approach entails a number of problems too. First of all, there is no text by Maitreya or Asaṅga that says that there are three vehicles ultimately, or that the teachings that there is a single yāna are of expedient meaning or entail some intention. On the contrary, at least as far as the presentations in the *Abhisamayālaṃkāra* and the *Uttaratantra* go, they are both clearly from the perspective of a single yāna. Among the works of Vasubandhu, Sthiramati, and Asvabhāva, the stance that the single yāna was taught with certain intentions is only found in their above-mentioned commentaries on the same two verses in the *Mahāyānasūtrālaṃkāra* and the *Mahāyānasaṃgraha*. Among these commentaries, it is only the one by Sthiramati which says that these teachings are of expedient meaning. However, in several other places in the same commentaries and other texts by these masters, there are passages that suggest only a single yāna, which eventually is entered by all śrāvaka and pratyekabuddha arhats as well. I am not going to provide a new commentary here on verses IX.53–54 of the *Mahāyānasūtrālaṃkāra*, but on their own, they could very well be read as giving the reasons for why there in fact *is* only a single yāna (see also Yamabe 1997, 200–203). In particular, the first reason in XI.53 is literally the same as in *Abhisamayālaṃkāra* I.40ab and verse 21 of Nāgārjuna's *Niraupamyastava*, which, however, is taken by these texts as the reason for why there in fact *is*, respectively, only a single *gotra* or yāna ultimately. In addition, these latter two verses are usually quoted by the very same scholars above as two of *the* classical scriptural supports for there being only a single *gotra* and yāna. Also, one cannot but wonder how this reason (1) of the dharmadhātu's being the same in śrāvakas and all others is supposed to establish the *ultimate* existence of three yānas, or how it could serve as a proof for the expediency of the single yāna (if anything, it only proves the opposite). In fact, it would then absurdly follow that these ultimately existing three yānas have three ultimately different fruitions, which could consequently only come from three ultimately different kinds of dharmadhātu. In the same vein, reasons (2)–(3) also speak about a single yāna by virtue of certain features from an ultimate point of view (lack of a self and irreversible liberation from afflictions) being the same for the three yānas, and (7) speaks about a single yāna by virtue of there being no higher destination than the one arrived at through the mahāyāna, so how can there be three different yānas ultimately? In fact, looking at Vasubandhu's above-concluding remarks in his commentary on IX.53, one could easily read them as stating that there is only a single yāna from the perspective of buddhahood, but, relatively speaking, from the perspective of those in the śrāvakayāna and the pratyekabuddhayāna, it is not that their yānas do not exist at all. Padma Karpo's commentary on the *Abhisamayālaṃkāra* (*mngon par rtogs pa'i rgyan gyi 'grel pa rje btsun byams pa'i gzhal lung*, fol. 107a.4–107b.3) says that Asaṅga and his followers, for the sake of guiding different beings, taught, for those whose dispositions are individually certain, that the yānas are real as different ones and, for those whose dispositions are not certain, that there is a single yāna. Statements such as those in *Mahāyānasūtrālaṃkāra* XI.54 and teachings about the single yāna taught in the *Daśabhūmikasūtra*, the *Ratnameghasūtras*, and so on being of expedient meaning are given only in order to dispel the fear of certain people, while Asaṅga's *Ratnagotravibhāgavyākhyā* establishes a single yāna. As for the sometimes chameleonlike notion of "intention" (Skt. abhiprāya/saṃdhi, Tib. dgongs pa), in general, as Ngülchu Togmé's commentary on *Mahāyānasūtrālaṃkāra* XII.16 18 (Dngul chu thogs med bzang po dpal 1979, fol. 133b.5–6) points out, "expedient meaning" on the one hand and the two categories of "intention" and "indirect intention" (Tib. ldem dgongs) on the other hand are not coextensive, since *Mahāyānasaṃgraha* II.31 states that all teachings of the Buddha (and not just the portions of expedient meaning) have to be understood in terms of the four intentions and also says that the indirect intention of a remedy teaches all the remedies that consist of the eighty-four thousand teachings of the Buddha. Also, as is often pointed out, if everything with an intention is necessarily of expedient meaning, then all Buddhist teachings would be of expedient meaning, because they were all given with certain intentions, including the ones with regard to emptiness. To conclude, the *Laṅkāvatārasūtra* (II, vv. 131–32 and 204–5; D107, fols. 127b.2–3 and 173b.7–174a.1) says that even the teachings on a single yāna are just for those of weak insight, but are not the definitive meaning. Rather, in ultimate reality, any presentations of any yānas are obsolete.

> On account of the differences between childish beings,
> Those of weak insight, and the noble ones,
> I speak of three yānas,
> One yāna, and no yāna.
> This is the door to the ultimate—
> Freedom from the duality of cognizance.
> Within the state of nonappearance, how could there be
> A presentation of three yānas?
> . . .
> As long as sentient beings are to be engaged,
> There is no limit for yānas.
> But once mind as such fundamentally changes state,
> There are no yānas and no one to progress.
> There is no presentation of yānas,
> But in order to guide childish beings,
> I explained different yānas,
> Being taught as a single yāna.

For further details, see the bibliography, especially Ruegg 1969, 73–86, 97–100, and 185–88; Kunst 1977; Hakamaya 1980; Prasad 1991,1–45; Lopez 1992, 16–70; Yamabe 1997; and D'Amato 2003.

174 D107, fol. 292a.

175 These are (1) causal features (*nimitta*), (2) names (*nāma*), (3) conception/imagination (*vikalpa/parikalpa*), (4) suchness (*tathatā*), and (5) perfect wisdom (*samyagjñāna*). For more details, see the translation of OED.

176 These are the five chapter headings of the *Madhyāntavibhāga*.

177 These are the five chapter headings of the *Uttaratantra*.

178 Pp. 490.2–491.2; 492.1–3; and 494.1–495.2.

179 Tib. sangs rgyas mnyan pa bkra shis dpal 'byor. The Sangyé Nyenpas are regarded as incarnations of the Indian paṇḍita Smṛtijñānakīrti (eleventh century), who stayed in Tibet for

many years as a teacher and translator, being instrumental in initiating the later spread of the dharma there. According to Krang dbyi sun 1985, 3249 and 3255, the First Sangyé Nyenpa was born in 1457 and his next incarnation appeared in 1520. This fits with the biography of the Eighth Karmapa in Chos kyi 'byung gnas and 'Be lo tshe dbang kun khyab 1972 (vol. 2, p. 20.7), which says that Dashi Baljor passed away in 1519. However, the latter's biography in Dpa' bo gtsug lag phreng ba 2003, 1200–1206 gives his year of birth as 1445 and says that he passed away at sixty-five. In the table of contents of Chos kyi 'byung gnas and 'Be lo tshe dbang kun khyab 1972, the editors Gyaltsan and Legshay say, "The work in hand gives the dates for this teacher as 1445–1509. These seem not to be in accordance with his relationship with the 7th and 8th Zhwanag Karma-pa." TBRC gives 1145/1457–1510/1525.

180 Literally, the Tibetan says *sems tsam* ("Mere Mentalism"), which is ever so often used in Tibetan texts to refer to the Yogācāra school in general or a specific part of it. What is meant in this context is clearly the classical Yogācāra system as presented by Maitreya, Asaṅga, and Vasubandhu, and not "Mere Mentalism" in its somewhat pejorative sense as what is refuted, and subordinated to, Madhyamaka in the default Tibetan doxographical hierarchies.

181 Mi bskyod rdo rje 1996, 40.

182 Kong sprul blo gros mtha' yas 2005b, fol. 6b.5–7a.1.

183 What follows is partly based on and confirms the preliminary remarks on Rangjung Dorje's view and his DSC in Brunnhölzl 2007b (see also for a number of different presentations of what *shentong* is).

184 1308 and 1332 were other Monkey Years, but the first one seems too early, while during the latter one, Rangjung Dorje was on his long journey to, and stay at, the Chinese court and not in Upper Dechen.

185 In the *Blue Annals* ('Gos lo tsā ba gzhon nu dpal. 1996, 492), Chos kyi 'byung gnas 1972, 210.7), and Tshal pa kun dga' rdo rje 1981, 100, the entry of the year 1326 is followed by a number of events, the last one being the composition of DSC. The next explicit dates are 1328 in the first two texts and 1329 in the latter.

186 There is some unclarity here, since both the commentaries by Jamgön Kongtrul and the Fifteenth Karmapa gloss this as the Pig Year of the sixth sixty-year cycle of the Tibetan calendar, which would make it 1335, since this is the only Pig Year within that cycle during Rangjung Dorje's lifetime. However, as this date is contradicted by NY's being explicitly referred to in AC, 1323 is the only Pig Year before AC's indubitable composition in 1325 and after ZMND's in 1322, which fits well with the overall chronology. Of course, there are still earlier Pig Years in Rangjung Dorje's life (1311 and 1299), but it seems highly unlikely that he composed NY eleven or even twenty-three years (at age fifteen) before ZMND. Also, while NY says itself that it was composed at Upper Dechen in Tsurpu (Central Tibet), all sources agree that, upon his return from the Chinese court, Rangjung Dorje went through Minyag and other areas of Kham in eastern Tibet in 1335, teaching the dharma extensively. Tshal pa kun dga' rdo rje 1981, 103; Dpa' bo gtsug lag phreng ba 2003 (vol. 2, 941); and Chos kyi 'byung gnas (fol. 111a) all say that he returned to Tsurpu only during the ninth month of that Pig Year (November/December) and then stayed at Chimpu in Samyé during that winter for six months.

187 Except for the two texts on the *Abhisamayālaṃkāra* and OED, all of these other texts are unfortunately lost. However, there is a commentary preserved on the *Uttaratantra* (Rang byung rdo rje 2006a, vol. ja, pp. 126–262) by Tülmo Dashi Öser (Tib. dul mo bkra shis 'od zer; born 1474), a close disciple of the Seventh Karmapa and teacher of the Eighth. This text is

basically Rangjung Dorje's own summary of the text with a few added clarifications and also exhibits many of the typical traits of his view as presented below.

188 See bibliography.

189 The last line in OED's colophon is not only remarkable because of this, but because the term "freedom from extremes" also stands for the view of "the earlier Mādhyamikas" in Tibet (meaning what was understood as the correct Madhyamaka view before Tsongkhapa). This view was proclaimed by masters such as Patsab Lotsāwa and his four main disciples; the Sakya masters Rendawa, Gorampa Sönam Senge, and Dagtsang Lotsāwa; the Eighth Karmapa Mikyö Dorjé; Pawo Rinpoche, and others. Said approach uses Madhyamaka analysis that results in an unqualified negation of all four positions of the typical Madhyamaka tetralemma without asserting anything instead, in order to completely overcome all conceptualizations and reference points. In this way, it is certainly an accurate characterization of the Indian Madhyamaka approach. However, "the later Mādhyamikas"—the Gelugpa school—criticized this view by saying that "lack of real existence" is the correct Madhyamaka view and thus not to be negated. At the same time, there were attempts to discredit "the Madhyamaka of freedom from extremes" through associating it with the notorious stereotype of the Chinese Hvashang Mahāyāna.

190 At times, NTC and NYC also pick up this approach. The contemporary eminent Kagyü scholar and meditation master Thrangu Rinpoche says on NT and NY that they combine scholasticism and reasoning within the *shentong* approach with the Mahāmudrā tradition of directly familiarizing with the nature of the mind. Thus, in terms of the more theoretical instructions, they present the definitive meaning, and in terms of practice, they correspond to the Mahāmudrā approach to meditation.

191 The Eighth Situpa's commentary (Chos kyi 'byung gnas n.d., 24–31) on this verse says that the ground for everything in saṃsāra and nirvāṇa is the purity of mind, that is, the Tathāgata heart. This is the basis of purification but not what is to be purified, since in its own essence, there is nothing whatsover to be purified. Also, mind's nature is the unity of being lucid and empty, since there is no being lucid apart from being empty and no being empty apart from being lucid. Those who explain lucidity and emptiness as two separate things and their union as these two things becoming associated stand outside the teachings of the Tathāgata. In terms of Mahāmudrā, this commentary justifies the Kagyü approach of pointing out instructions with or without tantric empowerment and clarifies that it is in full accord with Madhyamaka. Adventitious stains are identified as the dualistic phenomena of apprehender and apprehended produced by the adventitious mistakenness of mind about itself. The dharmakāya is the manifestation of the fundamental nature of the basis of purification in which all such adventitious dualistic phenomena are relinquished.

192 In the translated sections of AC, a few tantras are quoted too, but Rangjung Dorje's predominant reliance on Indian sūtrayāna treatises is remarkable for a text that is a commentary on the tantras, further underlining his stance that the fundamental view of the mahāyāna is the same in the sūtras and the tantras.

193 Rang byung rdo rje 2006c.

194 DSC, fol. 50b.

195 Even in Jamgön Kongtrul's NTC and NYC, the terms "Mere Mentalists" and "Mere Mentalism" do not appear at all (while he constantly uses these terms in his other works), but he too uses "Yogācāra."

196 Rang byung rdo rje 2006a, vol. ja, p. 128.

197 See Brunnhölzl 2007b, 159–93.

198 Tib.chos grags rgya mtsho.

199 ZDKT, pp. 396–97.

200 Ka rma 'phrin las pa 1975, vol. cha, pp. 90–92.

201 The sixty-four qualities are the thirty-two qualities of freedom of the dharmakāya (the ten powers, four fearlessnesses, and eighteen unique qualities of a buddha) and the thirty-two qualities of maturation of the rūpakāyas (the major marks). ZDKT (pp. 46.1–47.3) explains the above further: "Others say, 'If this Heart had the sixty-four qualities from the very beginning, the qualities of perfect buddhahood would exist in the mind streams of sentient beings, and in that case, does the buddha wisdom in the mind stream of a hell being experience the sufferings of hell?' Such is indeed said, but it is precisely for this reason that we speak about [wisdom or luminous mind] by making the distinction that it is stained during the phase of sentient beings and stainless in the state of a buddha. In other words, perfect buddhahood and its powers and so on do not exist in the mind streams of sentient beings. This is definitely how it is, but it will be understood through saying again and again, '*Stained* buddhahood and its powers and so on exist [in their mind streams].'"

202 These are Kalkin Puṇḍarīka's commentary on the *Kālacakratantra*, called *Vimalaprabhā* (Tib. 'grel chen dri med 'od); Vajragarbha's commentary on the *Hevajratantra*, called *Hevajrapiṇḍārthaṭīkā* (Tib. rdo rje'i snying 'grel); and Vajrapāṇi's commentary on the *Cakrasaṃvaratantra*, called *Lakṣābhidānāduddhṛtalaghutantrapiṇḍārthavivaraṇa* (Tib. phyag rdor stod 'grel). Note that Mipham Rinpoche's *Lion's Roar Proclaiming Other-Emptiness* starts by listing the sources of the *shentong* view as the sūtras of the third turning of the wheel of dharma, which teach the definitive meaning; Maitreya's *Uttaratantra*; the profound teachings by Asaṅga and Vasubandhu; the commentaries on the definitive meaning by Nāgārjuna, such as his collection of praises; the tantras, such as the *Kālacakratantra*; and the commentaries on their intention, such as the trilogy of bodhisattva commentaries.

203 These four lines list the key terms at the beginning of the first chapter of ZMND and AC (see the translations below).

204 The Tibetan has *stong byed*, but following the standard pair of "the basis of being empty" (*stong gzhi*) and "what it is empty/to be emptied of" (*stong bya*), this should be the latter.

205 Tib. gar dbang chos kyi dbang phyug.

206 Tib. rtogs brjod lta sgom spyod 'bras kyi glu (lines 132–35).

207 Tib. bdud 'dul rdo rje.

208 Tib. go nyams lta ba'i glu (lines 73–90). For complete translations of these two songs and more details, see Brunnhölzl 2007a.

209 Chos grags rgya mtsho 1985, vol. I, pp. 196–97.

210 Ibid., vol. 2, pp. 516–19.

211 Dpa' bo gtsug lag phreng ba 2003, 1109.

212 JNS, vol. 1, pp. 221 and 223.

213 Ibid., p. 210.

214 Ibid., pp. 33–34.

215 Kong sprul blo gros mtha' yas 1982, vol. III, p. 24.

216 JNS (vol. 2, pp. 297) identifies those who only realize the lack of nature of the apprehended as the Real Aspectarian Mere Mentalists, while the False Aspectarians are said to realize the lack of nature of both apprehender and apprehended. Thus, though there is no explicit division here into Real and False Aspectarians and the latter's doxographical place is not spelled out, the latter thus seem not to be included under the label Mere Mentalists. Also, though Mikyö Dorje does not explicitly call Maitreya and Asaṅga "Mādhyamikas" (or label them "False Aspectarians") here, he seems to suggest below that they (at least de facto) are. JNS explicitly refers to them as Mādhyamikas several times.

217 "The sevenfold collection" refers to Dharmakīrti's texts on valid cognition (such as the *Pramāṇavārttika*) and "the sūtra" refers to Dignāga's *Pramāṇasamucchaya*.

218 These are the *Madhyāntavibhāga*, the *Dharmadharmatāvibhāga*, and the *Uttaratantra*.

219 This is quite a remarkable early analysis of Dignāga's and Dharmakīrti's approach, since it already outlines the model called "ascending/sliding scales of analysis," with which the contemporary Western scholars Dreyfus and McClintock describe Dharmakīrti's system. I do not at all mean to diminish their merits in conducting excellent and detailed analyses of said approach (in fact, I greatly admire it), but—as the above passage shows—the principle obviously has been recognized before.

220 Chos grags rgya mtsho 1985, vol. 4, pp. 406–8.

221 JNS, pp. 22–26.

222 Ruegg 2000, 80–81.

223 This refers to the tantras.

224 As quoted in TOK vol. 2, p. 553.

225 Audio recording of an oral commentary on the *Dharmadharmatāvibhāga* in Samye Ling, Scotland (April 1990).

226 See my forthcoming translation of the major portions of this text.

227 *Dbu ma sogs gzhung spyi'i dka' gnad* (in 'Ju mi pham rgya mtsho 1990a, vol. 22, p. 450.3) and *Dam chos dogs sel* (in 'Ju mi pham rgya mtsho 1992, 521).

228 JNS, 218 says that what is called "uncontaminated consciousness" is the unconditioned naturally abiding disposition (the very nature of the mind associated with stains), which is definitely the cause for perfect buddhahood and primordially exists in all beings.

229 In Buddhism, by definition, only conditioned phenomena can be causes since unconditioned phenomena are permanent and cannot perform any active function. Cessation refers to the absence of a previously existent conditioned phenomenon, but in itself, an absence cannot be a cause for anything (the most famous counterexamples to this pan-Buddhist position are Tsongkhapa and his followers, who hold that cessation is a functional entity that serves as the operational agent that links karmic causes and effects).

230 ZDC (p. 29) adds that the immediate mind, once it becomes associated with the immaculate dharmas of the path, is also the cause for a buddha's qualities of freedom. The afflicted mind does not represent valid cognition, since it is the root of all saṃsāric mistakenness and of producing all mental states of noncognition, wrong cognition, and doubt.

231 Hsüan-tsang's *Vijñaptimātratāsiddhi* (La Vallée Poussin 1928–1948, 442) speaks about uncontaminated and contaminated mentation as referring to the minds of bodhisattvas when being engaged in, and rising from, meditative equipoise, respectively, with pure mentation being related to the wisdom of equality.

232 As explained above, the sixth consciousness is said to have two functions—the conceptual mind and mental perception, which perceives outer objects just like the five sense consciousnesses.

233 ZDKT calls this "the internally oriented aspect" of the mental consciousness as opposed to its externally oriented aspects—mental perception and thoughts.

234 No early biography of either Rangjung Dorje or Dölpopa records any such meeting. Three considerably later sources by Mangtö Ludrub Gyatso (1523–1596), Tāranātha, and the Eighth Situpa (Chos kyi 'byung gnas and 'Be lo tshe dbang kun khyab 1972, 208.1–2) report a single meeting of the two, saying that the former made a prophesy about the latter coming to realize a particularly sublime view unlike his present one (for details, see Stearns 1999, 47–48). However, there is no mention of Dölpopa being a student of Rangjung Dorje.

235 I am not attempting to make any judgments as to whose view is better or "higher"—both being undoubtedly highly erudite scholars and realized meditation masters.

236 All these terms come from several sūtras on buddha nature, and some are also found in the *Uttaratantra*. Dölpopa also often qualifies his descriptions, such as by saying that, when making distinctions between what is permanent and impermanent in the context of giving explanations, buddha nature, nondual wisdom, and so on are permanent, enduring etc., whereas all seeming phenomena are impermanent. However, within profound meditative equipoise, all reference points need to be let go of. As for the above terms, given his overall explanations on buddha nature, it seems that Rangjung Dorje wishes to avoid expressions that bear strong absolutist connotations.

237 Dol po pa shes rab rgyal mtshan 1998, 128, 430, and 454.

238 Though Rangjung Dorje never mentions the specific term "ālaya-wisdom," one could read certain passages in his texts as implying the above distinction, such as OED (pp. 501.4–502.2) describing "ālaya" as a general label for the three natures, while referring to the imaginary and other-dependent natures as "ālaya-consciousness." The eight consciousnesses are the obscurations, while the four wisdoms are the stainlessness of these consciousnesses, thus being the perfect nature, with dharmadhātu wisdom being the matrix of all of these (see also AC, pp. 26ff.). Note, however, that some later Kagyü commentators on Rangjung Dorje's texts use this terminology (such as Tagramba and Jamgön Kongtrul).

239 Dol po pa shes rab rgyal mtshan 1998, 97, lines 15–17.

240 Just as an aside, the fact that JNS refutes this position (which is no doubt still maintained by many Kagyüpas today and is regarded as the epitome of the *shentong* view) twice and also negates the claim that the ālaya-consciousness transforms into mirrorlike wisdom (as mentioned above) is quite remarkable (to say the least) for a text that is supposedly written to uphold the *shentong* view.

241 JNS, vol. 1, p. 223 (interestingly and unlike with other opponents, the Eighth Karmapa uses honorific terms when he quotes Dölpopa). What Dölpopa is reported here as saying is a paraphrase of a passage in his *Mountain Dharma* (Dol po pa shes rab rgyal mtshan 1998, 121), which concludes, "If [existence] were to establish being [something], since excrement exists in

humans, are humans then excrement or what?" Note that Hopkins (2006, 188), probably due to his Tibetan original reading *bshad pa* instead of *bshang ba*, has "explanations" instead of "excrement," which, of course, makes the argument much less poignant.

242 See, for example, DSC, fols. 14a, 16b, 25b–26a; NT lines 89–90 and 94; *A Song on the Ālaya*.

243 See his *Fourth Council* (Tib. bka' bsdus bzhi pa) in *Collected Works*, vol. 1. Paro, Bhutan: 1984, 404–5.

244 For further details, see Schaeffer 1995, 25–36; Stearns 1995 and 1999; Hopkins 2002, 273–315 and 2006, 8–39; Mathes 1998 and 2004; and Burchardi 2007.

245 Tib. khrims khang lo tsā ba, aka bsod nams rgya mtsho.

246 Tib. bya bral rin chen bzang po.

247 Tib. dvags po rab 'byams pa chos rgyal bstan pa.

248 Tib. ngo khro rab 'byams pa dbang phyug dpal (also known as ngo khro rab 'byams bshes gnyen rnam rgyal).

249 Tib. dkon mchog yan lag.

250 Tib. mkha' khyab rdo rje.

251 The most extensive commentaries among these are those by Tagbo Rabjampa (353 folios) and Ngotro Rabjampa (337 folios). For a complete list of these commentaries on ZMND (including their size and short biographies of their authors), see Rang byung rdo rje 2006a, vol. ka, pp. 22–39.

252 Tib. chos kyi byung gnas (also known as bstan pa'i nyin byed).

253 TOK, vol. 1, p. 461; vol. 2, p. 544.

254 Chos kyi 'byung gnas n.d., 20–22 (trans. Sherab Dorje 1995, 48–49).

255 Ibid., 24–26, and 30–31 (trans. 52–54 and 59–60).

256 Ibid., 32–39 (trans. 62–70).

257 Against common usage in Western translations, as indicated by Peter Roberts, Cyrus Streans, Elizabeth Callahan, and others, the above (and not *nāḍī*, *prāṇa*, and *bindu*) are the Sanskrit equivalents for the Tibetan *rtsa rlung thig le* in the Buddhist tantras and their Indian commentaries. This is also confirmed by the Sanskrit dictionary by Monier-Williams and the Tibetan-Sanskrit dictionary by J. S. Negi.

258 Ibid., 92 (trans. 127–28).

259 Thrangu Rinpoche 1990, 2–7.

260 Thrangu Rinpoche 2002, 20–51.

261 The translation consists of parts of the introduction, chapter 1, and parts of chapters 6 and 9. Numbers in "[ ]" refer to the page numbers in AC (Rang byung rdo rje n.d.[a]).

262 Lines 2–5 correspond almost literally to *Uttaratantra* I.147.

263 Chatral Rinchen Sangpo's commentary (Rang byung rdo rje 2006a, vol. āḥ, p. 16) glosses "rests upon buddha enlightenment" as follows. The meanings of cause, path, and fruition, respectively, refer to that which becomes enlightened, that through which it becomes

enlightened, and that which has become enlightened. All of them are resting upon the Sugata heart. In other words, buddha nature is the ground whose essence is buddhahood. It is also the path and the fruition in the sense of mind's nature respectively being in the process of becoming aware of itself and having become fully aware of itself.

264 ZDKT (pp. 51–52) says that, according to the Seventh Karmapa, the two types of purity of the buddha heart are its natural purity and its having become pure of adventitious stains. The former refers to mind as such being free from all identification and characteristics, while the latter means mind as such being free from the imaginary constructions of apprehender and apprehended. Therefore, wishing to point out ordinary mind as being endowed with such twofold purity at the time of the ground, Rangjung Dorje speaks here of "the stainless Heart of the victors."

265 Lit. "produced" (*bskyed*).

266 ZZB (pp. 452ff.) explains that the buddha heart is just single, but can be expressed by many different names in terms of how it may appear as certain aspects of seeming reality and ultimate reality, such as "heart" in terms of being the essence of everything; "space-pervading vajra" in terms of its nature being all-encompassing; "nāda" or "vāyu" in terms of its movement; "nāḍī" in terms of being a support; "tilaka" in terms of the qualities that are supported; "ashé" in terms of being unborn; "appropriating consciousness" in terms of temporary function; "the five afflictions" in terms of impurity; "the five wisdoms" in terms of purity; or "bodhicitta," "vajra body," "great bliss," and so on in terms of certain other situations and functions (see also appendix 1 for the many labels of inexpressible buddhahood). Chatral Rinchen Sangpo's commentary on ZMND (Rang byung rdo rje 2006a, vol. āḥ, p. 16) says that the enlightened activity that gives rise to all benefit and happiness of sentient beings is spontaneously present, but lacks any conceptions of agent and recipient.

267 I.25. A number of the quotations in AC and the other texts translated below show variant readings when compared to the canonical versions in the *Kangyur* and *Tengyur* (or the Sanskrit, if available), which I followed throughout.

268 On this, AC's introduction (pp. 18–19) says: "Non-Buddhist śrāvakas (such as the Parivrājakas and Carakas) and Buddhist śrāvakas (such as the Vaibhāṣikas) think that a self and the person are real and are ignorant about the nature of the mind. Also, this dharma is even difficult to realize by those who partially engage in the pāramitās. Therefore, it is self-secret. This is stated extensively in the *Śrīmālādevīsūtra*: 'Those who are outside of [the ranks of those who see] the Heart of the Bhagavat, the Tathāgata, are childish ordinary beings, śrāvakas, pratyekabuddhas, and beginner bodhisattvas whose minds are distracted by emptiness.' As for what is difficult to realize in this way, it is said that the stainless vajra-body—which is a natural outflow appearing from the Tathāgata heart, that is, the very profound rūpakāya endowed with the major and minor marks—dwells within the body that has stains. As for this mind with stains, which is ensnared by many cocoons of afflictions, it abides as the buddha heart that is endowed with the qualities of the powers (such as knowing what is the case and what is not), the fearlessnesses, and the unique dharmas." Later AC (pp. 86–87) quotes *Uttaratantra* I.28 and explains that the stained minds of ordinary beings, which appear as the five skandhas, are tainted forms of the buddhakāyas. Thus, upon the stains disappearing, the dharmakāya as well as, physically, the supreme nirmāṇakāya of a buddha radiate. As for the above quote from the *Śrīmālādevīsūtra*, this sūtra repeatedly speaks about the buddha heart not being the sphere of śrāvakas and pratyekabuddhas, but the passage as it stands is not found in it (the *Mahābherīsūtra* contains a very similar passage on not realizing the Buddha's parinirvāṇa; see Wayman and Wayman 1974, 45). Rather, the above passage is a paraphrase that combines

parts of Asaṅga's *Ratnagotravibhāgavyākhyā* on *Uttaratantra* I.32–33 and I.153–55 (J 29, 74, 76; P5526, fols. 92a.6–b.3, 117a.1–3, 118b.4–8). As for the "distraction of beginner bodhisattvas," it contains a nice ambiguity. In all the passages of Asaṅga's commentary where this expression appears, it is always the Sanskrit compound *śūnyatāvikṣiptacitta*, which can mean either a mind distracted by emptiness, from emptiness, or toward emptiness. From the various contexts in this commentary, it can be gathered that the ambiguity of this compound is probably not by chance. For, the point is always that beginner bodhisattvas are distracted *by* a wrong understanding of emptiness (either misconceiving it as destroying phenomena or as some separate entity to be focused on deliberately) and thus distracted *from* its correct understanding, which is explicitly identified as the principle of what emptiness means in terms of the Tathāgata heart. This ambiguity is reflected in the various Tibetan versions of Asaṅga's commentary in the *Tengyur* and its quotations in other texts (such as AC), which (in a rather inconsistent manner) take this Sanskrit compound to have either one of the above meanings (using *la*, *las*, or *gyis* after *stong pa nyid*).

269 At this point, AC obviously uses the traditional Indian theme of the wish-fulfilling gem, which is said to unfold its activity upon being supplicated and so on.

270 Since AC was written before the time of Tsongkhapa and his followers (who are well known to hold that buddha nature is nothing but sentient beings' emptiness in the sense of a nonimplicative negation), it must refer to the position of Ngog Lotsāwa and some of his followers, as it explicitly appears in the former's *Theg pa chen po'i rgyud bla ma'i don bsdus pa* (Dharamsala 1993, fol. 4a.2–3).

271 The Sanskrit of this verse is found in Asaṅga's *Ratnagotravibhāgavyākhyā* (J 37.6), though not attributed to any particular text. It is also quoted at the beginning of NT, and NTC identifies it as being from the *Abhidharmasūtra* (for details, see below).

272 This is the actual beginning of chapter 1 of ZMND.

273 I.55–57.

274 Lines 166–69.

275 Ed. Vaidya, 3.18 (D12, fol. 3a.3).

276 D4049, fol. 53a.5.

277 D107, fol. 137b.3–4.

278 I.8ab.

279 As explained below, from among the fifty-one mental factors, the ālaya-consciousness is constantly and solely associated with the five omnipresent ones. Among these, in terms of feelings, the ālaya is accompanied only by indifference, and not by any pleasant or unpleasant feelings. Just as the ālaya itself, all its accompanying mental factors too are unobscured by afflictions and neutral (that is, neither virtuous nor nonvirtuous).

280 Lines 2cd–5a (AC omits lines 3ab, 4c).

281 A typical example for the latter is Rangjung Dorje's *Song on the Ālaya* below.

282 The consciousnesses are called "collections" in order to highlight that mind (or any of its facets) is not a singular, permanent, and independent entity or self. From an ordinary point of view, we may think, "I see a dog," "I hear music," "I think about my home," and so on, always implying that our mind is one single unchanging entity that does all these things. However, not only are there eight different kinds of consciousness, but each one of them is

not a single consciousness either, such as one eye consciousness perceiving all kinds of visual objects. Rather, what is called "eye consciousness" is just a continuum of distinct moments of perception, with the moment of an eye consciousness that sees a dog not being the same as the moments of eye consciousnesses that see a table or a flower. Likewise, the different moments of looking at a dog for a while are all distinct, as is the momentarily changing dog looked at. Thus, for each one of the eight consciousnesses, both the object and the perceiving subject change in every instant. In this way, a "collection of consciousness" is a sample name for a being's infinite sequence of different momentary perceptions of the same general type (such as visual or auditory perceptions).

283 AC explains elsewhere (pp. 178.5–181.6) that śrāvaka and pratyekabuddha arhats do not relinquish the ālaya-consciousness. Rather, according to the common presentation, śrāvaka arhats realize one type of identitylessness (personal identitylessness), pratyekabuddha arhats one and a half of the two types of identitylessness (the personal one as well as the lack of nature of the apprehended aspect), and bodhisattvas both types. Accordingly, in the two kinds of arhats, there are residues of the ālaya-consciousness that respectively correspond to the obscurations of taking phenomena in general to be real and, among these, taking the apprehender to be real.

284 The Sanskrit verb root *ālī*, from which the word *ālaya* derives, means "to come close, settle down upon, stoop, stick."

285 D106, fol. 21b.1–2.

286 I.1–5 (P5549, fols. 3b.5–4a.3).

287 I.14 (ibid., fol. 6a.7–b.3).

288 This probably refers to various substances, such as tannin, applied to a cloth before it is dipped into a developing bath, which then causes the various colors to come forth. Likewise, as long as the latent tendencies in the ālaya are dormant, they do not manifest as distinctly experienced phenomena (such as sense objects and their respective consciousnesses), but do so only upon becoming karmically matured.

289 This kind of dependent origination is described in *Mahāyānasaṃgraha* I.19 (together with "the dependent origination of differentiating what is desired and undesired," which represents the twelve links of dependent origination; see below and OED, p. 503). *Mahāyānasaṃgraha* I.28 mentions a third kind of dependent origination, "the dependent origination of experience," without elaborating on it. According to TOK (vol. 2, pp. 427–28), this describes the way in which the six consciousnesses (the primary minds) arise and cease based on the four conditions. Here, the experiencer is the mental factor of feeling, and what is experienced is the mental factor of contact between object and consciousness. Feeling further produces the mental factor of impulse in the following way. In the case of a pleasant object, a pleasant feeling arises, which in turn leads to desire and the impulse of not wishing for the mind to become separated from that object. In the case of unpleasant or neutral objects, respectively, aversion and the wish to be separated from such objects, or indifference and no such wish arise. Together, the three mental factors of feeling, contact, and impulse are said to blemish the primary minds.

290 I.9. The above paragraph including this verse is a greatly abbreviated paraphrase of *Mahāyānasaṃgraha* I.15–26 (P5549, fols. 6b.4–8a.7).

291 Skt. samudānīta, Tib. yang dag blangs pa (an equivalent of "unfolding disposition").

292 I.149–50.

293 Asvabhāva's *Mahāyānasaṃgrahopanibandhana* (P5552, fol. 262a) gives the further example of the ālaya-consciousness being like an attic in which all kinds of things are jumbled up, such as a panacea amid all kinds of poison. Although these might abide next to each other for a long time, the medicine is not identical with the poison, nor are any of the poisons its seed. The same applies for the latent tendencies for listening.

294 Here, as in the Yogācāra system in general, the distinction between the vimuktikāya and the dharmakāya is that the former designates the removal of only the afflictive obscurations as attained by śrāvaka and pratyekabuddha arhats, while the latter refers to the removal of both afflictive and cognitive obscurations. The *Uttaratantra* describes these two kāyas as the two aspects of the complete relinquishment of the two obscurations in perfect buddhahood, without relating these kāyas to the distinction between bodhisattvas and arhats. Thus, when talking about the dharmakāya as the actual state of buddhahood in general, it is understood that both types of obscurations have been relinquished in it. In this sense, it then includes the vimuktikāya. See also appendix 1.

295 I.45–48 (P5549, fols. 11b.1–12a.4). As for the Sanskrit term *śrutavāsanā*, in itself, it can be understood as either "latent tendencies *of* or *through* listening" or "latent tendencies *for* listening" (the Tibetan *thos pa'i bag chags* seems rather to suggest the former). Accordingly, one finds a range of explanations of this term. In the above quote from the *Mahāyānasaṃgraha*, the latent tendencies for listening are described in both of the above senses. On the one hand, they are said to be a "remedy," "mundane," and increasing " by virtue of being associated with listening, reflection, and meditation that are performed many times." On the other hand, the term refers to "the seeds of supramundane mind," "the natural outflow of the pure dharmadhātu," "the seeds of the dharmakāya," and is "included in the dharmakāya." The comments on all these expressions in JNS (pp. 212–14) account for the latent tendencies for listening being thus said to be both mundane and supramundane, but clearly treat them primarily from an ultimate perspective. JNS says that they are "not something that must be input newly under the influence of conditions"; "what allows one to listen to all the twelve branches of a buddha's speech"; "the capacity of uncontaminated cognition that is active through the power of the nature of phenomena"; and "allowing the enlightened activity of the dharmakāya to engage the mind streams of sentient beings." Also, they do not really increase, but "it is only the power of the decline of the factors to be relinquished that appears as if the latent tendencies for listening, which are the natural outflow of the completely pure dharmadhātu, increase from small to medium and so on." The meaning of their being "mundane" is explained as referring only to their being the remedy for what is mundane, but, in being the natural outflow of the supramundane dharmadhātu, they are not contained in mundane mind streams. The gist of their being a "natural outflow of the dharmadhātu" is said to lie in this term addressing the need for some factor that is other than the completely pure dharmadhātu itself and at the same time outside of all impure phenomena. Thus, from the perspective of this factor of the natural outflow being associated with a mind stream on the path, it is presented as a bodhisattva and yet also as being included in the dharmakāya. In this way, "in the single body of a yogin that appears as the other-dependent nature, there are two modes of engagement—the mode of engagement of the continuum of consciousness, and the mode of engagement of the power of wisdom." Thus, depending on whether the latent tendencies for listening are regarded from the perspective of seeming reality, the path, and ordinary consciousness or from the perspective of ultimate reality, the ground/fuition, and nonconceptual supramundane wisdom (both perspectives are found in the *Mahāyānasaṃgraha* and JNS), these tendencies can be described as either mundane, conditioned, and acquired (being a remedy, increasing, associated with

listening, reflection, and meditation) or as supramundane, unconditioned, and innate (being the capacity of uncontaminated cognition that is active through the power of the nature of phenomena, being an outflow of the dharmadhātu, and belonging to the dharmakāya). According to JNS, said tendencies are the spontaneous impulses and habits of listening to and engaging in the dharma that are the natural expression of one's own buddha nature as the causal condition. Thus, the facts of the dharma, teachers, and texts appearing for oneself as well as being attracted to and engaging them come about through the main cause that consists of the revival of these internal tendencies appearing as if external, with the compassion and the enlightened activities of buddhas and bodhisattvas aiding as the dominant or contributing conditions. Fundamentally speaking, all of this happens nowhere else and as nothing else than appearances in the minds of the disciples, which in these cases are not stained by obscurations. See also *Mahāyānasaṃgraha* III.12 (as quoted in the Introduction under "Mind Only?"); OED (p. 504) below; and Schmithausen 1987, 80–81.

296 I.16cd.

297 IX.23ab.

298 This refers to the chapter 6 of ZMND and AC (see the translation below). JNS comments: "Those present-day followers of [Mahā]mudrā whose confusion is even a hundred thousand times bigger than this exclaim, 'Through refining the ālaya-consciousness into something pure, it turns into the result of mirrorlike wisdom.' This is not justified for the following reasons. Something like this does not appear in any of the traditions of the mahāyāna, and what does not appear [there also] does not appear in the sense of something that is obtained through reasoning. A presentation of the ālaya-consciousness as the cause and mirrorlike wisdom as its result is not something that is obtained through reasoning. Rather, with respect to the mode of being of causes and results in terms of [such] causes and results in the abhidharma that actually fulfill these functions (that is, what [actually and not just nonimally] produces and what is produced), the ālaya-consciousness and mirrorlike wisdom are not adequate as a cause and a result that fully qualify as such. Also, since the very nature of the ālaya-consciousness is [nothing but] the adventitious stains, it is presented as impure. No matter how it may be refined by something else, it will not turn into something pure. It is not possible within the sphere of knowable objects that something impure turns into something pure, or that something pure turns into something impure. Some assert that there is the mere factor of lucid and aware mind, and that this is what comprises all the seeds of saṃsāra as well as the seeds of nirvāṇa. This is not tenable. That just one single [phenomenon] should function as the seminal cause for all of saṃsāra and nirvāṇa is not something that appears in the Buddhist tradition. That such does not appear [in this tradition is shown by the fact that] this is put forward as the assertion of non-Buddhists ('just one single awareness-consciousness, which is the cause or seed of both bondage and liberation') by the great guardians of the Buddha's teaching, glorious Dignāga and Dharmakīrti, and then refuted. Most Tibetans in this land of snow say, 'The twofold distiction between ālaya-consciousness and [ālaya-]wisdom is the system of the Mere Mentalists' and also, 'The twofold distinction between ālaya-wisdom and [ālaya]-consciousness does not appear in any system whatsoever.' Their own words are self-contradictory, because if [this distinction] appeared in the system of the Mere Mentalists, it contradicts not appearing in any system at all (vol. 1, pp. 210–11) . . . As for the nature of the dharmakāya specifically being wisdom, it is the ultimate knowledge that represents *the change of* all *states* of stains having been completely relinquished {in this and the next sentence, JNS obviously plays on the crucial expression 'change of state'}. Some proponents of inferior philosophical systems say, 'The ālaya-consciousness exists on the buddhabhūmi, and "having relinquished it" just means *the change* through having relinquished its stains—the impregnations *of* negative *states*—so that

the ālaya-consciousness has *changed* into mirrorlike nondual wisdom.' Though this is invalidated through infinite scriptures and reasonings, I will not elaborate these here {for more details, see the beginning of JNS's general topic on the disposition (translated in Brunnhölzl 2007b, 83–102)}. Suffice it to say that such explanations are nothing but self-invented" (vol. 2, pp. 450–51).

299 III.6 (D106, fol. 14b.2).

300 Lines 14cd–15.

301 Verse 37.

302 Lines 5b–6ab.

303 I.9 (D4211, fol. 158a.6). The Sanskrit reads "mental consciousness" instead of "mentation" and lacks "is [valid] perception." This passage is part of the *Pramāṇaviniścaya*'s explanation on mentation being understood as the nonconceptual aspect of the sixth consciousness, which perceives outer objects (also known as mental valid perception). Thus, Rangjung Dorje seems to equate this with the immediate mind here, which is explicitly stated that way by Tagramba Chögyal Denba's commentary on ZMND (Dvags po rab 'byams pa mkhas grub chos rgyal bstan pa 2005, 104). However, as will be seen below, in most of the other parts of AC's presentation of the immediate mind, it is not so equated. Thus, the point of AC quoting the above passage seems to be mainly to establish the immediate mind as an undeceiving aspect or function of mind, in order to set it off from the afflicted mind, which is essentially mistaken and deceiving.

304 As ZDKT (p. 67) explicitly affirms, Rangjung Dorje explains here that the first line in the above quote from the *Triṃśikā* refers to the immediate mind and the remaining four to the afflicted mind.

305 I.6 (D4048, fols. 3b.5–4a.1).

306 The meditative absorption without discrimination is the highest level of three within the fourth dhyāna of the form realm, during which primary minds and mental factors with an unstable continuum (the five sense consciousnesses, the mental consciousness, and their accompanying mental factors) temporarily cease. However, the latent tendencies for the arising of these consciousnesses are not eliminated. Thus, mistaken appearances will occur again, once one rises from this meditative absorption. When performed for a long time, it leads to an actual rebirth as a "god without discrimination" on the corresponding highest level of the form realm. As mentioned above, the meditative absorption of cessation represents the cessation of all primary minds and mental factors with an unstable continuum (the first six consciousnesses) as well as one of the two consciousnesses with a stable continuum (the seventh consciousness with its mental factors, but not the ālaya-consciousness).

307 This refers to the *amalavijñāna* held by the Indian Yogācāra Paramārtha and some of his Chinese followers (see introduction).

308 ZDKT (pp. 64–67) elaborates on the above as follows: "What mind is ignorant about is its own empty essence (the dharmakāya), lucid nature (the sambhogakāya), and resultant power to appear as anything (the nirmāṇakāya), which means to be ignorant of just this being nothing but the play of these three kāyas. Mind is ignorant about its own essence, which is not established as anything whatsoever, through imagining one aspect of its unity—its fundamental unborn nature—as being oneself and the other aspect—its unimpeded radiance—as being everything that is other than oneself, thus appearing through its unimpeded creative display

as if there were a separate subject and object. The way this happens is that, when mind as such—uncontrived ordinary mind free from being identifiable—becomes associated with what is called 'sentient beings,' under the sway of dependent origination, it is stirred by the wind of mentation—the 'mover'—through which the seventh consciousness rises and conceives of self and others. Then, through focusing on the fundamental nature of mind as such and grasping at it as 'me' and a self, the afflicted mind comes about, with it and the ālaya-consciousness keeping stirring and shaping each other like waves on water. This entire process is false imagination. By virtue of this, the phenomena of saṃsāra, which do not exist by any nature of their own, are established as these appearances that look as if they were solidly real. Therefore, this is the manner in which mind is ignorant. Here, innate ignorance is identified through referring to the lucid aspect of mind as such with the term 'seventh consciousness,' and to not recognizing its own essence as ignorance. This also means that the formation of immaculate karma through the movement of the seventh consciousness is correct imagination. What abides as its own stainless essence is stainless mentation. Since this is included in a particular aspect of the Sugata heart—the unfolding disposition—it is the wisdom of equality at the time of the ground. Hence, it is the wisdom that entails the purity of the seventh consciousness. This should be understood as being of the same meaning as the explanation in chapter 6 that the wisdom of equality is the change of state of the afflicted mind and the internally oriented part of the sixth—the mental—consciousness. Therefore, the seventh consciousness that is explained here—which causes mind to form objects—is taken to be mentation in general, without differentiating between the afflicted mind and pure mentation. It is the mentation that is the immediate condition for the six collections of consciousness explained below. Therefore, the autocommentary says again and again that its synonym is the 'immediate mind.' My guru, the Seventh Karmapa holds that mentation has three parts. From the perspective of immediacy, it is presented as the seventh consciousness of mentation; from the perspective of being embraced by the set of four afflictions, it is the afflicted mind; and from the perspective of being embraced by the immaculate dharmas, it is stainless mentation. These days, many Tibetans who discuss the abhidharma only include the afflicted mind as the seventh of the eight consciousnesses, without ever presenting the immediate mind as the seventh consciousness. This approach is even followed in some commentaries on this text [ZMND], but Rangjung Dorje himself holds that the seventh consciousness is the immediate mind, which is asserted to be the afflicted mind from the perspective of being ignorant about the immediate mind's own essence and thus conceiving of it as a self, therefore functioning as the root of all mistakenness in saṃsāra with its three realms."

309 Vasubandhu's *Mahāyānasaṃgrahabhāṣya* (D4050, fols. 129a.8ff) defines isolated ignorance as "that which obscures the realization of true reality, if its remedy has not arisen." Asvabhāva's *Mahāyānasaṃgrahopanibandhana* (D4051, fols. 196b.5ff.) gives a similar definition, and both enter into a lengthy argument as to why this ignorance cannot be located in any of the five sense consciousnesses or the mental consciousness, but only in the afflicted mind. Consequently, the afflicted mind must exist, since there is no saṃsāric existence without this kind of ignorance.

310 The *Mahāyānasaṃgrahopanibandhana* (fol. 197b.6–7) says that the afflicted mind is called *manas* (the Sanskrit term for mentation) due to its being self-centeredness (*asmimāna*). So, if the afflicted mind did not exist, the term *manas* would not apply to anything. It is not tenable to apply it to the six other consciousnesses, since they have already ceased (once self-centeredness appears).

311 The *Mahāyānasaṃgrahopanibandhana* (fol. 198a.5) comments that self-conceit can never occur without ignorance. Since ignorance is a mental factor, it must have a primary

mind as the matrix in which it rests. There is no other such matrix than the afflicted mind—a virtuous mental state is not suitable as a matrix for ignorance.

312 I.7 (P5549, fol. 6a.7–b.8).

313 D4059, fol. 16b.1–2. The *Abhidharmasamucchaya* (D4049, fol. 53b.1) agrees: "Mentation . . . is the consciousness of any one of the six consciousnesses having just ceased." ZDC (pp. 28–29) concludes: "In brief, from the ocean of the ālaya, wave-like mentation stirs and forms, by virtue of which saṃsāra becomes established. The ālaya-consciousness is the ground or cause of saṃsāra, while mentation is the condition. The *Mahāyānasaṃgraha* presents [mentation] as two aspects—the first one is the immediate mind, which is the locus of the arising of the consciousnesses, and the second one is the afflicted mind, which afflicts these [consciousnesses]. Accordingly, Tagramba [Chögyal Denba]'s extensive explanation by dividing mentation into two is contained in this meaning. The former [aspect of] mentation serves as the locus of the arising of the six collections [of consciousness] from the ālaya, and, by virtue of being associated with the immaculate dharmas, it is the cause for a buddha's qualities of freedom. The latter [aspect of] mentation [—the afflicted mind—] does not serve as valid cognition, since it is the root of mistakenness in saṃsāra and of producing all mental states of noncognition, wrong cognition, and doubt. It should be understood that when consciousness is classified as eight collections, these two [aspects] are joined into one [as the seventh consciousness]."

314 Lines 8bc. In this text, Vasubandhu speaks about three kinds of basic modulations (Skt. pariṇāma), through which saṃsāric mind evolves or displays, which are the ālaya-consciousness, the afflicted mind, and the remaining six consciousnesses.

315 Lines 8d–9 (the delimiting mental factors are better known as the five object-determining ones).

316 D480, fol. 155a.3–4.

317 *Ālambanaparīkṣāvṛtti* (D4206, fol. 87a.1–2) on verse 6.

318 Verse 7. In very terse form, Dignāga's commentary explains that this verse answers two objections. First, under the premise that both object and subject are mind, neither the simultaneity of object and subject is contradictory, nor is taking them as being related as a cause (the object) preceding its result (the subject). The first line hinges on the unmistaken fact of positive and negative concomitance, that is, whenever there is an object, there necessarily is a subject perceiving it, and whenever there is no object, there is no subject either. The second line says that the traces or latent tendencies of certain objects, which are input into the mind stream by previous experiences, may be considered as the causes that precede the present perception of the actual objects as which these dormant potentials eventually surface. The last two lines answer the second objection that in the process of one aspect of mind simply cognizing another, any sense faculties, such as the eyes (which are taught to be material in many Buddhist teachings) would be superfluous. The answer is that the result caused by what appears as a sense faculty is a perception. However, all that can be properly inferred from this result is that there is just this power of what appears as a sense faculty that contributes to the arising of this perception, but not that this power is something material (as this power too is nothing but a manifested latent tendency or potential of a different type than the object). For more details, see Tola and Dragonetti 1982, 114–16, 122, and 126–28.

319 ZDKT says that the order of the five skandhas here (proceeding from consciousness to form) refers to the sequence of cause and effect in terms of the respective latter ones arising from

the former ones. The usual—reverse—order (as presented, for example, in the *Abhidharmakośa*) is given in terms of being more or less coarse and in terms of causing afflictions.

320 The three phrases above are usually given as the definitions of skandhas, dhātus, and āyatanas (in different places, the *Pañcaskandhaprakaraṇa* states almost literally the same thing as this paragraph, but apart from going into the classificatory details of skandhas, dhātus, and āyatanas, the text does not really elaborate on this particular point). In general, it is often said that the presentations of these three formats are given for three reasons. (1) They are remedies against the three types of ignorance: the skandhas remedy the wrong idea that mind is a single unit; the āyatanas remedy the notion that form (or matter) is a single unit; and the dhātus remedy the notion that both mind and form are single units. (2) In the above order, they are presented for those with highest faculties (who understand through a brief division), those with medium faculties, and those with inferior faculties. (3) They are presented for those who are inclined toward brief, medium, and extensive classifications, respectively.

321 The authorship of this text has been disputed by many, mainly based on the grounds that it speaks about the three natures and the ālaya-consciousness, which are assumed by these critics to be later Yogācāra notions. However, that Nāgārjuna was familiar with the three natures is also evidenced by his *Acintyastava* (whose authorship is undisputed) mentioning the first two natures in verses 44–45. As Lindtner 1992, 253 points out, lines 45cd are moreover identical to *Laṅkāvatārasūtra* II.191ab. His article presents detailed evidence that, throughout Nāgārjuna's texts, he not only knew, but also greatly relied on, an early version of this sūtra. No doubt, the sūtra is a major source for later Yogācāras (as well as Mādhyamikas), but it also seems to criticize (earlier?) reifying versions of Yogācāra/Vijñānavāda. Furthermore, verses 33–35 of the *Bodhicittavivaraṇa* on the ālaya-consciousness correspond almost literally to three verses from the *Ghanavyūhasūtra* (P778, fols. 49b.7–50a.2), which is also a major Yogācāra source.

322 Verses 59–60.

323 ZDKT (p. 74) remarks that these six are obviously not the six causes as explained in the abhidharma teachings, but the six main causes of the vajra body.

324 P5549, fol. 13b.7–8 (AC omits the beginning of this passage up to "likeness," and the phrase, "Therefore, it must exist" is not found in the *Tengyur* versions).

325 Some other sources speak of the fine down on such a bird.

326 Skt. mana āyatana, Tib. yid kyi skye mched. For example, the *Viniścayasaṃgrahaṇī* (D4038, fol. 16a.2–3) explicitly equates the immediate condition (as either one of the six consciousnesses' having ceased, and thus being the condition for the following ones to arise), mentation, the dhātu of mentation, and the āyatana of mentation.

327 ZDKT (p. 75) states that this explanation hinges on the same essential point as what is said about the immediate mind.

328 AC has *rnam par rig pa* for the last entry, obviously referring to *rnam par rig byed kyi gzugs* (Skt. vijñaptirūpa). This is defined as encompassing all inner and outer material forms, which is basically just another way of saying, "the four elements and their derivatives." As for the above sentence as a whole, in a way, it sounds like a brief statement on the two meanings of "form" in Buddhist terminology. In general, the term refers to the skandha of form, which is further classified as "causal form" (the four elements) and "resultant form" (whatever derives from these elements). In other words, this designates the sum total of matter, including visible forms, sounds, smells, tastes, tangible objects (outer forms), and the five sense faculties (inner forms). In addition, the skandha of form contains "imperceptible form" (Skt.

avijñaptirūpa, Tib. rnam par rig byed ma yin pa'i gzugs). This refers to five groups of phenomena that appear as aspects of form, which are considered as matter (in the Vaibhāṣika schools), but solely experienced by the mental consciousness, not demonstrable to the eye consciousness, and intangible. However, in the format of the twelve āyatanas, which is used above, these five are grouped under the "form of the āyatana of phenomena" (Skt. dharmāyatanarūpa, Tib. chos kyi skye mched kyi gzugs; for details, see entries (1)–(5) under "unconditioned phenomena" just below). The second and narrower meaning of "form" just refers to visible forms, that is, colors and shapes.

329 Among these five "imperceptible forms," aggregational form refers to the form of the minutest material particle. Examples for circumstantial form include the space in between things and reflections. Form originating from correct commitment and symbols refers to vows. Examples for imputed form include appearances in a dream and skeletons appearing through the samādhi of repulsiveness. Mastered form appears through mastering certain samādhis, for example, the entire universe appearing as earth, red, and so on due to the samādhis of the totality (Skt. kṛtsnāyatana, Tib. zad par kyi skye mched) of earth, red, and so on.

330 Analytical cessation (Skt. pratisaṃkhyānirodha, Tib. so sor brtags pa'i 'gog pa) refers to the result of freedom from the factors to be relinquished on the path of seeing through prajñā having thoroughly analyzed and realized all the aspects of the four realities of the noble ones. Nonanalytical cessation (Skt. apratisaṃkhyānirodha, Tib. so sor brtags pa ma vin pa'i 'gog pa) means that something is temporarily not happening by virtue of its specific causes and conditions not being complete.

331 The eight unconditioned phenomena are space; the two cessations; the suchness of virtuous, nonvirtuous, and neutral phenomena, respectively; the meditative absorption of cessation; and the meditative absorption without discrimination. This list originated with the Mahīśāsakas and is later found in Asaṅga's *Yogācārabhūmi* and the *Abhidharmasamucchaya*. In accordance with the Sarvāstivāda system, Vasubandhu's *Abhidharmakośa* lists only the two cessations and space, while his *Pañcaskandhaprakaraṇa* gives the same plus suchness in general.

332 AC omits the last line.

333 As mentioned before, in Buddhism, only conditioned phenomena can be causes, since unconditioned phenomena are permanent and cannot perform any active function. Cessation refers to the absence of a previously existent conditioned phenomenon, but in itself, an absence cannot be a cause for anything (the famous counterexamples to this pan-Buddhist position are Tsongkhapa and his followers, who hold that cessation is a functional entity that serves as the operational agent connecting karmic causes and effects).

334 In discussing this passage of AC that refers to the *Saṃdhinirmocanasūtra*, ZDKT (p. 76) glosses the immediate mind as the potential for the arising of the next consciousness, which is a powerful latent tendency in the ālaya and subsequently serves as the immediate condition for the arising of the respective next moments of consciousness. In other words, the immediate mind is the mentation that dwells in the ālaya and is the capacity for the arising of consciousnesses (this explanation is literally copied by ZDC, p. 33). In fact, both explanations come down to the same, since both the tendencies of the six consciousnesses as well as mentation in the sense of the immediate mind are input into and reemerge together from the ālaya. As mentioned in the introduction, the immediate mind (referring to mind's lucidity, as explained before) is nothing but the propelling force intrinsic to each moment of consciousness, which

makes it arise from, and sink down into, the ālaya (similar to the force through which waves move, which cannot be separated from the water of the waves).

335 The Tibetan *nye bar sbyor ba* renders the Sanskrit words *upayoga* or *upanaya*, which mean to apply, employ, make contact, draw near, or provide (all of which are implied here). As mentioned in the introdcution, the immediate mind triggers the latent tendencies of the six consciousnesses to manifest from within the ālaya as perceiving their respective objects, thus sustaining a continuous flow of subject-object interactions. Likewise, the immediate mind represents the energy to redirect and store the imprints of these interactions back into the ālaya, just to "revive" them at a later point. Per se, this "infinite loop" movement is neutral, but constitutes the actual driving force behind our saṃsāric travels, while the afflicted mind decides on the pleasant or unpleasant destinations to which this journey takes us.

336 Verse 15 (AC omits the last line).

337 In the Yogācāra tradition, these are the three conditions for the arising of a sense consciousness—the immediate condition, dominant condition, and object condition. Different from the presentation of these conditions in the Vaibhāṣika and Sautrāntika schools (in which the latter two are considered to be material), here, all of them are considered to be latent tendencies in the ālaya that become manifest and shape the particular features of the sense consciousnesses. Thus, the immediate condition is the power in the stream of the ālaya-consciousness that directly produces any phenomenon mainly as having the nature of lucid awareness (never as matter). The dominant condition is the potential that produces a sense consciousness mainly as being the apprehender of its object. The object condition is the potential that produces a sense consciousness mainly as that which possesses the apprehended mental aspect that appears as its specific object.

338 Verse 16. In general, as presented in the *Yogācārabhūmi* (D4035, fols. 160b.5–161a.2), there is a list of six "states without mind" (Skt. acittikābhūmi, Tib. sems med pa'i sa). These consist of (1) sleep, (2) fainting, (3) the meditative absorption of cessation, (4) the meditative absorption without discrimination, (5) the state of a god without discrimination (the result of (4), which is rebirth on the highest level of the fourth dhyāna of the form realm), and (6) the expanse of the nirvāṇa without remainder (which is what "the state without mind" in line 16d refers to). Among these, during the first five, only the first six or seven primary minds and their mental factors cease temporarily, but not the ālaya-consciousness. The expanse of the nirvāṇa without remainder is said to be the ultimate state without mind, because the ālaya-consciousness has ceased. As explained above (AC, p. 28), from a strictly mahāyāna point of view, even in the nirvāṇas without remainder of śrāvakas and pratyekabuddhas, there are still remainders of the ālaya-consciousness, but one can say that the cessation of the afflicted mind, which clings to a personal self, represents the cessation of one part of the ālaya-consciousness.

339 The text seems to count (4) and (5) among the above six states without mind as one, since their manner of primary minds and mental factors having ceased is the same.

340 As explained above, "the mentation that rests in the ālaya" is the seventh consciousness.

341 Both the Sanskrit *bhava* and the Tibetan *srid pa* for the ninth link of dependent origination can mean either "becoming" (the usual translation) or "existence." As the following shows, AC obviously takes it to mean the three realms of saṃsāric existence.

342 ZDKT (p. 87) emphasizes that "adventitious" refers to being separable and not to something that did not exist before and then arises newly.

343 Part 2, IV.69. The Sanskrit has four pādas, with the last two saying, "Due to the removal of these, no doubt, beings are buddhas indeed" (*tasyāpakarṣanāt sattvā buddhā eva na saṃśayaḥ*).

344 As they stand, theses two lines are unidentified. Most probably, they are a paraphrase of a similar passage in the *Tathāgatotpattisaṃbhavaṃbhāva* chapter of the *Avataṃsakasūtra* (P761, as quoted in Asaṅga's *Ratnagotravibhāgavyākhyā*; J 22, P5526, fol. 88a.2–3): "Within the hosts of sentient beings, there is no being whatsoever into which Tathāgata wisdom has not entered in its entirety" (*na sa kaścit sattvaḥ sattvanikāye saṃvidyate yatra tathāgatajñānaṃ na sakalam anupraviṣṭam*). Also, both Dharmamitra's *Prasphuṭapadā* (P5194, fol. 54a.7) and Abhayākaragupta's *Munimatālaṃkāra* (P5299, fol. 186a.8–186b.1) present a similar quote as stemming from the *Samādhirājasūtra* (or its early and shorter version, known as the *Candrapradīpasūtra*), saying, "All these beings will be enlightened, and there is no sentient being here who is not a vessel" (I could not, however, locate this passage in the sūtra).

345 These are the states of deep sleep, dreaming, sexual union, and ordinary waking life.

346 The following comments are from ZDKT (pp. 349ff.), which relates the first three lines to the dharmakāya, sambhogakāya, and nirmāṇakāya at the time of the ground, that is, mind's essence, nature, and capacity of reaching-out (Tib. ngo bo, rang bzhin, thugs rje; in other words emptiness, luminosity, and their indivisible play).

347 According to ZDKT, these three are innate ignorance and ignorance by virtue of the conditions of formation and imputations, respectively.

348 This refers to the outer world and the beings who inhabit it.

349 ZDKT says that pure mentation is the wisdom of equality, which means to accomplish the welfare of others in an unmoving way. "Imagination" refers to the sixth consciousness.

350 X.5 (D4048, fol. 38a.4–8).

351 AC explains elsewhere (p. 178.1–2) that the purification of the state of deep sleep pertains mainly to the ālaya-consciousness and results in mirrorlike wisdom, which is also said to be the essence of the dharmakāya free from reference points, that is, the nature of the dharmadhātu.

352 Likewise, the purification of the dream state mainly pertains to the afflicted mind and the immediate mind, thus resulting in the wisdom of equality and discriminating wisdom, which correspond to the sambhogakāya—lucid appearance and emptiness inseparable (ibid., pp. 183.3–184.3).

353 This is exactly what the quote from the *Trikāyanāmasūtra* on the first four wisdoms in NTC and NYC and OED (p. 600.3–4) says (see below).

354 IX.68–69.

355 Vasubandhu's *Bhāṣya* (Limaye 1992, 139) says that mirrorlike wisdom is not directed toward knowable objects, because it is without perceptual aspects (*anākāratvāt*). Both Sthiramati's and Asvabhāva's commentaries (D4034, fol. 139b.5–6; D4029, fol. 74a.5–6) explain this further, saying that mirrorlike wisdom neither operates through splitting knowable objects into the particulars of focal objects (such as form) or the particulars of perceptual aspects (such as blue), nor does it delimit or label distinct objects. Rather, in being the nonconceptual wisdom that is equal in terms of what is focused on and what focuses being equal, it is the nature of focusing on the dharmadhātu or suchness. Therefore, it is immovable.

356 ZDKT elaborates that, when a clear mirror and a face meet, a reflection of that face appears in it. Likewise, when mirrorlike wisdom meets beings to be guided, all the other wisdoms appear in it in the manner of reflections.

357 X.7 (D4048, fol. 38b.3).

358 Another tantric example is the *Mañjuśrīnāmasaṃgīti* (chaps. VI–X), which treats the five wisdoms by extensively praising the five related buddhas (Vairocana, Akṣobhya, Ratnasambhava, Amitābha, and Amoghasiddhi).

359 ZDKT (p. 353) elaborates the intention behind all this as follows. Ultimately, all five wisdom have the same nature, but are merely divided in terms of conceptual isolates. As for how the nature of buddhahood appears for buddhas themselves, it appears as the five wisdoms and the five buddha families not being different. As an appearance for others, buddhahood displays as the rūpakāyas. Therefore, though mirrorlike wisdom is not contradictory to the sambhogakāya, when making the conventional classification of three kāyas, it is explained as the dharmakāya and not the sambhogakāya.

360 IX.70–71.

361 ZDKT calls this the "internally oriented aspect" of the sixth consciousness.

362 There are four kinds of dhāraṇī (Tib. gzungs). (1) Bodhisattvas who have entered the bhūmis possess the dhāraṇī of words or dharma—immediately upon hearing great numbers of names, words, or letters, they do not forget them. (2) The dhāraṇī of meaning is to realize the meanings of these words and to not forget them. (3) The dhāraṇī of poised readiness refers to familiarizing with and realizing all phenomena as being unborn. (4) The dhāraṇī of secret mantra refers to feats such as bodhisattvas on the bhūmis blessing the letters of mantras, by virtue of which these mantras are able to overcome epidemics and so on. The first two among these are the actual dhāraṇīs, while the latter two are presented from the perspective of the mind streams of bodhisattvas retaining these respective powers. Thus, most commonly, in terms of (1) and (2), dhāraṇī refers to the power of total recall. Its nature is special recollection and prajñā, and its function is the power to retain virtuous dharmas and to eliminate nonvirtue. As for (3) and (4), there are many varieties. Sometimes, "dhāraṇī" is even used as a name for texts, such as the *Avikalpapraveśadhāraṇī*.

363 IX.72–73.

364 This refers to mental valid perception, which perceives outer objects just like the five sense consciousnesses (called the "externally oriented aspect" of the sixth consciousness by ZDKT).

365 This presentation corresponds to what *Mahāyānasūtrālaṃkāra* IX.42–44 and XI.45 (see NYC below) say about the correspondence of fourfold mastery with the change of state of mentation, perception, and conception, respectively. As discussed in the introduction and as NYC explains in more detail, actually, it is neither the conceptual nor the perceptual part of the sixth consciousness that changes state as discriminating wisdom, but the immediate mind as its underlying dynamic function.

366 IX.74–75.

367 When commenting on the "fundamental sphere free from reference points"—the nature of the mind—at the beginning of the chapter 5 of ZMND, AC (pp. 152–53), by quoting verses 43–47 of the *Dharmadhātustava*, discusses how the three kāyas are related to the present experiences of sentient beings and the meditation to realize this (see also the Third Karmapa's

Wisdom Lamp below). The connate wisdom of our own mind is empty in essence, lucid in nature, and unimpeded in its manifestation. All these three being free from reference points is the dharmakāya, lucidity is the sambhogakāya, and the compassionate display that can show as anything is the nirmāṇakāya. The indications that the three kāyas in this sense are present right now are as follows. The indication of the dharmakāya is that all entities appear as empty now too, since their nature never goes beyond emptiness. The indication of the sambhogakāya is the appearance of the ten signs of expanse and awareness inseparable as visual objects. The indication of the nirmāṇakāya is that the distinct energies of the appearances of the objects of the six consciousnesses manifest individually. The indication that all three are undeceiving appears in objects right now, since wisdom (the perceiving subject) is the very nature of the consciousnesses connected with these objects. Nonconceptual yogic valid perception right within these consciousnesses means to sustain the continuum of nonconceptual direct perception, which is given the conventional term "meditation."

368 IX.76. This is the classic presentation of the four wisdoms and their causes in the Yogācāra system—mirrorlike wisdom arises from the prajñā of studying and retaining the dharma; the wisdom of equality comes from cultivating a mindset of sentient beings being equal; discriminating wisdom arises from teaching the dharma to others; and all-accomplishing wisdom is the culmination of accomplishing what is beneficial for others. According to Thrangu Rinpoche, only four causes are taught, since the fifth wisdom—dharmadhātu wisdom—pervades the other four. Alternatively, the cause of this fifth wisdom may be said to be the realization of the nature of phenomena.

369 ZDKT glosses disposition and purpose as cause and result, respectively (note that both AC and this gloss differ from the first line in the following quote from the *Mahāyānasūtrālaṃkāra*).

370 IX.77. As mentioned in the introduction, on the five wisdoms "in action" in realized beings during all situations, AC (p. 326) says that, when embraced by the correct yoga, sense perception, mental direct perception, and self-aware direct perception are all yogic valid perception, which is connate wisdom's own nature. Through all aspects of knowing and what is to be known being embraced by the perfect view, in terms of its functions, this wisdom then manifests as the five wisdoms. These are the wisdom that discriminates all causes and results; the wisdom of being empty of a nature of its own (mirrorlike wisdom); all-accomplishing wisdom, which means to display wisdom's power by virtue of having gained mastery over it; the wisdom of seeing the equality of all this; and the principle of not moving away from suchness, which pervades all of this (dharmadhātu wisdom). JNS (vol. 2, p. 451) says that wisdom is fivefold—the four wisdoms clearly stated in *Mahāyānasūtrālaṃkāra* IX.67–76 and, by implication, the dharmadhātu wisdom. Among these, the dharmadhātu wisdom is the essence of all kāyas—the svābhāvikakāya, the basic element of all wisdoms, the wisdom of the nature of phenomena—whose nature it is to be free from all factors to be free from and to be endowed with all qualities. Some explain this from the point of view of a mere negation, but that is mistaken. Still, this very wisdom is divided into four in terms of its distinct functions. Mirrorlike wisdom refers to the appearance of the aspects of a Tathāgata's own unshared dharmas within luminous dharmadhātu wisdom through the power of the ālaya-consciousness having become pure. The wisdom of equality refers to being endowed with great love and compassion in an equal way for all beings by virtue of the afflicted mind having become completely pure. Discriminating wisdom refers to having become a treasury of samādhis and dhāraṇīs that are unimpeded with regard to all knowable objects by virtue of the flux of the mental consciousness having been stopped. All-accomplishing wisdom refers to having attained the power to creatively manifest as, and transform into, favorable circumstances in accordance with the

respective objects of enlightened activity in infinite realms of sentient beings by virtue of being free from the five sense consciousnesses. Among these four, the first two are primarily the knowledges that perform activities from a buddha's own perspective, while the latter two are primarily the knowledges that perform activities from the perspective of others. Through the power of a buddha's knowledge through previous aspirations, the kāyas of the two latter wisdoms appear. From the perspective of others (those to be guided), these kāyas are conceived as being endowed with three distinctive features—the characteristics of minds and mental factors are complete in them, since they appear as the duality of apprehender and apprehended; they perform activities, such as teaching the dharma; and they involve the change of state of the latent tendencies of dualistic appearance. As can be seen from these passages in AC and JNS, they represent two of the rare examples that explicitly state the crucial point of the division into the four or five wisdoms not being a static one, but one in terms of the operational dynamics of the single fundamental wisdom of buddhahood.

371 In chapter 10 of AC (p. 286), form is said to correspond to mirrorlike wisdom, feeling to the wisdom of equality, discrimination to discriminating wisdom, formation to all-accomplishing wisdom, and consciousness to dharmadhātu wisdom.

372 I.34 (the same four are found in *Mahāyānasūtrālaṃkāra* IV.11).

373 Following this, AC presents a quote by the Indian master Vīravajra, the gist of which is aptly summarized in ZDC (p. 200, based on ZDKT, pp. 358–59). The nirmāṇakāya is attained through purifying the stains of the waking state. Therefore, you should bind thoughts through the practice of the dharmamudrā. Although there are numerous ways of explaining the dharmamudrā, the intention in this context is the key instruction to take whatever appearances are encountered as the path. When appearances of various objects (such as forms) arise, you do not cling to them through thinking, "This is such and such," but bind them as the mudrā of being without fixation. This is called "sustaining whatever comes up, without fabrication and nakedly." It has been unanimously said by all the previous Kagyü masters that this is the genuine essential point of practice.

374 ZDC (p. 227) glosses this as self-arisen wisdom.

375 ZDC (p. 227) comments on the above two lines: "Its essence is being endowed with the union of the two [realities], with ultimate reality being its lack of stains (the mistakenness of the eight collections) and its natural purity, and seeming reality being its wisdom's own light."

376 ZDKT (pp. 396–97) comments on the last two paragraphs of AC as follows: "The meaning of this is that unconditioned and spontaneously present mind as such, the dharmakāya beyond the entire web of reference points, which has the nature of being all-pervading like space, exists as ultimate reality. However, this does not teach that the Sugata heart is really established, permanent, enduring, and eternal. Also the [Seventh Karmapa's] statement in his *Ocean of Texts on Reasoning* that nondual wisdom is established as ultimate reality has the meaning of 'established as being ultimate reality,' but he does not assert that it is really established, permanent, enduring, and eternal. Some think, 'If something is established as ultimate reality, it must be really established,' but they have not examined [this issue properly], since [their objection] comes down to nothing but being mistaken about the mere name 'reality.' For example, though something may be established as seeming reality, [that does not mean that] it needs to be really established. Therefore, most present-day proponents of *shentong* and the position of glorious Rangjung [Dorje] differ. Also the statement by my omniscient guru [the Seventh Karmapa] that '*rangtong* and *shentong* are not contradictory' is an excellent explanation, [which shows] that he has realized this meaning. Thus, [AC] says that what

is to be expressed is the mode of being of the buddha heart that exists as the great freedom from extremes, the inseparability of appearance and emptiness, and the union of the two realities. The Sugata heart is nothing but the unmistaken own essence of the eight collections [of consciousness] explained in chapter 1. Here, the distinct and unmixed eight collections are the seeming, and their unmistaken own essence is the ultimate, the two realities thus being a union. However, those who do not realize the meaning of the two realities are ignorant about the dependent origination that is only satisfying when not examined, thus circling in saṃsāra through their views of clinging to extremes, such as permanence and extinction. By stating the shortcomings of not realizing the two realities, [Rangjung Dorje] teaches that one needs to train in the mode of being of the two realities in union."

377 Verses 9–12.

378 Verses 13–14ac.

379 In fact, this text starts with the above quote from the *Guhyasamājatantra*.

380 Verse 2.

381 The *Vajrajñānasamucchayatantra* (D447) is an explanatory tantra of the *Guhyasamājatantra*. DSC, fol. 5a renders this passage as, "The seeming is dualistic appearance. [Its] reality is like [a reflection of] the moon [in] water. Ultimate reality is free from all characteristics, and its abode consists of the eighteen emptinesses." There are two more—somewhat differing—versions in TOK (vol. III, p. 40) and ZDC (p. 227). In addition, the *Hevajratantra* has a similar verse (part 2, III.36). For a list and explanation of the eighteen emptinesses, see Brunnhölzl 2004, 117–22.

382 I.3.

383 *Pramāṇavārttika* I.166ab and *Pramāṇaviniścaya* II.56ab.

384 T3881, lines 3cd.

385 Ibid., verse 12. ZDKT (pp. 400–401) says that the appearances of seeming reality are classified here as twofold—from the perspective of the noble ones on the path, they are the mere seeming, and from the perspective of ordinary beings, they are seeming reality. Furthermore, in terms of "correct and false seeming," the common explanation in the traditions of Madhyamaka and valid cognition is that water and a mirage both appear in a very similar way to be water, but the one actually performs the function of water, while the other does not. Thus, the former is the correct seeming and the latter is the false one. The way in which this classification was made by the former masters of the Kagyü lineage is as follows. In terms of being mere appearances, seeming appearances are similar for both noble ones and ordinary beings. However, since the noble ones know that they appear but are without nature, [for them,] they are able to perform the function of [yielding] the result of nirvāṇa. Therefore, for the noble ones, they are the correct seeming. Ordinary beings take these appearances to be real and cling to them, so that they are not able to perform said function. Consequently, for them, they are the false seeming.

386 Both Avalokitavrata's *Prajñāpradīpaṭīkā* (D3859, fol. 5b) and Atiśa's *Bodhipathapradīpapañjikā* (D3948, fol. 280b) explicitly identify the text as Nāgārjuna's autocommentary. However, in both the Tibetan tradition and Western scholarship, his authorship is often denied (and the text is usually neglected altogether), mainly on the grounds that it quotes a verse that is also found in Āryadeva's *Catuḥśataka*. However, given the well-known tendency of Indian texts to freely use verses from other authors, Āryadeva's text may equally have

incorporated it from some common earlier source. Tsongkhapa (1357–1419) says that it cannot be Nāgārjuna's work, since if it were, it would have to be quoted by later Mādhyamikas, such as Buddhapālita, Bhāvaviveka, and Candrakīrti, which it is not. In itself, this is not a very conclusive argument. For, it (a) contradicts the above attribution by at least two Indian masters generally (and also by Tsongkhapa) considered reliable, and (b) Buddhapālita's commentary on the *Mūlamadhyamakakārikā*—which is referred to and quoted at length in Bhāvaviveka's and Candrakīrti's commentaries—incorporates large parts of the *Akutobhayā* (on this, see the excellent documentation in Huntington 1995). Of course, (b) in itself is no proof that the text actually *was* authored by Nāgārjuna. Thus, the *Akutobhayā* no doubt existed in the mainstream of early Madhyamaka exegesis and, via Buddhapālita's text, exerted a considerable influence upon later commentators as well. Hence, a more thorough study of the *Akutobhayā* and its influence on the Madhyamaka approach to reasoning seems overdue.

387 *Akutobhayā* has "relying" (*brten par*).

388 D3829, fols. 88b.6–89a.5.

389 The Rumtek version of AC (p. 238.5) and Tagramba's commentary (pp. 497, 501) have *rtogs byed pa'i rtog pa*, but ZMND, the version of AC in the *Collected Works*, and all other available commentaries read and explain as *rtog byed pa'i rtog pa*. Thus, the translation follows the latter.

390 ZDC (p. 228) explains these two lines as follows: "Based on this mode of being of the two realities being an inseparable connate union, **what is produced by the correct conceptions that** discriminate **this** basic nature will be clearly realized as the unmistaken view. **The remedial** wisdom that is realized or produced in this way is the **means of purifying** the conceptions of apprehender and apprehended. This **is** also **explained** in the texts of mantra, Yogācāra, and Madhyamaka."

391 This is also the order of the words in this line in Narthang, P, and DSC, with most commentaries matching it with the order of afflictions in the next verse. D has *sprin dang khug rna du ba dang*, which correponds to the order in Sanskrit.

392 In ancient Indian cosmology, solar and lunar eclipses are regarded as the sun or moon being swallowed by the demon Rahu, since he envies them for their light. However, he is not able to retain them in his body and thus has to release them quickly.

393 Interestingly, the *Aṅguttaranikāya* (I, pp. 253–54, 275; III, p. 16) also speaks about mind needing to be freed from the same five obscuring stains in order to regain its natural state. Also, Vasubandhu's *Mahāyānasūtrālaṃkārabhāṣya* says that mind is similar to the sky by virtue of its luminosity, since all manifold phenomena are as adventitious with regard to the mind as are dust, smoke, clouds, and mist with regard to the sky (ed. Nagao, 18.43–44).

394 Verses 16–22. In this vein, AC says elsewhere (p. 227.2–5) that emptiness, which is usually stated to be the ultimate and prajñā, may also be expressed as the means (*upāya*), as is the case in Nāgārjuna's *Mahāyānaviṃśikā* 15:

> Whoever sees dependent origination,
> Just as it is, as true actuality
> Realizes the world to be empty,
> Relinquishing beginning, middle, and end.

Also the *Śrīmālādevīsūtra* states, "This attainment of liberation in dependence on the nature of all phenomena being emptiness is the means to engage the Tathāgata heart." To wit, as it stands, this passage is not found in the sūtra, but it most probably refers to the sutra's statement that "the wisdom of the Tathāgata heart is the emptiness-wisdom of the Tathāgatas" (Wayman and Wayman 1974, 99), which Rangjung Dorje also adduces in DSC by citing the passage in Asaṅga's *Ratnagotravibhāgavyākhyā* in which it appears too.

395 The *Uttaratantra* does not contain the first line as it stands here, the closest is I.49c (*sems kyi rang bzhin dri med dbyings*). The following two lines are I.144ab.

396 Lines 22–25ab (AC omits line 22b). As an aside, in the light of such explicit statements, the Gelugpa claim that Nāgārjuna and the Prāsaṅgikas do not only not refute, but even *assert* the existence of outer objects is all the more unbelievable (especially since no proper scriptural support for this claim is provided). Further evidence to the contrary of this claim includes *Mūlamadhyamakakārikā* V.7:

> Thus, space is neither an entity nor a nonentity,
> Neither what is to be characterized
> Nor a defining characteristic.
> The other five elements are analogous to space.

397 This refers to the inexpressible self or person claimed by the Vātsīputrīyas.

398 XX.92–103.

399 Lines 25cd–29.

400 VI.8. See also NYC on NY lines 60–61.

401 ZDKT (pp. 408–9) explains that the gradual stages of relinquishing the factors to be relinquished (the stains of clinging to duality) and the arising of the remedy (the wisdom that realizes nonduality) are to be understood as the former masters have taught them. Having meditated on the lack of a self as the remedy for conceiving of a self, the remedy for being mistaken in terms of outer referents other than mind is to realize them as being mere mental appearances. Again, this taking them to be mere cognizance is realized as freedom from all reference points. Thus, one should engage in the correct path in a gradual manner. In accordance with *Bodhicaryāvatāra* 4ab ("Also the yogins, due to differences in insight, are overruled by successively superior ones"), the four levels of yoga (that is, the four yogic practices) are held to be increasingly superior.

402 This is a partial translation of Rang byung rdo rje 2006b, with this first section being pp. 496.6–498.1.

403 D4028, fol. 27b.

404 XXV.19 (OED condenses this into three lines).

405 V.19.

406 The following sections are pp. 501.1–516.3 (numbers in "[ ]" refer to the page numbers of the Tibetan text).

407 D107, fol. 292a.5–6 (the third line in OED says "and the nature of the two realities").

408 (1) "Names" are mere designations, such as "book." (2) "Causal features" (Skt. *nimitta* can mean both "cause" and "characteristic" and is to be understood in this double sense here) refer to the bases for such designations with names, that is, dualistically appearing entities that perform functions and have certain characteristics. (3) "Imagination" refers here to the eight kinds of consciousness. (4) "Perfect wisdom" bears this name, because it is the nonconceptual

perceiving subject of suchness. (5) "Suchness" is the ultimate object to be focused on through the path—the dharmadhātu. Thus, (4)–(5) are the perfect nature in terms of subject and object (or the unmistaken and unchanging perfect nature), respectively. Needless to say, this explanation of the perfect nature as two is a pedagogical device to describe what is realized and what realizes it from the dualistic perspective of ordinary beings, but in no way implies any notion of a separate subject and object at the level of a buddha's mind realizing, or rather constituting, ultimate reality.

409 As AC (p. 35 above) explicitly says, the unfolding disposition is nothing but the four wisdoms, which are the stainless essence of the eight consciousnesses.

410 I.2 (P5549, fol. 3b.7).

411 I.17 (ibid., fol. 7a.3–4).

412 As DSC and OED explain, the former is the dharmakāya that is the stainless dharmadhātu, and the latter is the very profound dharmakāya—the two rūpakāyas—that is the natural outflow of this stainless dharmadhātu.

413 I.45 (ibid., fol. 11b.1–3).

414 I.46 (ibid., fol. 11b.4–5).

415 Note that OED comments on the prose version of the *Dharmadharmatāvibhāga*. Since the present focus of translating the excerpts from OED here is not on its being a commentary on Maitreya's text, but on presenting the Third Karmapa's view in general, I omit the references to the respective lines of the *Dharmadharmatāvibhāga* as well as highlighting its text in OED's comments.

416 As it stands, this passage is not found in any of Maitreya's texts, but the first line is an abbreviation of lines 86–87 of the *Dharmadharmatāvibhāga* and also resembles *Abhisamayālaṃkāra* V.7ab. In general, the meaning of these two lines is not only found throughout the texts of Maitreya, Asaṅga, Vasubandhu, and other Yogācāras, but also in some Madhyamaka works, such as Nāgārjuna's *Bodhicittavivaraṇa* (verses 39–40) and Candrakīrti's *Madhyamakāvatāra* VI.96.

417 D4206 (fol. 87a.1–2) on verse 6.

418 XI.40.

419 The former (Tib. rnam grangs pa'i kun brtags) refers to mental images of conventionally existent phenomena (such as when thinking of a book or a person), dualistic appearances for nonconceptual consciousnesses, and nonexistents that still seem to appear clearly (such as purple mice when drunk). The latter (Tib. mtshan nyid chad pa'i kun brtags) refers to sheer mental imputations of what does not exist at all in any way, such as a truly existent self or external material substances.

420 The Tibetan of OED mistakenly repeats here the above passage "are not at all established as having the natures of such [referents] . . . In brief, it consists of names and causal features."

421 XI.38. The causal features of appearances and their latent tendencies are presented as the imaginary nature, because they are the bases for imputing names and the causes for these features to appear, respectively. The actual essence of the imaginary nature is only what is stated in the third line of this verse—mere appearances being made into names and reference points.

422 OED has *'di lta bu'o*, which can only be a corruption of *'di bum pa'o* (given the preceding phrase "a round belly and so on," which represents the classical Tibetan way of presenting the characteristics of a vase).

423 XI.39. The objects of false imagination are the misconception of referents as if they existed just as they are labeled, and the misconception of names as existing in the same way as the referents they label.

424 XI.41. According to Vasubandhu's *Bhāṣya*, the defining characteristics of the perfect nature are threefold. The perfect nature is suchness, which is the nonexistence of all imaginary phenomena and exists in the sense of them being nonexistent. The equality of this existence and nonexistence means that they are not different. Its (seeming) lack of peace occurs through adventitious afflictions, and its (fundamental) peace is by virtue of it being natural purity. Nonconceptuality means that it is not the sphere of conceptions.

425 I.14–15.

426 V.13cd–14ab. The detailed explanation of these ten areas to be investigated and resolved through the prajñā cultivated during the meditation of superior insight follows in verses 14cd–22. According to Mipham Rinpoche's commentary on the *Madhyāntavibhāga* ('Ju mi pham rgya mtsho c. 1990c, 756–57), the ten kinds of unmistakenness are about (1) letters as the means of expression (being comprehensible only by virtue of their being properly connected and the listener/reader being familiar with such connections), (2) the meaning to be expressed (the imaginary being without a nature of its own), (3) mental engagement in the fact that the cause of dualistic appearances is mere other-dependent cognizance, (4) not straying into the two extremes by virtue of realizing that, just as illusions, phenomena appear in a dualistic manner, but are not real, (5) the specific characteristic—the perfect nature free from apprehender and apprehended, (6) the general characteristic of phenomena—the realization that all phenomena do not go beyond the true reality of being empty of duality, (7) purity and impurity derive from realizing and not realizing true reality, (8) the realization that purity and impurity appear, but are adventitious, because the true nature is pure in character, (9) no aversion toward accomplishing the decrease of afflicted phenomena, because they are primordially pure, and (10) lacking arrogance resulting from excellent qualities, because there is no increase of purified phenomena.

427 These three are divisions of the twelve links of dependent origination: (a) the afflictedness of afflictions consists of ignorance, craving, and grasping, (b) the afflictedness of karma consists of karmic formations and becoming, and (c) the afflictedness of birth consists of the remaining seven links. According to Mipham Rinpoche's commentary on the *Madhyāntavibhāga* V.24c ('Ju mi pham rgya mtsho c. 1990c, 769–70), (a) has three further aspects: view, the three main afflictions (ignorance, hatred, and desire), and striving for rebirth. Their respective remedies are emptiness, signlessness, and wishlessnes. (b) means committing virtuous and nonvirtuous deeds. The remedy for this is not committing any such deeds. (c) also has three aspects. The first one is rebirth in a further existence. The second one means that, after having been reborn until death, primary minds and mental factors arise in each moment. The third one is the continuum of being reborn, that is, the processes of dying, being alive, and being in the intermediate state. Their respective remedies are to realize the nonexistence of birth, arising, and any nature.

428 This paragraph is a summary of *Mahāyānasaṃgraha* II.2–3. The other-dependent nature—false imagination or mere cognizance—expresses itself in eleven forms: (1) refers to the five sense faculties (the first five inner dhātus), (2) refers to the afflicted mind, (3) is

mentation (the sixth inner dhātu), (4) are the six external objects (the six outer dhātus), (5) are the six consciousnesses (the dhātus of consciousness), (6) refers to the stream of saṃsāra being uninterrupted, (7) is the perception of numbers, (8) is the perception of the outer world, (9) means speech that uses conventional terms which refer to what is seen, heard, felt, and known, (10) refers to views about a self, "mine," and others, and (11) are the different ways in which all six kinds of beings manifest. As outlined above, the three types of latent tendencies are the respective causes of these eleven sets, which are all just various modulations (Skt. pariṇāma) of mind, without any of them existing as something other than mind.

429 These two lines are found in both his *Pramāṇavārttika* (III. 283ab) and *Pramāṇaviniścaya* (I.32ab).

430 Verses 37–38.

431 Verse 9.

432 VI.4cd.

433 Verse 35.

434 Verse 4.

435 XI.34.

436 Verse 20.

437 Lines 21ab.

438 Lines 21cd–22.

439 Verse 28.

440 The following section is a summary of pp. 516.4–526.3.

441 Pp. 520.6–526.3 (in a more classical format, these four steps are explained again on pp. 585.2–587.3). This section also includes an example for seemingly common appearances (521.3–4): Two people both dream about a golden vase and when they wake up, there seems to be a common color and shape of this vase, and a common sense of referring to me and mine. This is called "seemingly common."

442 Pp. 525.5–526.2.

443 I.21–22ab.

444 Lines 14cd–15.

445 This section is pp. 526.6–528.1.

446 This section is pp. 528.1–529.2.

447 II.32 (P5549, fol. 24b.1).

448 Note that the *Mahāyānasaṃgraha* above only says that the imaginary nature is not observed and that the perfect nature is observed. However, as OED explained several times before (in perfect harmony with many Indian Yogācāra texts), the other-dependent nature is unreal and a part of the obscurations. Also, mere cognizance (*vijñaptimātra*) is not the same as the other-dependent nature. By definition, the latter entails apprehender and apprehended, while the former is often explained as standing for nondual pure awareness without apprehender and apprehended, that is, nonconceptual wisdom as one of the two aspects of the perfect nature. Thus, there is no problem in saying that both the imaginary and the other-

dependent are not seen in such nonconceptual wisdom, while the nature of phenomena, or suchness, as the other aspect of the perfect nature is seen.

449 P. 552.4.

450 P. 553.5–6. In due order, the four phases correspond to the paths of preparation, seeing, and familiarization, and the vajralike samādhi.

451 This section is pp. 555.1–556.3.

452 XIII.18–19.

453 Verses 36–37.

454 Part 2, IV.69.

455 This section is pp. 562.5–563.1.

456 VIII.21 (P5549, fol. 41a.8–b.1).

457 This section is a paraphrasing summary of pp. 564.4–566.5.

458 In this text (D142), the first and fourth characteristics are called "nature" (Skt. prakṛti; indicating the five skandhas as what is to be relinquished) and "attainment" (Skt. prāpti), respectively (see also NTC, NYC, and DSC). It says that bodhisattvas have to gradually relinquish all four characteristics on the path in order to enter the sphere of nonconceptuality.

459 These are mastery over nonconceptuality, pure buddha realms, wisdom, and activity, which are attained on the eighth, ninth, and tenth bhūmis, respectively (see NY, lines 122–133).

460 The next paragraph is a paraphrasing summary of pp. 570.2–574.2.

461 This section is pp. 577.2–578.6.

462 In due order, this means that (1) nonconceptual wisdom is not just the mere absence of any mental engagement. Otherwise, being asleep, drunk, or just absent-minded would qualify as such wisdom too. Rather, in this wisdom's direct seeing of the true nature of phenomena, all reference points have vanished. Thus, since there is no reference point on the object side for it to engage in anymore, on the subject side, any mental engagement in such reference points naturally subsides. This does not mean, however, that this wisdom lacks wakefulness and one-pointed sharp mindfulness. It is also not without any cognitive capacity, since it directly and nondually realizes the nature of phenomena, that is, without a split into perceiver and perceived. (2) Nonconceptual wisdom is not just a state without any coarse or subtle conceptual analysis, since this likewise applies to all mundane meditative states from the second dhyāna of the form realm onward. (3) "The cessation of discrimination and feeling" (Skt. saṃjñāveditanirodha, Tib. 'du shes dang tshor ba 'gog pa) is another name of the meditative absorption of cessation. It is a more advanced state than any of the eight meditative absorptions of the form and formless realms, but it is not nonconceptual wisdom, since it is devoid of any active types of consciousness, and thus of corresponding mental factors (wisdom or prajñā being considered a mental factor), just as there are no light rays without the sun. (4) Nonconceptual wisdom is not something like matter, which simply lacks conceptions by its very nature. (5) This means completely letting go of all discursiveness and reference points, in particular with regard to true reality, such as trying to pinpoint a certain meditative experience, thinking, "This is nonconceptuality." Naturally, this means not just a state of trying not to think or imagine anything either, since such is just another subtle thought or grasping. These five aspects to be excluded are also found in other Yogācāra texts, such as Asaṅga's

Mahāyānasaṃgraha VIII.2 (P5549, fols. 39b.5–40a.1; for a translation of this chapter, see Brunnhölzl 2007a, 35–42).

463 This section is a paraphrasing summary of pp. 605.1–608.4.

464 This section is pp. 610.5–613.1.

465 This is followed by the classical nine examples found in the *Tathāgatagarbhasūtra* and *Uttaratantra* I.95cd–152 (such as a buddha statue in a withering lotus) for buddha nature being obscured by adventitious stains. These correspond to increasingly subtler obscurations and the respective natural qualities of buddha nature that are revealed (for details, see Arya Maitreya 2000, 148–73).

466 I.154–55.

467 The last sentence corresponds to an almost identical passage in Asaṅga's *Ratnagotravibhāgavyākhyā* on these two verses (P5526, fol. 118b.4–5). As for the emptiness endowed with the supreme of all aspects, "aspects" indicate all its excellent remedial qualities, such as the six pāramitās. Thus, it is both emptiness and that which makes one attain unsurpassable buddhahood. Another way to understand this expression is that it refers to the inseparability of appearance and emptiness, or luminosity and emptiness. ZDKT (p. 329; copied in ZDC, p. 183) says, "Here, my guru, the mighty victor [Chötra Gyatso] holds the following. Since the emptiness endowed with the supreme of all aspects and the Sugata heart are equivalent, being endowed with the supreme of all aspects refers to the Sugata heart being actually endowed with the sixty-four qualities of freedom and maturation, and the meaning of emptiness is that this is not established as anything identifiable or as any characteristics. Therefore, he asserts that making it a living experience—cultivating this lucid yet nonconceptual [state]—is Mahāmudrā meditation."

468 P. 613.3–4.

469 This is a partial translation of Rang byung rdo rje 2006f , 37–40.

470 The last two lines could also be understood as "[For] yogins who realize these to be one, everything is the three kāyas and five wisdoms."

471 Tib. rdzogs pa. This can mean "complete" or "perfect," and both seem to apply here, as this refers to Dzogchen, the "great perfection."

472 Tib. blo 'das, lit. "beyond [ordinary] states of mind."

473 This is a partial translation of Rang byung rdo rje 2006d, 101.

474 This is a translation of Rang byung rdo rje 2006e.

475 This echoes the two opening verses of Nāgārjuna's *Mūlamadhyamakakārikā*.

476 The text has *ming yang gzugs* (em. to *ming dang gzugs*).

477 The text has "impure" (*dag ma yin*), which seems not to make any sense, especially when considering what follows.

478 The last two lines almost literally correspond to *Madhyāntavibhāga* I.16cd.

479 The text has *'di 'ong*; one would rather expect *'gro 'ong*.

480 These five examples for the skandhas are found in *Saṃyutta Nikāya* III.141–42.

481 The last two verses describe the fourfold application of mindfulness of body, feelings, mind, and phenomena (the first set of four among the thirty-seven dharmas concordant with enlightenment).

482 This verse speaks about the second and third set of four among the thirty-seven dharmas. These first three sets correspond to the lesser, medium, and greater path of accumulation, respectively. As for the four correct exertions, while *prahāṇa* can mean either "relinquishment" or "exertion," it is always rendered as the former in Tibetan (*spong ba*). However, here, the term clearly refers to four activities in which one exerts effort.

483 The five faculties correspond to the first two phases of the path of preparation (heat and peak), and the five powers to the latter two (poised readiness and supreme mundane dharma). In due order, coarse conceptions about the apprehended and the apprehender are relinquished.

484 These are perfect mindfulness, prajñā, vigor, joy, complete suppleness, samādhi, and equanimity. Together, they refer to the path of seeing.

485 The last six lines on the eightfold path of the noble ones refer to the path of familiarization.

486 These are the "three doors to liberation" (Skt. vimokṣadvāra, Tib. rnam par thar pa'i sgo). In brief, the nature of phenomena is emptiness; causes lack any signs or defining characteristics; and the appearance of results is not bound to expectations or wishes.

487 Skt. pratisaṃvedanā, Tib. so so yang dag par rig pa. These are usually presented as a set of four. (1) The discriminating awareness of the dharma is to teach the eighty-four thousand doors of dharma as various remedial means in accordance with the different ways of thinking of sentient beings. (2) The discriminating awareness of meaning is to know the meanings that are expressed by the words and statements about the general characteristics of phenomena (impermanence, suffering, emptiness, and identitylessness) and their ultimate characteristic (the lack of arising and ceasing). (3) The discriminating awareness of semantic explanation (Skt. nirukti, Tib. nges tshig) is not to be ignorant about any of all beings' designations and languages as well as their meanings. (4) The discriminating awareness of self-confidence (Skt. pratibhāna, Tib. spobs pa) is to be unobstructed in teaching the dharma and cutting through doubts.

488 Tib. ka rma lha steng. This is a monastery in eastern Tibet founded by the First Karmapa in 1185.

489 This is a translation of an untitled song in Rang byung rdo rje 1983, fols. 97.5–98.5.

490 The entire outline of NTC is actually Rangjung Dorje's own outline of NT (Rang byung rdo rje 2006c).

491 Based on *tathāgata* being rendered *de bzhin gshegs pa* in Tibetan, its hermeneutical etymology as presented here in NTC differs slightly from the Sanskrit, with *de bzhin* being split up and taken as "that" (*de*) and "as it is" (*bzhin*) (while *tathā*—"thus"—is just a single word). Still, the overall explanation in NTC corresponds to the meaning of the Sanskrit term as explained above.

492 Tib. 'brel sgra. This refers to the particle for the sixth case in Tibetan, here referring to the genitive in "heart *of* a Tathāgata."

493 This explanation of "treatise" (*śāstra*) follows both the Sanskrit (*śās* meaning "teaching," "correcting," "controlling," and *trā* "protecting") and Tibetan (*bstan* meaning "teaching,"

and *bcos* "restoring"). It is based on a verse quoted in Vasubandhu's *Vyākhyāyukti* (P5562, fol. 143a.4) and Candrakīrti's *Prasannapadā* (ed. La Vallée Poussin, 3.3–4):

> What corrects the enemies of the afflictions without exception
> And protects from existences in lower realms
> Is a treatise by virtue of the qualities of correcting and protecting.
> These two [qualities] do not exist in other systems.

For an explanation of the term *śāstra* in relation to consciousness and wisdom, see the beginning of NYC.

494 From a Buddhist point of view, as presented in Asaṅga's *Viniścayasaṃgrahaṇī* (P5539, fol. 205a.3–7), there are six types of specious and three kinds of proper treatises. The former include meaningless ones (on topics such as whether crows have teeth), those with wrong meanings (from a Buddhist perspective, such as discussing an eternal soul), treatises on cheating others, heartless ones (such as on warfare or killing animals), and those that mainly focus on study or debate. Proper treatises are meaningful ones (in a Buddhist sense), those that lead to relinquishing suffering, and those that mainly focus on practice.

495 Traditionally, in Tibetan Buddhist texts (translated from Sanskrit or indigenous), the opening homage indicates to which one among the three scriptural collections (Skt. piṭaka, Tib. sde snod) of the sūtrayāna—sūtra, vinaya, or abhidharma—a work belongs. Paying homage to the buddhas and bodhisattvas (as above) shows that a text belongs to the category of sūtra, because this category is primarily related to the training in samādhi, and both buddhas and bodhisattvas know and engage in it. Paying homage to the Buddha alone indicates the category of the vinaya, since it is related to the training in ethics, and only a buddha can fully understand all the implications and reasons for this codex of discipline. Paying homage to Mañjuśrī refers to the category of the abhidharma, since it is related to the training in prajñā, which is embodied by Mañjuśrī.

496 The Sanskrit word *buddha* ("awake," "realized," "intelligent," "wise," "unfolded") is explained here through the two syllables of its Tibetan rendering (*sangs* meaning "purified" or "awakened," and *rgyas* "unfolded").

497 In Sanskrit, *bodhi* means "realization," "awakening," or "enlightenment," and *sattva* has many meanings (the most important ones here are "a being," "disposition of mind," "spiritual essence," "(strength of) character," "courage," "resolution," "magnanimity"). In Tibetan, this is translated as *byang chub sems dpa'*, with *byang chub* meaning "purified and realized" and *sems dpa'* "brave mind." Thus, bodhisattvas are those who have given rise to bodhicitta, the mental disposition of having enough courage and magnanimity for the resolve of setting their minds solely on the goal of buddhahood for the sake of all sentient beings. The bravery of this lies in being neither afraid of the infinite number of sentient beings to be liberated, nor the infinite time it takes to liberate them, nor the great hardships one has to go through in order to help these beings.

498 There are two kinds of bodhicitta—relative and ultimate. Here, the latter is meant, being an equivalent of the true nature of the mind, dharmadhātu, emptiness and so on.

499 These are the five sense consciousnesses and the mental consciousness.

500 The *Abhidharmasūtra* is frequently quoted in Indian and Tibetan texts, but not preserved in any language. The Sanskrit of the above verses is, for example, found in Asaṅga's *Ratnagotravibhāgavyākhyā* (J 37.6 and 72.13), though not attributed to any particular text. The

second verse is explicitly attributed to the *Abhidharmasūtra* in other sources, but apart from NTC's attribution here, so far, I could not find such an attribution for the first verse.

501 Since both NT and NY are written in meter, but not in actual four-line verses, the numbers in "[ ]" simply indicate the lines of the text (not considering the title and the above line of paying homage).

502 Most Tibetan commentators on this verse gloss its first line as pertaining to saṃsāra, which makes sense. Note however, that the first line in the Sanskrit (*anādibhūto 'pi hi cāvasānikaḥ*) clearly pertains to what is said in the second one (*svabhāvaśuddho dhruvadharmasaṃhitaḥ*), thus indicating that what is beginningless and yet entails an end is that which is naturally pure and so on (the dharmadhātu). In terms of the meaning, there is no difference, since "end" can only mean the end of the obscurations in relation to the naturally pure and unchanging dharmadhātu.

503 NTKY glosses this as "stains that are connate ignorance."

504 The two other kinds of enlightenment are the arhathoods of śrāvakas and pratyekabuddhas.

505 *Uttaratantra* I.55a (for the full quote of I.55–57, see AC, chapter 1 above).

506 Verse 17. Buddha nature is also described as a seed in the sixth of the nine examples in the *Tathāgatagarbhasūtra* (D258, fols. 252a.1–b.3) and *Uttaratantra* I.115–117.

507 Part 2, IV.69.

508 I.16.

509 Verses 18–19.

510 This passage on the five obscurations is almost literally taken from DSC (fol. 14b; see Brunnhölzl 2007b, 230), which adds that, consequently, the luminosity of sentient beings is not seen. In order to make it clearly manifest, it is to be realized through studying, reflecting, and meditating on the manner in which all phenomena are dependent origination.

511 NTKD glosses this as the time of mind itself being ignorant about or unaware of itself. According to NTKY, the end refers to the point when mind recognizes its own face or essence.

512 As it stands, this quote is not found in any of Nāgārjuna's texts. The first three lines resemble verse 60 his *Bodhicittavivaraṇa*, while the last two are almost literally lines 63ab.

513 NTKD glosses this as bearing these qualities through its own characteristic—its changeless essence.

514 In general, *dhātu* (Tib. khams) is defined as, "That which bears its own defining characteristics."

515 This term, found in both the *Śrīmālādevīsūtra* and the *Uttaratantra* (I.138 and III.34), is an equivalent of the ālaya, remainders of which are even present in arhathood (personal nirvāṇa) and on the ten bhūmis of bodhisattvas.

516 I.57 (see also above). The Eighth Karmapa's JNS (vol. 1, pp. 215–16) says the following on this: "The explanation in the *Uttaratantra* that these [phenomena] rest on or are supported by the [following ones] is merely a presentation from a conventional perspective that, with the intention that all phenomena are emptiness, they are suitable to arise, suitable to appear, and [may relate as] support and supported. That the nature of the mind—or the unconditioned dhātu free from stains—could be supported by or rest on another phenomenon is primordially

impossible. Therefore, it is neither justified that the very dharmadhātu supports something else, nor that the dharmadhātu itself is supported by something else. Furthermore, [*Uttaratantra* I.56–57] speak explicitly only of a being supported by or resting on the purity of mind, but they do not explain a being supported by the nature of the mind, the dhātu without stains. To identify 'the purity of mind' in this context as the dharmadhātu is not necessarily correct. Since the mind that is improper mental engagement never existed in this way, it does not change into something other than just its pure mode of being. Hence, this is the meaning of 'resting.'"

517 Lines 25–28 echo *Madhyāntavibhāga* I.1.

518 Lines 29–30 echo *Dharmadharmatāvibhāga* lines 24–27 and *Mahāyānasūtrālaṃkāra* VI.4cd.

519 Verse 24.

520 Verse 46.

521 I.60–61ab.

522 NTKD comments, "Since objects are the appearances of your own mind, through not desiring and rejecting them, where should they cease?"

523 NTKD glosses this as "the remedy for clinging thoughts."

524 IX.139cd–140.

525 The *Ratnakūṭa* is a large collection of sūtras in the *Tengyur*, one of them being the *Kāśyapaparivarta*, from which this quote stems (NTC cites only the first sentence).

526 XXIV.11ab.

527 XIII.8 (the last line in NTC reads "are incurable").

528 VI.8.

529 IX.32. Pawo Rinpoche Tsugla Trengwa's commentary on the *Bodhicaryāvatāra* (Dpa' bo gtsug lag phreng ba n.d., 675–76) explains this and the following verse ("Once this 'utter nonexistence'—the entity to be determined—cannot be observed, how should a nonentity without a basis remain before the mind?") as follows: "One should cultivate the discriminating notion that all phenomena are illusionlike. Once one is familiar with this [notion], [phenomena] will not even be observed as mere illusions [but] will be seen as empty aspects. **Through familiarity with the latent tendencies of emptiness, the latent tendencies of entities**—which apprehend all such varieties as the same and different—**will be relinquished.** All phenomena will be seen as nothing at all. You might wonder, 'Is this very "utter nonexistence" the ultimate?' Also this ['utter nonexistence'] is just some kind of discriminating notion, [a step in] a remedial sequence. However, it is not the perfect nature [itself], because it does not even abide as this very 'utter nonexistence.' Venerable Nāgārjuna [said] in [verse 23 of his] *Lokātītastava*:

> In order to relinquish all imagination,
> You taught the nectar of emptiness.
> However, those who cling to it
> Are blamed by you as well.

Nevertheless, this laxative of seeing nothing at all is applied as the remedy for the disease of apprehending reference points, [which exists] in sentient beings who are in trouble merely because of these reference points. **Utter nonexistence**, such as attaining something or not attaining it, being bound or being released, seeing or not seeing, means seeing [emptiness] as the aspect that is the extinction of all reference points. **Through** becoming increasingly accustomed to and **familiar with** exactly this [notion of utter nonexistence], **this** cognition that apprehends utter nonexistence **will be relinquished later on too.** Through one's seeing all phenomena as illusionlike, the reification that is entailed in the conception of reality is reversed. Then, even **this 'utter** and complete **nonexistence'**—the very nonexistence that is **the entity to be determined** [here]—**cannot be observed. Once** [such is the case,] all phenomena do not exist as any entities or nonentities whatsoever, and there is freedom from all flux of discriminating notions, such as [notions] about a basis and something based on it. However, **how should** even this firewoodlike entity—**a** mere **nonentity without a basis—remain before the** immaculate prajñā of true reality that is a **mind** similar to the conflagration at the end of time? Once the firewood is consumed, the fire also subsides on its own. Likewise, also this very mind of immaculate prajñā subsides in this way within the expanse of true reality, which is always at peace in that it is the very nature of primordial nonarising and nonceasing."

530 *Dohākośopadeśagīti* ("Queen Dohā"), lines 21–22.

531 Lines 48–49 summarize *Yuktiṣaṣṭikā*, verse 45.

532 Part 2, III.36.

533 I.51cd.

534 I.157.

535 For the answers of the Eighth Karmapa to the claim that *Uttaratantra* I.157 proves the teachings on buddha nature to be of expedient meaning, see Brunnhölzl 2004, 488ff.

536 The emptiness referred to here is emptiness in the sense of a nonimplicative negation, which can by definition be ascertained only through inferential valid cognition. This means that it appears in the minds of ordinary beings, belongs only to seeming reality, and is thus very much unlike the actual emptiness that is directly perceived by the yogic valid perception of noble ones. In other words, to claim that a conceptual object—the absence of real existence through the negation of real existence—is the fully qualified ultimate means simply to confuse the pointing finger with the moon to which it points. Since a nonimplicative negation, by definition, cannot appear to any kind of nonconceptual perception (not even of ordinary beings), how could it possibly appear for the wisdom minds of noble ones or a buddha, in whom even the most subtle reference points have vanished?

537 Verse 22.

538 Lines 60–64 are a condensation of *Uttaratantra* III.5–6, which compares the ten powers to a vajra, since they are indestructible and very powerful, eliminating the ignorance of both oneself and others.

539 This means to know that nonvirtue leads to unpleasant karmic maturations and never to pleasant ones.

540 Skt. adhyāśaya, Tib. lhag pa'i bsam pa. This is a term for the superior altruistic attitude of bodhisattvas, indicating that they have solely the welfare of others in mind. They do so in the same spontaneous and heartfelt intensity in which ordinary beings usually strive for their own well-being. This attitude is said to be the immediate prerequisite for the arising of uncontrived genuine bodhicitta.

541 This is brief for "the knowledge of termination and nonarising" (Skt. kṣayānutpattijñāna, Tib. zad dang mi skye shes pa), which means to realize that and how one's own karma and afflictions have been utterly exhausted and will never arise again.

542 The Sanskrit term *vaiśāradya* (translated as "fearlessness" into Tibetan) literally means self-confidence (also skill, expertise, wisdom, infallibility).

543 Lines 65–67 echo *Uttaratantra* III.8, which compares the four fearlessnesses to a lion's intrepidity in the midst of all other animals.

544 Lines 68–77 correspond to *Uttaratantra* III.11–13, which compares the eighteen unique qualities to space, since it is unique in that it, unlike the other four elements (earth, water, fire, and wind), is never mixed with any of them and shares none of their attributes.

545 During standing, walking, sitting, and lying, buddhas are completely free from any flaws in their physical, verbal, and mental conduct, whereas even arhats may sometimes bump into something or step on a snake. Some are reported to have yelled after women, guffawing with laughter. Udāyin still had some attachment and preferred to teach dharma in the neighborhood brothel. Nanda used to stare at the women in the audience when giving a dharma talk. High-caste Mahākāśyapa could not rid himself of habitual snobbery and—despite his renown for ascetism—could not help jigging to a tune because of his former lives spent as a monkey. Gavāmpati—because of his many lifetimes as an ox—habitually regurgitated his food to chew the cud. Madhuvasiṣṭha—another ex-monkey—could not resist climbing walls and trees. There are also stories about a pratyekabuddha—who had been a courtesan in past lives—still dressing like a coquette. As for being in constant meditative equipoise, even bodhisattvas on the ten bhūmis rise from their samādhis between their meditation sessions.

546 NTKY glosses this as examining which beings are suitable to be guided or not.

547 NTKY glosses this as (effortless vigor) without having to think about the welfare of those to be guided.

548 Buddhas are always aware of which beings are to be guided, knowing the exact place, time, and manner to do so.

549 These refer to the sixty aspects of Brahmā's melodious voice, which include being gentle, pleasant, clear, worthy to listen to, understandable by all, pervasive, making everything known, having the force of a lion's roar, and resounding within any kind of retinue. For details, see the *Mahāvyutpatti* (sec. 20, nos. 445–504, which are explained in detail in Abhayākaragupta's *Munimatālaṃkāra*).

550 This means that all physical, verbal, and mental actions of buddhas are purposeful in that they serve, in one way or the other, as means to guide certain beings. In other words, buddhas never act, speak, or think in any meaningless or nonbeneficial ways.

551 "Unattached and unhindered" usually refer to being free from afflictive and cognitive obscurations, respectively.

552 The last sentence contains the reason why these thirty-two qualities are called the "qualities of freedom." They are inseparable from buddha nature even at the time of sentient beings, but obscured by adventitious stains. Once they are freed from these stains, they become clearly manifest.

553 NTKD adds "as the dualistic appearances of apprehender and apprehended."

554 VI.4cd (NTC only quotes the last line).

555 In other words, through being unaware of the perfect nature due to ignorance (or false imagination), seemingly outer and inner appearances (the duality of apprehender and apprehended), afflictions, and karmic actions appear, all of which are the other-dependent nature.

These mere appearances are then labeled, clung to, and reified, thinking they are really existent, inside, outside, good or bad. The labeling mind itself is also part of the other-dependent nature, while all the notions and labels it produces are the imaginary nature.

556 Lines 11–12ab.

557 Lines 91–98 correspond to *Uttaratantra* I.154–55.

558 P36, fol. 34a.6–7. To provide a bit more of the context of these three lines in said tantra, the lines immediately preceding and following them are as follows:

> Once identitylessness in phenomena is realized
> Mind will be realized.
> Everything is filled with the flavor of being empty—
> This is called "mahāsukhakāya."
>
> It is prajñāpāramitā—
> In this, there is nothing to be removed
> And not the slightest to add on.
> Who sees true reality is released.
>
> Be it a single disposition, three dispositions,
> Five dispositions, a hundred dispositions and so on,
> In this true reality, there is no difference.
>
> Once you have found an ox,
> You don't search for the traces of that ox.
> Likewise, if you have found the true reality of mind,
> You don't search for any thoughts at all.

The last four lines also represent a very common example in the Mahāmudrā tradition. Obviously, the above three lines quoted in NTC correspond to *Uttaratantra* I.154.abd. The full verse represents one of the most famous and often cited stanzas in the literature of the mahāyāna. Gampopa's *Ornament of Liberation* (Sgam po pa 1990, 289) says that it is found in the *Gaganagañjaparipṛcchāsūtra* (P815). The verse is one of the most essential in both the *Uttaratantra* and the *Abhisamayālaṃkāra* (V.21). To my knowledge, there are at least nine more works in which it appears: Buddhaghoṣa's *Sumaṅgalavisāraṇī* I.12 (in Pāli; attributes the contents to the Buddha); Nāgārjuna's *Kāyatrayastotranāmasyavivaraṇa* (P2016, fol. 83a.7) and *Pratītyasamutpādahṛdayakārikā* (P5467, verse 7; some hold that it does not belong to the original Sanskrit stanzas, being added later, but it is found in this text as it appears in the Tibetan canon as well as in an eighth-century Tibetan manuscript from Dunhuang [PT 769]); Aśvaghoṣa's *Saundarananda* (paraphrase XIII.44) and *Śuklavidarśana* (a summary of the *Śālistambasūtra* that begins with this verse); Nāgamitra's *Kāyatrayāvatāramukha* (paraphrase verse 106); Sthiramati's *Madhyāntavibhāgaṭīkā* (P5534, fol. 36a.5); the *Nāmasaṃgītiṭīkā* ad VI.5 (which attributes it to Nāgārjuna); the *Bodhisattvabhūmi* (Wogihara ed., 48; prose); and the *Mahāyānaśraddhotpāda* (Suzuki's trans., 57; prose).

559 NTC has *rnam par byung ba*, but NTKD has the correct *rnam par byang ba*.

560 III.17–25.

561 VIII.13–17.

562 The source for the enumeration in the *Uttaratantra* is the *Ratnādārikāparipṛcchasūtra*, which also includes some of the minor marks. The sources for the list in the *Abhisamayālaṃkāra* (VIII.21–32) are the prajñāpāramitā sūtras. Nāgārjuna's *Ratnāvalī* (II.77–96) gives basically

the same list as the *Abhisamayālaṃkāra*. For a detailed comparison of these sources, including Nāgārjuna's * *Mahāprajñāpāramitāśāstra*, see the footnotes in Takasaki 1966 on the translation of the *Uttaratantra*'s above-mentioned verses. For the most detailed presentation of the major marks, see the *Lakkhaṇasutta* (*Dīgha Nikāya* III.142ff; trans. in Walshe 1995, 441–60), the *Arthaviniścayasūtra* (Samtani 2002, 205–16; which however lists thirty-three), and the prajñāpāramitā sūtras (Conze 1975, 657–61 and 583–85). See also the *Mahāvyutpatti* (sec. 17, nos. 236–67; trans. in Thurman 1997, 156); Pawo Tsugla Trengwa's commentary on the *Bodhicaryāvatāra* (Dpa' bo gtsug lag phreng ba n.d., 720–23); and TOK (vol. 3, pp. 619–22; except for minor differences in counting, this corresponds to the *Uttaratantra*).

563 In different texts, there are sometimes considerable variations in the list of the minor marks. Besides the above-mentioned, see Conze 1975, 661–65; Samtani 2002, 217–18; *Mahāvyutpatti* (sec. 18, nos. 269–349); Dpa' bo gtsug lag phreng ba n.d., 723–26; and TOK (vol. III, pp. 622–25). All of the major and minor marks are called "qualities of maturation," because they appear only as the results of having practiced the path of bodhisattvas.

564 Lines 102–4 almost literally correspond to NY lines 8–11.

565 Lines X.1–2.

566 Skt. antarābhava, Tib. bar do. These are the intermediate states of dying, dharmatā, and becoming (being in the process of approaching a new birth). During these states, one has a mental body, which is similar to how one experiences having a body in dreams.

567 Line II.7.

568 IX.41.

569 For the progressive numbers of these qualities, see NYC on NT lines 147–154.

570 IX.75.

571 Verse 48.

572 X.5 (D4048, fol. 38a.4–5). "The invisible mark" is the uṣṇīṣa on a buddha's head.

573 Part 2, II.41.

574 The causes of the major and minor marks are also discussed in the prajñāpāramitā sūtras (Conze 1975, 659–64), the commentaries on *Abhisamayālaṃkāra* VIII.13–32, and Nāgārjuna's *Ratnāvalī* II.77–96.

575 Introduction, line 5.

576 Lines II.133–36.

577 NTC *bsnyen par rdzogs pa*. AC has "complete realization" (*rtogs par rdzogs pa*), but "ordination" seems to fit better with the next two entries. Among the other available commentaries on ZMND, ZDC and Tagramba's commentary are the only ones that quote this passage from AC, but the entry in question is missing. Karma Trinlépa's commentary just quotes similar passages from the tantras, where this entry is missing too. All others do not refer to it at all.

578 NTC has "recitation" (*bzlas pa*).

579 AC, pp. 85.3–86.1.

580 This is another name of Vārāṇasī, traditionally the place in India where the finest cloths and brocades are produced.

581 This example of cleansing a blue beryl as related to the dharmadhātu is found in the *Dhāraṇīśvararājasūtra* (P814, fol. 176bff.), which is also quoted in Asaṅga's *Ratnagotravibhāgavyākhyā* on I.2 (J 6) and Nāgārjuna's *Sūtrasamucchaya* (D3934, fols. 189b–190a). The example is also found in the *Daśabhūmikasūtra*.

582 The three spheres refer to the notions of agent, recipient, and action as being distinct entities.

583 These are the four applications of mindfulness, the four correct exertions, and the four limbs of miraculous powers on the lesser, medium, and greater stages of the path of accumulation, respectively.

584 These are the four stages of heat, peak, poised readiness, and supreme mundane dharma.

585 These are clinging to the characteristics of what is to be relinquished, remedies, suchness, and fruition (they are treated in the following lines 122–26). DSC also mentions these same four characteristics several times and likewise uses the example of the beryl, referring to the *Avikalpapraveśadhāraṇī* for both. As mentioned before, in the latter, the first and fourth characteristics are called "nature" (indicating the five skandhas as what is to be relinquished) and "attainment," respectively, while the example is that of a wish-fulfilling jewel instead of a beryl. However, as can be seen in AC quoted right below, this text simply equates the beryl with a wish-fulfilling jewel.

586 Verses 9–10.

587 I.25. For details on these four inconceivable points, see the translation of AC's introduction above.

588 AC, pp. 21.6–23.4.

589 Lines 129–32 correspond to *Uttaratantra* I.147.

590 Lines 134–35 correspond to *Uttaratantra* I.51cd (exchanging "nature of phenomena" for "buddha heart"), and also resemble *Mahāyānasūtrālaṃkāra* IX.22ac.

591 Buddhas do not only know the true nature of all phenomena, but they also have the altruistic motivation to share this liberating knowledge with all beings and are actually able to do so in many efficient ways.

592 Dedication, lines 80–81.

593 IX.22.

594 NTC has "understanding" (*shes pa*) here, but "certainty" (*nges pa*) in the corresponding heading below (as do Rangjung Dorje's own outline and NTKD).

595 Verse 16.

596 IX.37.

597 These are the ancient Indian hedonistic materialists know as Lokāyatas or Cārvākas. In an attempt to base their teachings on scriptural authority, they claimed that Bṛhaspati, the accomplished Indian guru of the gods and mythological founder of the philosophy of state, was also the founder of their school (he is said to have composed the *Bṛhaspatisūtra*, later propagated on earth by Vālmīki).

598 Skt. saṃskāra, Tib. 'du byed. In general, the term refers to forming, creating, or putting something together, in particular, various mental configurations, functions, or activities.

In ordinary beings, this refers to the momentary and dualistic movement of the mind in general, or, more specifically, to the fourth skandha (that is, the last forty-nine among the fifty-one mental factors). However, in a buddha's mind, it means the effortless flux of nonconceptual nondual wisdom operating for the sake of all beings.

599 Here, mentation primarily refers to the immediate mind, as explained in NYC and AC.

600 In terms of how they appear to beings, the continua of sambhogakāyas and nirmāṇakāyas are in themselves momentarily changing displays, and the mind streams of the beings who perceive them are momentarily changing as well. So, one aspect of the momentariness of the rūpakāyas is that their wisdom (especially its discriminating part) and their enlightened activities must entail movement and change in order to perceive countless different beings to be guided and perform beneficial functions for them. The other aspect is that, in order to be perceptible to the momentarily changing minds of beings, the rūpakāyas and their activities must be momentary too, because, by definition, it is not possible for a momentarily impermanent subject to perceive a permanent object.

601 As mentioned before, Hsüan-tsang's *Vijñaptimātratāsiddhi* (La Vallée Poussin 1928–48, 442) speaks about uncontaminated and contaminated mentation as referring to the minds of bodhisattvas when being engaged in, and rising from, meditative equipoise, respectively, with pure mentation being related to the wisdom of equality.

602 Lines VI.147–48. In the second line, NTC has "consciousnesses" (*rnam shes*) instead of "objects" (*yul rnams*), but ZDC has both (the former obviously being implied here).

603 D283, fol. 56b.6–8 (NTC has some variant readings in this passage).

604 In the vajrayāna, it is said that the actual natures of the above five sense objects are the five principal buddhas (Vairocana, Akṣobhya, Ratnasaṃbhava, Amitābha, and Amoghasiddhi), respectively, while the natures of the five elements (the above four plus space) are their five female consorts (Dhātvīśvarī, Māmakī, Locanā, Paṇḍaravāsinī, and Samayatārā). In the above order, the five buddhas also correspond to the five wisdoms—dharmadhātu wisdom, mirror-like wisdom, the wisdom of equality, discriminating wisdom, and all-accomplishing wisdom. For a detailed description, see Thrangu Rinpoche 2002, 88–91.

605 IX.43.

606 Verse 9.

607 Verse 54.

608 I could not locate this quote in the Sanskrit version of the sūtra.

609 Rangjung Dorje's own outline has *dgos pa* instead of *dgod pa*.

610 IV.29.

611 These examples are treated in great detail in *Uttaratantra* IV.13–98.

612 V.8cd (D13, fol. 5b.3).

613 I.8ab.

614 Verse 101. In ancient India, captains who set sail to retrieve precious jewels from the ocean or islands in it, thus becoming rich, are a very common theme. However, in most commentaries on the *Dharmadhātustava*, "variegated jewel" is taken to refer to a wish-fulfilling jewel.

615 In other words, if wisdom and kāyas were solely something in the mind streams of ordinary beings, they would lack the power to actually perform the liberating activities of the rūpakāyas (for more details on the rūpakāyas not just being appearances in the minds of beings, nor being made to appear by either the dharmakāya or previous aspiration prayers alone, see appendix 1).

616 This is an offshoot of the discussion of mirrorlike wisdom in NYC on NY, lines 110–14.

617 Lines 166–68 summarize *Uttaratantra* I.53–57 and 62.

618 NTC reads *'khrul pa'i snang ba ji snyed pa rnams kyi ye shes yul du* ... ("the appearances of the mistakenness of sentient beings appears as the object of the wisdom of [their] varieties, ..."; NTKD even has *kyis* in the above phrase, which is hard to make sense of). Since the above *kyi* and the resulting meaning is somewhat awkward, and in order to follow the words of NT more closely, the phrase is translated as above.

619 Verse 45.

620 I was unable to locate this quote in Āryadeva's nontantric texts.

621 IX.32.

622 IX.74

623 I.16cd.

624 IX.70cd–71.

625 Lines 180–82 correspond to *Mahāyānasūtrālaṃkāra* IX.66cd.

626 See NYC on NY line 141.

627 From the perspective of those to be guided, different nirmāṇakāyas, such as Buddha Śākyamuni, appear and disappear, but at any given time, there are always *some* nirmāṇakāyas somewhere, and their enlightened activities as a whole are considered to be a single uninterrupted continuum.

628 IX.66cd. *Uttaratantra* II.62–68 gives ten reasons why the three kāyas are permanent. The three reasons pertaining to the dharmakāya are that (1) the lord of death has been vanquished, (2) the nature of the dharmakāya is not the one of conditioned phenomena, and (3) it is the ultimate protector and refuge for all beings. The seven reasons pertaining to the rūpakāyas are (1) their causes, such as the two accumulations, are infinite, (2) the number of beings to be guided is infinite, (3) great loving-kindness and compassion always strive for the benefit of these beings, (4) due to their miraculous powers, they are able to remain for the sake of beings' benefit as long as saṃsāra lasts, (5) seeing the oneness of saṃsāra and nirvāṇa, there is no need for rejecting the one or adopting the other, (6) they are unassailable by saṃsāra's suffering due to constantly dwelling in blissful samādhi, and (7) having mastered all qualities, they are not sullied by any saṃsāric phenomena, such as karma and afflictions. Usually, as in the *Ornament of Liberation* (Sgam po pa 1990, 346–47), the feature of how the three kāyas are permament is presented together with two more features. Their feature of equality is that the dharmakāyas of all buddhas are equal, since their foundation—the dharmadhātu—is not different; the sambhogakāyas are equal, since their intention is not different; and the nirmāṇakāyas are equal, since they represent a common enlightened activity (*Mahāyānasūtrālaṃkāra* IX.66ab). The feature of appearance is that the dharmakāya, the sambhogakāya, and the nirmāṇakāya appear by virtue of the cognitive obscurations, the afflictive obscurations, and the karmic obscurations, respectively, of one's mind stream having become pure within the dharmadhātu.

629 See AC (1.3.2. Instruction on the four conditions).

630 Verse 24.

631 Verse 95.

632 In other words, the nirvāṇa of arhats is attained solely for their own well-being, and it is a formless meditative state of their personal freedom from saṃsāra, in which they are of no benefit to other beings. Unlike that, motivated by the bodhisattva vow, buddhahood is attained primarily for the welfare of all other beings, which finds its expression in the limitless compassion that gives rise to the rūpakāyas with their enlightened activities.

633 I could not locate the quote as it stands, but such statements are found in many texts (not only Yogācāra works). A similar passage in prose is found in Asaṅga's *Mahāyānasaṃgraha* VIII.21 and elaborated on in the commentaries by Vasubandhu and Asvabhāva. Also, the first two lines above are almost identical to *Abhisamayālaṃkāra* III.10ab.

634 These particular ways of birth, aging, sickness, and death are all based on the "ground of the latent tendencies of ignorance," which is still present in śrāvaka and pratyekabuddha arhats as well as bodhisattvas on the bhūmis. These issues are discussed in the *Śrīmālādevīsūtra* (Wayman and Wayman 1974, 82ff.), the *Uttaratantra* (I.80–83), and the *Ratnagotravibhāgavyākhyā* (J 33 and 54).

635 I.81–82.

636 NTC and NTKD have *kyi*.

637 II.210cd–211ab (NTC omits the first line).

638 Ibid., II.141ab (in the first line, NTC omits "about a self"). This objection is basically just the reverse of the preceding one. A traditional example is to first mistake a mottled rope for a snake, and then to indubitably identify it as a rope. Once the rope is recognized in an incontrovertible manner, the thought that it is a snake—which obscured that recognition—will not happen again.

639 I.112–113.

640 Lines 203–06 correspond to *Mahāyānasūtrālaṃkāra* IX.25.

641 As before, NTC glosses the two syllables—"clear away/awaken" and "unfold"—of the Tibetan word (*sangs rgyas*) for buddha separately.

642 Verses 2–3.

643 II.32.

644 Skt. aṣṭavimokṣa, Tib. rnam thar brgyad. (1) One looks at outer forms with the notion that inner consciousness possesses form, and then (2) one looks at outer forms with the notion that inner consciousness does not possesses form. (3) "The liberation of notions of beauty" means having manifested the nature of pleasure through the body, which remedies the afflictions of liking to emanate beautiful forms and not liking to emanate ugly forms. (4)–(7) The next four liberations are the four formless meditative absorptions, and (8) the last one is the meditative absorption of cessation.

645 This phrase or very similar ones are found in many texts, sūtras and tantras as well as Madhyamaka and Yogācāra. Examples include many places in the *Laṅkāvatārasūtra* and *Saṃdhinirmocanasūtra*; Nāgārjuna's *Kāyatrayastotra* (line 1d); Bhāvaviveka's *Prajñāpradīpa* (D3853, fols. 190a.3 and 269a.2); Candrakīrti's *Prasannapadā* (D3860, fol.

163b.4) and *Madhyamakāvatārabhāṣya* (D3862, fols. 255a.6 and 314b.2–3); Vasubandhu's *Dharmadharmatāvibhāgavṛtti* (D4028, fol. 32a.1); and throughout the *Uttaratantra* (lines I.7a, 9b, 17b, 70b, V.1d) and the *Ratnagotravibhāgavyākhya*.

646 This line paraphrases *Uttaratantra* I.153ab, which is quoted just below in NTC.

647 Rangjung Dorje's own outline says, "The manner of obtaining the buddha heart from prajñā, love, and compassion" (which are embodied by Mañjuśrī, Maitreya, and Avalokiteśvara, respectively).

648 Tib. 'jam dbyangs don grub 'od zer, better known as Trimkang Lotsāwa. A student of the great Indian paṇḍita Vanaratna (1385–1468), Gö Lotsāwa (1392–1481), and Goshrī Töndrub Öser (Tib. go shrī don grub 'od zer), he lived for forty-three years at Tsurphu and wrote an important commentary on Rangjung Dorje's ZMND. NTC seems to suggest that there existed a commentary on NY by this author, but none is preserved today.

649 Tib. ka rma ngag dbang yon tan rgya mtsho blo gros mtha' yas pa'i sde.

650 Tib. dpal spungs thub bstan chos 'khor gling. This is the main seat of the Tai Situpas near Dergé in Kham, where Jamgön Kongtrul Lodrö Tayé stayed in retreat for most of his life and wrote all his major texts.

651 Tib. mdo khams.

652 The physical appearance of youthfulness is taught to be a mark of spiritual attainment.

653 The three planes are those of humans and others who live upon the earth, gods who dwell above the earth, and the beings who abide below it.

654 As at the beginning of NTC, this explanation is based on the two syllables of the Sanskrit term *śāstra* for "treatise" (*śās* meaning "teaching," "correcting," "mending," and *tra* "protecting"). Thus, the purpose for writing this treatise is to facilitate the full realization of the nature of one's mind through remedying the eight kinds of consciousness (the adventitious stains) by demonstrating their seeming functions and ultimate lack of existence, and by sustaining the glimpses of the true nature of these consciousnesses so as to become an uninterrupted stream of wisdom mind.

655 Lines 5cd.

656 As at the beginning of NTC, the word *buddha* is explained through the two syllables of its Tibetan rendering (*sangs* meaning "purified" or "awakened", and *rgyas* "unfolded").

657 These are the afflictive and cognitive obscurations.

658 This refers to the two wisdoms of knowing suchness and variety.

659 This refers to liberation from saṃsāra, either as an arhat or a buddha.

660 VI.5ab.

661 Lines 7cd.

662 I.25 (D4048, fol. 7b.3).

663 XXXII.4 (D13, fol. 19b.3–4).

664 II.36.

665 D3924, fol. 81b.4 (however, the above quote is just a quote in that text too).

666 This is another large collection of sūtras.

667 In the mahāyāna, the preparation for meditation is to take refuge in the three jewels and give rise to bodhicitta; the main part, no matter which specific kind of meditation one engages in, is to cultivate it in a nonreferential manner; and the conclusion is to dedicate the merit derived from the former two stages for all sentient beings attaining buddhahood.

668 Lines 6–7 are of course well known from many Madhyamaka texts, such as *Mūlamadhyamakakārikā* I.1ab.

669 As mentioned above, lines 8–11 almost literally correspond to NT lines 102–4.

670 Skt. rajas, tamas, sattva; Tib. rdul, mun pa, snying stobs.

671 Skt. prakṛti, Tib. gtso bo.

672 As listed in *Madhyamakāvatāra* VI.121ab, the five characteristics of the self are being eternal in nature, the experiencer, without qualities, inactive, and not an agent.

673 Also known as Cārvākas, a school of hedonistic materialists in ancient India.

674 Tib. sgam po phyva (sometimes translated as "fortune").

675 The Sautrāntika model of perception attempts to bridge the gap between mind and matter left unexplained by the Vaibhāṣikas. This "gap" refers to the inability of consciousness to experience a material object directly, which is due to the fact that mind and matter are held to be mutually exclusive in their characteristics in Buddhism, and consequently cannot be said to interact with one another (see also NYC on NY lines 35–41). Thus, the Sautrāntikas assert that consciousness is able to experience an object only via a third party, called "aspect" (Skt. ākāra, Tib. rnam pa). Though such an "aspect" is an image of the material object, this image itself is said to be of a mental nature, thus supposedly explaining its capacity to meet with the apprehending consciousness. In the metaphor of "an image drawn in ashes," the ashes stand for the consciousness and the image drawn represents the "aspect." Thus, the object merely "draws" a pattern into the consciousness, which the consciousness then reflexively experiences. Needless to say, this explanation does not solve said perceptual gap between mind and matter, but just shifts it from the level of the relationship between an outer material object and consciousness to the level of the relationship between this object and the mental aspect it supposedly casts.

676 According to the Sautrāntikas, a specifically characterized phenomenon is defined as impermanent, conditioned, and existing as ultimate reality. Generally characterized phenomena (such as the objects of the thinking mind) bear the opposite characteristics.

677 Line 14 is of course well known from the *Laṅkāvatārasūtra*, the *Daśabhūmikasūtra*, and other texts. Lines 12–14 together echo the first two lines of the opening stanza of Kambala's *Ālokamālā*.

678 Lines 17, 20, and 21 closely resemble *Yuktiṣaṣṭikā* 45abc.

679 Chapter 6 (Rahder ed., 49).

680 D107, fol. 207a.5–7 (NYC omits lines 3–4).

681 Ibid., fol. 185b.3–4.

682 Lines 3cd.

683 NYC mistakenly has *ye shes snying po kun las btus pa* (*Jñānasārasamucchaya*), which does not contain the following quote (see AC, chap. 9 above).

684 The detailed presentation of the eight flaws that would be entailed if the two realities were either one or different is found in this sūtra's chapter 3, called "The Questions of Suviśuddhamati" (D107, fol. 10a–14b; for details, see Brunnhölzl 2004, 88–94). The verse above is that chapter's concluding verse (NYC gives only the first two lines).

685 Verse 59.

686 Lines 66–69.

687 NY *chos* (Rumtek blockpr. *ches*), NYC and NYKD *tshul.*

688 As mentioned in the introduction, this is one of the cases in which mentation stands for the sixth—the mental—consciousness (and not the seventh). In particular, here, it indicates mental valid perception of outer objects (as opposed to thinking, which is the other part of the sixth consciousness).

689 Lines 32–34 are, of course, found in more or less the same way in many Yogācāra texts (such as *Ālambanaparīkṣā* 6ac), and also resemble *Bodhicittavivaraṇa* 22–23.

690 NYC has *skul snang* (which makes no sense and should be *'khrul snang*).

691 Verse 26.

692 Buddhism reduces all possible types of connection between phenomena to these two.

693 Skt. vastusatpadārthavādin, Tib. dngos po (yod pa)r smra ba. In particular from a Madhyamaka perspective, "realists" are all those who accept any kind of independently existing entities, such as outer material particles or some ultimately and truly existing kind of mind.

694 Lines 5–11. Here, one of the Yogācāra school's main arguments against the existence of real outer objects is stated. It says that there are no objects outside of the mind, because all our perceptions and what they perceive are alike since they are nothing but immaterial clear appearances in our mind. In other words, objects are not different from the cognizing consciousness by virtue of the very fact of being cognized. The reason is that consciousness—lucid awareness that neither consists of particles nor has spatial extension—can cognize only what has the same nature as consciousness, and thus cannot cognize material objects that have an altogether different nature (that is, lacking cognizance, consisting of particles, and possessing spatial dimensions). In Western scholarship, following Iwata 1984, this is often referred to as "the *saṃvedana* inference." It is found, for example, in Dignāga's *Pramāṇasamucchaya* (I.9–10) and its autocommentary, Dharmakīrti's *Pramāṇaviniścaya* (I.55bff), and Śāntarakṣita's *Tattvasaṃgraha* (lines 2001, 2003, and 2029–33).

695 Lines 42–43 are, of course, found in many Yogācāra texts and also resemble *Bodhicittavivaraṇa* lines 22bd.

696 Lines 46–48 represent the standard way in which Mādhyamikas such as Bhāvaviveka (*Madhyamakahṛdaya* V28.ab) and Candrakīrti (*Madhyamakāvatāra* VI. 87–90 and *Bhāṣya* [D3862, fols. 276b–277a]) explain the reason for the Buddha having taught "mere mind."

697 Also these four lines are found, in more or less the same ways, in several Yogācāra texts (such as *Viṃśikākārikā*, lines 16ab and 17a).

698 Lines 53–56 are an expansion of *Madhyāntavibhāga* I.3ab.

699 V.7.

700 Lines 10ab.

701 I.1.

702 Lines 166–69.

703 Depending on the level of the path, such nonobservation can be conceptual (as a result of inference), or a nonconceptual direct experience of self-aware valid cognition, which eventually becomes completely nonreferential yogic valid perception.

704 I.6–7ab (NYC omits lines 6d–7a).

705 VI.8.

706 V.9–11.

707 I.10–11.

708 For the eight conditioned and unconditioned phenomena, see AC (1.3.2.3. Instruction on the object condition). As for summarizing unconditioned phenomena into three or four, as mentioned above, Vasubandhu's *Abhidharmakośa* (in accordance with the Sarvāstivāda system) lists only the two cessations and space, while his *Pañcaskandhaprakaraṇa* adds suchness in general.

709 The sense faculties are explained to be manifestations of invisible subtle matter that, upon being destroyed and ceasing to function, disappear without a trace. Though technically consisting of minute particles, they are also said to be somewhat closer to the nature of consciousness. Nevertheless, the actual perceivers of sense objects are not these physical faculties, but the respective sense consciousnesses facilitated by them.

710 Skt. mano dhātu, Tib. yid kyi khams.

711 Skt. mana āyatana, Tib. yid kyi skye mched.

712 Lines 70–71 correspond to *Ālambanaparikṣā* VIIbc.

713 Lines 72–73 correspond to *Madhyāntavibhāga* I.8cd.

714 Here, NYC has *'du shes* (discrimination) and also explains accordingly, while NY says *'du byed* (formation). NYKD keeps the latter, glossing it as *mngon par 'du byed* (as does a contemporary commentary by the present Karma Trinlépa).

715 I.8cd.

716 Verse 16.

717 Lines 75–77 correspond to *Mahāyānasaṃgraha* I.6 (D4048, fol. 3b.5–6; see below).

718 Lines 82–86 continue *Mahāyānasaṃgraha* I.6 (D4048, fol. 3b.6–7; see below).

719 "Views about the perishable collection" (Tib. 'jig tshogs la lta ba) is the Tibetan rendering of Skt. *satkāyadṛṣṭi* (otherwise translated throughout the text as "views about a real personality"). Since NYC glosses the Tibetan, the English follows that.

720 Lines 5b–6ab.

721 As said in the introduction, in itself, the afflicted mind is neutral in the sense of being neither virtuous nor nonvirtuous. However, since the clinging to a self is the opposite of the prajñā that realizes the lack of a self, it obscures liberation.

722 These afflictions refer to the "innate" or deeply ingrained afflictive tendencies as opposed to the more superficial "imputed afflictions," which are relinquished on the path of seeing.

723 Lines 87–91 are also from *Mahāyānasaṃgraha* I.6 (D4048, fols. 3b.6–4a.1; see below).

724 I.6 (D4048, fols. 3b.5–4a.1).

725 Lines 92–93 resemble the last two lines in the verse from the *Abhidharmasūtra* and the first and last lines of the verse from the *Saṃdhinirmocanasūtra* quoted just below.

726 Lines 2cd–5a (NYC omits lines 3ab, 4c).

727 This is the concluding verse of the sūtra's chapter 5 (D106, fol. 21b.1–2).

728 Lines 94–104 are found and explained in chapter 1 of the *Mahāyānasaṃgraha.*

729 Tib. rab tu mi gnas pa'i rgyud. The *Tengyur* does not contain a tantra by this name.

730 X.5 (D4048, fol. 38a.4–8).

731 IX.76.

732 D283, fol. 56b.6–8. NYC has *sku gsum la 'jug pa'i mdo* as the title (which is not found in the *Tengyur*), and in the quote, replaces *gnas su dag pa* with *gnas gyur pa*, has *kun gzhi la gnas pa'i yid* instead of *nyon yid*, and does not mention the three kāyas.

733 Verse 39.

734 These lines are not found in the above text (nor could I locate them elsewhere). Bhāvaviveka's *Madhyamakaratnapradīpa* (D3854, fol. 284b.3–4) says, "Buddhahood means to have awoken from the sleep of ignorance, while the bodhicitta of the nature of phenomena—great self-sprung wisdom—knows and fully realizes the entire maṇḍala of knowable objects in a single instant." In terms of verses, the closest (also fitting the general context here), are two passages in two texts by Candrakīrti, the first one being the last two lines of *Triśaraṇasaptati* 14:

> Any nature of phenomena
> Does not exist at all.
> Therefore, it is held that the Sugata
> Knows all [of them] in a single instant.

The second one is the last line of *Madhyamakāvatāra* XI.11:

> Just as there are no divisions in space through the divisions of vessels,
> There are no divisions produced by entities in true reality.
> Therefore, once they are fully realized as being of equal taste,
> You, excellent knower, realize [all] knowable objects in a single instant.

735 Lines 112–15 correspond to *Mahāyānasūtrālaṃkāra* IX.68–69a (also including IX.67bd) quoted below.

736 IX. 69d.

737 IX.68.

738 IX.67.

739 IX.69 (NYC omits the last line).

740 X.7 (D4048, fol. 38b.3).

741 In the Tibetan tradition, this verse is often said to come from Rāhulabhadra's *Prajñāpāramitāstotra.* Though some lines in verses 1–2 of this text show similarities to the above verse, as it stands, it is neither contained in the available Sanskrit nor the equivalent

Tibetan versions of this text in the *Tengyur* (where it is moreover wrongly attributed to Nāgārjuna; P2018). Alternatively, it is held that this verse was spoken by Rāhula, the Buddha's son, to his mother.

742 Uusually, "the samādhi of the heroic stride" is defined as bodhisattvas experiencing and mastering the entire range of mundane and supramundane samādhis (for details, see Lamotte 1998).

743 Lines 120–121 resemble *Mahāyānasūtrālaṃkāra* IX.70cd quoted below.

744 IX.70.

745 Detailed presentations of these factors to be relinquished are found in the *Abhidharmakośa*, the *Abhidharmasamucchaya*, and the *Abhisamayālaṃkāra* with their respective commentaries. Note that the above presentation represents the mahāyāna presentation (as in the *Abhidharmasamucchaya* and the commentaries on the *Abhisamayālaṃkāra*) of only the afflictive obscurations to be relinquished through seeing and familiarization. The number of cognitive obscurations to be relinquished on the paths of seeing and familiarization are 108 on each one of these two paths (for details, see my forthcoming translations of the commentaries on the *Abhisamayālaṃkāra* by the Eighth Karmapa and the Fifth Shamarpa).

746 IX.72ab.

747 Lines 128–32 correspond to *Mahāyānasūtrālaṃkāra* IX.43ac and 44, quoted below.

748 Skt. anutpattidharmakṣānti, Tib. mi skye ba'i chos la bzod pa (more literally, *kṣānti* means patience, endurance). In a general mahāyāna sense, the term refers to being mentally ready for the direct realization of emptiness (also known as "the dharma of nonarising"). Thus, in this context, "poised readiness" does not mean passively enduring or bearing something, but rather indicates an active openness and receptiveness to integrate the experience of emptiness into one's mind stream and to be able to live within this utter groundlessness. In a more specific sense, "poised readiness" can also refer to the third of the four levels of the path of preparation (heat, peak, poised readiness, and supreme dharma), on which the practitioner newly attains some degree of openness and calm in the sense of not being afraid of profound emptiness (according to the *Abhidharmakośabhāṣya* [D4090, vol. khu, fol.13a.7–13b.1], this refers to undeclining readiness for the four realities of the noble ones). Strictly speaking, the full extent of this kind of poised readiness is attained only from the path of seeing onward (see NYC on line 144 below), when the nature of phenomena is directly seen for the first time. For the most part, the path of familiarization then consists of increasing and stabilizing one's familiarity with this realization in all situations. The culmination of this is reached on the eighth bhūmi, which results in all the kinds of mastery described in the following.

749 IX.42. The following two verses quoted are IX.43–44.

750 XI.45–46.

751 Lines 137–40 correspond to *Mahāyānasūtrālaṃkāra* IX.71, 72cd, and 73abd quoted below.

752 IX.71.

753 IX.73.

754 IX. 72cd.

755 This means that each sambhogakāya, despite being a momentary appearance, will remain as the continuity of such an appearance until the end of saṃsāra.

756 IX.61.

757 As mentioned before, the mental consciousness has two parts—(1) thinking and (2) what is called "mental valid perception." The latter refers to the capacity of the mental consciousness to not only think but, just as the sense consciousnesses, directly perceive the five kinds of outer objects (such as forms and sounds). However, this function of the mental consciousness cannot operate on its own, but must be triggered by a preceding sense consciousness (otherwise, blind people would be able to see via that "channel").

758 This presentation of the four times four wisdoms of the path of seeing follows the *Abhidharmasamucchaya* (D4049, fol. 93a.6–b.4), which says: "(1) What is readiness? It is the uncontaminated prajñā in which the reality of suffering becomes revealed as one's own personal experience by virtue of prior analysis [on the path of preparation]. Through this [prajñā] of seeing suffering, the [respective] afflictions to be relinquished are relinquished. This is called 'the readiness for the dharma cognition of suffering.' (2) What is the dharma cognition of suffering? It is the cognition that manifests liberation [from the respective afflictions] right after the end of the readiness [for the dharma cognition of suffering]. (3) What is the readiness for the subsequently realizing cognition of suffering? It is the uncontaminated prajñā right after the end of the dharma cognition of suffering in which it becomes revealed as one's own personal experience that the two [cognitions that consist] of the readiness for the dharma cognition of suffering and the dharma cognition of suffering are the causes for the qualities of the noble ones. (4) What is the subsequently realizing cognition of suffering? It is the cognition that definitely seizes the readiness for the subsequently realizing cognition. The readinesses and cognitions that correspond to the remaining three realities should be understood in the same way. Here, through the readinesses for dharma cognition and the [dharma] cognitions, the apprehended is realized [to be empty]. Through the subsequently realizing readinesses and the [subsequent] cognitions, the apprehender is realized [to be empty]. It should be understood that all readinesses and cognitions entail the yoga of dwelling in signlessness. These sixteen moments of mind constitute the path of seeing. A moment of mind should be understood as the complete arising of a cognition with regard to what is to be cognized [by it]." Thus, the sixteen wisdoms or "moments" of the path of seeing refer to said sixteen insights, with "moment" meaning the time it takes to complete each one of them. The *Abhisamayālaṃkāra* and its commentaries largely follow the above mahāyāna presentation of the *Abhidharmasamucchaya*, while the Vaibhāṣika presentation of the moments of the path of seeing is found in the *Abhidharmakośa*.

759 Lines 147–54 correspond to *Mahāyānasūtrālaṃkāra* IX.41 and 74 quoted below.

760 These qualities vary slightly in different sources. For example, both JNS (vol. 1, p. 343) and Dpal sprul 'jigs med chos kyi dbang po 1997, 162 explain that (2) is being blessed by a hundred buddhas, (5) means engaging through wisdom from the beginning to the end of one hundred eons, (6) corresponds to both (6) and (7) above, and (7) is maturing one hundred sentient beings. Here, (5) means that bodhisattvas, for the sake of helping sentient beings to become free from their negative actions, demonstrate the way in which ordinary beings wander in saṃsāra through their karma. Through (8) shaking a hundred realms, bodhisattvas induce aspiration in those to be guided. Through (9) seeing the illumination of realms, sentient beings are matured, and (10) opening a hundred gates of dharma means that bodhisattvas, for the sake of ripening their own insight, reflect about the meaning of the various specifications of dharma.

761 IX.41 (NYC omits line 2).

762 These numbers vary greatly in different sources (the main one being the *Daśabhūmikasūtra*).

763 IX.74

764 IX.64

765 Lines 159–60 resemble *Mahāyānasūtrālaṃkāra* IX.77bd quoted below.

766 IX.77.

767 IX.65.

768 X.1 (D4048, fol. 37a.4).

769 These are listed in *Abhisamayālaṃkāra* VIII.2–6 and include all major Buddhist samādhis, the thirty-seven dharmas concordant with enlightenment, omniscience, and so on (for details, see my forthcoming translation of this text).

770 VIII.1.

771 Sections 26a–b. The translation follows the Sanskrit as quoted in Makransky 1997, 375. NYC varies somewhat, "The buddhas are dharmakāya—the guides are the dharma view."

772 IX.26

773 For more details on different presentations of the three kāyas, see appendix 1.

774 Part 2, IV.70.

775 Verse 2.

776 This greatly resembles OED (p. 502.1), which states that the eight consciousnesses are the obscurations, while the four wisdoms are the stainlessness of these eight. Dharmadhātu wisdom is said to be the matrix of all of them.

777 I.51.

778 Verses 18–19.

779 I.32–33b.

780 I.33cd (I.34 lists all four remedies and their respective examples as explained right below in NYC; see AC, p. 206 above).

781 I.47.

782 The seven greatnesses of the mahāyāna are found in *Mahāyānasūtrālaṃkāra* XIX.59–60: (1) Greatness of focus means that bodhisattvas focus on the vast collection of mahāyāna scriptures. (2) Greatness of accomplishment is the benefit of both oneself and others. (3) Greatness of wisdom is the realization of both kinds of identitylessness. (4) Greatness of applying diligence is to make efforts on the path for three incalculable eons. (5) Greatness of skill in means refers to bodhisattvas from the first bhūmi onward being permitted to commit the seven negative actions of body and speech, because they, due to their stainless bodhicitta, never forsake any sentient being and are not subject to afflictions. (6) Greatness of perfect accomplishment means to attain the thirty-two qualities of the dharmakāya of a perfect buddha. (7) Greatness of enlightened activity is effortless, spontaneous, and ceaseless activity for the sake of all beings.

783 I.21bd (D13, fol. 3a.3).

784 The three mains seats of the Karma Kagyü lineage in Tibet are Kambo Kangra (Tib. kam po gangs rva; also known as Kambo Nenang, Tib. kam po gnas nang), Karma Gön (Tib. ka rma dgon; both in eastern Tibet), and Tsurpu (Tib. tshur phu; near Lhasa). They were founded by the First Karmapa, Tüsum Khyenba, in 1164, 1185, and 1189 CE, respectively. In due order, these seats are said to correspond to the maṇḍalas of the enlightened body, speech, and mind of Cakrasaṃvara. An alternative explanation for this is that Kambo Kangra had a large saṃgha (body aspect), Karma Gön many scholars (speech aspect), and Tsurpu many meditators (mind aspect).

785 Tib. shes rab rin chen. He was one of the main students of Rangjung Dorje.

786 Tib. rlung ban lha lung pa; he is mentioned in Jamgön Kongtrul's record of received teachings (Tib. gsan yig).

787 This refers to AC, many passages of which are incorporated in NYC.

788 The major text is ZMND (with AC), and the two minor are NT and NY.

789 Tib. kun bzang bde chen 'od gsal gling.

790 ZDKT, pp. 35–50.

791 NT, lines 48–51.

792 ZZB (pp. 450 and 453) explains this term as a synonym for the buddha heart (with further synonyms including Mahāmudrā, connate wisdom, dharmadhātu, and prajñāpāramitā). It is "indestructible" through any dualistic phenomena and a "sphere" in the sense of its nature never changing from the states of ordinary sentient beings up through buddhahood. It is "great," since all phenomena never go beyond its nature. Since it cannot be pointed out through anything within the webs of reference points, such as "having an identity" or "identitylessness," it is not asserted to be any of the many forms of appearance in saṃsāra or nirvāṇa, whose root it is. At the same time, it is what may appear as anything and everything without exception. Thus, it is inconceivable.

793 This is a paraphrase of parts of DSC, that is, heading 2.2.1.3. ("Brief introduction to the modes of being of what is to be relinquished and its remedy"; fol. 14b) and the subsequent explanation (fol. 17a) on *Dharmadhātustava*, verses 24–26 ("The manner in which the dharmadhātu is empty of something to be relinquished and a remedy"). For details, see Brunnhölzl 2007b, 231 and 233–35.

794 Like OED, ZDKT uses the prose version of the *Dharmadharmatāvibhāga* (this passage corresponds to lines 26–29 in the Mathes edition).

795 Tib. lus.

796 This and the following quote are from I.48 (P5549, fols. 11b.6–12a.2).

797 This quote is not found in the *Ratnāvalī*, but it is nearly identical to Āryadeva's *Catuḥśataka* VIII.5.

798 Lines 52–53.

799 Ibid., lines 54–55.

800 Ibid., lines 13–14.

801 Ibid., lines 17–18.

802 Ibid., lines 56–59.

803 Ibid., lines 108–10.

804 Ibid., lines 127–32.

805 I.39cd.

806 I.16cd.

807 AC, p. 35.

808 Tib. shes pa. This is the same Tibetan word as in *tha mal gyi shes pa*, rendered as "ordinary mind." Otherwise, *shes pa* is translated as "consciousness," but since the argument here is about the term "mind" in "ordinary mind," for the sake of consistency, *shes pa* is rendered here as mind too.

809 I.103ab (ZDKT quotes only the second line). The rendering "basic element of awareness" mirrors the Tibetan (*rig khams*). The Sanskrit has *sarvajñacakṣur viditaṃ maharṣir madhūpamaṃ dhātuṃ imaṃ vilokya*, which translates as, "The great sage with his omniscient eye, seeing this dhātu known to be honeylike."

810 I.104c. Again, the rendering "consciousness" mirrors primarily the Tibetan. The Sanskrit says *jñāna*, which can mean either "consciousness" or "wisdom."

811 I.6ab.

812 III.11. For a discussion of what this verse means, see below.

813 I.149–50.

814 Of course, the exact Sanskrit equivalent for "disposition" (Tib. rigs) is *gotra*. However, in this context here, all these terms are taken to be equivalent anyway.

815 In Tibetan debate, this is an expression for the utter defeat of opponents, that is, their being left without any of the three possible answers to an absurd consequence, since they can neither accept the thesis in this consequence, nor refute that the reason entails the predicate, nor refute the reason, since they have already accepted it before (if this happens, the challenger would circle his hand three times above the opponent's head). In the above case, the absurd consequence is, "The gathering of the accumulation of wisdom is the naturally abiding disposition, because the accomplishing of the roots of virtue is the unfolding disposition." If this statement is accepted by the opponents, technically speaking, they accept that whatever is the reason entails whatever is the predicate. Thus, the unfolding disposition (or its equivalent, the accomplishing of virtue) is included in the naturally abiding disposition, so there must be something that is a common locus. However, this contradicts the opponents' original position of the naturally abiding disposition being present right from the beginning, whereas the unfolding disposition is something newly accomplished, which excludes a common locus. By the same token, the opponents can in fact not accept the thesis that the accumulation of wisdom is the naturally abiding disposition (since the former is newly accumulated and the latter not). Also, the reason in the above consequence is exactly what the opponents claim themselves, so they cannot deny it.

816 I.115–17.

817 The dharmas that unfold the basic element are listed in *Dharmadhātustava* verses 66–68. Confidence is not explicitly mentioned there, but appears several times in DSC as the starting point in terms of such dharmas.

818 Dpa' bo gtsug lag phreng ba n.d., 683–87 and 692–93.

819 II.4.

820 *Uttaratantra* V.14.

821 See NTC on NT, lines 113–15.

822 These phrases are supported by extensive quotes from many sūtras, such as the *Sarvabuddhaviśayāvatārajñānālokālaṃkārasūtra*, the *Ghanavyūhasūtra*, the *Laṅkāvatārasūtra*, the *Samādhirājasūtra*, the *Tathāgatajñānamudrāsamādhisūtra*, the *Mahāparinirvāṇasūtra*, *Gaganagañjaparipṛcchāsūtra*, the *Sāgaramatiparipṛcchasūtra*, the *Anavataptanāgarājaparipṛcchāsūtra*, the *Vimalakīrtinirdeśasūtra*.

823 IX.6a, IX.15, IX.22, IX.24, and IX.79cd.

824 JNS (vol. 2, p. 435) attributes this expression to Dölpopa, while Dpa' bo gtsug lag phreng ba (n.d., 692) gives the *Bodhisattvabhūmi* as the source of this number. Usually, *Abhisamayālaṃkāra* VIII.2–6 is explained as describing the twenty-one sets of uncontaminated dharmas or wisdoms of buddhahood.

825 This section is Dpa' bo gtsug lag phreng ba n.d., 694–701.

826 XI.11.

827 IX.4.

828 III.1ab.

829 Ibid., I.145a.

830 Ibid., II.21 and 30ab.

831 This is followed by a virtually identical passage from the *Trikāyanāmasūtra*.

832 IX.60 and 65ab.

833 I.17ab.

834 Hsüan-tsang's *Vijñaptimātratāsiddhi* (La Vallée Poussin 1928–48, 703–16) reports Dharmapāla explaining that the svābhāvikakāya is one of the three aspects of the dharmakāya, and represents the foundation of the other two kāyas. In other words, the dharmakāya is the consummate makeup of buddhahood, the svābhāvikakāya represents its essence, and the sambhogakāya and nirmāṇakāya are its manifestations.

835 II.43.

836 Ibid., I.145.

837 D275, fol. 44a.6–7.

838 Ibid., fol. 37a.5–6. The *Tengyur* versions of this passage do not have "dharmadhātu wisdom" but "pure dharmadhātu" (for the full quote, see below), but it is always possible that there have been different editions.

839 For example, this is explained in Gyaltsab Darma Rinchen's (1364–1432) influential Gelugpa commentary on the *Uttaratantra*.

840 The phrases in "( )" are the *Uttaratantra*'s famous lines I.28a–c on why all sentient beings are endowed with buddha nature.

841 Ibid., I.144ab.

842 Ibid., I.146.

843 Ibid., I.147ab.

844 Ibid., I.147cd.

845 Ibid., I.150.

846 This section is Dpa' bo gtsug lag phreng ba n.d., 757–69.

847 XI.17.

848 A more modern example for the completion of former aspiration prayers and the two accumulations of merit and wisdom being the causes for the ongoing impetus of the dharmakāya's enlightened activity would be the flight of a rocket. Initially, it requires a lot of energy to lift off the ground, but the higher the rocket ascends, the easier and faster its motion becomes and the less energy it needs. Finally, once it glides in the vacuum of outer space, it moves on forever without needing any further energy, just through the power of the fuel that has already been spent.

849 These are lines XI.17d, 10cd, and 11d.

850 D283, fol. 56b.6–8.

851 D275, fol. 37a.5–6.

852 Ibid., fol. 37a.7ff.

853 I could not locate this exact phrase in the *Tengyur* versions of the sūtra. The sūtra does, however, speak of wisdom in connection with the dharmadhātu several times, the closest being the recurring phrase, "When the dharmadhātu has become pure, the complete enjoyment of wisdom . . ." (ibid., fol. 43a.3ff.).

854 IX.45.

855 D275, fol. 40a.4–40b.1.

856 Ibid., fols. 40b.1–41b.1.

857 In ancient Indian cosmology, the ocean that represents the periphery of the disk which is this world is surrounded by a gigantic wall of volcanic mountains that dam it in.

858 Ibid., fol. 41a.3–4.

859 Ibid., fols. 41b.1ff.

860 IX.41.

861 IX.42–45.

862 IX.46.

863 IX.47.

864 The change of state of the skandha of form is fivefold in terms of the five sense faculties.

865 IX.68–69.

866 I could not locate a sūtra by that name in the *Kangyur*.

867 The *Buddhabhūmivyākhyāna* and *Buddhabhūmyupadeśa* (Keenan 2002, 79–80) give partly corresponding lists of eleven qualities for mirrorlike wisdom, six for the wisdom of equality, five for discriminating wisdom, and two for all-accomplishing wisdom.

868 This section is Dpa' bo gtsug lag phreng ba n.d., 769–78.

869 IV.1.

870 XI.43ab.

871 This accords with JNS's detailed demonstration that buddha nature (or the dharmadhātu) are not actually connected in any way and that "sentient beings" are in fact nothing but what is called "adventitious stains." JNS (vol. 1, pp. 220–21) says: "In brief, no matter which reasoning you may put forward to prove that the buddha heart exists in the mind streams of sentient beings, it is impossible to establish a direct connection between the reason and the predicate [in such a reasoning]. Also, as far as the assertion by others that sentient beings possess the Heart is concerned, it is [only] suitable to assert that they possess [such a Heart] in the sense of the factors to be relinquished. However, in that case, the factors to be relinquished are nothing but mistakenness, which never existed from the start. The assertion that either a connection of identity or a causal connection is established between this Heart and sentient beings as well as the assertion that they are some kind of support and supported that actually fulfill these functions are not in accord with the Buddha and the successor to his throne, the protector Maitreya, and so forth. Therefore, they should be discarded. . . . Some fools say, 'The Omniscient Karmapa Rangjung [Dorje] asserts the intention of the *Mahāyānottaratantra* to be that the Tathāgata heart exists in the dharmadhātu of the mind of sentient beings in an inseparable manner.' This wise being did not assert such. In his autocommentary on *The Profound Inner Reality* he makes a twofold classification [of mind as such], saying, 'what is pure is expressed as mind, and what is impure is [also] expressed as mind' {see the beginning of AC's chapter 1 above}. By explaining that those who possess impure mental impulses are sentient beings, he elucidates that the dharmadhātu does not exist in such sentient beings. He presents these very sentient beings as *being* the adventitious stains that are produced by false imagination, which mistakenly strays from the dharmadhātu. By giving the pure mind names such as 'ordinary mind,' 'original protector,' and 'original buddha,' he says that it is exactly this [mind] that possesses the mode of being inseparable from the buddha qualities. This kind of [pure mind] is also the [buddha] heart that actually fulfills this function."

872 Often translated as "immeasurably negative or heinous action" (the other four are killing one's father, one's mother, or an arhat, and creating a schism in the saṅgha). They are called "without interval" because their result is the unavoidable rebirth in a hell realm immediately after death, without the interval of an intermediate state (bardo) before the next rebirth.

873 Sgam po pa 1990, 339–40.

874 I list here important works relevant to the current study, but for reasons of space I do not include Buddhist sūtras and some of the other canonical works cited in the text or notes.

Index